SEVEN VERDI

LIBRETTOS

English translations by
William Weaver

WITH THE ORIGINAL ITALIAN

W · W · NORTON & COMPANY

New York · London

To my sister, Jane Weaver Poulton

W. W. Norton & Company, Inc.
500 Fifth Avenue, New York, N.Y. 10110
www.wwnorton.com

W. W. Norton & Company Ltd.
Castle House, 75/76 Wells Street, London W1T 3QT

First published in the Norton Library 1977
by arrangement with Doubleday and Company, Inc.

Library of Congress Cataloging in Publication Data
Verdi, Giuseppe, 1813–1901.
    Seven Verdi librettos.
    Includes an introduction and synopsis to each opera.
    1. Operas—Librettos.   I. Title.
ML49.V45062   1975   782.1'2   74–19084

Printed in the United States of America

9 0

ISBN 0-393-00852-5

CONTENTS

FOREWORD

Whenever I see that William Weaver is preparing a paper, translating a libretto, or editing a book touching on the life or work of Giuseppe Verdi, I know I'm in for a treat. Mr. Weaver is not only a profound scholar and one of the world's experts on that great Italian master, but he puts forth his ideas with such style and freshness that no opera lover—indeed, no one who possesses an interest in music—can resist turning the pages to see what comes next. He is, in fact, a veritable Verdian Sherlock Holmes. In *Seven Verdi Librettos*, Weaver reveals new insights and fascinations for the opera lover by providing a sure and sensitive rendering of the Italian language into English. It is a rare and wonderful thing to have a literato as well as literal translation of a libretto and one's musical appreciation and comprehension of the opera is thereby enormously enhanced. By his skill with the word and his understanding of the music, William Weaver makes a real contribution to our enjoyment of Verdi's operas.

Schuyler G. Chapin
New York, June 1974

AN INTRODUCTORY NOTE

Though at times, especially in the early years of his career, Verdi was forced to compose operas in haste, he was seldom hasty about choosing his librettos. The only text he seems to have set without demanding alterations was Felice Romani's libretto of *Un Giorno di regno*, his second opera, written during a tragic period of his life when, after having lost his two children, his beloved wife Margherita also died. The disastrous failure then of this *opera buffa* was another blow: later, Verdi said that he had determined to end his theater career. But he was soon tempted back to the opera house, when the impresario of La Scala thrust a good libretto in his pocket. This was *Nabucco*. Verdi read it, was gripped by its dramatic possibilities, and promptly began writing what was to be the first great success in his long list of operas.

In a half century or so of activity, Verdi wrote hundreds of letters, a large part of them to his librettists, harrying them for new verses, demanding changes, explaining the requirements of a given scene or the subtleties of a hero or heroine. These letters are a guide to Verdi's taste in drama and to his requirements as a composer. To Chislanzoni, the librettist of *Aida*, Verdi was explicit: "Forgive this heresy, but I believe that in the theater it is sometimes praiseworthy for composers to have the talent for *not* making music and for knowing how to *s'effacer;* and by the same token, as far as the poets are concerned, the immediate, theatrical world° is better than a beautiful line of verse. I say this only for myself . . ."

Sometimes Verdi tried to secure acknowledged poets as collaborators, but the results were not satisfactory; and — at least until he began to work with Arrigo Boito — he preferred hack writers, men of the theater, whom he could bend easily to his will. What he sought in a libretto was rich situations, the "colors," as he called them. The words should be simple, but the characters should be complex, and the progress of his career is a continuing search for heroes and heroines who would be different from the old operatic stand-bys, the noble tenor, the ill-starred soprano, the villainous baritone. He defied convention by writing an opera about a hunchback (with a very ignoble tenor), then one about a prostitute. In *Il Trovatore* the character who most fascinated him was Azucena, the old and half-crazed gypsy.

For a poor young man of his day, Verdi received a sound formal education, but he liked to consider himself a self-made man. And it is undeniably true that much of his formation was based on his private, constant reading. He truly loved literature, and he had very catholic tastes. His library, still preserved in his villa at Sant'Agata, is respectably large, and the books look as if they have been read. Shakespeare and Schiller

° *La parola scenica* ("theatrical" but also "dramatic," "vivid").

are at his bedside, dog-eared and copiously annotated in the composer's hand. He was also a theatergoer, and even when he was an old man he made long and tiring trips to hear new operas. His adoration of Italy's great novelist Alessandro Manzoni is well-known, and his respect for the actress Adelaide Ristori led him to call her one of the glories of Italy.

Only specialists sit down to read a libretto for pleasure; to the ordinary reader a volume of librettos in translation, divorced from their music, may seem a peculiar enterprise. But Verdi, like Wagner and all other great opera composers, attached supreme importance to the words he was setting to music, and this means that the listener, if he is to understand the opera fully, must understand the situations, the shades of emotion that the music is describing. As Verdi's operas are generally given in Italian in English-speaking countries, the opera listener who doesn't know Italian should be able to follow the operas with a faithful guide in hand. Unfortunately, such guides have been virtually nonexistent. This volume is intended to fill that particular gap.

At one time or other nearly all of Verdi's operas have been translated, to be sure, but the translations are generally not faithful and, in some cases, are based on incorrect Italian texts. Many of the old translations sold in opera houses or printed in bilingual scores were made to be sung, so that the necessity to fit words to notes and to give the English some kind of style, however deplorable, resulted in translations that gave only an approximate idea of what the Italian words meant. An example, taken almost at random from a cheap score of *Il Trovatore*: "*Tacea la notte placida e bella in ciel sereno*" becomes in English "No star shone in the heav'nly vault, In silence all was sleeping." Try to find the words for "star," "vault," and "sleeping" in the original Italian.

Obviously, for Verdi each word had its own shading, its own music (listen to the way he sets key words: "*gelosia*" in *Otello* or "*vendetta*" in *Rigoletto*, for example). If we are to get to the heart of his operas, we must be able to follow them almost word by word. The translations in this volume, therefore, are printed facing the original Italian, and as fas as possible, the English follows the Italian line for line.

The translations have no literary pretensions, and, whenever necessary, English style has been sacrificed to faithfulness, even to literalness. The translator's hardest task was fighting the constant temptation to prettify the English. No attempt has been made to imitate the nineteenth-century diction of the original. Characters do not call each other "thou," and "*ali*" are "wings," not "pinions." Verdi's dictum about "the immediate word" has been the translator's motto. In the case of Verdi's Shakespearean librettos, no effort has been made to return to the poetry of the English original. Thus, when Shakespeare's Mr. Brook becomes, in *Falstaff*, "Signor Fontana," he subsequently becomes, in this English version, "Mister Fountain."

The translation of *Il Trovatore* was commissioned by Dorle and Dario Soria for Angel Records and is reprinted here (somewhat revised) with Angel's kind permission. The note on *Un ballo in maschera*, in a different form, appeared originally in the booklet accompanying the London recording of the opera; again it is reprinted through London's kind permission.

Five of the following translations were included in the volume *Verdi Librettos*, published as a Doubleday Anchor Book in 1963. At that time, the translator expressed his thanks to Miss Elizabeth Berlin and to the late Herbert Weinstock for their acute and patient help. That gratitude is undimmed. Now the translator must thank also his long-suffering editor at Norton, Mrs. Claire Brook ("Cara Signora Fontana"). Translating—and especially translating texts as tricky as these librettos—is a process strewn with pitfalls; many hands make more accurate, if never light, work.

William Weaver
Rome, 1962
Monte San Savino, May, 1974

BIBLIOGRAPHICAL NOTE

The Italian texts were all taken from the printed piano scores rather than from the printed librettos, which are often inaccurate. The stage directions, in the interest of greater completeness, have generally been based on the first edition of the librettos, with occasional additions also from the score.

In writing the introductory notes to the individual operas, the author consulted the following works:

Abbiati, Franco, *Giuseppe Verdi*, 4 vols. (Milan: Ricordi, 1959).

Baldini, Gabriele, *Abitare la battaglia* (Milan: Garzanti, 1970).

Budden, Julian, *The Operas of Verdi, from Oberto to Rigoletto*, vol. I (New York: Praeger, 1973).

Cesari, Gaetano, and Alessandro Luzio, eds., *I Copialettere di Giuseppe Verdi* (Milan, 1913).

Gatti, Carlo, *Verdi*, rev. ed. (Milan: Mondadori, 1953).

Luzio, Alessandro, ed., *Carteggi verdiani*, 4 vols. (Rome: Reale Accademia d'Italia, 1935, 1947).

Martin, George, *Verdi* (New York: Dodd, Mead, 1963).

Osborne, Charles, *The Complete Operas of Verdi* (New York: Knopf, 1970).

Smith, Patrick J., *The Tenth Muse* (New York: Knopf, 1970).

Verdi, Giuseppe, *Giuseppe Verdi: Autobiografia dalle lettere*, Aldo Oberdorfer, ed. (Milan: Rizzoli, 1951).

The author has also consulted the various publications of the Istituto di studi verdiani of Parma, all of them invaluable reading for students of Verdi's work.

Rigoletto

After the triumph of *Nabucco* (1842) and *I Lombardi* (1843) at La Scala in Milan, Verdi was invited to write for the great Venetian theater La Fenice, where in 1844 he had yet another success with *Ernani*. His success was social as well as musical, and in the fascinating city of the Doges, Verdi was lionized by their nineteenth-century descendants, as well as by a small and active group of opera fans, who were to encourage and assist him throughout the rest of his career.

A member of this Venetian band was *Ernani's* librettist, Francesco Maria Piave. Piave was a native of the nearby island of Murano, where his father had been a well-to-do glass manufacturer. But the elder Piave lost his fortune, and Francesco Maria — or "Checco," as he was familiarly called — had to adapt himself to the idea of making a living. He was not a particularly industrious young man, and though he found a job as proofreader, he spent most of his time writing verses, especially songs that were sung by Venice's gondoliers.

If Piave was no worker, he was apparently very good company and had many friends, including the secretary of La Fenice, who had proposed him to Verdi as the ideal librettist for the composer's Venetian debut.

Piave was inexperienced but willing and enthusiastic; he and Verdi worked well together on *Ernani*, and after that Verdi continued to use him for other librettos: *I Due Foscari, Macbeth, Il Corsaro, Stiffelio*, and *Rigoletto* (which was also commissioned by La Fenice).

Based on Victor Hugo's play *Le Roi s'amuse*, the libretto of *Rigoletto* was written under enormous difficulties. In 1851 Italy was still a divided country, and Venice's Austrian overlords were nervous about any subject that might seem subversive. Verdi's reputation as a patriot made him doubly suspect in their eyes, and the Austrians could hardly fail to read subversion into a story in which the hero is a humble jester and the villain a royal libertine. The censors, on reading the first draft of Piave's libretto, then called *La Maledizione* (The Curse), also objected to various "obscenities" and to the fact that in the last scene a corpse was carried onto the stage in a sack.

Piave and Verdi fought back. "The King *must* be a libertine," Verdi wrote, and, "I can't understand why the sack has been removed . . . I note that they have avoided making Triboletto [the character later to be called Rigoletto] ugly and hunchbacked! A hunchback who sings? Why not? . . . Will it be effective? I don't know. But if I don't know, then neither does the person who suggested this change. I find it very beautiful to portray this character, extremely deformed and ridiculous, yet within full of passion and of love. I chose this subject precisely because of all these qualities and these original features. If they are removed, I cannot write the music. An original, powerful drama, in short, has been turned into something quite cold and commonplace . . ."

With the help of the impresario of La Fenice, librettist and

composer won a victory — but with losses. The French king
of Hugo's original play had to be changed to an anonymous
Duke of Mantua, the splendid court of Francis I became
a more provincial model, but the sack was allowed, and
Triboletto-Rigoletto remained ugly and deformed.

"Will it be effective?" Verdi was sincerely in doubt about
the public's reaction to his unusual protagonist, but again he
won. The opera was performed on March 11, 1851, and was
a triumph. Applause, curtain calls, and — as the famous story
goes — the audience humming "*La donna è mobile*" on its way
out of La Fenice. Some critics found the opera "in bad taste"
and "banal," and one Milanese writer even accused Verdi of
imitating Mozart, but their dissent was inaudible in the roar
of praise.

The opera was immediately performed in other theaters all
over Italy and the rest of Europe. And Verdi himself remained
pleased with it. Years later he referred to *Rigoletto* as "my
best opera," and in a letter to a Neapolitan friend he praised
the libretto, too. "One of the most beautiful librettos that
exist," he wrote, then added a slight jab at his friend Piave:
"except for the verses."

THE PLOT

ACT ONE

A ball is in progress in the palace of the corrupt and frivo-
lous Duke of Mantua. Seconded by the mocking barbs of his
hunchbacked jester, Rigoletto, the Duke woos the wife of one
of his courtiers, Count of Ceprano. But the gaiety is interrupted by the sudden appearance of an elderly nobleman,
Monterone, whose daughter has been seduced by the Duke.
Monterone hurls his anathema at the heartless ruler, who has
the old man arrested. And when Rigoletto taunts the grief-
stricken father, the old man curses him.

Later, as he is returning home, the superstitious Rigoletto
broods over Monterone's curse. His thoughts are broken in
upon by a mysterious stranger, Sparafucile, a professional
assassin, who offers his services to Rigoletto, warning the jester
that he has enemies. Rigoletto dismisses the assassin, but is
still more disturbed by the man's hints. For a moment the
hunchback's gloom disappears as he goes into his house and
meets his beloved daughter, Gilda, whom he keeps in jealous
seclusion. Warning both Gilda and her nurse never to leave
the house nor to admit anyone, Rigoletto leaves them again.

As Rigoletto is taking his leave, the Duke himself slips into
the garden and learns to his amazement that Gilda, whom he
has noticed in church and followed, is the jester's daughter.
When Rigoletto has gone, Gilda expresses her remorse at
having deceived him by not mentioning the young man who
has captured her girlish fancy. The Duke comes from his
hiding place and quickly banishes her qualms by declaring his
love, but not his identity. He says that he is a poor student
named Gualtier Maldè.

There are noises in the street outside. The Duke goes out, leaving Gilda to muse on her new-found love, whose very name seems to breathe poetry.

In the street the courtiers are assembled, led by Count of Ceprano. They believe that Gilda is Rigoletto's mistress and plan to abduct her to revenge themselves for the jester's gibes. Rigoletto unexpectedly returns. Ceprano conceals himself in the darkness, and the courtiers explain to Rigoletto that they are going to carry off Ceprano's wife. Rigoletto is given a mask — in reality, a blindfold — and told to hold the ladder. The courtiers seize Gilda and carry her off. After a moment, Rigoletto realizes that he is blindfolded; he rips the mask from his face and discovers his daughter's disappearance. Immediately he remembers old Monterone's curse.

ACT TWO

The Duke has also discovered Gilda's disappearance, but when the courtiers come in and announce that they have brought Rigoletto's mistress to the palace, the Duke realizes her true identity and rushes to her.

Rigoletto comes in, looking for Gilda, but the courtiers taunt him until he finally reveals that she is his daughter, and he excoriates them. Gilda rushes from the next room and confesses her shame to her father. The courtiers leave Rigoletto and his daughter alone, and as the jester is consoling Gilda, old Monterone is led past, on his way to prison. Rigoletto vows that the old nobleman's vengeance will be one with his own.

ACT THREE

Sparafucile's attractive sister, Maddalena, has lured the Duke to their lonely tavern on the banks of the Mincio. It is a dark night and a storm is brewing. Outside the tavern, Rigoletto forces Gilda to observe her lover's treachery, then sends her away to put on male attire and leave for Verona, where he will join her.

Meanwhile he makes the final arrangements with Sparafucile, who is to kill the Duke and consign the body later to the jester, who will throw it in the river with his own hands.

Rigoletto leaves. Sparafucile prepares to murder the Duke, who has retired to an upstairs room. Captivated by the young man's charm, Maddalena pleads for his life, and her brother agrees to murder another in the Duke's stead, if a substitute turns up at the tavern. Outside, the horrified Gilda has overheard. She knocks on the door and goes in, making the final sacrifice for her lover.

At midnight Sparafucile gives Rigoletto a sack containing a body, then goes back inside and bars the door. Rigoletto suddenly hears the Duke singing from the upper room. Aghast, he opens the sack, and a flash of lightning reveals the dying Gilda, who asks forgiveness for herself and for the Duke. She dies, and again Rigoletto cries out: "The curse!"

RIGOLETTO

libretto by Francesco Maria Piave

First performed at the Teatro La Fenice, Venice
March 11, 1851

CHARACTERS

The Duke of Mantua	*Tenor*
Rigoletto, his jester, a hunchback	*Baritone*
Sparafucile, a bravo	*Bass*
Count Monterone	*Baritone*
Marullo	*Baritone*
Borsa	*Tenor*
Count of Ceprano	*Bass*
An usher	*Bass*
Gilda, Rigoletto's daughter	*Soprano*
Giovanna, her nurse	*Mezzo-soprano*
Maddalena, Sparafucile's sister	*Contralto*
Countess of Ceprano	*Mezzo-soprano*
A Page	*Mezzo-soprano*

Courtiers, Pages, Servants

The scene is laid in Mantua and environs
during the sixteenth century.

ATTO PRIMO

PARTE PRIMA

Sala magnifica nel palazzo ducale con porte nel fondo che mettono ad altre sale, pure splendidamente illuminate; folla di cavalieri e dame in gran costume nel fondo delle sale; paggi che vanno e vengono. La festa è nel suo pieno. Musica interna da lontano e scrosci di risa di tratto in tratto.

Il Duca e Borsa vengono da una porta del fondo.

DUCA	Della mia bella incognita borghese Toccare il fin dell'avventura io voglio.
BORSA	Di quella giovin che vedete al tempio?
DUCA	Da tre mesi ogni festa.
BORSA	La sua dimora?
DUCA	In un remoto calle; Misterioso un uom v'entra ogni notte.
BORSA	E sa colei chi sia L'amante suo?
DUCA	Lo ignora.

Un gruppo di dame e cavalieri attraversano la sala.

BORSA	Quante beltà!... Mirate.
DUCA	Le vince tutte di Ceprano la sposa.
BORSA (*piano*)	Non v'oda il Conte, o Duca.
DUCA	A me che importa?
BORSA	Dirlo ad altra ei potria.
DUCA	Nè sventura per me certo saria. Questa o quella per me pari sono A quant'altre d'intorno mi vedo; Del mio core l'impero non cedo Meglio ad una che ad altra beltà. La costoro avvenenza è qual dono Di che il fato ne infiora la vita; S'oggi questa mi torna gradita, Forse un'altra doman lo sarà. La costanza, tiranna del core, Detestiamo qual morbo crudele, Sol chi vuole si serbi fedele; Non v'ha amor, se non v'è libertà. De' mariti il geloso furore, Degli amanti le smanie derido; Anco d'Argo i cent'occhi disfido Se mi punge una qualche beltà.

Entra il Conte di Ceprano che segue da lungi la sua sposa servita da altro cavaliere. Dame e signori entrano da varie parti. Il Duca si rivolge alla signora di Ceprano movendo ad incontrarla con molta galanteria.

DUCA	Partite?... Crudele!

ACT ONE

SCENE ONE

A magnificent apartment in the ducal palace. Doors at the back open into other halls, also splendidly illuminated. An elegantly dressed crowd of courtiers and ladies moves through the inner rooms; pages come and go. The festivities are at their peak. Music from within, and occasional bursts of laughter.

The Duke and Borsa come through a door at the back.

DUKE	I want to conclude my flirtation With my lovely, unknown commoner.
BORSA	The young girl you see in church?
DUKE	Every holy day, for the last three months.
BORSA	Where is her house?
DUKE	In a remote little street; A mysterious man enters there every night.
BORSA	Does she know Who her admirer is?
DUKE	She doesn't know.

A group of ladies and courtiers crosses the room.

BORSA	How many beauties! . . . Look.
DUKE	Ceprano's wife outshines them all.
BORSA (*softly*)	Don't let the Count hear you, O Duke.
DUKE	What does that matter to me?
BORSA	He might tell it to another woman.
DUKE	That would surely be no misfortune for me. For me, this woman or that is the same As the many others I see around me; I don't surrender the rule of my heart More easily to one beauty than to another. Their loveliness is like a gift With which fate bedecks life; If today this woman pleases me, Perhaps tomorrow it will be another. Fidelity, the tyrant of the heart, We detest, like a cruel disease, Let only those who wish remain faithful; There is no love, if there is no freedom. I deride the jealous fury of husbands, And the ravings of lovers; I defy even Argus's hundred eyes When some beauty attracts me.

The Count of Ceprano comes in, following his wife at a distance, escorted by another courtier. Ladies and lords come in from various sides. The Duke addresses the Countess of Ceprano, going toward her with great courtliness.

DUKE	You're leaving? . . . Cruel one!

CONTESSA   Seguire lo sposo
                M'è forza a Ceprano.
DUCA   Ma dee luminoso
                In corte tal astro qual sole brillare,
                Per voi qui ciascuno dovrà palpitare.
                Per voi già possente la fiamma d'amore
                Inebria, conquide, distrugge mio core.
CONTESSA   Calmatevi.
DUCA   La fiamma d'amore
                Inebria, conquide, distrugge mio core!

Dà il braccio alla Contessa e esce con lei. Entra Rigoletto,
incontrandosi col Conte di Ceprano.

RIGOLETTO   In testa che avete, signor di Ceprano?

Ceprano fa un gesto d'impazienza e segue il Duca.

RIGOLETTO (*ai cortigiani*)
                Ei sbuffa! Vedete?

BORSA e CORO   Che festa!
RIGOLETTO   Oh sì

BORSA e CORO   Il Duca qui pur si diverte!
RIGOLETTO   Così non è sempre? Che nuove scoperte!
                Il giuoco ed il vino, le feste, la danza,
                Battaglia, conviti, ben tutto gli sta.
                Or della Contessa l'assedio egli avanza,
                          (*ridendo*)
                E intanto il marito fremendo ne va.

Rigoletto esce. Entra Marullo premuroso.

MARULLO   Gran nuova! gran nuova!
TUTTI   Che avvenne? Parlate!
MARULLO   Stupir ne dovrete ...
TUTTI   Narrate ... narrate ...
MARULLO   Ah! ah! Rigoletto ...
TUTTI   Ebben?
MARULLO   Caso enorme!
TUTTI   Perduto ha la gobba?
                Non è più difforme?
MARULLO   Più strana è la cosa! Il pazzo possiede —
TUTTI   Infine?
MARULLO   — un'amante!
TUTTI   Un amante! Chi il crede?
MARULLO   Il gobbo in Cupido or s'è trasformato.
TUTTI   Quel mostro? Cupido! Cupido beato!

Entra il Duca, seguito da Rigoletto.

DUCA (*a Rigoletto*)
                Ah più di Ceprano importuno non v'è!

COUNTESS	I'm forced to follow
	My husband to Ceprano.
DUKE	But such a star must shine at court,
	Radiant, like the sun,
	Every heart here must beat for you.
	For you, love's powerful flame
	Already intoxicates, wins, destroys my heart.
COUNTESS	Calm yourself.
DUKE	The flame of love
	Intoxicates, wins, destroys my heart!

He gives his arm to the Countess and goes out with her. Rigoletto enters, encountering the Count of Ceprano.

RIGOLETTO   What have you on your head, My Lord of
               Ceprano?

Ceprano makes an impatient gesture and follows the Duke.

RIGOLETTO (*to the courtiers*)
               He's huffy! You see?

BORSA and CHORUS
               What festivity!

RIGOLETTO   Oh yes!

BORSA and CHORUS
               The Duke is also enjoying himself here!

RIGOLETTO   Isn't it always like this? What a new discovery!
               Gaming and wine, feasting and dancing,
               Battles and banquets, everything suits him.
               Now he's laying siege to the Countess,
                       (*laughing*)
               And the husband meanwhile is raging about it.

Rigoletto goes out. Marullo hastens in.

MARULLO	Great news! Great news!
ALL	What's happened? Speak!
MARULLO	You'll be amazed . . .
ALL	Tell us . . . tell us!
MARULLO	Ha! Ha! Rigoletto . . .
ALL	Well?
MARULLO	Something enormous!
ALL	Has he lost his hump?
	Is he no longer misshapen?
MARULLO	It's even stranger! The madman has —
ALL	Finish!
MARULLO	— a mistress!
ALL	A mistress! Who'd believe it?
MARULLO	The hunchback's transformed into Cupid.
ALL	That monster? Cupid! Cupid the blessed!

The Duke enters, followed by Rigoletto.

DUKE (*to Rigoletto*)
               Ah, there's no one more bothersome than
               Ceprano!

La cara sua sposa è un angiol per me!

RIGOLETTO   Rapitela.

DUCA   È detto; ma il farlo?

RIGOLETTO   Stasera.

DUCA   Non pensi tu al Conte?

RIGOLETTO   Non c'è la prigione?

DUCA   Ah no.

RIGOLETTO   Ebben ... s'esilia.

DUCA   Nemmeno, buffone.

RIGOLETTO   Allora ... allora la testa.

                 (*indicando di farla tagliare*)

CEPRANO (*da sè*)

       (Oh l'anima nera!)

DUCA (*battendo colla mano una spalla al Conte*)

       Che di', questa testa?

RIGOLETTO   È ben naturale! Che far di tal testa?

       A cosa ella vale?

CEPRANO (*infuriato, brandendo la spada*)

       Marrano!

DUCA (*a Ceprano*)

       Fermate!

RIGOLETTO   Da rider mi fa.

MARULLO e CORO (*tra loro*)

       In furia è montato!

DUCA (*a Rigoletto*)

       Buffone, vien qua.

TUTTI   (In furia è montato!)

DUCA (*a Rigoletto*)

       Ah! sempre tu spingi lo scherzo all'estremo.

CEPRANO (ai cortigiani)

       Vendetta del pazzo! Contr'esso un rancore

       Di noi chi non ha? Vendetta!

RIGOLETTO   Che coglier mi puote?

       Di loro non temo.

DUCA (*a Rigoletto*)

       Quell'ira che sfidi, colpirti potrà.

MARULLO, BORSA e CORO (*a Ceprano*)

       Ma come?

CEPRANO   In armi chi ha core,

       Doman sia da me.

MARULLO, BORSA e CORO

       Sì!

CEPRANO   A notte.

MARULLO, BORSA e CORO

       Sarà!

RIGOLETTO   Del Duca il protetto nessun toccherà!

       Che cogliermi puote, ecc.

CORO   Vendetta, ecc.

His beloved wife is an angel for me!

RIGOLETTO Carry her off.

DUKE Easily said; but to do it?

RIGOLETTO This evening.

DUKE You're not thinking of the Count?

RIGOLETTO Isn't there a prison?

DUKE Ah no.

RIGOLETTO Well then . . . exile him.

DUKE Not that either, buffoon.

RIGOLETTO Then . . . then his head.
(*making gesture of beheading*)

CEPRANO (*aside*)
(Oh, what a black soul!)

DUKE (*slapping the Count's shoulder with his hand*)
What are you saying, this head?

RIGOLETTO It's quite natural. What's to be done with that head?
What good is it?

CEPRANO (*infuriated, brandishing his sword*)
Scoundrel!

DUKE (*to Ceprano*)
Stop!

RIGOLETTO He makes me laugh.

MARULLO and CHORUS (*among themselves*)
He's in a fury!

DUKE (*to Rigoletto*)
Buffoon, come here.

ALL (He's in a fury!)

DUKE (*to Rigoletto*)
Ah! You always force the jest to extremes.

CEPRANO (*to the courtiers*)
Revenge on that madman! Who of us doesn't
Feel some bitterness against him? Revenge!

RIGOLETTO What can touch me?
I don't fear them.

DUKE (*to Rigoletto*)
The wrath you provoke can strike you.

MARULLO, BORSA, and CHORUS (*to Ceprano*)
But how?

CEPRANO Those who have hearts,
Come to me, armed, tomorrow.

MARULLO, BORSA, and CHORUS
Yes!

CEPRANO At night.

MARULLO, BORSA, and CHORUS
So it shall be!

RIGOLETTO No one will touch whom the Duke protects!
What can touch me? etc.

CHORUS Revenge, etc.

DUCA   Ah sempre tu spingi lo scherzo, ecc.

BORSA   Sì, vendetta!

MARULLO e CORO
                Sì, vendetta!

DUCA e RIGOLETTO
                Tutto è gioia!

La folla dei danzatori invade la sala.

TUTTI   Tutto è festa!
                Tutto è gioia, tutto è festa;
                Tutto invitaci a godere!
                Oh guardate, non par questa
                Or la reggia del piacer!

MONTERONE (*dall'interno*)
                Ch'io gli parli.

DUCA   No!

MONTERONE (*entrando*)
                Il voglio.

TUTTI   Monterone!

MONTERONE (*fissando il Duca, con nobile orgoglio*)
                Sì, Monteron ...
                La voce mia qual tuono
                Vi scuoterà dovunque.

RIGOLETTO (*al Duca, contraffacendo la voce di Monterone*)
                Ch'io gli parli.
                        (*Si avanza con ridicola gravità.*)
                Voi congiuraste contro noi, signore.
                E noi clementi invero, perdonammo ...
                Qual vi piglia or delirio a tutte l'ore
                Di vostra figlia a reclamar l'onore?

MONTERONE (*guardando Rigoletto con ira sprezzante*)
                Novello insulto! Ah sì, a turbare
                Sarò vostr'orgie ... verrò a gridare
                Fino a che vegga restarsi inulto
                Di mia famiglia l'atroce insulto;
                E se al carnefice pur mi darete,
                Spettro terribile mi rivedrete,
                Portante in mano il teschio mio,
                Vendetta a chiedere al mondo, a Dio.

DUCA   Non più, arrestatelo!

RIGOLETTO   È matto!

BORSA, MARULLO, e CEPRANO
                Quai detti!

MONTERONE (*al Duca e Rigoletto*)
                Ah siate entrambi voi maledetti!

TUTTI   Ah!

MONTERONE   Slanciare il cane a leon morente
                È vile, o Duca ...
                                (*a Rigoletto*)
                E tu serpente,

DUKE   Ah, you always force the jest, etc.

BORSA   Yes, revenge!

MARULLO and CHORUS
         Yes, revenge!

DUKE and RIGOLETTO
         All is joy!

    The crowd of dancers invades the room.

ALL   All is feasting!
         All is joy, all is feasting;
         All invites us to enjoy ourselves!
         Ah look, doesn't this now seem
         The palace of pleasure!

MONTERONE (*from within*)
         Let me speak to him.

DUKE   No!

MONTERONE (*entering*)
         I wish it.

ALL   Monterone!

MONTERONE (*looking at the Duke, with noble pride*)
         Yes, Monterone . . .
         My voice like thunder
         Will strike you in any place.

RIGOLETTO (*to the Duke, imitating the voice of Monterone*)
         Let me speak to him.
            (*He comes forward with mock gravity.*)
         You plotted against us, sir.
         And we, truly clement, forgave you . . .
         What folly now seizes you, to make you
         Complain at all hours about your daughter's
           honor?

MONTERONE (*looking at Rigoletto, with contemptuous wrath*)
         A new affront! Ah yes, I'll come
         To disturb your orgies . . . I'll come to shout
         As long as I see the terrible insult
         To my family remain unavenged;
         And even if you give me to the executioner,
         You'll see me again, a terrible specter,
         Carrying my own skull in my hand,
         To ask vengeance of the world, of God.

DUKE   No more, arrest him!

RIGOLETTO   He's mad!

BORSA, MARULLO, and CEPRANO
         What words!

MONTERONE (*to the Duke and Rigoletto*)
         Ah, may you both be cursed!

ALL   Ah!

MONTERONE   To unleash the dog on a dying lion
         Is cowardly, O Duke . . .
            (*to Rigoletto*)
         And you, serpent,

Tu che d'un padre ridi al dolore,
Sii maledetto!

RIGOLETTO (*da sè, colpito*)
(Che sento! orrore!)

TUTTI   Oh tu che la festa audace hai turbato,
                     Da un genio d'inferno qui fosti guidato.

RIGOLETTO   (Orrore!)

TUTTI   È vano ogni detto, di qua t'allontana ...
                     Va, trema, o vegliardo, dell'ira sovrana,
                     Tu l'ha provocata, più speme non v'è,
                     Un'ora fatale fu questa per te.

RIGOLETTO   (Che orrore! che orrore!)

MONTERONE   Sii maledetto!
                     E tu serpente, ecc.

*Monterone parte fra due alabardieri. Tutti gli altri seguono
il Duca in altra stanza.*

ATTO PRIMO

PARTE SECONDA

*L'estremità d'una via cieca. A sinistra, una casa di discreta
apparenza con una piccola corte circondata da mura. Nella
corte un grosso ed alto albero ed un sedile di marmo; nel
muro, una porta che mette alla strada; sopra il muro, un terrazzo praticabile, sostenuto da arcate. La porta del primo piano
dà sul detto terrazzo, a cui si ascende per una scala di fronte.
A destra della via è il muro altissimo del giardino e un fianco
del palazzo di Ceprano. È notte.*
*Entra Rigoletto chiuso nel suo mantello. Sparafucile lo
segue, portando sotto il mantello una lunga spada.*

RIGOLETTO   (Quel vecchio maledivami!)

SPARAFUCILE   Signor ...

RIGOLETTO   Va, non ho niente.

SPARAFUCILE   Nè il chiesi ... A voi presente
                     Un uom di spada sta.

RIGOLETTO   Un ladro?

SPARAFUCILE   Un uom che libera
                     Per poco da un rivale.
                     E voi ne avete ...

RIGOLETTO   Quale?

SPARAFUCILE   La vostra donna è là.

RIGOLETTO   (Che sento!)
                     E quanto spendere
                     Per un signor dovrei?

SPARAFUCILE   Prezzo maggior vorrei.

RIGOLETTO   Com'usasi pagar?

                         Who laugh at a father's grief,
                         Be cursed!
RIGOLETTO (*to himself, stricken*)
                         (What do I hear? Oh, horror!)
ALL   Oh, you who have boldly disturbed the festivity,
                         Were led here by a demon from hell.
RIGOLETTO   (Horror!)
ALL   Any word is in vain, go away from here . . .
                         Go, tremble, old man, at the sovereign's wrath,
                         You provoked it, there's no hope for you now.
                         This was a fatal hour for you.
RIGOLETTO   (What horror! What horror!)
MONTERONE   Be cursed!
                         And you, serpent, etc.

*Monterone goes out between two halberdiers. All the others
follow the Duke into another room.*

ACT ONE

SCENE TWO

*The end of a blind alley. To the left, a modest-looking
house with a little courtyard surrounded by walls. In the
courtyard a tall, thick tree and a marble bench; in the wall a
door giving on the street; above the wall, a usable balcony,
supported by arches. The door of the upper floor opens onto
this balcony, which one reaches by a stairway opposite us.
To the right of the street are the very high wall of the garden
of Ceprano's palace and one flank of the building. It is night.*
   *Rigoletto enters, wrapped in his cloak. Sparafucile is follow-
ing him, with a long sword under his cloak.*

RIGOLETTO   (That old man cursed me!)
SPARAFUCILE   Sir . . .
RIGOLETTO   Go, I have nothing.
SPARAFUCILE   Nor did I ask anything . . . A swordsman
                Stands before you.
RIGOLETTO   A thief?
SPARAFUCILE   A man who can free you for little
                From a rival.
                And you have one . . .
RIGOLETTO   What?
SPARAFUCILE   Your woman is in there.
RIGOLETTO   (What do I hear!)
                And how much would I have to spend
                For a gentleman?
SPARAFUCILE   I would want a higher price.
RIGOLETTO   How are you usually paid?

SPARAFUCILE   Una metà s'anticipa,
               Il resto si dà poi ...
RIGOLETTO   (Demonio!) E come puoi
               Tanto securo oprar?
SPARAFUCILE   Soglio in cittade uccidere,
               Oppure nel mio tetto.
               L'uomo di sera aspetto ...
               Una stoccata, e muor.
RIGOLETTO   (Demonio!)
               E come in casa?
SPARAFUCILE   È facile ...
               M'aiuta mia sorella ...
               Per le vie danza ... è bella ...
               Chi voglio attira ... e allor ...
RIGOLETTO   Comprendo ...
SPARAFUCILE   Senza strepito ...
RIGOLETTO   Comprendo ...
SPARAFUCILE   (*mostra la spada*)
               È questo il mio strumento.
               Vi serve?
RIGOLETTO   No, al momento.
SPARAFUCILE   Peggio per voi ...
RIGOLETTO   Chi sa?
SPARAFUCILE   Sparafucil mi nomino ...
RIGOLETTO   Straniero?
SPARAFUCILE   (*per andarsene*)
               Borgognone.
RIGOLETTO   E dove, all'occasione?...
SPARAFUCILE   Qui sempre a sera.
RIGOLETTO   Va.
SPARAFUCILE   Sparafucil. Sparafucil.
RIGOLETTO   Va, va, va, va.

Sparafucile parte. Rigoletto gli guarda dietro.

RIGOLETTO   Pari siamo!... io la lingua, egli ha il pugnale;

               L'uomo son io che ride, ei quel che spegne!
               Quel vecchio maledivami!...
               O uomini!... o natura!
               Vil scellerato mi faceste voi!
               Oh rabbia! esser difforme!
               Oh rabbia! esser buffone!
               Non dover, non poter altro che ridere!...

               Il retaggio d'ogni uom m'è tolto: il pianto ...

               Questo padrone mio,
               Giovin, giocondo, sì possente, bello
               Sonnecchiando mi dice:
               Fa ch'io rida, buffone ...
               Forzarmi deggio e farlo!

SPARAFUCILE	One half is given in advance,
	The rest is given afterwards . . .
RIGOLETTO	(Demon!) And how are you able
	To work with such security?
SPARAFUCILE	I usually kill in the city,
	Or else under my roof.
	I wait for the man at evening . . .
	A thrust, and he dies.
RIGOLETTO	(Demon!)
	And how is he brought to your house?
SPARAFUCILE	It's easy . . .
	My sister helps me . . .
	She dances in the streets . . . she's beautiful . . .
	She attracts the one I want . . . and then . . .
RIGOLETTO	I understand . . .
SPARAFUCILE	Without any noise . . .
RIGOLETTO	I understand . . .
SPARAFUCILE	*(showing his sword)*
	This is my instrument.
	Do you need it?
RIGOLETTO	No, not at the moment.
SPARAFUCILE	So much the worse for you . . .
RIGOLETTO	Who knows?
SPARAFUCILE	Sparafucile is my name . . .
RIGOLETTO	A foreigner?
SPARAFUCILE	*(about to go)*
	Burgundian.
RIGOLETTO	And where, if the occasion rises? . . .
SPARAFUCILE	Always here in the evening.
RIGOLETTO	Go.
SPARAFUCILE	Sparafucil. Sparafucil.
RIGOLETTO	Go, go, go, go.

Sparafucile leaves. Rigoletto watches him go.

RIGOLETTO	We are equals! . . . I have my tongue, he has the dagger;
	I am the man who laughs, he, the one who kills!
	That old man cursed me! . . .
	O mankind! . . . O Nature!
	You made me base and wicked!
	Oh, fury! To be deformed!
	Oh, fury! To be a buffoon!
	Not allowed, not able to do anything but laugh! . . .
	Every man's release — weeping — is denied me . . .
	This master of mine,
	Young, gay, so powerful, handsome,
	Says to me, as he dozes:
	Make me laugh, buffoon . . .
	I must force myself, and do it!

Oh dannazione!
Odio a voi, cortigiani schernitori!...
Quanta in mordervi ho gioia!
Se iniquo son, per cagion vostra è solo.
Ma in altr'uomo qui mi cangio!
Quel vecchio maledivami ...
Tal pensiero perchè conturba ognor
La mente mia?...
Mi coglierà sventura?
Ah no! è follia!

Apre con chiave ed entra nel cortile. Gilda esce dalla casa
e si getta nelle sue braccia.

RIGOLETTO	Figlia!
GILDA	Mio padre!
RIGOLETTO	A te d'appresso Trova sol gioia il core oppresso.
GILDA	Oh quanto amore!
RIGOLETTO	Mia vita sei! Senza te in terra qual bene avrei?
GILDA	Oh quanto amore! Padre mio!
RIGOLETTO	Oh figlia mia!
	(*Sospira.*)
GILDA	Voi sospirate!... che v'ange tanto? Lo dite a questa povera figlia. Se v'ha mistero ... per lei sia franto ... Ch'ella conosca la sua famiglia ...
RIGOLETTO	Tu non le hai ...
GILDA	Qual nome avete?
RIGOLETTO	A te che importa?
GILDA	Se non volete di voi parlarmi ...

RIGOLETTO (*interrompendola*)
              Non uscir mai.

GILDA	Non vo che al tempio.
RIGOLETTO	Oh ben tu fai.
GILDA	Se non di voi, almen chi sia Fate ch'io sappia la madre mia.
RIGOLETTO	Deh non parlate al misero Del suo perduto bene ... Ella sentia, quell'angelo, Pietà, pietà delle mie pene ... Solo, difforme, povero, Per compassion mi amò. Ah! Moria ... moria ... Le zolle coprano Lievi quel capo amato. Sola or tu resti ... Sola or tu resti al misero. Dio, sii ringaziato!

Oh, damnation!
I hate you, scornful courtiers! . . .
What joy I feel in stinging you!
If I'm wicked, it's only because of you.
But here I'm changed into another man!
That old man cursed me . . .
Why does such a thought keep troubling
My mind? . . .
Will misfortune strike me?
Ah no! That is folly!

He unlocks the door and goes into the courtyard. Gilda comes out of the house and throws herself into his arms.

RIGOLETTO	Daughter!
GILDA	My father!
RIGOLETTO	My oppressed heart finds joy Only near you.
GILDA	Oh, such love!
RIGOLETTO	You are my life! Without you, what love would I have on earth?
GILDA	Oh, what love! My father!
RIGOLETTO	Oh, my daughter! (*He sighs.*)
GILDA	You sigh! . . . What worries you so? Tell your poor daughter. If there's some mystery . . . reveal it to her . . . Let her know about her family . . .
RIGOLETTO	You have none . . .
GILDA	What is your name?
RIGOLETTO	What does it matter to you?
GILDA	If you don't want to speak to me about yourself . . .

RIGOLETTO (*interrupting her*)
                    Never go out.

GILDA	I go only to church.
RIGOLETTO	Oh, that is well.
GILDA	If not of yourself, then at least Let me know who my mother is.
RIGOLETTO	Ah, don't speak to a poor wretch About his lost love . . . She, that angel, Felt pity for my sufferings . . . Alone, deformed, poor, She loved me out of compassion. Oh! . . . She died . . . she died . . . May the clods lightly cover That beloved head. Now only you remain . . . Only you remain to the wretch. God, be thanked!

GILDA   Oh quanto dolor! quanto dolor!
               Che spremere sì amaro pianto può?
               Padre, non più, non più, calmatevi ...
               Mi lacera tal vista!
               Il nome vostro ditemi,
               Il duol che sì v'attrista.

RIGOLETTO   A che nomarmi? è inutile.
               Padre ti sono, e basti.
               Me forse al mondo temono,
               D'alcuno ho forse gli asti ...
               Altri mi maledicono ...

GILDA   Patria, parenti, amici
               Voi dunque non avete?

RIGOLETTO   Patria! parenti! amici!
               Culto, famiglia, la patria,
               Il mio universo è in te!

GILDA   Ah se può lieto rendervi,
               Gioia è la vita a me!
               Già da tre lune son qui venuta,
               Nè la cittade ho ancor veduta;
               Se il concedete, farlo or potrei ...

RIGOLETTO   Mai, mai!...
               Uscita, dimmi, unqua sei?

GILDA   No.

RIGOLETTO   Guai!

GILDA   (Ah! che dissi!)

RIGOLETTO   Ben te ne guarda!
               (Potrien seguirla, rapirla ancora!
               Qui d'un buffone si disonora la figlia
               E se ne ride ... Orror!)
                                      (*verso la casa*)
               Olà?

Giovanna esce dalla casa.

GIOVANNA   Signor?

RIGOLETTO   Venendo mi vede alcuno?
               Bada, di' il vero.

GIOVANNA   Ah no, nessuno.

RIGOLETTO   Sta ben ...
               La porta che dà al bastione
               È sempre chiusa?

GIOVANNA   Ognor si sta.

RIGOLETTO (*a Giovanna*)
               Ah! veglia, o donna, questo fiore
               Che a te puro confidai;
               Veglia attenta, e non sia mai
               Che s'offuschi il suo candor.
               Tu dei venti dal furore,
               Ch'altri fiori hanno piegato,
               Lo difendi, e immacolato
               Lo ridona al genitor.

GILDA   Quanto affetto! quali cure!
               Che temete, padre mio?

GILDA	Oh, how much grief! How much grief! What can force such bitter tears? Father, no more, no more, be calm . . . This sight breaks my heart! Tell me your name. The grief that saddens you so.
RIGOLETTO	Why tell my name? It's useless. I'm your father; let that suffice. Perhaps people in the world fear me, Some perhaps may resent me . . . Others curse me . . .
GILDA	Have you then no homeland, No relatives or friends?
RIGOLETTO	Homeland! Relatives! Friends! Religion, family, and home, My universe is in you!
GILDA	Ah, if it can make you happy, Then my life is joy for me! I came here three months ago, And I still haven't seen the city; If you allow it, I could do so now . . .
RIGOLETTO	Never, never! . . . Tell me, have you gone out then?
GILDA	No.
RIGOLETTO	Beware!
GILDA	(Ah! What have I said?)
RIGOLETTO	Take care! (They could follow her, seize her even! Here they dishonor a jester's daughter And laugh about it . . . Horror!) (*toward the house*) Hola?

Giovanna comes out of the house.

GIOVANNA	Sir?
RIGOLETTO	When I come does anyone see me? Mind you, tell the truth.
GIOVANNA	Ah no, no one.
RIGOLETTO	Very well . . . The door that leads to the bastion Is always locked?
GIOVANNA	Always so.
RIGOLETTO (*to Giovanna*)	
	Ah! Woman, watch over this flower That I entrusted, pure, to you; Watch carefully, that her innocence Never be stained. From the fury of the winds That have bent other flowers, Defend her, and give her back, Untouched, to her father.
GILDA	Such affection! So much care! What do you fear, Father?

Lassù in cielo, presso Dio
Veglia un angiol protettor.
Da noi stoglie le sventure
Di mia madre il priego santo:
Non fia mai disvelto o franto
Questo a voi diletto fior.

RIGOLETTO   Ah! veglia, o donna, questo fiore
Che a te puro confi —
Alcun v'è fuori ...

*Il Duca compare nella strada in costume borghese. Rigo-
letto apre la porta della corte e, mentre esce a guardar sulla
strada, il Duca guizza furtivo nella corte e si nasconde dietro
l'albero; gettando a Giovanna una borsa, la fa tacere.*

GILDA   Cielo! Sempre novel sospetto.
RIGOLETTO *(a Giovanna, tornando)*
                 Alla chiesa vi seguiva mai nessuno?
GIOVANNA   Mai.
DUCA   (Rigoletto!)
RIGOLETTO   Se talor qui picchian,
                 Guardatevi d'aprire.
GIOVANNA   Nemmeno al Duca?
RIGOLETTO   Non che ad altri a lui!
                 Mia figlia, addio.
DUCA   (Sua figlia!)
GILDA   Addio, mio padre!
RIGOLETTO   Ah! veglia, o donna, ecc.
GILDA   Oh quanto affetto! ecc.
                 Padre, mio padre, addio!
RIGOLETTO   Figlia, mia figlia, addio!

S'abbracciano e Rigoletto parte, chiudendosi dietro la porta.

GILDA   Giovanna, ho dei rimorsi ...
GIOVANNA   E perchè mai?
GILDA   Tacqui che un giovin
                 Ne seguiva al tempio.
GIOVANNA   Perchè ciò dirgli?...
                 L'odiate dunque cotesto giovin, voi?
GILDA   No, no, chè troppo è bello
                 E spira amore ...
GIOVANNA   E magnanimo sembra ...
                 E gran signore.
GILDA   Signor nè principe io lo vorrei;
                 Sento che povero più l'amerei.
                 Sognando o vigile sempre lo chiamo,
                 E l'alma in estasi le dice, t'a —

*Il Duca esce improvviso, fa cenno a Giovanna d'andarsene,
e inginocchiandosi ai piedi di Gilda, termina la frase.*

Up in heaven, next to God
A protecting angel keeps watch.
The holy prayer of my mother
Keeps misfortunes from us:
May this flower that you love
Never be uprooted or broken.

RIGOLETTO   Ah! Woman, watch over this flower,
That I entrust —
Someone's outside . . .

The Duke appears in the street in humble clothes. Rigoletto opens the door of the courtyard and, as he goes out to look in the street, the Duke slips furtively into the courtyard and hides behind a tree; he silences Giovanna, throwing her a purse.

GILDA   Heavens! Always new suspicion.

RIGOLETTO (*to Giovanna, coming back*)
Did anyone ever follow you to church?

GIOVANNA   Never.

DUKE   (Rigoletto!)

RIGOLETTO   If they ever knock here,
Mind you don't open.

GIOVANNA   Not even to the Duke?

RIGOLETTO   To him least of all!
Farewell, Daughter.

DUKE   (His daughter!)

GILDA   Farewell, Father!

RIGOLETTO   Ah! Woman, watch over this flower, etc.

GILDA   Oh, such affection! etc.
Father, my father, farewell!

RIGOLETTO   Daughter, my daughter, farewell!

They embrace, then Rigoletto leaves, closing the door after him.

GILDA   Giovanna, I feel remorse . . .

GIOVANNA   And why?

GILDA   I didn't say that a young man
Followed us to church.

GIOVANNA   Why tell him that? . . .
Do you hate this young man, then?

GILDA   No, no, for he's too handsome
And he inspires love . . .

GIOVANNA   He seems magnanimous . . .
And a great gentleman.

GILDA   I wouldn't want him a gentleman or a prince;
I feel that I'd love him more if he were poor.
Dreaming or waking, I call him always,
And my soul in ecstasy says to him, I lo —

The Duke suddenly comes out, motions to Giovanna to go away, and kneels at Gilda's feet, concluding the phrase.

DUCA   T'amo!
                T'amo, ripetilo, sì caro accento
                Un puro schiudimi ciel di contento!

GILDA   Giovanna? Giovanna? Ahi misera!
                Non v'è più alcuno
                Che qui rispondami!
                Oh Dio!... nessuno?

DUCA   Son io coll'anima che ti rispondo ...
                Ah due che s'amano
                Son tutto un mondo!

GILDA   Chi mai, chi giungere vi fece a me?

DUCA   Se angelo o demone,
                Che importa a te? Io t'amo ...

GILDA   Uscitene ...

DUCA   Uscire! adesso!
                Ora che accendene un fuoco istesso!
                Ah inseparabile d'amore il dio
                Stringeva, o vergine, tuo fato al mio!
                È il sol dell'anima, la vita è amore,
                Sua voce è il palpito del nostro core ...
                E fama e gloria, potenza e trono,
                Umane, fragili qui cose sono:
                Una pur avvene, sola, divina,
                È amor che agl'angeli più ne avvicina!
                Adunque amiamoci, donna celeste,
                D'invidia agl'uomini sarò per te.

GILDA   (Ah de' miei vergini sogni son queste
                Le voci tenere, sì care a me!)

DUCA   Che m'ami, deh! ripetimi.

GILDA   L'udiste.

DUCA   Oh me felice!

GILDA   Il nome vostro ditemi;
                Saperlo non mi lice?

Ceprano e Borsa compaiono nella via.

CEPRANO (*a Borsa*)
                Il loco è qui ...

DUCA (*pensando*)
                Mi nomino ...

BORSA (*a Ceprano*)
                Sta ben!...

Borsa e Ceprano partono.

DUCA   ... Gualtier Maldè.
                Studente sono ... e povero.

GIOVANNA (*tornando spaventata*)
                Rumor di passi è fuori.

GILDA   Forse mio padre ...

DUCA   (Ah cogliere potessi il traditore
                Che sì mi sturba!)

GILDA (*a Giovanna*)
                Adducilo di qua al bastione ... or ite ...

DUKE   I love you!
      I love you: repeat it! Such beloved words
      Open a pure heaven of happiness to me!

GILDA   Giovanna? Giovanna? Ah, wretched me!
      Is there no one here
      Who will answer me!
      Oh, God! . . . No one?

DUKE   I am here, who answer you with my soul . . .
      Ah, two who love each other
      Are a whole world!

GILDA   Who, who made you come to me?

DUKE   Were it angel or devil,
      What does it matter to you? I love you . . .

GILDA   Leave . . .

DUKE   Leave? Now?
      Now that the same flame consumes us!
      Ah, the god of love, O maiden,
      Joined your fate inseparably to mine!
      Love is the sun of the soul, love is life,
      His voice is the beat of our hearts . . .
      And fame, glory, power, and throne,
      Here are human, fragile things:
      One thing alone is divine,
      It is love that brings us closest to the angels!
      So then let us love each other, heavenly girl,
      For you I'll be the envy of all men.

GILDA   (Ah, these are the tender words,
      So dear to me, of my virginal dreams!)

DUKE   Ah, say again that you love me.

GILDA   You heard it.

DUKE   How happy I am!

GILDA   Tell me your name;
      Am I not allowed to know it?

Ceprano and Borsa appear in the street.

CEPRANO (*to Borsa*)
      Here is the place . . .
DUKE (*thinking*)
      My name is . . .
BORSA (*to Ceprano*)
      Very well! . . .

Borsa and Ceprano leave.

DUKE   . . . Gualtier Maldè.
      I am a student . . . and poor.
GIOVANNA (*coming back, frightened*)
      There's a sound of footsteps outside.
GILDA   Perhaps my father . . .
DUKE   (Ah, if I could strike the traitor
      Who disturbs me thus!)
GILDA (*to Giovanna*)
      Lead him from here to the bastion...Go now...

DUCA   Di': m'amerai tu?
GILDA   E voi?
DUCA   L'intera vita ... poi ...
GILDA   Non più, non più ... partite ...

DUCA e GILDA   Addio, addio ... speranza ed anima
                Sol tu sarai per me!
                Addio, addio ... vivrà immutabile
                L'affetto mio per te.
                Addio! Addio!

*Il Duca esce scortato da Giovanna. Gilda resta fissando la
porta ond'è partito.*

GILDA   Gualtier Maldè!
                Nome di lui sì amato,
                Ti scolpisci nel core innamorato!
                Caro nome che il mio cor
                Festi primo palpitar,
                Le delizie dell'amor
                Mi dèi sempre rammentar!
                Col pensier il mio desir
                A te sempre volerà,
                E fin l'ultimo sospir,
                Caro nome, tuo sarà.
                Il mio desir a te
                Ognora volerà
                Fin l'ultimo sospiro
                Tuo sarà.

Sale al terrazzo con una lanterna.

                Gualtier Maldè ... Gualtier Maldè!
                Caro nome che il mio cor
                Festi primo palpitar ...

*Marullo, Ceprano, Borsa, cortigiani, armati e mascherati,
entrano nella via. Borsa indica Gilda agli altri.*

BORSA   È là.
GILDA   E fin l'ultimo sospir,
                Caro nome tuo sarà.
CEPRANO   Miratela.
CORTIGIANI   Oh quanto è bella!
MARULLO   Par fata od angiol.
GILDA   Gualtier Maldè! Gualtier Maldè ...
                                 (*entra in casa*)
CORTIGIANI   L'amante è quella di Rigoletto!
                Oh! quanto è bella!

Rigoletto viene per la via, concentrato.

RIGOLETTO   (Riedo!... perchè?)
BORSA (*agli altri*)
                Silenzio ... all'opra ... badate a me.

DUKE   Say: will you love me?
GILDA   And you?
DUKE   My whole life . . . then . . .
GILDA   No more, no more . . . leave . . .
DUKE and GILDA
                 Farewell, farewell . . . only you will be
                 Hope and spirit for me!
                 Farewell, farewell . . . my love for you
                 Will live unchangeable.
                 Farewell! Farewell!

*The Duke goes out, led by Giovanna. Gilda stands, looking
at the door by which he has left.*

GILDA   Gualtier Maldè!
                 Name of him I love so,
                 You are carved in my loving heart!
                 Dear name who first
                 Made my heart beat,
                 You must always remind me
                 Of the delights of love!
                 In my thoughts, my desire
                 Will always fly to you,
                 And even my last sigh
                 Will be yours, dear name.
                 My desire will always
                 Fly to you
                 And even my last sigh
                 Will be yours.

She goes up to the balcony with a lantern.

                 Gualtier Maldè . . . Gualtier Maldè!
                 Dear name who first
                 Made my heart beat . . .

*Marullo, Ceprano, Borsa, and courtiers, armed and wearing
masks, come into the street. Borsa points out Gilda to the
others.*

BORSA   There she is.
GILDA   And even my last sigh
                 Will be yours, dear name.
CEPRANO   Look at her.
COURTIERS   Oh, how beautiful she is!
MARULLO   She seems a fairy or an angel.
GILDA   Gualtier Maldè! Gualtier Maldè . . .
                      (*She goes into the house.*)
COURTIERS   That's the mistress of Rigoletto!
                 Oh! How beautiful she is!

Rigoletto comes along the street, pensive.

RIGOLETTO   (I'm returning! . . . Why?)
BORSA (*to the others*)
                 Silence . . . to our task . . . heed me.

RIGOLETTO   (Ah da quel vecchio fui maledetto!)
                    (*Urta in Borsa.*)
                 Chi va là?
BORSA (*ai compagni*)
                 Tacete ... c'è Rigoletto!
CEPRANO   Vittoria doppia!... l'uccideremo ...
BORSA   No, che domani più rideremo ...
MARULLO   Or tutto aggiusto ...
RIGOLETTO   Chi parla qua?
MARULLO   Ehi! Rigoletto ... Di'...
RIGOLETTO (*con voce terribile*)
                 Chi va là?
MARULLO   Eh non mangiarci! Son ...
RIGOLETTO   Chi?
MARULLO   Marullo.
RIGOLETTO   In tanto buio lo sguardo è nullo.
MARULLO   Qui ne condusse ridevol cosa ...
                 Torre a Ceprano vogliam la sposa.
RIGOLETTO   (Ahimè, respiro!)
                 Ma come entrare?
MARULLO (*a Ceprano*)
                 (La vostra chiave?)
                                      (*a Rigoletto*)
                 Non dubitare.
                 Non dee mancarci lo stratagemma ...
                    (*Gli dà la chiave avuta da Ceprano.*)
                 Ecco la chiave ...
RIGOLETTO (*palpando*)
                 Sento il suo stemma.
                 (Ah terror vano fu dunque il mio!)
                 N'è là il palazzo ... con voi son io.
MARULLO   Siam mascherati ...
RIGOLETTO   Ch'io pur mi mascheri;
                 A me una larva.
MARULLO   Sì, pronta è già.
                 Terrai la scala.

*Gli mette una maschera e nello stesso tempo lo benda con
un fazzoletto, e lo pone a reggere una scala, che avranno
appostata al terrazzo.*

RIGOLETTO   Fitta è la tenebra ...
MARULLO (*ai compagni*)
                 La benda cieco e sordo il fa.
BORSA, MARULLO, CEPRANO, e CORTIGIANI
                 Zitti, zitti moviamo a vendetta,
                 Ne sia colto or che men l'aspetta.
                 Derisore sì audace, costante
                 A sua volta schernito sarà!
                 Cheti, cheti, rubiamgli l'amante,
                 E la corte doman riderà.

RIGOLETTO   (Ah, I was cursed by that old man!)
            (*He bumps into Borsa.*)
            Who goes there?

BORSA (*to his companions*)
            Be quiet . . . it's Rigoletto!

CEPRANO   A double victory! . . . we'll kill him . . .

BORSA   No, for tomorrow we'll laugh all the more . . .

MARULLO   Now I'll arrange everything . . .

RIGOLETTO   Who's talking here?

MARULLO   Hey! Rigoletto . . . Tell me . . .

RIGOLETTO (*in a terrible voice*)
            Who goes there?

MARULLO   Eh, don't eat us! I'm . . .

RIGOLETTO   Who?

MARULLO   Marullo.

RIGOLETTO   In such darkness one's eyes are useless.

MARULLO   An amusing thing brought us here . . .
            We want to take Ceprano's wife from him.

RIGOLETTO   (Alas, I can breathe!)
            But how to enter?

MARULLO (*to Ceprano*)
            (Your key?)
                        (*to Rigoletto*)
            Never fear.
            Our stratagem shouldn't fail us . . .
            (*He gives him the key received from Ceprano.*)
            Here is the key . . .

RIGOLETTO (*feeling it*)
            I feel his coat-of-arms.
            (Ah, so my terror was useless!)
            His palace is there . . . I'm with you.

MARULLO   We are masked . . .

RIGOLETTO   Let me be masked too;
            Give me a disguise.

MARULLO   Yes, it's already prepared.
            You will hold the ladder.

He puts a mask on Rigoletto, and at the same time blind-folds him with a handkerchief, then sets him to hold a ladder, which the others have placed against the balcony.

RIGOLETTO   The darkness is thick . . .

MARULLO (*to his companions*)
            The blindfold makes him blind and deaf.

BORSA, MARULLO, CEPRANO, and COURTIERS
            Silent, silent, we move to our vengeance,
            Let it strike him now when he least expects it.
            The mocker, so bold and so constant,
            Will in his turn be mocked!
            Quiet, quiet, we will steal his mistress,
            And tomorrow the court will laugh.

Zitti, zitti, cheti, cheti,
Attenti all'opra, attenti all'opra.

*Alcuni salgono al terrazzo, rompono la porta del primo
piano, scendono, aprono ad altri che entrano dalla strada e
riescono trascinando Gilda, la quale avrà la bocca chiusa da
un fazzoletto. Nel traversare la scena ella perde una sciarpa.*

GILDA (*da lontano*)
            Soccorso, padre mio!
CORTIGIANI (*da lontano*)
            Vittoria!
GILDA (*più lontano*)
            Aita!
RIGOLETTO   Non han finito ancor!... qual derisione!
                        (*Si tocca gli occhi.*)
            Sono bendato!...

*Si strappa impetuosamente la benda e la maschera, ed al
chiarore d'una lanterna scordata riconosce la sciarpa, vede la
porta aperta. Entra, ne trae Giovanna spaventata; la fissa con
istupore, si strappa i capelli senza poter gridare. Finalmente,
dopo molti sforzi, esclama:*

RIGOLETTO   Ah! la maledizione!

Sviene.

ATTO SECONDO

*Salotto nel palazzo ducale. Vi sono due porte laterali, una
maggiore nel fondo che si chiude. Ai suoi lati pendono i ri-
tratti, in tutta figura, a sinistra del Duca, a destra della sua
sposa. V'ha un seggiolone presso una tavola coperta di velluto,
e altri mobili.*

Entra il Duca dal mezzo, agitato.

DUCA   Ella mi fu rapita!
            E quando, o ciel? Ne' brevi istanti,
            Prima che il mio presagio interno
            Sull'orma corsa ancora mi spingesse!
            Schiuso era l'uscio!...
            E la magion deserta!
            E dove ora sarà quel'angiol caro?
            Colei che prima potè in questo core
            Destar la fiamma di costanti affetti?
            Colei sì pura, al cui modesto sguardo
            Quasi spinto a virtù talor mi credo!
            Ella mi fu rapita!
            E chi l'ardiva?
            Ma ne avrò vendetta: lo chiede
            Il pianto della mia diletta.
            Parmi veder le lagrime

> Silent, silent, quiet, quiet,
> Mind the task, mind the task.

Some climb up to the balcony, break in the door of the upper floor, then come down and open to others, who enter from the street and come out dragging Gilda, her mouth bound with a handkerchief. Crossing the stage, she loses a scarf.

GILDA (*from a distance*)
> Help, Father!

COURTIERS (*from a distance*)
> Victory!

GILDA (*farther away*)
> Help!

RIGOLETTO   They still haven't finished! . . . What a joke!
> (*He touches his eyes.*)
> I'm blindfolded! . . .

He quickly rips off blindfold and mask, and in the light of a forgotten lantern recognizes the scarf, sees the open door. He goes in, and draws out the frightened Giovanna; he stares at her, stunned, tearing his hair, unable to shout. Finally, after many efforts, he exclaims:

RIGOLETTO   Ah! The curse!

He faints.

ACT TWO

Drawing room in the ducal palace. There are doors at either side, and a larger one in the back, which can be shut. To the left of it hangs a full-length portrait of the Duke; to the right, one of his wife. There is a large chair near a velvet-covered table, and other furniture.

The Duke comes in at the back, agitated.

DUKE   She was stolen from me!
> And when, O heaven? In the brief moments,
> Before my inner foreboding
> Drove me to retrace my footsteps!
> The door was open! . . .
> And the house deserted!
> And where can that beloved angel be now?
> She who could waken for the first time
> The flame of constant affection in this heart?
> She, so pure, by whose innocent gaze
> I believe myself almost impelled toward virtue!
> She was stolen from me!
> And who dared do it?
> But I'll have revenge:
> My beloved's weeping demands it.
> I seem to see the tears

Scorrenti da quel ciglio,
Quando fra il dubbio e l'ansia
Del subito periglio,
Dell'amor nostro memore,
Il suo Gualtier chiamò.
Ned ei potea soccorrerti,
Cara fanciulla amata;
Ei che vorria dell'anima
Farti quaggiù beata;
Ei che le sfere agl'angeli
Per te non invidiò.

Entrano Marullo, Ceprano, Borsa, ed altri cortigiani dal mezzo.

TUTTI	Duca, duca!
DUCA	Ebben?
TUTTI	L'amante fu rapita a Rigoletto!
DUCA	Come? e donde?
TUTTI	Dal suo tetto.
DUCA	Ah, ah! dite, come fu?

Siede.

TUTTI   Scorrendo uniti remota via,
Brev'ora dopo caduto il dì,
Come previsto ben s'era in pria,
Rara beltà ci si scoprì.
Era l'amante di Rigoletto,
Che, vista appena, si dileguò.
Già di rapirla s'avea il progetto,
Quando il buffon vêr noi spuntò,
Che di Ceprano noi la contessa
Rapir volessimo, stolto, credè;
La scala quindi all'uopo messa,
Bendato ei stesso ferma tenè.
Salimmo e rapidi la giovinetta
A noi riusciva quindi asportar.

DUCA   (Cielo! è dessa la mia diletta!)
TUTTI   Quand'ei s'accorse della vendetta
Restò scornato ad imprecar!

DUCA (*ai cortigiani*)
        Ma dove or trovasi la poveretta?

TUTTI   Fu da noi stessi addotta or qui.

DUCA (*alzandosi con gioia*)
        (Ah tutto il ciel non mi rapì!)
        * [Possente amor mi chiama,
Volar io deggio a lei;
Il serto mio darei
Per consolar quel cor.
Ah! sappia alfin chi l'ama,
Conosca alfin chi sono,
Apprenda ch'anco in trono

* Brackets denote passages often omitted in performance.

Flowing from those eyelids,
When between doubt and anguish
At the sudden danger,
Remembering our love,
She called for her Gaultier.
Nor could he help you,
Dear, beloved maiden;
He who with all his soul
Would like to make you blissful on earth;
He who, thanks to you, did not envy
The angels their heavenly spheres.

Enter Marullo, Ceprano, Borsa, and other courtiers from the back.

ALL	Duke, Duke!
DUKE	Well?
ALL	Rigoletto's mistress was carried off!
DUKE	How? From where?
ALL	From under his roof.
DUKE	Ha, ha! Tell me, how did it go?

He sits down.

ALL   Running together along a remote street,
A short time after day was done,
As we had clearly foreseen,
A rare beauty was revealed to us.
This was the mistress of Rigoletto,
Who, barely seen, disappeared.
We had already planned to seize her,
When the buffoon turned up, coming toward us.
The fool believed that we
Wanted to steal Ceprano's countess;
So, blindfolded, he himself
Held fast the ladder placed for the task.
We climbed up and then quickly
Were enabled to carry off the young girl.

DUKE   (Heaven! She is my beloved!)

ALL   When he realized our vengeance
He was left, cheated, and cursing!

DUKE *(to the courtiers)*
But where is the poor girl now?

ALL   We have brought her here now ourselves.

DUKE *(rising with joy)*
(Ah, heaven didn't take all from me!)
Powerful love summons me,
I want to fly to her;
I would give my crown
To console that heart.
Ah! Let her know at last who loves her,
Let her know at last who I am,
Let her learn that even on thrones

Ha degli schiavi Amor.
TUTTI   (Oh qual pensiero l'agita?
                     Come cangiò d'umor!)]

Il Duca esce frettoloso dal mezzo. Rigoletto entra dalla
destra cantarellando con represso dolore.

MARULLO   Povero Rigoletto!
RIGOLETTO   La rà, la rà, la rà, la rà ...
TUTTI   Ei vien! Silenzio!
RIGOLETTO   La rà, la rà, la rà, la rà ...
TUTTI   Oh buon giorno, Rigoletto!
RIGOLETTO   (Han tutti fatto il colpo!)
CEPRANO   Ch'hai di nuovo, buffon?
RIGOLETTO (*imitandolo*)
                     Ch'hai di nuovo, buffon?
                     Che dell'usato più noioso voi siete.
TUTTI   Ah! ah! ah!
RIGOLETTO (*spiando inquieto dovunque*)
                     La rà, la rà, la rà, la rà ...
                     (Ove l'avran nascosta?)
TUTTI   (Guardate com'è inquieto!)
RIGOLETTO (*a Marullo*)
                     Son felice che nulla a voi nuocesse
                     L'aria di questa notte.
MARULLO   Questa notte!
RIGOLETTO   Sì ... Oh fu il bel colpo!
MARULLO   S'ho dormito sempre.
RIGOLETTO   Ah voi dormiste!
                     Avrò dunque sognato!
                     La rà, la rà, la rà ...

S'allontana e vedendo un fazzoletto sopra una tavola ne
osserva inquieto la cifra.

TUTTI   (Ve', come tutto osserva!)
RIGOLETTO (*gettando il fazzoletto*)
                     (Non è il suo.)
                     Dorme il Duca tuttor?
TUTTI   Sì, dorme ancora.

Entra un paggio della Duchessa.

PAGGIO   Al suo sposo parlar vuol la Duchessa.
CEPRANO   Dorme.
PAGGIO   Qui or or con voi non era?
BORSA   È a caccia.
PAGGIO   Senza paggi! Senz'armi!
TUTTI   E non capisci che per ora
                     Vedere non può alcuno.

Il paggio esce. Rigoletto a parte è stato attentissimo al
dialogo. Balzando improvviso tra loro prorompe:

| | Love has slaves. |
| ALL | (Oh, what thought disturbs him? How his mood changed!) |

The Duke goes quickly out of the door at the back. Rigoletto comes in at right, singing softly, with repressed grief.

MARULLO	Poor Rigoletto!
RIGOLETTO	La rà, la rà, la rà, la rà . . .
ALL	He's coming! Silence!
RIGOLETTO	La rà, la rà, la rà, la rà . . .
ALL	Oh, good day, Rigoletto!
RIGOLETTO	(They all did the deed!)
CEPRANO	What's new, buffoon?
RIGOLETTO (*imitating him*)	What's new, buffoon? That you're even more tiresome than usual.
ALL	Ha! Ha! Ha!
RIGOLETTO (*looking nervously everywhere*)	La rà, la rà, la rà, la rà . . . (Where can they have hidden her?)
ALL	(Look how uneasy he is!)
RIGOLETTO (*to Marullo*)	I'm happy that last night's air Did you no harm.
MARULLO	Last night!
RIGOLETTO	Yes . . . Ah, it was a fine jest!
MARULLO	But I slept all night.
RIGOLETTO	Ah, you slept! I must have dreamed then! La rà, la rà, la rà . . .

He leaves. Seeing a handkerchief on a table, he nervously examines the initials.

ALL	(Look, how he observes everything!)
RIGOLETTO (*throwing down the handkerchief*)	(It's not hers.) Is the Duke still asleep?
ALL	Yes, he's still sleeping.

A page of the Duchess enters.

PAGE	The Duchess wishes to speak to her husband.
CEPRANO	He's asleep.
PAGE	Wasn't he with you here just now?
BORSA	He's gone hunting.
PAGE	Without pages? Without arms?
ALL	Don't you understand He can't see anyone for the moment?

The page goes out. Rigoletto, to one side, has followed the dialogue closely. He suddenly leaps into their midst and cries out:

RIGOLETTO	Ah, ella è qui dunque! Ella è col Duca!...
TUTTI	Chi?
RIGOLETTO	La giovin che stanotte Al mio tetto rapiste ... Ma la saprò riprender ... Ella è là ...
TUTTI	Se l'amante perdesti, La ricerca altrove.
RIGOLETTO	Io vo' mia figlia ...
TUTTI	La sua figlia!
RIGOLETTO	Sì, la mia figlia ... d'una tal vittoria ... Che?... adesso non ridete?

Egli corre verso la porta di mezzo, ma i cortigiani gli attraversano il passaggio.

RIGOLETTO Ella è là ... La voglio!
La renderete!
Cortigiani, vil razza dannata,
Per qual prezzo vendeste il mio bene?
A voi nulla per l'oro sconviene!...
Ma mia figlia è impagabil tesor.
La rendete ... o, se pur disarmata,
Questa man per voi fora cruenta;
Nulla in terra più l'uomo paventa,
Se dei figli difende l'onor.

Si getta ancor sulla porta che gli è nuovamente contesa dai gentiluomini.

Quella porta, assassini, assassini,
M'aprite, la porta, la porta, m'aprite!

Lotta alquanto, poi ritorna spossato sul davanti della scena.

Ah! voi tutti ... a me contro ... venite!
Tutti contro me! Ah!

Egli piange.

Ebben, piango ... Marullo ... signore ...
Tu ch'hai l'alma gentil come il core,
Dimmi tu dove l'hanno nascosta?
Marullo ... signore ...
Dimmi tu dove l'hanno nascosta?
E là? non è vero? E là? non è vero?
Tu taci! ohimè!
Miei signori ... perdono, pietate ...
Al vegliardo la figlia ridate ...
Ridonarla a voi nulla ora costa,
Tutto, tutto al mondo è tal figlia per me.
Signori, perdon, pietà ...
Ridate a me la figlia;
Tutto al mondo è tal figlia per me!
Pietà, signori, pietà!

Gilda esce dalla stanza a sinistra e si getta nelle braccia del padre.

RIGOLETTO	Ah, she is here then! She is with the Duke! . . .
ALL	Who?
RIGOLETTO	The young girl that you stole From under my roof last night . . . But I'll get her back . . . She is there . . .
ALL	If you've lost your mistress, Seek her elsewhere.
RIGOLETTO	I want my daughter . . .
ALL	His daughter!
RIGOLETTO	Yes, my daughter . . . What? Aren't you laughing now, at such a victory?

He runs toward the door in the center, but the courtiers block his way.

RIGOLETTO	She is there . . . I want her! You will give her back! Courtiers! Vile, damned race, For what price did you sell my happiness? There is nothing you won't do for gold! . . . But my daughter is a priceless treasure. Give her back . . . or, even disarmed, This hand will be bloodstained because of you; A man no longer fears anything on earth, If he is defending his children's honor.

He throws himself again toward the door, which is again blocked by the courtiers.

> That door, murderers, murderers,
> Open that door for me! Open the door!

He struggles for a while, then, exhausted, comes downstage.

> Ah! All of you . . . against me . . . come!
> All against me! Ah!

He weeps.

> Very well, I weep . . . Marullo . . . Lord . . .
> You, whose spirit is kind, like your heart,
> You, tell me where they've hidden her?
> Marullo . . . Lord . . .
> Tell me where they've hidden her?
> She's there, isn't she? She's there, isn't she?
> You're silent! Alas!
> My Lords . . . forgive me, have pity . . .
> Give the old man back his daughter . . .
> To give her back now costs you nothing,
> This daughter is all the world to me.
> Lords, forgive me, pity . . .
> Give me back my daughter;
> This daughter is all the world to me!
> Pity, Lords, pity!

Gilda comes out of the room at left and throws herself into her father's arms.

GILDA   Mio padre!
RIGOLETTO Dio! mia Gilda!
Signori ... in essa ... è tutta
La mia famiglia ...
        (a Gilda)
Non temer più nulla, angelo mio ...
        (ai cortigiani)
Fu scherzo!... non è vero?
Io che pur piansi or rido ...
        (a Gilda)
E tu a che piangi?
GILDA   Ah! l'onta, padre mio!
RIGOLETTO Cielo! che dici?
GILDA   Arrossir voglio innanzi a voi soltanto ...
RIGOLETTO *(volgendosi autoritario ai cortigiani)*
Ite di qua, voi tutti ...
Se il Duca vostro d'appressarsi osasse,
Ch'ei non entri, gli dite,
E ch'io ci sono.

Si abbandona sul seggiolone.

TUTTI   (Coi fanciulli e co' dementi
Spesso giova simular;
Partiam pur, ma quel ch'ei tenti
Non lasciamo d'osservar.)

Escono dal mezzo e chiudono la porta.

RIGOLETTO Parla, siam soli.
GILDA   (Ciel! dammi coraggio!)
Tutte le feste al tempio
Mentre pregava Iddio,
Bello e fatale un giovane
Offriasi al guardo mio ...
Se i labbri nostri tacquero,
Dagl'occhi il cor parlò.
Furtivo fra le tenebre
Sol ieri a me giungeva ...
Sono studente, povero,
Commosso mi diceva,
E con ardente palpito
Amor mi protestò.
Partì ... partì ...
Il mio core aprivasi
A speme più gradita,
Quando improvvisi apparvero
Color che m'han rapita,
E a forza qui m'addussero
Nell'ansia più crudel.
RIGOLETTO Ah!
(Solo per me l'infamia
A te chiedeva, o Dio ...
Ch'ella potesse ascendere
Quanto caduto er'io ...

GILDA	Father!

RIGOLETTO	God! My Gilda!
	Lords . . . in her . . . lies
	All my family . . .
	     (to Gilda)
	Fear no more, my angel . . .
	     (to the courtiers)
	It was a joke! . . . Wasn't it?
	I, who also wept, now laugh . . .
	     (to Gilda)
	And why are you weeping?

GILDA	Ah! The shame, Father!
RIGOLETTO	Heaven! What are you saying?
GILDA	I want to blush before you alone . . .
RIGOLETTO *(turning authoritatively to the courtiers)*	Get away from here, all of you . . . If your Duke dares approach, Tell him not to enter, And that I am here.

He sinks back on the ducal chair.

ALL	(With children and madmen It often helps to feign; Let us leave then, but we won't stop Observing what he may attempt.)

They go out at the back, closing the door.

RIGOLETTO	Speak, we are alone.
GILDA	(Heaven! Give me courage!) Every holiday, at the church, As I was praying to God, A young man, handsome and fatal, Presented himself to my gaze . . . If our lips were silent, Our hearts spoke through our eyes. Furtively, in the darkness, Only yesterday he came to me . . . I am a student, and poor, He said to me, moved, And with ardent impulsiveness He protested his love for me. He left . . . he left . . . My heart opened To most welcome hope, When suddenly there appeared The men who carried me off, And brought me here by force In the most cruel anxiety.
RIGOLETTO	Ah! (For myself alone, O God, I asked this infamy of you . . . So that she could rise up As far as I had fallen . . .

Ah! presso del patibolo
Bisogna ben l'altare!...
Ma tutto, tutto ora scompare ...
L'altare si rovesciò!)
Ah! piangi, piangi, fanciulla!

GILDA   Padre!

RIGOLETTO   Scorrer fa il pianto sul mio cor.

GILDA   Padre, in voi parla un angel
             Per me consolator.

RIGOLETTO   Compiuto pur quanto a fare mi resta,
             Lasciare potremo quest'aura funesta.

GILDA   Sì.

RIGOLETTO   (E tutto un sol giorno cangiare potè!)

*Entra un Usciere e il Conte di Monterone, che dalla destra
attraversa il fondo della sala fra gli alabardieri.*

USCIERE   Schiudete ... ire al carcere
             Monteron dee.

Monterone si ferma verso il ritratto del Duca.

MONTERONE   Poichè fosti invano da me maledetto,
             Nè un fulmine o un ferro colpiva il tuo petto,
             Felice pur anco, o Duca, vivrai.

Esce fra le guardie dal mezzo.

RIGOLETTO   No, vecchio, t'inganni ...
             Un vindice avrai.
             Sì, vendetta, tremenda vendetta
             Di quest'anima è solo desio ...
             Di punirti già l'ora affretta
             Che fatale per te tuonerà.
             Come fulmine scagliato da Dio,
             Te colpire il buffone saprà.

GILDA   O mio padre, qual gioia feroce
             Balenarvi negli'occhi vegg'io!...

RIGOLETTO   Vendetta!

GILDA   Perdonate, a noi pure una voce
             Di perdono dal cielo verrà.
             Perdonate!

RIGOLETTO   No!

GILDA   (Mi tradiva, pur l'amo, gran Dio!
             Per l'ingrato ti chiedo pietà.)

RIGOLETTO   Come fulmin scagliato da Dio, ecc.

GILDA   Perdonate, a noi pure, ecc.

Escono dal mezzo.

ATTO TERZO

*La sponda destra del Mincio. A sinistra è una casa a due
piani, mezzo diroccata, la cui fronte, volta allo spettatore,*

Ah! Beside the gallows
There must surely be an altar! . . .
But now all, all disappears . . .
The altar is overturned!)
Ah! Weep, weep, child!

GILDA   Father!

RIGOLETTO   Let your tears flow on my heart.

GILDA   Father, in you a consoling angel
            Speaks for me.

RIGOLETTO   When what I must do is done,
            We can leave this fatal air.

GILDA   Yes.

RIGOLETTO   (And a single day could change everything!)

*A footman enters with Count Monterone, who crosses the
back of the room from the right between halberdiers.*

FOOTMAN   Open . . . Monterone must go
            To the prison.

Monterone stops before the portrait of the Duke.

MONTERONE   Since you were cursed by me in vain,
            And no thunderbolt or sword struck your breast,
            You will live happily still, O Duke.

He goes out at the back between guards.

RIGOLETTO   No, old man, you are wrong . . .
            You will have an avenger.
            Yes, vengeance, terrible vengeance
            Is the sole desire of my spirit . . .
            To punish you, already the hour presses
            That will strike fatally for you.
            Like a thunderbolt hurled by God,
            The buffoon will be able to strike you.

GILDA   O Father, what fierce joy
            I see flashing in your eyes! . . .

RIGOLETTO   Vengeance!

GILDA   Forgive him, and a voice of forgiveness
            Will come for us, too, from heaven.
            Forgive him!

RIGOLETTO   No!

GILDA   (He betrayed me, yet I love him, God!
            I ask your mercy on the ungrateful one.)

RIGOLETTO   Like a thunderbolt hurled by God, etc.

GILDA   Forgive him, and a voice, etc.

They go out at the back.

ACT THREE

*The right bank of the Mincio. To the left, a half-ruined,
two-story house; the front of it, facing the spectator, has a*

lascia vedere per una grande arcata l'interno d'una rustica
osteria al pian terreno, ed una rozza scala che mette al gra-
naio, entro cui, da un balcone senza imposte, si vede un
lettuccio. Nella facciata che guarda la strada è una porta che
s'apre per di dentro; il muro poi è sì pieno di fessure, che dal
di fuori si può facilmente scorgere quanto avviene nell'interno.
Il resto del teatro rappresenta la deserta parte del Mincio, che
nel fondo scorre dietro un parapetto in mezza ruina; di là
dal fiume è Mantova. È notte.
    Gilda e Rigoletto inquieto sono sulla strada. Sparafucile
nell'interno dell'osteria, seduto presso una tavola, sta ripu-
lendo il suo cinturone senza nulla intendere di quanto accade
al di fuori.

RIGOLETTO	E l'ami?
GILDA	Sempre.
RIGOLETTO	Pure tempo a guarirne t'ho lasciato.
GILDA	Io l'amo!
RIGOLETTO	Povero cor di donna!...
	Ah il vile infame!
	Ma ne avrai vendetta, o Gilda!
GILDA	Pietà, mio padre!
RIGOLETTO	E se tu certa fossi
	Ch'ei ti tradissi, l'ameresti ancora?
GILDA	Nol so ... ma pur m'adora.
RIGOLETTO	Egli?
GILDA	Sì.

    Rigoletto la conduce presso una della fessure del muro, ed
ella vi guarda.

RIGOLETTO	Ebben, osserva dunque.
GILDA	Un uomo vedo.
RIGOLETTO	Per poco attendi.

    Il Duca, in assisa di semplice ufficiale di cavalleria, entra
nella sala terrena per una porta a sinistra.

GILDA *(trasalendo)*	
	Ah padre mio!
DUCA *(a Sparafucile)*	
	Due cose, e tosto ...
SPARAFUCILE	Quali?
DUCA	Una stanza e del vino ...
RIGOLETTO	(Son questi i suoi costumi!)
SPARAFUCILE	(Oh il bel zerbino!)

    Egli entra nella stanza vicina.

DUCA	La donna è mobile
	Qual piùm al vento,
	Muta d'accento
	E di pensiero.
	Sempre un amabile
	Leggiadro viso,

great arch through which one can see a rustic inn on the ground floor, and a rough stair that leads to the loft, where a bed can be seen, beyond a balcony without shutters. In the side toward the road there is a door that opens in; the wall is full of crevices, so that from outside one can easily see what is going on within. The rest of the scene represents a deserted part of the Mincio, which flows in the back beyond a half-ruined parapet; beyond the river lies Mantua. It is night.

Gilda and the uneasy Rigoletto are on the road. Sparafucile, inside the inn, is sitting at a table, polishing his belt. He can hear nothing of what happens outside.

RIGOLETTO	And you love him?
GILDA	Forever.
RIGOLETTO	Yet I gave you time to be cured of it.
GILDA	I love him!
RIGOLETTO	Poor woman's heart! . . . Ah, the vile wretch! But you'll have revenge, O Gilda!
GILDA	Have pity, Father!
RIGOLETTO	And if you were certain He betrayed you, would you love him still?
GILDA	I don't know . . . but anyway he adores me.
RIGOLETTO	He?
GILDA	Yes.

Rigoletto leads her to one of the crevices in the wall, and she looks inside.

RIGOLETTO	Very well, watch then.
GILDA	I see a man.
RIGOLETTO	Wait a little.

The Duke, in a simple cavalry officer's uniform, comes into the ground-floor room through a door at left.

GILDA (*starting*)
      Ah, Father!
DUKE (*to Sparafucile*)
      Two things, and quickly . . .

SPARAFUCILE	What?
DUKE	A room and some wine . . .
RIGOLETTO	(These are his ways!)
SPARAFUCILE	(Oh the handsome wastrel!)

He goes into the next room.

DUKE
      Woman is fickle
      Like a feather in the wind,
      She changes her words
      And her thoughts.
      Always a lovable
      And lovely face,

In pianto o in riso,
È menzognero.
È sempre misero
Chi a lei s'affida,
Chi le confida
Mal cauto il core!
Pur mai non sentesi
Felice appieno
Chi su quel seno
Non liba amore!
La donna è mobil, ecc.

*Sparafucile rientra con una bottiglia di vino e due bicchieri
che depone sulla tavola; quindi batte col pomo della sua
lunga spada due colpi al soffitto. A quel segnale una ridente
giovane, in costume da zingara, scende a salti la scala: il
Duca corre per abbracciarla, ma ella gli sfugge. Frattanto
Sparafucile, uscito sulla via, dice a parte a Rigoletto:*

SPARAFUCILE   È là il vostr'uomo ...
                Viver dee o morire?
RIGOLETTO   Più tardi tornerò l'opra a compire.

*Sparafucile si allontana dietro la casa verso il fiume. Gilda
e Rigoletto rimangono sulla via, il Duca e Maddalena nel
piano terreno.*

DUCA   Un dì, se ben rammentomi,
                O bella, t'incontrai ...
                Mi piacque di te chiedere,
                E intesi che qui stai.
                Or sappi, che d'allora
                Sol te quest'alma adora!
GILDA   Iniquo!
MADDALENA   Ah, ah!... e vent'altre appresso
                Le scorda forse adesso?
                Ha un'aria il signorino
                Da vero libertino ...
DUCA (*per abbracciarla*)
                Sì ... un mostro son ...
GILDA   Ah padre mio!
MADDALENA   Lasciatemi, stordito.
DUCA   Ih, che fracasso!
MADDALENA   Stia saggio.
DUCA   E tu sii docile,
                Non fare tanto chiasso.
                Ogni saggezza chiudesi
                Nel gaudio e nell'amore.
                    (*Le prende la mano.*)
                La bella mano candida!
MADDALENA   Scherzate voi, signore.
DUCA   No, no.
MADDALENA   Son brutta.

Weeping or laughing,
Is lying.
The man's always wretched
Who believes in her,
Who recklessly entrusts
His heart to her!
And yet one who never
Drinks love on that breast
Never feels
Entirely happy!
Woman is fickle, etc.

Sparafucile comes back in with a bottle of wine and two glasses, which he sets on the table; then he strikes the ceiling twice with the hilt of his long sword. At this signal, a laughing young girl, in gypsy dress, leaps down the stairs: the Duke runs to embrace her, but she escapes him. Meanwhile Sparafucile has gone out into the road, where he says softly to Rigoletto:

SPARAFUCILE Your man is there . . .
Must he live or die?

RIGOLETTO I'll return later to complete the deed.

Sparafucile goes off behind the house toward the river. Gilda and Rigoletto remain in the street, the Duke and Maddalena on the ground floor.

DUKE One day, if I remember right,
I met you, O beauty . . .
I was pleased to ask about you,
And I learned that you live here.
Know then, that since that time
My soul adores only you!

GILDA Villain!

MADDALENA Ha, ha! . . . And does it now perhaps
Forget twenty others?
The young gentleman looks like
A true libertine . . .

DUKE (*starting to embrace her*)
Yes . . . I'm a monster . . .

GILDA Ah, Father!

MADDALENA Let me go, foolish man!

DUKE Ah, what a fuss!

MADDALENA Be good.

DUKE And you, be yielding,
Don't make so much noise.
All wisdom concludes
In pleasure and in love.
      (*He takes her hand.*)
What a lovely, white hand!

MADDALENA You're joking, sir.

DUKE No, no.

MADDALENA I'm ugly.

DUCA	Abbracciami.
GILDA	Iniquo!
MADDALENA	Ebro!
DUCA	D'amor ardente.
MADDALENA	Signor l'indifferente,
	Vi piace canzonar?
DUCA	No, no, ti vo' sposar.
MADDALENA	Ne voglio la parola.
DUCA (*ironico*)	Amabile figliuola!

RIGOLETTO (*a Gilda che avrà tutto osservato e inteso*)
            E non ti basta ancor?

GILDA	Iniquo traditor!
MADDALENA	Ne voglio la parola.
DUCA	Amabile figliuola!
RIGOLETTO	E non ti basta ancor?
DUCA	Bella figlia dell'amore,
	Schiavo son de' vezzi tuoi;
	Con un detto sol tu puoi
	Le mie pene consolar.
	Vieni, e senti del mio core
	Il frequente palpitar ...
	Con un detto sol tu puoi
	Le mie pene consolar.
MADDALENA	Ah! ah! rido ben di core,
	Chè tai baie costan poco.
GILDA	Ah! così parlar d'amore ...
MADDALENA	Quanto valga il vostro gioco,
	Mel credete, so apprezzar.
GILDA	... a me pur l'infame ho udito!

RIGOLETTO (*a Gilda*)
            Taci, il piangere non vale.

GILDA	Infelice cor tradito,
	Per angoscia non scoppiar. Ah, no!
MADDALENA	Son avvezza, bel signore,
	Ad un simile scherzare.
	Mio bel signor!
DUCA	Bella figlia dell'amore, ecc.
	Vieni!
RIGOLETTO	Ch'ei mentiva sei sicura.
	Taci, e mia sarà la cura
	La vendetta d'affrettar.
	Sì, pronta fia, sarà fatale,
	Io saprollo fulminar.
	Taci, taci ...
	M'odi!... ritorna a casa ...
	Oro prendi, un destriero,
	Una veste viril che t'apprestai,
	E per Verona parti,
	Sarovvi io pur doman.
GILDA	Or venite.

DUKE	Embrace me.
GILDA	Villain!
MADDALENA	You're drunk!
DUKE	With ardent love!
MADDALENA	My indifferent sir, Do you enjoy teasing?
DUKE	No, no, I want to marry you.
MADDALENA	I want your word.
DUKE (*ironic*)	Lovable maiden!
RIGOLETTO (*to Gilda, who has seen and heard all*)	
	Isn't that enough for you yet?
GILDA	Villainous betrayer!
MADDALENA	I want your word.
DUKE	Lovable maiden!
RIGOLETTO	Isn't that enough for you yet?
DUKE	Beautiful daughter of love, I am the slave of your charms; With a single word you can Console my sufferings. Come, and feel the quick beating Of my heart . . . With a single word you can Console my sufferings.
MADDALENA	Ha! Ha! I laugh heartily, For such tales cost little.
GILDA	Ah! To speak thus of love . . .
MADDALENA	Believe me, I can judge How much your game is worth.
GILDA	. . . I too have heard the villain so!
RIGOLETTO (*to Gilda*)	
	Hush, weeping is of no avail.
GILDA	Unhappy, betrayed heart, Do not burst with anguish. Ah, no!
MADDALENA	I'm accustomed, handsome sir, To similar joking. My handsome sir!
DUKE	Beautiful daughter of love, etc. Come!
RIGOLETTO	You are sure that he was lying. Hush, and I will take care To hasten vengeance. Yes, it will be swift and fatal, I will know how to strike him down. Hush, hush . . . Hear me! . . . Go back home . . . Take gold, a horse, Man's clothing that I prepared for you, And leave for Verona, I too will be there tomorrow.
GILDA	Come now.

RIGOLETTO   Impossibil.
GILDA   Tremo.
RIGOLETTO   Va!

Gilda parte. Durante questa scena e la seguente il Duca e
Maddalena stanno fra loro parlando, ridendo, bevendo. Partita
Gilda, Rigoletto va dietro la casa, e ritorna parlando con
Sparafucile e contandogli delle monete.

RIGOLETTO   Venti scudi, hai tu detto?...
              Eccone dieci; e dopo l'opra il resto.
              Ei qui rimane?
SPARAFUCILE   Sì.
RIGOLETTO   Alla mezzanotte ritornerò.
SPARAFUCILE   Non cale.
              A gettarlo nel fiume basto io solo.
RIGOLETTO   No, no, il vo' far io stesso.
SPARAFUCILE   Sia! Il suo nome?
RIGOLETTO   Vuoi saper anche il mio?
              Egli è *Delitto, Punizion* son io.

Parte. Il cielo si oscura e tuona.

SPARAFUCILE   La tempesta è vicina!...
              Più scura fia la notte!
DUCA (*per prenderla*)
              Maddalena!
MADDALENA (*sfuggendogli*)
              Aspettate ... mio fratello viene ...
DUCA   Che importa?
MADDALENA   Tuona!
SPARAFUCILE (*entrando*)
              E pioverà fra poco.
DUCA   Tanto meglio!
                        (*a Sparafucile*)
              Tu dormirai in scuderia ...
              All'inferno ... ove vorrai ...
SPARAFUCILE   Oh grazie!
MADDALENA (*piano al Duca*)
              Ah no, partite.
DUCA (*a Maddalena*)
              Con tal tempo?
SPARAFUCILE (*piano a Maddalena*)
              Son venti scudi d'oro.
                        (*al Duca*)
              Ben felice d'offrirvi una stanza,
              Se a voi piace,
              Tosto a vederla andiamo.
DUCA   Ebben! sono con te ... presto ... vediamo ...

Dice una parola all'orecchio di Maddalena e segue Spara-
fucile.

RIGOLETTO	Impossible.
GILDA	I tremble.
RIGOLETTO	Go!

Gilda leaves. During this scene and the following one, the Duke and Maddalena are speaking between themselves, laughing, drinking. When Gilda has gone, Rigoletto goes behind the house and comes back with Sparafucile, talking and counting out some coins for him.

RIGOLETTO	Did you say twenty crowns? . . . Here are ten of them; the rest after the deed. Is he staying here?
SPARAFUCILE	Yes.
RIGOLETTO	I will return at midnight.
SPARAFUCILE	It's not necessary. I myself can throw him into the river.
RIGOLETTO	No, no, I want to do it myself.
SPARAFUCILE	Very well. His name?
RIGOLETTO	Do you want to know mine, too? He is *Crime,* I am *Punishment.*

He leaves. The sky darkens. Thunder.

SPARAFUCILE	The storm is near! . . . The night will be darker!
DUKE (*about to grasp her*)	Maddalena!
MADDALENA (*escaping him*)	Wait . . . my brother is coming . . .
DUKE	What does it matter?
MADDALENA	It's thundering!
SPARAFUCILE (*entering*)	And it will rain in a little while.
DUKE	So much the better! (*to Sparafucile*) You will sleep in the stable . . . In hell . . . wherever you like . . .
SPARAFUCILE	Oh, thank you!
MADDALENA (*softly to the Duke*)	Ah no, leave.
DUKE (*to Maddalena*)	With such weather?
SPARAFUCILE (*softly to Maddalena*)	There are twenty gold crowns. (*to the Duke*) Very happy to offer you a room, If you like, Let us go and see it at once.
DUKE	Very well! I'm with you . . . quickly . . . let's see . . .

He whispers something into Maddalena's ear and follows Sparafucile.

MADDALENA   Povero giovin! grazioso tanto!
              Dio, qual notte è questa!
DUCA (*giunto al granaio, vedendone il balcone senza imposte*)
              Si dorme all'aria aperta?
              Bene, bene!... Buona notte.
SPARAFUCILE   Signor, vi guardi Iddio!

Il Duca depone il cappello, la spada e si stende sul letto.

DUCA   Breve sonno dormiam ... stanco son io.
              La donna è mobile
              Qual piuma al vento,
              Muta d'accento
              E di pensiero ...
              Muta d'accento,
              E di pen ...
                    (*s'addormenta*)

*Maddalena frattanto siede presso la tavola. Sparafucile beve
dalla bottiglia lasciata dal Duca. Rimangono ambidue taciturni
per qualche istante, e preoccupati da gravi pensieri.*

MADDALENA   È amabile invero cotal giovinotto!
SPARAFUCILE   Oh sì, venti scudi ne dà di prodotto.
MADDALENA   Sol venti? Son pochi!
              Valeva di più.
SPARAFUCILE   La spada, s'ei dorme, va ...
              Portami giù.

*Maddalena sale al granaio e contempla il dormente. Gilda
comparisce nel fondo della via in costume virile, con stivali e
speroni, e lentamente si avanza verso l'osteria, mentre Sparafucile continua a bere. Spessi lampi e tuoni.*

GILDA   Ah più non ragiono ... Amor mi trascina!
              Mio padre, perdono ...
              Qual notte d'orrore!...
              Gran Dio, che accadrà!

Maddalena discende e posa la spada del Duca sulla tavola.

MADDALENA   Fratello?
GILDA   Chi parla?

Osserva per la fessura.

SPARAFUCILE (*frugando in un credenzone*)
              Al diavol ten va ...
MADDALENA   Somiglia un Apollo quel giovine ...
              Io l'amo ... ei m'ama ...
              Riposi ... nè più l'uccidiamo!
GILDA (*ascoltando*)
              Oh cielo!
SPARAFUCILE (*gettandole un sacco*)
              Rattoppa quel sacco!

MADDALENA   Poor youth! So handsome!
             God, what a night this is!
DUKE (*reaching the loft, seeing the balcony without shutters*)
             You sleep in the open air?
             Very well! . . . Good night.
SPARAFUCILE   God keep you, sir!

The Duke sets down his hat and sword and stretches out on the bed.

DUKE   Let's sleep a little . . . I'm tired.
             Woman is fickle
             Like a feather in the wind,
             She changes her words
             And her thoughts . . .
             Changes her words,
             And her thou . . .
                    (*falls asleep*)

Maddalena in the meanwhile has sat down at the table. Sparafucile drinks from the bottle the Duke has left. Both are silent for a few moments, filled with grave thoughts.

MADDALENA   That young man is really lovable!
SPARAFUCILE   Oh yes, he brings in twenty crowns for us.
MADDALENA   Only twenty? That's very few!
             He was worth more.
SPARAFUCILE   If he is sleeping, go . . .
             Bring me down his sword.

Maddalena goes up to the loft and gazes at the sleeping man. Gilda appears at the end of the street in man's dress, with boots and spurs and slowly she comes toward the inn, as Sparafucile continues to drink. Frequent thunder and lightning.

GILDA   Ah, I can reason no more . . . Love draws me on!
             Father, forgive me . . .
             What a night of horror! . . .
             Great God, what will happen!

Maddalena comes down and sets the Duke's sword on the table.

MADDALENA   Brother?
GILDA   Who is speaking?

She peers through the crevice.

SPARAFUCILE (*rummaging in a large chest of drawers*)
             Go to the devil . . .
MADDALENA   That youth looks like an Apollo . . .
             I love him . . . he loves me . . .
             Let him rest . . . let's not kill him!
GILDA (*listening*)
             Heaven!
SPARAFUCILE (*throwing her a sack*)
             Mend that sack!

MADDALENA	Perchè?
SPARAFUCILE	Entr'esso il tuo Apollo, sgozzato da me, Gettar dovrò al fiume ...
GILDA	L'inferno qui vedo!
MADDALENA	Eppure il danaro salvarti scommetto, Serbandolo in vita.
SPARAFUCILE	Difficile il credo.
MADDALENA	M'ascolta ... anzi facil ti svelo un progetto. De' scudi già dieci dal gobbo ne avesti;

Venire cogl'altri più tardi il vedrai ...
Uccidilo, e venti allora ne avrai,
Così tutto il prezzo goder si potrà.

GILDA	Che sento! mio padre!
SPARAFUCILE	Uccider quel gobbo!... che diavol dicesti!

Un ladro son forse? Son forse un bandito?
Qual altro cliente da me fu tradito?
Mi paga quest'uomo, fedele m'avrà.

MADDALENA	Ah grazia per esso.
SPARAFUCILE	E d'uopo ch'ei muoia.
MADDALENA	(*va per salire*) Fuggire il fo adesso!
GILDA	Oh buona figliuola!
SPARAFUCILE	(*trattenendola*) Gli scudi perdiamo.
MADDALENA	È ver ...
SPARAFUCILE	Lascia fare ...
MADDALENA	Salvarlo dobbiamo.
SPARAFUCILE	Se pria ch'abbia il mezzo la notte toccato Alcuno qui giunga, per esso morrà.
MADDALENA	È buia la notte, il ciel troppo irato, Nessuno a quest'ora da qui passerà.
GILDA	O qual tentazione!... morir per l'ingrato! Morire ... e mio padre!... Oh cielo! pietà!

MADDALENA	È buia la notte, ecc.
SPARAFUCILE	Se pria ch'abbia il mezzo, ecc.
GILDA	Oh cielo! pietà!

Battono le undici e mezzo.

SPARAFUCILE	Ancor c'è mezz'ora.
MADDALENA	(*piangendo*) Attendi, fratello.
GILDA	Che! piange tal donna!... Nè a lui darò aita! Ah s'egli al mio amore divenne rubello, Io vo' per la sua gettar la mia vita.

Picchia alla porta.

MADDALENA	Why?
SPARAFUCILE	I'll have to throw your Apollo into the river In it, when I have cut his throat . . .
GILDA	I see hell here!
MADDALENA	And still I wager I can save you the money, If you allow him to live.
SPARAFUCILE	That's hard, I think.
MADDALENA	Listen to me . . . I'll reveal an easy plan to you. You've had ten of the crowns from the hunch- back already; You'll see him coming with the others later . . . Kill him, and then you'll have twenty, Thus we can enjoy the full price.
GILDA	What do I hear? My father!
SPARAFUCILE	Kill that hunchback! . . . What the devil did you say! Am I a thief perhaps? Am I perhaps a bandit? What other customer was ever betrayed by me? This man pays me, and I'll be true to him.
MADDALENA	Ah, have mercy on him.
SPARAFUCILE	He has to die.
MADDALENA	*(starts to go upstairs)* I'll make him flee now!
GILDA	Oh, good maiden!
SPARAFUCILE	*(restraining her)* We'll lose the crowns.
MADDALENA	That's true . . .
SPARAFUCILE	Let it go . . .
MADDALENA	We must save him.
SPARAFUCILE	If before it has struck midnight Someone comes here, he'll die in his stead.
MADDALENA	The night is dark, the sky too wrathful, No one will pass by here at this hour.
GILDA	Oh, what temptation! . . . to die for the ingrate! To die . . . and my father! . . . Oh, heaven! Have mercy!
MADDALENA	The night is dark, etc.
SPARAFUCILE	If before it has struck, etc.
GILDA	Oh, heaven! Have mercy!

It strikes half-past eleven.

SPARAFUCILE	There's still half an hour.
MADDALENA	*(weeping)* Wait, Brother.
GILDA	What! such a woman weeps! . . . And I will not give him aid! Ah, though he refused my love, I want to cast away my life for his.

She knocks at the door.

MADDALENA   Si picchia?
SPARAFUCILE Fu il vento ...

Gilda torna a bussare.

MADDALENA   Si picchia, ti dico.
SPARAFUCILE È strano ... Chi è?
GILDA   Pietà d'un mendico;
             Asil per la notte a lui concedete.
MADDALENA   Fia lunga tal notte.
SPARAFUCILE (*va a cercare nel credenzone*)
             Alquanto attendete.
MADDALENA   Su, spicciati, presto, fa l'opra compita:
             Anelo una vita con altra salvar.
SPARAFUCILE Ebbene ... son pronto, quell'uscio dischiudi,
             Più ch'altro gli scudi mi preme salvar.
GILDA   Ah! presso alla morte, sì giovane sono!
             Oh ciel, per quegl'empì ti chieggo perdono!

             Perdona tu, o padre, a quest'infelice!
             Sia l'uomo felice ch'or vado a salvar.
             Perdona, perdona, o padre!
MADDALENA   Su, spicciati, ecc.
SPARAFUCILE Bene, son pronto, ecc.

Gilda bussa ancora.

MADDALENA   Spicciati ...
SPARAFUCILE Apri ...

*Sparafucile va a postarsi con un pugnale dietro alla porta;
Maddalena apre e poi corre a chiudere la grande arcata di
fronte, mentre entra Gilda, dietro a cui Sparafucile chiude la
porta e tutto resta sepolto nel silenzio e nel buio.*

MADDALENA e SPARAFUCILE
             Entrate ...
GILDA   Dio! loro perdona ...

*Rigoletto solo si avanza dal fondo della scena chiuso nel
suo mantello. La violenza del temporale è diminuita; nè
più si vede e sente che qualche lampo e tuono.*

RIGOLETTO   Della vendetta alfin giunge l'istante!
             Da trenta dì l'aspetto
             Di vivo sangue a lagrime piangendo,
             Sotto la larva del buffon ...
                  (*esaminando la casa*)
             Quest'uscio ... è chiuso!
             Ah non è tempo ancor! S'attenda.
             Qual notte di mistero!
             Una tempesta in cielo!
             In terra un omicidio!
             Oh come invero qui grande mi sento!...
                  (*Suona mezzanotte.*)

MADDALENA   Is someone knocking?
SPARAFUCILE It was the wind . . .

Gilda knocks again.

MADDALENA   Someone's knocking, I tell you.
SPARAFUCILE That's strange . . . Who is it?
GILDA   Have pity on a beggar;
             Grant him shelter for the night.
MADDALENA   May that night be a long one.
SPARAFUCILE (*goes to search in the chest of drawers*)
             Wait a moment.
MADDALENA   Go, hurry, quickly, complete the deed.
             I long to save one life with another.
SPARAFUCILE Very well . . . I'm ready, open that door.
             I want to save the money above all.
GILDA   Ah! So young, I am near my death!
             Oh, heaven, I ask forgiveness for those wicked
                 ones!
             And you, O Father, forgive this unhappy child!
             May the man I go to save be happy.
             Forgive me, forgive me, O Father!
MADDALENA   Go, hurry, etc.
SPARAFUCILE Very well, I'm ready, etc.

Gilda knocks again.

MADDALENA   Hurry . . .
SPARAFUCILE Open . . .

*Sparafucile goes and stands, with his dagger, behind the
door; Maddalena opens it, then runs to close the great arched
door opposite, as Gilda enters; Sparafucile closes the door
after her, and all is buried in silence and darkness.*

MADDALENA and SPARAFUCILE
             Enter . . .
GILDA   God! Forgive them . . .

*Rigoletto, alone, comes forward from the back, wrapped
in his cloak. The violence of the storm has lessened; only
occasional thunder can be heard and occasional lightning seen.*

RIGOLETTO   The moment of vengeance comes at last!
             For thirty days I have waited,
             Weeping my life's blood in tears,
             Under the buffoon's disguise . . .
                 (*examining the house*)
             This door . . . is locked!
             Ah, it is not time yet! I'll wait.
             What a mysterious night!
             A storm in heaven!
             A murder on earth!
             Oh, how truly great I feel myself here! . . .
                 (*Midnight strikes.*)

Mezzanotte ...
                    (*Bussa alla porta.*)
SPARAFUCILE   Chi è là?
RIGOLETTO (*per entrare*)
                    Son io.
SPARAFUCILE   Sostate ...
                    (*Rientra e torna trascinando un sacco.*)
                    È qua spento il vostr'uomo.
RIGOLETTO   Oh gioia! Un lume!
SPARAFUCILE   Un lume?... No, il danaro.
                    (*Rigoletto gli dà una borsa.*)
                    Lesti all'onda il gettiam.
RIGOLETTO   No, basto io solo.
SPARAFUCILE   Come vi piace ... Qui men atto è il sito.
                    Più avanti è più profondo il gorgo ...
                    Presto, che alcun non vi sorprenda.
                    Buona notte.

Rientra in casa.

RIGOLETTO   Egli è là! morto! oh sì! vorrei vederlo!
                    Ma che importa?... è ben desso! Ecco i suoi
                        sproni.
                    Ora mi guarda, o mondo!
                    Quest'è un buffone, ed un potente è questo!
                    Ei sta sotto i miei piedi! È desso! oh gioia!
                    È giunta alfine la tua vendetta, o duolo!
                    Sia l'onda a lui sepolcro,
                    Un sacco il suo lenzuolo!
                    All'onda! all'onda!

*Rigoletto fa per trascinare il sacco verso la sponda, quando
è sorpreso dalla lontana voce del Duca, che nel fondo attraversa la scena.*

DUCA   La donna è mobile
                    Qual piuma al vento,
                    Muta d'accento
                    E di pensiero.
RIGOLETTO   Qual voce!
DUCA   Sempre un amabile
                    Leggiadro viso,
                    In pianto o in riso,
                    È menzognero.
RIGOLETTO   Illusion notturna è questa!
                    No, no!... egli è desso! Maledizione!
                            (*verso la casa*)
                    Olà ... dimon ... bandito!
DUCA   Muta d'accento
                    E di pensier ...
RIGOLETTO   Chi è mai, chi è qui in sua vece?
                            (*Taglia il sacco.*)
                    Io tremo ... È umano corpo!...
                            (*Lampeggia.*)

                        Midnight ...
                            (*He knocks at the door.*)
SPARAFUCILE Who's there?
RIGOLETTO (*about to enter*)
                        It is I.
SPARAFUCILE Stay there ...
                        (*He goes back in, then returns, dragging a sack.*)
                        Your man is here, dead.
RIGOLETTO   Oh joy! A light!
SPARAFUCILE A light? ... No, the money.
                            (*Rigoletto gives him a purse.*)
                        Quickly, let's throw him into the water.
RIGOLETTO   No, I can do it alone.
SPARAFUCILE As you please ... Here the place is less suited.
                        Farther on the current is deeper ...
                        Quickly, let no one take you by surprise.
                        Good night.

He goes back into the house.

RIGOLETTO   He is there! Dead! Oh yes! I'd like to see him!
                        But what does it matter? ... It is truly he!
                            There are his spurs.
                        Now look at me, O world!
                        This is a buffoon, and this a mighty man!
                        He is under my feet! It's he! Oh, joy!
                        Your revenge has come at last, O grief!
                        Let the wave be his tomb,
                        A sack his shroud!
                        Into the water! Into the water!

*Rigoletto starts to drag the sack toward the bank, when
he is surprised by the distinct voice of the Duke, who crosses
the scene at back.*

DUKE   Woman is fickle
                        Like a feather in the wind,
                        She changes her words
                        And her thoughts.
RIGOLETTO   That voice!
DUKE   Always a lovable
                        And lovely face,
                        Weeping or laughing,
                        Is lying.
RIGOLETTO   This is an illusion of the night!
                        No, no! ... It's he! Curses!
                            (*toward the house*)
                        Hola ... demon ... bandit!
DUKE   She changes her words
                        And her thoughts ...
RIGOLETTO   Who, who can be here in his stead?
                            (*He cuts the sack.*)
                        I tremble ... It's a human body! ...
                            (*Lightning flashes.*)

Mia figlia!... Dio! mia figlia!...
Ah no!... è impossibil!
Per Verona è in via!
Fu vision ...
      (*inginocchiandosi*)
È dessa!
Oh mia Gilda!... fanciulla ... a me rispondi!
L'assassino mi svela ...
Olà!?
      (*Picchia disperatamente alla porta.*)
Nessuno? Nessun!
Mia figlia ... mia Gilda ... oh mia figlia!

GILDA   Chi mi chiama?

RIGOLETTO   Ella parla!... si move!... è viva!... oh Dio!

Ah mio ben solo in terra
Mi guarda ... mi conosce ...

GILDA   Ah padre mio!

RIGOLETTO   Qual mistero!... che fu!... sei tu ferita?

Dimmi ...

GILDA   L'acciar ... qui ... qui mi piagò ...
      (*indicando al core*)

RIGOLETTO   Chi t'ha colpita?...

GILDA   V'ho ingannato ... colpevole fui ...
L'amai troppo ... ora muoio per lui.

RIGOLETTO   (Dio tremendo! ella stessa fu colta
Dallo stral di mia giusta vendetta!)
Angiol caro ... mi guarda, m'ascolta ...
Parla ... parlami, figlia diletta!

GILDA   Ah ch'io taccia!... a me ... a lui perdonate!
Benedite ... alla figlia ... o mio padre ...
Lassù in cielo, vicina alla madre ...
In eterno per voi pregherò.

RIGOLETTO   Non morir ... mio tesoro ... pietade ...
Mia colomba ... lasciarmi non dèi ...
Non morir ... lasciarmi non dèi ...

GILDA   Lassù in cielo, ecc.

RIGOLETTO   Se t'involi, qui sol rimarrei ...
Non morire, o qui teco morrò!

GILDA   Non più ... A lui ... perdonate ... mio padre ...

RIGOLETTO   Oh mia figlia ... oh mia Gilda!
Lasciarmi non dèi ...

GILDA   Addio ... Lassù in ciel ...
Lassù in ciel ... pregherò ...

RIGOLETTO   Non morir!

GILDA   Per voi preghe ...

RIGOLETTO   Gilda! mia Gilda!... È morta!
Ah! la maledizione!

Strappandosi i capelli, cade sul cadavere della figlia.

My daughter! . . . God! My daughter! . . .
Ah no! . . . It's impossible!
She's on her way to Verona!
It was a vision . . .
                    (*kneeling*)
It is she!
Oh my Gilda! . . . Child . . . answer me!
Reveal the assassin to me . . .
Hola?
    (*He knocks desperately at the door.*)
No one? No one!
My daughter . . . my Gilda . . . oh my daughter!

GILDA Who calls me?

RIGOLETTO She speaks! . . . She moves! . . . She's alive! . . .
Oh God!
Ah, my only love on earth
Looks at me . . . knows me . . .

GILDA Ah, Father!

RIGOLETTO What mystery is this! . . . What was it? . . .
Are you wounded?
Tell me . . .

GILDA The blade . . . here . . . struck me here . . .
                    (*pointing to her heart*)

RIGOLETTO Who struck you? . . .

GILDA I deceived you . . . I was guilty . . .
I loved him too much . . . now I die for him.

RIGOLETTO (Terrible God! She herself was struck
By the arrow of my just revenge!)
Dear angel . . . look at me, listen to me . . .
Speak . . . speak to me, beloved Daughter!

GILDA Ah, let me be silent! . . . Forgive me . . . and him!
Bless . . . your daughter . . . O Father . . .
Up in heaven, near my mother . . .
I'll pray for you in eternity.

RIGOLETTO Do not die . . . my treasure . . . have mercy . . .
My dove . . . you must not leave me . . .
Do not die . . . you must not leave me . . .

GILDA Up in heaven, etc.

RIGOLETTO If you fly away, I'd be left here alone . . .
Do not die, or I will die with you here!

GILDA No more . . . Forgive . . . him . . . Father . . .

RIGOLETTO Oh, my daughter . . . oh, my Gilda!
You must not leave me . . .

GILDA Farewell . . . Up in heaven . . .
Up in heaven . . . I will pray . . .

RIGOLETTO Do not die!

GILDA For you I will pr . . .

RIGOLETTO Gilda! My Gilda! . . . She is dead!
Ah! The curse!

Tearing his hair, he falls across his daughter's dead body.

Il Trovatore

Even more than Venice, Naples was for Verdi a city of good friends and good times. Though he had quarrels with the various managers of the Teatro San Carlo, though his first Neopolitan opera, *Alzira*, was a fiasco ("downright ugly," he is supposed to have said of it later), though gossiping journalists and a rival composer with the evil eye bedeviled his visits to the city, still he succumbed to its charm and kept up a long and interesting correspondence with his closest friends there, especially the De Sanctis family and the painter Domenico Morelli, many of whose works hung in the Verdi villa.

Again the local librettist was a friend, though the relationship between Verdi and Salvatore Cammarano was less intimate than the composer's friendship with Piave. Cammarano was considerably older than Verdi, and when he wrote the libretto for *Alzira*, he was already well known as the author of other successful librettos, including Pacini's *Saffo* and Donizetti's *Lucia di Lammermoor*. In fact, the tone of Verdi's letters to Cammarano is much more deferential than it is in those to poor, browbeaten Piave.

Cammarano was Naples-born, scion of a long line of actors, writers, and painters. He had virtually grown up in the theater, and in addition to writing librettos he was often responsible for staging them (Verdi wrote him at length with suggestions for the Neapolitan production of his *Macbeth*, which Cammarano supervised). After the ill-fated *Alzira*, poet and composer collaborated on more fortunate works: *La Battaglia di Legnano* (1849) and *Luisa Miller* (1849).

The production of *Luisa Miller* took place amid grave and bitter arguments between Verdi and the slipshod management of the San Carlo, and though the composer was supposed to write another opera for Naples (he had planned a *King Lear*), he determined to give the new work elsewhere. As no theater could muster a suitable cast for *Lear*, Verdi shelved the idea and decided to work with Cammarano on *Il Trovatore*, which was based on a successful play by the Spaniard Antonio García Gutiérrez, with a subject Verdi found filled with "novelty and *bizzarria*."

While *Rigoletto* had been completed in record time — forty days — *Il Trovatore* was dragged out over more than a year, again because a suitable company of singers couldn't be found and because Cammarano, in poor health, took his time writing the verses. On July 17, 1852, Cammarano died. Verdi was grief-stricken, as he wrote to De Sanctis in Naples: "I was thunderstruck by the sad news of our Cammarano. It's impossible for me to describe my profound grief! I read of this death not in a friend's letter, but in a stupid theatrical journal! You, who loved him as I did, will understand all the things I cannot say. Poor Cammarano! What a loss! . . ." Verdi, promptly and generously, sent the poet's widow, left in straitened circumstances, six hundred ducats, a hundred more than he was to have paid for the libretto. Another Neapolitan,

Leone Emanuele Bardare, completed the versification of the third act and wrote all of the fourth. In cutting down the sprawling Spanish play to libretto dimensions, Cammarano had to eliminate minor characters and also a good deal of exposition and background material. The result is a work that is at times confusing and disjointed, though the overwhelming impetus of Verdi's music somehow carries us over the weak parts of the plot, hardly giving us time to ask embarrassing questions (such as why Di Luna doesn't burn Azucena, when he has the stake all prepared). The librettists had no time to tighten the story, but, thanks to the composer's genius, it makes a kind of dramatic sense anyway.

Rejecting offers from Florence, Bologna, and La Scala, Verdi chose to give the opera in Rome at the Teatro Apollo. After the first night, January 19, 1853, the composer sent De Sanctis a laconic telegram: "*Il Trovatore* didn't go badly." This was a Verdian understatement; the first night had been an enormous success.

But Verdi was tired and unwell, still oppressed by the death of his mother (some of Azucena's music is said to express his sense of loss). And at the same time he had other things to think about. The libretto of *La Traviata* was already in his hands.

THE PLOT

ACT ONE

The retainers of Count di Luna listen to old Ferrando, their captain, who tells how the Count's father once burned an old gypsy at the stake for witchcraft. In revenge, the gypsy's daughter stole the infant brother of the present Count and burned the child to death. As the clock strikes midnight, Ferrando finishes his weird tale, and the frightened men rush outside.

In the gardens of the palace, the beautiful Leonora is confiding in her companion, Ines, telling her how she has fallen in love with an unknown troubador-knight who comes to serenade her. Ines has misgivings, but Leonora is fascinated by her mysterious admirer. After the two women enter the palace, the Count appears. He too is in love with Leonora and plans to marry her. His thoughts are interrupted by the strains of a serenade, and the troubador enters. Leonora comes out of the palace in time to witness the knight's defiance as he reveals himself to be Manrico, follower of a rebel prince and therefore Di Luna's enemy. The two men rush off to fight a duel.

ACT TWO

A gypsy camp in the mountains. Old Azucena is crouched by a fire, Manrico lying at her feet. As day breaks, the gypsies take up their usual tasks, hammering on their anvils and singing. Azucena sings a strange song, the story of her mother's execution, the abduction of the Count's child, and the burning — not of Di Luna's brother, but of her own son.

Manrico, who has always believed himself her son, is puzzled, but she refuses to explain and insists that he is indeed her son, reminding him that Di Luna is his mortal enemy.

A messenger arrives. Manrico is summoned to defend the fortress of Castellor. Meanwhile Leonora is in a nearby convent, about to take the veil. Manrico rushes away to carry her off. In the cloister of the convent Di Luna and his men are planning the same thing. As Leonora comes in, so does Manrico, followed by his band, who fight off the Count's retainers, allowing Manrico to rescue his beloved.

ACT THREE

The Count is besieging Castellor. A gypsy woman is brought into the camp, and old Ferrando recognizes her as the murderess of Di Luna's brother. In despair she utters the name "Manrico," doubling the Count's fury.

Inside the fortress of Castellor, Manrico and Leonora are about to be married, but Ruiz, Manrico's friend, brings word that Azucena has been captured and is to be burned at the stake. Manrico hurries off to save her.

ACT FOUR

Now both Manrico and Azucena are imprisoned. Outside the tower, Leonora has come to save her lover, whom she hears singing inside. When the Count appears, Leonora offers herself to him in exchange for Manrico's life. Di Luna accepts the proposal and gives orders to the guards. Leonora swallows poison from her ring, so that Di Luna's reward will be only her lifeless corpse.

Inside the dungeon, Manrico tries to comfort Azucena, who dreams of their mountains in Biscaya. Leonora comes in and tells Manrico that he is free, but he suspects the price of his freedom and curses her. Leonora is dying, and as the Count appears, she tells Manrico that she preferred death to life with another. She dies and the Count sends Manrico to his death. Azucena, also close to death, wakes and tells the Count that he has executed his own brother. Azucena's mother has been avenged at last.

IL TROVATORE

libretto by Salvatore Cammarano
(completed by Leone Emanuele Bardare)

First performed at the Teatro Apollo, Rome

January 19, 1853

CHARACTERS

Count di Luna, a young noble of Aragon	Baritone
Ferrando, Di Luna's captain of the guard	Bass
Manrico, a chieftain under the Prince of Biscaya, and reputed son of Azucena	Tenor
Ruiz, a soldier in Manrico's service	Tenor
An old gypsy	Baritone
Leonora, noblewoman, lady-in-waiting to the Princess of Aragon	Soprano
Ines, confidante of Leonora	Soprano
Azucena, a Biscayan gypsy woman	Mezzo-soprano

Followers of Count di Luna and of Manrico,
a Messenger, Jailer, Soldiers, Nuns, Gypsies

The scenes are laid in the provinces of Aragon and Biscaya,
in Northern Spain, during a border war in the fifteenth century.

ATTO PRIMO

Il Duello

PARTE PRIMA

Atrio nel palazzo dell'Aliaferia: porta da un lato, che mette agli appartamenti del conte di Luna. Ferrando e molti famigliari del conte, che giacciono presso la porta; alcuni uomini d'arme che passeggiano in fondo.

FERRANDO (*parla ai famigliari, vicini ad assopirsi*)
All'erta! all'erta! Il Conte
N'è d'uopo attender vigilando;
Ed egli talor, presso i veroni
Della sua cara,
Intere passa le notti.

FAMIGLIARI Gelosia le fiere serpi
Gli avventa in petto.

FERRANDO Nel Trovator, che dai giardini
Move notturno il canto,
D'un rivale a dritto ei teme.

FAMIGLIARI Dalle gravi palpebre
Il sonno a discacciar,
La vera storia ci narra
Di Garzia, germano al nostro Conte.

FERRANDO La dirò: venite
Intorno a me.

ARMIGERI (*accostandosi*)
Noi pure ...

FAMIGLIARI Udite, udite.

FERRANDO Di due figli vivea padre beato ...
Il buon Conte di Luna.
Fida nutrice del secondo nato ...
Dormia presso la cuna.
Sul romper dell'aurora
Un bel mattino
Ella dischiude i rai;
E chi trova d'accanto
A quel bambino?

FAMIGLIARI ed ARMIGERI
Chi?... Favella ... Chi? Chi mai?

FERRANDO Abbietta zingara, fosca vegliarda!
Cingeva i simboli di maliarda;
E sul fanciullo, con viso arcigno,
L'occhio affiggea torvo, sanguigno!
D'orror compresa è la nutrice ...
Acuto un grido all'aura scioglie;
Ed ecco, in meno che labbro il dice,
I servi accorrono in quelle soglie;

ACT ONE

The Duel

SCENE ONE

A hall in the Aliaferia palace; a door at one side that leads into the Count di Luna's apartments. Ferrando and a number of the Count's retainers are resting near the door; some soldiers are pacing back and forth in the background.

FERRANDO (*to the retainers, who are about to fall asleep*)
Look sharp there! The Count
Must be served with vigilance;
Sometimes, near the balconies
Of his beloved,
He spends whole nights.

RETAINERS Jealousy's fierce serpents
Are writhing in his breast.

FERRANDO In the Troubadour, whose song
Rises at night from the gardens,
He rightly fears a rival.

RETAINERS To drive off the sleep
That hangs heavy on our eyelids,
Tell us the real story
Of Garzia, our Count's brother.

FERRANDO I'll tell you: gather
Around me.

SOLDIERS (*approaching*)
We too . . .

RETAINERS Listen, listen.

FERRANDO There lived a happy father of two sons . . .
The good Count di Luna.
The second boy's faithful nurse . . .
Slept next to his cradle.
As dawn was breaking
One fine morning
She opened her eyes;
And whom did she find
Next to that baby?

RETAINERS and SOLDIERS
Who? . . . Speak . . . Who? Who was it?

FERRANDO A dark, despicable gypsy crone!
Wearing the symbols of a scorceress;
And with a sullen face, over the boy,
She cast her bloody, baleful eye!
The nurse is seized with horror . . .
She utters a sharp cry in the air;
And, in less time than it takes to tell,
The servants hasten into the room;

E fra minaccie, urli, percosse,
La rea discacciano ch'entrarvi osò.

FAMIGLIARI ed ARMIGERI
Giusto quei petti sdegno commosse;
L'insana vecchia lo provocò!

FERRANDO
Asserì che tirar del fanciullino ...
L'oroscopo volea ... Bugiarda!...
Lenta febbre del meschino
La salute struggea!
Coverto di pallor, languido,
Affranto ei tremava la sera,
Il dì traeva in lamentevol pianto ...
Ammaliato egl'era!
(*Il coro inorridisce.*)
La fattucchiera perseguitata,
Fu presa e al rogo fu condannata:
Ma rimaneva la maledetta
Figlia, ministra di ria vendetta!...
Compì quest'empia nefando eccesso!...
Sparve il fanciullo,
E si rinvenne mal spenta brage
Nel sito istesso
Ov'arsa un giorno la strega venne ...
E d'un bambino, ahimè!... l'ossame
Bruciato a mezzo, fumante ancor!

FAMIGLIARI ed ARMIGERI
Ah scellerata! Oh donna infame!
Del par m'investe odio ed orror!
E il padre?

FERRANDO
Brevi e tristi giorni visse,
Pur ignoto del cor presentimento
Gli diceva che spento
Non era il figlio; ed, a morir vicino,
Bramò che il signor nostro
A lui giurasse di non cessar
Le indagini ... ah! fur vane!

ARMIGERI
E di colei
Non s'ebbe contezza mai?

FERRANDO
Nulla contezza.
Oh! dato mi fosse
Rintracciarla un dì!

FAMIGLIARI
Ma ravvisarla potresti?

FERRANDO
Calcolando gli anni trascorsi ...
Lo potrei.

ARMIGERI
Sarebbe tempo presso la madre
All'inferno spedirla.

FERRANDO
All'inferno?...
È credenza che dimori ancor
Nel mondo l'anima perduta
Dell'empia strega, e quando
Il cielo è nero
In varie forme altrui si mostri.

> And with shouts, blows, threats,
> They expel the wretch who dared enter.

RETAINERS and SOLDIERS
> Righteous scorn moves those hearts;
> The mad crone provoked it!

FERRANDO
> She claimed that she wanted to cast . . .
> The boy's horoscope . . . The liar! . . .
> A slow fever began to destroy
> The poor child's health!
> Covered with pallor, languid,
> Broken, he trembled at night,
> He moaned piteously all day long . . .
> He was bewitched!
> > (*All are horrified.*)
> The witch was pursued,
> Seized and condemned to the stake:
> But her cursed daughter was left,
> Instrument of a horrible revenge! . . .
> This criminal committed a terrible act! . . .
> The child disappeared,
> And they found still-glowing embers
> On the very same spot
> Where the witch had once been burned . . .
> And alas! . . . A child's skeleton,
> Half-burned, still smoking!

RETAINERS and SOLDIERS
> Ah, the wicked, infamous woman!
> It fills me with both hatred and horror!
> And the father?

FERRANDO
> His remaining days were few and sad,
> Yet an undefined presentiment
> At heart told him that his son
> Was not dead; and, when he lay dying,
> He desired that our master
> Should swear to him not to stop
> His search . . . ah! it was in vain!

SOLDIERS
> And was no news
> Ever received of her?

FERRANDO
> No news.
> Oh! that it should be granted me
> To track her down someday!

RETAINERS
> But could you recognize her?

FERRANDO
> Considering the years that have passed . . .
> I could.

SOLDIERS
> It would be time to send her
> To her mother in hell.

FERRANDO
> In hell? . . .
> It's a common belief that
> The wicked witch's damned soul
> Still lives in the world, and when
> The sky is black
> She shows herself in various shapes.

RETAINERS and SOLDIERS (*with terror*)
> It's true! It's true! It's true!
> On the edges of roof tops
> Some people have seen her!
> Sometimes she changes
> Into a hoopoe or screech-owl!
> At other times, a raven;
> More often, an owl,
> Flying through the dawn
> Like an arrow!

FERRANDO
> One of the Count's men died of fear,
> Because he had struck
> The gypsy's forehead!

FERRANDO and CHORUS
> Ah! . . . He died, he died, he died of fear!

FERRANDO
> She appeared to him
> In the form of an owl,
> In the deep calm of a silent room! . . .
> She stared, with gleaming eye . . .
> Stared, grieving the heavens
> With a bestial cry!
> Midnight was just striking . . .

Suddenly a bell strikes midnight.

ALL
> Ah! Ah! A curse on her,
> The infernal witch! Ah!

The retainers run toward the door and the soldiers hurry to the back.

ACT ONE

SCENE TWO

The gardens of the palace: at the right, a marble staircase leads up to the private apartments. It is late at night: thick clouds conceal the moon. Leonora and Ines are strolling.

INES
> Why stay here any longer? . . .
> It's late, come:
> The Queen asked about you;
> You heard her.

LEONORA
> Yet another night
> Without seeing him!

INES
> You're nursing a dangerous flame! . . .
> Oh, how, where
> Did its first spark
> Strike you?

LEONORA
> At the tourney. There appeared,
> In dark armor and dark helmet,

FAMIGLIARI ed ARMIGERI (*con terrore*)
    È vero! È vero! È ver!
    Sull'orlo dei tetti
    Alcun l'ha veduta!
    In upupa o strige
    Talora si muta!
    In corvo tal'altra;
    Più spesso in civetta,
    Sull'alba fuggente
    Al par di saetta!

FERRANDO
    Morì di paura un servo del Conte,
    Che avea della zingara
    Percossa la fronte!

FERRANDO e CORO
    Ah! Morì, morì, morì di paura!

FERRANDO
    Apparve a costui
    D'un gufo in sembianza,
    Nell'alta quiete di tacita stanza!...
    Con occhio lucente guardava ...
    Guardava, il cielo attristando
    D'un urlo feral!
    Allor mezzanotte appunto suonava ...

Una campana suona improvvisamente a disteso la mezzanotte.

TUTTI
    Ah! Ah! Sia maledetta
    La strega infernal! Ah!

I famigliari corrono verso la porta, gli uomini d'armo accorrono in fondo.

ATTO PRIMO

PARTE SECONDA

Giardini del palazzo: sulla destra, marmorea scalinata che mette agli appartamenti. La notte è inoltrata: dense nubi cuoprono la luna. Leonora ed Ines passeggiano.

INES
    Che più t'arresti?...
    L'ora è tarda, vieni:
    Di te la regal donna chiese,
    L'udisti.

LEONORA
    Un'altra notte ancora
    Senza vederlo!

INES
    Perigliosa fiamma tu nutri!...
    Oh come, dove
    La primiera favilla
    In te s'apprese?

LEONORA
    Ne' tornei. V'apparve,
    Bruno le vesti ed il cimier,

Lo scudo bruno e di stemma ignudo,
Sconosciuto guerrier,
Che dell'agone gli onori ottenne ...
Al vincitor sul crine
Il serto io posi ...
Civil guerra intanto arse —
Nol vidi più!...
Come d'aurato sogno
Fuggente immago!... ed era volta
Lunga stagion, ma poi ...

INES   Che avvenne?...

LEONORA   Ascolta!
Tacea la notte placida
E bella in ciel sereno;
La luna il viso argenteo
Mostrava lieto e pieno ...
Quando suonar per l'aere,
Infino allor sì muto,
Dolci s'udiro e flebili
Gli accordi d'un liuto,
E versi melanconici
Un trovator cantò.
Versi di prece, ed umile,
Qual d'uom che prega Iddio:
In quella ripeteasi
Un nome, il nome mio!...
Corsi al veron sollecita ...
Egli era, egli era desso!...
Gioia provai che agl'angeli
Solo è provar concesso!...
Al core, al guardo estatico
La terra un ciel sembrò!

INES   Quanto narrasti di turbamento
M'ha piena l'alma!...
Io temo ...

LEONORA   Invano!...

INES   Dubbio ma tristo presentimento
In me risveglia
Quest'uomo arcano!...
Tenta obbliarlo ...

LEONORA   Che dici?...
Oh basti!...

INES   Cedi al consiglio dell'amistà.
Cedi.

LEONORA   Obbliarlo!...
Ah! tu parlasti detto
Che intender l'alma non sa.
Di tale amor, che dirsi
Mal può dalla parola,
D'amor, che intendo io sola,
Il cor s'innebriò.
Il mio destino compiersi
Non può che a lui dappresso ...

With dark shield and without crest,
An unknown warrior,
Who won the honors of the arena . . .
On the victor's head
I placed the crown . . .
Then civil war raged —
I saw him no more! . . .
Like the fleeting image
Of a golden dream! . . . and a long
Time passed, but then . . .

INES What happened? . . .

LEONORA Listen!
The serene night was silent
And lovely in the calm sky;
The moon happily revealed
Its full and silvery face . . .
When resounding in the air,
Until then so quiet,
Sweet and sad were heard
The sounds of a lute,
And a troubadour
Sang melancholy verses.
Verses beseeching, and humble,
Like a man praying to God:
And in them was repeated
A name, my name! . . .
I ran eagerly to the balcony . . .
There he was, it was he! . . .
I felt a joy that only the angels
Are allowed to feel! . . .
To my heart, my ecstatic gaze
The earth seemed like heaven!

INES What you've told me has filled
My soul with anguish! . . .
I fear . . .

LEONORA Needlessly! . . .

INES A sad but vague presentiment
Is stirred in me
By this mysterious man! . . .
Try to forget him . . .

LEONORA What are you saying? . . .
Enough! . . .

INES Give way to a friend's advice.
Do give way!

LEONORA Forget him! . . .
Ah! you've spoken a word
That my soul cannot understand.
With such a love
That words can scarcely tell,
Of a love that only I know,
My heart is intoxicated.
My fate can be fulfilled
Only at his side . . .

S'io non vivrò per esso,
Per esso morirò, ah sì,
Per esso morirò.

INES (*da sè*)   * [(Non debba mai pentirsi
Chi tanto un giorno amò!)]

Ascendono agli appartamenti. Poi viene il Conte di Luna.

CONTE   Tace la notte!...
Immersa nel sonno è, certo,
La regal signora ...
Ma veglia la sua dama ...
Oh Leonora!... tu desta sei ...
Mel dice da quel verone
Tremolante un raggio
Della notturna lampa ...
Ah!... l'amorosa fiamma
M'arde ogni fibra!
Ch'io ti vegga è d'uopo ...
Che tu m'intenda ... vengo ...
A noi supremo è tal momento.
                (*Cieco d'amore, avviasi verso la gradinata.*)
Il Trovator! Io fremo!

MANRICO (*fuori scena*)
Deserto sulla terra,
Col rio destino in guerra,
È sola speme un cor,
È sola speme un cor,
Un cor al Trovator!

CONTE   Oh detti!... Io fremo!

MANRICO   Ma s'ei quel cor possiede,
Bello di casta fede,
È d'ogni re maggior ...

CONTE   Oh detti! Oh gelosia!...

MANRICO   È d'ogni re maggior,
Maggior il Trovator!

CONTE   Non m'inganno ...
Ella scende!

Il Conte si avvolge nel suo mantello. Leonora corre verso il Conte.

LEONORA   Anima mia!

CONTE   (Che far?)

LEONORA   Più dell'usato
È tarda l'ora;
Io ne contai gl'istanti
Co' palpiti del core!...
Alfin ti guida pietoso amor
Fra queste braccia ...

MANRICO (*una voce fra le piante*)
Infida!

LEONORA   Qual voce!

* Brackets denote passages often omitted in performance.

                 If I can't live for him,
                 Then I'll die for him, ah yes,
                 I'll die for him.

INES (*to herself*)
                 (May one who once loved so
                 Never have to regret it one day!)

They go up to their rooms. Then Count di Luna comes in.

COUNT   The night is still! . . .
                 The Queen, surely, is
                 Immersed in sleep . . .
                 But her lady is wakeful . . .
                 Oh, Leonora! . . . you're awake . . .
                 I'm told from that balcony
                 By the quavering ray
                 Of your night lamp . . .
                 Ah! . . . The flame of love
                 Burns my every fiber!
                 I must see you . . .
                 You must hear me . . . I'm coming . . .
                 This is our supreme moment.
                    (*Blind with love, he goes toward the steps.*)
                 The Troubadour! I tremble with rage!

MANRICO (*within*)
                 All alone on the earth,
                 At war with his evil fate,
                 His only hope is in one heart,
                 His only hope is in one heart,
                 A heart for the Troubadour!

COUNT   These words! . . . I tremble with rage!

MANRICO   But if he possesses that heart,
                 Lovely with its chaste promise,
                 He's greater than any king . . .

COUNT   Those words! What jealousy! . . .

MANRICO   He's greater than any king,
                 Greater is the Troubadour!

COUNT   I'm not mistaken . . .
                 She's coming down!

The Count wraps himself in his cloak. Leonora runs toward the Count.

LEONORA   My soul!

COUNT   (What to do?)

LEONORA   The hour
                 Is later than usual;
                 I counted its instants
                 By the beating of my heart! . . .
                 At last merciful love
                 Leads you to my arms . . .

MANRICO (*his voice coming from the trees*)
                 Faithless!

LEONORA   That voice!

La luna mostrasi dai nugoli, e lascia scorgere una persona,
di cui la visiera nasconde il volto.

LEONORA (*riconoscendo entrambi, e gettandosi ai piedi di*
    Manrico)
                Ah! dalle tenebre
                Tratta in errore io fui!
                    (*a Manrico agitatissima*)
                A te credei rivolgere
                L'accento, e non a lui ...
                A te, che l'alma mia
                Sol chiede, sol desia ...
                Io t'amo, il giuro, t'amo
                D'immenso, eterno amor!

CONTE   Ed osi!

MANRICO (*sollevando Leonora*)
                Ah, più non bramo!

CONTE   Avvampo di furor!

LEONORA   Io t'amo! Io t'amo!

CONTE   Se un vil non sei,
                Discovriti!

LEONORA   (Ohimè!)

CONTE   Palesa il nome!

LEONORA (*piano a Manrico*)
                Deh, per pietà!

MANRICO (*sollevando la visiera dell'elmo*)
                Ravvisami,
                Manrico io son.

CONTE   Tu!... Come?...
                Insano, temerario!
                D'Urgel seguace,
                A morte proscritto, ardisci
                Volgerti a queste regie porte?

MANRICO   Che tardi?...
                Or via, le guardie appella,
                Ed il rivale al ferro
                Del carnefice consegna!

CONTE   Il tuo fatale istante
                Assai più prossimo è,
                Dissennato!... Vieni ...

LEONORA   Conte!...

CONTE   Al mio sdegno vittima,
                È d'uopo ch'io ti sveni ...

LEONORA   Oh ciel, t'arresta!

CONTE   Seguimi!...

MANRICO   Andiam!...

LEONORA   (Che mai farò?
                Un sol mio grido
                Perdere lo puote!)
                M'odi!...

*The moon comes from behind the clouds and reveals a man
whose face is hidden by his visor.*

LEONORA (*recognizing both, and throwing herself at Manrico's
   feet*)

        Ah! The darkness
        Deceived me!
               (*to Manrico in agitation*)
        I thought that I was speaking
        To you, not to him . . .
        To you, whom alone
        My soul wants, desires . . .
        I love you, I swear it, love you
        With immense, eternal love!

COUNT   You dare!

MANRICO (*taking Leonora in his arms*)
        Ah! I ask no more!

COUNT   I'm burning with fury!

LEONORA   I love you! I love you!

COUNT   If you're not a coward,
        Reveal yourself!

LEONORA   (Oh, God!)

COUNT   Tell your name!

LEONORA (*softly to Manrico*)
        Ah, have mercy!

MANRICO (*lifting the visor of his helmet*)
        Know me, then,
        I'm Manrico!

COUNT   You! . . . What? . . .
        Mad, foolhardy man!
        A follower of Urgel,
        Sentenced to death, you dare
        Approach these royal gates?

MANRICO   Why do you delay? . . .
        Come, call the guards,
        And hand your rival over
        To the executioner's blade!

COUNT   Your last moment
        Is much nearer than that,
        Madman! . . . Come . . .

LEONORA   Count! . . .

COUNT   I must draw your blood,
        Victim of my contempt . . .

LEONORA   Oh heaven, stop!

COUNT   Follow me! . . .

MANRICO   Let's go! . . .

LEONORA   (What shall I do?
        One cry from me
        Could undo him!)
        Hear me!

CONTE
No!
Di geloso amor sprezzato
Arde in me tremendo il fuoco!
Il tuo sangue, o sciagurato,
Ad estinguerlo fia poco!
(*a Leonora*)
Dirgli, o folle,
Io t'amo, ardisti!...
Ei più vivere non può ...
Un accento proferisti
Che a morir lo condannò!

LEONORA
Un istante almen dia loco
Il tuo sdegno alla ragione:
Io, sol io, di tanto foco
Son, pur troppo, la cagione!
Piombi, piombi il tuo furore
Sulla rea che t'oltraggiò ...
Vibra il ferro in questo core
Che te amar non vuol nè può.

MANRICO
Del superbo è vana l'ira;
Ei cadrà da me trafitto:
Il mortal, che amor t'inspira,
Dall'amor fu reso invitto.
(*al Conte*)
La tua sorte è già compita ...
L'ora omai per te suonò!
Il suo core e la tua vita
Il destino a me serbò!

CONTE
Dirgli, o folle, ecc.

I due rivali si allontanano con le spade sguainate. Leonora cade, priva di sentimento.

ATTO SECONDO

La Gitana

PARTE PRIMA

Un diruto abituro sulle falde di un monte della Biscaglia; nel fondo, quasi tutto aperto, arde un gran fuoco. I primi albori. Azucena siede presso il fuoco. Manrico le sta disteso accanto sopra una coltrice, ed avviluppato nel suo mantello: ha l'elmo ai piedi, e fra le mani la spada, su cui figge immobilmente lo sguardo. Una banda di zingari è sparsa all'intorno.

ZINGARI
Vedi! le fosche notturne spoglie
De' cieli sveste l'immensa vôlta;
Sembra una vedova che alfin si toglie
I bruni panni ond'era involta.
(*danno di piglio ai ferri del mestiere*)

COUNT	No!
	My spurned and jealous love
	Burns in me with a terrible flame!
	Your blood, wretch, would be
	Hardly enough to put it out!
	(to Leonora)
	Foolish girl, you dared
	To tell him, "I love you"! . . .
	He can live no longer . . .
	You uttered a word
	That condemned him to die!
LEONORA	At least for a moment let your scorn
	Make room for reasoning:
	I, and only I, am unhappily
	The cause of all your fire!
	So let your fury fall, fall
	On the guilty girl who offended you . . .
	Plunge your sword into this heart
	That cannot, will not love you.
MANRICO	The haughty man's wrath is in vain;
	He'll fall, run through by me:
	The mortal who inspires your love
	Is made invulnerable by love.
	(to the Count)
	Your fate is already sealed . . .
	Your hour has struck now!
	Destiny has given to me
	Her heart and your life!
COUNT	Foolish girl, you dared, etc.

The two men leave, swords in hand. Leonora falls senseless.

ACT TWO

The Gypsy

SCENE ONE

A ruined dwelling on the slope of a mountain in Biscay; at the back, almost entirely open, a great fire burns. Early dawn. Azucena is sitting by the fire. Manrico is lying near her, on a blanket, wrapped in his cloak, his helmet is at his feet, and in his hands his sword, at which he is staring, motionless. A band of gypsies is scattered around them.

GYPSIES	See! The heavens' great vault
	Removes its gloomy, nighttime tatters;
	Like a widow who takes off at last
	The dark clothes that enfolded her.
	(picking up their tools)

All'opra, all'opra! Dagli. Martella.
Chi del gitano i giorni abbella?
La zingarella!
(*Si fermano un poco dal lavoro, e dicono alle
donne!*)
Versami un tratto: lena e coraggio
Il corpo e l'anima traggon dal bere.
(*Le donne mescono in rozze coppe.*)
Oh, guarda, guarda!... Del sole un raggio
Brilla più vivido nel mio (tuo) bicchiere!
All'opra, all'opra!...
Chi del gitano i giorni abbella?
La zingarella!

AZUCENA (*Gli zingari le si fanno allato.*)
Stride la vampa!
La folla indomita
Corre a quel foco,
Lieta in sembianza!
Urli di gioia
Intorno echeggiano;
Cinta di sgherri
Donna s'avanza;
Sinistra splende
Sui volti orribili
La tetra fiamma
Che s'alza, che s'alza al ciel!

Stride la vampa!
Giunge la vittima
Nero vestita,
Discinta e scalza;
Grido feroce
Di morte levasi;
L'eco il ripete
Di balza in balza.
Sinistra splende, ecc.

ZINGARI   Mesta è la tua canzon!
AZUCENA   Del pari mesta
Che la storia funesta
Da cui tragge argomento!
(*Rivolge il capo dalla parte di Manrico
e mormora sommessamente.*)
Mi vendica!... Mi vendica!

MANRICO   (L'arcana parola ognor!)
UNO ZINGARO   Compagni, avanza il giorno;
A procacciarci un pan,
Su, sul scendiamo
Per le propinque ville.

ZINGARI   Andiamo! Andiamo!
(*Ripongono sollecitamente nei sacchi i loro ar-
nesi e discendono giù alla rinfusa per la china.*)
Chi del gitano i giorni, ecc.

MANRICO (*sorgendo*)
Soli or siamo. Deh, narra
Quella storia funesta.

> To work, to work! At it. Hammer.
> Who brightens the gypsy man's days?
> The gypsy maid!
> (*They interrupt their work briefly, saying to the women:*)

> Pour me a draught: strength and courage
> The body and soul draw from drinking.
> (*The women pour wine into crude cups.*)
> Oh, look, look! . . . A ray of the sun
> Sparkles brighter in my (your) glass!
> To work, to work! . . .
> Who brightens the gypsy man's days?
> The gypsy maid!

AZUCENA (*The gypsies gather around her.*)
> The flame crackles!
> The unrestrained mob
> Runs to that fire,
> Their faces happy!
> Shouts of joy
> Re-echo around;
> Surrounded by killers,
> A woman comes forward;
> Sinister, shining
> On the horrible faces,
> The ghastly flame
> Rises, rises toward heaven!

> The flame crackles!
> The victim arrives
> Dressed in black,
> Disheveled, barefoot;
> A fierce shout
> Of death is raised;
> Its echo repeats it
> From hill to hill.
> Sinister, shining, etc.

GYPSIES   Your song's a sad one!

AZUCENA   Just as sad
> As the terrible story
> That inspired it!
> (*She turns her head toward Manrico and murmurs softly.*)

> Avenge me! . . . Avenge me!

MANRICO   (That mysterious word again!)

A GYPSY   Companions, day is approaching;
> To forage for our bread,
> Come, come! Let's go down
> To the nearby villages.

GYPSIES   Let's go! Let's go!
> (*Hastily replacing their tools in their
> sacks, they swarm down the slopes.*)
> Who brightens, etc.

MANRICO (*rising*)
> We're alone now. Ah, tell me
> That terrible story.

AZUCENA   E tu la ignori, tu pur!...
               Ma, giovinetto, i passi tuoi
               D'ambizion lo sprone
               Lungi traea!
               Dell'ava il fine acerbo
               È quest'istoria ...
               La incolpò superbo conte
               Di malefizio,
               Onde asseria côlto un bambin,
               Suo figlio ... essa bruciata venne
               Ov'arde quel foco!
MANRICO *(rifuggendo con raccapriccio dalla fiamma)*
               Ahi! sciagurata!
AZUCENA   Condotta ell'era in ceppi
               Al suo destin tremendo;
               Col figlio sulle braccia,
               Io la seguia piangendo.
               Infino ad essa un varco tentai,
               Ma invano, aprirmi ...
               Invan tentò la misera
               Fermarsi e benedirmi!
               Chè, fra bestemmie oscene,
               Pungendola coi ferri,
               Al rogo la cacciavano,
               Gli scellerati sgherri!...
               Allor, con tronco accento,
               "Mi vendica!" sclamò!...
               Quel detto un eco eterno
               In questo cor lasciò.
MANRICO   La vendicasti?
AZUCENA   Il figlio giunsi
               A rapir del conte;
               Lo trascinai qui meco ...
               La fiamme ardean già pronte.
MANRICO *(con raccapriccio)*
               Le fiamme?... Oh ciel!...
               Tu forse?...
AZUCENA   Ei distruggeasi in pianto ...
               Io mi sentiva il core
               Dilaniato, infranto!...
               Quand'ecco agl'egri spirti,
               Come in un sogno, apparve
               La vision ferale
               Di spaventose larve!...
               Gli sgherri!... ed il supplizio!...
               La madre smorta in volto ...
               Scalza, discinta!...
               Il grido!... il grido!
               Il noto grido ascolto!...
               "Mi vendica!"
               La mano convulsa stendo ...
               Stringo la vittima ...
               Nel foco la traggo, la sospingo!
               Cessa il fatal delirio ...

AZUCENA   You, even you don't know it! . . .
But, as a boy,
The spur of ambition
Drove your steps far from here!
This is the story
Of your grandmother's bitter end . . .
A haughty count accused her
Of witchcraft,
And said that a child, his son,
Had been bewitched; she was burned
Where that fire gleams!

MANRICO (*starting back in horror from the flame*)
Ah! The wretch!

AZUCENA   She was led in irons
To her terrible fate;
With my baby in my arms,
I followed her, weeping.
I tried to make my way
To her, but in vain . . .
And in vain the poor woman
Tried to stop and bless me!
Then, amid obscene curses,
Pricking her with their swords,
They forced her to the stake,
Those wicked killers! . . .
Then, in a broken voice,
"Avenge me!" she cried! . . .
Those words left an eternal echo
In my heart.

MANRICO   Did you avenge her?

AZUCENA   I managed to steal
The Count's son;
I dragged him here with me . . .
The flames were ready, burning.

MANRICO (*with horror*)
The flames? . . . Oh heaven! . . .
Did you perhaps? . . .

AZUCENA   He was racked with sobs . . .
I felt my heart
Torn, broken! . . .
When, lo, to my weak spirits,
As in a dream, appeared
The bestial vision
Of frightful forms! . . .
The killers! . . . and the torture! . . .
My mother, with blanched face . . .
Barefoot, disheveled!
Her cry! . . . Her cry! . . .
I hear the familiar cry! . . .
"Avenge me!"
I stretch out my shaking hand . . .
Seize the victim . . .
Draw him to the fire, and push!
The fatal madness ends . . .

L'orrida scena fugge ...
La fiamma sol divampa,
E la sua preda strugge!...
Pur volgo intorno il guardo
E innanzi a me vegg'io
Dell'empio Conte il figlio!

MANRICO   Ah, che dici?

AZUCENA   Il figlio mio, mio figlio
Avea bruciato!

MANRICO   Ah! quale orror!

AZUCENA   Sul capo mio le chiome
Sento drizzarsi ancor!

*Azucena ricade, trambasciata sul proprio seggio. Manrico
ammutolisce, colpito d'orrore e di sorpresa.*

MANRICO   Non son tuo figlio! ...
E chi son io? Chi dunque?

AZUCENA (*interrompendo*)
Tu sei mio figlio!

MANRICO   Eppur dicesti ...

AZUCENA   Ah forse? Che vuoi!
Quando al pensier s'affaccia
Il truce caso
Lo spirto intenebrato pone
Stolte parole sul mio labbro.
Madre, tenera madre,
Non m'avesti ognora?

MANRICO   Potrei negarlo?

AZUCENA   A me, se vivi ancora,
Nol dèi?
Notturna, nei pugnati campi
Di Pelilla, ove spento fama
Ti disse, a darti sepoltura
Non mossi?
La fuggente aura vital
Non iscovrì? Nel seno
Non t'arrestò materno affetto?
E quante cure non spesi
A risanar le tante ferite!...

MANRICO (*con* nobile orogoglio)
Che portai nel dì fatale ...
Ma tutte qui, nel petto ...
Io sol, fra mille già sbandati,
Al nemico volgendo ancor la faccia!...
Il rio Di Luna su me piombò
Col suo drappello: io caddi,
Però, da forte io caddi!

AZUCENA   Ecco mercede ai giorni,
Che l'infame nel singolar certame
Ebbe salvi da te!
Qual t'accieccava
Strana pietà per esso?

	The horrible scene disappears . . . Only the flame rages, And destroys its prey! . . . And yet, I look around And before me I see The wicked Count's son!
MANRICO	Ah, what are you saying?
AZUCENA	My own, my own son I had burned!
MANRICO	Ah! how horrible!
AZUCENA	I can still feel the hair Stand up on my head!

Exhausted, Azucena sinks back on her stool. Manrico is silent, astonished, and horror-stricken.

MANRICO	I'm not your son! Who am I? Who, then?
AZUCENA (*interrupting*)	
	You are my son!
MANRICO	Yet you said . . .
AZUCENA	Perhaps I did. You know how it is! When the ghastly event Comes into my mind My clouded spirit sets Foolish words on my lips. Haven't I always been a mother, A tender mother, to you?
MANRICO	Could I deny it?
AZUCENA	If you're still alive, Don't you owe it to me? At night, over the battlefields Of Pelilla, where the story was That you were dead, didn't I come To give you burial? Didn't I discover your fleeting Breath of life? And didn't maternal Love hold it in your breast? And what care I devoted To healing all those wounds! . . .
MANRICO (*with noble pride*)	
	That I bore on that fatal day . . . But all of them, here, in my chest . . . Only I, among the retreating thousand, Turned my face still toward the foe! . . . The evil Di Luna fell upon me With his escort: I fell, But I fell like a strong man!
AZUCENA	That was the thanks for his life, Which in that single combat The monster was given by you! What strange pity for him Blinded you?

MANRICO   Oh madre!
              Non saprei dirlo a me stesso!
AZUCENA   Strana pietà! Strana pietà!
MANRICO   Mal reggendo all'aspro assalto,
              Ei già tocco il suolo avea:
              Balenava il colpo in alto
              Che trafiggerlo dovea ...
              Quando arresta un moto arcano
              Nel discender questa mano!
              Le mie fibre acuto gelo
              Fa repente abbrividir!
              Mentre un grido vien dal cielo,
              Che mi dice: Non ferir!
AZUCENA   Ma nell'alma dell'ingrato
              Non parlò del ciel un detto!
              Oh se ancor ti spinge il fato
              A pugnar col maledetto,
              Compi, o figlio, qual d'un Dio,
              Compi allora il cenno mio:
              Sino all'elsa questa lama
              Vibra, immergi all'empio in cor!
MANRICO   Sì, lo giuro, questa lama
              Scenderà dell'empio in cor!

Odesi un prolungato suono di corno.

              L'usato messo Ruiz invia!...
              Forse ...

Dà fiato anch'esso al suo corno.

AZUCENA (*resta concentrata, quasi inconsapevole di ciò che
    succede.*)
              "Mi vendica!"

Entra il messo.

MANRICO   Inoltra il piè ...
              Guerresco evento, dimmi, seguia?
MESSO   Risponda il foglio
              Che reco a te.
MANRICO (*leggendo la lettera*)
              "In nostra possa è Castellor;
              Ne dêi tu, per cenno del Prence,
              Vigilar le difese.
              Ove ti è dato, affrettati a venir.
              Giunta la sera, tratta in inganno
              Di tua morte al grido,
              Nel vicin chiostro della Croce,
              Il velo cingerà Leonora."
                  (*con dolorosa esclamazione*)
              Oh giusto cielo!
AZUCENA (*scuotendosi*)
                  (Che fia?)
MANRICO (*al messo*)
              Veloce scendi la balza,

MANRICO	Oh, Mother,
	I can't explain it to myself!
AZUCENA	A strange pity! Strange pity!
MANRICO	Fighting off poorly my fierce attack,
	He had already fallen to the ground:
	The thrust that was to pierce him
	Already flashed in the air . . .
	When a mysterious feeling
	Stays my hand, as it decends!
	Suddenly a sharp chill
	Runs shuddering through me!
	As a cry comes down from heaven,
	That says to me: Don't strike.
AZUCENA	But to that ingrate's spirit
	Heaven said not a word!
	Oh, if fate should drive you
	To fight that cursed man again,
	Then follow, my son, like a God,
	Follow then what I tell you to do:
	Strike, plunge that blade
	Up to its hilt in the villain's heart!
MANRICO	Yes, I swear it, this blade
	Will plunge into the villain's heart!

A prolonged sound of a horn is heard.

Ruiz sends the usual messenger!
Perhaps . . .

He also blows on his horn.

AZUCENA (*still lost in thought, almost oblivious of what is happening*)
"Avenge me!"

The messenger enters.

MANRICO	Come in. Tell me . . .
	Did more fighting follow?
MESSENGER	Let this letter I bear you
	Give the answer.

MANRICO (*reading the letter*)
"Castellor is in our hands;
The Prince's orders are that you
Shall supervise its defense.
When you are able, hurry here.
This evening, deceived by the cry
Of your death,
In the nearby Holy Cross Convent,

Leonora will take the veil."
(*crying out, grief-stricken*)
Oh, merciful heaven!

AZUCENA (*stirring*)
(What is it?)

MANRICO (*to the messenger*)
Hurry down the hill,

E d'un cavallo a me provvedi.

MESSO   Corro.

AZUCENA (*frapponendosi*)
           Manrico!

MANRICO (*al messo*)
           Il tempo incalza ...
           Vola ... m'aspetta del colle
           Ai piedi.

Il messo parte frettolosamente.

AZUCENA   E speri? e vuoi?

MANRICO   (Perderla! Oh ambascia!
           Perder quell'angel!)

AZUCENA   (È fuor di sè!)

MANRICO (*postosi l'elmo sul capo ed afferrando il mantello*)
           Addio!

AZUCENA   No, ferma, odi ...

MANRICO   Mi lascia!

AZUCENA   Ferma!
           Son io che parlo a te!
           Perigliarti ancor languente
           Per cammin selvaggio ed ermo!
           Le ferite vuoi, demente!
           Riaprir del petto infermo?
           No, soffrirlo non poss'io ...
           Il tuo sangue è sangue mio!
           Ogni stilla che ne versi
           Tu la spremi dal mio cor!

MANRICO   Un momento può involarmi
           Il mio ben, la mia speranza!
           No, che basti ad arrestarmi,
           Terra e ciel non han possanza.

AZUCENA   Demente!

MANRICO   Ah! mi sgombra, o madre, i passi ...
           Guai per te s'io qui restassi!
           Tu vedresti, a' piedi tuoi
           Spento il figlio di dolor!

AZUCENA   No, soffrirlo, ecc.
           Deh! ferma! ferma!

MANRICO   Mi lascia, addio!

Manrico si allontana, indarno trattenuto de Azucena.

ATTO SECONDO

PARTE SECONDA

*Atrio interno di un luogo di ritiro in vicinanza di Castellor.
Alberi in fondo. È notte. Il Conte, Ferrando, ed alcuni seguaci
innoltrandosi cautamente, avviluppati nei lori mantelli.*

And prepare a horse for me.

MESSENGER I'll run.

AZUCENA (*blocking his way*)
Manrico!

MANRICO (*to the messenger*)
Time presses!
Fly . . . Wait for me
At the foot of the hill.

The messenger hurries off.

AZUCENA What do you want or hope to do?

MANRICO (To lose her! Oh, woe!
To lose that angel!)

AZUCENA (He's beside himself!)

MANRICO (*putting on his helmet and seizing his cloak*)
Farewell!

AZUCENA No, stop, hear me . . .

MANRICO Let me go!

AZUCENA Stop!
It is I who speak to you!
To risk yourself, still sickly,
On a wild and steep road!
Madman, do you mean to reopen
The wounds in your unhealed breast?
No, I cannot bear it . . .
Your blood is my blood!
Every drop you shed of it
You're pressing from my heart!

MANRICO A moment can steal from me
My love, my hope!
No, heaven and earth haven't
The strength to stop me.

AZUCENA Madman!

MANRICO Ah! Mother. Get out of my way . . .
Woe to you if I remain here!
You would see, at your feet,
Your son, dead of grief!

AZUCENA No, I cannot bear it, etc.
Ah! Stop! Stop!

MANRICO Let me go, farewell!

Manrico leaves as Azucena tries in vain to hold him back.

ACT TWO

SCENE TWO

*Inner courtyard of a retreat in the neighborhood of Castel-
lor. Trees at the back. It is night. The Count, Ferrando, and
some retainers come in cautiously, wrapped in their cloaks.*

CONTE	Tutto è deserto;
	Nè per l'aure ancora
	Suona l'usato carme.
	In tempo io giungo!
FERRANDO	Ardita opra, o signore,
	Imprendi.
CONTE	Ardita, e qual furente amore
	Ed irritato orgoglio
	Chiesero a me.
	Spento il rival, caduto
	Ogni ostacol sembrava
	A' miei desiri;
	Novello e più possente
	Ella ne appresta ... l'altare ...
	Ah no! Non fia d'altri Leonora!
	Leonora è mia!
	Il balen del suo sorriso
	D'una stella vince il raggio;
	Il fulgor del suo bel viso
	Novo infonde a me coraggio.
	Ah! l'amor, l'amore ond'ardo
	Le favelli in mio favor,
	Sperda il sole d'un suo sguardo
	La tempesta del mio cor.
	(*Odesi il rintocco de' sacri bronzi.*)
	Qual suono! Oh ciel!
FERRANDO	La squilla
	Vicino il rito annunzia.
CONTE	Ah! pria che giunga all'altar ...
	Si rapisca!
FERRANDO	Ah bada!
CONTE	Taci!...
	Non odo!... Andate.
	Di quei faggi all'ombra
	Celatevi.
	(*Ferrando ed i seguaci si allontanano.*)
	Ah! fra poco mia diverrà!...
	Tutto m'investe un foco!

Ansioso e guardingo, osserva dalla parte ove deve giungere Leonora.

FERRANDO e SEGUACI	Ardir! andiam,
	Celiamoci fra l'ombre,
	Nel mister! ardir! andiam ...
	Silenzio!
	Si compia il suo voler!
CONTE	Per me ora fatale,
	I tuoi momenti affretta, affretta:
	La gioia che m'aspetta,
	Gioia mortal non è, no!
	Invano un Dio rivale
	S'oppone all'amor mio ...

COUNT   All is deserted;
                 Nor has the usual hymn
                 Yet resounded on the air.
                 I've come in time!

FERRANDO   O master, you are undertaking
                 A bold errand.

COUNT   Bold, yes, it's what furious love
                 And provoked pride
                 Have demanded of me.
                 My rival killed, every obstacle
                 To my wishes
                 Seemed to have fallen;
                 Now she prepares a new
                 And more powerful one . . . the altar . . .
                 Ah no! Leonora shall not belong to others!
                 Leonora is mine!
                 The flashing of her smile
                 Is brighter than a star's ray;
                 The splendor of her fair face
                 Instills new courage in me.
                 Ah! Let the love that enflames me
                 Speak to her in my favor,
                 Let the sun of her glance
                 Dispel the storm in my heart.
                        (*A church bell is heard.*)
                 That sound! Oh, heaven!

FERRANDO   Its tolling
                 Announces the approaching rite.

COUNT   Ah! Before she reaches the altar . . .
                 She shall be seized!

FERRANDO   Watch out!

COUNT   Silence! . . .
                 I am not listening! . . . Go.
                 And in the shade of those beeches
                 Conceal yourselves.
                 (*Ferrando and the retainers leave.*)
                 Ah! Soon she'll become mine! . . .
                 A fire rages through me!

*Anxious and cautious, he looks toward the spot where
Leonora is to appear.*

FERRANDO and RETAINERS
                 Courage! Let's go,
                 And hide in the shadows,
                 In mystery! Courage! Let's go . . .
                 Silence!
                 His will be done!

COUNT   Hour, fatal for me,
                 Speed, speed on your moments:
                 The joy that awaits me
                 Is not mortal joy, no!
                 In vain a rival God
                 Opposes my love . . .

                    Non può nemmen un Dio,
                    Donna, rapirti a me!

FERRANDO e SEGUACI
                    Ardir! andiam, ecc.

*S'allontana a poco a poco e si nasconde col coro fra gli
alberi. Si sentono le voci delle religiose dentro.*

CONTE   Per me ora fatale, ecc.

RELIGIOSE   Ah! se l'error t'ingombra,
                O figlia d'Eva, i rai,
                Presso a morir, vedrai
                Che un'ombra, un sogno fu,
                Anzi del sogno un'ombra
                La speme di quaggiù!

CONTE (*nascosto fra le piante*)
                    (No, no, non può
                    Nemmen un Dio, ecc.)

FERRANDO e SEGUACI (*nascosti fra le piante*)
                    Coraggio, ardir!, ecc.

RELIGIOSE   Vieni, e t'asconda il velo
                Ad ogni sguardo umano;
                Aura o pensier mondano
                Qui vivo più non è!
                Al ciel ti volgi, e il cielo
                Si schiuderà per te.

Leonora con Ines e seguito muliebre.

LEONORA   Perchè piangete?

INES   Ah! dunque tu per sempre
                Ne lasci!

LEONORA   O dolci amiche,
                Un riso, una speranza, un fior
                La terra non ha per me!
                Degg'io volgermi
                A Quei che degli afflitti
                È solo sostegno,
                E dopo i penitenti giorni,
                Può fra gli eletti
                Al mio perduto bene
                Ricongiungermi un dì.
                Tergete i rai,
                E guidatemi all'ara ...

CONTE (*irrompendo ad un tratto*)
                    No! giammai!

INES e DONNE   Il Conte!

LEONORA   Giusto ciel!

CONTE   Per te non havvi
                Che l'ara d'imeneo.

INES e DONNE   Cotanto ardia!

> Not even a God is able,
> O woman, to steal you from me!

FERRANDO and RETAINERS
> Courage! Let's go, etc.

The Count hides with the others. Inside the church the nuns' voices are heard.

COUNT
> Hour, fatal for me, etc.

NUNS
> Ah! if error blinds your eyes,
> Daughter of Eve,
> As death nears, you'll see
> That it was a shadow, a dream,
> Nay, but the shadow of a dream
> Is our yearning here below!

COUNT (*hidden among the trees*)
> (No, no, not even a God
> Is able, etc.)

FERRANDO and RETAINERS (*hidden among the trees*)
> (Courage, be bold!, etc.)

NUNS
> Come, let the veil hide you
> From every human eye;
> No worldly air or thought
> Can live in here any longer!
> Turn to heaven, and heaven
> Will be disclosed to you.

Leonora and Ines enter with a train of women.

LEONORA
> Why are you weeping?

INES
> Ah! Then you are leaving us
> Forever!

LEONORA
> O sweet friends,
> Earth no longer has for me
> Laughter, hope, or flowers!
> I must turn now
> To Him who is the only support
> Of the grieving,
> Who after my days of penance,
> Can join me
> To my lost love
> One day among the blessed!
> Dry your eyes,
> And lead me to the altar . . .

COUNT (*bursting in suddenly*)
> No! Never!

INES and WOMEN
> The Count!

LEONORA
> Merciful heaven!

COUNT
> The only altar for you
> Is the nuptial altar.

INES and WOMEN
> He dared go so far!

LEONORA	Insano! E qui venisti?
CONTE	A farti mia!

Comparisce Manrico.

TUTTI	Ah!
LEONORA	E deggio e posso crederlo?
	Ti veggo a me d'accanto!
	È questo un sogno, un'estasi,
	Un sovrumano incanto!
	Non regge a tanto giubilo
	Rapito il cor, sorpreso!
	Sei tu dal ciel disceso,
	O in ciel son io con te?
CONTE	Dunque gli estinti lasciano
	Di morte il regno eterno!
MANRICO	Nè m'ebbe il ciel nè l'orrido
	Varco infernal sentiero.
CONTE	A danno mio rinunzia
	Le prede sue l'inferno!
MANRICO	Infami sgherri vibrano
	Mortali colpi, è vero!
CONTE	Ma se non mai si fransero
	De' giorni tuoi gli stami,
	Se vivi e viver brami,
	Fuggi da lei, da me.
MANRICO	Potenza irresistibile
	Hanno de' fiumi l'onde!
	Ma gli empi un Dio confonde!
	Quel Dio soccorse a me.
LEONORA	O in ciel son io con te?
INES e DONNE (*a Leonora*)	
	Il cielo in cui fidasti, ah!
	Pietade avea di te.
FERRANDO e SEGUACI (*al Conte*)	
	Tu col destin contrasti,
	Suo difensore egli è.

Ruiz entra con uomini armati.

RUIZ e SEGUACI DI MANRICO	
	Urgel viva!
MANRICO	Miei prodi guerrieri!
RUIZ	Vieni!
MANRICO (*a Leonora*)	
	Donna, mi segui.
CONTE (*opponendosi*)	
	E tu speri?
LEONORA	Ah!
MANRICO (*al Conte*)	
	T'arresta!
CONTE	Involarmi costei! No!

*Il Conte sguaina la spada ma viene disarmato da Ruiz e da
i suoi uomini.*

LEONORA	Madman? You've come here?
COUNT	To make you mine!

Manrico appears.

ALL	Ah!
LEONORA	Must I, can I believe it? I see you at my side! This is a dream, an ecstasy, A supernatural enchantment! My heart surprised, transported, Cannot bear such joy! Have you come down from heaven, Or am I in heaven with you?
COUNT	Then the dead can leave Death's eternal realm!
MANRICO	Heaven did not hold me, nor did The horrid path of hell.
COUNT	Hell gives up its prey In order to do me harm!
MANRICO	Your foul killers struck Mortal blows, it's true!
COUNT	But if they never broke The stalk of your days, If you live and want to live, Flee from her, and from me.
MANRICO	The waves of the rivers Have an irresistible force! But a God confounds the wicked! And that God succored me.
LEONORA	Or am I in heaven with you?
INES and WOMEN (*to Leonora*)	
	Ah! The heaven that you trusted Had mercy on you.
FERNANDO and RETAINERS (*to the Count*)	
	You're fighting against fate, Which is his defender.

Ruiz enters with armed men.

RUIZ and MANRICO'S FOLLOWERS	
	Long live Urgel!
MANRICO	My brave fighters!
RUIZ	Come!
MANRICO (*to Leonora*)	
	My lady, follow me.
COUNT (*blocking his way*)	
	You dare hope?
LEONORA	Ah!
MANRICO (*to the Count*)	
	Stop!
COUNT	To steal her from me? No!

The Count draws his sword but is disarmed by Ruiz and his men.

RUIZ ed UOMINI (*accerchiando il Conte*)
            Vaneggi!
FERRANDO e SEGUACI
            Che tenti, signor?
CONTE (*con gesti ed accenti di maniaco furore*)
            Di ragione ogni lume perdei!
LEONORA   M'atterrisce!

INES e DONNE Ah, sì, il ciel
            Pietade avea di te!
MANRICO   Fia supplizio la vita per te!
CONTE   Ho le furie nel cor!
RUIZ ed UOMINI
            Vieni, la sorte sorride per te.
FERRANDO e SEGUACI
            Cedi; or ceder
            Viltade non è!
LEONORA   Sei tu dal ciel, ecc.

Manrico tragge seco Leonora. Il Conte è respinto, le donne
rifuggono al cenobio. Scende subito la tela.

ATTO TERZO

Il Figlio della zingara

PARTE PRIMA

Accampamento. A destra padiglione del Conte di Luna, su
cui sventola la bandiera in segno di supremo comando. Da
lungi torreggia Castellor.

ALCUNI SOLDATI
            Or co' dadi, ma fra poco
            Giocherem ben altro gioco!
            Quest'acciar, dal sangue or terso,
            Fia di sangue in breve asperso!
            (*Un grosso drappello di Balestrieri traversa*
                      il campo.)
            Il soccorso dimandato!
            Han l'aspetto del valor!
            Più l'assalto ritardato
            Or non fia di Castellor.
FERRANDO   Sì, prodi amici: al dì novello,
            È mente del capitan la rôcca
            Investir da ogni parte.
            Colà pingue bottino
            Certezza è rinvenir più che speranza.
            Si vinca; è nostro.
SOLDATI   Tu c'invita a danza!

RUIZ and MEN (*surrounding the Count*)
>You rave!

FERRANDO and RETAINERS
>What are you attempting, sir?

COUNT (*wild fury in his words and movements*)
>I lost all reason!

LEONORA   He terrifies me!

INES and WOMEN
>Ah, yes, heaven
>Had mercy on you!

MANRICO   May your life be a torment!

COUNT   My heart is raging!

RUIZ and MEN
>Come, fate smiles on you.

FERRANDO and RETAINERS
>Surrender; to surrender now
>Is not cowardice!

LEONORA   Have you come down, etc.

Manrico drags Leonora off with him. The Count is driven back, the women flee into the convent. The curtain falls at once.

ACT THREE

The Gypsy's Son

SCENE ONE

Military camp. At right the Count di Luna's tent, over which the banner indicating the supreme command is flying. In the distance stand the towers of Castellor.

SOME SOLDIERS
>Now we're dicing, but before long
>We'll play a very different game!
>This sword, now wiped clean of blood,
>Will soon be bathed in blood again!
>(*A large detachment of archers crosses the camp.*)

>The reinforcements asked for!
>They look brave!
>May the attack on Castellor
>Be put off no longer.

FERRANDO   Yes, brave friends: at dawn,
>The captain plans to attack
>The fort from every side.
>There we'll surely find
>Booty rich beyond our hopes.
>Conquer then; it's ours.

SOLDIERS   You're inviting us to a party!

102

TUTTI
Squilli, echeggi la tromba guerriera,
Chiami all'armi, alla pugna, all'assalto;
Fia domani la nostra bandiera
Di quei merli piantata sull'alto.
No, giammai non sorrise vittoria
Di più liete speranze finor!
Ivi l'util ci aspetta e la gloria,
Ivi opimi la preda e l'onor.
Squilli, echeggi, ecc.

Si disperdono.

Il Conte, uscito dalla tenda, volge uno sguardo bieco a Castellor.

CONTE
In braccio al mio rival!
Questo pensiero come persecutor demone
Ovunque m'insegue.
In braccio al mio rival!
Ma corro, surta appena l'aurora,
Io corro a separarvi.
Oh Leonora!
     (*Odesi tumulto. Entra Ferrando.*)
Che fu?

FERRANDO
Dappresso al campo
S'aggirava una zingara:
Sorpresa da' nostri esploratori,
Si volse in fuga; essi, a ragion
Temendo una spia nella trista,
L'inseguîr.

CONTE
Fu raggiunta?

FERRANDO
È presa.

CONTE
Vista l'hai tu?

FERRANDO
No. Della scorta il condottier
M'apprese l'evento.

Tumulto più vicino.

CONTE
Eccola.

Con le mani legate, Azucena è trascinata dagli esploratori.

SOLDATI
Innanzi, o strega, innanzi!

AZUCENA
Aita! Mi lasciate!...
Ah furibondi!
Che mal fec'io?

CONTE
S'appressi.
     (*Azucena è tratta innanzi al Conte.*)
A me rispondi,
E trema dal mentir!

AZUCENA
Chiedi.

CONTE
Ove vai?

AZUCENA
Nol so.

CONTE
Che?

AZUCENA
D'una zingara è costume

ALL	Let the warlike trumpet sound and echo, Call to arms, to the fray, the attack; May our flag be planted tomorrow On the highest of those ramparts. No, victory has never smiled On happier hopes before! There glory awaits us, and the needful, There wait spoils, booty, and honor. Let the warlike trumpet, etc.

They disperse.

The Count, coming out of his tent, looks grimly at Castellor.

COUNT	In my rival's arms! This thought pursues me everywhere Like a persecuting demon. In my rival's arms! But as soon as dawn breaks, I'll run, I'll run to separate you. Oh Leonora! *(Noise is heard. Ferrando enters.)* What is it?
FERRANDO	Near the camp A gypsy was wandering: Surprised by our scouts, She started to flee; rightfully Fearing the wretch was a spy, They followed her.
COUNT	Did they overtake her?
FERRANDO	She's been taken.
COUNT	Have you seen her?
FERRANDO	No. The commander of the patrol Gave me the news.

Noise is nearer.

COUNT	Here she is.

Her hands bound, Azucena is dragged by the scouts.

SOLDIERS	Forward, you witch, forward!
AZUCENA	Help! Let me go! . . . Ah, you raving men! What wrong have I done?
COUNT	Approach. *(Azucena is dragged before the Count.)* Answer me, And don't dare lie!
AZUCENA	Question me.
COUNT	Where are you going?
AZUCENA	I don't know.
COUNT	What?
AZUCENA	It's a gypsy's custom

	Mover senza disegno
	Il passo vagabondo,
	Ed è suo tetto il ciel,
	Sua patria il mondo.

CONTE   E vieni?

AZUCENA   Da Biscaglia, ove finora
           Le sterili montagne ebbi a ricetto.

CONTE   (Da Biscaglia!)

FERRANDO   (Che intesi!
           Oh! Qual sospetto!)

AZUCENA   Giorni poveri vivea,
           Pur contenta del mio stato;
           Sola speme un figlio avea.
           Mi lasciò, m'obblia l'ingrato!
           Io, deserta, vado errando
           Di quel figlio ricercando,
           Di quel figlio che al mio core
           Pene orribili costò!
           Qual per esso provo amore
           Madre in terra non provò!

FERRANDO   (Il suo volto!)

CONTE   Di', traesti lunga etade
           Fra quei monti?

AZUCENA   Lunga, sì.

CONTE   Rammenteresti un fanciul,
           Prole di conti,
           Involato al suo castello,
           Son tre lustri,
           E tratto quivi?

AZUCENA   E tu ... parla ... sei?

CONTE   Fratello del rapito!

AZUCENA   (Ah!)

FERRANDO (*notando il terrore di Azucena*)
           (Sì!)

CONTE   Ne udivi mai novella?

AZUCENA   Io! no!... Concedi
           Che del figlio l'orme io scopra.

FERRANDO   Resta, iniqua!...

AZUCENA   (Ohimè!)

FERRANDO (*al Conte*)
           Tu vedi chi l'infame,
           Orribil opra commettea!

CONTE   Finisci.

FERRANDO   È dessa!

AZUCENA (*piano a Ferrando*)
           Taci!

FERRANDO   È dessa
           Che il bambino arse!

CONTE   Ah, perfida!

SOLDATI   Ella stessa!

	To move her wandering steps Without any plan, The sky is her roof, And the world is her country.
COUNT	Where have you come from?
AZUCENA	From Biscay, whose barren mountains Housed me until now.
COUNT FERRANDO	(From Biscay!) (What do I hear! Oh! What a suspicion!)
AZUCENA	I lived days of poverty, Yet happy in my condition; My only hope was my son. The ingrate left and forgot me! Abandoned, I wander about Hunting for that son, For that son who cost my heart Horrible pangs! The love I feel for him No other mother on earth has felt!
FERRANDO	(Her face!)
COUNT	Tell me, did you stay a long time In those mountains?
AZUCENA	Yes, a long time.
COUNT	Can you remember a child, A son of a count, Stolen from his castle, Fifteen years ago, And brought there?
AZUCENA	You . . . speak . . . who are you?
COUNT	The stolen boy's brother!
AZUCENA	(Ah!)
FERRANDO *(seeing Azucena's terror)*	(Yes!)
COUNT	Did you ever have word of him?
AZUCENA	Not I! . . . Let me Trace my son's footsteps.
FERRANDO	Wait, foul wretch! . . .
AZUCENA	(Alas!)
FERRANDO *(to the Count)*	You see who committed The horrible, ghastly deed!
COUNT	Go on.
FERRANDO	She's the one!
AZUCENA *(softly to Ferrando)*	Be silent!
FERRANDO	She's the one Who burned the child!
COUNT	Ah, monster!
SOLDIERS	She's the one!

AZUCENA   Ei mentisce!...
CONTE   Al tuo destino
              Or non fuggi!
AZUCENA   Deh!
CONTE   Quei nodi più stringete!

I soldati eseguiscono.

AZUCENA   Oh Dio! Oh Dio!
SOLDATI   Urla pur!
AZUCENA (*con disperazione*)
              E tu non vieni, o Manrico,
              O figlio mio?
              Non soccorri all'infelice
              Madre tua?
CONTE   Di Manrico genitrice!
FERRANDO   Trema!
CONTE   Oh sorte! In mio poter!
AZUCENA   Ah! Deh, rallentate, o barbari,
              Le acerbe mie ritorte ...
              Questo crudel martirio
              È prolungata morte!
              D'iniquo genitore
              Empio figliuol peggiore,
              Trema! V'è Dio pei miseri
              E Dio ti punirà!

CONTE   Tua prole, o turpe zingara,
              Colui, quel traditore?
              Potrò col tuo supplizio
              Ferirlo in mezzo al cor!
              Gioia m'innonda il petto,
              Cui non esprime il detto!
              Ah, meco il fraterno cenere
              Piena vendetta avrà!

FERRANDO e SOLDATI
              Infame, pira sorgere, ah sì, vedrai
              Vedrai tra poco ...
              Nè solo tuo supplizio
              Sarà terreno foco!
              Le vampe dell'inferno
              A te fian rogo eterno!
              Ivi penare ed ardere
              L'alma dovrà!

*Al cenno del Conte i soldati traggono seco loro Azucena.
Egli entra nella tenda, seguito da Ferrando.*

AZUCENA	He's lying! . . .
COUNT	Now you won't escape Your fate!
AZUCENA	I beg you!
COUNT	Tie those knots tighter!

The soldiers obey.

AZUCENA	Oh, God! Oh, God!
SOLDIERS	Go ahead and shout!
AZUCENA (*in desperation*)	
	Why don't you come, Manrico, O my son? Won't you aid your Wretched mother?
COUNT	Manrico's mother!
FERRANDO	Tremble!
COUNT	Oh, luck! She's in my power!
AZUCENA	Ah! Pray, barbarians, loosen My harsh chains . . . This cruel torture Is like a drawn-out death! Oh, wicked son, worse Than your wicked father, Beware! There is a God for the helpless, And God will punish you!
COUNT	Your brood, foul gypsy, He, that traitor? With your torture then I can wound his heart! Joy that no words can express Floods my breast! Ah, through me my brother's ashes Will have complete vengeance!

FERRANDO and SOLDIERS

        Wretch, you'll see a pyre, ah yes,
        Rise here in a little while . . .
        Nor will that earthly fire
        Be your only punishment!
        For you the flames of hell
        Will be an eternal stake!
        There your soul will have
        To suffer and to burn!

*At a sign from the Count the soldiers drag Azucena away
with them. He goes into his tent, followed by Ferrando.*

ATTO TERZO

PARTE SECONDA

Sala adiacente alla cappella in Castellor, con verone in fondo. Manrico, Leonora e Ruiz sono in scena.

LEONORA   Quale d'armi fragor
Poc'anzi intesi?

MANRICO   Alto è il periglio ...
Vano dissimularlo fora!
Alla novella aurora
Assaliti saremo.

LEONORA   Ahimè! Che dici?

MANRICO   Ma de' nostri nemici
Avrem vittoria. Pari
Abbiamo al loro ardir,
Brando e coraggio.
    (a Ruiz)
Tu va. Le belliche opre,
Nell'assenza mia breve,
A te commetto.
Che nulla manchi!
    (Ruiz parte.)

LEONORA   Di qual tetra luce
Il nostro imen risplende!

MANRICO   Il presagio funesto
Deh, sperdi, o cara!

LEONORA   E il posso?

MANRICO   Amor, sublime amore,
In tale istante
Ti favelli al core.
Ah sì, ben mio, coll'essere
Io tuo, tu mia consorte.
Avrò più l'alma intrepida,
Il braccio avrò più forte.
Ma pur, se nella pagina
De' miei destini è scritto
Ch'io resti fra le vittime,
Dal ferro ostil trafitto,
Fra quegli estremi aneliti
A te il pensier verrà,
E solo in ciel precederti
La morte a me parrà.

Si sente l'organo della vicina cappella.

LEONORA e MANRICO
    L'onda de' suoni mistici
Pura discende al cor!
Vieni, ci schiude il tempio
Gioie di casto amor!

ACT THREE

SCENE TWO

A hall at Castellor next to the chapel, with a balcony at the back. Manrico, Leonora, and Ruiz.

LEONORA	What was that sound of arms I heard a moment ago?
MANRICO	The danger is great . . . It is vain to pretend! At dawn tomorrow We'll be attacked.
LEONORA	Alas! What are you saying?
MANRICO	But we will vanquish Our enemies. Our daring, Our arms, and our courage Are equal to theirs. *(to Ruiz)* Go. During my short absence, I commit to your care The war preparations. Let nothing be wanting. *(Ruiz leaves.)*
LEONORA	What a grim light Shines on our wedding!
MANRICO	Ah, my dear, rid yourself Of gloomy foreboding!
LEONORA	How can I?
MANRICO	Let love, sublime love, At this moment Speak to your heart. Ah yes, my love, when I am Yours and you are mine, My spirit will be more fearless, My arm will be stronger. And yet, if on the page Of my destiny it's written That I must be among the victims, Pierced by the foe's steel, As I draw my last breath My thoughts will come to you, And death will seem to me Only preceding you to heaven.

The organ is heard in the nearby chapel.

LEONORA and MANRICO

> Let the wave of holy sounds
> Descend pure into our hearts!
> Come, the altar opens to us
> The joys of chaste love!

Ruiz entra frettoloso.

RUIZ   Manrico?
MANRICO   Che?
RUIZ   La zingara ... vieni ...
             Tra' ceppi mira ...
MANRICO   Oh Dio!
RUIZ   Per man de' barbari
             Accesa è già la pira ...
MANRICO (*accostandosi al verone*)
             Oh ciel ... Mie membra oscillano.
             Nube mi copre il ciglio!
LEONORA   Tu fremi!
MANRICO   E il deggio!
             Sappilo: io son —
LEONORA   Chi mai?
MANRICO   Suo figlio!
LEONORA   Ah!
MANRICO   Ah, vili! Il rio spettacolo
             Quasi il respir m'invola!
             Raduna i nostri! Affrettati,
             Ruiz! Va, va ...
             Torna, vola!
                 (*Ruiz parte frettoloso.*)
             Di quella pira l'orrendo foco
             Tutte le fibre m'arse, avvampò!
             Empi, spegnetela, o ch'io fra poco
             Col sangue vostro la spegnerò!
             Era già figlio prima d'amarti;
             Non può frenarmi il tuo martir ...
             Madre infelice, corro a salvarti,
             O teco almeno corro a morir!
LEONORA   ° [Non reggo a colpi tanto funesti ...
             Oh quanto meglio saria morir!
MANRICO   Di quella pira, ecc.]

Ruiz torna con gli armati.

RUIZ ed ARMATI
             All'armi! All'armi!
             Eccone presti a pugnar teco,
             O teco a morir!
MANRICO   All'armi! All'armi!

*Manrico parte frettoloso, seguito da Ruiz e dagli armati,
mentre odesi dall'interno fragor d'armi e di bellici strumenti.*

° Brackets denote passages often omitted in performance.

Ruiz hurries in.

RUIZ	Manrico?
MANRICO	What is it?
RUIZ	The gypsy . . . come . . . In irons . . . look . . .
MANRICO	Oh, God!
RUIZ	Those barbarians' hands Have already lighted the pyre . . .

MANRICO (*approaching the balcony*)
> Oh, heaven . . . My legs fail me.
> My eyes are clouding over!

LEONORA	You're raging!
MANRICO	I should! Learn then: I am —
LEONORA	Who?
MANRICO	Her son!
LEONORA	Ah!
MANRICO	Ah, cowards! This wicked sight Almost robs me of my breath! Get our men together! Hurry, Ruiz! Go, go . . . And fly back! (*Ruiz leaves hastily.*) The horrible blaze of that pyre Burns, enflames all of my being! Monsters, put it out, or very quickly I'll put it out with your blood! Before I loved you, I was already her son; Your suffering cannot restrain me . . . Unhappy mother, I hasten to save you, Or at least hasten to die with you!
LEONORA	I can't bear these grievous blows . . . How much better it would be to die!
MANRICO	The horrible blaze, etc.

Ruiz comes back with the soldiers.

RUIZ and SOLDIERS
> To arms! To arms!
> Here we are, ready to fight with you,
> Or to die with you!

MANRICO	To arms! To arms!

*Manrico leaves hastily, followed by Ruiz and the soldiers,
as the sound of arms and instruments of war is heard within.*

ATTO QUARTO

Il Supplizio

PARTE PRIMA

Un'ala del palazzo dell'Aliaferia: all'angolo una torre, con
finestre assicurate da spranghe di ferro. Notte oscurissima.
Si avanzano due persone ammantellate: sono Leonora e Ruiz.

RUIZ (*sommessamente*)
       Siam giunti; ecco la torre,
       Ove di Stato gemono i prigionieri ...
       Ah, l'infelice ivi fu tratto!

LEONORA   Vanne ... lasciami;
       Nè timor di me ti prenda.
       Salvarlo io potrò, forse.
          (*Ruiz si allontana.*)
       Timor di me?... Sicura,
       Presta è la mia difesa.
        (*I suoi occhi figgonsi ad una gemma*
         che fregia la sua destra.)
       In quest'oscura notte ravvolta,
       Presso a te son io,
       E tu nol sai!
       Gemente aura, che intorno spiri,
       Deh, pietosa gli arreca i miei sospiri.
       D'amor sull'ali rosee
       Vanne, sospir dolente,
       Del prigioniero misero
       Conforta l'egra mente ...
       Com'aura di speranza
       Aleggia in quella stanza,
       Lo desta alle memorie,
       Ai sogni, ai sogni dell'amor!...
       Ma, deh, non dirgli improvvido
       Le pene, le pene del mio cor!

FRATI (*dall'interno*)
       Miserere d'un'alma già vicina
       Alla partenza che non ha ritorno;
       Miserere di lei, bontà divina;
       Preda non sia dell'infernal soggiorno.

LEONORA   Quel suon, quelle preci,
       Solenni, funeste,
       Empiron quest'aere
       Di cupo terror!
       Contende l'ambascia,
       Che tutta m'investe,
       Al labbro il respiro,
       I palpiti al cor!

ACT FOUR

The Torture

SCENE ONE

A wing of the palace of Aliaferia: at one corner a tower, its windows secured by iron bars. A very dark night. Two cloaked figures come forward: they are Leonora and Ruiz.

RUIZ (*softly*)   We've arrived; there's the tower,
Where the State's prisoners languish . . .
Ah, the hapless man was brought here!

LEONORA   Go . . . leave me;
And don't fear for me.
I can save him, perhaps.
        (*Ruiz leaves.*)
Fear for me? . . . Sure,
And ready is my protection.
(*Her eyes fix upon a ring that adorns her right hand.*)

Shrouded in this dark night,
I'm near you,
And you don't know it!
Moaning wind, you who blow here,
Ah, mercifully take my sighs to him.
On the roseate wings of love
Go, oh mournful sigh,
Comfort the flagging spirits
Of the wretched prisoner . . .
Like a breath of hope
Waft in that room,
Waken in him the memories
The dreams, the dreams of love! . . .
But, pray, don't imprudently tell him
The sufferings of my heart!

MONKS (*from within*)

Have mercy upon a spirit approaching
The departure that has no return;
Have mercy on him, divine goodness;
Keep him from being the prey of hell.

LEONORA   That sound, those prayers,
Solemn and dire,
Fill the air
With baleful terror!
The anguish that fills me
Almost deprives
My lips of their breath,
My heart of its beating!

MANRICO (*dalla torre*)
  Ah!... che la morte ognora
  È tarda nel venir,
  A chi desia morir!
  Addio, addio, Leonora, addio!

LEONORA
  Oh ciel!
  Sento mancarmi!

FRATI
  Miserere, ecc.

LEONORA
  Sull'orrida torre,
  Ahi, par che la morte
  Con ali di tenebre
  Librando si va ...
  Ah forse dischiuse
  Gli fian queste porte
  Sol quando cadaver
  Già freddo sarà!

MANRICO
  Sconto col sangue mio
  L'amor che posi in te!
  Non ti scordar,
  Non ti scordar di me, Leonora,
  Addio, Leonora, addio!

LEONORA
  Di te, di te scordarmi!
  Sento, mancarmi!
  * [Tu vedrai che amore in terra
  Mai del mio non fu più forte:
  Vinse il fato in aspra guerra,
  Vincerà la stessa morte.
  O col prezzo di mia vita
  La tua vita salverò,
  O con te per sempre unita
  Nella tomba scenderò!
  Tu vedrai che amore in terra, ecc.]

S'apre una porta; n'escono il Conte ed alcuni seguaci.
Leonora è in disparte.

CONTE (*ad alcuni seguaci*)
  Udiste?
  Come albeggi, la scure al figlio,
  Ed alla madre il rogo.
    (*I seguaci entrano nella torre.*)
  Abuso forse quel poter
  Che pieno in me trasmise il Prence!
  A tal mi traggi,
  Donna per me funesta!
  Ov'ella è mai?
  Ripreso Castellor,
  Di lei contezza non ebbi,
  E furo indarno
  Tante ricerche e tante!
  Ah! dove sei, crudele?

Leonora, avanzandosi, si rivela.

LEONORA A te davante.

* Brackets denote passages often omitted in performance.

MANRICO (*from the tower*)
>   Ah! . . . how slow death is
>   In its coming,
>   To him who longs to die!
>   Farewell, farewell, Leonora, farewell!

LEONORA   Oh, heaven!
>   I feel faint!

MONKS   Have mercy, etc.

LEONORA   Over the horrid tower,
>   Ah, death seems
>   With wings of darkness
>   To be poised . . .
>   Ah, perhaps these doors
>   Will be opened for him
>   Only when he will be
>   Already a cold corpse

MANRICO   I'm paying with my blood
>   For the love I bore you!
>   Don't forget,
>   Don't forget me, Leonora.
>   Farewell, Leonora, farewell!

LEONORA   Forget you! Forget you!
>   I feel faint!
>   You will see that no love stronger than mine
>   Ever existed on earth;
>   Fate won in a fierce battle,
>   It will conquer even death.
>   Either with the price of my life
>   I shall save your life,
>   Or united with you forever
>   I shall descend to the tomb!
>   You will see that no love on earth, etc.

*A door opens; the Count comes in with some retainers.
Leonora is off to one side.*

COUNT (*to some of his men*)
>   Did you hear?
>   As dawn breaks, the son to the block,
>   And the mother to the stake.
>   (*The guards go into the tower.*)
>   Perhaps I'm abusing the power
>   That the Prince gave me fully!
>   That's what you drive me to,
>   O woman fatal to me!
>   Where can she be?
>   When Castellor was retaken,
>   I had no word of her,
>   And all our searching
>   Was in vain!
>   Ah! Where are you, cruel one?

Leonora comes forward and reveals herself.

LEONORA   Before you.

CONTE	Qual voce! Come! Tu, donna?
LEONORA	Il vedi.
CONTE	A che venisti?
LEONORA	Egli è già presso All'ora estrema, E tu lo chiedi?
CONTE	Osar potresti?
LEONORA	Ah sì, per esso pietà domando!
CONTE	Che? Tu deliri!
LEONORA	Pietà! Pietà!
CONTE	Ah! io del rival sentir pietà?
LEONORA	Clemente Nume a te l'ispiri ...
CONTE	È sol vendetta mio Nume.
LEONORA	Pietà! Pietà! Domando pietà!
CONTE	Va! va!

LEONORA (*si getta disperatamente a' suoi piedi*)
      Mira, d'acerbe lagrime
      Spargo al tuo piede un rio:
      Non basta il pianto?
      Svenami, ti bevi il sangue mio ...
      Calpesta il mio cadavere,
      Ma salva il Trovator

CONTE   Ah! dell'indegno rendere
      Vorrei peggior la sorte ...
      Fra mille atroci spasimi
      Centuplicar sua morte.
      Più l'ami, e più terribile
      Divampa il mio furor!

Il Conte vuol partire. Leonora si avviticchia ad esso.

LEONORA	Conte!
CONTE	Nè cessi?
LEONORA	Grazia!
CONTE	Prezzo non avvi alcuno Ad ottenerla. Scostati.
LEONORA	Uno ve n'ha, sol uno! Ed io te l'offro.
CONTE	Spiegati, Qual prezzo, di'?

LEONORA (*stendendogli la destra con dolore*)
      Me stessa!

CONTE	Ciel! Tu dicesti?
LEONORA	E compiere saprò la mia promessa.
CONTE	È sogno il mio?
LEONORA	Dischiudimi la via Fra quelle mura ... Ch'ei mi oda, Che la vittima fugga, E son tua.

COUNT	That voice! What? You, woman?
LEONORA	As you see.
COUNT	Why have you come?
LEONORA	His last hour Is approaching, And you ask me?
COUNT	Could you dare?
LEONORA	Ah yes, I ask mercy for him!
COUNT	What? You're raving!
LEONORA	Mercy! Mercy!
COUNT	I? Show mercy to my rival?
LEONORA	May a clement God inspire you . . .
COUNT	Vengeance is my only god.
LEONORA	Pity! Pity! I ask pity!
COUNT	Go! go!

LEONORA (*throwing herself desperately at his feet*)
Look, at your feet I shed
A river of bitter tears;
Isn't my weeping enough?
Then stab me and drink my blood . . .
Trample upon my corpse,
But save the Troubadour!

COUNT
Ah! I would like to make worse
The unworthy man's fate . . .
Make him die a hundred deaths
In a thousand horrible spasms.
The more you love him, the more terribly
My fury flames up!

The Count starts to leave. Leonora clings to him.

LEONORA	Count!
COUNT	Won't you stop?
LEONORA	Pardon!
COUNT	At no price could you Gain that. Move away.
LEONORA	There is one price, just one! And I offer it to you.
COUNT	Explain yourself, Tell me, what is this price?

LEONORA (*holding out her hand sadly*)
Myself!

COUNT	Heaven! What did you say?
LEONORA	And I will know how to keep my promise.
COUNT	Am I dreaming?
LEONORA	Open the way for me Though those walls . . . Let him hear me, Let the victim flee, And I am yours.

CONTE   Lo giura.
LEONORA   Lo giuro a Dio,
                 Che l'anima tutta mi vede!
CONTE   Olà?

*Si presenta un custode: il Conte gli parla all'orecchio. Leo-
nora sugge il veleno chiuso nell'anello.*

LEONORA   (M'avrai ...
                 Ma fredda, esanime spoglia.)
CONTE *(a Leonora, tornando innanzi)*
                 Colui vivrà.
LEONORA *(da sè con giubilo)*
                 (Vivrà! Contende il giubilo i detti a me, Signore,
                      *(alzando gli occhi cui fanno
                           velo lagrime di gioia)*
                 Ma coi frequenti palpiti
                 Mercè ti rende il core!
                 Or il mio fine, impavida,
                 Piena di gioia attendo,
                 Potrò dirgli, morendo:
                 Salvo tu sei per me!)
CONTE   Fra te che parli? Volgimi,
                 Mi volgi il detto ancora,
                 O mi parrà delirio
                 Quanto ascoltai finora ...
                 Tu mia! tu mia! ripetilo,
                 Il dubbio cor serena ...
                 Ah! ch'io lo credo appena
                 Udendolo da te!
LEONORA   Andiam!
CONTE   Giurasti ... pensaci!
LEONORA   È sacra la mia fè!
                 Vivrà, ecc.
CONTE   Tu mia, ecc.

Entrano nella torre.

ATTO QUARTO

PARTE SECONDA

*Orrido carcere: in un canto finestra con inferriata, porta nel
fondo, smorto fanale pendente dalla vôlta. Azucena giacente
sovra rozza coltre, Manrico seduto a lei dappresso.*

MANRICO   Madre, non dormi?
AZUCENA   L'invocai più volte,
                 Ma fugge il sonno a queste luci!
                 Prego.

COUNT   Swear it.

LEONORA   I swear it before God,
               Who can see my whole soul!

COUNT   Ho there!

A guard appears: the Count whispers to him. Leonora drains the poison contained in the ring.

LEONORA   (You'll have me . . .
               But a cold and lifeless corpse.)

COUNT (*to Leonora, coming back*)
               He shall live.

LEONORA (*aside, joyfully*)
               (He'll live! My joy deprives me
               Of words, O Lord,
               (*looking up with tears of joy in her eyes*)
               But with its hurried beating
               My heart renders thanks to you!
               Now, fearless, filled with joy,
               I can await the end,
               Dying I can tell him:
               I have saved you!)

COUNT   What are you whispering? Turn,
               Turn your words to me again,
               Or it will all seem a dream,
               What I heard before . . .
               You're mine! Mine! Repeat it,
               Reassure my doubting heart . . .
               Ah! I can scarcely believe it
               When I hear it from you!

LEONORA   Let us go!

COUNT   You've sworn . . . remember!

LEONORA   My word is sacred!
               He'll live, etc.

COUNT   You're mine, etc.

They go into the tower.

ACT FOUR

SCENE TWO

A grim prison: in one corner a barred window, a door at the back, a dim light hangs from the vaulted ceiling. Azucena lies on a rough blanket, with Manrico seated by her.

MANRICO   Mother, can't you sleep?

AZUCENA   I've invoked sleep time and again,
               But it flees from my eyes!
               I'm praying.

MANRICO   L'aura fredda è molesta
               Alle tue membra, forse?
AZUCENA   No; da questa tomba di vivi
               Solo fuggir vorrei,
               Perchè sento il respiro
               Soffocarmi.
MANRICO (*torcendosi le mani*)
               Fuggir!
AZUCENA (*sorgendo*)
               Non attristarti.
               Far di me strazio
               Non potranno i crudi!
MANRICO   Ahi, come?
AZUCENA   Vedi? Le sue fosche impronte
               M'ha già segnato in fronte
               Il dito della morte!
MANRICO   Ahi!
AZUCENA   Troveranno un cadavere
               Muto, gelido!
                    (*con gioia feroce*)
               Anzi uno scheletro!
MANRICO   Cessa!
AZUCENA   Non odi?
               Gente appressa ...
               I carnefici son!...
               Vogliono al rogo trarmi!
               Difendi tua madre!
MANRICO   Alcuno, ti rassicura,
               Alcuno qui non volge.
AZUCENA (*senza badare a Manrico*)
               Il rogo! il rogo!
               Parola orrenda!
MANRICO   Oh madre! oh madre!
AZUCENA   Un giorno turba feroce
               L'ava tua condusse al rogo!
               Mira la terribil vampa!
               Ella n'è tocca già!
               Già l'arso crine al ciel
               Manda faville!
               Osserva le pupille
               Fuor dell'orbita loro!
               Ahi! chi mi toglie
               A spettacolo sì atroce!

          Cade tutta convulsa tra le braccia di Manrico.

MANRICO   Se m'ami ancor,
               Se voce di figlio
               Ha possa d'una madre in seno,
               Ai terrori dell'alma
               Oblio cerca nel sonno,
               E posa e calma.

MANRICO   Perhaps the cold air
               Is painful on your limbs?

AZUCENA   No; I would only like
               To flee from this tomb of the living,
               Because I feel that my breath
               Is choking me.

MANRICO (*wringing his hands*)
               Flee!

AZUCENA (*rising*)
               Don't be sad.
               The barbarians won't be able
               To torture me!

MANRICO   What?

AZUCENA   The finger of death, you see?
               Has already set its dark prints
               On my forehead!

MANRICO   Ah!

AZUCENA   They'll find a corpse
               Mute and cold!
                        (*with fierce joy*)
               No, a skeleton!

MANRICO   Stop!

AZUCENA   Don't you hear?
               People are coming . . .
               The executioners! . . .
               They want to drag me to the stake!
               Defend your mother!

MANRICO   Nobody, rest assured,
               Nobody's coming here.

AZUCENA (*ignoring Manrico*)
               The stake! The stake!
               That horrible word!

MANRICO   Oh, Mother! Mother!

AZUCENA   One day a ferocious mob
               Led your grandmother to the stake!
               Look at the terrible flames!
               They're touching her already!
               Her burning hair already
               Sends sparks up to heaven!
               Look at her eyes,
               Hanging out of their sockets!
               Ah! Who will save me
               From this horrible sight!

She falls, overcome, into Manrico's arms.

MANRICO   If you love me still,
               If a son's voice
               Has power in a mother's breast,
               Seek oblivion in sleep
               From the spirit's terrors,
               And rest and calm.

La conduce presso alla coltre.

AZUCENA   Sì; la stanchezza m'opprime,
                   O figlio ...
                   Alla quiete io chiudo il ciglio ...
                   Ma se del rogo
                   Arder si veda l'orrida fiamma,
                   Destami allor.
MANRICO   Riposa, o madre; Iddio conceda
                   Men tristi immagini al tuo sopor.
AZUCENA *(tra il sonno e la veglia)*
                   Ai nostri monti ritorneremo,
                   L'antica pace ivi godremo!
                   Tu canterai ... sul tuo liuto,
                   In sonno placido io dormirò.
MANRICO   Riposa, o madre, io prono
                   E muto la mente al cielo rivolgerò.
AZUCENA   Tu canterai, ecc.
MANRICO   Riposa, o madre, ecc.

Manrico resta genuflesso accanto alla madre. Si addormenta.
La porta si apre e Leonora entra.

MANRICO   Che! Non m'inganna
                   Quel fioco lume?
LEONORA   Sono io, Manrico, mio Manrico!
MANRICO   Oh! mia Leonora!
                   Ah, mi concedi, pietoso Nume,
                   Gioia sì grande
                   Anzi ch'io mora?
LEONORA   Tu non morrai ...
                   Vengo a salvarti ...
MANRICO   Come! A salvarmi?
                   Fia vero?
LEONORA   Addio!
                   Tronca ogni indugio ...
                   T'affretta ... Parti!
                                 (accenandogli la porta)
MANRICO   E tu non vieni?
LEONORA   Restar degg'io.
MANRICO   Restar!
LEONORA   Deh, fuggi!
MANRICO   No ...
LEONORA   Guai se tardi!
MANRICO   No!
LEONORA *(correndo verso l'uscio)*
                   La tua vita!
MANRICO   Io la disprezzo!
LEONORA   Parti, parti!
MANRICO   No!
LEONORA   La tua vita!

He takes her to her blanket.

AZUCENA	Yes; weariness overcomes me, My son . . . I'll close my eyes in peace . . . But if you see burning The stake's terrible flames, Then waken me.
MANRICO	Rest now, Mother; may God Grant less grievous images to your sleep.

AZUCENA (*between sleep and waking*)
    We'll go back to our mountains,
    And there enjoy our former peace!
    You'll sing . . . with your lute,
    And I'll sleep serenely.

MANRICO	Rest, Mother. Prone and silent, I'll turn my thoughts to heaven.
AZUCENA	You'll sing, etc.
MANRICO	Rest, Mother, etc.

Manrico remains kneeling beside his mother. She falls asleep. The door opens and Leonora comes in.

MANRICO	What! Is that feeble light Deceiving me?
LEONORA	It's I, Manrico, my Manrico!
MANRICO	Oh! My Leonora! Ah, piteous Heaven, do you grant me Such a great joy Before I die?
LEONORA	You won't die . . . I've come to save you . . .
MANRICO	What? To save me? Can it be true?
LEONORA	Farewell! Don't delay . . . Hurry . . . Leave! (*pointing to the door*)
MANRICO	And you're not coming?
LEONORA	I must stay.
MANRICO	Stay!
LEONORA	Ah, flee!
MANRICO	No . . .
LEONORA	Woe if you delay!
MANRICO	No!

LEONORA (*running toward the door*)
    Your life!

MANRICO	I scorn it!
LEONORA	Leave, leave!
MANRICO	No!
LEONORA	Your life!

MANRICO   Io la disprezzo!
               Pur ... figgi, o donna,
               In me gli sguardi ...
               Da chi l'avesti?
               Ed a qual prezzo?
               Parlar non vuoi?
               Balen tremendo!
               Dal mio rivale!
               Intendo, intendo!
               Ha quest'infame l'amor venduto ...

LEONORA   Oh quant'ingiusto!

MANRICO   Venduto un core che mio giurò!

LEONORA   Oh come l'ira ti rende cieco!
               Oh quanto ingiusto, crudel
               Sei meco! T'arrendi, fuggi,
               O sei perduto,
               Nemmeno il cielo salvar ti può!

MANRICO   Infame!
               Ha quest'infame, ecc.

LEONORA   Oh come l'ira, ecc.

AZUCENA (*in sogno*)
               Ai nostri monti ritorneremo, ecc.

Leonora cade ai piedi di Manrico.

MANRICO   Ti scosta!

LEONORA   Non respingermi ...
               Vedi? languente,
               Oppressa, io manco.

MANRICO   Va ... ti abomino!
               Ti maledico ...

LEONORA   Ah cessa, cessa!
               Non d'imprecar,
               Di volgere per me la prece
               A Dio è questa l'ora!

MANRICO   Un brivido corse nel petto mio!

LEONORA (*cade boccone*)
               Manrico!

MANRICO (*accorendo a sollevarla*)
               Donna! svelami ... narra ...

LEONORA   Ho la morte in seno.

MANRICO   La morte!

LEONORA   Ah! fu più rapida
               La forza del veleno
               Ch'io non pensava!

MANRICO   Oh, fulmine!

LEONORA   Senti ... la mano è gelo,
                              (*toccandosi il petto*)
               Ma qui, qui foco
               Terribil arde!

MANRICO   Che festi, o cielo!

MANRICO	I scorn it!
	Still . . . O woman,
	Look into my eyes . . .
	Who gave it to you?
	And at what price?
	You won't speak?
	A terrible thought!
	From my rival!
	I understand!
	This infamous woman sold her love . . .
LEONORA	Oh, how unjust!
MANRICO	Sold a heart she swore was mine!
LEONORA	Oh, how your wrath blinds you!
	Oh, how unjust and cruel you are
	To me! Give in to me, flee,
	Or you're lost,
	Not even Heaven can save you!
MANRICO	Infamous woman!
	This infamous woman, etc.
LEONORA	Oh, how your wrath, etc.
AZUCENA (*dreaming*)	
	We'll go back to our mountains, etc.

Leonora sinks at Manrico's feet.

MANRICO	Go away!
LEONORA	Don't drive me off . . .
	You see? my strength fails,
	I'm overcome, weak.
MANRICO	Go . . . I detest you!
	I curse you . . .
LEONORA	Ah, stop, stop!
	Don't curse me,
	This is the hour
	To pray to God for me!
MANRICO	A shudder runs through my breast!
LEONORA (*falling prone*)	
	Manrico!
MANRICO (*running to help her up*)	
	Woman! Reveal . . . tell me . . .
LEONORA	I have death in my breast.
MANRICO	Death!
LEONORA	Ah! The poison's strength
	Was more rapid
	Than I thought!
MANRICO	Oh, horror!
LEONORA	Feel . . . my hand is icy,
	(*touching her breast*)
	But here, here a terrible
	Fire is burning!
MANRICO	Heaven, what have you done!

LEONORA   Prima che d'altri vivere
                 Io volli tua morir!
MANRICO   Insano! ed io
                 Quest'angelo osava maledir!
LEONORA   Più non resisto!
MANRICO   Ahi misera!
LEONORA   Ecco l'istante!...
                 Io moro, Manrico!

Stringendogli la destra in segno d'addio.

MANRICO   Ciel!

Entra il Conte, e si ferma sulla soglia.

CONTE   Ah!
LEONORA   Or la tua grazia,
                 Padre del cielo, imploro!
CONTE   (Ah volle me deludere,
                 E per costui morir!)
LEONORA   Prima che d'altri vivere
                 Io volli tua morir!
MANRICO   Insano! ed io
                 Quest'angelo osava maledir!
LEONORA   Manrico ... addio ... Io moro!
                                 (*Spira.*)
MANRICO   Leonora!
CONTE (*indicando agli armati Manrico*)
                 Sia tratto al ceppo!
MANRICO (*partendo fra gli armati*)
                 Madre! oh madre, addio!
AZUCENA (*destandosi*)
                 Manrico!
                 Ov'è mio figlio!
CONTE   A morte corre.
AZUCENA   Ah ferma! M'odi!
CONTE (*la trascina alla finestra*)
                 Vedi?
AZUCENA   Cielo!
CONTE   È spento.
AZUCENA   Egl'era tuo fratello!
CONTE   Ei! quale orror!
AZUCENA (*cade a piè della finestra*)
                 Sei vendicata, o madre!
CONTE (*inorridito*)
                 E vivo ancor!

LEONORA	Rather than live as another's I wanted to die yours!
MANRICO	And I, like a madman, Dared curse this angel!
LEONORA	I can bear no more!
MANRICO	Ah, unhappy girl!
LEONORA	The moment has come . . . I'm dying, Manrico.

Pressing his hand in farewell.

MANRICO	Heaven!

The Count enters, stopping on the threshhold.

COUNT	Ah!
LEONORA	Father in heaven, I beg your forgiveness!
COUNT	(Ah, she wanted to deceive me And die for him!)
LEONORA	Rather than live as another's I wanted to die yours!
MANRICO	And I, like a madman, Dared curse this angel!
LEONORA	Manrico, farewell! I'm dying! (*She dies.*)
MANRICO	Leonora!

COUNT (*indicating Manrico to the soldiers*)
Take him to the block!

MANRICO (*leaving among the soldiers*)
Mother! Ah, Mother, farewell!

AZUCENA (*waking*)
Manrico!
Where is my son?

COUNT	Hastening to his death.
AZUCENA	Ah, stop! Hear me!

COUNT (*draws her to the window*)
Do you see?

AZUCENA	Heaven!
COUNT	He's dead.
AZUCENA	He was your brother!
COUNT	He! What horror!

AZUCENA (*falling at the window*)
Mother, you are avenged!

COUNT (*horrified*)
And I still live!

La Traviata

In 1844, when Verdi was in Venice for the first performance of *Ernani*, an old friend wrote him, suggesting that Victor Hugo's *Marion Delorme* would make a good libretto. Verdi's reply was curt: "I know the subject you suggest. The heroine is a character I don't like. I don't like prostitutes on the stage . . ."

In March 1852, Verdi was in Paris with his mistress, Giuseppina Strepponi, later his second wife. One evening they went to the Théâtre-Vaudeville to see the sensational hit play of the season, Alexandre Dumas *fils*'s stage adaptation of his popular novel, *La Dame aux camélias*. Like almost everyone else in Paris, Verdi was deeply impressed by the play, and a few months later, when he was arranging to write a new opera for Venice, he thought at once of the Dumas play, a subject that was "ready and surely effective."

What had happened between 1844 and 1852 to make Verdi change his mind about prostitutes as heroines? In those eight years, Verdi had become internationally famous, and he had become a man of the world. In Giuseppina Strepponi, he had come to know and love a sophisticated, cultivated woman, whose past life (which she was quietly trying to live down) had points in common with that of the Dumas heroine, Marguerite Gauthier (soon to be rechristened Violetta by Verdi and the faithful Piave).

Of all of Verdi's famous operas, *La Traviata* is the one about whose creation we know least. This is partly because, like *Rigoletto*, it was written in a brief space of time (less than two months), and partly because Piave wrote the libretto in Verdi's house, with the composer standing over him, so there is none of the usual correspondence over revisions.

Much, however, has been written about the opening night: Sunday, March 6, 1853. The première was a fiasco such as Verdi had not known since the very first years of his career: the tenor was without voice, the baritone listless, the consumptive heroine sung by an unsuitably fat soprano. The audience laughed and at the same time was shocked at the bold subject and at the fact that the singers were in modern dress — something unheard of on the operatic stage at that time.

In his usual terse style, Verdi wrote a series of letters reporting the event, with no attempt to sugar-coat the bitter pill he had swallowed. To his former pupil and amanuensis Muzio: "*La Traviata* last night: fiasco. Is the fault mine or the singers'? Time will judge."

To his publisher Ricordi: "I'm sorry to give you sad news. *La Traviata* was a fiasco. Let's not investigate the causes. So it is. Good-bye . . ."

And, two days later, to a friend in Rome: "I didn't write you after the first performance of *La Traviata;* I am writing now after the second. The outcome was a fiasco, a decided fiasco! I don't know whose fault it is, best not to talk about it . . ."

He seems almost to derive a kind of grim satisfaction from repeating the word *fiasco*. But at the same time he wrote to a musician friend: "I don't think the last word on *La Traviata* was said last night. They will see it again, and then we will see!"

Verdi was right. The last word had not been said. In the unruly Venetian first-night audience there were several of Verdi's little band of admirers, including a music dealer and sometime impresario named Tonino Gallo, who did not share the general contempt for this revolutionary work. On May 6, 1854, Gallo had the courage to present *La Traviata* again to the same public that had laughed it off the stage the preceding season. There were minor changes, the cast was now dressed in early-eighteenth-century costumes, but, as Verdi wrote after this second version's triumphant reception: "The *Traviata* now performed at the Teatro San Benedetto is the same, the very same that was given last year at La Fenice, except for some changes of key and a little touching-up . . ."

And this time it is Verdi's friends who write the news to him: "The enthusiasm is incredible . . ." "The same people who condemned it before now boast of having considered it a beautiful opera also last year . . ." "Venice has never seen a success like *La Traviata*'s . . ."

As Verdi had said the year before: "Time will judge." In this case time moved swiftly, reversing its decision after only fourteen months.

THE PLOT

ACT ONE

A gay party is in progress in the house of Violetta, a beautiful Paris courtesan. Her protector, Baron Douphol, arrives with Violetta's friend Flora and others. A few moments later, another friend, Gaston, comes in with a young man who has long wanted to meet Violetta. His name is Alfredo Germont. As all sit down to dinner, Gaston reveals that during Violetta's illness a year before, Alfredo asked every day for news of her. Violetta is amused and touched. She and Alfredo drink a toast, then, as the others go into the next room to dance, Violetta remains behind, seized with a fit of coughing. Alfredo stays with her and tells her of his concern for her health, declaring his sincere love. She dismisses the idea but invites him to return to her the next day. When she is alone, she ponders his words, then insists to herself that hers can be a life only of fleeting pleasures.

ACT TWO

Contrary to her own predictions, Violetta has been living simply and happily in the country with Alfredo. But when Alfredo discovers that, to pay for this retreat, she has sold all her belongings, he rushes to Paris to ask his father for his patrimony.

Monsieur Germont, in the meanwhile, comes to the house and persuades Violetta to give up his son, whose behavior is compromising not only the young man's own future but also the happiness of his innocent sister. Though impressed by Violetta's obvious sincerity, Germont nevertheless insists.

Violetta knows that there is only one way to make Alfredo give her up. She goes away, leaving him a letter indicating that she is going back to the Baron and her former life.

Germont tries to persuade Alfredo to come home to Provence, but instead the young man pursues Violetta to Flora's house, where still another party is being given. There he insults Violetta violently and provokes a duel with the Baron.

ACT THREE

Violetta is alone, ill, destitute. In the duel, the Baron was wounded and Alfredo has had to go abroad. The elder Germont, however, has promised to reveal Violetta's noble sacrifice to his son, and it is this hope — and the hope of Alfredo's return — that keeps Violetta alive. Alfredo does return, but it is too late. Violetta dies in his arms.

LA TRAVIATA

libretto by Francesco Maria Piave

First performed at the Teatro La Fenice, Venice
March 6, 1853

CHARACTERS

Alfredo Germont, lover of Violetta	*Tenor*
Giorgio Germont, his father	*Baritone*
Gastone, Viscount de Letorières	*Tenor*
Baron Douphol, a rival of Alfredo	*Baritone*
Marchese d'Obigny	*Bass*
Dr. Grenvil	*Bass*
Giuseppe, servant to Violetta	*Tenor*
Violetta Valery, a courtesan	*Soprano*
Flora Bervoix, her friend	*Mezzo-soprano*
Annina, confidante of Violetta	*Soprano*

Friends and Guests of Violetta and Flora,
Servants, Maskers

The scenes are laid in Paris and environs, around 1850.
The first act takes place in August,
the second in January, the third in February.

ATTO PRIMO

*Salotto in casa di Violetta. Nel fondo è la porta che mette
ad altra sala; ve ne sono altre due laterali; a sinistra, un caminetto con sopra uno specchio. Nel mezzo è una tavola riccamente imbandita.*

*Violetta, seduta sopra un divano, sta discorrendo col
Dottore e con alcuni amici, mentre altri vanno ad incontrare
quelli che sopraggiungono, tra i quali sono il Barone e Flora
al braccio del Marchese.*

CORO I   Dell'invito trascorsa è già l'ora ...
     Voi tardaste ...
CORO II   Giocammo da Flora,
     E giocando quell'ora volâr.

VIOLETTA (*andando loro incontro*)
     Flora, amici, la notte che resta
     D'altre gioie qui fate brillar ...
     Fra le tazze più viva è la festa ...

FLORA e MARCHESE
     E goder voi potrete?
VIOLETTA Lo voglio;
     Al piacer m'affido, ed io soglio
     Con tal farmaco i mali sopir.
TUTTI   Sì, la vita s'addoppia al gioir.

*Entra il Visconte Gastone de Letorières con Alfredo Ger-
mont. Servi affaccendati intorno alla mensa.*

GASTONE In Alfredo Germont, o signora,
     Ecco un altro che molto v'onora;
     Pochi amici a lui simili sono.
VIOLETTA (*dà la mano ad Alfredo, che gliela bacia*)
     Mio Visconte, mercè di tal dono.
MARCHESE Caro Alfredo ...
ALFREDO Marchese ...

Si stringono la mano.

GASTONE (*ad Alfredo*)
     T'ho detto:
     L'amistà qui s'intreccia al diletto.

I servi frattanto avranno imbandite le vivande.

VIOLETTA (*ai servi*)
     Pronto è il tutto?
       (*Un servo accenna di sì.*)
     Miei cari, sedete;
     E al convito che s'apre ogni cor.
TUTTI   Ben diceste ... le cure segrete
     Fuga sempre l'amico licor.

ACT ONE

Salon in Violetta's house. At back a door leading to another room; there are two more doors, one at either side. Left, a fireplace with a mirror over it. In the center, a richly laid table.

Violetta, sitting on a sofa, is conversing with the Doctor and some friends. Others are going to meet some guests who are just arriving, among them the Baron and Flora, on the arm of the Marquis.

CHORUS I The time of the invitation is already past . . .
You are late . . .

CHORUS II We were gambling at Flora's,
And as we played, those hours flew.

VIOLETTA (*going toward them*)
Flora, friends, you make
What's left of the night shine with other
joys . . .
The party is livelier, among the cups . . .

FLORA and MARQUIS
Are you able to enjoy it?

VIOLETTA I want to;
I entrust myself to pleasure, and with that drug
I dull my sufferings.

ALL Yes, life is doubled by enjoyment.

Viscount Gastone de Letorières enters with Alfredo Germont. Servants are busy around the table.

GASTONE Here's Alfredo Germont, madame:
Another who esteems you greatly;
There are few friends like him.

VIOLETTA (*gives her hand to Alfredo, who kisses it*)
My dear Viscount, thank you for such a gift.

MARQUIS Dear Alfredo . . .

ALFREDO Marquis . . .

They shake hands.

GASTONE (*to Alfredo*)
As I told you:
Here friendship and pleasure are joined.

The servants in the meanwhile have set out the food.

VIOLETTA (*to the servants*)
Is everything ready?
(*A servant nods yes.*)
Dear friends, be seated;
At table all hearts are opened.

ALL Well said . . . our friend drink
Always dispels secret troubles.

Siedono in modo che Violetta resti tra Alfredo e Gastone; di fronte vi sarà Flora, tra il Marchese ed il Barone; gli altri siedono a piacere. V'ha un momento di silenzio, frattanto passano i piatti, e Violetta e Gastone parlano sottovoce tra loro, poi:

GASTONE   Sempre Alfredo a voi pensa.

VIOLETTA   Scherzate?

GASTONE   Egra foste, e ogni dì con affanno
Qui volò, di voi chiese ...

VIOLETTA   Cessate,
Nulla son io per lui ...

GASTONE   Non v'inganno ...

VIOLETTA (*ad Alfredo*)
Vero è dunque?... onde è ciò?...
Nol comprendo.

ALFREDO (*sospirando*)
Sì, egli è ver.

VIOLETTA (*ad Alfredo*)
Le mie grazie vi rendo.
(*al Barone*)
Voi, Barone, non feste altrettanto ...

BARONE   Vi conosco da un anno soltanto.

VIOLETTA   Ed ei solo da qualche minuto.

FLORA (*piano al Barone*)
Meglio fora se aveste taciuto.

BARONE (*piano a Flora*)
M'è increscioso quel giovin ...

FLORA   Perchè?
A me invece simpatico egli è.

GASTONE (*ad Alfredo*)
E tu dunque non apri più bocca?

MARCHESE (*a Violetta*)
È a madama che scuoterlo tocca.

VIOLETTA (*mesce ad Alfredo*)
Sarò l'Ebe che versa ...

ALFREDO (*con galanteria*)
E ch'io bramo
Immortal come quella.

TUTTI   Beviamo, beviamo ...

GASTONE   O Barone, nè un verso, nè un viva
Troverete in quest'ora giulia?

Il Barone accenna di no.

GASTONE (*ad Alfredo*)
Dunque a te ...

TUTTI   Sì, sì, un brindisi.

ALFREDO   L'estro non m'arride ...

GASTONE   E non sei tu maestro?

They sit down in such a way that Violetta is between Alfredo and Gastone; opposite her, Flora, between the Marquis and the Baron; the others sit as they please. A moment of silence, as the plates are passed, and Violetta and Gastone talk softly between themselves, then:

GASTONE   Alfredo thinks of you constantly.

VIOLETTA   You're joking?

GASTONE   When you were ill, every day he rushed
Here anxiously, and asked about you . . .

VIOLETTA   Stop,
I am nothing to him . . .

GASTONE   I'm not deceiving you . . .

VIOLETTA (*to Alfredo*)
Is it true then? . . . Why is this? . . .
I don't understand.

ALFREDO (*sighing*)
Yes, it's true.

VIOLETTA (*to Alfredo*)
I thank you.
(*to the Baron*)
You, Baron, didn't do as much . . .

BARON   I've known you only for a year.

VIOLETTA   And he only for a few minutes.

FLORA (*softly to the Baron*)
You'd have done better to remain silent.

BARON (*softly to Flora*)
That young man annoys me . . .

FLORA   Why?
I find him likable, on the contrary.

GASTONE (*to Alfredo*)
Aren't you going to open your mouth any
more?

MARQUIS (*to Violetta*)
It's up to Madame to stir him.

VIOLETTA (*pouring wine for Alfredo*)
I'll be Hebe and pour . . .

ALFREDO (*chivalrous*)
And I hope
As immortal as she.

ALL   Let's drink, let's drink . . .

GASTONE   Oh, Baron, can't you find a verse
Or a toast, at this festive hour?

The Baron shakes his head no.

GASTONE (*to Alfredo*)
You then . . .

ALL   Yes, yes, a toast.

ALFREDO   Inspiration isn't favoring me . . .

GASTONE   But aren't you a master?

ALFREDO (*a Violetta*)
>   Vi fia grato?

VIOLETTA   Sì.

ALFREDO (*s'alza*)
>   Sì?... L'ho già in cor.

MARCHESE   Dunque attenti ...

TUTTI   Sì, attenti al cantor ...

ALFREDO   Libiamo, libiamo ne' lieti calici
>   Che la bellezza infiora;
>   E la fuggevol ora
>   S'innebrii a voluttà.
>   Libiam ne' dolci fremiti
>   Che suscita l'amore,
>   (*indicando Violetta*)
>   Poichè quell'occhio al core
>   Onnipotente va ...
>   Libiamo, amore, amor fra i calici
>   Più caldi baci avrà.

TUTTI   Ah! Libiam, amor fra' calici
>   Più caldi baci avrà.

VIOLETTA (*s'alza*)
>   Tra voi saprò dividere
>   Il tempo mio giocondo;
>   Tutto è follia nel mondo
>   Ciò che non è piacer.
>   Godiam, fugace e rapido
>   È il gaudio dell'amore;
>   È un fior che nasce e muore,
>   Nè più si può goder ...
>   Godiam ... c'invita un fervido
>   Accento lusinghier.

TUTTI   Ah!... godiam ... la tazza e il cantico
>   Le notte abbella e il riso;
>   In questo paradiso
>   Ne scopra il nuovo dì.

VIOLETTA (*ad Alfredo*)
>   La vita è nel tripudio ...

ALFREDO (*a Violetta*)
>   Quando non s'ami ancora ...

VIOLETTA (*ad Alfredo*)
>   Nol dite a chi l'ignora.

ALFREDO (*a Violetta*)
>   È il mio destin così ...

TUTTI   Godiamo ... la tazza e il cantico
>   La notte abbella e il riso;
>   Godiamo ... in questo paradiso
>   Ne scopra il nuovo dì.

S'ode musica dall'altra sala.

TUTTI   Che è ciò?

VIOLETTA   Non gradireste ora le danze?

TUTTI   Oh, il gentil pensier!...
>   Tutti accettiamo.

ALFREDO (*to Violetta*)
Would you like it?

VIOLETTA   Yes.

ALFREDO (*gets up*)
Yes? . . . It's in my heart already.

MARQUIS   Pay attention then . . .

ALL   Yes, attention to the singer . . .

ALFREDO   Let us drink, drink from the happy goblets
That beauty embellishes;
And let the fleeting hour
Intoxicate itself with pleasure.
Let us drink in the sweet trembling
That love arouses,
(*pointing to Violetta*)
Since that eye goes
All-powerful to the heart . . .
Let us drink, among the cups,
Love will have warmer kisses.

ALL   Ah! Let us drink, among the cups
Love will have warmer kisses.

VIOLETTA (*rising*)
Among you I will share
My time of joy;
All is folly in the world
That isn't pleasure.
Let us enjoy ourselves, love's joy
Is quick and fleeting;
It's a flower that is born and dies,
Nor can it be enjoyed again . . .
Let us enjoy ourselves . . . feverish,
Enchanting words invite us.

ALL   Ah! . . . Let us enjoy ourselves . . . cup and song
Night embellishes, and laughter;
In this paradise
Let the new day find us.

VIOLETTA (*to Alfredo*)
Life is pleasure . . .

ALFREDO (*to Violetta*)
When one isn't yet in love . . .

VIOLETTA (*to Alfredo*)
Don't speak of it to one who doesn't know it.

ALFREDO (*to Violetta*)
That is my destiny . . .

ALL   Let us enjoy ourselves . . . cup and song
Night embellishes, and laughter;
In this paradise
Let the new day find us.

Music is heard from the other room.

ALL   What is that?

VIOLETTA   Wouldn't you like to dance now?

ALL   Oh, what a pleasant thought! . . .
We all accept.

VIOLETTA   Usciamo dunque ...

S'avviano alla porta di mezzo, ma Violetta è colta da subito pallore.

VIOLETTA   Ohimè!...
TUTTI   Che avete?
VIOLETTA   Nulla, nulla.
TUTTI   Che mai v'arresta?...
VIOLETTA   Usciamo ...

Fa qualche passo, ma è obbligata a nuovamente fermarsi e sedere.

VIOLETTA   Oh Dio!...
TUTTI   Ancora!
ALFREDO   Voi soffrite.
TUTTI   Oh ciel! ch'è questo?
VIOLETTA   Un tremito che provo!...
               Or ... là ... passate ...
                           (*indica l'altra sala.*)
               Fra poco anch'io sarò.
TUTTI   Come bramate.

Tutti passano all'altra sala, meno Alfredo, che resta indietro.

VIOLETTA (*si alza e va a guardarsi allo specchio*)
               Oh qual pallor!
                           (*Si volge e s'accorge d'Alfredo.*)
               Voi qui!
ALFREDO   Cessata è l'ansia
               Che vi turbò?
VIOLETTA   Sto meglio.
ALFREDO   Ah in cotal guisa
               V'ucciderete ... aver v'è d'uopo cura
               Dell'esser vostro ...
VIOLETTA   E lo potrei?
ALFREDO   Oh! se mia foste,
               Custode veglierei
               Pe' vostri soavi dì.
VIOLETTA   Che dite?... ha forse alcuno
               Cura di me?
ALFREDO (*con fuoco*)
               Perchè nessuno al mondo v'ama ...
VIOLETTA   Nessun?...
ALFREDO   Tranne sol io.
VIOLETTA (*ridendo*)
               Gli è vero!...
               Sì grande amor dimenticato avea.
ALFREDO   Ridete!... e in voi v'ha un core?
VIOLETTA   Un cor?... sì ... forse ...
               E a che lo richiedete?

VIOLETTA   Let us go then . . .

They start toward the door in the center, but Violetta suddenly turns pale.

VIOLETTA   Alas! . . .
ALL   What is it?
VIOLETTA   Nothing, nothing.
ALL   Whatever made you stop? . . .
VIOLETTA   Let us go . . .

She takes a few steps, but then is again forced to stop and sit down.

VIOLETTA   Oh, God! . . .
ALL   Again!
ALFREDO   You're ill.
ALL   Heaven! What is this?
VIOLETTA   I feel a trembling! . . .
       Now . . . go in . . . there . . .
       (*pointing to the other room*)
       I will be there too, shortly.
ALL   As you wish.

All go into the other room, except Alfredo, who remains behind.

VIOLETTA (*stands up and goes to look at herself in the mirror*)
       Oh, what pallor!
       (*She turns, seeing Alfredo.*)
       You here!
ALFREDO   Is the trouble
       That upset you past?
VIOLETTA   I am better.
ALFREDO   Ah, in this fashion
       You will kill yourself . . . You must take care
       Of yourself.
VIOLETTA   How could I?
ALFREDO   Oh! If you were mine,
       Like a guardian, I'd watch over
       Your peaceful days.
VIOLETTA   What are you saying? . . . Does anyone
       Really care for me?
ALFREDO (*with fire*)
       Because no one in the world loves you . . .
VIOLETTA   No one? . . .
ALFREDO   Only I, I alone.
VIOLETTA (*laughing*)
       That's true! . . .
       I had forgotten such a great love.
ALFREDO   You laugh! . . . Have you a heart?
VIOLETTA   A heart? . . . Yes . . . perhaps . . .
       Why do you ask?

ALFREDO   Ah se ciò fosse ...
               Non potreste allora celiar ...
VIOLETTA   Dite davvero?
ALFREDO   Io non v'inganno.
VIOLETTA   Da molto è che mi amate?
ALFREDO   Ah sì, da un anno.
               Un dì felice, eterea
               Mi balenaste innante,
               E da quel dì tremante
               Vissi d'ignoto amor.
               Di quell'amor, quell'amor ch'è palpito
               Dell'universo, dell'universo intero,
               Misterioso, altero,
               Croce e delizia al cor.
VIOLETTA   Ah se ciò è ver, fuggitemi ...
               Solo amistade io v'offro;
               Amar non so, nè soffro
               Un così eroico amore.
               Io sono franca, ingenua;
               Altra cercar dovete;
               Non arduo troverete
               Dimenticarmi allor.
ALFREDO   Oh amore misterioso,
               Misterioso, altero,
               Croce e delizia al cor.
VIOLETTA   Non arduo troverete
               Dimenticarmi allor.

Gastone si presenta sulla porta di mezzo.

GASTONE   Ebben? che diavol fate?
VIOLETTA   Si folleggiava ...
GASTONE   Ah! ah!... sta ben ... restate ...

Rientra.

VIOLETTA   Amor dunque non più ...
               Vi garba il patto?
ALFREDO   Io v'obbedisco ... Parto ...
VIOLETTA (*si toglie un fiore dal seno*)
               A tal giungeste?
               Prendete questo fiore.
ALFREDO   Perchè?
VIOLETTA   Per riportarlo.
ALFREDO (*tornando*)
               Quando?
VIOLETTA   Quando sarà appassito.
ALFREDO   Oh ciel!... Domani ...
VIOLETTA   Ebben ... domani.
ALFREDO (*prende con trasporto il fiore*)
               Io son, io son felice!
VIOLETTA   D'amarmi dite ancora?
ALFREDO (*per partire*)
               Oh, quanto, quanto v'amo!

ALFREDO	Ah, if that were so . . .
	Then you wouldn't be able to mock . . .
VIOLETTA	Are you speaking the truth?
ALFREDO	I'm not deceiving you.
VIOLETTA	Have you loved me for a long time?
ALFREDO	Ah yes, for a year.
	One day, happy and ethereal,
	You appeared before me,
	And since that day I've lived,
	Trembling, in an unknown love.
	In that love which is the pulse
	Of the universe, the whole universe,
	Mysterious, aloof,
	The heart's cross and delight.
VIOLETTA	Ah, if that is true, flee from me . . .
	I offer you only friendship;
	I cannot love, nor can I bear
	Such a heroic love.
	I am frank, simple;
	You must look for another woman;
	You won't find it difficult
	To forget me then.
ALFREDO	Oh, mysterious love,
	Mysterious, aloof,
	The heart's cross and delight.
VIOLETTA	You won't find it difficult
	To forget me then.

Gastone appears at the door in the center.

GASTONE	Well? What the devil are you doing?
VIOLETTA	We were talking nonsense . . .
GASTONE	Ha! Ha! . . . very well . . . stay . . .

He goes back in.

VIOLETTA	No more love then . . .
	Does this agreement suit you?
ALFREDO	I obey you . . . I'm leaving . . .
VIOLETTA (*takes a flower from her bosom*)
	You go that far?
	Take this flower.
ALFREDO	Why?
VIOLETTA	To bring it back.
ALFREDO (*coming back*)
	When?
VIOLETTA	When it has withered.
ALFREDO	Heaven! . . . Tomorrow . . .
VIOLETTA	Very well . . . tomorrow.
ALFREDO (*ecstatically taking the flower*)
	I . . . I am happy!
VIOLETTA	You still say you love me?
ALFREDO (*about to leave*)
	Ah, how much, how much, I love you!

VIOLETTA   Partite?
ALFREDO (*torna a lei e le bacia la mano*)
            Parto.
VIOLETTA   Addio.
ALFREDO   Di più non bramo.
VIOLETTA e ALFREDO
            Addio. Addio.

*Alfredo esce. Ritornano tutti gli altri dalla sala riscaldati
dalle danze.*

TUTTI   Si ridesta in ciel l'aurora,
            E n'è forza di partire;
            Mercè a voi, gentil signora,
            Di sì splendido gioir.
            La città di feste è piena,
            Volge il tempo dei piacer;
            Nel riposo ancor la lena
            Si ritempri per goder.

Partono dalla destra. Violetta è sola.

VIOLETTA   È strano!... è strano!... in core
            Scolpiti ho quegli accenti!
            Saria per me sventura un serio amore?
            Che risolvi, o turbata anima mia?
            Null'uomo ancor t'accendeva ...
            Oh gioia ch'io non conobbi,
            Esser amata amando!...
            E sdegnarla poss'io
            Per l'aride follie del viver mio?...
            Ah fors'è lui che l'anima
            Solinga ne' tumulti
            Godea sovente pingere
            De' suoi colori occulti ...
            Lui, che modesto e vigile
            All'egre soglie ascese,
            E nuova febbre accese
            Destandomi all'amor.
            A quell'amor, quell'amor ch'è palpito
            Dell'universo, dell'universo intero,
            Misterioso, altero,
            Croce e delizia al cor.
            ° [A me, fanciulla, un candido
            E trepido desire
            Quest'effigiò dolcissimo
            Signor dell'avvenire,
            Quando ne' cieli il raggio
            Di sua beltà vedea,
            E tutta me pascea
            Di quel divino error.
            Sentia che amore è palpito
            Dell'universo intero,
            Misterioso, altero,
            Croce e delizia al cor.]

° Brackets denote *passages often omitted in performance.*

VIOLETTA   Are you going?

ALFREDO *(comes back to her and kisses her hand)*
            I go.

VIOLETTA   Good-by.

ALFREDO   I long for nothing more.

VIOLETTA and ALFREDO
            Good-by, good-by.

Alfredo goes out. The others, flushed from their dancing, come back from the other room.

ALL   Dawn is reawakening in the sky,
            And we must leave;
            Our thanks to you, kind lady,
            For such splendid entertainment.
            The city is filled with parties,
            The season of pleasures is coming;
            We must restore our vigor by resting
            So that we can enjoy ourselves more.

They go out at right. Violetta is alone.

VIOLETTA   It's strange! . . . strange! . . . those words
              Are carved in my heart!
            Would a serious love be a misfortune for me?
            What are you resolving, O my anguished spirit?
            No man ever aroused you before . . .
            O joy I did not know,
            To be loved and to love! . . .
            And can I spurn it
            For the barren follies of my life? . . .
            Ah, perhaps he is the one whom my spirit,
            Alone amid tumults,
            Often enjoyed painting
            With its mysterious colors . . .
            He who, modest and constant,
            Came to my sickroom door,
            And kindled a new fever
            Waking me to love.
            To that love which is the pulse
            Of the universe, the whole universe,
            Mysterious, aloof,
            The heart's cross and delight.
            When I was a girl, an innocent
            And timid desire
            Depicted him, the tender
            Lord of my future,
            When I saw in the skies
            The glow of his beauty,
            And I fed myself wholly
            On that divine fancy.
            I felt that love is the pulse
            Of the whole universe,
            Mysterious, aloof,
            The heart's cross and delight.

Resta concentrata un istante, poi si scuote.

> Follie!... follie!...
> Delirio vano è questo!...
> Povera donna, sola,
> Abbandonata in questo
> Popoloso deserto
> Che appellano Parigi,
> Che spero or più?...
> Che far degg'io?... Gioire!
> Di voluttà ne' vortici perir!
> Gioir!... gioir!...
> Sempre libera degg'io
> Folleggiare di gioia in gioia,
> Vo' che scorra il viver mio
> Pe' sentieri del piacer.
> Nasca il giorno, o il giorno muoia,
> Sempre lieta ne' ritrovi,
> A diletti sempre nuovi
> Dee volar il mio pensier.

ALFREDO (*sotto al balcone*)
> Amor è palpito dell'universo, ecc.

VIOLETTA   Dee volar, ah! il mio pensier!

Entra a sinistra.

ATTO SECONDO

PARTE PRIMA

Casa di campagna presso Parigi. Salotto terreno. Nel fondo, in faccia agli spettatori, è un camino, sopra il quale uno specchio ed un orologio, fra due porte chiuse da cristalli che mettono ad un giardino. Al primo piano due altre porte, una di fronte all'altra. Sedie, tavolini, qualche libro, l'occorrente per scrivere.

Alfredo entra in costume da caccia. Depone il fucile.

ALFREDO   Lunge da lei per me non v'ha diletto!...
> Volaron già tre lune
> Dacchè la mia Violetta
> Agi per me lasciò, dovizie, amori
> E le pompose feste,
> Ov'agli omaggi avvezza,
> Vedea schiavo ciascun di sua bellezza ...
> Ed or contenta in questi ameni luoghi
> Tutto scorda per me. Qui presso a lei
> Io rinascer mi sento,
> E dal soffio d'amor rigenerato
> Scordo ne' gaudi suoi tutto il passato.
> De' miei bollenti spiriti
> Il giovanile ardore

She is lost in thought for a moment, then she recovers herself.

> Folly! . . . folly! . . .
> This is vain raving! . . .
> A poor woman, alone,
> Abandoned in this
> Crowded desert
> That they call Paris,
> What more can I hope for now? . . .
> What must I do? . . . Enjoy myself!
> Perish in the giddy whirl of pleasure!
> Enjoy myself! . . . Enjoy! . . .
> Always free I must
> Dart lightheadedly from joy to joy,
> I want my life to glide
> Along the paths of pleasure.
> Whether the day is born or dying,
> Always gay at parties,
> My thought must fly
> Always to new delights.

ALFREDO *(below the balcony)*
> Love is the pulse of the universe, etc.

VIOLETTA   Ah! My thought must fly!

She leaves through the door, left.

ACT TWO

SCENE ONE

A country house near Paris. Drawing room on the ground floor. In the back, facing the audience, there is a fireplace, with a clock and a mirror over it, between two French windows that give onto a garden. Downstage, two other doors, facing each other. Chairs, tables, some books, and writing materials.

Alfredo comes in, wearing hunting clothes. He puts down his gun.

ALFREDO   Away from her, there's no joy for me! . . .
> Three months have flown past already
> Since for me my Violetta
> Abandoned comforts, riches, loves
> And the elaborate parties,
> Where, accustomed to admiration,
> She saw every man enslaved by her beauty . . .
> And now, content in these pleasant surroundings,
> She forgets it all for me. Here with her
> I feel myself reborn,
> And regenerated by the breath of love,
> In its ecstasies, I forget all the past.
> The youthful ardor
> Of my ebullient spirits

Ella temprò col placido
Sorriso dell'amor!...
Dal dì che disse: "Vivere
Io voglio a te fedel,"
Dell'universo immemore
Io vivo quasi in ciel.

Annina entra affannosa in arnese da viaggio.

ALFREDO	Annina, donde vieni?
ANNINA	Da Parigi.
ALFREDO	Chi tel commise?
ANNINA	Fu la mia signora.
ALFREDO	Perchè?
ANNINA	Per alienar cavalli, cocchi E quanto ancor possiede.
ALFREDO	Che mai sento!
ANNINA	Lo spendio è grande a viver qui solinghi ...
ALFREDO	E tacevi?
ANNINA	Mi fu il silenzio imposto.
ALFREDO	Imposto?!... or v'abbisogna?...
ANNINA	Mille luigi.
ALFREDO	Or vanne ... Andrò a Parigi ... Questo colloquio non sappia la signora; Il tutto valgo a riparar ancora. Va! va!

Annina parte.

ALFREDO	° [Oh mio rimorso! oh infamia! Io vissi in tale errore!... Ma il turpe sonno a frangere Il ver mi balenò!... Per poco in seno acquetati, O grido dell'onore; M'avrai securo vindice; Quest'onta laverò. Oh mio rossor! oh infamia! Ah sì, quest'onta laverò!]

Esce. Violetta entra con alcune carte, parlando con Annina.

VIOLETTA	Alfredo?
ANNINA	Per Parigi or or partiva.
VIOLETTA	E tornerà?
ANNINA	Pria che tramonti il giorno ... Dirvel m'impose ...
VIOLETTA	È strano!

Giuseppe entra e le presenta una lettera.

GIUSEPPE	Per voi.

° Brackets denote passages often omitted in performance.

> She tempered with the calm
> Smile of love! . . .
> Since the day she said:
> "I want to live, faithful to you,"
> Not heeding the universe,
> I live as if in heaven.

Annina comes in hastily, in traveling attire.

ALFREDO	Annina, where are you coming from?
ANNINA	From Paris.
ALFREDO	Who sent you there?
ANNINA	It was my mistress.
ALFREDO	Why?
ANNINA	To sell off her horses, carriages And everything she still owns.
ALFREDO	What's this I hear!
ANNINA	The expense is great, living here alone . . .
ALFREDO	And you were silent?
ANNINA	I was ordered to be silent.
ALFREDO	Ordered?! . . . Now how much is needed? . . .
ANNINA	A thousand louis.
ALFREDO	Go now . . . I'll go to Paris . . . Madame must not know of this talk; I can still set everything right. Go! Go!

Annina goes out.

ALFREDO	Oh, my remorse! Oh, disgrace! I lived in such ignorance! . . . But the truth appeared to me To break off my shameful slumber! . . . Be silent in my breast a little while, O cry of honor; I'll be your certain avenger; I'll wash away this shame. Oh, my blushes! Oh, shame! Ah yes, I'll wash away this shame!

He goes out. Violetta comes in with some papers, talking with Annina.

VIOLETTA	Alfredo?
ANNINA	He just left for Paris.
VIOLETTA	When will he come back?
ANNINA	Before sunset . . . He told me to tell you . . .
VIOLETTA	That's strange!

Giuseppe comes in and hands her a letter.

GIUSEPPE	For you.

VIOLETTA (*sedendo, la prende*)
> Sta ben ... In breve
> Giungerà un uom d'affari ...
> Entri all'istante.

Annina e Giuseppe partono. Violetta apre la lettera.

VIOLETTA   Ah, ah! scopriva Flora il mio ritiro,
> E m'invita a danzar per questa sera!...
> Invan m'aspetterà ...

Getta il foglio sul tavolino e siede. Giuseppe rientra.

GIUSEPPE   È qui un signore.
VIOLETTA   Sarà lui che attendo.

Accena a Giuseppe d'introdurlo. Entra il Signor Germont, introdotto da Giuseppe che avanza due sedie e parte.

GERMONT   Madamigella Valery?...
VIOLETTA   Son io.
GERMONT   D'Alfredo il padre in me vedete!
VIOLETTA (*sorpresa, gli accenna di sedere*)
> Voi!
GERMONT (*sedendo*)
> Sì, dell'incauto, che a ruina corre,
> Ammaliato da voi.
VIOLETTA (*alzandosi, risentita*)
> Donna son io, signore, ed in mia casa;
> Ch'io vi lasci assentite,
> Più per voi, che per me.

Per uscire.

GERMONT   (Quai modi!) Pure ...
VIOLETTA   Tratto in error voi foste ...

Torna a sedere.

GERMONT   De' suoi beni
> Dono vuol farvi ...
VIOLETTA   Non l'osò finora ...
> Rifiuterei.
GERMONT (*guardando intorno*)
> Pur tanto lusso ...
VIOLETTA (*gli dà una carta*)
> A tutti è mistero quest'atto ...
> A voi nol sia ...
GERMONT (*scorre le carte*)
> Ciel! che discopro!
> D'ogni vostro avere
> Or volete spogliarvi?
> Ah il passato perchè, perchè v'accusa?...

VIOLETTA (*sits down, taking it*)
Very well . . . Shortly
A man will come on business . . .
Show him in at once.

Annina and Giuseppe go out. Violetta opens the letter.

VIOLETTA   Ha, ha! Flora has discovered my retreat,
And she invites me to a dance this evening! . . .
She'll wait for me in vain . . .

She throws the letter on the table and sits down. Giuseppe comes back in.

GIUSEPPE   A gentleman is here.

VIOLETTA   It will be the one I'm expecting.

She nods to Giuseppe to show him in. Monsieur Germont enters, preceded by Giuseppe, who draws up two chairs and leaves.

GERMONT   Mademoiselle Valery? . . .

VIOLETTA   I am she.

GERMONT   In me you see Alfredo's father!

VIOLETTA (*surprised, motions him to be seated*)
You!

GERMONT (*sitting down*)
Yes, father of the heedless boy, who rushes
To his ruin, bewitched by you.

VIOLETTA (*rising, offended*)
I am a woman, sir, and in my own house;
Allow me to leave you,
More for your sake, than for mine.

She starts to go.

GERMONT   (What manners!) And yet . . .

VIOLETTA   You were mistaken . . .

She sits down again.

GERMONT   He wants to make you a gift
Of his possessions . . .

VIOLETTA   He never dared before . . .
I would refuse.

GERMONT (*looking around*)
Still, all this luxury . . .

VIOLETTA (*gives him a paper*)
This deed is a secret from everyone . . .
But not from you . . .

GERMONT (*glancing over the papers*)
Heavens! What's this I discover!
You mean to deprive yourself
Of everything you own?
Ah, why, why does the past accuse you? . . .

VIOLETTA (*con entusiasmo*)
Più non esiste ...
Or amo Alfredo, e Dio
Lo cancellò col pentimento mio!
GERMONT Nobili sensi invero!
VIOLETTA Oh come dolce
Mi suona il vostro accento!
GERMONT (*alzandosi*)
Ed a tai sensi
Un sacrifizio chieggo.
VIOLETTA (*alzandosi*)
Ah no ... tacete ...
Terribil cosa chiedereste certo ...
Il previdi ... v'attesi ...
Era felice troppo ...
GERMONT D'Alfredo il padre
La sorte, l'avvenir domanda or qui
De' suoi due figli!...
VIOLETTA Di due figli!
GERMONT Sì.
Pura siccome un angelo
Iddio mi diè una figlia;
Se Alfredo nega riedere
In seno alla famiglia,
L'amato e amante giovine,
Cui sposa andar dovea,
Or si ricusa al vincolo
Che lieti ne rendeva.
Deh non mutate in triboli
Le rose dell'amor ...
A' prieghi miei resistere
Non voglia il vostro cor, no, no.
VIOLETTA Ah! comprendo ...
Dovrò per alcun tempo
Da Alfredo allontanarmi ... doloroso
Fora per me ... pur ...
GERMONT Non è ciò che chiedo ...
VIOLETTA Cielo! che più cercate?...
Offersi assai!...
GERMONT Pur non basta.
VIOLETTA Volete che per sempre
A lui rinunzi?
GERMONT È d'uopo.
VIOLETTA Ah no! giammai!... no, mai!
Non sapete quale affetto
Vivo, immenso m'arda in petto?
Che nè amici, nè parenti
Io non conto tra' viventi?
E che Alfredo m'ha giurato
Che in lui tutto troverò?
Non sapete che colpita
D'atro morbo è la mia vita?

VIOLETTA (*with enthusiasm*)
It exists no more . . .
Now I love Alfredo, and God
Erased it, with my repentance!

GERMONT Noble feelings, indeed!

VIOLETTA Ah, how sweet your words
Sound to me!

GERMONT (*rising*)
And I ask a sacrifice
Of those feelings.

VIOLETTA (*rising*)
Ah no . . . don't speak . . .
You'd surely ask something terrible . . .
I foresaw it . . . I was expecting you . . .
I was too happy . . .

GERMONT Alfredo's father here
Asks of you the destiny, the future
Of his two children! . . .

VIOLETTA Two children!

GERMONT Yes.
Pure as an angel
God gave me a daughter;
If Alfredo refuses to return
To his family's bosom,
The beloved and loving youth
Whose bride she was to be,
Will now reject the tie
That made them so happy.
Ah, don't change into trials
The roses of love . . .
Your heart must not resist
My entreaties, no, no.

VIOLETTA Ah! I understand· . . .
I'll have to go away
From Alfredo for a while . . .
It will be painful for me . . . still . . .

GERMONT That isn't what I'm asking . . .

VIOLETTA Heaven! What more do you want? . . .
I've offered so much! . . .

GERMONT And yet it's not enough.

VIOLETTA You want me to give him up
Forever?

GERMONT It's necessary.

VIOLETTA Ah no! Never! . . . no, never!
Don't you know the love,
Vital, immense, that burns in my heart?
That I have no friends,
No relatives among the living?
And that Alfredo has sworn to me
That in him I'll find everything?
Don't you know that my life
Is stricken by a dire disease?

Che già presso il fin ne vedo?...
Ch'io mi separi da Alfredo!...
Ah il supplizio è sì spietato,
Che a morir preferirò.

GERMONT   È grave il sagrifizio;
Ma pur tranquilla uditemi.
Bella voi siete e giovine ...
Col tempo ...

VIOLETTA   Ah più non dite ...
V'intendo ... m'è impossibile ...
Lui solo amar vogl'io ...

GERMONT   Sia pure ... ma volubile
Sovente è l'uom ...

VIOLETTA (*colpita*)
Gran Dio!

GERMONT   Un dì, quando le veneri
Il tempo avrà fugate,
Fia presto il tedio a sorgere ...
Che sarà allor?... Pensate ...
Per voi non avran balsamo
I più soavi affetti!
Poichè dal ciel non furono ...
Tai nodi benedetti ...

VIOLETTA   È vero! è vero!

GERMONT   Ah dunque sperdasi
Tal sogno seduttore ...
Siate di mia famiglia
L'angel consolatore ...
Violetta, deh pensateci,
Ne siete in tempo ancor ...
È Dio che ispira, o giovine,
Tai detti a un genitor.

VIOLETTA (*da sè, con estremo dolore*)
(Così alla misera, ch'è un di caduta,
Di più risorgere speranza è muta!
Se pur benefico le indulga Iddio,
L'uomo implacabile per lei sarà.)

GERMONT   Siate di mia famiglia
L'angiol consolator.

VIOLETTA (*piangendo*)
Dite alla giovine sì bella e pura,
Ch'avvi una vittima della sventura,
Cui resta un unico raggio di bene ...
Che a lei il sacrifica a che morrà.

GERMONT   Piangi, piangi, o misera.
Supremo, il veggo, è il sagrifizio
Ch'ora ti chieggo ...
Sento nell'anima già le tue pene ...
Coraggio, e il nobil tuo cor
Vincerà!

VIOLETTA   Dite alla giovine, ecc.

Silenzio.

	That I can already see its end near? . . .
	For me to leave Alfredo! . . .
	Ah, the torment is so merciless,
	That I'd prefer to die.
GERMONT	The sacrifice is hard;
	Yet listen to me calmly.
	You are beautiful and young . . .
	In time . . .
VIOLETTA	Ah, say no more . . .
	I understand you . . . it's impossible for me . . .
	I want to love only him . . .
GERMONT	That may be . . . But men
	Are often fickle . . .
VIOLETTA *(stricken)*	
	Good God!
GERMONT	One day, when time has put
	Carnal desire to flight,
	Boredom will follow quickly . . .
	Then what will happen? . . . Think . . .
	You won't have the solace
	Of tenderer affections!
	Since these bonds were not . . .
	Blessed by heaven . . .
VIOLETTA	It's true! It's true!
GERMONT	Ah, then let this seductive dream
	Be dispelled . . .
	Be the consoling angel
	Of my family . . .
	Violetta, ah, think it over,
	You are still in time . . .
	Ah, young lady, it is God
	Who inspires a father's words.
VIOLETTA *(to herself, with great grief)*	
	(So, for the wretched girl, who one day fell,
	Any hope of rising again is silent!
	Even if God is kind and indulgent to her,
	Mankind will always be implacable.)
GERMONT	Be the consoling angel
	Of my family.
VIOLETTA *(weeping)*	
	Tell the young girl, so beautiful and pure,
	That there is a victim of misfortune
	Who has a single ray of happiness . . .
	Which she sacrifices to her, and who will die.
GERMONT	Weep, weep, O unhappy girl.
	I am asking, I see,
	The supreme sacrifice of you now . . .
	Already in my spirit I feel your sufferings . . .
	Courage, your noble heart
	Will win out!
VIOLETTA	Tell the young girl, etc.

Silence.

	Imponete.
GERMONT	Non amarlo ditegli.
VIOLETTA	Nol crederà.
GERMONT	Partite ...
VIOLETTA	Seguirammi.
GERMONT	Allor ...
VIOLETTA	Qual figlia m'abbraciate ...
	Forte così sarò.

(*Si abbracciano.*)

Tra breve ei vi fia reso,
Ma afflitto oltre ogni dire ...
A suo conforto di colà volerete.

Violetta gli indica il giardino, poi va per iscrivere.

GERMONT	Che pensate?
VIOLETTA	Sapendol, v'opporreste
	Al pensier mio ...
GERMONT	Generosa!... e per voi che far poss'io?

VIOLETTA (*tornando a lui*)
Morrò!... morro!... la mia memoria
Non fia ch'ei maledica,
Se le mie pene orribili
Vi sia chi almen gli dica.

GERMONT
No, generosa vivere
E lieta voi dovrete ...
Mercè di queste lagrime
Dal cielo un giorno avrete.

VIOLETTA
Conosca il sagrifizio
Ch'io consumai d'amore ...
Che sarà suo fin l'ultimo
Sospiro del mio cor.

GERMONT
Premiato il sagrifizio
Sarà del vostro amore,
D'un'opra così nobile
Sarete fiera allor, sì, sì.

VIOLETTA	Qui giunge alcun: partite.
GERMONT	Oh grato v'è il cor mio!
VIOLETTA	Partite.
	Non ci vedrem più forse ...

VIOLETTA e GERMONT (*s'abbracciano*)
Siate felice ... Addio!

Germont è sulla porta.

VIOLETTA (*piangendo*)
Conosca il sagrifizio
Che consumai d'amore ...
Che sarà suo fin l'ultimo ...
(*Il pianto le tronca la parola.*)
Addio!

VIOLETTA e GERMONT
Felice siate ... Addio!

	Command me.
GERMONT	Say you don't love him.
VIOLETTA	He won't believe it.
GERMONT	Leave . . .
VIOLETTA	He will follow me.
GERMONT	Then . . .
VIOLETTA	Embrace me as a daughter . . . Then I will be strong.

(They embrace.)

He will be given back to you soon,
But unspeakably grieved . . .
From there you will hasten to console him.

Violetta points to the garden, then goes to write.

GERMONT	What are you thinking of?
VIOLETTA	If you knew, you would oppose My idea . . .
GERMONT	Generous girl! . . . What can I do for you?

VIOLETTA *(coming back to him)*
I'll die . . . I'll die . . . Don't allow him
To curse my memory,
Let someone at least tell him
Of my horrible sufferings.

GERMONT
No, you must live,
Generous and happy . . .
One day you'll receive from heaven
A reward for these tears.

VIOLETTA
Let him know the sacrifice
That I made for love . . .
And that even the last sigh
Of my heart will be his.

GERMONT
The sacrifice of your love
Will be rewarded,
You'll be proud then
Of such a noble deed, yes, yes.

VIOLETTA   Someone is coming; leave.

GERMONT   Oh, my heart is grateful to you!

VIOLETTA   Leave.
Perhaps we won't see each other again . . .

VIOLETTA and GERMONT *(embracing)*
Be happy . . . farewell!

Germont is at the door.

VIOLETTA *(weeping)*
Let him know the sacrifice
That I made for love . . .
And that even the last sigh . . .
(Her tears choke her words.)
Farewell!

VIOLETTA and GERMONT
Be happy . . . farewell!

Germont esce per la porta del giardino. Violetta siede e scrive.

VIOLETTA   Dammi tu forza, o cielo!

Suona il campanello. Annina entra.

ANNINA   Mi richiedeste?...
VIOLETTA   Sì, reca tu stessa
                Questo foglio.
ANNINA (*ne guarda la direzione e se ne mostra sorpresa*)
                Oh!
VIOLETTA   Silenzio ... va all'istante.

                                    (*Annina parte.*)

                Ed or si scriva a lui ...
                Che gli dirò?...
                Chi men darà il coraggio?

Scrive, poi suggella. Entra Alfredo.

ALFREDO   Che fai?
VIOLETTA (*nascondendo la lettera*)
                Nulla.
ALFREDO   Scrivevi?
VIOLETTA (*confusa*)
                Sì ... no ...
ALFREDO   Qual turbamento!...
                A chi scrivevi?...
VIOLETTA   A te ...
ALFREDO   Dammi quel foglio.
VIOLETTA   No, per ora.
ALFREDO   Mi perdona ... son io preoccupato.
VIOLETTA (*alzandosi*)
                Che fu?
ALFREDO   Giunse mio padre ...
VIOLETTA   Lo vedesti?
ALFREDO   Ah no; severo scritto mi lasciava!
                Però l'attendo ...
                T'amerà in vederti ...
VIOLETTA (*agitata*)
                Ch'ei qui non mi sorprenda ...
                Lascia che m'allontani ...
                Tu lo calma ... Ai suoi piedi
                Mi getterò ...
                            (*male frenando il pianto*)
                Divisi ei più ... non ne vorrà ...
                Sarem felici ... sarem felici ...
                Perchè tu m'ami, Alfredo,
                Tu m'ami, non è vero? Tu m'ami?
                Alfredo, non è vero?
ALFREDO   Oh quanto! Perchè piangi?

Germont goes out of the door into the garden. Violetta sits down and writes.

VIOLETTA   Give me the strength, O heaven!

She rings the bell. Annina comes in.

ANNINA   You sent for me? . . .
VIOLETTA   Yes,
             Take this letter yourself.
ANNINA (*looks at the address and shows her surprise*)
             Oh!
VIOLETTA   Silence . . . go at once.

                         (*Annina goes.*)

             And now I must write to him . . .
             What will I tell him? . . .
             Who will give me the courage?

She writes, then seals the letter. Alfredo enters.

ALFREDO   What are you doing?
VIOLETTA (*hiding the letter*)
             Nothing.
ALFREDO   Were you writing?
VIOLETTA (*confused*)
             Yes . . . no.
ALFREDO   What agitation! . . .
             To whom were you writing? . . .
VIOLETTA   To you . . .
ALFREDO   Give me that paper.
VIOLETTA   No, not now.
ALFREDO   Forgive me . . . I'm worried.
VIOLETTA (*rising*)
             What is it?
ALFREDO   My father came . . .
VIOLETTA   Did you see him?
ALFREDO   Ah, no; he left me a stern note!
             However, I expect him . . .
             When he sees you, he'll love you . . .
VIOLETTA (*agitated*)
             He mustn't surprise me here . . .
             Let me go away . . .
             You calm him . . . I'll throw myself
             At his feet . . .
                         (*controlling her tears with effort*)
             He won't want us . . . separated any more . . .
             We will be happy . . . we will be happy . . .
             Because you love me, Alfredo,
             You love me, don't you? You love me?
             Alfredo, don't you?
ALFREDO   Oh, so much! Why are you crying?

VIOLETTA   Di lagrime avea d'uopo ...
Or son tranquilla ... lo vedi?...
        (*sforzandosi*)
Or son tranquilla ... ti sorrido ...
Sarò là, tra quei fior,
Presso a te sempre, sempre ...
Amami, Alfredo, amami quant'io t'amo ...
Addio!...

Corre in giardino.

ALFREDO   Ah, vive sol quel core
All'amor mio!

*Siede, prende a caso un libro, legge alquanto, quindi si
alza, guarda l'ora sull'orologio sovrapposto al camino.*

È tardi ... ed oggi forse
Più non verrà mio padre.

Giuseppe entra frettoloso.

GIUSEPPE   La signora è partita ...
L'attendeva un calesse,
E sulla via già corre di Parigi ...
Annina pure prima di lei spariva ...

ALFREDO   Il so ... ti calma.

GIUSEPPE   (Che vuol dir ciò?)

Parte.

ALFREDO   Va forse d'ogni avere
Ad affrettar la perdita ...
Ma Annina lo impedirà.

Si vede il padre attraversare in lontananza il giardino.

Qualcuno è nel giardino ...
Chi è là?...

Fa per uscire, ma un commissionario compare sulla porta.

COMMISSIONARIO
Il signor Germont?

ALFREDO   Son io.

COMMISSIONARIO
Una dama da un cocchio,
Per voi, di qua non lunge,
Mi diede questo scritto ...

Dà una lettera ad Alfredo, riceve una moneta, e parte.

ALFREDO   Di Violetta!... Perchè son io commosso!...
A raggiungerla forse ella m'invita ...
Io tremo!... Oh ciel!... Coraggio!...
        (*Apre e legge.*)
"Alfredo, al giungervi di questo foglio ..."
        (*Come fulminato, grida.*)

VIOLETTA   I needed tears . . .
              Now I'm calm . . . you see? . . .
                          (*forcing herself*)
              Now I'm calm . . . I'm smiling at you . . .
              I'll be there, among those flowers,
              Near you always, always . . .
              Love me, Alfredo, love me as I love you . . .
              Farewell! . . .

She runs into the garden.

ALFREDO   Ah, that heart lives only
              For love of me!

*He sits down, picks up a book at random, reads a bit, then
stands up, looks at the time on the clock over the fireplace.*

              It's late . . . and perhaps my father
              Will not come today.

Giuseppe hurries in.

GIUSEPPE   Madame has gone . . .
              A coach was waiting for her,
              And it is already hurrying toward Paris . . .
              Annina also disappeared, before her . . .
ALFREDO   I know . . . calm yourself.
GIUSEPPE   (What can this mean?)

He goes out.

ALFREDO   Perhaps she is going
              To hasten the loss of all her possessions . . .
              But Annina will prevent that.

His father is seen crossing the garden in the distance.

              Someone is in the garden . . .
              Who is there? . . .

He starts to go out, but a messenger appears in the doorway.

MESSENGER   Monsieur Germont?
ALFREDO   I am he.

MESSENGER   A lady in a carriage,
              Not far from here,
              Gave me this letter for you . . .

He gives a letter to Alfredo, accepts a tip, and leaves.

ALFREDO   From Violetta! . . . Why am I upset! . . .
              Perhaps she's inviting me to join her . . .
              I'm trembling . . . O heaven! . . . Courage! . . .
                          (*He opens and reads the letter.*)
              "Alfredo, when you receive this letter . . ."
                          (*He shouts, thunderstruck.*)

Ah!
(*Volgendosi si trova a fronte del padre, nelle
     cui braccia si abbandona esclamando:*)
Padre mio!

GERMONT   Mio figlio! Oh quanto soffri!...
               Oh tergi il pianto,
               Ritorna di tuo padre orgoglio e vanto.

*Alfredo disperato siede presso il tavolino col volto tra le
mani.*

GERMONT   Di Provenza il mar, il suol
               Chi dal cor ti cancellò?
               Al natio fulgente sol
               Qual destino ti furò?
               Oh rammenta pur nel duol
               Ch'ivi gioia a te brillò,
               E che pace colà sol
               Su te splendere ancor può ...
               Dio mi guidò ... Dio mi guidò!
               Ah il tuo vecchio genitor
               Tu non sai quanto soffrì!
               Te lontano, di squallor
               Il suo tetto si coprì ...
               Ma se alfin ti trovo ancor,
               Se in me speme non fallì,
               Se la voce dell'onor
               In te appien non ammutì
               Dio m'esaudì ... Dio m'esaudì.

                         (*scuotendo Alfredo*)
               Ne rispondi d'un padre all'affetto?

ALFREDO   Mille serpi divoranmi il petto ...
                    (*respingendo il padre*)
               Mi lasciate ...

GERMONT   Lasciarti!

ALFREDO (*risoluto*)
               (Oh vendetta!)

GERMONT   Non più indugi, partiamo ...
               T'affretta ...

ALFREDO   (Ah fu Douphol!)

GERMONT   M'ascolti tu?

ALFREDO   No!

GERMONT   Dunque invano trovato t'avrò?
               ° [No, non udrai rimproveri;
               Copriam d'oblio il passato;
               L'amor che m'ha guidato
               Sa tutto perdonar.
               Vieni, i tuoi cari in giubilo
               Con me rivedi ancora;
               A chi penò finora
               Tal gioia non negar.
               Un padre ed una suora
               T'affretta a consolar.]

° Brackets denote passages often omitted in performance.

Ah!

(*Turning, he finds himself facing his father,
into whose arms he falls, crying:*)

Father!

GERMONT My son! Oh how you are suffering! . . .
Oh, dry your tears,
Come back, your father's pride and boast.

Alfredo, in despair, sits at the table, his face in his hands.

CERMONT Who erased the sea, the land
Of Provence from your heart?
What fate stole you
From your splendid native sun?
Ah, recall even in your grief
That joy glowed for you there,
And that only there
Can peace still shine on you . . .
God led me . . . God led me!
Ah, you don't know how much
Your old father suffered!
With you far away, his roof
Was covered with shame . . .
But if I've found you at last,
If my hope didn't fail,
If the voice of honor
Isn't completely dumb in you
God answered my prayer . . . God answered
my prayer.

(*shaking Alfredo*)

Don't you respond to your father's love?

ALFREDO A thousand serpents are devouring my breast . . .

(*rejecting his father*)

Leave me . . .

GERMONT Leave you!

ALFREDO (*resolved*)

(Oh, vengeance!)

GERMONT No more delay, we are leaving . . .
Hurry . . .

ALFREDO (Ah, it was Douphol!)

GERMONT Are you listening to me?

ALFREDO No!

GERMONT Then have I found you in vain?
No, you will hear no reproaches;
Let us cover the past with oblivion;
The love that has guided me
Can pardon everything.
Come, you will see with me
Your loved ones rejoice again;
Don't deny such joy
To those who have suffered till now.
Hasten to console
A father and a sister.

*Alfredo, scuotendosi, getta a caso gli occhi sulla tavola, vede
la lettera di Flora, esclama:*

ALFREDO   Ah!... ell'è alla festa! volisi
                 L'offesa a vendicar.

Egli fugge precipitosamente inseguito dal padre.

GERMONT   Che dici? ah ferma!

ATTO SECONDO

PARTE SECONDA

*Galleria nel palazzo di Flora, riccamente addobbata ed
illuminata. Una porta nel fondo e due laterali. A destra, più
avanti, un tavoliere con quanto occorre pel giuoco; a sinistra,
ricco tavolino con fiori e rinfreschi; varie sedie e un divano.*

*Flora, il Marchese, il Dottore, ed altri invitati entrano
dalla sinistra, discorrendo fra loro.*

FLORA   Avrem lieta di maschere la notte;
                 N'è duce il Viscontino ...
                 Violetta ed Alfredo anco invitai ...
MARCHESE   La novità ignorate?
                 Violetta e Germont sono disgiunti.
FLORA e DOTTORE
                 Fia vero?
MARCHESE   Ella verrà qui col Barone.
DOTTORE   Li vidi ieri ancor ... parean felici.

S'ode rumore a destra.

FLORA   Silenzio ... Udite?...

Vanno verso la destra.

FLORA, DOTTORE, e MARCHESE
                 Giungono gli amici.

Molte signore mascherate da zingare entrano dalla destra.

ZINGARELLE   Noi siamo zingarelle
                 Venute da lontano;
                 D'ognuno sulla mano
                 Leggiamo l'avvenir.
                 Se consultiam le stelle
                 Null'avvi a noi d'oscuro,
                 E i casi del futuro
                 Possiamo altrui predir.
                 Vediamo!

Una prima parte del coro osserva la mano di Flora.

Alfredo, recovering himself, glances at the table and sees Flora's letter, exclaims:

ALFREDO   Ah! . . . She is at the ball! Let me fly
To avenge the offense.

He rushes out, followed by his father.

GERMONT   What are you saying? Ah, stop!

ACT TWO

SCENE TWO

A salon in Flora's town house, richly decorated and lighted. A door in the back, and one at either side. Downstage, right, a table equipped for gambling; at left, a table richly laden with flowers and refreshments; various chairs and a sofa.

Flora, the Marquis, the Doctor, and other guests come in from the left, conversing.

FLORA   We'll have a gay night, with masquers;
The Viscount is the leader . . .
I invited Violetta and Alfredo, too . . .
MARQUIS   Don't you know the news?
Violetta and Germont have separated.

FLORA and DOCTOR
Can it be true?
MARQUIS   She'll come here with the Baron.
DOCTOR   I saw them just yesterday . . . they seemed
happy.

A noise is heard at right.

FLORA   Silence . . . You hear? . . .

They go toward the right.

FLORA, DOCTOR, and MARQUIS
Our friends are coming.

Many ladies disguised as gypsies come in at right.

GYPSIES   We are gypsy girls
Who've come from afar;
In everyone's hand
We read the future.
If we consult the stars
Nothing is dark to us,
And future events
We can predict for others.
Let's see!

A first part of the chorus looks at Flora's hand.

ZINGARELLE I Voi, signora ...
              Rivali alquanti avete ...
ZINGARELLE II (*osservando la mano del Marchese*)
              Marchese, voi non siete
              Model di fedeltà.
FLORA (*al Marchese*)
              Fate il galante ancora?
              Ben, vo' me la paghiate.
MARCHESE (*a Flora*)
              Che diamin vi pensate?...
              L'accusa e falsità.
FLORA   La volpe lascia il pelo,
              Non abbandona il vizio ...
              Marchese mio, giudizio,
              O vi farò pentir ...
TUTTI   Su via, si stenda un velo

              Sui fatti del passato;
              Già quel ch'è stato è stato,
              Badate (badiamo) all'avvenir.

*Flora e il Marchese si stringono la mano. Gastone ed altri,
mascherati da mattadori e piccadori spagnuoli, entrano viva-
cemente dalla destra.*

GASTONE e MATTADORI
              Di Madride noi siam mattadori,
              Siamo i prodi del circo dei tori,
              Testè giunti a godere del chiasso
              Che a Parigi si fa pel Bue grasso;
              E una storia, se udire vorrete,
              Quali amanti noi siamo saprete.
GLI ALTRI   Sì, sì bravi; narrate, narrate,
              Con piacere l'udremo.

GASTONE e MATTADORI
              Ascoltate.
              È Piquillo un bel gagliardo
              Biscaglino mattador;
              Forte il braccio, fiero il guardo,
              Delle giostre egli è signor.
              D'andalusa giovinetta
              Follemente innamorò;
              Ma la bella ritrosetta
              Così al giovine parlò:
              "Cinque tori in un sol giorno
              Vo' vederti ad atterrar;
              E, se vinci, al tuo ritorno
              Mano e cor ti vo' donar."
              "Sì," gli disse, e il mattadore
              Alle giostre mosse il piè;
              Cinque tori, vincitore,
              Sull'arena egli stendè.
GLI ALTRI   Bravo, bravo il mattadore,
              Ben gagliardo si mostrò,

GYPSIES I   You, madame . . .
                   Have many rivals . . .
GYPSIES II (*looking at the Marquis's hand*)
                   Marquis, you are not
                   A model for faithfulness.
FLORA (*to the Marquis*)
                   Are you still playing the swain?
                   Well, you'll pay me for it.
MARQUIS (*to Flora*)
                   Whatever are you thinking? . . .
                   The charge is a falsehood.
FLORA   A fox will leave his skin,
                   But not his wickedness . . .
                   My dear Marquis, be careful,
                   Or I'll make you regret it . . .
ALL   Come, let's draw a curtain

                   Over the deeds of the past;
                   What has been has been,
                   Look (let us look) only to the future.

Flora and the Marquis shake hands. Gastone and others, disguised as Spanish matadors and picadors, come running in from the right.

GASTONE and MATADORS
                   We are matadors from Madrid,
                   We're the heroes of the bull ring,
                   Just arrived to enjoy the fuss
                   They're making in Paris for Mardi Gras;
                   And if you care to hear a story,
                   You'll learn what lovers we are.
THE OTHERS   Yes, yes, good for you; tell us, tell,
                   We'll hear it with pleasure.

GASTONE and MATADORS
                   Listen.
                   Piquillo's a bold and handsome
                   Matador from Biscay;
                   Strong of arm, fierce of eye,
                   He's the lord of the arena.
                   He fell madly in love
                   With an Andalusian maiden;
                   But the pretty, coy girl
                   Spoke to the young man thus:
                   "I want to see you bring down
                   Five bulls in a single day;
                   If you win, at your return
                   I'll give you my hand and heart."
                   "Yes," he said, and the matador
                   Went off to the arena;
                   And, a winner, five bulls then
                   He laid out on the sand.
THE OTHERS   Good for him, the matador,
                   He showed how bold he was,

Se alla giovane l'amore
In tal guisa egli provò!

GASTONE e MATTADORI

Poi, tra plausi, ritornato
Alla bella del suo cor,
Colse il premio desiato
Tra le braccia dell'amor.

GLI ALTRI   Con tai prove i mattadori
San le belle conquistar.

GASTONE e MATTADORI

Ma qui son più miti i cori;
A noi basta folleggiar.

TUTTI   Sì, allegri, or pria tentiamo
Della sorte il vario umor;
La palestra dischiudiamo
Agli audaci giuocator.

Gli uomini si tolgono la maschera, chi passeggia e chi si accinge a giuocare. Entra Alfredo.

TUTTI   Alfredo!... Voi!...

ALFREDO   Sì, amici ...

FLORA   Violetta?

ALFREDO   Non ne so.

TUTTI   Ben disinvolto!... bravo!...
Or via, giuocar si può.

Gastone si pone a tagliare, Alfredo ed altri puntano. Entra Violetta a braccio del Barone. Flora va loro incontro.

FLORA   Qui desiata giungi ...

VIOLETTA   Cessi al cortese invito.

FLORA   Grata vi son, Barone,
D'averlo pur gradito.

BARONE (*piano a Violetta*)

Germont è qui!... il vedete?

VIOLETTA   (Cielo! gli è vero!)
                              (*piano al Barone*)
Il vedo.

BARONE   Da voi non un sol detto
Si volga a questo Alfredo ...
Non un detto!

VIOLETTA   (Ah perchè venni, incauta!
Pietà, gran Dio, pietà di me!)

Flora fa sedere Violetta presso di sè sul divano; il Dottore si avvicina ad esse; il Marchese si trattiene a parte col Barone; Gastone taglia, Alfredo ed altri puntano, altri passeggiano.

FLORA (*a Violetta*)

Meco t'assidi; narrami:
Quai novità vegg'io?...

If that was how he proved
His love to the young girl!

GASTONE and MATADORS
Then, amid applause, he went
Back to his heart's beauty,

He took the prize he wanted
In the arms of love.

THE OTHERS   With such exploits matadors
Know how to win the fair.

GASTONE and MATADORS
But here the hearts are milder;
We have only to amuse.

ALL   Yes, be merry . . . first let's test
Luck's fickle mood;
Let's open the arena
To the bold gamblers.

The men take off their masks; some walk up and down and others prepare to gamble. Alfredo enters.

ALL   Alfredo! . . . You! . . .
ALFREDO   Yes, friends.
FLORA   Violetta?
ALFREDO   I know nothing about her.
ALL   Such nonchalance! . . . Bravo! . . .
Come, now we can gamble.

Gastone starts to cut the cards. Alfredo and others place bets. Violetta comes in, on the Baron's arm. Flora goes toward them.

FLORA   We hoped you would come . . .
VIOLETTA   I accepted the kind invitation.
FLORA   I'm grateful to you, Baron,
Also for having accepted it.

BARON (*softly to Violetta*)
Germont is here! . . . Do you see him?
VIOLETTA   (Heaven! It's true!)
(*softly to the Baron*)
I see him.
BARON   Don't you say a single word
To this Alfredo . . .
Not a word!
VIOLETTA   (Ah, reckless me, why did I come!
Have mercy on me, God!)

Flora has Violetta sit down near her on the sofa. The Doctor comes over to them; the Marquis stays to one side with the Baron; Gastone cuts the cards, Alfredo and the others bet, other guests stroll about.

FLORA (*to Violetta*)
Sit with me; tell me:
What do I see that's new? . . .

Flora e Violetta parlano fra loro.

ALFREDO   Un quattro!
GASTONE   Ancora hai vinto!
ALFREDO   Sfortuna nell'amore
             Fortuna reca al giuoco ...

Punta e vince.

TUTTI   È sempre vincitore!...
ALFREDO   Oh vincerò stasera; e l'oro guadagnato
             Poscia a goder tra' campi tornerò beato.
FLORA   Solo?
ALFREDO   No ... no ...
             Con tale che vi fu meco ancora,
             Poi mi sfuggia ...
VIOLETTA   (Mio Dio!...)
GASTONE *(ad Alfredo, indicando Violetta)*
             (Pietà di lei!)
BARONE *(ad Alfredo, con mal frenata ira)*
             Signor!
VIOLETTA *(piano al Barone)*
             (Frenatevi, o vi lascio.)
ALFREDO *(disinvolto)*
             Barone, m'appellaste?
BARONE   Siete in sì gran fortuna,
             Che al giuoco mi tentaste ...
ALFREDO *(ironico)*
             Sì?... La disfida accetto.
VIOLETTA   (Che fia?... morir mi sento!...
             Pietà, gran Dio, pietà di me!)
BARONE *(puntando)*
             Cento luigi a destra.
ALFREDO *(puntando)*
             Ed alla manca cento ...
GASTONE *(tagliando)*
             Un asso ... un fante ...
                              (ad Alfredo)
             Hai vinto!
BARONE   Il doppio?...
ALFREDO   Il doppio sia.
GASTONE *(tagliando)*
             Un quattro ... un sette ... .
TUTTI   Ancora!...
ALFREDO   Pur la vittoria è mia!
TUTTI   Bravo davver!... la sorte è tutta per Alfredo!...
FLORA   Del villeggiar la spesa
             Farà il baron, già il vedo.
ALFREDO *(al Barone)*
             Seguite pur!

Entra un servo.

Flora and Violetta talk together.

ALFREDO	A four!
GASTONE	You've won again!
ALFREDO	Misfortune in love Brings luck in gambling . . .

He bets and wins.

ALL	He's still the winner! . . .
ALFREDO	Oh, I'll win this evening; and then I'll go Back to the country to enjoy the gold I've won.
FLORA	Alone?
ALFREDO	No . . . no . . . With her who was with me before, Then ran away from me . . .
VIOLETTA	(My God! . . .)
GASTONE (*to Alfredo, pointing at Violetta*)	(Have pity on her!)
BARON (*to Alfredo, with ill-concealed wrath*)	Sir!
VIOLETTA (*softly to the Baron*)	(Control yourself, or I'll leave you.)
ALFREDO (*nonchalant*)	Did you call me, Baron?
BARON	You're so lucky, That you've tempted me to gamble . . .
ALFREDO (*ironic*)	Yes? . . . I accept the challenge.
VIOLETTA	(What is this? . . . I feel as if I were dying! . . . Have mercy on me, God!)
BARON (*betting*)	A hundred louis on the right.
ALFREDO (*betting*)	And a hundred on the left . . .
GASTONE (*cutting*)	An ace . . . a knave . . . (*to Alfredo*) You've won!
BARON	Double? . . .
ALFREDO	Double it is.
GASTONE (*cutting*)	A four . . . a seven . . .
ALL	Again! . . .
ALFREDO	The victory is still mine!
ALL	Good for him! . . . Luck is all with Alfredo! . . .
FLORA	The Baron will pay his holiday's expenses, I see that already.
ALFREDO (*to the Baron*)	Continue!

A servant comes in.

SERVO	La cena è pronta.
FLORA	Andiamo.
TUTTI	Andiamo.
VIOLETTA	(Che fia?... morir mi sento! Pietà, gran Dio, pietà di me!)

Tutti partono, restando indietro Alfredo ed il Barone.

ALFREDO	Se continuar v'aggrada ...
BARONE	Per ora nol possiamo: Più tardi la rivincita.
ALFREDO	Al giuoco che vorrete.
BARONE	Seguiam gli amici ... poscia ...
ALFREDO	Sarò qual bramerete. Andiam.
BARONE	Andiam.

Si allontanano. La scene rimane un istante vuota. Poi Violetta ritorna affannata.

VIOLETTA	Invitato a qui seguirmi, Verrà desso?... vorrà udirmi? Ei verrà ... chè l'odio atroce Puote in lui più di mia voce ...

Entra Alfredo.

ALFREDO	Mi chiamaste?... che bramate?...
VIOLETTA	Questi luoghi abbandonate; Un periglio vi sovrasta ...
ALFREDO	Ah comprendo!... Basta, basta ... E sì vile mi credete?
VIOLETTA	Ah no, no, mai ...
ALFREDO	Ma che temete?
VIOLETTA	Tremo sempre del Barone ...
ALFREDO	È fra noi mortal quistione ... S'ei cadrà per mano mia, Un sol colpo vi torria Coll'amante il protettore ... V'atterrisce tal sciagura?
VIOLETTA	Ma s'ei fosse l'uccisore!... Ecco l'unica sventura Ch'io pavento a me fatale.
ALFREDO	La mia morte!... che ven cale?...
VIOLETTA	Deh, partite ... e sull'istante.
ALFREDO	Partirò, ma giura innante Che dovunque seguirai I passi miei ...
VIOLETTA	Ah no, giammai.
ALFREDO	No!... giammai!...
VIOLETTA	Va, sciagurato! Scorda un nome ch'è infamato ...

SERVANT	Supper is ready.
FLORA	Let's go.
ALL	Let's go.
VIOLETTA	(What is this? I feel as if I were dying!
	Have mercy on me, God!)

All go out, only Alfredo and the Baron remain behind.

ALFREDO	If you care to go on ...
BARON	We can't for the moment:
	I'll have my return chance later.
ALFREDO	At any game you wish.
BARON	Let us follow our friends ... then ...
ALFREDO	I will be yours to command.
	Let us go.
BARON	Let us go.

They go off. The stage is deserted for a moment. Then Violetta comes back, distressed.

VIOLETTA	Will he come after me here,
	As I've asked him? ... Will he listen to me?
	He'll come ... for his terrible hatred
	Has more power over him than my voice.

Alfredo enters.

ALFREDO	You called me? ... What do you want?
VIOLETTA	Leave this place;
	Danger threatens you ...
ALFREDO	Ah, I understand! ... Enough, enough ...
	You think I'm so cowardly?
VIOLETTA	Ah, no, no, never ...
ALFREDO	But what do you fear?
VIOLETTA	I'm always afraid the Baron ...
ALFREDO	It's a life-and-death matter between us ...
	If he falls by my hand,
	A single blow would deprive you
	Of lover and keeper ...
	Does such a disaster terrify you?
VIOLETTA	But if he were the killer! ...
	That is the only misfortune
	I fear, a fatal one for me.
ALFREDO	My death! What does it matter to you? ...
VIOLETTA	Please, leave ... and at once.
ALFREDO	I'll leave, but swear first
	That you'll follow my steps
	Anywhere ...
VIOLETTA	Ah no, never.
ALFREDO	No! ... never! ...
VIOLETTA	Go, unhappy man!
	Forget a name that is dishonored ...

Va, mi lascia sul momento ...
Di fuggirti un giuramento
Sacro io feci ...

ALFREDO   A chi?... Dillo ... Chi potea?...

VIOLETTA   A chi dritto pien n'avea.

ALFREDO   Fu Douphol?...

VIOLETTA (*con supremo sforzo*)
                 Sì.

ALFREDO   Dunque l'ami?

VIOLETTA   Ebben ... l'amo ...

Alfredo corre furente a spalancare la porta.

ALFREDO   Or tutti a me.

Tutti entrano confusamente.

TUTTI   Ne appellaste?... che volete?

Alfredo addita Violetta, che abbattuta si appoggia al tavo-lino.

ALFREDO   Questa donna conoscete?

TUTTI   Chi? Violetta?

ALFREDO   Che facesse non sapete?

VIOLETTA   (Ah! taci.)

TUTTI   No.

ALFREDO   Ogni suo aver tal femmina
                 Per amor mio sperdea ...
                 Io cieco, vile, misero,
                 Tutto accettar potea.
                 Ma è tempo ancora!... tergermi
                 Da tanta macchia bramo ...
                 Qui testimon vi chiamo,
                 Or testimon vi chiamo
                 Che qui pagata io l'ho.

Getta con furente sprezzo una borsa a' piè di Violetta, che sviene fra le braccia di Flora. All'ultime parole entra il signor Germont.

TUTTI   Oh, infamia orribile
                 Tu commettesti!
                 Un cor sensibile
                 Così uccidesti!...
                 Di donne ignobile
                 Insultatore,
                 Di qua allontanati,
                 Ne desti orror!
                 Va! Va! Ne desti orror!

GERMONT (*con dignitoso fuoco*)
                 Di sprezzo degno sè stesso rende
                 Chi pur nell'ira la donna offende.
                 Dov'è mio figlio?... più non lo vedo;
                 In te, in te più Alfredo trovar non so.

     Go, leave me at once.
     I took a sacred oath
     To flee from you . . .

ALFREDO   To whom? . . . Tell me . . . Who could make
     you? . . .

VIOLETTA   One who had every right.

ALFREDO   Was it Douphol? . . .

VIOLETTA (*making a supreme effort*)
     Yes.

ALFREDO   Then you love him?

VIOLETTA   Very well . . . I love him . . .

Furious, Alfredo runs and flings open the door.

ALFREDO   Everyone come here to me.

All come in, confused.

ALL   You called us? . . . What do you want?

*Alfredo points to Violetta, who leans against the table,
crushed.*

ALFREDO   You know this woman?

ALL   Who? Violetta?

ALFREDO   You don't know what she did?

VIOLETTA   (Ah! Be silent!)

ALL   No.

ALFREDO   This woman squandered
     All she owned for love of me . . .
     Blind, cowardly, wretched,
     I could accept it all.
     But I'm still in time! . . . I want
     To cleanse myself of such a stain . . .
     I call you here as witnesses,
     Now I call you as witnesses
     That here I have repaid her.

*With furious contempt he throws a purse at the feet of
Violetta, who faints in Flora's arms. At the last words Monsieur Germont comes in.*

ALL   Oh, you've committed
     A horrible infamy!
     In this way, you've killed
     A sensitive heart! . . .
     Ignoble insulter
     Of women,
     Go away from here,
     You fill us with horror!
     Go! Go! You fill us with horror!

GERMONT (*with dignity and fire*)
     A man who, even in anger, offends a woman
     Renders himself deserving of contempt.
     Where is my son? . . . I see him no more;
     I cannot discover Alfredo in you.

ALFREDO   (Ah sì! che feci!... ne sento orrore!

                 Gelosa smania, deluso amore
                 Mi strazian l'alma ... più non ragiono ...
                 Da lei perdono più non avrò.
                 Volea fuggirla ... non ho potuto ...
                 Dall'ira spinto son qui venuto!
                 Or che lo sdegno ho disfogato,
                 Me sciagurato! rimorso n'ho!)

GERMONT   (Io sol fra tanti so qual virtude
                 Di quella misera il sen racchiude ...
                 Io so che l'ama, che gli è fedele;
                 Eppur crudele tacer dovrò!)

BARONE (*piano ad Alfredo*)
                 A questa donna l'atroce insulto
                 Qui tutti offese, ma non inulto
                 Fia tanto oltraggio ... provar vi voglio
                 Che il vostro orgoglio fiaccar saprò.

FLORA, GASTONE, DOTTORE, MARCHESE e CORO (*a Violetta*)
                 Oh quanto peni! ma pur fa cor ...
                 Qui soffre ognuno del tuo dolor;
                 Fra cari amici qui sei soltanto,
                 Rasciuga il pianto che t'inondò.

VIOLETTA (*riavendosi*)
                 Alfredo, Alfredo, di questo core
                 Non puoi comprendere tutto l'amore ...
                 Tu non conosci che fino a prezzo
                 Del tuo disprezzo provato io l'ho.
                 Ma verrà tempo, in che il saprai ...
                 Come t'amassi confesserai ...
                 Dio dai rimorsi ti salvi allor ...
                 Ah! io spenta ancora t'amerò.

ALFREDO   (Ohimè! che feci! ne sento orror! ecc.)

BARONE   Provar vi voglio, ecc.

TUTTI   Quanto peni! fa cor! ecc.

*Germont trae seco il figlio. Il Barone lo segue. Violetta è
condotta in altra stanza dal Dottore e da Flora; gli altri si
disperdono.*

ATTO TERZO

*Camera da letto di Violetta. Nel fondo è un letto con cortine
mezzo tirate; una finestra chiusa da imposte interne; presso il
letto uno sgabello su cui una bottiglia di acqua, una tazza di
cristallo, diverse medicine. A metà della scena una toilette,
vicino un canapè; più distante un altro mobile su cui arde un
lume da notte; varie sedie ed altri mobili. La porta è a sinistra;
di fronte v'è un caminetto con fuoco acceso.*

*Violetta dorme sul letto. Annina, seduta presso il caminetto,
è pure addormentata.*

ALFREDO   (Ah yes! What have I done? . . . I feel horror
         at it!
        Jealous raving, disappointed love
        Tear my soul . . . I can reason no more . . .
        I'll never receive her pardon now.
        I wanted to flee her, but I wasn't able to . . .
        Driven by anger, I came here!
        Now that I've unburdened my scorn,
        Wretched, I feel remorse for it!)

GERMONT   (Only I, among them all, know what virtue
        Is contained in the heart of that poor girl . . .
        I know she loves him, that she is faithful to him;
        And yet I must be cruelly silent!)

BARON (*softly to Alfredo*)
        The terrible insult to this woman
        Offended all here, but such an outrage
        Must not go unpunished . . . I want to prove
        That I can humble your pride.

FLORA, GASTONE, DOCTOR, MARQUIS and CHORUS (*to Violetta*)
        Ah, how you suffer! But still, take heart . . .
        Here everyone suffers at your grief;
        Here you are among dear friends only;
        Dry the tears that bathed you.

VIOLETTA (*coming around*)
        Alfredo, Alfredo, you can't understand
        All the love in this heart . . .
        You don't know that I have subjected it
        Even to the price of your contempt.
        But the time will come, when you will know . . .
        You will admit how much I loved you . . .
        May God save you from remorse then . . .
        Ah! Even when I'm dead, I'll love you still.

ALFREDO   (Alas, what have I done? I feel horror at it! etc.)

BARON   (I want to prove, etc.)

ALL   How you suffer! Take heart! etc.

*Germont takes his son away with him. The Baron follows.
Violetta is led into another room by the Doctor and Flora;
the others disperse.*

ACT THREE

*Violetta's bedroom. In the back there is a bed with curtains
half-drawn; a window with shut blinds on the inside; near the
bed a stool with a carafe of water on it, a crystal cup, and
various medicines. Halfway downstage there is a dressing
table near a sofa; farther away another piece of furniture with
a night light burning on it; various chairs and other pieces.
The door is at left; opposite, a fireplace with a fire burning.*

*Violetta is sleeping in the bed. Annina, sitting near the
fire, is also asleep.*

VIOLETTA (*destandosi*)
    Annina?
ANNINA (*svegliandosi confusa*)
    Comandate?
VIOLETTA   Dormivi? poveretta!
ANNINA   Sì, perdonate.
VIOLETTA   Dammi d'acqua un sorso.

Annina eseguisce.

VIOLETTA   Osserva ... È pieno il giorno?
ANNINA   Son sett'ore.
VIOLETTA   Dà accesso a un po' di luce.

Annina apre le imposte e guarda nello via.

ANNINA   Il signor di Grenvil ...
VIOLETTA   Oh il vero amico!
            Alzar mi vo'... M'aita.

*Fa per alzarsi, ma ricade; poi, sostenuta da Annina, va lenta-
mente verso il canapè, ed il Dottore entra in tempo per assis-
terla ad adagiarvisi. Annina vi aggiunge dei cuscini.*

VIOLETTA   Quanta bontà!... Pensaste a me per tempo!
DOTTORE (*le tocca il polso*)
            Sì ... Come vi sentite?
VIOLETTA   Soffre il mio corpo, ma tranquilla ho l'alma.
            Mi confortò iersera un pio ministro ...
            Ah! religione è sollievo ai sofferenti.
DOTTORE   E questa notte?
VIOLETTA   Ebbi tranquillo il sonno.
DOTTORE   Coraggio adunque ...
            La convalescenza non è lontana ...
VIOLETTA   Oh, la bugia pietosa
            Ai medici è concessa!
DOTTORE (*le stringe la mano*)
            Addio ... a più tardi!
VIOLETTA   Non mi scordate.

*Il Dottore parte. Annina lo accompagna, dicendogli presto e
piano:*

ANNINA   Come va, signore?
DOTTORE   La tisi non le accorda che poche ore.

Esce.

ANNINA   Or fate cor ...
VIOLETTA   Giorno di festa è questo?
ANNINA   Tutta Parigi impazza ... è carnevale.
VIOLETTA   Ah nel comun tripudio, sallo Iddio
            Quanti infelici soffron!
                    (*indicandolo*)

VIOLETTA (*waking*)
> Annina?

ANNINA (*waking, confused*)
> Yes, Madame?

VIOLETTA   Were you asleep? Poor thing!

ANNINA   Yes, forgive me.

VIOLETTA   Give me a sip of water.

Annina obeys.

VIOLETTA   Look . . . Is it broad daylight?

ANNINA   It's seven o'clock.

VIOLETTA   Let a little light in.

Annina opens the shutters and looks into the street.

ANNINA   Monsieur de Grenvil . . .

VIOLETTA   Oh, a true friend!
> I want to get up . . . Help me.

*She starts to rise, but falls back, then, with Annina support-
ing her, she goes slowly to the sofa. The Doctor enters in
time to help settle her on it. Annina adds some cushions.*

VIOLETTA   How kind! . . . You thought of me early!

DOCTOR (*touching her wrist*)
> Yes . . . How do you feel?

VIOLETTA   My body suffers, but my spirit is serene.
> A priest comforted me yesterday evening . . .
> Ah! Religion is a relief to those who suffer.

DOCTOR   And last night?

VIOLETTA   My sleep was peaceful.

DOCTOR   Courage then . . .
> Your convalescence isn't far off . . .

VIOLETTA   Ah, doctors are allowed
> Merciful lies!

DOCTOR (*shaking her hand*)
> Good-by . . . until later.

VIOLETTA   Don't forget me.

*The Doctor leaves. Annina accompanies him to the door,
saying softly and hastily:*

ANNINA   How is she, sir?

DOCTOR   Her consumption grants her only a few hours
> more.

He goes out.

ANNINA   Now take heart . . .

VIOLETTA   Is this a holiday?

ANNINA   All Paris is going mad . . . it's carnival.

VIOLETTA   Ah, God knows, in the general festivity,
> How many unfortunates are suffering!
> > (*pointing*)

Quale somma v'ha in quello stipo?

ANNINA (*apre e conta*)
Venti luigi.

VIOLETTA   Dieci ne reca a' poveri tu stessa.

ANNINA   Poco rimanvi allora ...

VIOLETTA   Oh mi saran bastanti!...
Cerca poscia mie lettere.

ANNINA   Ma voi?

VIOLETTA   Null'occorrà ...
Sollecita, se puoi.

Annina esce. Violetta trae dal seno una lettera e legge.

VIOLETTA   "Teneste la promessa ... La disfida
Ebbe luogo! Il Barone fu ferito,
Però migliora ... Alfredo
È in stranio suolo. Il vostro sagrifizio
Io stesso gli ho svelato.
Egli a voi tornerà pel suo perdono;
Io pur verrò ... Curatevi ... mertate
Un avvenir migliore.
Giorgio Germont."
È tardi!
                    (*Si alza.*)
Attendo, attendo, nè a me giungon mai!...
          (*Si guarda nello specchio.*)
Oh come son mutata!...
Ma il Dottore a sperar pure m'esorta!...
Ah con tal morbo ogni speranza è morta!
Addio, del passato bei sogni ridenti,
Le rose del volto già sono pallenti;
L'amore d'Alfredo perfino mi manca,
Conforto, sostegno dell'anima stanca ...
Ah! della traviata sorridi al desio,
A lei, deh perdona, tu accoglila, o Dio!
Ah! tutto ... or tutto finì.
* [Le gioie, i dolori tra poco avran fine;
La tomba ai mortali di tutto è confine!
Non lagrima o fiore avrà la mia fossa!
Non croce col nome che copra quest'ossa!
Ah! della traviata sorridi al desio,
A lei, deh perdona, tu accoglila, o Dio!
Ah! tutto ... or tutto finì.]

Siede.

CORO DI MASCHERE (*esterno*)
Largo al quadrupede sir della festa,

Di fiori e pampini cinta la testa ...
Largo al più docile d'ogni cornuto,
Di corni e pifferi abbia il saluto.
Parigini, date passo
Al trionfo del Bue grasso.

* Brackets denote passages often omitted in performance.

How much is there in that cupboard?

ANNINA (*opens and counts*)

Twenty louis.

VIOLETTA Take ten to the poor yourself.

ANNINA Little is left then . . .

VIOLETTA Oh, it will be enough for me! . . .
Then see if I have any letters.

ANNINA But what about you?

VIOLETTA I won't need anything . . .
Hurry, if you can.

Annina leaves. Violetta takes a letter from her bosom and reads.

VIOLETTA "You kept the promise . . . The duel
Took place! The Baron was wounded,
But is improving . . . Alfredo
Is in a foreign land. I myself
Revealed your sacrifice to him.
He will come back to you for your forgiveness;
I too will come . . . Take care of yourself . . .
You deserve a better future.
Giorgio Germont."
It's late!
    (*She rises.*)
I wait and wait, but they never come to me! . . .
   (*She looks at herself in the mirror.*)
Oh, how I've changed! . . .
Still the Doctor urges me to hope! . . .
Ah, with this disease, all hope is dead!
Farewell, lovely, happy dreams of the past,
The roses in my face are fading already;
And I am without Alfredo's love also,
The comfort and support of my weary soul . . .
Ah! Smile at the wish of the lost one,
Forgive her, and receive her, O God!
Ah! All . . . now all is finished.
The joys, the griefs will soon have an end;
The tomb is the end of everything for mortals!
No tear or flower will my grave have!
Nor a cross with a name to cover these bones!
Ah! Smile at the wish of the lost one,
Forgive her, and receive her, O God!
Ah! All . . . now all is finished.

She sits down.

CHORUS OF MASQUERS (*outside*)

Make way for the quadruped lord of the feast,
His head garlanded with flowers and vine
 leaves . . .
Make way for the mildest of all horned beasts,
Let him be greeted by horns and fifes.
Parisians, step aside
For the triumph of the fat Ox.

L'Asia, nè l'Africa vide il più bello,
Vanto ed orgoglio d'ogni macello ...
Allegre maschere, pazzi garzoni,
Tutti plauditelo con canti e suoni.
Parigini, date passo
Al trionfo del Bue grasso.
Largo al quadrupede, ecc.

Annina torna frettolosa.

ANNINA (*esitando*)
    Signora ...
VIOLETTA   Che t'accadde?
ANNINA   Quest'oggi, è vero?... vi sentite meglio?
VIOLETTA   Sì, perchè?
ANNINA   D'esser calma promettete?...
VIOLETTA   Sì, che vuoi dirmi?
ANNINA   Prevenir vi volli ...
    Una gioia improvvisa ...
VIOLETTA   Una gioia!... dicesti?
ANNINA   Sì, o signora ...

Annina afferma col capo a va ad aprire la porta.

VIOLETTA   Alfredo!... Ah tu il vedesti!
    Ei vien!... t'affretta ...
    Alfredo?

*Comparisce Alfredo, pallido per la commozione, ed ambi-
due, gettandosi le braccia al collo, esclamano:*

VIOLETTA   Amato Alfredo, oh gioia!
ALFREDO   Oh mia Violetta, oh gioia!
    Colpevol sono ... so tutto, o cara ...
VIOLETTA   Io so che alfine reso mi sei!
ALFREDO   Da questo palpito
    S'io t'ami impara,
    Senza te esistere
    Più non potrei.
VIOLETTA   Ah s'anco in vita
    M'hai ritrovata,
    Credi che uccidere
    Non può il dolor.
ALFREDO   Scorda l'affanno, donna adorata,
    A me perdona e al genitor.
VIOLETTA   Ch'io ti perdoni? le rea son io:
    Ma solo amor tal me rendè.
ALFREDO e VIOLETTA
    Null'uomo o demon, angiol mio,
    Mai più dividermi potrà da te.
ALFREDO   Parigi, o cara, noi lasceremo,
    La vita uniti trascorreremo ...
    De' corsi affanni compenso avrai,
    La tua salute rifiorirà ...

Not Asia nor Africa ever saw a handsomer,
Pride and joy of every butcher shop . . .
Merry masquers, mad apprentices,
All applaud him with songs and music.
Parisians, step aside
For the triumph of the fat Ox.
Make way for the quadruped, etc.

Annina comes back, hurrying.

ANNINA (*hesitating*)	
	Madame . . .
VIOLETTA	What's happened to you?
ANNINA	You do feel better today, don't you?
VIOLETTA	Yes, why?
ANNINA	You promise to be calm? . . .
VIOLETTA	Yes, what do you want to tell me?
ANNINA	I wanted to prepare you . . .
	A sudden joy . . .
VIOLETTA	A joy! . . . you said?
ANNINA	Yes, madame . . .

Annina nods and goes to open the door.

VIOLETTA	Alfredo! . . . Ah, you saw him!
	He's coming! . . . Hurry . . .
	Alfredo?

*Alfredo appears, pale with emotion; they throw themselves
into each other's arms, exclaiming:*

VIOLETTA	Beloved Alfredo, oh joy!
ALFREDO	Oh, my Violetta, oh, joy!
	I'm to blame . . . I know all, my dear . . .
VIOLETTA	I know that at last you've been restored to me!
ALFREDO	See how I love you
	From my heart's beating,
	I could exist no longer
	Without you.
VIOLETTA	Ah, if you've found me
	Still alive,
	You must believe
	That grief cannot kill.
ALFREDO	Forget your grief, adored woman,
	Forgive me and my father.
VIOLETTA	I, forgive you? I'm the guilty one:
	But it was love alone that made me so.
ALFREDO and VIOLETTA	
	No man or demon, my angel,
	Will ever again separate me from you.
ALFREDO	We will leave Paris, O beloved,
	We'll spend our life together . . .
	You'll be rewarded for your past sufferings,
	Your health will bloom again . . .

> Sospiro e luce tu mi sarai,
> Tutto il futuro ne arriderà.

VIOLETTA (e ALFREDO)
> Parigi, o caro, noi lasceremo, ecc.
> La mia salute rifiorirà, ecc.

VIOLETTA
> Ah non più ... a un tempio ...
> Alfredo, andiamo,
> Del tuo ritorno grazie rendiamo.

Vacilla.

ALFREDO
> Tu impallidisci!...

VIOLETTA
> È nulla, sai?
> Gioia improvvisa non entra mai,
> Senza turbarlo, in mesto core.

Violetta si abbandona sfinita sopra una sedia. Alfredo, spaventato, la sorregge.

ALFREDO
> Gran Dio!... Violetta!

VIOLETTA
> È il mio malore!... fu debolezza ...
> Ora son forte ... vedi? sorrido ...

Sforzandosi.

ALFREDO (*desolato*)
> (Ahi cruda sorte!)

VIOLETTA
> Fu nulla!... Annina, dammi a vestire.

ALFREDO
> Adesso?... attendi ...

VIOLETTA (*alzandosi*)
> No!... voglio uscire.

Annina le presenta una veste, ch'ella fa per indossare, e impeditane dalla debolezza, la getta con dispetto e ricade sulla sedia.

VIOLETTA
> Gran Dio!... non posso!

ALFREDO
> (Cielo! che vedo!)
>   (*ad Annina*)
> Va pel Dottore ...

VIOLETTA (*ad Annina*)
> Ah! digli ... digli che Alfredo
> È ritornato ... all'amor mio ...
> Digli che vivere ... ancor vogl'io ...

Annina parte.

VIOLETTA (*ad Alfredo*)
> Ma se tornando non m'hai salvato,
> A niuno in terra salvarmi è dato.
>   (*sorgendo impetuosa*)
> Ah! gran Dio!... morir sì giovine,
> Io che penato ho tanto!
> Morir sì presso a tergere
> Il mio sì lungo pianto!
> Ah! dunque fu delirio
> La credula speranza!...
> Invano di costanza

                        You'll be my light, my breath,
                        All the future will smile on us.
VIOLETTA (and ALFREDO)
                        We will leave Paris, O beloved, etc.
                        My health will bloom again, etc.
VIOLETTA   Ah, no more . . . to a church . . .
                        Alfredo, let us go,
                        Let us give thanks for your return.

She falters.

ALFREDO   You're pale! . . .
VIOLETTA   It's nothing, you know.
                        Sudden joy never enters
                        A sad heart, without upsetting it.

*Violetta, exhausted, sinks into a chair. Frightened, Alfredo
holds her up.*

ALFREDO   Oh God! . . . Violetta!
VIOLETTA   It's my illness! . . . weakness . . .
                        Now I'm strong . . . you see? I'm smiling . . .

Making an effort.

ALFREDO (*desolate*)
                        (Alas, cruel fate!)
VIOLETTA   It was nothing! . . . Annina, give me my clothes.
ALFREDO   Now? . . . Wait . . .
VIOLETTA (*standing up*)
                        No! . . . I want to go out.

*Annina brings her a dress, which she starts to put on, but
her weakness prevents her, she throws it away crossly and
sinks back in the chair.*

VIOLETTA   Good God! . . . I can't!
ALFREDO   (Heaven! What do I see?!)
                                    (*to Annina*)
                        Go for the Doctor . . .
VIOLETTA (*to Annina*)
                        Ah! Tell him . . . tell him that Alfredo
                        Has come back . . . to my love . . .
                        Tell him . . . I want to live again . . .

Annina leaves.

VIOLETTA (*to Alfredo*)
                        But if, by coming back, you haven't saved me,
                        Then no one on earth has the power to save me.
                                    (*impetuously rising*)
                        Ah! Great God! . . . to die so young,
                        I who have suffered so much!
                        To die so close to drying
                        My many, many tears!
                        Ah! So my credulous hope
                        Was delirium! . . .
                        I've armed my heart

Armato avrò il mio cor!...

ALFREDO   Oh mio sospiro e palpito,
Diletto del cor mio!
Le mie colle tue lagrime
Confondere degg'io!...
Ma più che mai, deh! credilo
M'è d'uopo di costanza ...
Ah tutto alla speranza
Non chiudere il tuo cor!

VIOLETTA   Oh Alfredo, il crudo termine ...

ALFREDO   Ah! Violetta mia, deh! calmati.

VIOLETTA   ... serbato al nostro amor!

ALFREDO   M'uccide il tuo dolor.

*Violetta s'abbandona sul canapè. Entra il signor Germont,
seguito dal Dottore con Annina.*

GERMONT   Ah Violetta!...

VIOLETTA   Voi, signor!

ALFREDO   Mio padre!

VIOLETTA   Non mi scordaste?

GERMONT   La promessa adempio ...
A stringervi qual figlia al seno,
O generosa!

VIOLETTA   Ahimè! tardi giungeste!
                    (*abbracciandolo*)
Pure, grata ven sono ...
Grenvil, vedete? fra le braccia
Io spiro di quanti cari ho al mondo ...

GERMONT   Che mai dite!
                    (*osservando Violetta*)
(Oh cielo!... è ver!)

ALFREDO   La vedi, padre mio?

GERMONT   Di più non lacerarmi,
Troppo rimorso l'alma mi divora ...
Quasi fulmin m'atterra ogni suo detto ...
Ah mal cauto vegliardo!
Il mal ch'io feci ora sol vedo!

*Violetta frattanto avrà aperto a stento un ripostiglio della
toilette, e toltone un medaglione, dice:*

VIOLETTA   Più a me t'appressa ...
Ascolta, amate Alfredo.
Prendi: quest'è l'immagine
De' miei passati giorni,
A rammentar ti torni
Colei che sì t'amò.

ALFREDO   No, non morrai, non dirmelo ...
Dêi viver, amor mio ...
A strazio sì terribil
Qui non mi trasse Iddio.

GERMONT   Cara, sublime vittima
D'un disperato amore,

	With constancy, in vain! . . .
ALFREDO	Oh, my breath and pulse,
	Delight of my heart!
	I must mingle
	My tears with yours! . . .
	But more than ever, believe me,
	I need your constancy . . .
	Ah, don't close your heart
	To hope entirely!
VIOLETTA	Oh, Alfredo, the cruel end . . .
ALFREDO	Ah! My Violetta, please be calm!
VIOLETTA	. . . destined for our love!
ALFREDO	Your grief destroys me.

Violetta sinks back on the sofa. Monsieur Germont enters, followed by the Doctor, with Annina.

GERMONT	Ah, Violetta! . . .
VIOLETTA	You, monsieur!
ALFREDO	Father!
VIOLETTA	You haven't forgotten me?
GERMONT	I'm keeping my promise . . .
	To clasp you to my bosom as a daughter,
	O generous girl!
VIOLETTA	Alas. You've come late!
	(*embracing him*)
	Still I'm grateful to you . . .
	Grenvil, you see? I die in the arms
	Of those dearest to me in the world . . .
GERMONT	What are you saying?!
	(*observing Violetta*)
	(Oh heaven! . . . It's true!)
ALFREDO	You see her, Father?
GERMONT	Don't distress me further,
	Too much remorse is consuming my soul . . .
	Her every word strikes me like a thunderbolt . . .
	Ah, ill-advised old man!
	Only now do I see the harm I did!

Violetta meanwhile has painfully opened a drawer in the dressing table, and taking out a miniature, she says:

VIOLETTA	Come closer to me . . .
	Listen, beloved Alfredo.
	Take this: this is the picture
	Of my former days,
	Let it remind you again
	Of her who loved you so.
ALFREDO	No, you won't die, don't say it to me . . .
	You must live, my love . . .
	God didn't bring me here
	For such terrible torment.
GERMONT	Beloved, sublime victim
	Of a desperate love.

	Perdonami lo strazio Recato al tuo bel cor.
VIOLETTA	Se una pudica vergine, Degli anni suoi sul fiore, A te donasse il core ... Sposa ti sia ... Io vo' ... Le porgi quest'effigie; Dille che dono ell'è Di chi nel ciel fra gli angeli Prega per lei, per te.
ALFREDO	Sì presto, ah no, dividerti Morte non può da me. Ah vivi, o solo un feretro M'accoglierà con te.

GERMONT, DOTTORE, e ANNINA
Finchè avrà il ciglio lagrime
Io piangerò per te.
Vola a' beati spiriti,
Iddio ti chiama a sè.

VIOLETTA (*rialzandosi animata*)
È strano!

TUTTI   Che!

VIOLETTA   Cessarono gli spasimi del dolore ...
In me ... rinasce ... m'agita
Insolito vigor!...
Ah!... ma io ... ah! ma io ritorno a viver!
Oh gioia!

Ricade sul canapè.

TUTTI   Oh cielo!... muor!

ALFREDO   Violetta?

ANNINA e GERMONT
Oh Dio, soccorrasi ...

Il Dottore le tocca il polso.

DOTTORE   È spenta!

ANNINA   Oh rio dolor!

ALFREDO e GERMONT
Oh mio dolor!

	Forgive me for the torture I caused your noble heart.
VIOLETTA	If an innocent maiden, In the flower of her years, Should give her heart to you . . . Let her be your bride . . . I wish it . . . Give her this portrait; Tell her it is the gift Of one who, among the angels in heaven, Is praying for her, for you.
ALFREDO	Ah no, death cannot separate You from me so quickly. Ah, live . . . or a single coffin Will receive me, with you.
GERMONT, DOCTOR, and ANNINA	As long as my eyes have tears I will weep for you. Fly to the blessed spirits; God is calling you to Him.
VIOLETTA *(rising again, animated)*	It's strange!
ALL	What!
VIOLETTA	The seizures of pain have stopped . . . An unfamiliar strength Is born in me . . . stirs me! . . . Ah! . . . Why, I . . . I am returning to life! Oh joy!

She falls back on the sofa.

ALL	Oh, heaven! . . . She's dying!
ALFREDO	Violetta?
ANNINA and GERMONT	Oh, God, help her . . .

The Doctor touches her wrist.

DOCTOR	She's dead!
ANNINA	Oh, cruel grief!
ALFREDO and GERMONT	Oh, my grief!

Un ballo in maschera

° The opera Verdi really wanted to write in 1857 was *King Lear*. He had been corresponding with the poet Antonio Somma about the project for four years (and their partially published correspondence on the subject affords a fascinating insight into Verdi's dramaturgy). But like all Verdi's operas after his first, *Oberto*, and up to his last two, *Otello* and *Falstaff*, the 1857 work was being written to fulfill a commission, in this case from the Teatro San Carlo in Naples. For that season the Neapolitan opera house did not have a soprano to Verdi's liking. The composer wanted Maria Piccolomini, whom he had particularly admired in *Traviata*, for his Cordelia. Since she was not available, Verdi postponed the *Lear* project.

Even before Somma had completed the *Lear* libretto, Verdi asked him to suggest another opera idea. In 1855, the composer wrote from Paris: "Could you find another story for me, which you could then write at your leisure? A story that is beautiful, *original*, interesting, with beautiful situations, and impassioned. *Passions*, above all! . . ."

Somma suggested Lewis's novel *The Monk*, but Verdi wrote: "I want a story of feelings, not a spectacle." Finally Verdi found his own story, *Gustave III*, beautiful and impassioned, albeit not exactly original. Eugène Scribe had written this libretto for Auber, whose opera of that title was heard in Paris in 1833. A decade later, Cammarano (Verdi's future collaborator) adapted the story for Saverio Mercadante, entitling it *Il reggente*.

But these antecedents clearly did not disturb Verdi, who sent the proposal to Somma on October 9, 1857. Somma answered four days later, agreeing—on one condition: his work was to remain anonymous. Biographers of Verdi have said that Somma wanted this anonymity because he was ashamed of the libretto, but he made the condition before he had even begun work. Sommas's exact words are: "I would like, if you don't mind, to remain anonymous for this work, or sign it with a pseudonym. Thus I will write with greater freedom."

The last sentence is significant. Somma probably wanted to keep out of the public eye for political reasons. In the years 1848–49 he had participated in the Venetian rebellion against the Austrians, and he was still under police surveillance. Therefore, he would not want to sign a story involving a regicide.

Born in Udine in 1809, educated in Padua, Somma was a lawyer by profession. But he was also, by the time Verdi met him in Venice, a respected writer. After a youthful tragedy, entitled *Parisina*, Somma published another tragedy, *Marco Bozzari*, in 1847. His *La figlia dell'Appenino* was seen in

° This introductory note was originally written, in a somewhat different form, to accompany a complete recording of the opera by London Records. The material is reprinted here with their kind permission.

Milan, and in 1859—the year of *Un ballo in maschera*'s première—the great Adelaide Ristori performed his *Cassandra*
in Paris, where Théophile Gautier said, "it approached and, in
many places, equaled the *Oresteia* of Aeschylus."

As usual, Verdi worked hard on the new libretto himself,
sending Somma numerous suggestions ("we'll change Locu-
sta's name to Ulrica," he wrote at one point). The librettist
came to Verdi's Villa Sant'Agata for Christmas in 1857, and
apparently the libretto was completed then.

Before the libretto was finished, both Verdi and Somma
were already preparing themselves for battle with the censor
(who, in fact, proved still more difficult than his Venetian
counterpart who had made such trouble over *Rigoletto*). They
were willing to shift the scene from Sweden to Pomerania
and to make other alterations. But when Verdi reached Naples
in mid-January, he found himself faced with an intolerable
situation. The censor demanded (as Verdi informed Somma)
that the hero be made a private gentleman, not a sovereign;
his wife was to become his sister; there was to be no final
ball; the assassination had to take place off stage; the scene
of the drawing of Renato's name from the urn could not remain. The impresario of the San Carlo whipped up a new
libretto, entitled *Adelia degli Adimari*, which Verdi rejected.
A lawsuit resulted; it was settled out of court, but it was late
April before Verdi could leave Naples.

Meanwhile Vincenzo Jacovacci, the colorful and alert impresario of Rome's Teatro Apollo, had journeyed to Naples
and persuaded Verdi to give him *Gustave III* for his theater.
There were more censorship problems, but they were resolved
by shifting the scene this time to Boston and demoting the
king to the rank of count. The opera also was then given its
definitive title—*Un ballo in maschera*.

Although Verdi grumbled about the Roman cast (which
included, however, his favorite tenor Gaetano Fraschini), the
première of *Un ballo in maschera*, on February 17, 1859, was
an enormous success. The composer was called out on the
stage twenty times.

During the later years of the Fascist period, at the height
of Mussolini's Anglophobia, some anonymous revisions were
made in the libretto, and the words "Inghilterra" and "America" were replaced by the suitable noun "patria" (this version can be heard in a historic recording with Beniamino
Gigli). More recently, some theaters have tried to restore the
original Swedish setting, calling the characters Gustavus (Riccardo), Ankarstroem (Renato), Mamzell Arvidson (Ulrica),
and so on. The changes can be interesting, but they are not
really significant. In this opera it is the passions that count,
not the geography.

THE PLOT

ACT ONE

Boston. In the Governor's residence, some officers and various deputies are waiting for Count Riccardo, the Governor, to appear. A group of conspirators, headed by Samuel and Tom, is also present. Announced by Oscar, his page, Riccardo enters, and his just, noble nature is immediately evident. When Oscar hands him the invitation list for a forthcoming masked ball, the first name that strikes Riccardo's gaze is Amelia, the woman he secretly loves. She is the wife of his best friend and loyal adviser Renato, who comes in soon afterward. The Chief Justice arrives with some documents for the Governor to sign, including a banishment order for Ulrica, a soothsayer. Oscar defends the supposed prophetess, and Riccardo, as a lark, suggests that the whole court visit her in disguise. All agree; Samuel, Tom and their followers hope that the occasion will offer them an opportunity to assassinate Riccardo.

Ulrica, with a number of her believers around her, is invoking the King of Darkness. Riccardo arrives, disguised as a fisherman; then Silvano, a sailor, comes forward and has his fortune told. He is promised gold and a promotion, and Riccardo lightheartedly secretes a purse and a scribbled commission in the sailor's pocket, so the prophecy is proved correct. At a secret door a knocking is heard. A servant, whom Riccardo recognizes as Amelia's, asks for a private audience for his mistress. In hiding, the Count overhears Amelia's confession of her guilty love to Ulrica, who tells her of a magic herb that will cure this passion. It must be picked at midnight beneath the gallows on the city's outskirts.

Riccardo vows to go there, too. Now Oscar and the court arrive, and Riccardo demands to have his fortune told. Ulrica says he is a man of high rank. Then, with great reluctance, she tells him he will soon die, and by a friend's hand. Riccardo scoffs at the prophecy. Ulrica, pressed, then tells him that the murderer will be the man whose hand he next shakes. Riccardo's amusement is all the greater since Renato—his best friend—now arrives and, shaking his hand, reveals the Count's identity. Ulrica is pardoned, and she thanks the Governor, continuing to warn him, while Silvano, reappearing, leads the crowd in a song of praise for the generous Riccardo.

ACT TWO

Midnight. Filled with fear, Amelia comes to the horrid field to pluck the magic herb. Riccardo appears suddenly and, after declaring his love, forces her to admit that she, too, loves him. As she is reminding him of his duty toward his friend, Renato himself arrives to warn Riccardo that the conspirators are after him. Amelia is veiled, so her husband does not recognize her. Riccardo agrees to escape only after Renato has promised to accompany the unknown woman into the city, without seeking to know her identity. When the Count has gone, the conspirators arrive, and as Renato is about to duel with them, Amelia intervenes and her veil falls off. The conspirators mock the astonished Renato, who then invites them to his house the following morning. As they go off, still laughing at his discomfiture, he drags Amelia away.

ACT THREE

Renato's study. He enters with Amelia. Refusing to listen to her explanations, he announces that he will kill her; but as a final favor, he allows her first to go and embrace their only child. Then, alone, looking at Riccardo's portrait which dominates the room, he realizes that it is the Count he must kill. Samuel and Tom arrive, and Renato joins their plot, proving his intentions by destroying the evidence he has of their treason. The murderer is to be decided by lot, and Amelia, who now comes back, is made to draw a name from a vase. The name is Renato's, and as Oscar arrives to invite them to a masked ball that evening, the ideal opportunity for the assassination seems clear. Amelia guesses what is afoot and plans to forewarn Riccardo.

The Governor's study. Riccardo's sense of duty has conquered his passion. After a brief hesitation, he signs an order sending Renato (and with him, Amelia) back to England. Oscar delivers an anonymous note from an unknown woman, warning him that an attempt will be made on his life during the ball. Fearlessly, Riccardo decides to attend it anyway.

The ballroom is crowded with guests, many of them masked. Oscar discovers Renato's identity and is, in his turn, unmasked. After some jesting, Oscar describes the Count's disguise. As Renato goes off, Riccardo appears, joined by Amelia, who begs him to flee. As they are exchanging a last farewell, Renato returns and stabs the Count. Riccardo reveals Amelia's and his own innocence, pardons Renato and the other conspirators, and dies as all mourn him.

UN BALLO IN MASCHERA

libretto by Antonio Somma

First performed at the Teatro Apollo, Rome
February 17, 1859

CHARACTERS

Riccardo, Count of Warwick, Governor of Boston	*Tenor*
Renato, a Creole, Riccardo's adviser	*Baritone*
Amelia, Renato's wife	*Soprano*
Ulrica, a fortuneteller	*Contralto*
Oscar, Riccardo's page	*Soprano*
Silvano, a sailor	*Bass*
Samuel, enemy of the Count	*Bass*
Tom, enemy of the Count	*Bass*
Chief Justice	*Tenor*
Amelia's manservant	*Tenor*

Deputies, Officers, Sailors, Guards, Men, Women and Children
of the populace, Gentlemen, Followers of Samuel and Tom,
Servants, Maskers and Dancing Couples

The scene is laid in Boston and environs at the end of the
seventeenth century.

ATTO PRIMO

SCENA PRIMA

Una sala nella casa del Governatore. In fondo l'ingresso delle sue stanze. È il mattino. Deputati, Gentiluomini, Popolani, Uffiziali. Sul dinanzi Samuel, Tom e loro aderenti, tutti in attesa di Riccardo.

UFFIZIALI e GENTILUOMINI
> Posa in pace, a' bei sogni ristora,
> O Riccardo, il tuo nobile cor.
> A te scudo su questa dimora
> Sta d'un vergine mondo l'amor.

SAMUEL, TOM e loro ADERENTI
> E sta l'odio, che prepara il fio,
>
> Ripensando ai caduti per te.

UFFIZIALI e GENTILUOMINI
> Posa in pace.

SAMUEL, TOM e loro ADERENTI
> Come speri, disceso l'obblio
> Sulle tombe infelici non è.
> No, no, come speri, *ecc.*

UFFIZIALI e GENTILUOMINI
> Posa in pace, *ecc.*

Oscar entra dalle stanze del Conte.

OSCAR   S'avanza il Conte.

Entra Riccardo salutando gli astanti.

RICCARDO   Amici miei . . . Soldati . . .
> *(ai Deputati)*
> E voi del par diletti a me!
> *(riceve delle suppliche)*
> Porgete: a me, a me s'aspetta:
> Io deggio su' miei fidi vegliar,
> Perchè sia pago ogni voto, se giusto.
> Bello il poter non è, che de' soggetti
> Le lacrime non terge, e ad incorrotta
> Gloria non mira.

OSCAR *(a Riccardo)*
> Leggere vi piaccia
> Delle danze l'invito.

RICCARDO   Avresti alcuna beltà dimenticato?

OSCAR *(offrendogli un foglio)*
> Eccovi i nomi.

ACT ONE

SCENE ONE

A hall in the Governor's house. At the rear, the entrance to his rooms. It is morning. Delegates, Gentlemen, Commoners, Officers. In the foreground, Samuel, Tom, and their followers. All are waiting for Riccardo.

OFFICERS and GENTLEMEN

Repose in peace, with beautiful dreams refresh,
O Riccardo, your noble heart.
A shield for you over this house
Stands the love of a virgin world.

SAMUEL, TOM and their FOLLOWERS

And there stands hate, which prepares the penalty,
Reflecting on those who have fallen because of you.

OFFICERS and GENTLEMEN

Repose in peace.

SAMUEL, TOM and their FOLLOWERS

Oblivion has not descended,
As you hope, on the unhappy graves.
No, no, as you hope, *etc.*

OFFICERS and GENTLEMEN

Repose in peace, *etc.*

Oscar enters from the Count's rooms.

OSCAR   The Count is arriving.

Riccardo enters, greeting those present.

RICCARDO   My friends . . . Soldiers . . .
                (to the Delegates)
             And you, equally dear to me!
                (receives some petitions)
             Give me: to me, to me they are due.
             I must watch over my faithful subjects,
             So that every wish, if just, is granted.
             Power is not beautiful if it does not
             Dry its subjects' tears, and does not
             Aim at uncorrupted glory.

OSCAR *(to Riccardo)*

             May it please you read
             The invitation to the dances.

RICCARDO   Could you have forgotten some beauty?

OSCAR *(offering him a paper)*

             Here are the names.

RICCARDO (*leggendolo, tra sè*)
>Amelia . . . ah dessa ancor! dessa ancor!
>L'anima mia in lei rapita
>Ogni grandezza oblia!
>La rivedrà nell'estasi
>Raggiante di pallore
>E qui sonar d'amore
>La sua parola udrà sonar d'amore.
>O dolce notte, scendere
>Tu puoi gemmata a festa:
>Ah, ma la mia stella è questa,
>Che il ciel non ha!
>Quest'è mia stella!

SAMUEL, TOM e loro ADERENTI (*sommessamente*)
>L'ora non è, l'ora non è, chè tutto
>Qui d'operar ne toglie:
>Dalle nemiche soglie
>Meglio l'uscir sarà.
>Dalle nemiche soglie, *ecc.*

OSCAR, UFFIZIALI e GENTILUOMINI
>Con generoso affetto
>Entro sè stesso assorto,
>Il nostro bene oggetto
>De' suoi pensier farà.
>Il nostro bene, *ecc.*

RICCARDO   Ah! E qui sonar d'amore, *ecc.*

RICCARDO (*ad Oscar*)
>Il cenno mio di là con essi attendi.

>*Tutti s'allontanano. Oscar, l'ultimo, incontra Renato al limitare.*

OSCAR (*verso Renato che s'avanza*)
>Libero è il varco a voi.

RENITO (*tra sè*)
>Deh come triste appar!

RICCARDO (*tra sè*)
>Amelia!

RENATO (*chinandosi*)
>Conte . . .

RICCARDO   (Oh ciel! lo sposo suo!)

RENATO (*accostandosi*)
>Turbato il mio signor,
>Mentre dovunque il nome suo inclito suona?

RICCARDO   Per la gloria è molto,
>Nulla per cor. Segreta, acerba
>Cura m'opprime.

RENATO   E d'onde?

RICCARDO   Ah no . . . non più . . .

RENATO   Dirolla io la cagion.

RICCARDO   (Gran Dio!)

RENATO   So tutto . . .

RICCARDO *(reading it, aside)*
>Amelia . . . ah, she again! She again!
>My soul, enraptured by her,
>Forgets all grandeur!
>I shall see her again in ecstasy,
>Radiant in pallor,
>And here, resound with love,
>I shall hear her word resound with love.
>O sweet night, you may descend,
>Bejewelled festively:
>Ah! but this is my star,
>Which the sky does not have!
>This is my star!

SAMUEL, TOM and their FOLLOWERS *(softly)*
>It is not the hour, it is not the hour,
>For everything here prevents our operating.
>From the hostile threshold
>It will be better to leave.
>From the hostile threshold, *etc.*

OSCAR, OFFICERS and GENTLEMEN
>With generous affection,
>Absorbed in himself,
>He will make our welfare
>The object of his thoughts.
>Our welfare, *etc.*

RICCARDO   Ah, And here resound with love, *etc.*
RICCARDO *(to Oscar)*
>Wait for my signal with them, in there.

*All go away. Oscar, the last, encounters Renato at the door-
way.*

OSCAR *(toward Renato, who advances)*
>The way is open to you.

RENATO *(aside)*
>Ah! how sad he seems!

RICCARDO *(aside)*
>Amelia!

RENATO *(bowing)*
>Count . . .

RICCARDO   (Oh, heaven! Her husband!)
RENATO *(coming closer)*
>My lord upset,
>While everywhere his glorious name resounds?

RICCARDO   For glory it is much;
>For the heart, nothing. A secret, bitter
>Care oppresses me.

RENATO   And wherefore?
RICCARDO   Ah, no! . . No more . . .
RENATO   I shall say the reason.
RICCARDO   (Great God!)
RENATO   I know everything . . .

RICCARDO   E che?

RENATO   So tutto.
            Già questa soglia stessa
            Non t'è securo asilo.

RICCARDO   Prosegui.

RENATO   Un reo disegno
            Nell'ombre si matura,
            I giorni tuoi minaccia.

RICCARDO *(con gioia)*
            Ah! gli è di ciò che parli?
            Altro non sai? . . .

RENATO   Se udir ti piace i nomi . . .

RICCARDO   Che importa? io li disprezzo.

RENATO   Svelarli è mio dover.

RICCARDO   Taci: nel sangue
            Contaminarmi allor dovrei. Non fia,
            Nol vo'. Del popol mio
            L'amor mi guardi,
            E mi protegga Iddio.

RENATO   Alla vita che t'arride
            Di speranze e gaudio piena,
            D'altre mille e mille vite
            Il destino s'incatena!
            Te perduto, te perduto, ov'è la patria,

            Te perduto, ov'è la patria
            Col suo splendido avvenir?
            E sarà dovunque, sempre
            Chiuso il varco alle ferite,
            Perchè scudo del tuo petto
            È del popolo l'affetto?
            Dell'amor più desto è l'odio
            Le sue vittime a colpir.
            Te perduto, *ecc.*

OSCAR *(entra)* Il primo giudice.

RICCARDO   S'avanzi.

GIUDICE *(offrendogli dispacci a firmare)*
            Conte!

RICCARDO   Che leggo! . . .
            Il bando ad una donna; Or d'onde?
            Qual è il suo nome?
            Di che rea?

GIUDICE   S'appella Ulrica, dell'immondo
            Sangue dei negri.

OSCAR   Intorno a cui s'affollano
            Tutte le stirpi. Del futuro
            L'alta divinatrice . . .

GIUDICE   Che nell'antro abbietto
            Chiama i peggiori, d'ogni reo consiglio
            Sospetta già.

RICCARDO	And what?
RENATO	I know everything. Even this very threshold Is not a safe refuge for you.
RICCARDO	Continue.
RENATO	An evil plot Is ripening in the shadows; It threatens your days.

RICCARDO (*with joy*)
Ah! That is what you are speaking of?
You know nothing else? . . .

RENATO	If you care to hear the names . . .
RICCARDO	What does it matter? I scorn them.
RENATO	It is my duty to reveal them.
RICCARDO	Be silent: then I should Poison my blood. Let it not be, I do not wish it. Let my people's Love keep watch over me, And let God protect me.
RENATO	To the life that smiles at you, Full of hopes and joy, The fate of thousands and thousands Of others lives is linked! If you are lost, if you are lost, where is the fatherland, If you are lost, where is the fatherland With its splendid future? And will the way to wounds Be always, everywhere, blocked, Because a shield for your bosom Is the love of the people? Hatred is more alert than love To strike its victims. If you are lost, *etc.*

OSCAR (*enters*) The Chief Justice.

RICCARDO	Let him come forward.

JUSTICE (*giving him despatches to sign*)
Count!

RICCARDO	What do I read! . . . Banishment for a woman! Now why? What is her name? Of what guilty?
JUDGE	She is called Ulrica, of the foul Blood of the Negroes.
OSCAR	Around whom crowd All breeds. The lofty prophetess Of the future . . .
JUSTICE	Who to her squalid den Calls the worst, of every evil counsel Already suspect.

                 Dovuto è a lei l'esilio:
                 Nè muta il voto mio.

RICCARDO *(ad Oscar)*
                 Che ne di' tu?
                 Che ne di' tu?

OSCAR
                 Difenderla vogl'io.
                 Volta la terrea
                 Fronte alle stelle
                 Come sfavilla
                 La sua pupilla,
                 Quando alle belle
                 Il fin predice
                 Mesto o felice
                 Dei loro amor,
                 Mesto, felice, dei loro amor!
                 È con Lucifero
                 D'accordo ognor!
                 Ah! è con Lucifero, *ecc.*

RICCARDO
                 Che vaga coppia . . .
                 Che protettor! che protettor!
                 Che protettor!

OSCAR
                 Chi la profetica
                 Sua gonna afferra,
                 O passi 'l mare,
                 Voli alla guerra,
                 Le sue vicende
                 Soavi, amare
                 Da questa apprende
                 Nel dubbio cor.
                 Da questa apprende
                 Nel dubbio cor.
                 Ah! è con Lucifero, *ecc.*

GIUDICE
                 Sia condannata.

OSCAR *(verso il Conte)*
                 Assolverla degnate.

GIUDICE
                 Condannata.

RICCARDO
                 Ebben . . . tutti chiamate:
                 (Renato ed Oscar invitano a rientrare gli
                   usciti.)
                 Or v'apro un mio pensier.
                 Signori, oggi d'Ulrica
                 Alla magion v'invito,
                 Ma sotto altro vestito;
                 Io là sarò.

RENATO
                 Davver? davver?

RICCARDO
                 Sì, vo' gustar la scena.

RENATO
                 L'idea non è prudente.

OSCAR
                 La trovo anzi eccellente,
                 Feconda di piacer.

RENATO
                 Te ravvisar taluno
                 Ivi potria.

Exile is due her:
Nor does my vow change.

RICCARDO *(to Oscar)*
What do you say about it?
What do you say about it?

OSCAR
I wish to defend her.
Having turned her ashen
Brow to the stars,
How her eye
Flashes,
When to the beauties
She foretells the end,
Sad or happy,
Of their loves,
Sad, happy, of their loves!
She is with Lucifer
Always in league!
Ah! she is with Lucifer, *etc.*

RICCARDO
What a lovely couple . . .
What a protector! What a protector!
What a protector!

OSCAR
He who grasps
Her prophetical skirt
Whether he cross the sea,
Or fly to the war,
His vicissitudes,
Sweet, bitter,
He learns from this woman
In his suspecting heart.
He learns from this woman
In his suspecting heart.
Ah! she is with Lucifer, *etc.*

JUSTICE
Let her be condemned.

OSCAR *(toward the Count)*
Deign to absolve her.

JUSTICE
Condemned.

RICCARDO
Very well . . . call everybody:
*(Renato and Oscar invite those who went out
to come in again.)*
Now I shall reveal a thought of mine to you.
Gentlemen, today I invite you
To the dwelling of Ulrica,
But in another costume:
I shall be there.

RENATO
Really? Really?

RICCARDO
Yes, I want to relish the scene.

RENATO
The idea is not prudent.

OSCAR
On the contrary, I find it excellent,
Rich in pleasure.

RENATO
Some there could
Recognize you.

RICCARDO   Qual tema! . . .

SAMUEL, TOM e loro ADERENTI
                  Ve', ve', di tutto trema
                  Codesto consiglier.

RICCARDO *(ad Oscar)*
                  E tu m'appronta un abito
                  Da pescator.

SAMUEL, TOM e loro ADERENTI *(sotto voce)*
                  Chi sa che alla vendetta l'adito
                  Non s'apra alfin colà?

RICCARDO   Ogni cura si doni al diletto,
                  E s'accorra nel magico tetto:
                  Tra la folla de' creduli ognuno
                  S'abbandoni e folleggi con me.
                  Ed ognun . . . s'abbandoni, *ecc.*

RENATO   E s'accorra, ma vegli il sospetto
                  Sui perigli che fremono intorno,
                  Ma protegga il magnanimo petto
                  A chi nulla paventa per sè.

OSCAR   L'indovina ne dice di belle,
                  E sta ben che l'interroghi anch'io;
                  Sentirò se m'arridono le stelle,
                  Di che sorti benefica m'è.

RICCARDO   Ogni cura si doni, *ecc.*

RENATO   E s'accorra, *ecc.*

RICCARDO   Dunque, signori, aspettovi,
                  Signori, aspettovi, aspettovi,
                  Incognito, incognito, alle tre.
                  Nell'antro dell'oracolo,
                  Nell'antro dell'oracolo
                  Della gran maga al piè,
                  Della gran maga al piè.

OSCAR, UFFIZIALI e GENTILUOMINI
                  Teco sarem di subito,
                  Sarem di subito, incogniti,
                  Incogniti, alle tre,
                  Nell'antro dell'oracolo,
                  Della gran maga al piè.

SAMUEL, TOM e loro ADERENTI
                  Senza posa vegliamo all'intento,
                  Nè si perda ove scocchi il momento;
                  Forse l'astro che regge il suo fato
                  Nell'abisso là spegnersi de'.

RICCARDO   Ogni cura si doni al diletto,
                  E s'accorra al fatidico tetto:
                  Per un dì si folleggi, si scherzi;
                  Mai la vita più cara non è.
                  La vita mai sì cara non è, *ecc.*
                  Dunque, signori, aspettovi, *ecc.*

OSCAR   Sì! sì! sì! Sentirò,

RICCARDO   What fear! . . .

SAMUEL, TOM and their FOLLOWERS
                See, see, this counsellor
                Trembles at everything.

RICCARDO *(to Oscar)*
                And you prepare me a costume
                As a fisherman.

SAMUEL, TOM and their FOLLOWERS *(aside)*
                Who knows that the entry to revenge
                May not finally open there?

RICCARDO   Let every care be given to pleasure,
                And let us hasten to the magic roof:
                Amid the crowd of the credulous let each one
                Abandon himself and frolic with me.
                And let each one . . . abandon himself, *etc.*

RENATO   And let us hasten, but let suspicion keep watch
                On the dangers that rage around,
                But let us protect the magnanimous bosom
                Of him who fears nothing for himself.

OSCAR   The fortuneteller says some fine things,
                And it is well that I also question her.
                I shall hear if the stars smile on me,
                Of what fates she is beneficent with me.

RICCARDO   Let every care, *etc.*

RENATO   And let us hasten, *etc.*

RICCARDO   Then, gentlemen, I expect you,
                Gentlemen, I expect you, I expect you,
                Disguised, disguised, at three o'clock.
                In the den of the oracle,
                In the den of the oracle,
                At the foot of the great sorceress,
                At the foot of the great sorceress.

OSCAR, OFFICERS and GENTLEMEN
                We shall be with you promptly,
                We shall be promptly, disguised,
                Disguised, at three,
                In the den of the oracle,
                At the foot of the great sorceress.

SAMUEL, TOM and their FOLLOWERS
                Without rest let us attend to our purpose
                Nor miss the moment when it strikes;
                Perhaps the star that rules his destiny
                Must be extinguished in the abyss there.

RICCARDO   Let every care be given to pleasure,
                And let us hasten to the magic roof:
                For one day let us frolic, joke;
                Never is life more dear.
                Life is never so dear, *etc.*
                Then, gentlemen, I expect you, *etc.*

OSCAR   Yes! yes! yes! I shall hear,

Sentirò se m'arridon le stelle,
Qual presagio le dettan per me,
Sentirò, *ecc.*

UFFIZIALI e GENTILUOMINI
Sì! sì! sì! Alfin brilli,
Alfin brilli d'un po' di follia
Questa vita che il cielo ne diè,
Alfin brilli, *ecc.*

RICCARDO   Alle tre . . .

TUTTI   Alle tre! . . .

RICCARDO   Dureque, signori, *ecc.*

TUTTI   Teco sarem, *ecc.*

SCENA SECONDA

L'abituro dell'indovina. A sinistra un camino; il fuoco è acceso, e la caldaja magica fuma sovra un treppiè; dallo stesso lato l'uscio d'un oscuro recesso. Suf fianco a destra una scala che gira e si perde sotto la vôlta, e all'estremita della stessa sul davanti una piccola porta segreta. Nel fondo L'entrata della porta maggiore con ampia finestra da lato. In mezzo una rozza tavola e pendenti dal tetto e dalle pareti strumenti ed arredi analoghi al luogo. Nel fondo Uomini e Donne del Popolo. Ulrica presso la tavola; poco discosti un Fanciullo ed una Giovinetta che le domandano la buona ventura.

DONNE e FANCIULLI
Zitti . . . l'incanto non dèssi turbare . . .
Il dimonio tra breve halle a parlare!

ULRICA *(come ispirata)*
Re dell'abisso, affrettati,
Precipita per l'etra,
Senza libar la folgore
Il tetto mio penetra.
Omai tre volte l'upupa
Dall'alto sospirò;
La salamandra ignivora
Tre volte sibilò . . .
E delle tombe il gemito
Tre volte a me parlò!
E delle tombe il gemito, *ecc.*

Entra Riccardo vestito da pescatore, avanzandosi tra la folla, nè scorgendo alcuno de' suoi.

RICCARDO   Arrivo il primo!

DONNE e FANCIULLI *(lo respingono)*
Villano, dà indietro!
Villano, dà indietro!

Riccardo s'allontana ridendo. La scena s'oscura di più.

DONNE e FANCIULLI
Oh come tutto riluce di tetro!

> I shall hear if the stars smile on me,
> What prediction they dictate to her for me,
> I shall hear, *etc.*

OFFICERS and GENTLEMEN

> Yes! yes! yes! At last let there sparkle,
> At last let there sparkle with a bit of folly
> This life that heaven gave us,
> At last let there sparkle, *etc.*

RICCARDO   At three o'clock . . .

ALL   At three o'clock! . . .

RICCARDO   Then, gentlemen, *etc.*

ALL   We shall be with you, *etc.*

SCENE TWO

The fortuneteller's dwelling. At left, a fireplace; the fire is lighted, and the magic cauldron is steaming over a tripod. On the same side there is the door of a dark recess. On the right-hand side, there is a stairway that winds up and vanishes beneath the ceiling, and at the end of it, in the foreground, a little secret door. In the back there is the main doorway with a broad window to one side. In the center, a rough table; and hanging from the roof and from the walls, instruments and furnishings suited to the place. In the back, Men and Women of the populace. Ulrica is by the table. Nearby are a Youth and a Girl, who are asking her their fortune.

WOMEN and YOUNG PEOPLE

> Hush . . . the spell must not be disturbed . . .
> The demon is soon to talk to her!

ULRICA *(as if inspired)*

> King of the abyss, hasten,
> Plunge through the air;
> Without releasing the thunderbolt,
> Penetrate my roof.
> Three times now the owl
> Has sighed from on high;
> The fire-eating salamander
> Has hissed three times . . .
> And from the graves the moan
> Has three times spoken to me!
> And from the graves, *etc.*

Enter Riccardo, dressed as a fisherman, advancing through the crowd, not glimpsing any of his followers.

RICCARDO   I arrive first!

WOMEN and YOUNG PEOPLE *(pushing him back)*

> Boor, go back!
> Boor, go back!

Riccardo moves away, laughing. The scene becomes darker.

WOMEN and YOUNG PEOPLE

> Oh, how everything glows grimly!

ULRICA *(con esaltazione, declamando)*
È lui! è lui! ne' palpiti
Come risento adesso
La voluttà riardere
Del suo tremendo amplesso!
La face del futuro
Nella sinistra egli ha.
M'arrise al mio scongiuro,
Rifolgorar la fa:
Nulla più, nulla più, nulla ascondersi
Al guardo mio potrà.
Nulla ascondersi potrà, *ecc.*
(batte il suolo e sparisce)

TUTTI   Evviva la maga, evviva la maga!

ULRICA *(di sotterra)*
Silenzio! Silenzio!

SILVANO *(rompendo la calca)*
Su, fatemi largo,
Saper vo' il mio fato.
Son servo del Conte:
Son suo marinaro:
La morte per esso
Più volte ho sfidato,
La morte ho sfidato.
Tre lustri son corsi
Del vivere amaro,
Tre lustri che nulla
S'è fatto per me.
Tre lustri, *ecc.*

ULRICA *(ricomparendo)*
E chiedi?

SILVANO   Qual sorte pel sangue versato
M'attende.

RICCARDO   (Favella da franco soldato.)

ULRICA *(a Silvano)*
La mano.

SILVANO   Prendete.

ULRICA *(osservando la mano)*
Rallegrati omai: in breve
Dell'oro e un grado t'avrai.

Riccardo trae un rotolo e vi scrive su.

SILVANO   Scherzate?

ULRICA   Va pago.

Riccardo mette il rotolo nella tasca di Silvano, che non s'avvede.

RICCARDO   (Mentire non de'.)

SILVANO   A fausto presagio
Ben vuolsi mercè,
A fausto presagio, *ecc.*
(frugando trova il rotolo su cui legge estatico)

ULRICA *(with exaltation, declaiming)*
> It is he! It is he! In my heartbeats
> How I feel now
> Blazing again the voluptuousness
> Of his terrible embrace!
> The torch of the future
> He holds in his left hand.
> He has smiled on my spell;
> He makes it flash:
> Nothing more, nothing more, nothing
> Can be hidden from my gaze.
> Nothing can be hidden, *etc.*
> > *(strikes the ground and vanishes)*

ALL   Long live the sorceress, long live the sorceress!

ULRICA *(from underground)*
> Silence! Silence!

SILVANO *(breaking through the throng)*
> Come, make way for me,
> I want to know my fate.
> I the Count's servant:
> I am his sailor.
> Death, for his sake,
> I have defied many times,
> I have defied death.
> Fifteen years have passed
> Of bitter living,
> Fifteen years in which nothing
> Has been done for me.
> Fifteen years, *etc.*

ULRICA *(reappearing)*
> And you ask?

SILVANO   What destiny, for the blood shed,
> Awaits me.

RICCARDO   (He speaks like a straightforward soldier.)

ULRICA *(to Silvano)*
> Your hand.

SILVANO   Take it.

ULRICA *(observing the hand)*
> Rejoice at last: soon
> You will have gold and a commission.

Riccardo takes out a paper and writes on it.

SILVANO   You are joking?

ULRICA   Co content.

Riccardo puts the paper into the pocket of Silvano, who does not notice.

RICCARDO   (She must not lie.)

SILVANO   For a happy prediction
> A recompense is well deserved,
> For a happy prediction, *etc.*
> > *(digging, he finds the paper on which he reads, ecstatic)*

"Riccardo al suo caro
Silvano uffiziale."
Per bacco! non sogno!
Dell'oro ed un grado!
Evviva! evviva!

DONNE e FANCIULLI
Evviva la nostra Sibilla immortale,
Che spande su tutti ricchezze e piacer!

S'ode picchiare alla piccola porta; Ulrica va ad aprire, e v'entra un servo.

SILVANO, DONNE e FANCIULLI
Si batte!

RICCARDO   (Che veggo! sull'uscio segreto
Un servo d'Amelia!)

SERVO *(sommessamente ad Ulrica, ma inteso da Riccardo)*
Sentite: la mia signora,
Che aspetta là fuori, vorria
Pregarvi in segreto d'arcano parer.

RICCARDO   (Amelia!)

ULRICA   S'inoltri,
Ch'io tutti allontano.

RICCARDO   (Non me!)

Il servo parte. Riccardo si nasconde nel gabinetto.

ULRICA *(si volge agli astanti)*
Perchè possa rispondere a voi
È d'uopo che innanzi m'abbocchi a Satana.
Uscite: lasciate ch'io scruti nel ver.

SILVANO, DONNE e FANCIULLI
Usciamo: si lasci
Che scruti nel ver.

ULRICA   Uscite, uscite.

SILVANO, DONNE e FANCIULLI
Usciam, usciam.

Mentre tutti s'allontanano, Riccardo s'asconde. Entra Amelia.

ULRICA   Che v'agita così?

AMELIA   Segreta, acerba cura
Che amor destò . . .

RICCARDO *(nascosto)*
(Che ascolto!)

ULRICA   E voi cercate? . . .

AMELIA   Pace . . . svellermi dal petto
Chi sì fatale e desiato impera!
Lui, che su tutti
Il ciel arbitro pose.

RICCARDO *(con viva emozione di gioia)*
(Che ascolto! Anima mia!)

ULRICA   L'oblio v'è dato. Arcane
Stille conosco d'una magica erba,

"Riccardo, to his beloved
Officer, Silvano."
By Jove! I am not dreaming!
Gold and a commission!
Hurrah! Hurrah!

WOMEN and YOUNG PEOPLE
Long live our immortal Sibyl,
Who showers riches and pleasure on all!

*Knocking is heard at the little door. Ulrica goes to open,
and a manservant enters.*

SILVANO, WOMEN and YOUNG PEOPLE
Someone knocks!

RICCARDO   (What do I see! At the secret door
A servant of Amelia's!)

SERVANT *(softly to Ulrica, but overheard by Riccardo)*
Listen: my mistress,
Who is waiting outside there, would like
To ask you privately a secret counsel.

RICCARDO   (Amelia!)

ULRICA   Let her come in,
As I send all away.

RICCARDO   (Not me!)

The servant leaves. Riccardo hides in the recess.

ULRICA *(turns to those present)*
In order that I may answer you
It is first necessary that I confer with Satan.
Go out. leave me to peer into the truth.

SILVANO, WOMEN and YOUNG PEOPLE
We go out: let her be left
To peer into the truth.

ULRICA   Go out, go out.

SILVANO, WOMEN and YOUNG PEOPLE
We are going out, we are going out.

As all go off, Riccardo hides. Amelia enters.

ULRICA   What troubles you so?

AMELIA   A secret, bitter care
That love aroused . . .

RICCARDO *(hidden)*
(What do I hear!)

ULRICA   And you seek?

AMELIA   Peace . . . to uproot from my breast
Him who reigns, so fatal and desired!
He who, over all,
Heaven placed as ruler.

RICCARDO *(with lively emotion of joy)*
(What do I hear! My soul!)

ULRICA   Oblivion is granted you. I know
Mysterious drops of a magic herb,

Che rinnovella il cor.
Ma chi n'ha d'uopo
Spiccarla debbe di sua man
Nel fitto delle notti . . .
Funereo è il loco.

AMELIA   Ov'è?

ULRICA   L'osate voi?

AMELIA *(risoluta)*
Sì, qual esso sia.

ULRICA   Dunque ascoltate.
Della città all'occaso,
Là dove al tetro lato
Batte la luna pallida
Sul campo abbominato . . .
Abbarbica gli stami
A quelle pietre infami,
Ove la colpa scontasi
Coll'ultimo sospir!
Ove la colpa, *ecc.*

AMELIA   Mio Dio! qual loco!

ULRICA   Attonita e già tremante siete?

RICCARDO   (Povero cor!)

ULRICA   V'esanima?

AMELIA   Agghiaccio . . .

ULRICA   E l'oserete?

AMELIA   Se tale è il dover mio
Troverò possa anch'io.

ULRICA   Stanotte?

AMELIA   Sì.

RICCARDO   (Non sola: chè te degg'io seguir.)

AMELIA   Consentimi, o Signore,
Virtù ch'io lavi 'l core
E l'infiammato palpito
Nel petto mio sopir.
Ah! Consentimi, *ecc.*

ULRICA   Va, non tremar, l'incanto
Inaridisco il pianto.
Non tremar, non tremar.
Osa, e berrai nel farmaco
L'oblio de' tuoi martir.
Osa, *ecc.*

RICCARDO   (Ardo, e seguirla ho fisso
Se fosse nell'abisso.
Amelia, pur ch'io respiri, Amelia,
L'aura dei tuoi sospir.
Pur ch'io respiri, *ecc.*
Ah! Ardo, *ecc.*)

CORO *(dal fondo)*
Figlia d'averno, schiudi la chiostra,
E tarda meno a noi ti mostra.

                    Which renew the heart.
                    But whoever needs it
                    Must pluck it with his own hand
                    In the dead of night . . .
                    The place is lugubrious.

AMELIA   Where is it?

ULRICA   Do you dare do it?

AMELIA *(determined)*
                    Yes, whatever it may be.

ULRICA   Then listen.
                    To the west of the city,
                    There, where on the gloomy side
                    The pale moon strikes
                    The loathed field . . .
                    It puts down its threaded roots
                    In those infamous stones,
                    Where crime is expiated
                    With the final breath!
                    Where crime, *etc.*

AMELIA   My God! What a place!

ULRICA   Are you already stunned and trembling?

RICCARDO   (Poor heart!)

ULRICA   Does it dishearten you?

AMELIA   I freeze . . .

ULRICA   And you will dare it?

AMELIA   If such is my duty,
                    I too shall find strength.

ULRICA   Tonight?

AMELIA   Yes.

RICCARDO   (Not alone: for I must follow you.)

AMELIA   Grant me, O Lord,
                    Power that I may cleanse my heart,
                    And still the enflamed throb
                    In my bosom.
                    Ah! grant me, *etc.*

ULRICA   Go, do not tremble, the spell
                    Dries weeping.
                    Do not tremble, do not tremble.
                    Dare, and in the drug you will drink
                    Oblivion of your sufferings.
                    Dare, *etc.*

RICCARDO   (I am afire, and I have decided to follow her
                    Were it into the abyss.
                    Amelia, if I may breathe, Amelia,
                    The air of your sighs, *etc.*
                    Ah! I am afire, *etc.*)

CHORUS *(from the rear)*
                    Daughter of hell, open the gate,
                    And show yourself less slow toward us.

Spinte alla porta.

ULRICA *(ad Amelia)*
Presto, partite.

AMELIA   Stanotte . . .

ULRICA   Addio . . .

RICCARDO   (Non sola: chè te degg'io seguir!)

ULRICA   Partite, presto partite!

AMELIA   Addio!
(fugge per la porta segreta)

Ulrica apre l'entrata maggiore: entrano Samuel, Tom e Aderenti, Oscar, Gentiluomini e Uffiziali travestiti bizzarramente, ai quali s'unisce Riccardo.

SAMUEL, TOM e CORO
Su, profetessa, monta il treppiè;
Canta il futuro, monta il treppiè.

OSCAR   Ma il Conte ov'è?

RICCARDO *(fattosi presso a lui)*
Taci, nascondile che qui son io.
(poi vôlto rapidamente ad Ulrica)
Or tu, Sibilla, che tutto sai,
Della mia stella mi parlerai.

SAMUEL, TOM e CORO
Canta il futuro, canta il futuro.

RICCARDO   Di' tu se fedele
Il flutto m'aspetta,
Se molle di pianto
La donna diletta
Dicendomi addio, dicendomi addio,
Tradì l'amor mio,
Tradì l'amor mio.
Con lacere vele
E l'alma in tempesta
I solchi so franger
Dell'onda funesta,
L'averno ed il cielo
Irati sfidar.
L'averno ed il cielo
Irati sfidar.
Sollecita esplora,
Divina gli eventi,
Non possono i fulmin,
La rabbia de' venti,
La morte, l'amore
Sviarmi dal mar.

No, no, no, no . . .
La morte, *ecc.*

OSCAR, SAMUEL, TOM e CORO
Non posson i fulmin,
La rabbia de' venti,

Shoving at the door.

ULRICA *(to Amelia)*

    Quickly, go.

AMELIA   Tonight . . .

ULRICA   Farewell . . .

RICCARDO (Not alone: for I must follow you!)

ULRICA   Quickly, quickly go!

AMELIA   Farewell!

    (flees by the secret door)

Ulrica opens the main door. Enter Samuel, Tom and Followers, Oscar, Gentlemen and Officers in bizarre disguises. Riccardo joins them.

SAMUEL, TOM and CHORUS

    Come, prophetess, set up your tripod;

    Sing the future, set up your tripod.

OSCAR   But where is the Count?

RICCARDO *(having come over to him)*

    Be silent. Conceal from her that I am here.

    (then having turned quickly to Ulrica)

    Now you, Sibyl, who know all,

    Will speak to me of my star.

SAMUEL, TOM and CHORUS

    Sing the future, sing the future.

RICCARDO Tell me it, faithful,

    The wave awaits me,

    If, melting in tears,

    My beloved woman,

    In bidding me farewell, bidding me farewell,

    Betrayed my love,

    Betrayed my love.

    With tattered sails

    And my soul in a storm,

    I know how to break the furrows

    Of the dire wave,

    To defy enraged

    Hell and heaven.

    To defy enraged

    Hell and heaven.

    Promptly investigate,

    Divine the events;

    The thunderbolts,

    The winds' fury,

    Death, love cannot

    Turn me from the sea.

    No, no, no, no . . .

    Death, *etc.*

OSCAR, SAMUEL, TOM and CHORUS

    The thunderbolts,

    The winds' fury,

                     La morte, l'amor
                     Sviarlo dal mar.

RICCARDO   Sull'agile prora
                 Che m'agita in grembo,
                 Se scosso mi sveglio
                 Ai fischi del nembo,
                 Ripeto fra' tuoni,
                 Ripeto fra' tuoni
                 Le dolci canzoni.
                 Le dolci canzoni,
                 Le dolci canzoni
                 Del tetto natio,
                 Che i baci ricordan
                 Dell'ultimo addio,
                 E tutte raccendon
                 Le forze del cor,
                 E tutte raccendon, *ecc.*
                 Su dunque, risuoni
                 La tua profezia,
                 Di' ciò che può sorger
                 Dal fato qual sia;
                 Nell'anime nostre
                 Non entra terror.
                 Non entra terror, *ecc.*

OSCAR, SAMUEL, TOM e CORO
                 Nell'anime nostre
                 Non entra terror,
                 Non entra terror.

RICCARDO   Nell'anime nostre
                 Non entra terror.

ULRICA   Chi voi siate, l'audace parola
                 Può nel pianto prorompere un giorno,
                 Se chi sforza l'arcano soggiorno
                 Va la colpa nel duolo a lavar,
                 Se chi sfida il suo fato insolente
                 Deve l'onta nel fato scontar.

RICCARDO   Orsù, amici.

SAMUEL   Ma il primo chi fia?

OSCAR   Io!

RICCARDO *(offrendo la palma ad Ulrica)*
                 L'onore a me cedi.

OSCAR   E lo sia!

ULRICA *(esaminando la mano, solennemente)*
                 È la destra d'un grande,
                 Vissuto sotto gli astri di marte.

OSCAR   Nel vero ella colse.

RICCARDO   Tacete.

ULRICA *(staccandosi da lui)*
                 Infelice . . . va, mi lascia . . .
                 Non chieder di più!

                        Death, love cannot
                        Turn him from the sea.

RICCARDO   On the nimble prow
                        That jolts me in its womb,
                        If shaken, I wake
                        At the storm's whistles,
                        I repeat among thunder claps,
                        I repeat among thunder claps
                        The sweet songs.
                        The sweet songs,
                        The sweet songs
                        Of my native roof,
                        That recall the kisses
                        Of my last farewell,
                        And rekindle all
                        The forces of my heart.
                        And rekindle all, *etc.*
                        Come then, let
                        Your prophecy resound,
                        Say what may arise
                        From whatever fate may be;
                        In our souls
                        Terror does not enter.
                        Terror does not enter, *etc.*

OSCAR, SAMUEL, TOM and CHORUS
                        In our souls
                        Terror does not enter,
                        Terror does not enter.

RICCARDO   In our souls
                        Terror does not enter

ULRICA   Whoever you may be, your bold word
                        May burst into weeping one day;
                        If he who violates the mysterious realm
                        Goes to cleanse his guilt in suffering,
                        If he who insolently challenges fate
                        Must expiate the insult in his fate.

RICCARDO   Come, friends.

SAMUEL   But who is to be the first?

OSCAR   I!

RICCARDO (*offering his palm to Ulrica*)
                        Cede to me the honor.

OSCAR   So be it!

ULRICA (*examining his hand, solemnly*)
                        It is the right hand of a great man,
                        Who has lived under the stars of Mars.

OSCAR   She hit upon the truth.

RICCARDO   Be silent.

ULRICA (*breaking away from him*)
                        Unhappy man . . . go, leave me . . .
                        Do not ask any more!

RICCARDO   Su, prosegui.

ULRICA   No . . . lasciami.

RICCARDO   Parla.

ULRICA   Va.

RICCARDO   Parla.

ULRICA *(evitando)*
                Te ne prego.

OSCAR, SAMUEL, TOM e CORO *(ad Ulrica)*
                Eh finiscila omai!

RICCARDO   Te lo impongo.

ULRICA   Ebben, presto morrai.

RICCARDO   Se sul campo d'onor,
                Ti so grado.

ULRICA *(con più forza)*
                No . . . per man d'un amico . . .

OSCAR   Gran Dio!
                Quale orror!

SAMUEL, TOM e CORO
                Quale orror! Quale orror!

ULRICA   Così scritto è lassù . . .

SAMUEL, TOM e CORO
                Quale orror!

RICCARDO *(guardando intorno)*
                È scherzo od è follia
                Siffatta profezia,
                È scherzo od è follia
                Siffatta profezia.
                Ma come fa da ridere
                La lor credulità!
                Ma come fa, *ecc.*

ULRICA *(passando innanzi a Samuel e Tom)*
                Ah voi, signori, a queste
                Parole mie funeste,
                Voi non osate ridere;
                Che dunque in cor vi sta?

SAMUEL e TOM *(fissando Ulrica)*
                La sua parola è dardo,
                È fulmine lo sguardo,
                È fulmine, *ecc.*

OSCAR   Ah! e tal fia dunque il fato?
                Ch'ei cada assassinato?
                Al sol pensarci l'anima
                Abbrividendo va,
                Abbrividendo va, al sol pensarci, *ecc.*

RICCARDO   È scherzo od è follia, *ecc.*

SAMUEL e TOM
                La sua parola è dardo,
                È fulmine lo sguardo,
                Dal confidente demone

RICCARDO   Come, continue.

ULRICA   No . . . leave me.

RICCARDO   Speak.

ULRICA   Go.

RICCARDO   Speak.

ULRICA *(evading)*
    I beseech you.

OSCAR, SAMUEL, TOM and CHORUS *(to Ulrica)*
    Eh! put an end to it now!

RICCARDO   I command you.

ULRICA   Very well. You will die soon.

RICCARDO   If on the field of honor,
    I am grateful to you.

ULRICA *(more forcefully)*
    No . . . by a friend's hand . . .

OSCAR   Great God!
    How horrible!

SAMUEL, TOM and CHORUS
    How horrible! How horrible!

ULRICA   So it is written up above . . .

SAMUEL, TOM and CHORUS
    How horrible!

RICCARDO *(looking around)*
    It is a joke or it is madness,
    Such a prophecy.
    It is a joke or it is madness,
    Such a prophecy.
    But how laughable
    Is their credulity!
    But how, *etc.*

ULRICA *(passing in front of Samuel and Tom)*
    Ah, you, gentlemen, at these
    Dire words of mine,
    You dare not laugh.
    What then is in your heart?

SAMUEL and TOM *(staring at Ulrica)*
    Her word is an arrow;
    A thunderbolt is her gaze,
    A thunderbolt, *etc.*

OSCAR   Ah! and is fate thus then?
    That he fall, assassinated?
    At just thinking of it my soul
    Starts shuddering,
    Starts shuddering, at just thinking, *etc.*

RICCARDO   It is a joke or it is madness, *etc.*

SAMUEL and TOM
    Her word is an arrow;
    A thunderbolt is her gaze,
    From her devil-confidant

Tutto costei risà,
Tutto costei, risà, *ecc.*

ULRICA   Ah voi, signori, a queste
                  Parole mie funeste, *ecc.*

CORO   Tal fia dunque il fato? *ecc.*

RICCARDO   Finisci il vaticinio.
                  Di', chi fia dunque l'uccisor?

ULRICA   Chi primo tua man
                  Quest'oggi stringerà.

RICCARDO *(con vivacità)*
                  Benissimo!
                        *(offrendo la destra a' circostanti che non
                        osano toccare)*
                  Qual è di voi, che provi
                  L'oracolo bugiardo?
                  Nessuno!

*Renato appare all'entrata. Riccardo accorre a lui e gli stringe
la mano.*

RICCARDO   Eccolo.

OSCAR, SAMUEL, TOM e CORO
                  È desso!

SAMUEL e TOM *(ai suoi)*
                  Respiro: il caso ne salvò.

OSCAR e CORO *(contro Ulrica)*
                  L'oracolo mentiva.

RICCARDO   Sì: perchè la man che stringo
                  È del più fido amico mio!

RENATO   Riccardo!

ULRICA *(ravvisando il Governatore)*
                  Il Conte! . . .

RICCARDO *(ad Ulrica)*
                  Nè, chi fossi il genio tuo
                  Ti rivelò, nè che voleano
                  Al bando oggi dannarti.

ULRICA   Me?

RICCARDO *(gettandole una borsa)*
                  T'acqueta e prendi.

ULRICA   Magnanimo tu sei, ma v'ha fra loro
                  Il traditor: più d'uno forse . . .

SAMUEL e TOM
                  (Gran Dio!)

RICCARDO   Non più.

*Entra Silvano dal fondo. Marinai, Uomini e Donne del
Popolo s'affollano all'entrata.*

SILVANO e CORO DEL POPOLO
                  Viva Riccardo!

OSCAR, ULRICA, RICCARDO, RENATO, SAMUEL, TOM
                  Quai voci?

	She knows everything,
	She knows everything, *etc.*
ULRICA	Ah! you, gentlemen, at these
	Dire words of mine, *etc.*
CHORUS	Is fate thus then? *etc.*
RICCARDO	Finish the prophecy.
	Say, who then is the murderer?
ULRICA	He who today will first
	Clasp your hand.

RICCARDO *(brightly)*
> Very well!
>
> *(offering his right hand to those around him,*
> *who dare not touch it)*
> Which of you will prove
> The oracle a liar?
> No one!

Renato appears at the entrance. Riccardo hastens to him
and shakes his hand.

RICCARDO	Here he is.
OSCAR, SAMUEL, TOM and CHORUS	
	It is he!
SAMUEL and TOM *(to their men)*	
	I can breathe: chance saved us.
OSCAR and CHORUS *(against Ulrica)*	
	The oracle lied.
RICCARDO	Yes, because the hand I clasp
	Is my most faithful friend's!
RENATO	Riccardo!
ULRICA *(recognizing the Governor)*	
	The Count! . . .

RICCARDO *(to Ulrica)*
> Nor did your talent reveal to you
> Who I am, nor that they wanted
> To sentence you today to banishment.

ULRICA	Me?
RICCARDO *(throwing her a purse)*	
	Calm yourself and take this.
ULRICA	You are magnanimous, but there is among them
	The traitor. More than one perhaps . . .
SAMUEL and TOM	
	(Great God!)
RICCARDO	No more.

Enter Silvano from the back. Sailors, Men and Women of
the populace crowd at the door.

SILVANO and CHORUS OF THE PEOPLE
> Long live Riccardo!

OSCAR, ULRICA, RICCARDO, RENATO, SAMUEL, TOM
> What voices?

SILVANO e CORO DEL POPOLO
Viva!

SILVANO *(dalla soglia, volto a' suoi)*
È lui, ratti movete, è lui:
Il nostro, il nostro amico e padre.
(tutti entrano in scena)
Tutti con me chinatevi al suo piede
E l'inno suoni della nostra fè.

SILVANO e CORO
O figlio d'Inghilterra,
Amor di questa terra:
Reggi felice, arridano
Gloria e salute,
Gloria e salute a te.

OSCAR
Il più superbo alloro
Che vince ogni tesoro,
Alla tua chioma intrecciano
Riconoscenza e fè.

RICCARDO
E posso alcun sospetto
Alimentar nel petto,
Se mille cuori battono
Per immolarsi a me?

RENATO
Ma la sventura è cosa
Pur ne' trionfi ascosa,
Là dove il fato ipocrita
Veli una rea mercè.

ULRICA
Non crede al proprio fato
Ma pur morrà, morrà piagato;
Sorrise al mio presagio,
Ma nella fossa ha il piè.
Non crede, *ecc.*

SAMUEL, TOM e loro ADERENTI
Chiude al ferir la via
Questa servil genia,
Che sta lambendo l'idolo,
E che non sa il perchè.
Questa servil genia, *ecc.*

OSCAR
Ah! invidiato alloro, *ecc.*

RICCARDO
Ah! e posso alcun sospetto, *ecc.*

RENATO
Ah! ma la sventura è cosa, *ecc.*

SILVANO e CORO
O figlio d'Inghilterra, *ecc.*

ATTO SECONDO

Campo solitario nei dintorni di Boston, appiè d'un colle scosceso. A sinistra nel basso biancheggiano due pilastri: e la luna leggermente velata illumina alcuni punti della scena. S'alza subito la tela. Appare Amelia dalle eminenze. S'inginocchia e prega. Si alza, ed a poco a poco discende dal colle.

SILVANO and CHORUS OF THE PEOPLE
    Long life!

SILVANO *(from the door, turning to his friends)*
    It is he! Move quickly! It is he!
    Our friend and father.
        (all come on stage)
    All, with me, bow at his foot,
    And let the anthem of our devotion resound.

SILVANO and CHORUS
    O son of England,
    Love of this land,
    Reign happily, may
    Glory and health smile,
    Glory and health upon you.

OSCAR
    The proudest laurel
    Which surpasses every treasure
    On your brow
    Gratitude and devotion entwine.

RICCARDO
    And can I nourish
    Any suspicion in my breast,
    When a thousand hearts beat
    To sacrifice themselves for me?

RENATO
    But calamity is something
    Concealed even in triumphs,
    There where hypocritical fate
    Hides a wicked compensation.

ULRICA
    He does not believe in his own fate,
    But still he will die, die, wounded;
    He smiled at my prediction,
    But he has his foot in the grave.
    He does not believe, *etc.*

SAMUEL, TOM and their FOLLOWERS
    This servile rabble
    Blocks the path to wounding,
    As it is fawning on its idol,
    And does not know the reason.
    This servile rabble, *etc.*

OSCAR
    Ah! envied laurel, *etc.*

RICCARDO
    Ah! and can I nourish, *etc.*

RENATO
    Ah! but calamity is something, *etc.*

SILVANO and CHORUS
    O son of England, *etc.*

ACT TWO

Lonely field on the outskirts of Boston, at the foot of a steep hill. At left, below, two columns gleam whitely; and the slightly veiled moon illuminates some points of the scene. The curtain rises at once. Amelia appears from the heights. She kneels and prays. She rises, and gradually comes down from the hill.

AMELIA   Ecco l'orrido campo ove s'accoppia
Al delitto la morte!
Ecco là le colonne . . .
La pianto è là, verdeggia al piè.
S'inoltri.
Ah! mi si aggela il core!
Sino il rumor de' passi miei, qui
Tutto m'empie di raccappriccio
E di terrore!
E se perir dovessi? Perire!
Ebben! . . . quando la sorte mia,
Il mio dover tal è . . .
S'adempia, e sia!
     (fa per avviarsi)
Ma dall'arido stelo divulsa
Come avrò di mia mano quell'erba,
E che dentro la mente convulsa
Quell'eterea sembianza morrà:
Che ti resta, perduto l'amor . . .
Che ti resta, che ti resta,
Mio povero cor!
Oh! chi piange, qual forza m'arretra?
M'attraversa la squallida via?
Su coraggio . . . e tu fatti di pietra,
Non tradirmi, dal pianto ristà:
O finisci di battere e muor,
T'annienta, t'annienta,
Mio povero cor! . . .
     (s'ode un tocco d'ore lontano)
Mezzanotte! . . . Ah! che veggio?
Una testa di sotterra si leva . . .
E sospira!
Ha negli occhi il baleno dell'ira
E m'affisa e m'affisa
E terribile sta! Ah!
E m'affisa . . . e m'affisa . . .
Terribile sta!
     (cade in ginocchio)
Deh! mi reggi, m'aita, o Signor,
Miserere d'un povero cor.
O Signor, m'aita, o Signor.
Miserere, miserere,
Ah! miserere d'un povero cor!

Esce improvvisamente Riccardo.

RICCARDO   Teco io sto.

AMELIA   Gran Dio!

RICCARDO   Ti calma . . .

AMELIA   Ah!

RICCARDO   Di che temi?

AMELIA   Ah! mi lasciate . . .
Son la vittima che geme . . .

AMELIA   Here is the ghastly field where
Crime is paired with death!
There are the columns . . .
The plant is there, greening at their foot.
Let me go forward.
Ah! my heart freezes!
Even the sound of my footsteps, here
Everything fills me with horror
And with terror!
And if I were to die? To die!
Very well! . . . when such is my fate,
My duty . . .
Let it be carried out, and so be it!
    (starts to go on)
But from its dry stem
When my hand will have torn that herb,
And when in my distraught mind
That celestial image will die,
What is left you, when love is lost . . .
What is left you, what is left you,
My poor heart!
Oh! Who weeps? What power drives me back?
Crosses my grim path?
Come, be brave . . . and you, turn to stone,
Do not betray me, refrain from weeping;
Or cease beating and die,
Be annihilated, be annihilated,
My poor heart! . . .
    (a distant tolling of hours is heard)
Midnight! . . . Ah! what do I see?
A head rises from underground . . .
And it sighs!
It has the flash of wrath in its eyes
And it stares at me and it stares at me
And is terrifying; Ah!
And it stares at me . . . and it stares at me . . .
It is terrifying!
    (falls on her knees)
Ah! support me, assist me, O Lord,
Have mercy on a poor heart.
O Lord, assist me, O Lord.
Have mercy, have mercy,
Ah! have mercy on a poor heart!

Riccardo comes out suddenly.

RICCARDO	I am with you.
AMELIA	Great God!
RICCARDO	Calm yourself . . .
AMELIA	Ah!
RICCARDO	What do you fear?
AMELIA	Ah! leave me . . . I am the victim who groans . . .

Il mio nome almen salvate . . .
O lo strazio ed il rossore
La mia vita abbatterà.

RICCARDO   Io lasciarti? No, giammai:
                Non poss'io; chè m'arde in petto
                Immortal di te l'affetto.

AMELIA   Conte, abbiatemi pietà,
                Pietà, pietà.

RICCARDO   Così parli a chi t'adora?
                Pietà chiedi e tremi ancora?
                Il tuo nome intemerato,
                L'onor tuo sempre sarà.

AMELIA   Ma, Riccardo, io son d'altrui . . .
                Dell'amico più fidato . . .

RICCARDO   Taci, Amelia . . .

AMELIA   Io son di lui,
                Che daria la vita, la vita a te . . .

RICCARDO   Ah crudele, e mel rammemori,
                Lo ripeti innanzi a me!
                Non sai tu che se l'anima mia
                Il rimorso dilacera e rode,
                Quel suo grido non cura, non ode,
                Sin che l'empie di fremiti amor?
                Non sai tu che di te resteria,
                Se cessasse di battere il cor!
                Quante notti ho vegliato anelante!
                Come a lungo infelice lottai!
                Quante volte dal cielo implorai
                La pietà che tu chiedi da me!
                Ma per questo ho potuto un istante,
                Infelice, non viver di te?

AMELIA   Ah! deh soccorri tu, cielo, all'ambascia
                Di chi sta fra l'infamia e la morte;
                Tu pietoso rischiara le porte
                Di salvezza all'errante mio piè.
                    (a Riccardo)
                E tu va: ch'io non t'oda; mi lascia,
                Mi lascia . . .
                Son di lui, son di lui,
                Che il suo sangue ti diè.

RICCARDO   La mia vita . . . l'universo,
                L'universo per un detto . . .

AMELIA   Ciel pietoso!

RICCARDO   Di' che m'ami . . .

AMELIA   Va, Riccardo!

RICCARDO   Un sol detto, un sol detto . . .

AMELIA   Ebben . . . sì . . . t'amo . . .

RICCARDO   M'ami, Amelia!

AMELIA   Ma tu, nobile,
                Me difendi dal mio cor!

	Save my name at least . . . Or torment and shame Will destroy my life.
RICCARDO	I, leave you? No, never. I cannot, for in my breast Immortal love for you burns.
AMELIA	Count, have pity on me, Pity, pity.
RICCARDO	You speak thus to him who adores you? You ask for pity and tremble still? Your name, your honor Will be unblemished always.
AMELIA	But, Riccardo, I belong to another . . . To your most trusted friend . . .
RICCARDO	Be silent, Amelia . . .
AMELIA	I belong to him, Who would give his life, his life to you . . .
RICCARDO	Ah, cruel one, and you remind me of it! You repeat it before me! Do you not know that if remorse Tears and gnaws at my soul, It does not heed, does not hear that cry, Since love fills it with throbbings? Do you not know that it would remain yours If my heart stopped beating? How many nights have I lain awake, yearning! How long did I struggle, unhappy! How many times have I begged of heaven The pity that you ask of me! But for all this have I been for an instant Able, unhappy me, not to live for you?
AMELIA	Ah, pray, heaven, relieve the anguish Of one who is between infamy and death; In pity, illuminate the gates Of salvation to my straying foot. *(to Riccardo)* And you, go. Let me not hear you. Leave me, Leave me . . . I belong to him, I belong to him, Who shed his blood for you.
RICCARDO	My life . . . the universe . . . The universe for one word . . .
AMELIA	Merciful heaven!
RICCARDO	Say you love me . . .
AMELIA	Go, Riccardo!
RICCARDO	Just one word, just one word . . .
AMELIA	Very well . . . yes . . . I love you . . .
RICCARDO	You love me, Amelia!
AMELIA	But you, noble, Defend me from my heart!

RICCARDO	M'ami, Amelia!
AMELIA	Me difendi dal mio cor!
RICCARDO	M'ami, m'ami! . . . oh sia distrutto
	Il rimorso, l'amicizia
	Nel mio seno: estinto tutto,
	Tutto sia fuorchè l'amor,
	Fuorchè l'amor.
	Oh qual soave brivido
	L'acceso petto irrora!
	Ah ch'io t'ascolti ancora
	Rispondermi così!
	Astro di queste tenebre
	A cui consacro il core:
	Irradiami d'amore,
	E più non sorga, non sorga il dì.
	Irradiami d'amore, *ecc.*
AMELIA	Ahi sul funereo letto
	Ov'io sognava spegnerlo,
	Gigante torna in petto
	L'amor che mi ferì!
	Chè non m'è dato in seno
	A lui versar quest'anima?
	O nella morte almeno
	Addormentarmi qui?
	O nella morte, *ecc.*
RICCARDO	Amelia! tu m'ami, Amelia?
	Tu m'ami?
AMELIA	Sì . . . t'amo.
RICCARDO	Irradiami d'amor.
AMELIA	Ma tu, nobile,
	Me difendi dal mio cor,
	Me difendi dal mio cor.
RICCARDO	Tu m'ami, Amelia?
	Ah! Ah! qual soave brivido, *ecc.*
AMELIA	Ah sul funereo letto, *ecc.*

La luna illumina sempre più.

AMELIA *(in ascolto)*
           Ahimè! S'appressa alcun!

RICCARDO   Chi giunge in questo
           Soggiorno della morte?
           (fatti pochi passi)
           Ah, non m'inganno . . .
           (si vede Renato)
           Renato!

AMELIA *(abbassando il velo atterrita)*
           Il mio consorte!
RICCARDO *(incontrandolo)*
           Tu qui?
RENATO   Per salvarti da lor, che, celati
           Lassù, t'hanno in mira.

RICCARDO   You love me, Amelia!

AMELIA   Defend me from my heart!

RICCARDO   You love me, you love me! . . . Oh, let remorse,
Friendship be destroyed in my breast:
Let everything be killed,
Everything except love,
Except love.
Oh, what sweet thrill
Bedews my ardent bosom!
Ah, let me listen to you again
Answering me thus!
Star of this darkness
To whom I dedicate my heart,
Illuminate me with love,
And let day break no more, day break no more.
Illuminate me with love, *etc.*

AMELIA   Alas, on the lugubrious bed
Where I dreamed to extinguish it,
Gigantic, in my bosom
The love that wounded me returns!
Why am I not allowed to pour out
To him this soul in my bosom?
Or in death at least
Fall asleep here?
Or in death, *etc.*

RICCARDO   Amelia! You love me, Amelia?
You love me?

AMELIA   Yes . . . I love you.

RICCARDO   Illuminate me with love.

AMELIA   But you, noble,
Defend me from my heart,
Defend me from my heart.

RICCARDO   You love me, Amelia?
Ah, ah! what sweet thrill, *etc.*

AMELIA   Ah, on the lugubrious bed, *etc.*

The moon is brighter and brighter.

AMELIA *(listening)*
    Alas! Someone is approaching!

RICCARDO   Who is arriving in this
Abode of death?
    (having taken a few steps)
Ah! I am not mistaken . . .
    (Renato is seen)
Renato!

AMELIA *(lowering her veil, terrified)*
    My husband!

RICCARDO *(going to meet him)*
    You here?

RENATO   To save you from them, who, hidden
Up there, have you in their aim.

RICCARDO   Chi son?

RENATO   Congiurati.

AMELIA   (Oh ciel!)

RENATO   Trasvolai nel manto serrato,
               Così che m'han preso
               Per un dell'agguato,
               E intesi taluno proromper:
               L'ho visto: è il Conte:
               Un'ignota beltà è con esso.
               Poi altri qui vôlto: fuggevole acquisto!
               S'ei rade la fossa,
               Se il tenero amplesso
               Troncar, di mia mano,
               Repente saprò.

AMELIA   (Io muoio!)

RICCARDO *(ad Amelia)*
               Fa core!

RENATO *(coprendolo col suo mantello)*
               Ma questo ti do.
                    (poi additandogli un viottolo a destra)
               E bada, lo scampo t'è libero là.

RICCARDO *(presa per mano Amelia)*
               Salvarti degg'io! . . .

AMELIA *(sotto voce a lui)*
               Me misera! Va!

RENATO *(passando ad Amelia)*
               Ma voi non vorrete segnarlo, o signora,
               Al ferro spietato!

    Renato dilegua nel fondo a vedere se s'avanzano.

AMELIA *(a Riccardo)*
               Deh solo t'invola!

RICCARDO   Che qui t'abbandoni?

AMELIA   T'è libero ancora il passo,
               Deh! fuggi . . .

RICCARDO   E lasciarti qui sola con esso?
               Sola con esso? No, mai!
               Piuttosto morrò.

AMELIA   O fuggi, o che il velo
               Dal capo torrò.

RICCARDO   Che dici?

AMELIA   Risolvi.

RICCARDO   Desisti.

AMELIA   Lo vo'.

    *Riccardo esita, ma ella rinnova l'ordine colla mano; al ricom-
    parire di Renato, Riccardo gli va incontro.*

AMELIA   (Salvarlo a quest'alma se data sarà,
               Salvarlo se dato sarà,

RICCARDO   Who are they?

RENATO   Conspirators.

AMELIA   (Oh, heaven!)

RENATO   I rushed past, wrapped in my cloak,
So they took me
For one of the ambush,
And I heard one exclaim:
I saw him, it is the Count,
An unknown beauty is with him.
Then another, turned here: fleeting conquest!
If he brushes with the grave,
If the tender embrace
I shall be able promptly
To cut short, with my hand.

AMELIA   (I die!)

RICCARDO *(to Amelia)*
    Take heart!

RENATO *(covering him with his cloak)*
    But I give you this.
       (then pointing out to him a path on the right)
    And mind, escape is open to you there.

RICCARDO *(having taken Amelia by the hand)*
    I must save you! . . .

AMELIA *(in a low voice to him)*
    Wretched me! Go!

RENATO *(moving to Amelia)*
    But you will not want to mark him, O my lady,
For the merciless sword!

Renato vanishes at the rear, to see if they are advancing.

AMELIA *(to Riccardo)*
    Ah! flee alone!

RICCARDO   And abandon you here?

AMELIA   The way is still open to you.
Ah! flee . . .

RICCARDO   And leave you here alone with him?
Alone with him? No, never!
Rather I shall die.

AMELIA   Either you flee, or I will remove
The veil from my head.

RICCARDO   What are you saying?

AMELIA   Decide.

RICCARDO   Desist.

AMELIA   I wish it.

*Riccardo hesitates, but she repeats the order with her hand;
as Renato reappears, Riccardo goes toward him.*

AMELIA   (If it is granted to this soul to save him,
If it is granted to save him

Dal fiero, dal fiero suo fato
Più tema non ha,
No, più tema, *ecc.*)

RICCARDO *(a Renato solennemente)*
Amico. Gelosa t'affido una cura:
L'amor che mi porti
Garante mi sta.

RENATO Affidati, imponi.

RICCARDO *(indicando Amelia)*
Promettimi, giura
Che tu l'addurrai, velata, in città.
Nè un detto, nè un guardo
Su essa trarrai.

RENATO Lo giuro.

RICCARDO E che tocche le porte,
N'andrai da solo all'opposto.

RENATO Lo giuro, e sarà.

AMELIA Odi tu come fremono cupi
Per quest'aura gli accenti di morte?
Di lassù, da quei negri dirupi,
Il segnal de' nemici partì.
Ne' lor petti scintillano d'ira . . .
E già piomban, t'accerchiano fitti . . .

Al tuo capo già volser la mira . . .

Per pietà, va, t'invola di qui.
Va, va, *ecc.*

RENATO *(staccandosi dal fondo ove stava esplorando)*

Fuggi, fuggi: per l'orrida via
Sento l'orma de' passi spietati.
Allo scambio dei detti esecrati
Ogni destra la daga brandì

AMELIA Di lassù, da quei negri dirupi,
Il segnal de' nemici partì.
Va, va, *ecc.*

RENATO Va, ti salva, o che il varco all'uscita
Qui fra poco serrarsi vedrai;
Va, ti salva, del popolo è vita
Questa vita che getti così, va, va, *ecc.*
Riccardo, ti salva, va, va, *ecc.*
Ah fuggi . . . Va, fuggi . . .

AMELIA Ah fuggi . . . Va, fuggi . . .

RICCARDO (Traditor, congiurati son essi,
Che minacciano il vivere mio?
Ah! l'amico ho tradito pur io . . .
Son colui che nel cor lo ferì.
Innocente, sfidati gli avrei;
Or d'amore colpevole fuggo.

From his fierce, from his fierce fate,
It has no more fear,
No, no more fear, *etc.*)

RICCARDO *(to Renato, solemnly)*
Friend. I entrust to you a delicate mission:
The love that you bear me
Is guarantee for me.

RENATO   Rely on me. Command.

RICCARDO *(pointing to Amelia)*
Promise me, swear
That you will lead her, veiled, to the city.
Not a word, not a glance
Will you direct at her.

RENATO   I swear it.

And that, having reached the gates,
You will go off alone in the opposite direction.

RENATO   I swear it, and it shall be.

AMELIA   Do you hear how grimly resound
In this air the accents of death?
From up there, from those black crags,
The enemies' signal was fired
In their bosoms they flash with rage . . .
And they already plunge down, encircle you,
    closely . . .
They have already turned their aim at your
    head . . .
For pity's sage, go, flee from here.
Go, go, *etc.*

RENATO *(moving away from the rear where he was recon-
  noitering)*
Flee, flee: along the horrid path
I hear the print of merciless steps.
At the exchange of their loathed words
Each right arm brandished the dagger.

AMELIA   From up there, from those black crags,
The enemies' signal was fired.
Go, go, *etc.*

RENATO   Go, save yourself, or the avenue of escape
Here soon you will see blocked.
Go, save yourself, this life you thus cast away
Is the people's life, go, go, *etc.*
Riccardo, save yourself, go, go, *etc.*
Ah, flee! . . . Go, flee . . .

AMELIA   Ah, flee! . . . Go, flee . . .

RICCARDO   (Traitors, conpirators are they,
Who threaten my existence?
Ah! I too have betrayed my friend . . .
I am the one who wounded him in the heart.
Innocent, I would have defied them;
Now guilty of love, I flee.

La pietà del Signore su lei
Posi l'ale, protegga i suoi dì.)

AMELIA   Odi tu, *ecc.*

RENATO   Fuggi, fuggi, *ecc.*

RICCARDO   Innocente, *ecc.*

Riccardo esce.

RENATO   Seguitemi.

AMELIA   (Mio Dio!)

RENATO   Perchè tremate?
           Fida scorta vi son, l'amico accento
           Vi risollevi il cor!

Dalle alture compariscono Samuel, Tom con seguito.

CORO *(in lontananza, avvicinandosi a poco a poco)*
           Avventiamoci su lui,
           Chè scoccata è l'ultim'ora,
           Chè scoccata è l'ultim'ora,
           L'ultim'ora.
           Il saluto dell'aurora
           Pel cadavere sarà.

AMELIA   Eccoli.

RENATO   Presto, appoggiatevi a me.

AMELIA   Morir mi sento!

SAMUEL e TOM
           Avventiamoci su lui, *ecc.*

SAMUEL *(a Tom)*
           Scerni tu quel bianco velo
           Onde spicca la sua dea?

TOM   Si precipiti dal cielo
           All'inferno.

RENATO *(forte)*
           Chi va là?

SAMUEL   Non è desso!

TOM   O furor mio!

CORO   Non è il Conte!

RENATO   No, son io
           Che dinanzi a voi qui sta.

TOM *(beffardo)*
           Il suo fido!

SAMUEL   Men di voi
           Fortunati fummo noi:
           Chè il sorriso d'una bella
           Stemmo indarno ad aspettar.

TOM   Io per altro il volto almeno
           Vo' a quest'Iside mirar!

*Alcuni seguaci di Samuel e Tom reintrano con fiaccole
accese.*

RENATO *(colla mano sull'elsa)*
           Non un passo: se l'osate

>The Lord's pity set its wing on her,
>May it protect her days.)

AMELIA   Do you hear, *etc.*

RENATO   Flee, flee, *etc.*

RICCARDO   Innocent, *etc.*

Riccardo leaves.

RENATO   Follow me.

AMELIA   (My God!)

RENATO   Why do you tremble?
I am a trusted escort for you, let
A friendly voice relieve your heart!

From the heights appear Samuel, Tom with their following.

CHORUS *(in the distance, approaching little by little)*
Let us fling ourselves upon him,
For the last hour has struck,
For the last hour has struck,
The last hour.
The dawn's greeting
Will be for a corpse.

AMELIA   There they are.

RENATO   Quickly, lean on me.

AMELIA   I feel I am dying!

SAMUEL and TOM
Let us fling ourselves on him, *etc.*

SAMUEL. *(to Tom)*
Do you discern that white veil
Whereby his goddess is distinguished?

TOM   Let him plunge from heaven
To hell.

RENATO *(loud)*
Who goes there?

SAMUEL   It is not he!

TOM   O my rage!

CHORUS   It is not the Count!

RENATO   No, it is I,
Who stands before you here.

TOM *(mocking)*
His loyal friend!

SAMUEL   We were less fortunate
Than you:
For we were waiting in vain
For a beauty's smile.

TOM   I, however, want at least
To see the face of this Isis!

Some followers of Samuel and Tom come in again with lighted torches.

RENATO *(with his hand on his hilt)*
Not a step! If you dare it,

Traggo il ferro . . .

SAMUEL   Minacciate?

TOM   Non vi temo.

La luna è in tutto il suo splendore.

AMELIA   O ciel, aita!

CORO (*verso Renato*)
           Giù l'acciaro . . .

RENATO   Traditori! . . .

TOM (*mentre va per istrappare il velo ad Amelia*)
           Vo' finirla . . .

RENATO (*assalendolo*)
           E la tua vita
           Quest'insulto pagherà.

Nell'atto che tutti s'avventano contro Renato, Amelia fuori di sè inframmettendosi, lascia cadere il velo.

AMELIA   No: fermatevi . . .

RENATO (*colpito*)
           Che! . . . Amelia!

SAMUEL, TOM e CORO
           Lei! . . . lei! . . . sua moglie!

AMELIA   O ciel! pietà!

SAMUEL, TOM e CORO
           Sua moglie!

AMELIA   Oh ciel! pietà!

SAMUEL, TOM e CORO
           Sua moglie!

RENATO (*fremendo*)
           Amelia!

SAMUEL (*sogghignando*)
           Ve' se di notte qui colla sposa
           L'innamorato campion si posa,
           E come al raggio lunar del miele
           Sulle rugiade corcar si sa!

SAMUEL e TOM
           Ah! ah! ah! ah! ah! ah! ah! ah! ah!
           E che baccano sul caso strano,
           E che commenti per la città!
           E che baccano, *ecc.*

RENATO (*fisso alla via onde fuggì Riccardo*)
           Così mi paga, se l'ho salvato!
           Ei m'ha la donna contaminato!
           Per lui non posso levar la fronte,
           Sbranato il cor per sempre m'ha!
           Sbranato il cor, *ecc.*

AMELIA (*piangente*)
           A chi nel mondo crudel più mai,
           Misera Amelia, ti volgerai?
           La tua spregiata lacrima, quale,

                            I draw my sword . . .

SAMUEL   You threaten?

TOM   I do not fear you.

   The moon is in its full splendor.

AMELIA   O heaven, help!

CHORUS *(toward Renato)*
                            Put down your steel . . .

RENATO   Traitors! . . .

TOM *(as he goes to tear away Amelia's veil)*
                            I want to end it . . .

RENATO *(attacking him)*
                            And your life
                            Will pay for this insult.

   *At the moment when all fling themselves against Renato,
Amelia, beside herself, intervening, drops her veil.*

AMELIA   No! Stop . . .

RENATO *(stricken)*
                            What! . . . Amelia!

SAMUEL, TOM and CHORUS
                            She! . . . She! . . . His wife!

AMELIA   O heaven! Pity!

SAMUEL, TOM and CHORUS
                            His wife!

AMELIA   O heaven! Pity!

SAMUEL, TOM and CHORUS
                            His wife!

RENATO *(raging)*
                            Amelia!

SAMUEL *(sneering)*
                            See how at night, here with his wife,
                            The enamoured champion rests,
                            An how, in the honeyed moon's ray,
                            He knows how to recline on the dews!

SAMUEL and TOM
                            Ha! ha! ha! Ha! ha! ha! ha! ha! ha!
                            And what an uproar at the odd situation,
                            And what remarks in the city!
                            And what an uproar, *etc.*

RENATO *(staring at the path by which Riccardo fled)*
                            Thus he pays me, when I saved him!
                            He has dishonored my wife!
                            Because of him I cannot raise my head;
                            He has lacerated my heart for ever!
                            Lacerated my heart, *etc.*

AMELIA *(weeping)*
                            To whom in the cruel world ever,
                            Wretched Amelia, will you turn?
                            Your despised tear, what

Qual man pietosa rasciugherà?
Qual man pietosa?

SAMUEL e TOM

Ah! ah! ah! ah! ah! ah! ah! ah! ah!
E che baccano, *ecc.*

RENATO   Per lui non posso, *ecc.*

AMELIA   A chi nel mondo, *ecc.*

CORO   E che baccano, *ecc.*

SAMUEL, TOM e CORO

Ve' la tragedia mutò in commedia,
Ah, ah! ah! *ecc.*

*Renato poi si riscuote, e come chi ha preso un grave partito,
s'accosta a Samuel e Tom.*

RENATO   Converreste in casa mia
                Sul mattino di domani?

SAMUEL   Forse ammenda aver chiedete?

RENATO   No: ben altro in cor mi sta.

SAMUEL   Che vi punge?

RENATO   Lo saprete, se verrete.

SAMUEL e TOM

E ci vedrai, e ci vedrai.
    (sull'uscire seguiti dai loro)
Dunque andiamo: per vie diverse
L'un dall'altro s'allontani.
Il mattino di domani
Grandi cose apprenderem.

CORO   Il mattino di domani
                Grandi cose apprenderem.

SAMUEL e TOM

Andiam.

CORO   Andiam.

SAMUEL e TOM

Ve' la tragedia mutò in commedia . . .
Ah! ah! ah! *ecc.*
E che baccano, *ecc.*

CORO *(partendo)*

Ah, ah! ah! *ecc.*
E che baccano, *ecc.*

RENATO *(rimasto solo con Amelia le dice fremente)*

Ho giurato che alle porte
V'addurrei della città.

AMELIA   (Come sonito di morte
                La sua voce al cor mi va!)

SAMUEL, TOM e CORO

Ah! ah! ah! ah!

RENATO   Andiam!

AMELIA   Oh no! pietà!

RENATO   Andiam!

Partono dal piccolo viottolo.

What pitying hand will dry?
What pitying hand?

SAMUEL and TOM

Ha! ha! ha! Ha! ha! ha! Ha! ha! ha!
And what an uproar, *etc.*

RENATO   Because of him I cannot, *etc.*

AMELIA   To whom in the world, *etc.*

CHORUS   And what an uproar, *etc.*

SAMUEL, TOM and CHORUS

See, the tragedy is changed into comedy,
Ha! ha! ha! *etc.*

Renato then recovers himself, and, like someone who has made a grave decision, he approaches Samuel and Tom.

RENATO   Would you gather at my house
In the morning tomorrow?

SAMUEL   Perhaps you ask to have satisfaction?

RENATO   No. Something quite different is in my heart.

SAMUEL   What is goading you?

RENATO   You will know it, if you come.

SAMUEL and TOM

And you will see us, and you will see us.
(about to leave, followed by their men)
Let us go then. By different paths
Let one separate from the other.
Tomorrow morning
We shall learn great things.

CHORUS   Tomorrow morning
We shall learn great things.

SAMUEL and TOM

Let us go.

CHORUS   Let us go.

SAMUEL and TOM

See, the tragedy is changed into comedy . . .
Ha! ha! ha! *etc.*
And what an uproar *etc.*

CHORUS *(leaving)*

Ah! ah! ah! *etc.*
And what an uproar, *etc.*

RENATO *(left alone with Amelia, says to her, raging)*

I swore that I would lead you
To the gates of the city.

AMELIA   (Like a death knell
His voice goes to my heart!)

SAMUEL, TOM and CHORUS

Ha! ha! ha! ha!

RENATO   Let us go!

AMELIA   Oh, no! Pity!

RENATO   Let us go!

They go off along the little path.

SAMUEL, TOM e CORO (*in lontananza*)
    E che baccano, *ecc.*

ATTO TERZO

SCENA PRIMA

Una stanza da studio nell'abitazione di Renato. Sovra un caminetto di fianco due vasi di bronzo, rimpetto a cui la biblioteca. Nel fondo v'ha un magnifico ritratto del conte Riccardo in piedi, e nel mezzo della scena una tavola. Entrano Renato ed Amelia.

RENATO (*deposta la spada e chiusa la porta*)
    A tal colpa è nulla il pianto,
    Non la terge e non la scusa.
    Ogni prece è vana omai;
    Sangue vuolsi, e tu morrai.

AMELIA
    Ma se reo, se reo soltanto
    È l'indizio che m'accusa?

RENATO
    Taci, adultera.

AMELIA
    Gran Dio!

RENATO
    Chiedi a Lui misericordia.

AMELIA
    E ti basta un sol sospetto?

RENATO
    Sangue vuolsi.

AMELIA
    E vuoi dunque il sangue mio?

RENATO
    Tu morrai.

AMELIA
    E m'infami, e più non senti
    Nè giustizia, nè pietà?

RENATO
    Sangue vuolsi, e tu morrai.

AMELIA
    Un istante, è ver, l'amai,
    Ma il tuo nome non macchiai.

RENATO (*ripigliando la spada*)
    Hai finito!

AMELIA
    Sallo Iddio, che nel mio petto
    Mai non arse indegno affetto.

RENATO
    Hai finito! hai finito!
    Tardi è omai . . . sangue vuolsi,
    Sangue vuolsi, e tu morrai.

AMELIA
    Ah! ni sveni! . . .
    Ebbene sia . . . ma una grazia . . .

RENATO
    Non a me.
    La tua prece al ciel rivolgi.

AMELIA (*genuflessa*)
    Solo un detto ancora a te.
    M'odi, m'odi, l'ultimo,
    L'ultimo sarà.
    Morrò, ma prima in grazia
    Deh! mi consenti almeno
    L'unico figlio mio,
    L'unico figlio mio

SAMUEL, TOM and CHORUS *(in the distance)*
>And what an uproar, *etc.*

ACT THREE

SCENE ONE

A study in Renato's house. Over a mantelpiece to one side, two bronze vases, with the bookcase opposite them. In the back there is a magnificent, full-length portrait of Count Riccardo, and in the center of the stage, a table.

RENATO *(having set down his sword and closed the door)*
>For such guilt weeping is worthless,
>It does not cleanse it and does not excuse it.
>All pleading is vain now;
>Blood is demanded, and you will die.

AMELIA
>But if guilty, if guilty is only
>The appearance that accuses me?

RENATO
>Be silent, adulteress.

AMELIA
>Great God!

RENATO
>Ask mercy of Him.

AMELIA
>And one suspicion is enough for you?

RENATO
>Blood is demanded.

AMELIA
>And you want my blood then?

RENATO
>You will die.

AMELIA
>And you defame me, and hear no longer
>Neither justice nor pity?

RENATO
>Blood is demanded, and you will die.

AMELIA
>For an instant, it is true, I loved him;
>But I did not besmirch your name.

RENATO *(picking up his sword again)*
>You have finished!

AMELIA
>God knows that in my bosom
>An unworthy love never burned.

RENATO
>You have finished! You have finished!
>It is late now . . . Blood is demanded,
>Blood is demanded, and you will die.

AMELIA
>Ah! open my veins! . . .
>Very well, so be it . . . but one favor . . .

RENATO
>Not of me.
>Address your plea to heaven.

AMELIA *(kneeling)*
>Only one word more to you.
>Hear me, hear me, the last,
>It will be the last.
>I shall die, but first, out of pity,
>Ah! allow me at least
>To hold my only child,
>My only child

Avvincere al mio seno.
E se alla moglie nieghi
Quest'ultimo favor,
Non rifiutar ai prieghi,
Ai prieghi del mio materno cor.
Morrò, ma queste viscere
Consolini i suoi baci,
Or che l'estrema è giunta
Dell'ore mie fugaci.
Spenta per man del padre,
La man ei stenderà
Sugl'occhi d'una madre,
Sugl'occhi d'una madre
Che mai più non vedrà.
Che mai più, *ecc.*

RENATO *(lasciato il ferro, additandole, senza guardarla, un uscio)*

Alzati! là tuo figlio
A te concedo riveder.
Nell'ombra e nel silenzio, là,
Il tuo rossore e l'onta mia nascondi.

Amelia esce.

RENATO

Non è su lei, nel suo
Fragile petto che colpir degg'io.
Altro, ben altro sangue
A terger dèssi l'offesa . . .
(fissando il ritratto)
Il sangue tuo!
E lo trarrà il pugnale
Dallo sleal tuo core:
Delle lacrime mie vendicator,
Vendicator, vendicator!
Eri tu che macchiavi quell'anima,
La delizia dell'anima mia . . .
Che m'affidi e d'un tratto esecrabile
L'universo avveleni per me,
Avveleni per me!
Traditor! Che compensi in tal guisa
Dell'amico tuo primo,
Dell'amico tuo primo la fè!
O dolcezze perdute! o memorie
D'un amplesso che l'essere india!
Quando Amelia sì bella, sì candida
Sul mio seno brillava d'amor!
Quando Amelia, *ecc.*
È finita. non siede che l'odio,
Non siede che l'odio,
Che l'odio e la morte nel vedovo cor!
O dolcezze perdute! O speranze d'amor,
D'amor, d'amor!

Samuel e Tom entrano, salutandolo freddamente.

RENATO

Siam soli. Udite. Ogni disegno vostro
M'è noto. Voi di Riccardo

To my breast.
And if to your wife you deny
This last favor,
Do not refuse the prayers,
The prayers of my maternal heart.
I shall die, but let his kisses
Console this heart,
Now that the last
Of my fleeting hours has arrived.
Killed by the father's hand,
He will hold out his hand
On the eyes of a mother,
On the eyes of a mother
Whom he will never see again.
Whom never again, *etc.*

RENATO *(putting aside his sword, pointing, without looking at her, to a door)*

Rise! There I allow you
To see your son again.
In the darkness and in the silence, there,
Hide your blushing and my shame.

Amelia goes out.

RENATO

It is not upon her, in her
Fragile bosom that I must strike.
Other, quite other blood
Must cleanse the offense . . .
          (staring at the portrait)
Your blood!
And my dagger will draw it
From your treacherous heart,
Of my tears the avenger,
The avenger, the avenger!
It was you who besmirched that soul,
The delight of my soul . . .
You who trust me and suddenly loathesome
Poison the universe for me,
Poison for me!
Traitor! You who repay in such a fashion
The loyalty of your best friend,
Of your best friend!
O lost sweets; O memories
Of an embrace that composed my being!
When Amelia, so beautiful, so pure,
On my bosom glowed with love!
When Amelia, *etc.*
It is finished. Only hatred dwells,
Only hatred dwells,
Only hatred and death in my bereaved heart!
O lost sweets! O hopes of love,
Of love, of love!

Samuel and Tom come in, greeting him coldly.

RENATO

We are alone. Listen. Your every plan
Is known to me. You want

La morte volete.

TOM   È un sogno!

RENATO *(nostrando alcune carte che ha sul tavolo)*
Ho qui le prove!

SAMUEL *(fremendo)*
Ed ora la trama
Al Conte svelerai?

RENATO   No: voglio dividerla.

SAMUEL e TOM
Tu scherzi.

RENATO   E non co' detti:
Ma qui col fatto
Struggerò i sospetti.
Io son vostro, compagno m'avrete
Senza posa a quest'opra di sangue:
Arra il figlio vi sia. L'uccidete
Se vi manco.

SAMUEL   Ma tal mutamento
È credibile appena.

RENATO   Qual fu la cagion non cercate.
Son vostro, son vostro
Per la vita dell'unico figlio!

SAMUEL *(fra loro)*
Ei non mente.

TOM   No, non mente.

RENATO   Esitate?

SAMUEL e TOM
Non più.

RENATO, SAMUEL e TOM
Non più.

RENATO   Dunque l'onta di tutti sol una,
Uno il cor, la vendetta sarà, sarà,
Che tremenda, repente, digiuna
Su quel capo esecrato cadrà.

SAMUEL e TOM
Dunque l'onta di tutti, *ecc.*

RENATO   Uno il cor, *ecc.*
D'una grazia vi supplico.

SAMUEL   E quale?

RENATO   Che sia dato d'ucciderlo a me.

SAMUEL   No, Renato: l'avito castello
A me tolse, e tal dritto a me spetta.

TOM   Ed a me, cui spegneva il fratello,
Cui decenne agonia di vendetta
Senza requie divora, qual parte
Assegnaste?

RENATO   Chetatevi, solo
Qui la sorte decidere de'.

*Prende un vaso dal camino e lo colloca sulla tavola. Samuel
scrive tre nomi e getta entro i viglietti.*

                   Riccardo's death.

TOM   It is a dream!

RENATO *(showing some papers that he has on the table)*
                   I have the proofs here!

SAMUEL *(in a fury)*
                   And now you will reveal
                   The plot to the Count?

RENATO   No, I want to share it.

SAMUEL and TOM
                   You are joking.

RENATO   And not with words;
                   But here, with action,
                   I shall destroy the suspicions.
                   I am yours, you will have me as comrade
                   Without rest in this work of blood.
                   Let my son be the pledge. Kill him
                   If I fail you.

SAMUEL   But such a change
                   Is barely credible.

RENATO   Do not seek what was the cause.
                   I am yours, I am yours
                   By the life of my only son!

SAMUEL *(between themselves)*
                   He is not lying.

TOM   No, he is not lying.

RENATO   You hesitate?

SAMUEL and TOM
                   No longer.

RENATO, SAMUEL and TOM
                   No longer.

RENATO   Then the shame of all is one alone,
                   One heart, vengeance will be, will be
                   Which, terrible, swift, hungering,
                   On that loathed head will fall.

SAMUEL and TOM
                   Then the shame of all, *etc.*

RENATO   One heart, *etc.*
                   I beg a favor of you.

SAMUEL   And what?

RENATO   That killing him be assigned to me.

SAMUEL   No, Renato. My ancestral castle
                   He took from me; such a privilege is due me.

TOM   And to me, whose brother he killed,
                   Whom ten years' yearning for vengeance
                   Ceaselessly devours, what role
                   Did you assign?

RENATO   Be calm. Only
                   Chance must decide here.

    *He takes a vase from the mantelpiece and sets it on the
table. Samuel writes three names and throws the papers into it.*

RENATO   E chi vien?

Amelia entra.

RENATO *(incontrandola)*
            Tu?

AMELIA   V'è Oscarre che porta
            Un invito del Conte.

RENATO *(impallidendo)*
            Di lui! . . . Chi m'aspetti.
            E tu resta, lo dêi:
            Poichè parmi che il cielo t'ha scorta.

AMELIA   (Qual tristezza m'assale, qual pena!
            Qual terribile lampo balena!
            Qual terribile lampo, ah! *ecc.*)

RENATO *(additando sua moglie a Samuel e Tom)*
            Nulla sa: non temete. Costei
            Esser debbe anzi l'auspice lieto.
                (ad Amelia traendola verso la tavola)
            V'ha tre nomi in quell'urna:
            Un ne tragga l'innocente tua mano.

AMELIA *(tremante)*
            E perchè?

RENATO *(fulminandola dello sguardo)*
            Obbedisci: non chieder di più.

AMELIA   (Non è dubbio: il feroce decreto
            Mi vuol parte ad un'opra di sangue.)

*Amelia si avvicina lentamente e tremante al tavolo su cui
vi è il vaso. Renato fulminandola sempre dello sguardo, finalmente Amelia con mano tremante estrae un viglietto che suo
marito passa a Samuel.*

RENATO   Qual è dunque l'eletto?

SAMUEL *(con dolore)*
            Renato.

RENATO *(con esaltazione)*
            Il mio nome!
                (fremente di gioia)
            O giustizia del fato;
            La vendetta mi deleghi tu!

AMELIA   (Ah! del Conte la morte si vuole!
            Nol celâr le crudeli parole!
            Su quel capo snudati dall'ira
            I lor ferri scintillano già!
            Ah! del Conte la morte si vuole, *ecc.*)

RENATO, SAMUEL and TOM
            Sconterà dell'Americai il pianto
            Lo sleal che ne fece suo vanto.
            Se trafisse, soccomba trafitto,
            Tal mercede pagata gli va!
            Tal mercede, *ecc.*

RENATO   Il messaggio entri.

Entra Oscar.

OSCAR *(verso Amelia)*

RENATO   Now who is coming?

Amelia enters.

RENATO *(going toward her)*
          You?

AMELIA   There is Oscar, who is bearing
          An invitation from the Count.

RENATO *(blanching)*
          From him! . . . Let him wait for me.
          And you, remain. You must,
          For it seems that heaven has brought you.

AMELIA   (What sadness assails me, what suffering!
          What a terrible thought flashes!
          What a terrible thought, ah! *etc.*)

RENATO *(pointing out his wife to Samuel and Tom)*
          She knows nothing. Do not fear. She
          Must be, indeed, the happy augury.
              (to Amelia, drawing her toward the table)
          There are three names in that urn:
          Let your innocent hand extract one.

AMELIA *(trembling)*
          And why?

RENATO *(withering her with his glance)*
          Obey. Ask no further.

AMELIA   (There is no doubt: his fierce command
          Wants me a part of a deed of blood.)

*Amelia, slowly, trembling, approaches the table on which
the vase is set; Renato still withering her with his gaze.
Finally, with trembling hand, Amelia draws a paper out,
which her husband passes to Samuel.*

RENATO   Who is then the chosen one?

SAMUEL *(with sorrow)*
          Renato.

RENATO *(with exultation)*
          My name!
              (trembling with joy)
          O justice of destiny;
          You delegate vengeance to me!

AMELIA   (Ah! they want the Count's death!
          They did not conceal their cruel words!
          On that head, unsheathed by wrath,
          Their swords are already glinting!
          Ah! they want the Count's death, *etc.*)

RENATO, SAMUEL and TOM
          The traitor who made America's weeping
          His boast will pay.
          If he stabbed, let him die, stabbed.
          Such recompense should be paid him!
          Such recompense, *etc.*

RENATO   Let the messenger enter.

Enter Oscar.

OSCAR *(toward Amelia)*

Alle danze questa sera, se gradite,
Con lo sposo, il mio signore
Vi desidera.

AMELIA *(turbata)*
Nol posso.

RENATO *(ad Oscar)*
Anche il Conte vi sarà?

OSCAR   Certo.

SAMUEL e TOM *(fra loro)*
Oh sorte!

RENATO *(al Paggio, ma collo sguardo a Tom)*
Tanto invito so che valga.

OSCAR   È un ballo in maschera
Splendidissimo . . .

RENATO   Benissimo!
    (accennando Amelia)
Ella meco interverrà.

AMELIA   (Gran Dio!)

SAMUEL e TOM
E noi pur, se da quell'abito
Più spedito il colpo va.

OSCAR   Ah! di che fulgor, che musiche
Esulteran le soglie,
Ove di tante giovani
Bellezze il fior s'accoglie,
Di quante altrice palpita,
Ah! questa gentil, gentil città!

AMELIA   (Ed io medesma, io misera,
Lo scritto inesorato
Trassi dall'urna complice,
Pel mio consorte irato:
Su cui del cor più nobile,
Del cor più nobile
Ferma la morta sta.
Ah! ah! trassi dall'urna, *ecc.*)

RENATO   (Là fra le danze esanime
La mente mia sel pinge,
La mente mia sel pinge . . .
Ove del proprio sangue
Il pavimento tinge
Spira dator d'infamie
Senza trovar pietà,
Senta trovar pietà, *ecc.*
Là tra le danze, *ecc.*)

SAMUEL e TOM *(fra loro)*
Una vendetta in domino
È ciò che torna all'uopo.
Fra l'urto delle maschere
Non fallirà lo scopo:
Sarà una danza funebre
Con pallide, con pallide beltà.
Una vendetta in domino, *ecc.*

OSCAR   Di che fulgor, *ecc.*

At the dances this evening, if you like,
My master wishes you,
With your husband.

AMELIA *(upset)*
I cannot.

RENATO *(to Oscar)*
Will the Count be there also?

OSCAR   Of course.

SAMUEL and TOM *(aside)*
Oh, luck!

RENATO *(to the Page, but with his gaze on Tom)*
I know what such an invitation is worth.

OSCAR   It is a very splendid
Masked ball . . .

RENATO   Very well!
(pointing to Amelia)
She will attend with me.

AMELIA   (Great God!)

SAMUEL and TOM
And we too, if from that costume
The blow goes more swiftly.

OSCAR   Ah! With what splendor, what music
The halls will rejoice
Where the flower of so many
Young beauties is assembled,
Of all that, giving life,
Ah! this lovely, lovely city throbs!

AMELIA   (And I myself, wretched me,
The inexorable writing
Drew from the conspiratorial urn
For my enraged husband,
Wherein of the noblest heart,
Of the noblest heart
The death is fixed.
Ah! ah! I drew from the urn, *etc.*)

RENATO   (There amid the dances, lifeless,
My mind depicts him,
My mind depicts him . . .
Where with his own blood
He stains the floor,
The giver of infamy dies
Without finding mercy,
Without finding mercy, *etc.*
There amid the dances, *etc.*)

SAMUEL and TOM *(aside)*
A vengeance in domino
Is what suits our need.
Amid the jostle of the maskers
Our aim will not fail;
It will be a funereal dance
With pale, with pale beauties.
A vengeance in domino, *etc.*

OSCAR   With what splendor, *etc.*

AMELIA   (Prevenirlo potessi,
              E non tradir lo sposo mio! . . .)

OSCAR   Reina della festa sarete.

AMELIA   (Forse potrallo Ulrica.)

Renato, Samuel e Tom sono in disparte.

SAMUEL e TOM
              E qual costume indosserem?

RENATO   Azzurra la veste, e da vermiglio
              Nastro le ciarpe al manco lato attorte.

SAMUEL e TOM
              E qual accento a ravvisarci?

RENATO *(sottovoce)*
              Morte!

AMELIA   (Prevenirlo potessi!)

OSCAR   Regina sarete!

RENATO, SAMUEL e TOM
              Morte, morte!

SCENA SECONDA

Sontuoso gabinetto del Conte. Tavolo con l'occorrente per iscrivere; nel fondo un gran cortinaggio che scoprirà la festa da ballo.

RICCARDO   Forse la soglia attinse,
              E posa alfin. L'onore
              Ed il dover fra i nostri petti
              Han rotto l'abisso. Ah! sì,
              Renato rivedrà l'Inghilterra . . .
              E la sua sposa lo seguirà.
              Senza un addio, l'immenso
              Oceàn ne separi . . .
              E taccia il core.
                 (scrive e nel momento di appor la firma lascia cader la penna)
              Esito ancor? ma, oh ciel,
              Non lo degg'io?
                 (sottoscrive, e chiude il foglio in seno)
              Ah l'ho segnato, ah l'ho segnato
              Il sacrifizio mio!
              Ma se m'è forza perderti
              Per sempre, o luce mia,
              A te verrà il mio palpito
              Sotto qual ciel tu sia,
              Chiusa la tua memoria
              Nell'intimo del cor,
              Chiusa nell'intimo del cor.
              Ed or qual reo presagio
              Lo spirito m'assale,
              Che il rivederti annunzia
              Quasi un desio fatale . . .
              Come se fosse l'ultima
              Ora del nostro amor,

AMELIA   (If I could warn him,
                And not betray my husband! . . .)
OSCAR   You will be queen of the ball.
AMELIA   (Perhaps Ulrica will be able to do it.)

Renato, Samuel and Tom are off to one side.

SAMUEL and TOM
                And what costume shall we wear?
RENATO   A blue garment, and on the left side
                The scarves entwined with a scarlet ribbon.
SAMUEL and TOM
                And what word, to identify ourselves?
RENATO *(in a low voice)*
                Death!
AMELIA   (If I could warn him!)
OSCAR   You will be queen!
RENATO, SAMUEL and TOM
                Death, death!

SCENE TWO

The Count's sumptuous study. A table with writing materials; in the rear a great curtain that will reveal the ball.

RICCARDO   Perhaps she reached her door,
                And is resting at last. Honor
                And duty have opened the abyss
                Between our bosoms. Ah! yes,
                Renato will see England again . . .
                And his wife will accompany him.
                Without a farewell, let the immense
                Ocean separate us . . .
                And let my heart be silent.
                        *(writes, and at the moment he is about to
                        sign, he drops his pen)*
                Do I still hesitate? But, O heaven,
                Must I not do it?
                        (signs, and conceals the paper in his bosom)
                Ah! I have signed it! Ah! I have signed it,
                My sacrifice!
                But if I am forced to lose you
                Forever, O my light,
                My heartthrob will come to you
                Beneath whatever sky you may be,
                Your memory enclosed
                In the secrecy of my heart,
                Enclosed in the secrecy of my heart.
                And now what evil foreboding
                Assails my spirit,
                That heralds my seeing you again
                Like a fatal desire . . .
                As if it were the last
                Hour of our love,

> Come se fosse l'ultima,
> L'ultima ora, ora del nostro amor? *ecc.*
> *(musica di dentro)*
> Ah! dessa è là . . .
> Potrei vederla . . .
> Ancora riparlarle potrei . . .
> Ma no: chè tutto or mi strappa da lei.

Entra Oscar con una lettera.

OSCAR
> Ignota donna questo foglio diemmi.
> E pel Conte, diss'ella;
> A lui lo reca e di celato.

Riccardo legge il foglio.

RICCARDO *(dopo letto)*
> Che nel ballo alcuno
> Alla mia vita attenterà,
> Sta detto. Ma se m'arresto:
> Ch'io pavento diran.
> Nol vo': nessuno pur sospettarlo de'.
> Tu va: t'appresta,
> E ratto, per gioir meco alla festa.

Oscar parte. Riccardo rimasto solo vivamente prorompe:

RICCARDO
> Sì, rivederti, Amelia,
> E nella tua beltà,
> Anco una volta l'anima
> D'amor mi brillerà,
> Mi brillerà d'amor!

SCENA TERZA

Vasta e ricca sala da ballo splendidamente illuminata e parata a festa. Liete musiche preludiano alle danze, e già all'aprirsi delle cortine una moltitudine d'invitati empie la scena. Il maggior numero è in maschera, alcuni in domino, altri in costume di gala a viso scoperto; fra le coppie danzanti alcune giovani creole. Chi va in traccia, chi evita, chi ossequia e chi persegue. Il servizio è fatto dai neri, e tutto spira magnificenza ed ilarità.

CORO GENERALE
> Fervono amori e danze
> Nelle felici stanze,
> Fervono amori, onde la vita è solo
> Un sogno lusinghiero,
> Un sogno, un sogno lusinghier.
> Notte de' cari istanti,
> De' palpiti e de' canti,
> Perchè non fermi 'l volo
> Perchè non fermi 'l volo
> Sull'onda, sull'onda del piacer?

Samuel e Tom coi loro Aderenti in domino azzurro col cinto vermiglio. Renato, nello stesso costume, s'avanza lentamente.

As if it were the last,
The last hour, hour of our love? *etc.*
(*music within*)
Ah! she is there . . .
I could see her . . .
I could speak to her again . . .
But no! For everything tears me from her now.

Enter Oscar with a letter.

OSCAR   An unknown woman gave me this paper.
It is for the Count, she said,
Take it to him, and secretly.

Riccardo reads the paper.

RICCARDO (*after having read it*)
That during the ball someone
Will make an attempt on my life,
Is written. But if I stay away,
They will say I am afraid.
I do not want that. No one must even suspect it.
Go. Make yourself ready,
And quickly, to rejoice with me at the party.

Oscar leaves. Riccardo, left alone, bursts out intensely:

RICCARDO   Yes, to see you again, Amelia,
And in your beauty,
Once more my soul
Will glow with love,
Will glow with love!

SCENE THREE

A vast and rich ballroom, splendidly illuminated and decorated for the festivity. Gay music precedes the dances, and
already at the opening of the curtains a throng of guests fills
the stage. The majority are masked. Some are in dominoes;
others, in ball dress with their faces uncovered. Among the
dancing couples, some young Creole girls. Some are seeking;
some are eluding; some are bowing, and some chasing. The
service is carried out by blacks, and everything breathes mag-
nificence and good humor.

GENERAL CHORUS
Loves and dances rage
In the happy rooms,
Loves rage, where life is only
A seductive dream,
A dream, a seductive dream.
Night of dear moments,
Of thrills and of songs,
Why do you not stop your flight,
Why do you not stop your flight
On the wave, on the wave of pleasure?

*Samuel and Tom with the followers, in blue dominoes with
scarlet sashes. Renato, in the same costume, comes forward
slowly.*

SAMUEL *(additando Renato a Tom)*
>   Altro de' nostri è questo.
>   *(fattosi presso a Renato)*
>   Morte!

RENATO *(amaramente)*
>   Sì: morte!
>   Ma non verrà.

SAMUEL e TOM
>   Che parli?

RENATO   Qui l'aspettarlo è vano.

SAMUEL   Come?

TOM   Perchè?

RENATO   Vi basti saperlo altrove.

SAMUEL   O sorte ingannatrice!

TOM *(fremente)*
>   Sempre ne sfuggirà di mano!

RENATO   Parlate basso; alcuno lo sguardo
>   A noi fermò.

RENATO   Quello a sinistra dal breve domino.

Si disperdono tra la folla, ma Renato viene inseguito da Oscar in maschera.

OSCAR *(a Renato)*
>   Più non ti lascio, o maschera;
>   Mal ti nascondi.

RENATO *(cansandolo)*
>   Eh via!

OSCAR *(inseguendolo sempre, con vivacità)*
>   Tu se' Renato.

RENATO *(spiccandogli la maschera)*
>   E Oscarre tu sei.

OSCAR   Qual villania!

RENATO   Ma bravo, e ti par dunque
>   Convenienza questa,
>   Che mentre il Conte dorme,
>   Tu scivoli alla festa?

OSCAR   Il Conte è qui . . .

RENATO *(trasalendo)*
>   Che! . . . dove?

OSCAR   L'ho detto . . .

RENATO   Ebben! . . . qual è?

OSCAR   Non vel dirò! . . .

RENATO   Gran cosa!

OSCAR *(volgendogli le spalle)*
>   Cercatelo da voi.

RENATO *(con accento amichevole)*
>   Orsù!

OSCAR   È per fargli il tiro
>   Che regalaste a me?

RENATO   Via calmati: almen dirmi
>   Del suo costume puoi?

SAMUEL *(pointing out Renato to Tom)*
>This is another of ours.
>>*(having approached Renato)*
>Death!

RENATO *(bitterly)*
>Yes, death!
>But he will not come.

SAMUEL and TOM
>What are you saying?

RENATO   Awaiting him here is futile.

SAMUEL   What?

TOM   Why?

RENATO   Be satisfied to know he is elsewhere.

SAMUEL   O treacherous luck!

TOM *(raging)*
>He will always elude our grasp!

RENATO   Speak softly; someone has fixed
>His gaze on us.

RENATO   The one on the left in the short domino.

They scatter amid the crowd, but Renato is pursued by Oscar in costume.

OSCAR *(to Renato)*
>I am leaving you no more, O masker;
>You disguise yourself poorly.

RENATO *(avoiding him)*
>Ah, go away!

OSCAR *(still pursuing him, brightly)*
>You are Renato.

RENATO *(plucking off his mask)*
>And you are Oscar.

OSCAR   What rudeness!

RENATO   Why, bravo! And does this then
>Seem suitable to you:
>That while the Count sleeps,
>You slip off to the ball?

OSCAR   The Count is here . . .

RENATO *(starting)*
>What! . . . Where?

OSCAR   I told you . . .

RENATO   Well . . . which is he?

OSCAR   I will not tell you! . . .

RENATO   Fine thing!

OSCAR *(turning his back on him)*
>Seek him for yourself.

RENATO *(with a friendly tone)*
>Come now!

OSCAR   Is it to play on him
>The trick you pulled on me?

RENATO   Come, calm yourself. At least
>You can tell me about his costume?

OSCAR *(scherzando)*
Saper vorreste
Di che si veste,
Quando l'è cosa
Ch'ei vuol nascosa.
Oscar lo sa,
Ma nol dirà.
Tra la la, *ecc.*
Oscar lo sa,
Ma nol dirà,
Tra la la, *ecc.*
Pieno d'amor
Mi balza il cor,
Ma più discreto
Serba il segreto.
Nol rapirà
Grado o beltà,
Tra la la, *ecc.*
Oscar lo sa,
Ma nol dirà,
Tra la la, *ecc.*

*In questo momento gruppi di maschere e coppie danzanti
attraversano il dinanzi della scena e separano Oscar da Renato.*

CORO GENERALE
Fervono amori e danze, *ecc.*

*Rimontano di nuovo la scena e si perdono nel fondo. Renato
raggiunge di nuovo Oscar.*

RENATO   So che tu sai distinguere
                Gli amici suoi.

OSCAR   V'alletta interrogarlo,
                E forse celiar con esso un po'?

RENATO   Appunto.

OSCAR   E compromettere di poi
                Chi ve l'ha detto?

RENATO   M'offendi. È confidenza
                Che quanto importi so.

OSCAR   Vi preme assai . . .

RENATO   Degg'io di gravi cose ad esso,
                Pria che la notte inoltri,
                Qui favellar. Su te
                Farò cader la colpa,
                Se non mi fia concesso.

OSCAR   Dunque . . .

RENATO   Fai grazia a lui, se parli,
                E non a me.

OSCAR *(più d'appresso e rapidamente)*
                Veste una cappa nera,
                Con roseo nastro al petto.
                     (e fa per andarsene)

RENATO   Una parola ancora.

OSCAR *(joking)*

> You would like to know
> What he is wearing,
> When that is a thing
> That he wants hidden.
> Oscar knows it,
> But will not tell it.
> Tra la la, *etc.*
> Oscar knows it,
> But will not tell it,
> Tra la la, *etc.*
> Filled with love,
> My heart leaps up,
> But more discreet,
> It keeps the secret;
> Rank or beauty
> Will not steal it,
> Tra la la, *etc.*
> Oscar knows it,
> But will not tell it,
> Tra la la, *etc.*

At this moment groups of maskers and dancing couples cross the front of the stage and separate Oscar from Renato.

GENERAL CHORUS

> Loves and dances rage, *etc.*

They move back up the stage and are lost in the rear. Renato overtakes Oscar again.

RENATO
> I know that you can distinguish
> His friends.

OSCAR
> It amuses you to question him,
> And perhaps to tease him a bit?

RENATO
> Exactly.

OSCAR
> And then compromise
> The one who told you?

RENATO
> You offend me. That is a confidence
> The importance of which I know.

OSCAR
> It means much to you . . .

RENATO
> I must speak of serious things
> To him here, before
> The night grows later. On you
> I will place the blame,
> If it is not granted me.

OSCAR
> Then . . .

RENATO
> You do a favor to him, if you speak,
> And not to me.

OSCAR *(closer and rapidly)*
> He is wearing a black cloak,
> With a pink ribbon on the bosom.
> *(and he starts to leave)*

RENATO
> One word more.

OSCAR *(dileguandosi tra la folla)*
> Più che abbastanza ho detto.

CORO GENERALE
> Fervono amori e danze, *ecc.*

Danzatori e danzatrici s'intrecciano al proscenio; Renato scorge intanto taluno de' suoi e scompare di là. Poco dopo, al volger delle coppie nel fondo, Riccardo in domino nero col nastro di rosa, s'affaccia pensieroso, e dietro a lui Amelia in domino bianco.

AMELIA *(sottovoce in modo da non essere riconosciuta)*
> Ah! perchè qui! . . . fuggite . . .

RICCARDO
> Sei quella dello scritto?

AMELIA
> La morte qui v'accerchia . . .

RICCARDO
> Non penetra nel mio petto il terror.

AMELIA
> Fuggite, fuggite, o che trafitto
> Cadrete qui!

RICCARDO
> Rivelami il nome tuo.

AMELIA
> Gran Dio! nol posso!

RICCARDO
> E perchè piangi . . . mi supplichi
> Atterrita? . . .
> Onde cotanta senti pietà
> Della mia vita?

AMELIA *(tra singulti che svelano la sua voce naturale)*
> Tutto, per essa,
> Tutto il sangue mio darei!

RICCARDO
> Invan ti celi, Amelia:
> Quell'angelo tu sei!

AMELIA *(con disperazione)*
> T'amo, sì, t'amo, e in lagrime
> A' piedi tuoi m'atterro,
> Ove t'anela incognito
> Della vendetta il ferro.
> Cadavere domani
> Sarai se qui rimani:
> Salvati, va, mi lascia,
> Fuggi, fuggi dall'odio lor.

RICCARDO
> Sin che tu m'ami, Amelia,
> Non curo il fato mio.

AMELIA
> Fuggi.

RICCARDO
> Nòn ho che te nell'anima,
> E l'universo obblio.

AMELIA
> Salvati.

RICCARDO
> Nè so temer la morte,
> Perchè di lei più forte
> È l'aura che m'innebria
> Del tuo divino amor.

AMELIA
> Va. Ah! salvati!
> Cadavere domani
> Sarai se tu rimani, *ecc.*

OSCAR *(vanishing amid the crowd)*
> I have said more than enough.

GENERAL CHORUS
> Loves and dances rage, *etc.*

Dancers, male and female, weave together at the footlights. Renato meanwhile glimpses some of his associates and vanishes into the next room. A little later, as the couples at the back turn, Riccardo, in a black domino with a pink ribbon, appears, pensive, and behind him, Amelia in a white domino.

AMELIA *(in a low voice, so as not to be recognized)*
> Ah! why are you here? . . . Flee . . .

RICCARDO   You are the lady of the letter?

AMELIA   Death surrounds you here . . .

RICCARDO   Terror does not penetrate my breast.

AMELIA   Flee, flee, or you will fall
> Here, stabbed!

RICCARDO   Reveal your name to me.

AMELIA   Great God! I cannot!

RICCARDO   And why do you weep? . . . You beseech me,
> Terrified? . . .
> Why do you feel such concern
> For my life?

AMELIA *(amid sobs which reveal her natural voice)*
> For it, all,
> All my blood would I give!

RICCARDO   You conceal yourself in vain, Amelia!
> You are that angel!

AMELIA *(with despair)*
> I love you, yes, I love you, and in tears
> At your feet I prostrate myself,
> Where the disguised sword
> Of vengeance yearns for you.
> Tomorrow you will be a corpse
> If you remain here.
> Save yourself, go, leave me,
> Flee, flee from their hatred.

RICCARDO   As long as you love me, Amelia,
> I care not for my fate.

AMELIA   Flee.

RICCARDO   I have only you in my soul,
> And I forget the universe.

AMELIA   Save yourself.

RICCARDO   Nor can I fear death,
> Because stronger than it
> Is the breath that intoxicates me
> Of your divine love.

AMELIA   Go. Ah! save yourself!
> Tomorrow you will be a corpse
> If you remain, *etc.*

RICCARDO	Perchè di lei più forte, *ecc.*
AMELIA	Dunque vedermi vuòi D'affanno morta e di vergogna?
RICCARDO	Salva ti vo'. Domani Con Renato andrai . . .
AMELIA	Dove?
RICCARDO	Al natio tuo cielo.
AMELIA	In Inghilterra!
RICCARDO	Mi schianto il cor . . . Ma partirai . . . ma addio!
AMELIA *(con disperazione)*	
	Riccardo! Riccardo!
RICCARDO	Mi schianto il cor . . . Ti lascio, Amelia . . .
AMELIA	Riccardo!

Riccardo si stacca, ma dopo pochi passi tornando a lei e con tutta l'anima:

RICCARDO	Anco una volta addio!
AMELIA	Ohimè!
RICCARDO	L'ultima volta addio! Addio!
AMELIA	Addio!

RENATO *(lanciatosi inosservato fra loro, lo trafigge di pugnale)*

        E tu ricevi il mio!

RICCARDO	Ahimè!
AMELIA *(d'un grido)*	
	Soccorso! Soccorso!
OSCAR *(accorrendo)*	
	Oh ciel! Ei trucidato!

Entrano da tutte le parti Dame, Uffiziali e Guardie.

CORO	Da chi? Ov'è l'infame?

Veggonsi apparire nel fondo Samuel e Tom.

OSCAR *(accennando Renato)*
        Eccol! . . .

Tutti lo circondano e gli strappano la maschera.

AMELIA, OSCAR e CORO
        Renato!

CORO *(con furore)*
        Ah! morte . . . infamia,
        Infamia sul traditor, traditor!
        L'acciaro lo laceri,
        L'acciaro vendicator!
        Morte, morte al traditor!
        Morte, *ecc.*

RICCARDO   No, no . . . lasciatelo . . .
        Lasciatelo!
          (a Renato; e tratto il dispaccio, e fatto cenno
          a lui di accostarsi)

RICCARDO	Because stronger than it, *etc.*
AMELIA	So then you wish to see me Dead of sorrow and of shame?
RICCARDO	I want you saved. Tomorrow With Renato you will go . . .
AMELIA	Where?
RICCARDO	To your native sky.
AMELIA	To England!
RICCARDO	I am breaking my heart . . . But you will leave . . . but farewell!
AMELIA *(with desperation)*	
	Riccardo! Riccardo!
RICCARDO	I am breaking my heart . . . I leave you, Amelia . . .
AMELIA	Riccardo!

Riccardo moves away, but after a few steps, returning to her and with his whole soul:

RICCARDO	Once again, farewell!
AMELIA	Alas!
RICCARDO	The last time: farewell! Farewell!
AMELIA	Farewell!

RENATO *(having flung himself, unseen, between them, stabs him with a dagger)*

And you receive mine!

RICCARDO	Alas!

AMELIA *(with a cry)*

Help! Help!

OSCAR *(rushing up)*

Oh, heaven! He is slain!

From all sides enter Ladies, Officers and Guards.

CHORUS	By whom? Where is the murderer?

Samuel and Tom are seen, appearing at the back.

OSCAR *(pointing to Renato)*

There he is! . . .

They all surround him and rip off his mask.

AMELIA, OSCAR and CHORUS

Renato!

CHORUS *(with fury)*

Ah! death . . . infamy,
Infamy upon the traitor, the traitor!
Let the sword tear him,
The avenging sword!
Death, death to the traitor!
Death, *etc.*

RICCARDO	No, no . . . let him go . . . Let him go! *(to Renato; having taken out the despatch and having motioned him to approach)*

Tu . . . m'odi ancor.
Ella è pura; in braccio a morte
Te lo giuro, Iddio m'ascolta:
Io che amai la tua consorte,
Rispettato ho il suo candor.
   (gli dà il foglio)
A novello incarco asceso
Tu con lei partir dovevi . . .
Io l'amai, ma volli illeso
Il tuo nome ed il suo cor!

AMELIA   Oh rimorsi dell'amor
Che divorano il mio cor,
Fra un colpevole che sanguina
E la vittima che muor! Ah!

OSCAR   O dolor senza misura,
O terribile sventura!
La sua fronte è tutta rorida
Già dell'ultimo sudor!

RENATO   Ciel! che feci! e che m'aspetta

Esecrato sulla terra!
Esecrato sulla terra!
Di qual sangue e qual vendetta
M'assetò l'infausto error!

RICCARDO   Grazia a ognun: signor qui sono:
Tutti assolve il mio perdono . . .

Samuel e Tom occupano sempre il fondo della scena.

CORO   Cor sì grande e generoso
Tu ci serba, a Dio pietoso:
Raggio in terra a noi miserrimi
È del tuo celeste amor,
Raggio in terra, *ecc.*

RENATO, SAMUEL e TOM
Cor sì grande e generoso, ecc.

AMELIA e OSCAR
Dio pietoso, *ecc.*

RICCARDO   Addio per sempre, miei figli . . .

TUTTI   Ei muore!

RICCARDO   Addio, diletta America!

TUTTI   Ei muore!

RICCARDO   Addio . . . miei figli . . . per sempre . . . ah!
Ohime! . . . io moro! . . .
Miei figli . . . per sem . . .
   (la voce gli manca)
Addio!
   (cade e spira)

TUTTI   Notte, notte d'orror,
Notte, notte d'orror!

Cala la tela.

You . . . hear me still.
She is pure; in the embrace of death,
I swear it to you. God hears me.
I, who loved your wife,
Have respected her purity.
(gives him the paper)
Promoted to a new assignment,
You were to leave with her . . .
I loved her, but I wanted unharmed
Your name and her heart.

AMELIA   Oh, remorse for love
That devours my heart,
Between a guilty man, dripping blood,
An the victim who dies! Ah!

OSCAR   O grief beyond measure!
O terrible misfortune!
His brow is all bedewed
With his last sweat already!

RENATO   Heaven! What have I done! And what awaits
me,
Despised, on earth!
Despised on earth!
For what blood and what vengeance
Did my ill-omened error make me thirst!

RICCARDO   Pardon for all: I am master here.
My forgiveness absolves all . . .

Samuel and Tom still occupy the rear of the scene.

CHORUS   Preserve for us, O merciful God,
Such a great and generous heart;
On earth, for us most wretched,
It is a ray of your celestial love.
A ray on earth, *etc.*

RENATO, SAMUEL and TOM
Such a great and generous heart, *etc.*

AMELIA and OSCAR
Merciful God, *etc.*

RICCARDO   Farewell forever, my children . . .
ALL   He is dying!
RICCARDO   Farewell, beloved America!
ALL   He is dying!
RICCARDO   Farewell . . . my children . . . forever . . . ah!
Alas . . . I die! . . .
My children . . . forev . . .
(his voice fails him)
Farewell!
(falls and dies)
ALL   Night, night of horror!
Night, night of horror!

The curtain falls.

Aïda

After the feverish creation of his trio of masterpieces, *Rigoletto*, *Il Trovatore*, and *La Traviata*, Verdi's career assumed a calmer rhythm. There were no more operas written in forty days and orchestrated in ten, no assembly line of music running from the Villa Sant'Agata to La Fenice or the San Carlo. And the change in his pace of production reflected a change in his private, or nonmusical, life. Sant'Agata had been transformed from a simple rustic lodging to a comfortable and rather luxurious retreat. Italy, too, had changed; the revolutionary land of *Nabucco* and *Ernani* had become the united monarchy of Victor Emmanuel and Cavour. Its senate included — at everyone's insistence — Senatore Giuseppe Verdi, a reluctant and almost inactive parliamentarian.

Verdi was a world figure. He had written two more operas for Paris: the epic *Les Vêpres siciliennes* (1855) and the profound *Don Carlos* (1867). In Italy, he had also written *Simon Boccanegra* (Venice, 1857) and *Un Ballo in maschera* (Rome, 1859), and he had even written an opera for St. Petersburg, *La Forza del destino* (1862). In those years he also rewrote earlier works whose lack of success he felt was due to faulty librettos: the *Stiffelio* of 1850 became *Aroldo* in 1857, *Macbeth* (1847) was revised for a Paris production in 1865, and *La Forza del destino* was given a thorough overhauling before its first La Scala performance in 1869.

At the beginning of the summer of 1870 Verdi was back at Sant'Agata, and in a light-hearted letter to his old friend Countess Clarina Maffei he said: "The Maestro is not composing, and has no desire to compose . . ." This was a recurrent theme in the latter half of his life. After the period of intense musical activity which he called his "years as a galley slave," he wanted to write only when he felt like it, choosing his subjects, his singers, his theaters. And if he did not feel like writing, he could tend to his farms and his crops. The intervals between one opera and the next became longer and longer.

But a very short time after his letter to Countess Maffei, he was writing to his publisher: "I have the outline of an opera, amply laid out, with the characters, choruses, *mise en scène*. It lacks only the dialogue and the verses. If I were to make an opera of it, could Ghislanzoni write the libretto?"

The outline, called "Aida," was by a distinguished Egyptologist known as Mariette Bey. The Khedive of Egypt wanted Verdi (or, failing him, Gounod or Wagner) to write a work for the newly built opera house in Cairo, constructed to celebrate the opening of the Suez Canal in 1869. Verdi's French librettist Du Locle (Mariette's go-between) had already approached him twice about the offer, and twice Verdi had refused. But when he was sent the detailed outline, the story fascinated him, he saw the rich possibilities of the exotic subject (and he was not indifferent to the substantial sum offered him by the Egyptian authorities).

Antonio Ghislanzoni was a logical choice as librettist. Verdi's old friend and colleague Piave was mortally ill, in a physical and mental decline that prevented him from doing any work (he was dependent largely on Verdi's charity for his sustenance). The librettist of *Un Ballo in maschera* was dead. And Ghislanzoni, then in his late forties, was a man with considerable experience in the theater. As a youth he had been a singer, then a music critic and writer. He had worked satisfactorily with Verdi in adjusting the confused libretto of *La Forza del destino* (Piave's last effort) for its Italian debut.

Enchanted by the colorful story of *Aïda*, Verdi immediately wanted to know more about the historical background; Ricordi and Ghislanzoni were given a series of questions to investigate: Was ancient Egyptian worship restricted to men only? Was Ethiopia the same as Abyssinia? Which of the Ramses might the "great king" be, unnamed in the outline? Where and how were the rites of Isis performed? To Du Locle, Verdi wrote for information about ancient Egyptian instruments, and expressed his horror at the suggestion that he use the newly invented saxophone.

A few weeks after the contract had been signed and the libretto begun, the Franco-Prussian war broke out and correspondence stopped between Verdi and Ghislanzoni in Italy and Du Locle in Paris (where costumes and sets were being made). In those months the opera was completed, as Verdi worked along with the librettist, often writing the words himself, then telling Ghislanzoni to give them a meter.

On November 13, 1870, Giuseppina Verdi wrote in her daybook that the opera was finished, adding that now they had to "let Papà rest and put on some flesh."

Verdi went on changing and polishing until late in 1871, then sent the last of the completed work to Ricordi and wrote to a friend: "Amen, and *à la grâce de Dieu.*" Later Verdi went back to work, composing a long overture, which he subsequently discarded in favor of the present, brief prelude.

The war in France meant that the opera could not be given in Cairo on schedule, but finally, after tedious correspondence about the choice of singers and conductor (who was to be Giovanni Bottesini, the double-bass virtuoso), on Christmas Eve 1871, *Aïda* was performed in the presence of the Khedive and an international public, including critics from France and Italy. The success was enormous, but Verdi was more concerned about the European première at La Scala, for which he composed a new soprano aria *"O cieli azzurri."* He staged and conducted the opera himself, and on February 8, 1872, the Egyptian success was repeated in Milan.

Verdi himself received thirty-two curtain calls, which were interrupted as the composer left the stage to hunt for Ghislanzoni, wanting to give the librettist his share of the acclaim. But Ghislanzoni had left the theater so that Verdi could stand alone in his triumph.

THE PLOT

ACT ONE

Ancient Egypt. In a hall of the king's palace in Memphis, Ramfis, the High Priest, tells the young warrior Radamès that the King will soon announce the appointment of a general to lead the Egyptian forces against Amonasro, King of the invading Ethiopians. Left alone then, Radamès dreams of being that general so that, victorious, he can ask the King for the hand of Aïda, a young Ethiopian slave girl with whom he is secretly in love, unaware that she is the daughter of the enemy ruler. Princess Amneris, the Egyptian King's daughter, comes in. She is also in love with Radamès and is disturbed by his interest in her slave girl, who follows her.

The King and his court enter. A messenger confirms the Ethiopian invasion, and the King names Radamès supreme commander. Aïda is torn between love of her father and her country and her love for Radamès.

Later, in the temple of Ptah, Radamès is invested with the consecrated armor and the symbols of his high mission.

ACT TWO

Radamès is victorious. As Amneris's slaves prepare her for the triumphal celebration, she dreams of his return, then tricks Aïda into revealing her love. Princess and slave girl are rivals.

After the elaborate procession of the victorious troops, the King asks Radamès what he wants as a reward. The young general first has the prisoners brought in. Among them, unrecognized by all except Aïda, is her father, King Amonasro, disguised as a simple warrior. Radamès asks the Egyptian King to free them, believing Amonasro dead and the enemy spirit therefore broken. The priests object, but the King grants this request for clemency and at the same time announces that the young general will be given Amneris in marriage and that one day the royal couple will rule over Egypt together. Amneris is exultant, but Radamès and Aïda are aghast at this turn of events.

ACT THREE

Ramfis accompanies Amneris to the Temple of Isis, on the banks of the Nile, where she is to pray and keep vigil in preparation for her forthcoming marriage.

When they have gone inside, Aïda appears. She is to meet Radamès nearby, but before he comes her father suddenly confronts her and makes her promise to discover the road that the Egyptian army will take, so that the reassembled Ethiopian forces can fall on the enemy and destroy him.

Amonasro hides, and Aïda persuades Radamès to flee with her to Ethiopia, then to reveal the secret. Once the young general has spoken, Amonasro steps forward and reveals who he is. Radamès is horrified at his own treason and gives himself up to the High Priest, who appears with Amneris and with guards, who pursue Aïda and Amonasro.

ACT FOUR

Despite Radamès's act of treason, Amneris still loves him, and as the priests gather to decide his fate, she offers him a final opportunity to save himself by giving up Aïda. He refuses. The priests condemn him to be buried alive.

Two priests close the stone over the crypt where Radamès has been placed. But Aïda has already concealed herself in this tomb, and as the priests and priestesses chant in the temple above, where Amneris is praying for peace, Aïda is reunited with her lover and dies in his arms.

AÏDA

libretto by Antonio Ghislanzoni, based on a plot
by Mariette Bey and a prose sketch in French by
Camille du Locle

First performed at the Khedival Theater in Cairo

December 24, 1871

CHARACTERS

Aïda, Ethiopian princess, slave of Amneris	Soprano
Amneris, daughter of the King of Egypt	Mezzo-soprano
Amonasro, King of Ethiopia, Aïda's father	Baritone
Radamès, captain of the Egyptian guard	Tenor
Ramfis, High Priest of Egypt	Bass
King of Egypt	Bass
Messenger	Tenor

Priests, Soldiers, Ethiopian Slaves, Egyptians,
Dignitaries

The time is the epoch of the Pharaohs,
in Memphis and Thebes.

ATTO PRIMO

SCENA PRIMA

Sala nel palazzo del Re a Menfi. A destra e a sinistra una colonnata con statue e arbusti in fiori. Grande porta nel fondo, da cui appariscono i templii, i palazzi di Menfi e le Piramidi.

Radamès e Ramfis in scena, conversando fra loro.

RAMFIS	Sì: corre voce che l'Etiope
	Ardisca sfidarci ancora,
	E del Nilo la valle e Tebe
	Minacciar. Fra breve un messo
	Recherà il ver.
RADAMÈS	La sacra Iside consultasti?
RAMFIS	Ella ha nomato
	Dell'Egizie falangi
	Il condottier supremo.
RADAMÈS	Oh, lui felice!
RAMFIS	(*con intenzione, fissando Radamès*)
	Giovane e prode è desso.
	Ora, del Nume reco
	I decreti al Re.

Ramfis esce.

RADAMÈS	Se quel guerrier io fossi!
	Se il mio sogno si avverasse!...
	Un esercito di prodi
	Da me guidato ... e la vittoria ...
	E il plauso di Menfi tutta!
	E a te, mia dolce Aïda, tornar
	Di lauri cinto ...
	Dirti: per te ho pugnato,
	Per te ho vinto!
	Celeste Aïda, forma divina,
	Mistico serto di luce e fior,
	Del mio pensiero tu sei regina,
	Tu di mia vita sei lo splendor.
	Il tuo bel cielo vorrei ridarti,
	Le dolci brezze del patrio suol;
	Un regal serto sul crin posarti,
	Ergerti un trono vicino al sol.

Entra Amneris.

AMNERIS	Qual insolita gioia nel tuo sguardo!
	Di quale nobil fierezza
	Ti balena il volto!
	Degna d'invidia oh! quanto
	Saria la donna il cui bramato aspetto
	Tanta luce di gaudio in te destasse!

ACT ONE

SCENE ONE

Hall in the King's palace at Memphis. At left and right a colonnade with statues and flowering bushes. A great door at the back, through which appear the temples and palaces of Memphis and the Pyramids.

Radamès and Ramfis are on stage, talking to each other.

RAMFIS	Yes: there is a rumor that the Ethiopian
	Dares to challenge us again,
	And threaten the Nile valley
	And Thebes. A messenger soon
	Will bring the truth.
RADAMÈS	Did you consult holy Isis?
RAMFIS	She has named
	The supreme commander
	Of the Egyptian troops.
RADAMÈS	Oh, happy man!
RAMFIS (*looking meaningfully at Radamès*)
	He is young and brave.
	Now I am taking
	The Deity's decree to the King.

Ramfis goes out.

RADAMÈS	If I were that warrior!
	If my dream came true! ...
	An army of brave men
	Led by me ... and victory ...
	And the acclaim of all Memphis!
	And, my sweet Aïda, to come back to you
	Crowned with laurels ...
	Tell you: for you I fought,
	For you I have won!
	Heavenly Aïda, divine form,
	Mystic garland of light and flowers,
	You are the queen of my thoughts,
	You are the radiance of my life.
	I would like to give you back your lovely sky,
	The gentle breezes of your native land;
	Set a royal crown on your locks,
	Raise you a throne near the sun.

Amneris enters.

AMNERIS	What unaccustomed joy in your gaze!
	With what noble pride
	Your countenance flashes!
	Ah! How worthy of envy
	Would be the woman whose longed-for
	appearance
	Wakened such a light of joy in you!

RADAMÈS   D'un sogno avventuroso
            Si beava il mio cuore.
            Oggi la Diva profferse il nome
            Del guerrier che al campo
            Le schiere egizie condurrà ...
            Ah! s'io fossi a tal onor prescelto ...

AMNERIS   Nè un altro sogno mai
            Più gentil ... più soave ...
            Al core ti parlò?
            Non hai tu in Menfi desiderii ...
            Speranze?...

RADAMÈS   Io!
            (Quale inchiesta!
            Forse ... l'arcano amore
            Scoprì che m'arde in core ...)

AMNERIS   (Oh! guai se un altro amore
            Ardesse a lui nel core!)

RADAMÈS   (Della sua schiava il nome
            Mi lesse nel pensier!)

AMNERIS   (Guai se il mio sguardo penetra
            Questo fatal mister!
            Guai! oh, guai!...)

Entra in scena Aïda.

RADAMÈS *(vedendo Aïda)*
            Dessa!

AMNERIS *(da sè, osservando)*
            (Ei si turba ... e quale sguardo
            Rivolse a lei!...
            Aïda!... a me rivale ...
            Forse saria costei?)
               (volgendosi ad Aïda)
            Vieni, o diletta, appressati ...
            Schiava non sei nè ancella
            Qui dove in dolce fascino
            Io ti chiamai sorella ...
            Piangi?... delle tue lacrime
            Svela il segreto a me.

AÏDA   Ohimè! di guerra fremere
            L'atroce grido io sento ...
            Per l'infelice patria,
            Per me ... per voi pavento.

*Aïda abbassa gli occhi e cerca dissimulare il proprio turba-
mento.*

AMNERIS   Favelli il ver?
            Nè s'agita più grave cura in te?
               (fra sè, guardando Aïda)
            (Trema! o rea schiava,
            Ch'io nel tuo cor discenda!...)

RADAMÈS   (Nel volto a lei balena
            Lo sdegno ed il sospetto ...
            Guai se l'arcano affetto
            A noi leggesse in core!)

AMNERIS   (Trema che il ver m'apprenda
            Quel pianto e quel rossor!)

RADAMÈS   My heart was basking
             In a dream of adventure.
             Today the Goddess uttered the name
             Of the warrior who will lead
             The Egyptian troops into the field . . .
             Ah! If I were chosen for such honor . . .

AMNERIS   Has another dream
             Gentler . . . sweeter . . .
             Never spoken to your heart?
             Have you no desires in Memphis . . .
             No hopes? . . .

RADAMÈS   I!
             (What questioning!
             Perhaps . . . she has discovered
             The secret love that enflames my heart . . .)

AMNERIS   (Oh! Woe, if another love
             Should enflame his heart!)

RADAMÈS   (She has read in my thoughts
             The name of her slave!)

AMNERIS   (Woe if my gaze should pierce
             This fatal mystery!
             Woe! Ah, woe! . . .)

             Aïda comes in.

RADAMÈS (*seeing Aïda*)
             She!

AMNERIS (*to herself, observing*)
             (He is upset . . . and what a look
             He gave her! . . .
             Aïda! . . . My rival . . .
             Could it perhaps be she?)
                        (*turning to Aïda*)
             Come, beloved girl, approach . . .
             You are no slave, no handmaiden
             Here, where in your sweet spell
             I have called you my sister . . .
             You weep? . . . Reveal the secret
             Of your tears to me.

AÏDA   Alas! I hear the dreadful cry
             Of war ringing . . .
             I am afraid for my unhappy country,
             For myself . . . for your people.

             Aïda lowers her eyes, trying to conceal her inner turmoil.

AMNERIS   Are you speaking the truth?
             Is no deeper concern upsetting you?
                        (*to herself, looking at Aïda*)
             (Tremble! Oh base slave,
             Should I descend into your heart! . . .)

RADAMÈS   (Contempt and suspicion
             Flash in her countenance . . .
             Woe should she read
             The secret love in our hearts!)

AMNERIS   (Tremble, for those tears and that blushing
             Are telling me the truth!)

AÏDA
    (Ah no, sulla mia patria
    Non geme il cor soltanto;
    Quello ch'io verso è pianto
    Di sventurato amor!)

Entra il Re, preceduto dalle sue guardie e seguito da Ramfis, dai ministri, sacerdoti, capitani, ecc. Un uffiziale di palazzo, indi un messaggero.

IL RE
    Alta cagion v'aduna,
    O fidi Egizii,
    Al vostro Re d'intorno.
    Dai confin d'Etiopia un messaggero
    Dianzi giungea.
    Gravi novelle ei reca ...
    Vi piaccia udirlo ...
      (*ad un uffiziale*)
    Il messagger s'avanzi!

MESSAGGERO
    Il sacro suolo dell'Egitto
    È invaso dai barbari Etiopi ...
    I nostri campi fur devastati ...
    Arse le messi ...
    E baldi della facil vittoria
    I predatori già marciano su Tebe ...

TUTTI
    Ed osan tanto!

MESSAGGERO
    Un guerriero indomabile, feroce,
    Li conduce, Amonasro!

TUTTI
    Il Re!

AÏDA (*a parte*)
    (Mio padre!)

MESSAGGERO
    Già Tebe è in armi e dalle cento porte
    Sul barbaro invasore
    Proromperà, guerra recando e morte.

IL RE
    Sì: guerra e morte
    Il nostro grido sia.

TUTTI
    Guerra! guerra! tremanda, inesorata!

IL RE (*accostandosi a Radamès*)
    Iside venerata
    Di nostre schiere invitte
    Già designava il condottier supremo:
    Radamès.

TUTTI
    Radamès!

RADAMÈS
    Ah! Sien grazie ai Numi!
    Son paghi i voti miei!

AMNERIS
    (Ei duce!)

AÏDA
    (Io tremo.)

IL RE
    Or, di Vulcano al tempio
    Muovi, o guerrier;
    Le sacre armi ti cingi
    E alla vittoria vola.
    Su! del Nilo al sacro lido
    Accorrete, Egizii eroi;

AÏDA   (Ah no, my heart is not suffering
                        Only for my homeland;
                        The tears I shed are tears
                        Of unfortunate love!)

The King enters, preceded by his guards, and followed by Ramfis, with the ministers, priests, captains, etc. An official of the palace, and then a messenger.

THE KING   A lofty occasion,
                        O faithful Egyptians,
                        Gathers you around your King.
                        A messenger has just arrived
                        From the Ethiopian border.
                        He brings grave news . . .
                        May it please you to hear him . . .
                                (to an official)
                        Let the messenger come forward!

MESSENGER   The sacred soil of Egypt
                        Is invaded by the Ethiopian barbarians . . .
                        Our fields have been destroyed . . .
                        The harvests burned . . .
                        And emboldened by their easy victory
                        The vandals are already marching on
                           Thebes . . .

ALL   They dare so much!

MESSENGER   A fierce, unconquerable warrior
                        Is leading them, Amonasro!

ALL   The King!

AÏDA *(aside)*   (My father!)

MESSENGER   Thebes is already in arms, and will break forth
                        From its hundred gates against the barbarous
                             invader,
                        Bringing war and death.

THE KING   Yes: let war and death
                        Be our cry.

ALL   War! War! Terrible and merciless!

THE KING *(approaching Radamès)*
                        Isis, whom we worship,
                        Has already named the supreme general
                        Of our undefeated troops:
                        Radamès.

ALL   Radamès!

RADAMÈS   Ah! The Gods be thanked!
                        My prayers are answered!

AMNERIS   (He the general!)

AÏDA   (I tremble.)

THE KING   Now, go to the Temple of Vulcan,
                        O warrior;
                        Gird on the sacred weapons
                        And hasten to victory.
                        On! Hasten to the Nile's
                        Sacred shore, Egyptian heroes;

Da ogni cor prorompa il grido:
Guerra e morte,
Morte allo stranier!

RAMFIS   Gloria ai Numi! ognun rammenti
Ch'essi reggono gli eventi,
Che in poter de' Numi solo
Stan le sorti del guerrier.

TUTTI   Su! del Nilo al sacro lido, ecc.

RADAMÈS   Sacro fremito di gloria
Tutta l'anima m'investe.
Su, corriamo alla vittoria!
Guerra, guerra
E morte allo stranier.

AÏDA   (Per chi piango? per chi prego?
Qual poter m'avvince a lui!
Deggio amarlo ... ed è costui
Un nemico, uno stranier!)

AMNERIS (*consegnando una bandiera a Radamès*)
Di mia man ricevi, o duce,
Il vessillo glorioso;
Ti sia guida, ti sia luce
Della gloria sul sentier.

RAMFIS e SACERDOTI
Gloria ai Numi e ognun rammenti, ecc.

IL RE, MINISTRI e CAPITANI
Su! del Nilo al sacro lido, ecc.

RADAMÈS e MESSAGGERO
Su! corriamo alla vittoria!, ecc.

AÏDA   (Per chi piango?, ecc.)

RE e RAMFIS   Guerra!

TUTTI   Guerra! guerra! guerra!
Sterminio all'invasor.

AMNERIS (*a Radamès*)
Ritorna vincitor!

TUTTI   Ritorna vincitor!

Escono tutti, meno Aïda.

AÏDA   Ritorna vincitor!
E dal mio labbro
Uscì l'empia parola!
Vincitor del padre mio ...
Di lui che impugna l'armi per me ...
Per ridonarmi una patria, una reggia
E il nome illustre che qui
Celar m'è forza!
Vincitor de' miei fratelli ...
Ond'io lo vegga,
Tinto del sangue amato,
Trionfar nel plauso dell'Egizie coorti!

E dietro il carro, un re ...
Mio padre ... di catene avvinto!...

	Let this cry burst from every heart:
	War and death,
	Death to the foreigner!
RAMFIS	Glory to the Gods! Let all remember
	That they control events,
	That in the Gods' power alone
	Lies the fate of the warrior.
ALL	On! Hasten to the Nile's sacred shore, etc.
RADAMÈS	A holy yearning for glory
	Fills all my soul.
	On, let us rush on to victory!
	War, war
	And death to the foreigner.
AÏDA	(For whom do I weep? for whom, pray?
	What power binds me to him!
	I must love him . . . and he is
	An enemy, a foreigner!)

AMNERIS (*giving a banner to Radamès*)

Receive from my hand, O leader,
The glorious banner;
Let it be your guide, the light
Of glory on your path.

RAMFIS and PRIESTS

Glory to the Gods and let all remember, etc.

THE KING, MINISTERS, and CAPTAINS

On! Hasten to the Nile's sacred shore, etc.

RADAMÈS and MESSENGER

On! Let us rush on to victory!, etc.

AÏDA   (For whom do I weep?, etc.)

KING and RAMFIS

War!

ALL   War! War! War!

Destruction to the invader.

AMNERIS (*to Radamès*)

Return victorious!

ALL   Return victorious!

All go out, except Aïda.

AÏDA   Return victorious!
               And from my lips

               Came the wicked word!
               Victorious over my father . . .
               He who takes up arms for me . . .
               To give me again a homeland, a palace
               And the illustrious name that here
               I am forced to conceal!
               Victorious over my brothers . . .
               So that I may see him,
               Stained with their beloved blood,
               Triumph among the cheers of the Egyptian
                   cohorts!
               And behind his chariot, a king . . .
               My father . . . bound in chains! . . .

L'insana parola,
O Numi, sperdete!
Al seno d'un padre
La figlia rendete;
Struggete, struggete le squadre
Dei nostri oppressor!
Ah! sventurata! che dissi?
E l'amor mio?...
Dunque scordar poss'io
Questo fervido amore
Che, oppressa e schiava,
Come raggio di sol
Qui mi beava?
Imprecherò la morte a Radamès ...
A lui ch'amo pur tanto!
Ah! non fu in terra mai
Da più crudeli angoscie
Un core affranto!
I sacri nomi di padre ... d'amante
Nè profferir poss'io,
Nè ricordar ...
Per l'un ... per l'altro ... confusa ...
Tremante ... io piangere vorrei ...
Vorrei pregar.
Ma la mia prece in bestemmia
Si muta ... delitto è il pianto a me ...
Colpa il sospir ...
In notte cupa la mente è perduta ...
E nell'ansia crudel vorrei morir.
Numi, pietà del mio soffrir!
Speme non v'ha pel mio dolor ...
Amor fatal, tremendo amor,
Spezzami il cor, fammi morir!
Numi, pietà del mio soffrir!

Esce.

SCENA SECONDA

*Interno del Tempio di Vulcano a Menfi. Una luca misteriosa
scende dall'alto. Una lunga fila di colonne, l'una all'altra ad-
dossate, si perde fra le tenebre. Statue di varie Divinità. Nel
mezzo della scena, sovra un palco coperto da tappeti, sorge
l'altare sormontato da emblemi sacri. Dai tripodi d'oro si
innalza il fumo degli incensi. Ramfis ai piedi dell'altare.*

GRAN SACERDOTESSA *(nell'interno)*
Possente, possente Fthà, del mondo
Spirito animator, ah!
Noi t'invochiamo!
SACERDOTESSE *(nell'interno)*
Noi t'invochiamo!
RAMFIS e SACERDOTI
Tu che dal nulla hai tratto
L'onde, la terra, il ciel,
Noi t'invochiamo!

O Gods, obliterate
That insane word!
Restore a daughter
To her father's bosom;
Destroy, destroy the ranks
Of our oppressors!
Ah! Hapless me! What have I said?
And my love? . . .
Can I then forget
This ardent love
That, like a ray of sun,
Beamed on me here,
A slave and oppressed?
Shall I invoke death for Radamès . . .
For him whom I love so much!
Ah! Never was a heart on earth
Overcome by such
Cruel anguish!
The sacred names of father . . . of lover
I cannot utter,
Or remember . . .
For the one . . . the other . . . confused . . .
Trembling . . . I want to weep . . .
I want to pray.
But my prayer is changed
To blasphemy . . . my tears are a crime . . .
My sigh is guilty . . .
My mind is lost in darkest night . . .
And in this cruel anxiety I want to die.
Gods, have pity on my suffering!
There is no hope for my grief . . .
Fatal love, terrible love,
Break my heart, make me die!
Gods, have pity on my suffering!

She goes out.

SCENE TWO

Interior of the Temple of Vulcan in Memphis. A mysterious light falls from above. A long row of columns, one almost against the other, is lost in the shadows. Statues of various divinities. In the center of the scene, on a platform covered with rugs, rises the altar surmounted by sacred emblems. Smoke rises from incense in golden tripods. Ramfis is at the foot of the altar.

HIGH PRIESTESS (*within*)
Mighty, mighty Ptah,
Life-giving spirit of the world, ah!
We invoke thee!

PRIESTESSES (*within*)
We invoke thee!

RAMFIS and PRIESTS
Thou who from the void drew
The waves, the land, and the sky,
We invoke thee!

GRAN SACERDOTESSA
>Immenso, immenso Fthà, del mondo
>Spirito fecondator, ah!
>Noi t'invochiamo!

SACERDOTESSE
>Noi t'invochiamo!

RAMFIS e SACERDOTI
>Nume che del tuo spirito
>Sei figlio e genitor,
>Noi t'invochiamo!

GRAN SACERDOTESSA
>Fuoco increato, eterno,
>Onde ebbe luce il sol, ah!
>Noi t'invochiamo!

SACERDOTESSE
>Noi t'invochiamo!

RAMFIS e SACERDOTI
>Vita dell'Universo,
>Mito d'eterno amor,
>Noi t'invochiamo!

GRAN SACERDOTESSA e SACERDOTESSE
>Immenso Fthà!

RAMFIS e SACERDOTI
>Noi t'invochiamo!

Radamès viene introdotto senz'armi. Mentre va all'altare, le Sacerdotesse eseguiscono la danza sacra. Sul capo di Radamès viene steso un velo d'argento.

SACERDOTESSE
>Immenso Fthà! Noi t'invochiam!

RAMFIS *(a Radamès)* ....
>Mortal, diletto ai Numi,
>A te fidate
>Son d'Egitto le sorti.
>Il sacro brando dal Dio temprato,
>Per tua man diventi ai nemici
>Terror, fulgore, morte!

SACERDOTI   Il sacro brando, ecc.

RAMFIS *(volgendosi al nume)*
>Nume, custode e vindice
>Di questa sacra terra,
>La mano tua distendi
>Sovra l'egizio suol.

RADAMÈS   Nume, che duce ed arbitro
>Sei d'ogni umana guerra,
>Proteggi tu, difendi
>D'Egitto il sacro suol.

RAMFIS e SACERDOTI
>Nume, custode e vindice, ecc.
>Possente Fthà, spirito fecondator, ecc.

TUTTI   Noi t'invochiam!
>Immenso Fthà! Immenso Fthà!

HIGH PRIESTESS
> Great, great Ptah,
> Seed-giving spirit of the world, ah!
> We invoke thee!

PRIESTESSES
> We invoke thee!

RAMFIS and PRIESTS
> God who of thy spirit
> Are son and father,
> We invoke thee!

HIGH PRIESTESS
> Uncreated, eternal fire,
> From whence the sun had light, ah!
> We invoke thee!

PRIESTESSES   We invoke thee!

RAMFIS and PRIESTS
> Life of the Universe,
> Myth of eternal love,
> We invoke thee!

HIGH PRIESTESS and PRIESTESSES
> Mighty Ptah!

RAMFIS and PRIESTS
> We invoke thee!

Radamès, unarmed, is led in. As he goes to the altar, the priestesses perform the sacred dance. A silver veil is placed over Radamès' head.

PRIESTESSES   Mighty Ptah! We invoke thee!

RAMFIS (*to Radamès*)
> Mortal, beloved of the Gods,
> The fate of Egypt
> Is entrusted to you.
> May the holy sword, tempered by the God,
> Become in your hand
> Terror, lightning, death for our enemies!

PRIESTS   May the holy sword, etc.

RAMFIS (*turning to the god*)
> God, guardian and avenger
> Of this holy land,
> Hold out thy hand
> Over the Egyptian soil.

RADAMÈS
> God, thou who art leader
> And arbiter of all human wars,
> Protect and defend
> The holy soil of Egypt.

RAMFIS and PRIESTS
> God, guardian and avenger, etc.
> Mighty Ptah, seed-giving spirit, etc.

ALL
> We invoke thee!
> Mighty Ptah! Mighty Ptah!

ATTO SECONDO

SCENA PRIMA

*Una sala nell'appartamento di Amneris. Amneris circondata
dalle schiave che l'abbigliano per la festa trionfale. Dai tripodi
si eleva il profumo degli aromi. Giovani schiavi mori agitano
i ventagli di piume.*

SCHIAVE   Chi mai fra gl'inni e i plausi
                      Erge alla gloria il vol,
                      Al par d'un Dio terribile,
                      Fulgente al par del sol?
                      Vieni: sul crin ti piovano
                      Contesi ai lauri i fior;
                      Suonin di gloria i cantici
                      Coi cantici d'amor.

AMNERIS   (Ah! vieni, vieni, amor mio,
                      M'inebria ... fammi beato il cor!)

SCHIAVE   Or dove son le barbare
                      Orde dello stranier?
                      Siccome nebbia sparvero
                      Al soffio del guerrier.
                      Vieni: di gloria il premio
                      Raccogli, o vincitor;
                      T'arrise la vittoria,
                      T'arriderà l'amor.

AMNERIS   (Ah! vieni, vieni, amor mio,
                      Ravvivami d'un caro accento ancor!)

    Le schiave continuano sempre ad abbigliare Amneris. Danzano i piccoli schiavi mori.

SCHIAVE   Vieni: sul crin ti piovano
                      Contesti ai lauri, i fior;
                      Suonin di gloria i cantici
                      Coi cantici d'amor.

AMNERIS   (Ah! vieni, vieni amor mio,
                      M'inebria, fammi beato il cor!)
                      Silenzio! Aïda verso noi s'avanza ...
                      Figlia de' vinti,
                      Il suo dolor m'è sacro.

    *Ad un cenno d'Amneris le schiave s'allontanano. Entra Aïda
portando la corona.*

AMNERIS   (Nel rivederla, il dubbio
                      Atroce in me si desta ...
                      Il mistero fatal si squarci alfine!)
                        (ad Aïda con simulata amorevolezza)
                      Fu la sorte dell'armi a' tuoi funesta,
                      Povera Aïda! Il lutto
                      Che ti pesa sul cor teco divido.
                      Io son l'amica tua ...

ACT TWO

SCENE ONE

A room in the apartments of Amneris. Amneris is sur-
rounded by slave girls, who are dressing her for the triumphal
celebrations. Perfumed vapors rise from tripods. Young Moor-
ish slaves wave plume fans.

SLAVE GIRLS   Who amid anthems and cheers
　　　　　　Is taking flight toward glory,
　　　　　　Terrible as a God,
　　　　　　Radiant as the sun?
　　　　　　Come: let flowers rain on your hair,
　　　　　　Competing with the laurels;
　　　　　　Let the songs of glory sound
　　　　　　Along with songs of love.

AMNERIS   (Ah! Come, come, my love,
　　　　　　Intoxicate me . . . make my heart blissful!)

SLAVE GIRLS   Where now are the barbarian
　　　　　　Hordes of the foreigner?
　　　　　　Like mist they vanished
　　　　　　At the warrior's breath.
　　　　　　Come: receive, O victor,
　　　　　　The reward of glory;
　　　　　　Victory smiled on you,
　　　　　　Love will smile on you.

AMNERIS   (Ah! Come, come, my love,
　　　　　　Restore me with a cherished word again!)

The slave girls continue to dress Amneris. The little black-
amoor slaves perform a dance.

SLAVE GIRLS   Come: let flowers rain on your hair,
　　　　　　Competing with the laurels;
　　　　　　Let the songs of glory sound
　　　　　　Along with songs of love.

AMNERIS   (Ah! Come, come, my love,
　　　　　　Intoxicate me . . . make my heart blissful!)
　　　　　　Silence! Aïda is coming toward us . . .
　　　　　　Daughter of the vanquished,
　　　　　　Her grief is sacred to me.

At a sign from Amneris, the slave girls go off. Aïda enters,
carrying a crown.

AMNERIS   (As I see her again, the horrible
　　　　　　Suspicion is wakened in me . . .
　　　　　　Let the fatal mystery be rent at last!)
　　　　　　(*to Aïda, with feigned loving concern*)
　　　　　　The battle's outcome was dire for your people,
　　　　　　Poor Aïda! I share
　　　　　　The mourning that weighs on your heart.
　　　　　　I am your friend . . .

Tutto da me tu avrai ...
Vivrai felice!

AÏDA

Felice esser poss'io
Lungi dal suol natio,
Qui dove ignota
M'è la sorte del padre e dei fratelli?

AMNERIS

Ben ti compiango!
Pure hanno un confine
I mali di quaggiù ... Sanerà il tempo
Le angoscie del tuo core ...
E più che il tempo,
Un Dio possente ... amore.

AÏDA (*vivamente commossa*)

(Amore, amore! Gaudio ... tormento ...
Soave ebbrezza, ansia crudel ...
Ne' tuoi dolori la vita io sento ...
Un tuo sorriso mi schiude il ciel!)

AMNERIS (*guardano Aïda fissamente*)

(Ah! quel pallore ... quel turbamento
Svelan l'arcana febbre d'amor ...
D'interrogarla quasi ho sgomento ...
Divido l'ansie del suo terror.)

(*osservandola attentamente*)

Ebben: qual nuovo fremito
T'assal, gentil Aïda?
I tuoi segreti svelami,
All'amor mio t'affida ...
Tra i forti che pugnarono
Della tua patria a danno ...
Qualcuno ... un dolce affano ...
Forse ... a te in cor destò?

AÏDA

Che parli?

AMNERIS

A tutti barbara
Non si mostrò la sorte ...
Se in campo il duce impavido
Cadde trafitto a morte ...

AÏDA

Che mai dicesti? misera! ...

AMNERIS

Sì ... Radamès da' tuoi fu spento ...

AÏDA

Misera!

AMNERIS

E pianger puoi?

AÏDA

Per sempre io piangerò!

AMNERIS

Gli Dei t'han vendicata ...

AÏDA

Avvresi sempre a me furo i Numi ...

AMNERIS (*prorompendo con ira*)

Trema! in cor ti lessi ...
Tu l'ami ...

AÏDA

Io!...

AMNERIS

Non mentire!... Un detto ancora
E il vero saprò ...
Fissami in volto ...
Io t'ingannava ... Radamès vive ...

AÏDA (*con esaltazione, inginocchiandosi*)

Vive! ah grazie, o Numi!

                          You will receive everything from me . . .
                          You will live happily!
AÏDA   Can I be happy,
                          Far from my native land,
                          Here where I do not know
                          The fate of my father and brothers?
AMNERIS   I greatly pity you!
                          And yet there is an end
                          To the ills of this world . . . Time will heal
                          The anguish in your heart . . .
                          And more than time,
                          A mighty God . . . love.
AÏDA (*visibly moved*)
                          (Love, love! Bliss . . . torment . . .
                          Sweet ecstasy, cruel anxiety . . .
                          I feel life in your pain . . .
                          A smile from you opens heaven to me!)
AMNERIS (*observing Aïda closely*)
                          (Ah! That pallor . . . that turmoil
                          Reveal the mysterious fever of love . . .
                          I am almost afraid to question her . . .
                          I share her anxious terror.)
                          (*watching her with attention*)
                          Why, what now trembling
                          Seizes you, gentle Aïda?
                          Reveal your secrets to me,
                          Trust in my love . . .
                          Among the strong men who fought
                          Against your country . . .
                          Did one . . . perhaps . . . waken
                          A gentle longing in your heart?
AÏDA   What are you saying?
AMNERIS   Fate was not cruel
                          To all of them . . .
                          Even if the fearless general
                          Fell fatally wounded in the field . . .
AÏDA   What have you said? Wretched me! . . .
AMNERIS   Yes . . . Radamès was killed by your people . . .
AÏDA   Wretched me!
AMNERIS   And you can weep?
AÏDA   I shall weep forever!
AMNERIS   The Gods have avenged you . . .
AÏDA   The Gods have been against me always . . .
AMNERIS (*bursting out angrily*)
                          Tremble! I have read In your heart . . .
                          You love him . . .
AÏDA   I! . . .
AMNERIS   Do not lie! . . . Another word
                          And I will know the truth . . .
                          Look into my face . . .
                          I deceived you . . . Radamès is alive . . .
AÏDA (*beside herself, falling on her knees*)
                          Alive! Ah, the gods be thanked!

AMNERIS   E ancor mentir tu speri?
               (*nel massimo furore*)
               Sì... tu l'ami ... Ma l'amo
               Anch'io ... intendi tu?...
               Son tua rivale ... figlia de' Faraoni ...

AÏDA (*con orgoglio, alzandosi*)
               Mia rivale!... ebben sia pure ...
               Anch'io ... son tal ...
               (*reprimendosi e cadendo a' piedi d'Amneris*)
               Ah! che dissi mai?... pietà? perdono! ah!

               Pietà ti prenda del mio dolor ...
               È vero ... io l'amo d'immenso amor ...
               Tu sei felice, tu sei possente ...
               Io vivo solo per questo amor!
AMNERIS   Trema, vil schiava! Spezza il tuo core ...
               Segnar tua morte può quest'amore ...
               Del tuo destino arbitra sono,
               D'odio e vendetta le furie ho in cor.

AÏDA   Tu sei felice ... tu sei possente, ecc.
AMNERIS   Trema, vil schiava!, ecc.
CORO (*interno*)
               Su! del Nilo al sacro lido, ecc.
AMNERIS   Alla pompa che s'appresta,
               Meco, o schiava, assisterai;
               Tu prostrata nella polvere,
               Io sul trono accanto al Re.
AÏDA   Ah! pietà!... che più mi resta?
               Un deserto è la mia vita;
               Vivi e regna, il tuo furore
               Io tra breve placherò.
               Quest'amore che t'irrita
               Nella tomba spegnerò.
AMNERIS   Vien ... mi segui, apprenderai
               Se lottar tu puoi con me ...
AÏDA   Ah! pietà! Quest'amor
               Nella tomba io spegnerò, pietà!
CORO (*interno*)
               Guerra e morte allo stranier!

         Amneris parte.

AÏDA   Numi, pietà del mio martir,
               Speme non v'ha pel mio dolor.
               Numi, pietà del mio soffrir ...
               (*s'incammina verso la scena ... a stento ...*)
               Numi, pietà ... pietà!

Sull'ultima nota ... sarà scomparsa.

AMNERIS   And do you still hope to lie?
                   (at the peak of her fury)
                   Yes . . . you love him . . . But I love him
                   Also . . . do you understand? . . .
                   I am your rival . . . I, daughter of the
                        Pharaohs . . .

AÏDA *(with pride, standing up)*
                   My rival! . . . so be it then . . .
                   I too . . . am . . .
                   (checking herself and falling at Amneris's feet)
                   Ah! What have I said? . . . Pity! Forgiveness!
                        . . . Ah!
                   Have pity on my grief . . .
                   It's true . . . I love him with immense love . . .
                   You are happy, you are powerful . . .
                   I live only for this love!

AMNERIS   Tremble, base slave! Break your heart . . .
                   This love can mean your death . . .
                   I am the arbiter of your fate,
                   I have the furies of hate and revenge in my
                        heart.

AÏDA   You are happy . . . you are powerful, etc.

AMNERIS   Tremble, base slave! etc.

CHORUS *(within)*
                   On! Hasten to the Nile's sacred shore, etc.

AMNERIS   You, slave, will attend with me
                   The triumph that is being prepared;
                   You, prostrate in the dust,
                   And I on the throne beside the King.

AÏDA   Ah! Pity! . . . What have I left?
                   My life is a desert;
                   Live and reign, I will soon
                   Placate your fury.
                   I will extinguish in my grave
                   This love that annoys you.

AMNERIS   Come . . . follow me. You will learn
                   Whether you can compete with me . . .

AÏDA   Ah! Have pity! I will extinguish
                   This love in my grave, have pity!

CHORUS *(within)*
                   War and death to the foreigner!

Amneris goes out.

AÏDA   Gods, have pity on my torment,
                   There is no hope for my grief.
                   Gods, have pity on my suffering . . .
                   (She starts to walk off . . . painfully . . .)
                   Gods, pity . . . pity!

On the last note . . . she is gone.

SCENA SECONDA

Uno degli ingressi della città di Tebe. Sul davanti un
gruppo di palme. A destra il Tempio di Ammone. A sinistra
un trono sormontato da un baldacchino di porpora. Nel fondo
una porta trionfale. La scena è ingombra di popolo.

Entra il Re, seguito dai ministri, dai sacerdoti, capitani,
flabelliferi, porta insegne, ecc. Quindi, Amneris con Aïda e
schiave. Il Re va a sedere sul trono. Amneris prende posto
alla sinistra del Re.

POPOLO   Gloria all'Egitto, ad Iside
                Che il sacro suol protegge!
                Al Re che il Delta regge
                Inni festosi alziam!
                Gloria! Gloria! Gloria al Re!

DONNE   S'intrecci il loto al lauro
                Sui crin dei vincitori!
                Nembo gentil di fiori
                Stenda sull'armi un vel.
                Danziam, fanciulle egizie,
                Le mistiche carole,
                Come d'intorno al sole
                Danzano gli astri in ciel.

RAMFIS e SACERDOTI
                Della vittoria agli arbitri
                Supremi il guardo ergete;
                Grazie agli Dei rendete
                Nel fortunato dì.

Le truppe Egizie, precedute dalle fanfare, sfilano dinanzi
al Re. Seguono i carri di guerra, le insegne, i vasi sacri, le
statue degli Dei. Un drappello di danzatrici che recano i tesori
dei vinti. Da ultimo Radamès, sotto un baldacchino portato
da dodici uffiziali.

POPOLO   Vieni, o guerriero vindice,
                Vieni a gioir con noi;
                Sul passo degli eroi
                I lauri, i fior versiam! Gloria!

SACERDOTI   Agli arbitri supremi il guardo ergete.
                Grazie agli Dei rendete
                Nel fortunato dì. Grazie, grazie agli Dei!

Il Re scende dal trono per abbracciare Radamès.

IL RE   Salvator della patria, io ti saluto.
                Vieni, e mia figlia di sua man
                Ti porga il serto trionfale.

Radamès s'inchina davanti ad Amneris che gli porge la
corona.

IL RE (*a Radamès*)
                Ora, a me chiedi
                Quanto più brami.

SCENE TWO

One of the gates to the city of Thebes. In the foreground a group of palm trees. At right the Temple of Ammon. At left a throne beneath a purple canopy. In the background a triumphal arch. The scene is crowded with people.

The King enters, followed by his ministers, priests, captains, fan bearers, standard-bearers, etc. Then Amneris, with Aïda and slave girls. The King goes and sits on the throne. Amneris takes her place at his left.

PEOPLE   Glory to Egypt, to Isis,
Who protects the sacred soil!
To the King, who rules the Delta,
We raise our festive songs!
Glory! Glory! Glory to the King!

WOMEN   Let lotus be entwined with laurel
On the brows of the victors!
Let a gentle cloud of flowers
Cast a veil over the weapons.
Let us dance, Egyptian maidens,
Our mystic chants,
As the stars in heaven
Dance about the sun.

RAMFIS and PRIESTS
Lift up your eyes to the supreme
Arbiters of victory;
Give thanks to the Gods
On this day of good fortune.

The Egyptian troops, preceded by fanfares, parade past the King. They are followed by war chariots, standards, the sacred vessels, the statues of the Gods. A group of dancing girls carries the treasure of the conquered. Finally Radamès, under a canopy held up by twelve officers.

PEOPLE   Come, O avenging warrior,
Come and rejoice with us;
In the path of the heroes
Let us strew laurel and flowers! Glory!

PRIESTS   Lift up your eyes to the supreme arbiters.
Give thanks to the Gods
On this day of good fortune. Thanks, thanks, to
the Gods!

The King comes down from the throne to embrace Radamès.

THE KING   Savior of the country, I hail you.
Come, let my daughter give you
The triumphal crown with her own hands.

Radamès bows before Amneris, who gives him the crown.

THE KING *(to Radamès)*
Now, ask of me
What you want most.

Nulla a te negato sarà
In tal dì ... lo giuro
Per la corona mia, pei sacri Numi.

RADAMÈS   Concedi in pria che innanzi a te
Sien tratti i prigionier ...

Entrano fra le guardie i prigionieri Etiopi, ultimo Amonasro,
vestito da uffiziale Etiope.

RAMFIS e SACERDOTI
Grazie agli Dei rendete, ecc.

AÏDA *(lanciandosi verso Amonasro)*
Che veggo!... Egli?... Mio padre!

TUTTI   Suo padre!

AMNERIS   In poter nostro!...

AÏDA *(abbracciando il padre)*
Tu! prigionier!

AMONASRO *(piano ad Aïda)*
Non mi tradir!

IL RE *(ad Amonasro)*
T'appressa ... Dunque ... tu sei?...

AMONASRO   Suo padre. Anch'io pugnai ...
Vinti noi fummo ...
Morte invan cercai.
(accennando alla divisa che lo veste)
Quest'assisa ch'io vesto vi dica
Che il mio Re, la mia patria ho difeso;
Fu la sorte a nostr'armi nemica ...
Tornò vano de' forti l'ardir.
Al mio piè nella polve disteso
Giacque il Re da più colpi trafitto;
Se l'amor della patria è delitto
Siam rei tutti, siam pronti a morir!
(al Re con accento supplichevole)
Ma tu Re, tu signore possente,
A costoro ti volgi clemente ...
Oggi noi siam percossi dal fato,
Ah! doman voi potria il fato colpir.

AÏDA   Ma tu Re, tu signore possente, ecc.

SCHIAVE e PRIGIONIERI
Sì: dai Numi percossi noi siamo;
Tua pietà, tua clemenza imploriamo;
Ah, giammai di soffrir vi sia dato
Ciò che in oggi n'è dato soffrir!

RAMFIS e SACERDOTI
Struggi, o Re, queste ciurme feroci,
Chiudi il cor alle perfide voci;
Fur dai Numi votati alla morte,
Or de' Numi si compia il voler!
A morte! a morte! a morte!

POPOLO   Sacerdoti, gli sdegni placate;
L'umil prece dei vinti ascoltate;
E tu, o Re, tu possente, tu forte,
A clemenza dischiuda il pensier.
O Re, possente Re.

Nothing will be denied you
On such a day . . . I swear it
By my crown, by the sacred Gods.

RADAMÈS   First permit that the prisoners
Be brought before you . . .

Under guard the Ethiopian prisoners come in, Amonasro last, dressed as an Ethiopian officer.

RAMFIS and PRIESTS
Give thanks to the Gods, etc.

AÏDA *(rushing toward Amonasro)*
What do I see? . . . He? . . . My father!

ALL   Her father!

AMNERIS   In our power! . . .

AÏDA *(embracing her father)*
You! A prisoner!

AMONASRO *(softly to Aïda)*
Don't give me away!

THE KING *(to Amonasro)*
Approach . . . So . . . you are? . . .

AMONASRO   Her father. I also fought . . .
We were defeated . . .
I sought death, in vain.
(indicating the uniform he is wearing)
Let this uniform I am wearing tell you
That I defended my King and my country;
Fate was hostile to our arms . . .
The courage of the strong was useless.
At my feet in the dust
Lay the King, wounded many times;
If love of country is a crime
We are all guilty, we are ready to die!
(to the King in an entreating tone)
But you, O King, mighty lord,
Show clemency to them . . .
Today we have been buffeted by fate,
But tomorrow fate might strike you.

AÏDA   But you, O king, mighty lord, etc.

SLAVES and PRISONERS
Yes: we have been buffeted by the Gods;
We implore your pity, your clemency;
Ah, may you never be made to suffer
What we are made to suffer today!

RAMFIS and PRIESTS
Destroy, O King, these fierce hordes,
Shut your heart to their perfidious voices;
The Gods marked them for death,
Now let the will of the Gods be done!
To death! To death! To death!

PEOPLE   Priests, allay your scorn:
Hear the humble prayer of the defeated;
And you, O King, powerful and strong,
Open your thoughts to clemency.
O King, mighty King.

AMNERIS   (Quali sguardi sovr'essa ha rivolti!
Di qual fiamma balenano i volti!
Ed io sola, avvilita, rejetta?...
La vendetta mi rugge nel cor.)

RADAMÈS (*fissando Aïda*)
    (Il dolor che in quel volto favella
Al mio sguardo la rende più bella;
Ogni stilla del pianto adorato
Nel mio petto ravviva l'ardor.)

IL RE   Or che fausti ne arridon gli eventi
A costoro mostriamci clementi ...
La pietà sale ai Numi gradita
E rafferma de' prenci il poter.

RADAMÈS   Re: pei sacri Numi,
Per lo splendor della tua corona,
Compier giurasti il voto mio ...

IL RE   Giurai.

RADAMÈS   Ebbene: a te pei prigionieri Etiopi
Vita domando e libertà.

AMNERIS   (Per tutti!)

SACERDOTI   Morte ai nemici della patria!

POPOLO   Grazia per gl'infelici!

RAMFIS   Ascolta, o Re.
                 (*a Radamès*)
Tu pure, giovine eroe,
Saggio consiglio ascolta:
Son nemici e prodi sono ...
La vendetta hanno nel cor,
Fatti audaci dal perdono
Correranno all'armi ancor!

RADAMÈS   Spento Amonasro, il re guerrier,
Non resta speranza ai vinti.

RAMFIS   Almeno, arra di pace e securtà,
Fra noi resti col padre Aïda ...

IL RE   Al tuo consiglio io cedo.
Di securtà, di pace un miglior pegno
Or io vo' darvi.
Radamès, la patria
Tutto a te deve.
D'Amneris la mano premio ti sia.
Sovra l'Egitto un giorno
Con essa regnerai ...

AMNERIS   (Venga la schiava,
Venga a rapirmi l'amor mio ...
Se l'osa!)

RE e POPOLO   Gloria all'Egitto, ad Iside,
Che il sacro suol difende,
S'intrecci il loto al lauro
Sul crin del vincitor.

PRIGIONIERI e SCHIAVE
    Gloria al clemente Egizio,
Che i nostri ceppi ha sciolto,

AMNERIS (What looks he has turned toward her!
What flames flash in their faces!
And I, alone, sad, rejected? . . .
Vengeance roars in my heart.)

RADAMÈS (*looking at Aïda*)
(The grief that speaks in that face
Makes her more beautiful to my eyes;
Every adored teardrop
Rekindles the ardor in my heart.)

THE KING Now that events smile favorably on us,
Let us be clement toward those people . . .
Mercy rises, welcome, to the Gods
And strengthens the power of princes.

RADAMÈS King: by the sacred Gods,
By the splendor of your crown,
You swore to grant my wish . . .

THE KING I swore.

RADAMÈS Well then: I ask of you life and liberty
For the Ethiopian prisoners.

AMNERIS (For all!)

PRIESTS Death to the enemies of the fatherland!

PEOPLE Mercy for the unfortunates!

RAMFIS Hear me, O King.
(*to Radamès*)
And you too, young hero,
Listen to sage advice:
They are enemies and fighters . . .
They have revenge in their hearts,
Emboldened by this pardon,
They will hasten to arms again!

RADAMÈS With Amonasro dead, their warrior king,
No hope remains to the defeated.

RAMFIS As a pledge of peace and security,
At least let Aïda and her father stay with us . . .

THE KING I bow to your advice.
Now I want to give you a better pledge
Of security and peace.
Radamès, the fatherland
Owes you everything.
Let Amneris's hand be your reward.
With her one day
You will rule over Egypt . . .

AMNERIS (Let the slave come,
Let her come to steal my beloved . . .
If she dares!)

KING and PEOPLE
Glory to Egypt and to Isis,
Who protects the sacred soil,
Let lotus be entwined with laurel
On the brow of the victor.

PRISONERS and SLAVES
Glory to the clement Egyptian,
Who has undone our bonds,

Che ci ridona ai liberi
Solchi del patrio suol.

RAMFIS e SACERDOTI

Inni leviamo ad Iside,
Che il sacro suol difende!
Preghiam che i fati arridano
Fausti alla patria ognor.

AÏDA

(Qual speme omai più restami?
A lui la gloria, il trono ...
A me l'oblio ... le lacrime
D'un disperato amor.)

RADAMÈS

(D'avverso Nume il folgore
Sul capo mio discende ...
Ah no! d'Egitto il soglio
Non val d'Aïda il cor.)

AMNERIS

(Dall'inatteso giubilo
Inebbriata io sono;
Tutti in un dì si compiono
I sogni del mio cor.)

AMONASRO *(sottovoce ad Aïda)*

Fa cor: della tua patria
I lieti eventi aspetta;
Per noi della vendetta
Già prossimo è l'albor.

RE e POPOLO   Gloria all'Egitto, ecc.

RAMFIS e SACERDOTI

Inni leviam, ecc.

AÏDA   A me l'oblio, ecc.

AMNERIS   Tutte in un dì si compiono
Le gioie del mio cor.
Dall'inatteso gaudio
Inebbriata io sono, ecc.

RADAMÈS   Qual inatteso folgore!, ecc.

AMONASRO   Fa cor, ecc.

ATTO TERZO

Le rive del Nilo. Roccie di granito fra cui crescono dei palmizii. Sul vertice delle roccie il Tempio d'Iside per metà nascosto tra le fronde. È notte stellata. Splendore di luna.

CORO *(nel tempio)*

O tu che sei d'Osiride
Madre immortale e sposa,
Diva che i casti palpiti
Desti agli umani in cor;
Soccorri a noi pietosa,
Madre d'immenso amor.
Soccorri a noi, soccorri a noi.

Da una barca che approda alla riva, discendono Amneris, Ramfis, alcune donne coperte da fitto velo e guardie.

Who restores us to the free
Furrows of our native land.

RAMFIS and PRIESTS

Let us sing hymns to Isis,
Who defends the sacred soil!
Let us pray that fate will still
Smile favorably on the fatherland.

AÏDA

(What hope remains to me now?
For him, glory, the throne . . .
For me oblivion . . . the tears
Of a desperate love.)

RADAMÈS

(The thunderbolt of a hostile God
Descends upon my head . . .
Ah no! The throne of Egypt
Is not worth Aïda's heart.)

AMNERIS

(I am intoxicated
With this unexpected joy;
All in a single day
My heart's dreams are fulfilled.)

AMONASRO (*softly to Aïda*)

Take heart: await the happy days
Of your fatherland;
For us the dawn of revenge
Is already near.

KING and PEOPLE

Glory to Egypt, etc.

RAMFIS and PRIESTS

Let us sing hymns, etc.

AÏDA

For me oblivion, etc.

AMNERIS

All in a single day
My heart's joys are fulfilled.
With this unexpected bliss
I am intoxicated, etc.

RADAMÈS

The unexpected thunderbolt!, etc.

AMONASRO

Take heart, etc.

ACT THREE

The banks of the Nile. Granite cliffs, with palms growing among them. On the top of some cliffs the Temple of Isis, half hidden by palm fronds. A starry night. The moon is shining.

CHORUS (*in the temple*)

O thou who are the immortal
Mother and bride of Osiris,
Goddess who wakest the chaste
Beating of human hearts;
Succor us pityingly,
Mother of immense love.
Succor us, succor us.

From a boat that draws up to the bank, Amneris steps out, followed by Ramfis, some heavily veiled women, and guards.

RAMFIS (*ad Amneris*)
<blockquote>
Vieni d'Iside al tempio: alla vigilia
Delle tue nozze invoca
Della Diva il favore.
Iside legge de' mortali nel core;
Ogni mistero degli umani
A lei è noto.
</blockquote>

AMNERIS
<blockquote>
Sì, io pregherò che Radamès
Mi doni tutto il suo cor,
Come il mio cor a lui
Sacro è per sempre ...
</blockquote>

RAMFIS
<blockquote>
Andiamo. Pregherai fino all'alba;
Io sarò teco.
</blockquote>

Tutti entrano nel tempio.

CORO (*nel tempio*)
<blockquote>
Soccorri a noi, ecc.
</blockquote>

Aïda entra cautamente, coperta da un velo.

AÏDA
<blockquote>
Qui Radamès verrà! ...
Che vorrà dirmi? Io tremo! ...
Ah! se tu vieni a recarmi,
O crudel, l'ultimo addio,
Del Nilo i cupi vortici
Mi daran tomba ... e pace forse ...
E pace forse e oblio.
Oh, patria mia, mai più,
Mai più ti rivedrò!
O cieli azzurri, a dolci aure native,
</blockquote>

<blockquote>
Dove sereno il mio mattin brillò ...
O verdi colli ... o profumate rive ...
O patria mia, mai più ti rivedrò!
No ... no ... mai più, mai più!
O fresche valli, o queto asil beato
Che un dì promesso dall'amor mi fu ...
Or che d'amore il sogno è dileguato ...
O patria mia, non ti vedrò mai più!
</blockquote>

Aïda si volge verso Amonasro che compare.

AÏDA
<blockquote>
Ciel! mio padre!
</blockquote>

AMONASRO
<blockquote>
A te grave cagion
M'adduce, Aïda.
Nulla sfugge al mio sguardo.
D'amor ti struggi per Radamès ...
Ei t'ama ... qui lo attendi.
Dei Faraon la figlia è tua rivale ...
Razza infame, abborrita
E a noi fatale!
</blockquote>

AÏDA
<blockquote>
E in suo potere io sto! ...
Io, d'Amonasro figlia! ...
</blockquote>

AMONASRO
<blockquote>
In poter di lei! ... No! ... se lo brami
La possente rival tu vincerai,
E patria, e trono, e amor,
Tutto tu avrai.
</blockquote>

RAMFIS (*to Amneris*)
Come to the Temple of Isis: on the eve
Of your marriage implore
The Goddess's favor.
Isis reads the hearts of mortals;
Every human mystery
Is known to her.

AMNERIS   Yes, I will pray that Radamès
Give me all of his heart,
As my heart is consecrated
To him forever . . .

RAMFIS   Let us go. You will pray until dawn;
I will be with you.

They all go into the temple.

CHORUS (*in the temple*)
Succor us, etc.

Aïda enters cautiously, covered by a veil.

AÏDA   Radamès will come here! . . .
What can he want to say to me? I tremble! . . .
Ah! If you are coming,
O cruel one, to bid me a last farewell,
The dark eddies of the Nile
Will give me a grave . . . and perhaps peace . . .
And perhaps peace and forgetfulness.
O my country, never,
Never shall I see you again!
O blue skies, O gentle native breezes,
Where the morning of my life serenely
    shone . . .
O green hills . . . O perfumed shores . . .
O my country, never shall I see you again!
No . . . no . . . never, never again!
O cool valleys, O calm, happy refuge
That love promised me one day . . .
Now that the dream of love has vanished . . .
O my country, I'll never see you again!

Aïda turns toward Amonasro, who has appeared.

AÏDA   Heaven! My father!

AMONASRO   A serious matter brings me
To you, Aïda.
Nothing escapes my eyes.
You are consumed with love for Radamès . . .
He loves you . . . you are waiting for him here.
The daughter of the Pharaohs is your rival . . .
Infamous, detested race,
And fatal to us!

AÏDA   And I am in her power! . . .
I, daughter of Amonasro! . . .

AMONASRO   In her power! . . . No! . . . If you wish it
You will defeat your powerful rival,
And homeland, throne, love,
You will have them all.

Rivedrai le foreste imbalsamate,
Le fresche valli, i nostri templi d'ôr!...

AÏDA *(con trasporto)*

Rivedrò le foreste imbalsamate!...
Le fresche valli ... i nostri templi d'ôr!

AMONASRO   Sposa felice a lui che amasti tanto,
Tripudii immensi ivi potrai gioir ...

AÏDA *(con espansione)*

Un giorno solo di sì dolce incanto ...
Un'ora, un'ora di tal gioia, e poi morir!

AMONASRO   Pur rammenti che a noi l'Egizio immite
Le case, i templi e l'are profanò ...
Trasse in ceppi le vergini rapite ...
Madri ... vecchi ... fanciulli ei trucidò.

AÏDA   Ah! ben rammento quegl'infausti giorni!
Rammento i lutti che il mio cor soffrì!
Deh! fate, o Numi, che per noi ritorni
L'alba invocata de' sereni dì.

AMONASRO   Non fia che tardi. In armi ora si desta
Il popol nostro; tutto è pronto già ...
Vittoria avrem ... Solo a saper mi resta
Qual sentier il nemico seguirà ...

AÏDA   Chi scoprirlo potria? Chi mai?

AMONASRO   Tu stessa!

AÏDA   Io?...

AMONASRO   Radamès so che qui attendi ...
                              (con intenzione)
Ei t'ama ... ei conduce gli Egizii ...

Intendi?...

AÏDA   Orrore! Che mi consigli tu?
No! no! giammai!

AMONASRO *(con impeto selvaggio)*

Su, dunque, sorgete,
Egizie coorti!
Col fuoco struggete
Le nostre città ...
Spargete il terrore,
Le stragi, le morti ...
Al vostro furore
Più freno non v'ha.

AÏDA   Ah! padre!... padre!...

AMONASRO *(respingendola)*

Mia figlia ti chiami!

AÏDA *(atterrita e supplichevole)*

Pietà! pietà! pietà!

AMONASRO   Flutti di sangue scorrono
Sulle città dei vinti ...
Vedi?... dai negri vortici
Si levano gli estinti ...
Ti additan essi e gridano:
"Per te la patria muor!"

AÏDA   Pietà! pietà! padre, pietà!

You will see again the aromatic forests,
The cool valleys, our golden temples! . . .

AÏDA (*ecstatic*)
I'll see again the aromatic forests! . . .
The cool valleys . . . our golden temples!

AMONASRO
The happy bride of the man you love so,
Great bliss you will enjoy there . . .

AÏDA (*opening her heart*)
A single day of such sweet enchantment . . .
An hour, an hour of such joy, and then to die!

AMONASRO
Remember, then, that the cruel Egyptian
Profaned our houses, temples, and altars . . .
Dragged off in chains the captured maidens . . .
He slaughtered mothers . . . old men . . .
children.

AÏDA
Ah! Well I remember those unhappy days!
I remember the mourning my heart suffered!
Ah! Grant, O Gods, that the prayed-for dawn
Of peaceful days return to us.

AMONASRO
Let it not delay. Our people are rising
In arms now; now everything is ready . . .
We'll win the victory . . . I have only to learn
What road the enemy will take . . .

AÏDA
Who could ever discover that? Who?

AMONASRO
You yourself!

AÏDA
I? . . .

AMONASRO
I know you are waiting here for Radamès . . .
(*meaningfully*)
He loves you . . . He is leading the
Egyptians . . .
You understand? . . .

AÏDA
Horror! What are you suggesting to me?
No! No! Never!

AMONASRO (*with savage vehemence*)
On, then! Arise,
Egyptian cohorts!
With fire destroy
Our cities . . .
Sow terror,
Slaughter, death . . .
There is no obstacle
To your fury now.

AÏDA
Ah, Father! . . . Father! . . .

AMONASRO (*thrusting her away*)
You call yourself my daughter!

AÏDA (*terrified and pleading*)
Have pity! Pity! Pity!

AMONASRO
Rivers of blood flow
Over the cities of the defeated . . .
You see? . . . From their black eddies
Rise the dead . . .
They point to you and shout:
"Because of you, the fatherland dies!"

AÏDA
Pity! Pity! Father, have pity!

AMONASRO   Una larva orribile
              Fra l'ombre a noi s'affaccia ...
              Trema! le scarni braccia
              Sul capo tuo levò ...
AÏDA   Ah! padre!... No!... Ah!...
AMONASRO   Tua madre ell'è ... ravvisala ...
              Ti maledice ...
AÏDA (*nel massimo terrore*)
              Ah, no! ah, no!... padre, pietà, pietà!
AMONASRO (*respingendola*)
              Non sei mia figlia ...
              Dei Faraoni tu sei la schiava!
AÏDA (*con un grido*)
              Ah, pietà! pietà!
                  (*trascinandosi a stento ai piedi del padre*)
              Padre! ... a costoro ... schiava ... non sono ...
              Non maledirmi ... non imprecarmi ...
              Ancor tua figlia potrai chiamarmi ...
              Della mia patria degna sarò.
AMONASRO   Pensa che un popolo, vinto, straziato
              Per te soltanto risorger può ...
AÏDA   Oh patria! oh patria ...
              Quanto mi costi!
AMONASRO   Coraggio! ei giunge ...
              Là tutto udrò ...

       Si nasconde fra i palmizi. Arriva Radamès.

RADAMÈS   Pur ti riveggo, mia dolce Aïda ...
AÏDA   T'arresta, vanne ... che speri ancor?
RADAMÈS   A te dappresso l'amor mi guida.
AÏDA   Te i riti attendono d'un altro amor.
              D'Amneris sposo ...
RADAMÈS   Che parli mai?...
              Te sola, Aïda, te deggio amar.
              Gli Dei m'ascoltano,
              Tu mia sarai.
AÏDA   D'uno spergiuro non ti macchiar!
              Prode t'amai, non t'amerei spergiuro.

RADAMÈS   Dell'amor mio dubiti, Aïda?
AÏDA   E come speri sottrarti
              D'Amneris ai vezzi,
              Del Re al voler, del tuo popolo ai voti,
              Dei Sacerdoti all'ira?
RADAMÈS   Odimi, Aïda.
              Nel fiero anelito di nuova guerra
              Il suolo Etiope si ridestò ...
              I tuoi già invadono la nostra terra,
              Io degli Egizii duce sarò.
              Fra il suon, fra i plausi della vittoria,
              Al Re mi prostro, gli svelo il cor ...

AMONASRO	A horrible form
	Comes toward us from the shadows ...
	Tremble! Its wasted arms
	Are raised toward your head ...
AÏDA	Ah, father! ... No! ... Ah! ...
AMONASRO	It is your mother ... recognize her ...
	She curses you ...
AÏDA *(filled with terror)*	
	Ah, no! Ah, no! ... Father, pity, pity!
AMONASRO *(rejecting her)*	
	You are not my daughter ...
	You are the slave of the Pharaohs!
AÏDA *(with a cry)*	
	Ah, pity! Pity!
	(dragging herself painfully to her father's feet)
	Father! ... I am not ... their ... slave ...
	Don't curse me ... don't revile me ...
	You can still call me your daughter ...
	I shall be worthy of my country.
AMONASRO	Think, a martyred, defeated people
	Can rise again only through you ...
AÏDA	Oh, fatherland! ... Fatherland ...
	What you are costing me!
AMONASRO	Be brave! He is coming ...
	There I will hear everything ...

He hides among the palm trees. Radamès arrives.

RADAMÈS	I see you again, my sweet Aïda ...
AÏDA	Stop, Go away ... What can you hope for still?
RADAMÈS	Love leads me to you.
AÏDA	The rites of another love await you.
	Husband of Amneris ...
RADAMÈS	What are you saying? ...
	Only you, Aïda, can I love.
	May the Gods hear me.
	You will be mine.
AÏDA	Don't stain yourself with a false oath!
	I loved you as a brave man; I wouldn't love you
	in perjury.
RADAMÈS	Do you doubt my love, Aïda?
AÏDA	How can you hope to elude
	The charms of Amneris,
	The will of the King, the people's desire,
	And the wrath of the priests?
RADAMÈS	Hear me, Aïda.
	The Ethiopian soil has wakened again
	To the fierce impulse of a new war ...
	Your people are already invading our land,
	I will be leader of the Egyptians.
	In the din and cheers of victory,
	I'll prostrate myself before the King and open
	my heart ...

Sarai tu il serto della mia gloria,
Vivrem beati d'eterno amor.

AÏDA   Nè d'Amneris paventi
Il vindice furor? la sua vendetta,
Come folgor tremenda,
Cadrà su me, sul padre mio, su tutti.

RADAMÈS   Io vi difendo.

AÏDA   Invan! tu nol potresti ...
Pur ... se tu m'ami ... ancor s'apre
Una via di scampo a noi ...

RADAMÈS   Quale?

AÏDA   Fuggir ...

RADAMÈS   Fuggire!

AÏDA (*colla più viva espansione*)
Fuggiam gli ardori inospiti
Di queste lande ignude;
Una novella patria
Al nostro amor si schiude ...
Là ... tra foreste vergini,
Di fiori profumate,
In estasi beate
La terra scorderem.

RADAMÈS   Sovra una terra estrania
Teco fuggir dovrei!
Abbandonar la patria,
L'are de' nostri Dei!
Il suol dov'io raccolsi
Di gloria i primi allori,
Il ciel de' nostri amori,
Come scordar potrem?

AÏDA   Là ... tra foreste vergini, ecc.

RADAMÈS   Il ciel de' nostri amori, ecc.

AÏDA   Sotto il mio ciel più libero
L'amor ne fia concesso;
Ivi nel tempio istesso
Gli stessi Numi avrem.
Fuggiam, fuggiam.

RADAMÈS (*esitante*)
Aïda!

AÏDA   Tu non m'ami ... Va!

RADAMÈS   Non t'amo!

AÏDA   Va!

RADAMÈS   Mortal giammai nè Dio
Arse d'amor al par del mio possente.

AÏDA   Va ... va ... T'attende all'ara Amneris ...

RADAMÈS   No!... giammai!...

AÏDA   Giammai, dicesti? Allor piombi la scure
Su me, sul padre mio ...

RADAMÈS   Ah no! fuggiamo!
(*con appassionata risoluzione*)
Sì: fuggiam da queste mura,
Al deserto insiem fuggiamo;

> You will be the crown of my glory,
> We will live in the bliss of eternal love.

AÏDA
> Do you not fear the vindictive
> Fury of Amneris? Her vengeance,
> Like a terrible thunderbolt,
> Will fall on me, my father, on everyone.

RADAMÈS
> I will defend all of you.

AÏDA
> In vain! You couldn't . . .
> And yet . . . if you love me . . . there is still
> An escape open to us . . .

RADAMÈS
> What?

AÏDA
> To flee . . .

RADAMÈS
> To flee!

AÏDA (*with great excitement*)
> Let us flee the unfriendly heat
> Of these barren plains;
> A new fatherland
> Opens to our love . . .
> There . . . among the virgin forests,
> Perfumed with flowers,
> In blissful ecstasies
> We will forget the earth.

RADAMÈS
> Into a foreign country
> I should flee with you!
> Abandon my fatherland,
> The altars of our Gods!
> The land where I gathered
> The first laurels of glory,
> The sky of our love,
> How could we forget them?

AÏDA
> There . . . among the virgin forests, etc.

RADAMÈS
> The sky of our love, etc.

AÏDA
> Under my sky a freer love
> Would be granted us;
> There in the same temple
> We will have the same Gods.
> Let us flee, flee.

RADAMÈS (*hesitantly*)
> Aïda!

AÏDA
> You don't love me . . . Go!

RADAMÈS
> I don't love you!

AÏDA
> Go!

RADAMÈS
> No mortal or God
> Ever burned with a love as powerful as mine.

AÏDA
> Go . . . go . . . Amneris awaits you at the altar.

RADAMÈS
> No! . . . Never! . . .

AÏDA
> Never, you said? Then let the ax fall
> On me, on my father . . .

RADAMÈS
> Ah no! Let us flee!
> (*with passionate resolve*)
> Yes: let us flee from these walls,
> Let us flee together to the desert;

Qui sol regna la sventura,
Là si schiude un ciel d'amor.
I deserti interminati
A noi talamo saranno,
Su noi gli astri brilleranno
Di più limpido fulgor.

AÏDA   Nella terra avventurata
De' miei padri, il ciel ne attende;
Ivi l'aura è imbalsamata,
Ivi il suolo è aromi e fior.
Fresche valli e verdi prati
A noi talamo saranno,
Su noi gli astri brilleranno
Di più limpido fulgor.

AÏDA e RADAMÈS
Vieni meco, insiem fuggiamo
Questa terra di dolor.
Vieni meco ... t'amo, t'amo!
A noi duce fia l'amor.

S'allontanano rapidamente, ad un tratto Aïda s'arresta.

AÏDA   Ma, dimmi: per qual via
Eviterem le schiere degli armati?

RADAMÈS   Il sentier scelto dai nostri
A piombar sul nemico fia deserto
Fino a domani ...

AÏDA   E quel sentier?...

RADAMÈS   Le gole di Nàpata ...

Amonasro esce.

AMONASRO   Di Nàpata le gole!
Ivi saranno i miei ...

RADAMÈS   Oh! chi ci ascolta? . . .

AMONASRO   D'Aïda il padre e degli Etiopi il Re.

RADAMÈS (*nella massima agitazione e sorpresa*)
Tu!... Amonasro!... tu!... il Re?
Numi! che dissi?... No ... non è ver ...

No ... no ... non è ver ... no!
Sogno ... delirio è questo ....

AÏDA   Ah no! ti calma, ascoltami,
All'amor mio t'affida.

AMONASRO   A te l'amor d'Aïda
Un soglio innalzerà.

RADAMÈS   Io son disonorato! Io son disonorato!
Per te tradii la patria!

AÏDA   Ti calma!... Ah no!...

AMONASRO   No: tu non sei colpevole,
Era voler del fato ...
Vien: oltre il Nil ne attendono
I prodi a noi devoti.
Là del tuo core i voti
Coronerà l'amor.
(*trascinando Radamès*)

> Here only misfortune reigns,
> There a heaven of love opens.
> The boundless deserts
> Will be our marriage bed,
> The stars will shine over us
> With a clearer radiance.

AÏDA

> In the blessed land
> Of my fathers, heaven awaits us;
> There the air is perfumed,
> There the earth is aroma and flowers.
> Cool valleys and green meadows
> Will be our marriage bed,
> The stars will shine over us
> With a clearer radiance.

AÏDA and RADAMÈS

> Come with me, we will flee together
> From this land of grief.
> Come with me . . . I love you, I love you!
> Love will be our guide.

They start off quickly, but suddenly Aïda stops.

AÏDA

> But, tell me: on what road
> Can we avoid the hosts of soldiers?

RADAMÈS

> The road chosen by our armies
> To fall on the enemy will be deserted
> Until tomorrow . . .

AÏDA

> What road? . . .

RADAMÈS

> The gorge of Nàpata . . .

Amonasro comes out.

AMONASRO

> The gorge of Nàpata!
> My men will be there . . .

RADAMÈS

> Oh! Who is listening to us? . . .

AMONASRO

> Aïda's father, the Ethiopians' King.

RADAMÈS (*profoundly disturbed and surprised*)

> You! . . . Amonasro! . . . You! . . . The King?
> Gods! What have I said? . . . No . . . it's not
> true. . .
> No . . . no . . . it's not true . . . no!
> This is a dream . . . a nightmare . . .

AÏDA

> Ah no! Calm yourself, listen to me,
> Trust in my love.

AMONASRO

> Aïda's love will erect
> A throne for you.

RADAMÈS

> I am dishonored! I am dishonored!
> For you I betrayed the fatherland!

AÏDA

> Calm yourself! . . . Ah no! . . .

AMONASRO

> No: you are not guilty,
> It was the will of fate . . .
> Come: beyond the Nile
> Soldiers devoted to us are waiting.
> There love will fulfill
> The desires of your heart.
> (*drawing Radamès away*)

Vieni, vieni, vieni.

Amneris esce dal tempio, indi Ramfis, sacerdoti e guardie.

AMNERIS   Traditor!
AÏDA   La mia rival!
AMONASRO   L'opra mia a strugger vieni! Muori!

Si avventa ad Amneris con un pugnale. Radamès si frappone.

RADAMÈS   Arresta, insano!...
AMONASRO   Oh rabbia!
RAMFIS   Guardie, olà!
RADAMÈS (*ad Aïda e Amonasro*)
               Presto!... fuggite!...
AMONASRO (*trascinando Aïda*)
               Vieni, o figlia!
RAMFIS (*alle guardie*)
               L'inseguite!
RADAMÈS (*a Ramfis*)
               Sacerdote, io resto a te.

ATTO QUARTO

SCENA PRIMA

*Sala nel palazzo del Re. Alla sinistra, una gran porta che
mette alla sala sotterranea delle sentenze. Andito a destra che
conduce alla prigione di Radamès. Amneris mestamente atteg-
giata davanti la porta del sotterraneo.*

AMNERIS   L'abborrita rivale a me sfuggia ...
               Dai sacerdoti Radamès attende
               Dei traditor la pena ...
               Traditor egli non è ... Pur rivelò
               Di guerra l'alto segreto ...
               Egli fuggir volea ... con lei fuggire ...
               Traditori tutti! a morte! a morte!...
               Oh! che mai parlo?
               Io l'amo, io l'amo sempre ...
               Disperato, insano è quest'amor
               Che la mia vita strugge.
               Oh! s'ei potesse amarmi!...
               Vorrei salvarlo ... E come?
               Si tenti!
               Guardie: Radamès qui venga.

Radamès viene condotto dalle guardie.

AMNERIS   Già i sacerdoti adunansi
               Arbitri del tuo fato;
               Pur dell'accusa orribile
               Scolparti ancor t'è dato;
               Ti scolpa, e la tua grazia

Come, come, come.

*Amneris comes out of the temple, later followed by Ramfis,
the priests, and guards.*

AMNERIS   Traitor!
AÏDA   My rival!
AMONASRO   You come to destroy my work! Die!

*He hurls himself toward Amneris with a dagger. Radamès
stands between them.*

RADAMÈS   Stop, madman! . . .
AMONASRO   Oh rage!
RAMFIS   Here, guards!
RADAMÈS (*to Aïda and Amonasro*)
               Hurry! . . . Flee! . . .
AMONASRO (*dragging off Aïda*)
               Come, Daughter!
RAMFIS (*to the guards*)
               Follow them!
RADAMÈS (*to Ramfis*)
               Priest, I remain here, in your hands.

ACT FOUR

SCENE ONE

*A hall in the King's palace. At left, a great door that leads
to the underground judgment chamber. At right, a corridor
leading to Radamès's prison. Amneris is standing sadly outside
the dungeon door.*

AMNERIS   My detested rival escaped me . . .
               Radamès is awaiting the punishment
               Of traitors from the priests . . .
               He is no traitor . . . And yet he revealed
               The deep war secret . . .
               He wanted to flee . . . to flee with her . . .
               Traitors all! To death with them! Death! . . .
               Oh! What have I said?
               I love him, I love him still . . .
               Desperate, insane is this love·
               That is destroying my life.
               Oh! If he could love me! . . .
               I want to save him . . . But how?
               Let me try!
               Guards! Have Radamès come here.

Radamès is brought in by the guards.

AMNERIS   Already the priests are meeting,
               The arbiters of your fate;
               And yet you still are allowed
               To defend yourself against the horrible charge;
               Defend yourself, and I will plead

Io pregherò dal trono
E nunzia di perdono,
Di vita a te sarò.

RADAMÈS Di mie discolpe i giudici
Mai non udran l'accento;
Dinanzi ai Numi, agli uomini
Nè vil, nè reo mi sento.
Profferse il labbro incauto
Fatal segreto, è vero,
Ma puro il mio pensiero
E l'onor mio restò.

AMNERIS Salvati dunque e scolpati.

RADAMÈS No.

AMNERIS Tu morrai ...

RADAMÈS La vita abborro;
D'ogni gaudio la fonte inaridita,
Svanita ogni speranza,
Sol bramo di morir.

AMNERIS Morire!... Ah! tu dei vivere!...
Sì, all'amor mio vivrai;
Per te le angoscie orribili
Di morte io già provai;
T'amai, soffersi tanto ...
Vegliai le notti in pianto ...
E patria, e trono, e vita
Tutto darei, tutto darei per te.

RADAMÈS Per essa anch'io la patria
E l'onor mio tradia ...

AMNERIS Di lei non più ...

RADAMÈS L'infamia m'attende
E vuoi ch'io viva?...
Misero appien mi festi,
Aïda a me togliesti,
Spenta l'hai forse ...
E in dono offri la vita a me?

AMNERIS Io ... di sua morte origine!
No!... vive Aïda ...

RADAMÈS Vive!

AMNERIS Nei disperati aneliti
Dell'orde fuggitive
Sol cadde il padre ...

RADAMÈS Ed ella?...

AMNERIS Sparve, nè più novella s'ebbe ...

RADAMÈS Gli Dei l'adducano
Salva alle patrie mura,
E ignori la sventura
Di chi per lei morrà!

AMNERIS Ma, s'io ti salvo, giurami
Che più non la vedrai ...

RADAMÈS Nol posso!...

AMNERIS A lei rinunzia per sempre ...
E tu vivrai!...

	For your pardon from the throne,
	And for you I will be
	The messenger of forgiveness and life.
RADAMÈS	The judges will never hear
	A word of self-defense from me;
	Before the Gods and men,
	I do not feel base or guilty.
	My impulsive lips revealed
	A fatal secret, it's true,
	But my thoughts and my honor
	Remained pure.
AMNERIS	Save yourself, then, and defend yourself.
RADAMÈS	No.
AMNERIS	You will die . . .
RADAMÈS	I loathe life;
	The source of all joy has dried up,
	All hope vanished,
	I long only to die.
AMNERIS	Die! . . . Ah! You must live! . . .
	Yes, you will live, for my love;
	I have already experienced
	Death's horrible anguish because of you;
	I loved you, I suffered so . . .
	I lay awake nights in tears . . .
	And fatherland, throne, my life,
	All, all I would give for you.
RADAMÈS	For her I too betrayed the fatherland
	And my honor . . .
AMNERIS	No more of her . . .
RADAMÈS	Dishonor awaits me,
	And you want me to live? . . .
	You made me completely wretched,
	You took Aïda from me,
	Perhaps you have killed her . . .
	And you offer me life as a gift?
AMNERIS	I . . . cause of her death!
	No . . . Aïda is alive . . .
RADAMÈS	Alive!
AMNERIS	In the desperate race
	Of the fleeing hordes
	Only her father fell . . .
RADAMÈS	And she? . . .
AMNERIS	She vanished, nor was there news of her . . .
RADAMÈS	May the Gods lead her
	Safely to her native walls,
	And may she never know the misfortune
	Of him who will die for her!
AMNERIS	But, if I save you, swear to me
	That you will not see her again . . .
RADAMÈS	I cannot! . . .
AMNERIS	Give her up forever . . .
	And you will live! . . .

RADAMÈS	Nol posso!...
AMNERIS	Anco una volta: a lei rinunzia ...
RADAMÈS	È vano ...
AMNERIS	Morir vuoi dunque, insano?
RADAMÈS	Pronto a morir son già.
AMNERIS	Chi ti salva, sciagurato,
	Dalla sorte che t'aspetta?
	In furore hai tu cangiato
	Un amor ch'egual non ha.
	De' miei pianti la vendetta
	Or dal ciel si compirà.
RADAMÈS	È la morte un ben supremo
	Se per lei morir m'è dato;
	Nel subir l'estremo fato
	Gaudii immensi il cor avrà.
AMNERIS	Ah! chi ti salva?
	Dei miei pianti la vendetta, ecc.
RADAMÈS	L'ira umana più non temo,
	Temo sol la tua pietà.

Amneris cade desolata su un sedile. Radamès parte circondato dalle guardie.

AMNERIS	Ohimè!... morir mi sento ...
	Oh! chi lo salva?
	(*soffocata dal pianto*)
	E in poter di costoro
	Io stessa lo gettai!...
	Ora, a te impreco, atroce gelosia,
	Che la sua morte e il lutto eterno
	Del mio cor segnasti!

I sacerdoti attraversano la scena ed entrano nel sotterraneo.

AMNERIS (*vedendo i sacerdoti*)
      Ecco i fatali, gl'inesorati
      Ministri di morte ...
      Oh! ch'io non vegga
      Quelle bianche larve!
          (*si copre il volto colle mani*)
      E in poter di costoro
      Io stessa lo gettai!...

RAMFIS e SACERDOTI (*nel sotterraneo*)
      Spirto del Nume, sovra noi discendi!
      Ne avviva al raggio dell'eterna luce;
      Pel labbro nostro tua giustizia apprendi.

AMNERIS
      Numi, pietà del mio straziato core ...
      Egli è innocente, lo salvate, o Numi!
      Disperato, tremendo è il mio dolore!

Radamès fra le guardie attraversa la scena e scende nel sotterraneo. Amneris, al vederlo, mette un grido.

RAMFIS e SACERDOTI
      Spirto del Nume, sovra noi discendi!

AMNERIS   Oh, chi lo salva? Ohimè! mi sento morir!

RADAMÈS	I cannot! . . .
AMNERIS	Once more: give her up . . .
RADAMÈS	It's useless . . .
AMNERIS	You want to die then, madman?
RADAMÈS	I am already prepared to die.
AMNERIS	Who will save you, wretch,
	From the fate that awaits you?
	You have changed into fury
	A love that has no equal.
	Now revenge for my weeping
	Will be taken by heaven.
RADAMÈS	Death is the supreme boon,
	If I am to die for her;
	In submitting to my final destiny
	My heart will have immense joy.
AMNERIS	Ah! Who will save you?
	Revenge for my weeping, etc.
RADAMÈS	I fear human wrath no longer.
	I fear only your pity.

Amneris sinks on to a bench desolately. Radamès leaves, surrounded by guards.

AMNERIS	Alas! . . . I feel I'm dying . . .
	Oh! Who will save him?
	(*choked with tears*)
	And I myself cast him
	Into the power of those men! . . .
	Now I curse you, terrible jealousy,
	Which determined his death
	And the eternal mourning of my heart!

The priests cross the stage and go into the dungeon.

AMNERIS (*seeing the priests*)
    There are the fatal, inexorable
    Ministers of death . . .
    Oh! Let me not see
    Their white forms!
    (*covers her face with her hands*)
    And I myself cast him
    Into the power of those men! . . .

RAMFIS and PRIESTS (*in the dungeon*)
    Spirit of the God, descend unto us!
    Fill us with the ray of the eternal light;
    Express thy justice through our lips.

AMNERIS   Gods, have pity on my tormented heart . . .
    He is innocent, save him, O Gods!
    My grief is desperate, terrible!

Radamès, with his guards, crosses the stage and goes down into the dungeon. Seeing him, Amneris cries out.

RAMFIS and PRIESTS
    Spirit of the God, descend unto us!

AMNERIS   Oh, who will save him? Alas, I feel I'm dying!

RAMFIS	Radamès!... Radamès!... Radamès!... Tu rivelasti della patria I segreti allo straniero ... Discolpati!
SACERDOTI	Discolpati!
RAMFIS	Egli tace ... Traditor!
SACERDOTI	Traditor!
AMNERIS	Ah, pietà!... egli è innocente, Numi, pietà, Numi, pietà!
RAMFIS	Radamès!... Radamès!... Radamès!... Tu disertasti dal campo Il dì che precedea la pugna. Discolpati!
SACERDOTI	Discolpati!
RAMFIS	Egli taci ... Traditor!
SACERDOTI	Traditor!
AMNERIS	Ah, pietà! ah! lo salvate, Numi, pietà, Numi, pietà!
RAMFIS	Radamès!... Radamès!... Radamès!... Tua fe' violasti, Alla patria spergiuro, al Re, all'onor. Discolpati!
SACERDOTI	Discolpati!
RAMFIS	Egli tace! Traditor!
SACERDOTI	Traditor!
AMNERIS	Ah! pietà! Ah! lo salvate, Numi, pietà, Numi, pietà!

RAMFIS e SACERDOTI

> Radamès: è deciso il tuo fato;
> Degli infami la morte tu avrai;
> Sotto l'ara del Nume sdegnato
> A te vivo fia schiuso l'avel!

AMNERIS

> A lui vivo ... la tomba ...
> Oh! gl'infami! nè di sangue
> Son paghi giammai ...
> E si chiaman ministri del ciel!

I sacerdoti escono dal sotterraneo.

RAMFIS e SACERDOTI

> Traditor! traditor! traditor!

AMNERIS (*investendo i sacerdoti*)

> Sacerdoti; compiste un delitto!
> Tigri infami di sangue assetate ...
> Voi la terra ed i Numi oltraggiate ...
> Voi punite chi colpe non ha.

RAMFIS e SACERDOTI

> È traditor! morrà!

AMNERIS (*a Ramfis*)

> Sacerdote: quest'uomo che uccidi,
> Tu lo sai ... da me un giorno fu amato ...
> L'anatema d'un core straziato
> Col suo sangue su te ricadrà!

RAMFIS	Radamès! ... Radamès! ... Radamès! ... You revealed the fatherland's secrets To the foreigner ... Defend yourself!
PRIESTS	Defend yourself!
RAMFIS	He is silent ... Traitor!
PRIESTS	Traitor!
AMNERIS	Ah, have mercy! ... He is innocent, Gods, pity, pity!
RAMFIS	Radamès! ... Radamès! ... Radamès! ... You deserted the field The day before the battle. Defend yourself!
PRIESTS	Defend yourself!
RAMFIS	He is silent! Traitor!
PRIESTS	Traitor!
AMNERIS	Ah, pity! ... Ah! Save him! Gods, have pity ... pity!
RAMFIS	Radamès! ... Radamès! ... Radamès! ... You violated your oath, False to your country, your King, your honor. Defend yourself!
PRIESTS	Defend yourself!
RAMFIS	He is silent! Traitor!
PRIESTS	Traitor!
AMNERIS	Ah! Have pity! Ah! Save him! Gods, have pity ... pity ...
RAMFIS and PRIESTS	Radamès: your fate is sealed; You will die the death of the disgraced; Below the altar of the outraged God You will be entombed alive!
AMNERIS	For him alive ... the tomb ... Oh! The monsters! Nor are they ever sated With blood ... And they call themselves ministers of heaven!

The priests come out of the dungeon.

RAMFIS and PRIESTS	Traitor! Traitor! Traitor!
AMNERIS (*inveighing against the priests*)	Priests: you have committed a crime! Unspeakable tigers, thirsting for blood ... You outrage the earth and the Gods ... You punish an innocent man.
RAMFIS and PRIESTS	He is a traitor! He will die!
AMNERIS (*to Ramfis*)	Priest: this man you are killing, You know ... was loved one day by me ... The curse of a tormented heart Will fall on you with his blood!

RAMFIS e SACERDOTI (*allontanadosi lentamente*)
    È traditor! morrà!

AMNERIS   Voi la terra ed i Numi oltraggiate ...
    Voi punite chi colpe non ha.
    Ah no, ah no, non è traditor ...
    Pietà! pietà! pietà!

RAMFIS e SACERDOTI
    Traditor! traditor! traditor!

AMNERIS   Empia razza! Anatèma su voi!
    La vendetta del ciel scenderà!

Esce disperata.

SCENA SECONDA

La scena è divisa in due piani. Il piano superiore rappresenta l'interno del Tempio di Vulcano splendente d'oro e di luce; il piano inferiore, un sotterraneo. Lunghe file d'arcate si perdono nell'oscurità. Statue colossali d'Osiride colle mani incrociate sostengono i pilastri della vôlta.
Radamès è nel sotterraneo sui gradini per cui è disceso.
Al disopra, due sacerdoti intenti a chiudere la pietra del sotterraneo.

RADAMÈS   La fatal pietra sovra me si chiuse ...
    Ecco la tomba mia. Del dì la luce
    Più non vedrò ...
    Non rivedrò più Aïda ...
    Aïda, ove sei tu?
    Possa tu almeno viver felice
    E la mia sorte orrenda sempre ignorar!
    Qual gemito!... Una larva ... una visione ...
    No! forma umana è questa ...
    Ciel!... Aïda!

AÏDA   Son io ...

RADAMÈS   Tu ... in questa tomba!

AÏDA   Presago il core della tua condanna,
    In questa tomba che per te s'apriva
    Io penetrai furtiva ...

    E qui lontana da ogni umano sguardo
    Nella tue braccia desiai morire.

RADAMÈS   Morir! sì pura e bella!
    Morir per me d'amore ...
    Degli anni tuoi nel fiore,
    Fuggir la vita!
    T'avea il ciel per l'amor creata,
    Ed io t'uccido per averti amata!
    No, non morrai!
    Troppo t'amai! troppo sei bella!

AÏDA (*vaneggiando*)
    Vedi?... di morte l'angelo
    Radiante a noi s'appressa ...
    Ne adduce a eterni gaudii
    Sovra i suoi vanni d'ór.
    Già veggo il ciel dischiudersi,

RAMFIS and PRIESTS *(slowly going away)*
> He is a traitor! He will die!

AMNERIS
> You outrage the earth and the Gods . . .
> You punish an innocent man.
> Ah no, ah no, he is no traitor . . .
> Have pity! pity! pity!

RAMFIS and PRIESTS
> Traitor! Traitor! Traitor!

AMNERIS
> Wicked race! A curse upon you!
> Vengeance will come down from heaven!

She goes out in despair.

SCENE TWO

The scene is divided on two levels. The upper level repre-
sents the interior of the Temple of Vulcan, gleaming with
gold and light. The lower level, a tomb. Long rows of arches
disappear into the darkness. Colossal statues of Osiris, his
hands crossed over his breast, hold up the ceiling of the vault.

Radamès is in the crypt on the steps by which he has de-
scended into it. Above him, two priests are closing the stone
over the tomb.

RADAMÈS
> The fatal stone has closed over me . . .
> Here is my tomb. I'll never see again
> The light of day . . .
> I'll never see Aïda again . . .
> Aïda, where are you?
> May you at least live happily
> And never know of my terrible fate!
> That moan! . . . A form . . . a vision . . .
> No! That is a human shape . . .
> Heaven! . . . Aïda!

AÏDA
> It is I . . .

RADAMÈS
> You . . . in this tomb!

AÏDA
> My heart foresaw your sentence,
> I slipped furtively
> Into this tomb that was being opened for
>   you . . .
> Here, far from every human gaze,
> I wanted to die in your arms.

RADAMÈS
> To die! So pure and beautiful!
> To die, for love of me . . .
> In the bloom of your years,
> To flee from life!
> Heaven had created you for love,
> And I kill you because I loved you!
> No, you shall not die!
> I loved you too much! You are too beautiful!

AÏDA *(delirious)*
> You see? . . . The angel of death,
> Radiant, is approaching us . . .
> He leads us to eternal bliss
> On his golden wings.
> I see heaven opening already,

> Ivi ogni affanno cessa ...
> Ivi comincia l'estàsi
> D'un immortale amor.

SACERDOTESSE (*nel tempio*)
> Immenso, immenso Fthà ...

AÏDA   Triste canto!...

RADAMÈS   Il tripudio dei sacerdoti ...

SACERDOTESSE Del mondo spirito animator ...

AÏDA   Il nostro inno di morte ...

RADAMÈS (*cercando di smuovere la pietra del sotterraneo*)
> Nè le mie forti braccia
> Smuoverti potranno, o fatal pietra!

AÏDA   Invan!...

SACERDOTI e SACERDOTESSE
> Ah! noi t'invochiam ...

AÏDA   Tutto è finito sulla terra per noi ...

RADAMÈS (*con desolata rassegnazione*)
> È vero! è vero!...

AÏDA e RADAMÈS
> O terra addio; addio valle di pianti ...
> Sogno di gaudio che in dolor svanì ...
> A noi si schiude il ciel
> E l'alme erranti volano
> Al raggio dell'eterno dì.

SACERDOTI e SACERDOTESSE
> Immenso Fthà, noi t'invochiam!

Amneris in abito di lutto apparisce nel tempio e va a pros-
trari sulla pietra che chiude il sotterraneo.

AMNERIS   Pace t'imploro, salma adorata ...
> Isi placata ti schiuda il ciel ...

AÏDA e RADAMÈS
> Si schiude il ciel ... il ciel ...

Aïda cade e muore nelle braccia di Radamès.

AMNERIS   Pace t'imploro, pace, pace!

There all pain ceases . . .
There begins the ecstasy
Of immortal love.

PRIESTESSES (*in the temple*)
Mighty, mighty Ptah!

AÏDA   That sad chant! . . .

RADAMÈS   The celebration of the priests . . .

PRIESTESSES   Life-giving spirit of the world . . .

AÏDA   Our hymn of death . . .

RADAMÈS (*trying to move the stone of the vault*)
Nor can my strong arms
Move you, O fatal stone!

AÏDA   In vain! . . .

PRIESTS and PRIESTESSES
Ah! We invoke thee . . .

AÏDA   All is finished on earth for us . . .

RADAMÈS (*with desolate resignation*)
It's true! It's true! . . .

AÏDA and RADAMÈS
O earth, farewell; farewell, vale of tears . . .
Dream of joy that vanished in grief . . .
Heaven is opening to us
And our wandering spirits fly
To the glow of eternal day.

PRIESTS and PRIESTESSES
Mighty Ptah, we invoke thee!

*Amneris, dressed in mourning, appears in the temple. She
comes and prostrates herself on the stone that seals the tomb.*

AMNERIS   Peace, I beseech you, adored corpse . . .
May Isis, assuaged, open heaven to you . . .

AÏDA and RADAMÈS
Heaven is opening . . . heaven . . .

Aïda falls, dying, into the arms of Radamès.

AMNERIS   Peace, I beseech you, peace, peace!

Otello

In 1865, when Verdi's revised version of *Macbeth* was given its first performance in Paris, some of the French critics implied that he did not know his Shakespeare. This accusation struck a sensitive spot. "Oh, in this they are very wrong," he wrote his French publisher. "I may not have rendered *Macbeth* well, but to say that I do not know, do not understand, do not feel Shachspeare [sic] — no, by God, no. He is one of my favorite poets, whom I have been familiar with since my early youth, whom I read and reread continually . . ."

Verdi never gave himself intellectual airs, and though he could not spell the poet's name properly, he had truly read and reread all his works. After *Macbeth*, on several occasions the composer worked on the idea of a *King Lear*, and his long correspondence with Antonio Somma (librettist of *Un Ballo in maschera*) about the project is a fascinating summation of what Verdi wanted in a libretto, and, at the same time, proof of his profound penetration of Shakespeare's characters.

So in 1879, when Giulio Ricordi, Verdi's astute publisher, mentioned the idea of an opera based on *Othello*, it was only natural that the composer should be interested, especially as the proposed librettist was Arrigo Boito. But Verdi was sixty-five, he felt old and was unwilling to do battle with the public again. He was tempted to rest on his ample laurels. He would only say that, if Boito felt like writing a libretto, he, Verdi, would be happy to have a look at it. That was all the encouragement Boito needed. He wrote a draft, and Verdi was captivated by it. Once again the magic of a stimulating text had done its work, as it had with *Nabucco*, with *Aïda*, and with so many others. Verdi did not commit himself this time, but he began to suggest revisions.

Before he could get to work on *Otello*, Verdi had another job to do. He wanted to make a new version of *Simon Boccanegra*, whose lack of success, he felt, came from a grim and mixed-up story. Boito helped him adjust it into more logical shape, and Verdi began to get used to working with the younger man.

In many ways, Boito was the ideal collaborator. At the time they began to work on *Otello* and *Boccanegra*, the librettist was in his late thirties, composer of a successful opera on his own libretto (*Mefistofele*) and author of librettos for several other composers, including Ponchielli, for whom he had written *La Gioconda*. Verdi and Boito had met nearly twenty years before and had collaborated on *L'Inno delle nazioni*, one of Verdi's few occasional pieces (written for the London Exhibition of 1862). Boito, then a bright young graduate of the Milan Conservatory, had provided the text.

But in the years after that collaboration, the first acquaintance had not ripened into friendship, largely because Boito had been one of Wagner's leading Italian champions and the translator of some of his works in Italian. Though Verdi admired Wagner, he was suspicious of his Italian enthusiasts and was convinced that Wagnerian theories were fatal to Italian composers.

By 1879, however, Boito had outgrown his youthful brashness, and in various articles (he was an acute and industrious critic) had proved his sincere admiration of Verdi. Also Boito was an ardent Shakespearean, like the composer. In 1888, he translated *Antony and Cleopatra*, which was interpreted by Eleonora Duse, then his mistress. And, in his young days, he had also made a libretto from *Hamlet* for his friend Franco Faccio.

As work on *Otello* slowly progressed, Verdi warmed to Boito, who became a frequent visitor to Sant'Agata and remained the old man's close friend until his death. Their revised *Boccanegra* was not warmly received at La Scala in 1881, and a revised *Don Carlos* in 1884 was given an equally tepid reception. These near-failures helped dampen Verdi's enthusiasm for the *Otello* project.

But Boito did not despair, and by the summer of 1885, *Otello* was well under way. On October 5 of that year Verdi wrote: "I've finished the fourth act and I can breathe again."

Of course Verdi had not finished. Revisions went on, dozens of letters were exchanged between composer and librettist as the two of them — Ricordi helping — set about finding singers. Verdi traveled to Milan to hear the young Gemma Bellincioni (and rejected her), to Paris to hear how Victor Maurel was singing these days (he became the first Iago). Finally, on November 1, 1886, Verdi was able to write, after completing the orchestration: "*Otello* is completely finished!! Really finished!!! Finally!!!!!!!"

For the next few months Verdi was busy coaching his singers: Francesco Tamagno, the famous tenor, worried him because of an inability to sing mezza voce; Romilda Pantaleoni, the Desdemona, seemed more suited for heavier roles. Maurel pleased him, and Verdi had confidence in the conductor Franco Faccio, Boito's old friend. But the rehearsals were hard, inhuman.

Finally opening night came. February 5, 1887. All of Italy was there, and many literary and musical figures from France: Massenet, Reyer, Clemenceau. It was another triumph.

After the third performance Verdi went to say good-by to the directors of La Scala. For the occasion the mayor of Milan was also present, and, as Verdi was preparing to leave, the mayor said that everyone wanted to see the composer at La Scala again, "perhaps with an *opera buffa.*"

Verdi shook his head. "I've been looking for a good *opera buffa* libretto for forty years . . ." And he added: "My long career is closed." But two years later Boito sent Verdi another outline, that of *Falstaff*, and the magic of the *parola scenica* worked a final time.

THE PLOT

ACT ONE

On the island of Cyprus, Venetian officers and the Cypriot populace are awaiting the arrival of the Moor Othello, the new governor from Venice, whose ship is battling a violent storm. The storm subsides and Othello lands, to the joy of the crowd. Only Iago and Roderigo do not share the general happiness. Iago is bitter because Othello has named Cassio his lieutenant, instead of Iago; and Roderigo is unhappy because he is in love with Desdemona, Othello's wife.

Iago is already plotting his revenge, and when Cassio appears, Iago and Roderigo make him drunk, then provoke a duel. Othello, summoned by the brawling, dismisses Cassio from his service. Desdemona also comes out, and when all have gone, she and Othello again declare their love.

ACT TWO

Iago, now Othello's confidant, continues his plotting. He advises Cassio to ask Desdemona to intercede with Othello for the disgraced officer's pardon. The Moor sees Cassio with his wife, and Iago plants the seed of jealousy, which grows as Desdemona pleads with her husband to forgive their old friend Cassio.

Iago takes a handkerchief of Desdemona's from his wife, Emilia, who is Desdemona's companion. Later he will use it as evidence. When he and Othello are alone, he tells how he heard Cassio talk in his sleep about Desdemona, as if the two of them were lovers. Othello vows vengeance, and Iago swears to assist him and to furnish him proof.

ACT THREE

Ambassadors are coming from Venice. Before they arrive, Desdemona again broaches the subject of Cassio, and Othello openly accuses her of adultery. Later he spies on a meeting between Iago and Cassio, who displays a handkerchief he has mysteriously found in his room. It is Desdemona's, placed there by Iago. Othello cannot hear the two men's words, but the sight of the handkerchief convinces him. When he receives the ambassadors, he cannot restrain his jealous fury and, in front of all, insults his wife and hurls her to the floor. Iago feels that his triumph is near.

ACT FOUR

Desdemona is preparing for bed. As Emilia assists her, she sings "Willow, willow," a sad song about unhappy love. Emilia leaves; Desdemona prays, then goes to bed. Othello enters and warns her that he has come to kill her. Again she protests her innocence, but he refuses to believe her and strangles her. Emilia knocks, then bursts in to tell Othello that Roderigo, who — according to Iago's plot — was to kill Cassio, has been killed. Cassio lives.

Desdemona moans. Emilia cries out in horror, and others come in, including Iago, whose villainy is revealed. Iago flees, pursued by the others, and Othello kills himself over Desdemona's lifeless body.

OTELLO

libretto by Arrigo Boito

First performed at La Scala, Milan
February 5, 1887

CHARACTERS

Othello, a Moor, general in the Venetian Army	Tenor
Iago, his ensign	Baritone
Cassio, his lieutenant	Tenor
Roderigo, a Venetian gentleman	Tenor
Lodovico, ambassador of the Venetian Republic	Bass
Montano, Othello's predecessor in Cyprus	Bass
Desdemona, Othello's wife	Soprano
Emilia, Iago's wife and Desdemona's lady	Mezzo-soprano

Soldiers and Sailors of the Republic, Venetian
Ladies and Gentlemen, Cypriot Men and Women

The opera takes place in Cyprus at the end
of the fifteenth century.

ATTO PRIMO

L'esterno del castello. Una taverna con pergolato. Gli spaldi nel fondo e il mare. È sera. Lampi, tuoni, uragano.

Jago, Roderigo, Cassio, Montàno, Otello, Cipriotti e soldati Veneti.

S'alza subito il sipario.

CIPRIOTTI   Una vela! Una vela! Un vessillo! Un vessillo!
MONTÀNO   È l'alato Leon!

Un fulmine, lampi e tuoni.

CASSIO   Or la folgor lo svela.
ALTRI *(che sopraggiungono)*
               Uno squillo! Uno squillo!

Colpo di cannone.

TUTTI   Ha tuonato il cannon.
CASSIO   È la nave del Duce.
MONTÀNO   Or s'affonda, or s'inciela . . .
CASSIO   Erge il rostro dall'onda.
ALCUNI CIPRIOTTI
               Nelle nubi si cela e nel mar,
               E alla luce dei lampi ne appar.

Lampi e tuoni continui.

TUTTI   Lampi! tuoni! gorghi! turbi tempestosi e
               fulmini!
               Treman l'onde, treman l'aure, treman basi e
               culmini.
       (Entrano dal fondo molte donne del popolo.)
               Fende l'etra un torvo e cieco spirto di vertigine,
               Iddio scuote il cielo bieco, come un tetro vel.

               Tutto è fumo! tutto è fuoco! l'orrida caligine
               Si fa incendio, poi si spegne più funesta. Spasima

               L'universo, accorre a valchi l'aquilon fantasima,

               I titanici oricalchi squillano nel ciel.
TUTTI *(con gesti di spavento e di supplicazione e rivolti verso lo spaldo)*
               Dio, fulgor della bufera!
               Dio, sorriso della duna!
               Salva l'arca e la bandiera
               Della veneta fortuna!
               Tu, che reggi gli astri e il Fato!
               Tu, che imperi al mondo e al ciel!
               Fa che in fondo al mar placato
               Posi l'àncora fedel.

ACT ONE

Outside the castle. A tavern with a pergola. Ramparts in the background, and the sea. It is evening. Thunder, lightning, wind.

Iago, Roderigo, Cassio, Montano, Othello, Cypriots, and Venetian soldiers.

The curtain rises at once.

CYPRIOTS   A sail! A sail! A flag! A flag!

MONTANO   It's the winged lion!

Flashes of lightning, thunder.

CASSIO   The lightning reveals it now.

OTHERS (*arriving*)
     A trumpet blast! A trumpet blast!

A cannon is fired.

ALL   The cannon has thundered.

CASSIO   It's the General's ship.

MONTANO   First it sinks down, then it rears up . . .

CASSIO   Its prow rises from the waves.

SOME CYPRIOTS
     It is hidden in the clouds and the sea,
     Then appears in the lightning's flash.

Constant thunder and lightning.

ALL   Lightning! Thunder! Whirlpools! Storm winds
     and thunderbolts!
     The waves quake, the winds quake, foundations
     and pinnacles quake.
     (*Many women come in at the back.*)
     A grim, blind, whirling spirit cleaves the air,
     God shakes the white heavens like a gloomy
     curtain.
     All is smoke! All is fire! The horrible soot
     Turns to fire, then dies, still more ghastly, the
     universe
     Writhes, the phantom north wind rushes
     through the passes,
     Titanic trumpets blare out in the sky.

ALL (*with gestures of fear and supplication, facing the battlements*)
     God, lightning in the storm!
     God, the smile of the shore!
     Save the vessel and the flag
     Of Venetian destiny!
     Thou, who rulest the stars and Fate!
     Thou, who governest world and sky!
     Grant that the faithful anchor
     Rest on the bottom of the calmed sea.

JAGO   È infranto l'artimon!
RODERIGO   Il rostro piomba su quello scoglio!
CIPRIOTTI   Aita! Aita!
JAGO (*a parte a Roderigo*)
               (L'alvo frenetico del mar sia la sua tomba!)
CIPRIOTTI   È salvo! à salvo!

VOCI INTERNE   Gittate i palischermi!
               Mano alle funi! Fermi!
CIPRIOTTI   Forza ai remi! Alla riva!

VOCI INTERNE   All'approdo! allo sbarco!
TUTTI   Evviva! Evviva! Evviva!
OTELLO (*dalla scala della spiaggia salendo sullo spaldo con
    seguito di marinai e di soldati*)
               Esultate! L'orgoglio musulmano
               Sepolto è in mar, nostra e del cielo è gloria!

               Dopo l'armi lo vinse l'uragano.
TUTTI   Evviva Otello! Evviva! Evviva! Evviva!
               Vittoria! Vittoria!

    *Otello entra nella rôcca, seguito da Cassio, da Montàno e
dai soldati.*

CIPRIOTTI   Vittoria! Sterminio!
               Dispersi, distrutti, sepolti nell'orrido

               Tumulto piombâr.
               Avranno per requie la sferza dei flutti,
               La ridda dei turbini,
               L'abisso del mar.
               Vittoria! Vittoria! Vittoria! Vittoria!
               Dispersi, distrutti, sepolti nell'orrido

               Tumulto piombâr.
               Vittoria! Vittoria! Evviva! Vittoria! Evviva!

    Tuono lontano.

CIPRIOTTI   Si calma la bufera.
JAGO (*in disparte a Roderigo*)
               Roderigo, ebben, che pensi?
RODERIGO   D'affogarmi ...
JAGO   Stolto è chi s'affoga per amor di donna.

    *Nel fondo è un andirivieni della ciurma che sale dalla scala
della spiaggia ed entra nel castello portando armi e bagagli
mentre dei popolani escono da dietro la rôcca portando dei
rami da ardere presso lo spaldo; alcuni soldati con fiaccole
illuminano la via percorsa da questa gente.*

RODERIGO   Vincer nol so.

    *Alcuni del popolo formano da un lato una catasta di legna:
la folla s'accalca intorno turbolenta e curiosa.*

IAGO   The mainsail's ripped!
RODERIGO   The prow is hurtling at that rock!
CYPRIOTS   Help! Help!
IAGO (*aside to Roderigo*)
                (Let the frenzied bed of the sea be his grave!)
CYPRIOTS   He's safe! He's safe!
VOICES WITHIN
                Lower the small boats!
                All hands to the ropes! Make fast!
CYPRIOTS   Row with all your might! To the shore!
VOICES WITHIN
                To the landing place! Disembark!
ALL   Hurrah! Hurrah! Hurrah!
OTHELLO (*from the steps from the beach, climbing onto the
        ramparts with sailors and soldiers behind him*)
                Rejoice! The Mussulman's pride
                Is buried in the sea, the glory is ours and
                    heaven's!
                After our arms the storm defeated him.
ALL   Long live Othello! Hurrah! Hurrah! Hurrah!
                Victory! Victory!

*Othello goes into the castle, followed by Cassio, Montano,
and the soldiers.*

CYPRIOTS   Victory! Destruction!
                Scattered, destroyed, they sank and found
                    graves
                In the horrible, raging sea.
                The lash of the waves will be their rest,
                The riot of the whirlwinds,
                The abyss of the sea.
                Victory! Victory! Victory! Victory!
                Scattered, destroyed, they sank and were
                    buried
                In the horrible, raging sea.
                Victory! Victory! Hurrah! Victory! Hurrah!

Distant thunder.

CYPRIOTS   The storm is dying down.
IAGO (*aside to Roderigo*)
                Well, Roderigo, what are you thinking?
RODERIGO   Of drowning myself . . .
IAGO   He who drowns himself for a woman's love is
                    a fool.

*In the background the crew goes back and forth between
the beach and the castle carrying weapons and baggage,
while some of the people come from behind the castle, carrying firewood up near the ramparts; some soldiers with torches
light the way for them.*

RODERIGO   I cannot overcome it.

*Some of the people heap the wood in a pile to one side; the
crowd mills around, restless and curious.*

JAGO   Su via, fa senno, aspetta
L'opra del tempo; a Desdemona bella,
Che nel segreto de' tuoi sogni adori,
Presto in uggia verranno i foschi baci
Di quel selvaggio dalle gonfie labbra.
Buon Roderigo, amico tuo sincero
Mi ti professo, nè in più forte ambascia
Soccorrerti potrei. Se un fragil voto
Di femmina non è tropp'arduo nodo
Pel genio mio nè per l'inferno, giuro
Che quella donna sarà tua. M'ascolta,
Bench'io finga d'amarlo, odio quel Moro ...

Entra Cassio, poi s'unisce a un crocchio di soldati.

JAGO (*sempre in disparte a Roderigo*)
         E una cagion dell'ira, eccola, guarda.

         (*indicando Cassio*)
Quell'azzimato capitano usurpa
Il grado mio, il grado mio che in cento
Ben pugnate battaglie ho meritato;
(*Continua il passaggio della bassa ciurma nel fondo.*)

         Tal fu il voler d'Otello, ed io rimango
Di sua Moresca signoria l'alfiere!
(*Dalla catasta incominciano ad alzarsi dei
globi di fumo sempre più denso.*)
Ma, com'è ver che tu Roderigo sei,
Così è pur certo che se il Moro io fossi
Vedermi non vorrei d'attorno un Jago.
Se tu m'ascolti ...

Jago conduce Roderigo verso il fondo. Il fuoco divampa.
I soldati s'affollano intorno alle tavole della taverna.
  Mentre dura il canto intorno al fuoco di gioia, i tavernieri
appenderanno al pergolato dell'osteria delle lanterne veneziane
a vari colori che illumineranno gaiamente la scena. I soldati
si saranno adunati intorno alle tavole, parte seduti, parte in
piedi, ciarlando e bevendo.

CIPRIOTTI   Fuoco di gioia! l'ilare vampa
Fuga la notte col suo splendor,
Guizza, sfavilla, crepita, avvampa
Fulgido incendio che invade il cor.
Dal raggio attratti vaghi sembianti
Movono intorno mutando stuol,
E son fanciulle dai lieti canti,
E son farfalle dall'igneo vol.
Arde la palma col sicomoro,
Canta la sposa col suo fedel,
Sull'aurea fiamma, sul lieto coro
Soffia l'ardente spiro del ciel.
Fuoco di gioia rapido brilla!
Rapido passa fuoco d'amor!
Splende, s'oscura, palpita, oscilla,
L'ultimo guizzo lampeggia e muor.

IAGO   Come to your senses now, wait
For time to do its work; the lovely Desdemona,
Whom you adore in your secret dreams,
Will soon come to dislike the dark kisses
Of that savage with swollen lips.
Good Roderigo, I declare myself
Your sincere friend, nor could I help you
In greater distress. If a woman's fragile vow
Is not too tough a knot
For my wits or for hell's, I swear
That woman shall be yours. Listen to me.
Though I pretend to love him, I hate that
    Moor . . .

Cassio enters, then joins a group of soldiers.

IAGO *(still aside to Roderigo)*
And there is a reason for my wrath. There.
    Look.
        (pointing to Cassio)
That dandified captain usurps
My rank, the rank I have deserved
For fighting well in a hundred battles;
*(The crew continues to move back and forth in
the background.)*
This was Othello's wish, and I remain
His Moorish Lordship's ensign!
*(Denser and denser clouds of smoke begin to rise
from the pile of wood.)*
But, as surely as you are Roderigo,
So it is sure that if I were the Moor
I shouldn't want to see an Iago around me.
If you listen to me . . .

*Iago leads Roderigo toward the back. The fire leaps up. The
soldiers crowd around the tables of the tavern.*

*As the singing goes on around the fire of rejoicing, the
tavern-keepers hang varicolored Venetian lanterns from the
pergola, giving a festive illumination to the scene. The soldiers
gather around the tables, some sitting, some standing, chat-
tering and drinking.*

CYPRIOTS   Fire of rejoicing! The merry flame
Banishes night by its brightness,
It darts, sparkles, crackles, and blazes,
The shining fire that invades our hearts.
Drawn by the light, lovely forms
Move about, a changing mass,
Now they are maidens with joyful songs,
Now they are butterflies with fiery flights.
The palm log burns with the sycamore,
The bride sings with her faithful beloved,
Over the golden flame, over the happy chorus
Plays the ardent breath of heaven.
The joyful fire quickly gleams!
Quickly passes the fire of love!
It glows, darkens, throbs, and wavers,
The last flame flickers and dies.

Fuoco di gioia rapido brilla!
Splende, s'oscura, palpita, ecc.

Il fuoco si spegne a poco a poco; la bufera è cessata. Jago,
Roderigo, Cassio e parecchi altri uomini d'arme intorno a un
tavolo dove c'è del vino; parte in piedi, parte seduti.

JAGO   Roderigo, beviam! qua la tazza,
      Capitano.

CASSIO   Non bevo più.

JAGO *(avvicinando il boccale alla tazza di Cassio)*
      Ingoia questo sorso.

CASSIO *(ritirando il bicchiere)*
      No.

JAGO   Guarda! oggi impazza tutta Cipro!
      È una notte di gioia, dunque ...

CASSIO   Cessa. Già m'arde il cervello
      Per un nappo vuotato.

JAGO   Sì, ancora bever tu devi.
      Alle nozze d'Otello e Desdemona!

TUTTI *(tranne Roderigo)*
      Evviva!

CASSIO *(alzando il bicchiere e bevendo un poco)*
      Essa infiora questo lido.

JAGO *(sottovoce a Roderigo)*
      (Lo ascolta.)

CASSIO   Col vago suo raggiar chiama i cori a raccolta.

RODERIGO Pur modesta essa è tanto.

CASSIO   Tu, Jago, canterai le sue lodi!

JAGO *(piano a Roderigo)*
      (Lo ascolta.)
         (forte a Cassio)
      Io non sono che un critico.

CASSIO   Ed ella d'ogni lode è più bella.

JAGO *(come sopra, a Roderigo, a parte)*
      (Ti guarda da quel Cassio.)

RODERIGO (Che temi?)

JAGO   (Ei favella
      Già con troppo bollor, la gagliarda
      Giovinezza lo sprona, è un astuto
      Seduttor che t'ingombra il cammino.
      Bada ...)

RODERIGO (Ebben?)

JAGO   (S'ei s'innebbria è perduto!
      Fallo ber.)
         (ai tavernieri)
      Qua, ragazzi, del vino!

Jago riempie tre bicchieri: uno per se, uno per Roderigo,
uno per Cassio. I tavernieri circolano colle anfore.

JAGO *(a Cassio col bicchiere in mano: la folla gli si avvicina*
  e lo guarda curiosamente)
      Inaffia l'ugola!
      Trinca, tracanna!

The joyful fire quickly gleams!
It glows, darkens, throbs, etc.

*The fire slowly dies out; the storm is over. Iago, Roderigo,
Cassio, and several other armed men are around a table where
there is wine; some are standing, some sitting.*

IAGO   Roderigo, let's drink! Your cup here,
            Captain.

CASSIO   I'll drink no more.

IAGO (*holding the pitcher toward Cassio's cup*)
            Swallow this drop.

CASSIO (*drawing back his glass*)
            No.

IAGO   Look! All Cyprus is running riot!
            It's a night of joy. So . . .

CASSIO   Stop. My brain is already on fire
            From a glass I drained.

IAGO   Yes, you must drink more.
            To the marriage of Othello and Desdemona!

ALL (*except Roderigo*)
            Hurrah!

CASSIO (*raising his glass and drinking a little*)
            She bedecks this island like a flower.

IAGO (*whispering to Roderigo*)
            (Listen to him.)

CASSIO   With her sweet radiance she gathers all hearts.

RODERIGO   And yet she is very modest.

CASSIO   You, Iago, will sing her praises!

IAGO (*softly to Roderigo*)
            (Listen to him.)
                    (*aloud to Cassio*)
            I am only a critic.

CASSIO   And she is more beautiful than any praise.

IAGO (*as above, to Roderigo, aside*)
            (Beware of that Cassio.)

RODERIGO   (What do you fear?)

IAGO   (He speaks
            Already with too much ardor, his bold
            Youth spurs him on, your path is blocked
            By a clever seducer.
            Watch out . . .)

RODERIGO   (Yes?)

IAGO   (If he becomes drunk, he is lost!
            Make him drink.)
                    (*to the tavern waiters*)
            Here, boys, some wine!

*Iago fills three glasses: one for himself, one for Roderigo,
one for Cassio. The waiters move about with pitchers.*

IAGO (*to Cassio, glass in hand. The crowd gathers around and
    watches him with curiosity*)
            Wet your gullet!
            Drink up, gulp it down!

Prima che svampino
Canto e bicchier.

CASSIO (*a Jago, col bicchiere in mano*)
Questa del pampino
Verace manna
Di vaghe annugola
Nebbie il pensier.

JAGO (*a tutti*)
Chi all'esca ha morso
Del ditirambo
Spavaldo e strambo
Beva con me.

TUTTI   Chi all'esca ha morso
Del ditirambo
Spavaldo e strambo
Beve con te.

JAGO (*piano a Roderigo indicando Cassio*)
(Un altro sorso
E brillo egli è.)

RODERIGO (*a Jago*)
(Un altro sorso
E brillo egli è.)

JAGO (*ad alta voce*)
Il mondo palpita
Quand'io son brillo!
Sfido l'ironico
Nume e il destin!

CASSIO (*bevendo ancora*)
Come un armonico
Lïuto oscillo;
La gioia scalpita
Sul mio cammin!

JAGO   Chi all'esca ha morso, ecc.
TUTTI   Chi all'esca ha morso, ecc.
JAGO (*a Roderigo*)
(Un altro sorso
E brillo egli è.)

RODERIGO (*a Jago*)
(Un altro sorso
E brillo egli è.)

JAGO (*ad alta voce*)
Fuggan dal vivido
Nappo i codardi ...

CASSIO (*interrompendo*)
In fondo all'anima
Ciascun mi guardi!
(*beve*)

JAGO   ... che in cor nascondono frodi ...
CASSIO   Non temo, non temo il ver ...
(*barcollando*)
Non temo il ver ... e bevo ...

TUTTI (*ridendo*)
Ah! Ah! Ah!

Before song and glass
Disappear.
CASSIO (*to Iago, glass in hand*)
The vine's
Truth-giving manna
Beclouds my mind
With lovely mists.

IAGO (*to all*)   He who has taken the bait
Of the Bacchanalian song,
Bold and strange,
Drink with me.
ALL   He who has taken the bait
Of the Bacchanalian song,
Bold and strange,
Drinks with you.
IAGO (*softly to Roderigo, pointing at Cassio*)
(Another sip
And he's drunk.)
RODERIGO (*to Iago*)
(Another sip
And he's drunk.)

IAGO (*aloud*)   The world throbs
When I am drunk!
I defy the ironic
Deity and fate!
CASSIO (*drinking again*)
I sway like a
Tuned lute;
Joy is waiting impatiently
On my path!
IAGO   He who has taken, etc.
ALL   He who has taken, etc.
IAGO (*to Roderigo*)
(Another sip
And he's drunk.)
RODERIGO (*to Iago*)
(Another sip
And he's drunk.)

IAGO (*aloud*)   Cowards flee
From the glowing cup ...
CASSIO (*interrupting him*)
Let each man look
Into the depths of my soul!
(*drinks*)
IAGO   ... who hide deceit in their hearts ...
CASSIO   I don't fear, I don't fear the truth ...
(*staggering*)
I don't fear the truth ... and I drink ...
ALL (*laughing*)
Ha! Ha! Ha!

CASSIO   Del calice ...

Vorrebbe ripetere il primo motivo, ma non si sovviene.

JAGO (*a Roderigo*)
              (Egli è briaco fradicio.)
CASSIO   Del calice ... gl'orli ...
CIPRIOTTI (*ridono di Cassio*)
              Ah, ah!
JAGO (*sempre a Roderigo*)
              (Ti scuoti,
              Lo trascina a contesa;
              È pronto all'ira,
              T'offenderà ... ne seguirà tumulto!)
CASSIO (*ripiglia, ma con voce soffocata*)
              Del calice ... gl'orli ...
JAGO (*sempre a Roderigo*)
              (Pensa che puoi così del lieto Otello
              Turbar la prima vigilia d'amor!)
RODERIGO   (Ed è ciò che mi spinge.)
CASSIO   ... gl'orli ... s'impor ... s'impor ...
              s'imporporino ...
CIPRIOTTI   Ah, ah, ah, ah!
TUTTI   Bevi, bevi con me, bevi con me.
              (*tutti bevono*)
MONTÀNO (*venendo dal castello, si rivolge a Cassio*)
              Capitano,
              V'attende la fazione ai baluardi.
CASSIO (*barcollando*)
              Andiam!
MONTÀNO   Che vedo?
JAGO (*a Montàno*)
              (Ogni notte in tal guisa
              Cassio preludia al sonno.)
MONTÀNO   Otello il sappia.
CASSIO   Andiamo ai baluardi ...
RODERIGO, poi TUTTI
              Ah! ah!
CASSIO   Chi ride?
RODERIGO (*provocandolo*)
              Rido d'un ebbro ...
CASSIO (*scagliandosi contro Roderigo*)
              Bada alle tue spalle! Furfante!
RODERIGO (*difendendosi*)
              Briaco ribaldo!
CASSIO   Marrano! Nessun più ti salva.
MONTÀNO (*separandoli a forza e dirigendosi a Cassio*)
              Frenate la mano, signor, ve ne prego.
CASSIO (*a Montàno*)
              Ti spacco il cerèbro se qui t'interponi.
MONTÀNO   Parole d'un ebbro ...
CASSIO   D'un ebbro!

CASSIO The cup's . . .

Wants to repeat the first tune but cannot remember it.

IAGO (*to Roderigo*)
  (He's blind drunk.)
CASSIO The cup's . . . lips . . .
CYPRIOTS (*laugh at Cassio*)
  Ha! ha!
IAGO (*still to Roderigo*)
  (Bestir yourself,
  Draw him into an argument;
  He is quick to anger,
  He will insult you . . . a brawl will follow!)
CASSIO (*continues, but in a choked voice*)
  The cup's . . . lips . . .
IAGO (*still to Roderigo*)
  (Think that thus you can disturb happy
  Othello's first night of love!)
RODERIGO (And that is what drives me on.)
CASSIO . . . the lips . . . bepurp . . . bepurp . . .
  bepurpled . . .
CYPRIOTS Ha, ha, ha, ha!
ALL Drink, drink with me, drink with me.
  (*all drink*)
MONTANO (*coming from the castle, speaks to Cassio*)
  Captain,
  The watch awaits you on the ramparts.
CASSIO (*staggering*)
  Let's go!
MONTANO What do I see?
IAGO (*to Montano*)
  (Every night Cassio prepares for sleep
  In this fashion.)
MONTANO Othello must know this.
CASSIO Let's go to the ramparts . . .
RODERIGO, then ALL
  Ha! Ha!
CASSIO Who's laughing?
RODERIGO (*provoking him*)
  I'm laughing at a drunkard . . .
CASSIO (*hurling himself at Roderigo*)
  Guard your back! Scoundrel!
RODERIGO (*defending himself*)
  Drunken knave!
CASSIO Rogue! No one can save you now.
MONTANO (*forcing them apart and speaking to Cassio*)
  Restrain your hand, sir, I beseech you.
CASSIO (*to Montano*)
  I'll split your skull if you interfere here.
MONTANO The words of a drunkard . . .
CASSIO Of a drunkard!

344   *Otello*

*Cassio sguaina la spada. Montàno s'arma anch'esso. Assalto
furibondo. La folla si ritrae.*

JAGO (*a parte a Roderigo, rapidamente*)
                (Va al porto, con quanta più possa
                Ti resta, gridando: sommossa! sommossa!
                Va! spargi il tumulto, l'orror. Le campane
                Risuonino a stormo.)

*Roderigo esce correndo. Jago si rivolge rapidamente ai due
combattenti.*

JAGO   Fratelli! l'immane conflitto cessate!
MOLTE DONNE DEL CORO (*fuggendo*)
                Fuggiam!
JAGO   Ciel! già gronda
                Di sangue Montàno! Tenzon furibonda!

ALTRE DONNE   Fuggiam!
JAGO   Tregua!
TUTTI   Tregua!
DONNE (*fuggendo*)
                S'uccidono!
UOMINI (*ai combattenti*)
                Pace!
JAGO (*agli astanti*)
                Nessun più raffrena quel nembo pugnace!
                Si gridi l'allarme! Satàna li invade!
VOCI (*in scena e dentro*)
                All'armi!!

Campane a stormo.

TUTTI   Soccorso!!
OTELLO (*entra seguito da genti con fiaccole*)
                Abbasso le spade!
                (*I combattenti s'arrestano.*)
                Olà! che avvien?
                (*Le nubi si diradano a poco a poco.*)
                Son io fra i Saraceni?
                O la turchesca rabbia è in voi trasfusa
                Da sbranarvi l'un l'altro?... Onesto Jago,

                Per quell'amor che tu mi porti, parla.
JAGO   Non so ... qui tutti eran cortesi amici,
                Dianzi, e giocondi ... ma ad un tratto, come
                Se un pianeta maligno avesse a quelli
                Smagato il senno, sguainando l'arme
                S'avventano furenti ... avess'io prima

                Stroncati i piè che qui m'addusser!

OTELLO   Cassio, come obliasti te stesso a tal segno?...
CASSIO   Grazia ... perdon ... parlar non so ...
OTELLO   Montàno ...
MONTÀNO (*sostenuto da un soldato*)
                Son ferito ...

Cassio draws his sword. Montano also takes arms. A furious fight. The crowd draws back.

IAGO (*aside to Roderigo, quickly*)
>   (Go to the port, shouting with all the strength
>   You have left: rebellion, rebellion!
>   Go! Spread disorder, horror. Let the bells
>   Ring the alarm.)

Roderigo runs out. Iago turns rapidly to the two men who are fighting.

IAGO   Brothers! Stop this monstrous fight!

MANY WOMEN OF THE CHORUS (*fleeing*)
>   Let's flee!

IAGO   Heaven! Montano is already
>   Drenched in blood! O furious fight!

OTHER WOMEN
>   Let's flee!

IAGO   A truce!

ALL   A truce!

WOMEN (*fleeing*)
>   They're killing each other!

MEN (*to the two fighters*)
>   Peace!

IAGO (*to the bystanders*)
>   No one can now restrain that fighting tempest!
>   Give the alarm! Satan possesses them!

VOICES (*on stage and off*)
>   To arms!!

Bells toll the alarm.

ALL   Help!!

OTHELLO (*enters, followed by men with torches*)
>   Lower your swords!
>   (*The men stop fighting.*)
>   How now? What's happening?
>   (*The clouds gradually disperse.*)
>   Am I among the Saracens?
>   Or has Turkish fury filled you,
>   That you tear each other to pieces?... Honest
>   Iago,
>   By the love that you bear me, speak.

IAGO   I don't know ... here all were courteous friends,
>   Before, and merry ... but suddenly, as if
>   An evil planet had bewitched the minds
>   Of those two, drawing their weapons
>   They hurled themselves on each other
>   furiously ...
>   Would I had chopped off the feet that brought
>   me here!

OTHELLO   Cassio, how did you so far forget yourself?...

CASSIO   Mercy ... forgive me ... I cannot speak ...

OTHELLO   Montano ...

MONTANO (*supported by a soldier*)
>   I am wounded ...

OTELLO   Ferito!... pel cielo
Già il sangue mio ribolle. Ah! l'ira volge
L'angelo nostro tutelare in fuga!

Entra Desdemona.

OTELLO (*accorendo a Desdemona*)
         Che?... la mia dolce Desdemona anch'essa
Per voi distolta da' suoi sogni! Cassio,
Non sei più capitano.

Cassio lascia cadere la spada, che è raccolta da Jago.

JAGO (*porgendo la spada di Cassio a un ufficiale*)
         (Oh! mio trionfo!)
OTELLO   Jago, tu va nella città sgomenta
Con quella squadra a ricompor la pace.
         (*Jago esce.*)
Si soccorra Montàno.
    (*Montàno è accompagnato nel castello.*)
         Al proprio tetto
Ritorni ognun.
         (*a tutti, con gesto imperioso*)
Io da qui non mi parto
Se pria non vedo deserti gli spaldi.

*La scena si vuota. Otello fa cenno agli uomini colle fiaccole
che lo accompagnavano di rientrare nel castello.*

OTELLO   Già nella notte densa
S'estingue ogni clamor.
Già il mio cor fremebondo
S'ammansa in quest'amplesso e si risensa.
Tuoni la guerra e s'inabissi il mondo
Se dopo l'ira immensa
Vien questo immenso amor!

DESDEMONA   Mio superbo guerrier! quanti tormenti,
Quanti mesti sospiri e quanta speme
Ci condusse ai soavi abbracciamenti!
Oh! com'è dolce il mormorare insieme:
Te ne rammenti!
Quando narravi l'esule tua vita
E i fieri eventi e i lunghi tuoi dolor,
Ed io t'udia coll'anima rapita
In quei spaventi e coll'estasi in cor.

OTELLO   Pingea dell'armi il fremito, la pugna
E il vol gagliardo alla breccia mortal,
L'assalto, orribil edera, coll'ugna
Al baluardo e il sibilante stral.

DESDEMONA   Poi mi guidavi ai fulgidi deserti,
All'arse arene, al tuo materno suol,
Narravi allor gli spasimi sofferti
E le catene e dello schiavo il duol.

OTELLO   Ingentilìa di lacrime la storia
Il tuo bel viso e il labbro di sospir;
Scendean sulle mie tenebre la gloria,
Il paradiso e gli astri a benedir.

OTHELLO Wounded! . . . By heaven
My blood is already boiling. Ah! Anger
Puts our guardian angel to flight!

Desdemona enters.

OTHELLO (*hurrying to Desdemona*)
What? . . . My sweet Desdemona also roused
From her dreams on your account! Cassio,
You are no longer captain.

Cassio drops his sword, which is picked up by Iago.

IAGO (*handing Cassio's sword to an officer*)
(Oh! My triumph!)

OTHELLO Iago, go into the alarmed city
With that squad of soldiers and restore peace.
(*Iago goes out.*)
Assist Montano.
(*Montano is taken into the castle.*)
Let everyone
Return to his own home.
(*to all, with authoritative gesture*)
I will not leave here
Until I see the ramparts deserted.

The stage empties. Othello motions to the torch-bearers who accompanied him to go back into the castle.

OTHELLO Now in the dense night
Every noise is silenced.
Now my furious heart
Is appeased in this embrace and grows calm.
Let war thunder and the world be engulfed
If after such immense wrath
Comes this immense love!

DESDEMONA My superb warrior! How many torments,
How many sad sighs, and how much hope
Led us to these tender embraces!
Ah! How sweet it is to murmur together:
Do you remember?
When you told of your life in exile
The fierce events and your long sorrows,
And I listened to you with my soul enthralled
In those fears and with ecstasy in my heart.

OTHELLO I described the clang of arms, the fighting,
And the bold rush into the mortal breach,
The attack, hanging like horrible ivy on
The rampart by our nails, and the whistling
arrow.

DESDEMONA Then you led me to the shining deserts,
The burning sands, your native land,
Then you told me of the sufferings undergone,
The chains and the slave's sorrow.

OTHELLO Your lovely face ennobled the story
With tears and your lip with sighs;
On my darkness glory descended,
Paradise, and the stars to give their blessing.

DESDEMONA   Ed io vedea fra le tue tempie oscure
             Splender del genio l'eterea beltà.
OTELLO   E tu m'amavi per le mie sventure
             Ed io t'amavo per la tua pietà.
DESDEMONA   Ed io t'amavo per le tue sventure
             E tu m'amavi per la mia pietà.
OTELLO   Venga la morte! mi colga nell'estasi
             Di quest'amplesso
             Il momento supremo!
             (*Il cielo si sarà tutto rasserenato: si vedranno
             alcune stelle e sul lembo dell'orizzonte il
             riflesso ceruleo della nascente luna.*)
             Tale è il gaudio dell'anima che temo,
             Temo che più non mi sarà concesso
             Quest'attimo divino
             Nell'ignoto avvenir del mio destino.
DESDEMONA   Disperda il ciel gli affanni
             E Amor non muti col mutar degl'anni.
OTELLO   A questa tua preghiera
             Amen risponda la celeste schiera.
DESDEMONA   Amen risponda.
OTELLO (*appoggiandosi ad un rialzo degli spaldi*)
             Ah! la gioia m'innonda
             Sì fieramente ... che ansante mi giacio ...
             Un bacio ...
DESDEMONA   Otello!...
OTELLO   Un bacio ... ancora un bacio.
             (*alzandosi e mirando il cielo*)
             Già la pleiade ardente in mar discende.

DESDEMONA   Tarda è la notte.
OTELLO   Vien ...Venere splende.
DESDEMONA   Otello!

S'avviano abbracciati verso il castello.

ATTO SECONDO

*Una sala terrena nel castello. Una invetriata la divide da
un grande giardino. Un verone. Jago e Cassio.*

JAGO (*al di qua del verone*)
             Non ti crucciar. Se credi a me, tra poco,
             Farai ritorno ai folleggianti amori
             Di Monna Bianca, altiero capitano,
             Coll'elsa d'oro e col balteo fregiato.
CASSIO (*al di là del verone*)
             Non lusingarmi ...
JAGO   Attendi a ciò ch'io dico.
             Tu dèi saper che Desdemona è il Duce

             Del nostro Duce, sol per essa ei vive.

DESDEMONA	And at your dark temples I saw The ethereal beauty of genius shine.
OTHELLO	And you loved me for my misfortunes And I loved you for your pity.
DESDEMONA	And I loved you for your misfortunes And you loved me for my pity.
OTHELLO	Let death come! Let it take me in the ecstasy Of this embrace, The supreme moment!

(*The sky has become completely serene: some stars can*
be seen, and at one side of the horizon the azure
reflection of the rising moon.)
        Such is the joy of my soul that I am afraid,
        I am afraid that I will not be granted again
        This divine moment
        In the unknown future of my destiny.

DESDEMONA	Let heaven dispel all sorrows And may Love not change as the years change.
OTHELLO	To this prayer of yours May the heavenly host answer Amen.
DESDEMONA	May it answer Amen.

OTHELLO (*leaning against a step of the ramparts*)
        Ah! Joy engulfs me
        So fiercely . . . that I lie, breathless . . .
        A kiss . . .

DESDEMONA	Othello! . . .

OTHELLO   A kiss . . . another kiss.
        (*rising and looking at the sky*)
        The glowing Pleiades already descend to the
           sea.

DESDEMONA	The night is late.
OTHELLO	Come . . . Venus is shining.
DESDEMONA	Othello!

Embracing, they go toward the castle.

ACT TWO

A room on the ground floor of the castle. A glass-paneled
door separates it from a large garden. A balcony. Iago and
Cassio.

IAGO (*this side of the balcony*)
        Don't torment yourself. If you believe me, soon
        You will return to the frivolous loves
        Of Monna Bianca, a proud captain,
        With a gold hilt and embroidered belt.

CASSIO (*beyond the balcony*)
        Don't flatter me . . .

IAGO   Listen to what I say to you.
        You must know that Desdemona is the
           Commander
        Of our Commander, he lives only for her.

Pregala tu, quell'anima cortese
Per te interceda e il tuo perdono è certo.

CASSIO   Ma come favellarle?

JAGO   È suo costume
Girsene a meriggiar fra quelle fronde
Colla consorte mia. Quivi l'aspetta.
Or t'è aperta la via di salvazione;
Vanne.

Cassio s'allontana.

JAGO (*seguendo coll'occhio Cassio*)
Vanne; la tua meta già vedo.
Ti spinge il tuo dimone,
E il tuo dimon son io,
E me trascina il mio, nel quale io credo
Inesorato Iddio:
(*allontanandosi dal verone senza più guardar Cassio
che sarà scomparso fra gli alberi*)

Credo in un Dio crudel che m'ha creato
Simile a sè, e che nell'ira io nomo.

Dalla viltà d'un germe o d'un atòmo
Vile son nato.
Son scellerato
Perchè son uomo;
E sento il fango originario in me.
Sì! questa è la mia fè!
Credo con fermo cuor, siccome crede
La vedovella al tempio,
Che il mal ch'io penso e che da me procede

Per mio destino adempio.
Credo che il giusto è un istrïon beffardo
E nel viso e nel cuor,
Che tutto è in lui bugiardo:
Lagrima, bacio, sguardo,
Sacrificio ed onor.
E credo l'uom gioco d'iniqua sorte

Dal germe della culla
Al verme dell'avel.
Vien dopo tanta irrisïon la Morte.
E poi? La Morte è il Nulla,
È vecchia fola il Ciel.

*Si vede passare nel giardino Desdemona con Emilia. Jago
si slancia al verone, al di là del quale è appostato Cassio.*

JAGO (*a Cassio*)
Eccola ... Cassio ... a te ... Questo è il momento.

Ti scuoti ... vien Desdemona.
(*Cassio va verso Desdemona, la saluta, le s'accosta.*)

Beseech her, that kindly soul,
To intercede for you and your pardon is assured.

CASSIO   But how can I speak with her?

IAGO   It is her habit
To stroll among those trees at noontime
With my wife. Await her here.
Now the way to salvation is open to you;
Go.

Cassio leaves.

IAGO (*following Cassio with his eye*)
Go. I see your destination already.
Your demon drives you,
And I am your demon,
Mine drives me, and I believe in it,
An inexorable God:
(*moving away from the balcony without looking any
longer in the direction of Cassio, who has
disappeared among the trees*)
I believe in a cruel God who created me
Similar to Himself, and whom I name in my
wrath.
From the baseness of a germ or an atom,
Basely I was born.
I am wicked
Because I am a man;
And I feel the mud of my origin in me.
Yes! This is my creed!
I believe with a firm heart, just as
The little widow in church believes,
That the evil I think, the evil that comes from
me,
Is wrought by my destiny.
I believe the honest man is a mocking actor
In his face and in his heart,
That everything in him is falsehood:
His tears, kiss, gaze,
Sacrifice, and honor.
And I believe that man is the plaything of
unjust fate
From the germ of the cradle
To the worm of the grave.
After so much derision comes Death.
And then? Death is Nothingness
And heaven an old wives' tale.

*Desdemona is seen passing through the garden with Emilia.
Iago dashes to the balcony, beyond which Cassio has taken his
stand.*

IAGO (*to Cassio*)
There she is . . . Cassio . . . it's up to you . . .
This is the moment.
Bestir yourself . . . Desdemona's coming.
(*Cassio goes toward Desdemona, greets her,
walks beside her.*)

(S'è mosso; la saluta
E s'avvicina.
Or qui si tragga Otello!... aiuta, aiuta

Sàtana il mio cimento!...
(*Sempre al verone, osservando, ma un poco discosto*)
(*si vedono ripassare nel giardino Cassio e Desdemona.*)
Già conversano insieme ... ed essa inclina,

Sorridendo, il bel viso.
Mi basta un lampo sol di quel sorriso
Per trascinare Otello alla ruina.
Andiam ...
(*Fa per avviarsi rapido all'uscio del lato destro,
     ma s'arresta subitamente.*)
Ma il caso in mio favor s'adopra.
Eccolo ... al posto, all'opra.)

*Si colloca immoto al verone, guardando fissamente verso il
giardino, dove stanno Cassio e Desdemona.*

JAGO (*simulando di non aver visto Otello e fingendo di parlare
fra sè*)
                 Ciò m'accora ...
OTELLO (*avvicinandosi a Jago*)
                 Che parli?
JAGO   Nulla ... voi qui? una vana
                 Voce m'uscì dal labbro ...
OTELLO   Colui che s'allontana
                 Dalla mia sposa, è Cassio?
JAGO (*e l'uno e l'altro si staccano dal verone*)
                 Cassio? no ... quei si scosse
                 Come un reo nel vedervi.
OTELLO   Credo che Cassio ei fosse.
JAGO   Mio signore ...
OTELLO   Che brami?...
JAGO   Cassio, nei primi dì
                 Del vostro amor, Desdemona non conosceva?
OTELLO   Sì.
                 Perchè fai tale inchiesta?
JAGO   Il mio pensiero è vago
                 D'ubbìe, non di malizia.
OTELLO   Di' il tuo pensiero, Jago.
JAGO   Vi confidaste a Cassio?
OTELLO   Spesso un mio dono o un cenno
                 Portava alla mia sposa.
JAGO   Dassenno?
OTELLO   Sì, dassenno.
                           (*calmo*)
                 Nol credi onesto?
JAGO (*imitando Otello*)
                 Onesto?
OTELLO   Che ascondi nel tuo core?
JAGO   Che ascondo in cor, signore?

(He has moved; he's greeted her
And is approaching her.
Now let Othello be drawn here! ... Help,
    Satan,
Help my cause! ...
(Still at the balcony, observing, but slightly to one side)
(Cassio and Desdemona are seen crossing the garden again.)
They are already talking together ... And she
    inclines
Her beautiful face, smiling.
I need only one flash of that smile
To drag Othello to his ruin.
Let us go ...
*(He starts to go quickly toward the door at the right,
                but suddenly stops.)*
But chance is working in my favor.
There he is ... to my place, to work.)

He takes his place, motionless, on the balcony, staring toward the garden, where Cassio and Desdemona are.

IAGO *(pretending that he hasn't seen Othello and is talking to himself)*
    That distresses me ...
OTHELLO *(coming over to Iago)*
    What are you saying?
IAGO   Nothing ... you here? An idle
    Word escaped my lips ...
OTHELLO   That man going away from
    My wife, is it Cassio?
IAGO *(as the two of them move from the balcony)*
    Cassio? No ... that man started
    As if guilty, on seeing you.
OTHELLO   I believe it was Cassio.
IAGO   My Lord ...
OTHELLO   What do you want? ...
IAGO   In the first days of your love
    Didn't Cassio know Desdemona?
OTHELLO   Yes.
    Why do you ask such a question?
IAGO   My thought is vague,
    A whim, with no malice.
OTHELLO   Speak your thought, Iago.
IAGO   You confided in Cassio?
OTHELLO   Often he carried a gift or a word
    From me to my wife.
IAGO   Really?
OTHELLO   Yes, really.
            (calmly)
    Don't you believe him honest?
IAGO *(imitating Othello)*
    Honest?
OTHELLO   What are you hiding in your heart?
IAGO   What am I hiding in my heart, My Lord?

OTELLO   "Che ascondo in cor, signore?"
Per cielo! tu sei l'eco dei detti miei, nel chiostro

Dell'anima ricetti qualche terribil mostro.
Sì, ben t'udii poc'anzi mormorar: ciò m'accora.

Ma di che t'accoravi? nomini Cassio e allora

Tu corrughi la fronte. Suvvia, parla se m'ami.
JAGO   Voi sapete ch'io v'amo.
OTELLO   Dunque senza velami
T'esprimi e senza ambagi. T'esca fuor dalla gola

Il tuo più rio pensiero colla più ria parola!
JAGO   S'anco teneste in mano tutta l'anima mia
Nol sapreste.
OTELLO   Ah!
JAGO (*avvicinandosi molto ad Otello e sottovoce*)
Temete, signor, la gelosia!
È un'idra fosca, livida, cieca, col suo veleno

Sè stessa attosca, vivida piaga le squarcia il seno.

OTELLO   Miseria mia! No! il vano sospettar nulla giova.
Pria del dubbio l'indagine, dopo il dubbio la
    prova,
Dopo la prova (Otello ha sue leggi supreme),
Amore e gelosia vadan dispersi insieme!
JAGO (*con piglio più ardito*)
Un tal proposto spezza di mie labbra il suggello.
Non parlo ancor di prova; pur, generoso Otello,

Vigilate, soventi le oneste e ben create
Coscïenze non vedono la frode: vigilate.
Scrutate le parole di Desdemona, un detto
Può ricondur la fede, può affermare il
    sospetto ...
VOCI LONTANO
Dove guardi splendono
Raggi, avvampan cuori,
Dove passi scendono
Nuvole di fiori.
Qui fra gigli e rose
Come a un casto altare,
Padri, bimbi, spose
Vengono a cantar.

   Si vede ricomparire Desdemona nel giardino, dalla vasta apertura del fondo: essa è circondata da donne dell'isola, da fanciulli, da marinai cipriotti e albanesi, che si avanzano e le offrono fiori e rami fioriti ed altri doni. Alcuni s'accompagnano, cantando, sulla guzla (una specie di mandòla), altri hanno delle piccole arpe ad armacollo.

OTHELLO	"What am I hiding in my heart, My Lord?"
	By heaven! You are the echo of my words; in the cloister
	Of your soul you harbor some terrible monster.
	Yes, I clearly heard you murmur just now: that distresses me.
	But what distressed you? You mention Cassio and then
	You frown. Come, if you love me, speak.
IAGO	You know that I love you.
OTHELLO	Then without veils and without
	Ambiguous words express yourself. Let your worst thought
	Come from your throat with the worst words!
IAGO	Even if you held my whole soul in your hand
	You would not know it.
OTHELLO	Ah!

IAGO (*coming very close to Othello and whispering*)
Fear jealousy, My Lord!
It is a dark, leaden, blind hydra that poisons itself
With its own venom, tearing an open wound in its breast.

OTHELLO   O misery! No! Vain suspicions are no help.
Before doubt, enquiry. After doubt, the proof.

After the proof (Othello has his supreme laws),
Let love and jealousy be dispelled together!

IAGO (*with a bolder mien*)
Such a proposal breaks the seal on my lips.
I do not yet speak of proof; still, generous Othello,
Keep watch; often honest and well-disposed
Minds do not see deceit: keep watch.
Examine Desdemona's words; a remark
Can restore trust or confirm suspicion . . .

DISTANT VOICES
Where you glance bright rays
Shine, hearts are enflamed,
Where you pass clouds
Of flowers descend.
Here among lilies and roses
As if at a chaste altar,
Fathers, children, brides
Come to sing.

Desdemona is seen again in the garden, through the broad open window at the back: she is surrounded by women of the island, children, Cypriot and Albanian sailors, who come forward and offer her flowers and blossoming branches and other presents. Some sing, accompanying themselves on the guzla (a kind of mandolin), others have little harps slung over their shoulders.

JAGO (*come prima sottovoce*)
> Eccola ... vigilate.

CORO (*nel giardino*)
> Dove guardi splendono
> Raggi, avvampan cuori, ecc.

FANCIULLI (*spargendo al suolo fiori di giglio*)
> T'offriamo il giglio
> Soave stel
> Che in man degli angeli
> Fu assunto in ciel,
> Che abbella il fulgido
> Manto e la gonna
> Della Madonna
> E il santo vel.

DONNE e MARINAI
> Mentre all'aura vola
> Lieta la canzon,
> L'agile mandòla
> Ne accompagna il suon.

MARINAI (*offrendo a Desdemona dei monili di corallo e di perle*)
> A te le porpore,
> Le perle e gli ostri,
> Nella voragine
> Côlti del mar.
> Vogliam Desdemona
> Coi doni nostri
> Come un'immagine
> Sacra adornar.

FANCIULLI e DONNE
> Mentre all'aura vola
> Lieta la canzon,
> L'agile mandòla
> Ne accompagna il suon.

LE DONNE (*spargendo fronde e fiori*)
> A te la florida
> Messe dai grembi
> A nembi, a nembi,
> Spargiamo al suol.
> L'April circonda
> La sposa bionda
> D'un'etra rorida
> Che vibra al Sol.

FANCIULLI e MARINAI
> Mentre all'aura vola
> Lieta la canzon,
> L'agile mandòla
> Ne accompagna il suon.

TUTTI   Dove guardi splendono, ecc.

DESDEMONA   Splende il cielo, danza
> L'aura, olezza il fior ...

OTELLO   Quel canto mi conquide.
> S'ella m'inganna, il ciel se stesso irride!

IAGO (*whispering as before*)
     There she is . . . keep watch.
CHORUS (*in the garden*)
          Where you glance bright rays
          Shine, hearts are enflamed, etc.
CHILDREN (*scattering lilies on the ground*)
          We offer you the lily,
          The tender stalk
          That in the angels' hands
          Was borne up to heaven,
          That bedecks the gleaming
          Mantle and the gown
          Of the Madonna
          And her holy veil.
WOMEN and SAILORS
          As the happy song
          Is wafted on the air,
          The agile mandolin
          Accompanies its sound.
SAILORS (*offering pearl and coral jewels to Desdemona*)

          For you the purple conches,
          The pearls and the coral,
          Gathered in the abyss
          Of the sea.
          We wish to adorn
          Desdemona
          With our gifts
          Like a holy image.
MAIDENS and WOMEN
          As the happy song
          Is wafted on the air,
          The agile mandolin
          Accompanies its sound.
WOMEN (*scattering branches and flowers*)
          For you we scatter
          From our laps
          In clouds, in clouds,
          The harvest of flowers to the ground.
          April surrounds
          The blond bride
          With dewy air
          That shimmers in the Sun.
YOUNG MEN and SAILORS
          As the happy song
          Is wafted on the air
          The agile mandolin
          Accompanies its sound.
ALL   Where you glance, etc.
DESDEMONA   The sky is bright, the air
             Dances, the flowers are perfumed . . .
OTHELLO   That song overcomes me.
             If she is betraying me, heaven is mocking
                  itself!

JAGO (*a sè*)

> (Beltà ed amor in dolce inno concordi!
> I vostri infrangerò soavi accordi.)

DESDEMONA   Gioia, amor, speranza
               Cantan nel mio cor.

TUTTI   Vivi felice! vivi felice!
               Addio. Qui regna Amor.

OTELLO   Quel canto mi conquide.

Finito il coro, Desdemona bacia la testa d'alcuni tra i fan-
ciulli, e alcune donne le baciano il lembo della veste, ed essa
porge una borsa ai marinai. Il coro s'allontana. Desdemona,
seguita poi da Emilia, entra nella sala e s'avanza verso Otello.

DESDEMONA (*a Otello*)

> D'un uom che geme sotto il tuo disdegno
> La preghiera ti porto.

OTELLO   Chi è costui?

DESDEMONA   Cassio.

OTELLO   Era lui
               Che ti parlava sotto quelle fronde?

DESDEMONA   Lui stesso, e il suo dolor che in me s'infonde
               Tant'è verace che di grazia è degno.
               Intercedo per lui, per lui ti prego.
               Tu gli perdona.

OTELLO   Non ora.

DESDEMONA   Non oppormi il tuo diniego.
               Gli perdona.

OTELLO   Non ora.

DESDEMONA   Perchè torbida suona
               La voce tua? qual pena t'addolora?

OTELLO   M'ardon le tempie ...

DESDEMONA (*spiegando il suo fazzoletto come per fasciare la*
fronte d'Otello)

> Quell'ardor molesto
> Svanirà, se con questo
> Morbido lino la mia man ti fascia.

OTELLO (*getta il fazzoletto a terra*)

> Non ho d'uopo di ciò.

DESDEMONA   Tu sei crucciato, Signor.

OTELLO (*aspramente*)

> Mi lascia! mi lascia!

Emilia raccoglie il fazzoletto dal suolo.

DESDEMONA   Se inconscia, contro te, sposo, ho peccato,

              Dammi la dolce e lieta parola del perdono.

OTELLO (*a parte*)

> Forse perchè gl'inganni
> D'arguto amor non tendo ...

DESDEMONA   La tua fanciulla io sono
               Umile e mansueta;

IAGO (*to himself*)
                (Beauty and love united in sweet song!
                I will interrupt your tender chords.)

DESDEMONA   Joy, love, and hope
                Sing in my heart.

ALL   May you live happily! Live happily!
                Good-by. Here Love reigns.

OTHELLO   That song overcomes me.

When the chorus is over, Desdemona kisses the heads of some of the children, and some of the women kiss the hem of her dress; she hands a purse to the sailors. The chorus goes away. Desdemona, followed by Emilia, comes into the room and goes toward Othello.

DESDEMONA (*to Othello*)
                I bring you the plea of a man
                Who is suffering at your displeasure.

OTHELLO   Who is he?

DESDEMONA   Cassio.

OTHELLO   Was it he
                Who spoke to you under those trees?

DESDEMONA   He himself, and his grief, which I feel,
                Is so real that it merits forgiveness.
                I intercede for him. I beg you, on his behalf.
                Forgive him.

OTHELLO   Not now.

DESDEMONA   Don't deny me.
                Forgive him.

OTHELLO   Not now.

DESDEMONA   Why does your voice sound
                Shaken? What grief saddens you?

OTHELLO   My temples burn . . .

DESDEMONA (*unfolding her handkerchief, as if to bandage Othello's forehead*)
                That troublesome burning
                Will disappear if my hand bandages you
                With this soft linen.

OTHELLO (*throwing the handkerchief on the ground*)
                I do not need that.

DESDEMONA   You are worried, My Lord.

OTHELLO (*harshly*)
                Leave me! Leave me!

Emilia picks the handkerchief from the ground.

DESDEMONA   If, unwittingly, I have offended you, my
                      husband,
                Give me your sweet and happy word of pardon.

OTHELLO (*aside*)
                Perhaps because I do not understand
                The deceits of sly love . . .

DESDEMONA   I am your maiden
                Humble and obedient;

Ma il labbro tuo sospira,
Hai l'occhio fiso al suol.
Guardami in volto e mira
Come favella amor.
Vien ch'io t'allieti il core,
Ch'io ti lenisca il duol.
Guardami in volto e mira, ecc.

OTELLO (*sempre a parte*)
(Forse perchè discendo
Nella valle degli anni,
Forse perchè ho sul viso
Quest'atro tenebror ...
Forse perchè gl'inganni d'arguto
Amor non tendo, ecc.
Ella è perduta e irriso
Io sono e il core infrango
E ruinar nel fango
Vedo il mio sogno d'or.
Ella è perduta e irriso, ecc.)

JAGO (*a Emilia sottovoce*)
(Quel vel mi porgi
Ch'or hai raccolto.)

EMILIA (*sottovoce a Jago*)
(Qual frode scorgi?
Ti leggo in volto.)

JAGO   T'opponi a vôto
Quand'io comando.

EMILIA   Il tuo nefando
Livor m'è noto.

JAGO   Sospetto insano!

EMILIA   Guardia fedel
È questa mano.

JAGO   Dammi quel vel!
(*Afferra violentemente il braccio di Emilia.*)
Su te l'irosa mia man s'aggrava!

EMILIA   Son la tua sposa,
Non la tua schiava.

JAGO   La schiava impura
Tu sei di Jago.

EMILIA   Ho il cor presago
D'una sventura.

JAGO   Nè mi paventi?

EMILIA   Uomo crudel!

JAGO   A me.

EMILIA   Che tenti?

JAGO   A me quel vel!
(*Con un colpo di mano, Jago ha carpito il
fazzoletto ad Emilia.*)

EMILIA   Uomo crudel!

JAGO   (Già la mia brama
Conquido, ed ora

But your lip sighs,
Your eyes are on the ground.
Look into my face and see
How love speaks.
Come, let me gladden your heart,
Let me ease your suffering.
Look into my face and see, etc.

OTHELLO (*still aside*)
(Perhaps because I am declining
Into the valley of my years,
Perhaps because on my face
There is this darkness . . .
Perhaps because I do not understand
The deceits of sly love, etc.
She is lost and I
Am mocked and my heart breaks.
I see my golden dream
Ruined in the mire.
She is lost and I
Am mocked, etc.)

IAGO (*to Emilia in a low voice*)
(Give me that handkerchief
You just picked up.)

EMILIA (*to Iago in a low voice*)
(What deceit are you planning?
I can read your face.)

IAGO
You oppose me in vain
When I command.

EMILIA
I know
Your unspeakable rancor.

IAGO
Insane suspicion!

EMILIA
My hand
Is a loyal guard.

IAGO
Give me that handkerchief!
(*He violently seizes Emilia's arm.*)
My angry hand is poised over you!

EMILIA
I am your wife,
Not your slave.

IAGO
You are the unchaste
Slave of Iago.

EMILIA
My heart has a presentiment
Of misfortune.

IAGO
Do you not fear me?

EMILIA
Cruel man!

IAGO
Give it to me.

EMILIA
What are you attempting?

IAGO
Give me that handkerchief!
(*With a sudden movement, Iago seizes the
handkerchief from Emilia.*)

EMILIA
Cruel man!

IAGO
(I am already achieving
My desire, and now

Su questa trama
Jago lavora!)

EMILIA (Vinser gli artigli
Truci e codardi.
Dio dai perigli
Sempre ci guardi.)

DESDEMONA Dammi la dolce e lieta parola del perdon.

OTELLO Escite! Solo vo' restar.

JAGO (*sottovoce ad Emilia che sta per escire*)
Ti giova tacer. Intendi?

*Desdemona ed Emilia escono. Jago finge d'escire dalla porta
del fondo, ma giuntovi s'arresta.*

OTELLO (*accasciato, su d'un sedile*)
Desdemona rea!

JAGO (*nel fondo guardano di nascosto il fazzoletto, poi ripo-
nendolo con cura nel giustacuore*)
(Con questi fili tramerò la prova
Del peccato d'amor. Nella dimora
Di Cassio ciò s'asconda.)

OTELLO Atroce idea!

JAGO (*fissando Otello*)
(Il mio velen lavora.)

OTELLO Rea contro me! contro me!!!

JAGO (*cupo*) (Soffri e ruggi!)

OTELLO Atroce!!!... atroce!!!...

JAGO (*dopo essersi portato accanto ad Otello — bonariamente*)
Non pensateci più.

OTELLO (*balzando*)
Tu?! Indietro! fuggi!!
M'hai legato alla croce!...
Ahimè!... Più orrendo d'ogni orrenda ingiuria

Dell'ingiuria è il sospetto.
Nell'ore arcane della sua lussuria
(E a me furate!) m'agitava il petto
Forse un presagio? Ero baldo, giulivo ...

Nulla sapevo ancor; io non sentivo
Sul suo corpo divin che m'innamora
E sui labbri mendaci
Gli ardenti baci
Di Cassio! Ed ora!... ed ora ...
Ora e per sempre addio sante memorie,
Addio sublimi incanti del pensier!
Addio schiere fulgenti, addio vittorie,
Dardi volanti e volanti corsier!
Addio vessillo trïonfale e pio!
E dïane squillanti in sul mattin!
Clamori e canti di battaglia, addio!...
Della gloria d'Otello è questo il fin.

JAGO Pace, signor.

Iago is at work
On this plot!)

EMILIA (His grim and cowardly
Claws overpowered me.
God guard us always
From dangers.)

DESDEMONA Give me the sweet and happy word of pardon.

OTHELLO Go away! I want to remain alone.

IAGO (*in a low voice to Emilia, who is about to go*)
It's best for you to keep silent. Understand?

*Desdemona and Emilia go out. Iago pretends to leave by
the door at the back, but when he reaches it he stops.*

OTHELLO (*sinking into a chair*)
Desdemona guilty!

IAGO (*at the back, covertly looking at the handkerchief, then
carefully placing it in his doublet*)
(With these threads I will weave the proof
Of sinful love. It shall be hidden
In Cassio's house.)

OTHELLO Horrible idea!

IAGO (*gazing at Othello*)
(My poison is working.)

OTHELLO Guilty toward me! Toward me!!!

IAGO (*grimly*)
(Suffer and roar!)

OTHELLO Horrible!!! Horrible!!! ...

IAGO (*after coming up to Othello — in a kindly tone*)
Think no more about it.

OTHELLO (*springing up*)
You? Stand back! Flee!!
You have nailed me to the cross! ...
Alas! ... More horrible than any horrible
injury
Is the suspicion of injury.
In the secret hours of her lust
(And stolen from me!) did any presentiment
Perhaps stir in my breast? I was confident,
joyful ...
I knew nothing yet; I didn't feel
On her divine body that makes me love her
And on her false lips
The ardent kisses
Of Cassio! And now! ... And now ...
Now and forever, farewell sacred memories,
Farewell sublime enchantments of my thought!
Farewell, gleaming troops, farewell victories,
Flying arrows and flying chargers!
Farewell holy, triumphant banner!
And trumpets blaring at early morning!
Sounds and songs of battle, farewell! ...
This is the end of Othello's glory.

IAGO Peace, My Lord.

OTELLO   Sciagurato! mi trova
                Una prova secura
                Che Desdemona è impura —
                Non sfuggir! non sfuggir! nulla ti giova!
                Vo' una secura, una visibil prova!
                O sulla tua testa
                S'accenda e precipiti il fulmine
                Del mio spaventoso furor che si desta!
                (*Afferra Jago alla gola e lo atterra.*)
JAGO   Divina grazia difendimi!
                        (*alzandosi*)
                Il cielo vi protegga. Non son più vostro alfiere.
                Voglio che il mondo testimon mi sia
                Che l'onestà è periglio.

Fa per andarsene.

OTELLO   No ... rimani.
                Forse onesto tu sei.
JAGO (*sulla soglia fingendo d'andarsene*)
                Meglio varrebbe
                Ch'io fossi un ciurmador.
OTELLO   Per l'universo!
                Credo leale Desdemona e credo
                Che non lo sia; te credo onesto e credo

                Disleale ... La prova io voglio! voglio
                La certezza!!
JAGO (*ritornando verso Otello*)
                Signor, frenate l'ansie.
                E qual certezza v'abbisogna? Avvinti
                Vederli forse?
OTHELLO   Ah! Morte e dannazione!!
JAGO   Ardua impresa sarebbe; e qual certezza

                Sognate voi se quell'immondo fatto
                Sempre vi sfuggirà?... Ma pur se guida
                È la ragione al vero, una sì forte
                Congettura riserbo che per poco
                Alla certezza vi conduce. Udite:
                (*avvicinandosi molto ad Otello e sottovoce*)
                Era la notte, Cassio dormìa, gli stavo accanto.

                Con interrotte voci tradìa l'intimo incanto.

                Le labbra lente, lente, movea, nell'abbandono
                Del sogno ardente; e allor dicea, con flebil
                        suono:
                Desdemona soave! Il nostro amor s'asconda.
                Cauti vegliamo! l'estasi del ciel tutto m'innonda.

                Seguia più vago l'incubo blando; con molle
                        angoscia,
                L'interna imago quasi baciando, ei disse poscia:
                        (*parlando*)
                Il rio destino impreco che al Moro ti donò.

OTHELLO   Wretch! Find me
            Certain proof
            That Desdemona is unchaste —
            Don't flee! Don't flee! Nothing avails you!
            I want certain, visible proof!
            Or else on your head
            Let the thunderbolt of my fearful,
            Wakening fury kindle and fall!
     (*He seizes Iago by the throat and hurls him to the ground.*)

IAGO   Divine grace, defend me!
                    (*rising*)
            Heaven protect you. I am your ensign no longer.
            I want the world to be my witness
            That honesty is a danger.

     He starts to leave.

OTHELLO   No . . . stay.
            Perhaps you are honest.

IAGO (*on the threshold, pretending to go*)
            It would be better for me
            If I were a deceiver.

OTHELLO   By the universe!
            I believe Desdemona faithful, and I believe
            That she is not. I believe you honest, and I
              believe you
            Disloyal . . . I want the proof! I want
            Certainty!!

IAGO (*coming back toward Othello*)
            My lord, restrain your anxiety.
            What certainty do you need? To see them
            Embracing perhaps?

OTHELLO   Ah! Death and damnation!

IAGO   That would be a difficult undertaking; and of
              what certainty
            Do you dream, if that foul act
            Will always elude you? . . . But if reason
            Be the guide to truth, I have such a strong
            Conjecture that it leads almost
            To certainty. Listen:
     (*coming very close to Othello and in a low voice*)
            It was night, Cassio was sleeping, I was beside
              him.
            With faltering words he betrayed his inner
              enchantment.
            His lips moved very slowly in the abandon
            Of his ardent dream; And then he said, in a
              faint tone;
            Sweet Desdemona! Let our love be kept hidden.
            We must keep careful watch! Heavenly
              ecstasy engulfs me wholly.
            The tender nightmare continued more sweetly;
              with soft anguish,
            As if kissing the inner vision, he said then:
                    (*speaking*)
            I curse wicked fate, which gave you to the
              Moor.

E allora il sogno in cieco letargo si mutò.

OTELLO   Oh! mostruosa colpa!

JAGO   Io non narrai che un sogno.

OTELLO   Un sogno che rivela un fatto.

JAGO   Un sogno che può dar forma di prova
Ad altro indizio.

OTELLO   E qual?

JAGO   Talor vedeste
In mano di Desdemona un tessuto
Trapunto a fiori e più sottil d'un velo?

OTELLO   È il fazzoletto ch'io le diedi, pegno
Primo d'amor.

JAGO   Quel fazzoletto ieri
(Certo ne son) lo vidi in man di Cassio.

OTELLO   Ah! mille vite gli donasse Iddio!
Una è povera preda al furor mio!
Jago, ho il cor di gelo.
Lungi da me le pietose larve!
Tutto il mio vano amor esalo al cielo,
Guardami, ei sparve.
Nelle sue spire d'angue
L'idra m'avvince. Ah! sangue! sangue! sangue!!
    (*s'inginocchia*)
Sì, pel ciel marmoreo giuro! Per le attorte
    folgori!
Per la Morte e per l'oscuro mar sterminator!
D'ira e d'impeto tremendo presto fia che
    sfolgori
Questa man ch'io levo e stendo!

*Levando le mani al cielo, fa per alzarsi, Jago lo trattiene
inginocchiato.*

JAGO   Non v'alzate ancor!
    (*S'inginocchia anch'esso.*)
Testimon è il Sol ch'io miro, che m'irradia e
    innanima,
L'ampia terra e il vasto spiro del Creato inter,

Che ad Otello io sacro ardenti, core, braccio ed
    anima
S'anco ad opere cruenti s'armi il suo voler!

JAGO e OTELLO (*insieme, alzando le mani al cielo come chi
    giura*)
Sì, pel ciel marmoreo giuro! per le attorte
    folgori!
Per la Morte e per l'oscuro mar sterminator!
D'ira e d'impeto tremendo presto fia che
    sfolgori
Questa man ch'io levo e stendo. Dio vendicator!

	Then the dream turned into blind sleep.
OTHELLO	Oh! Monstrous guilt!
IAGO	I related only a dream.
OTHELLO	A dream that reveals an act.
IAGO	A dream that can make another clue Become proof.
OTHELLO	What clue?
IAGO	Have you seen sometimes In Desdemona's hand a handkerchief Embroidered with flowers and finer than gauze?
OTHELLO	It's the handkerchief I gave her, My first pledge of love.
IAGO	I saw that handkerchief yesterday (I'm certain of it) in Cassio's hand.
OTHELLO	Ah! If God gave him a thousand lives! One is a poor prey to my rage!! Iago, my heart is of ice. Far from me forms of pity! I breathe all my vain love to heaven. Look at me, it vanishes. In its serpent's coils The hydra grips me. Ah! Blood! Blood! Blood! 　　　　　(*kneels*) Yes, I swear by marble heaven! By the forked 　lightning! By Death and by the dark, murderous sea! With rage and terrible force let this hand

　　　　　That I raise and extend soon blaze out!

Raising his hands toward heaven, he starts to rise, but Iago keeps him on his knees.

| IAGO | Don't rise yet!
　　　　(*He kneels too.*)
Witness is the Sun that I see, that shines on me
　and animates me,
The broad earth and the vast breath of all
　Creation,
That to Othello I consecrate my ardent heart,
　arm, and soul
Even if his will arms itself for bloody tasks! |

IAGO and OTHELLO (*together, raising their arms to heaven, as if swearing*)
　　　　　Yes, I swear by marble heaven! By the forked
　　　　　　lightning!
　　　　　By Death and by the dark, murderous sea!
　　　　　With rage and terrible force let this hand

　　　　　That I raise and extend soon blaze out!
　　　　　　Avenging God!

ATTO TERZO

La gran sala del castello. A destra un vasto peristilio a colonne. Questo peristilio è annesso ad una sala di minori proporzioni; nel fondo della sala un verone. Otello, Jago, l'araldo.

ARALDO (*dal peristilio, a Otello che sarà con Jago nella sala*)

> La vedetta del porto ha segnalato
> La veneta galea che a Cipro adduce
> Gli ambasciatori.

OTELLO (*fa cenno all'araldo di allontanarsi*)
> Bene sta.

L'araldo esce.

OTELLO (*a Jago*)
> Continua.

JAGO
> Qui trarrò Cassio e con astute inchieste
> Lo adescherò a ciarlar.
> (*indicando il vano del verone*)
> Voi là nascosto
> Scrutate i modi suoi, le sue parole,
> I lazzi, i gesti. Paziente siate
> O la prova vi sfugge. Ecco Desdemona.
> Finger conviene ... io vado.

Dicendo io vado, s'allontana come per escire, poi s'arresta e si riavvicina ad Otello per dirgli l'ultima parola.

> Il fazzoletto ...

OTELLO
> Val volentieri obliato l'avrei.
> (*Jago esce.*)

DESDEMONA (*dalla porta di sinistra, ancora presso alla soglia*)
> Dio ti giocondi, o sposo dell'alma mia sovrano.

OTELLO (*andando incontro a Desdemona e prendendole la mano*)

> Grazie, madonna, datemi la vostra eburnea
>   mano.
> Caldo mador ne irrora la morbida beltà.

DESDEMONA
> Essa ancor l'orme ignora del duolo e dell'età.

OTELLO
> Eppur qui annida il demone gentil del mal
>   consiglio,
> Che il vago avorio allumina del piccioletto
>   artiglio.
> Mollemente alla prece s'atteggia e al pio
>   fervore ...

DESDEMONA
> Eppur con questa mano io v'ho donato il core.
> Ma riparlar vi debbo di Cassio.

OTELLO
> Ancor l'ambascia
> Del mio morbo m'assale; tu la fronte mi fascia.

ACT THREE

*The great hall of the castle. At right a vast court with a
colonnade. This court is connected to a smaller room; at the
back of the hall a balcony. Othello, Iago, the herald.*

HERALD (*from the courtyard, to Othello, who is in the hall
    with Iago*)
              The sentry at the harbor has sighted
              The Venetian galley that is bringing
              The ambassadors to Cyprus.
OTHELLO (*motioning to the herald to go*)
              Very well.

The herald leaves.

OTHELLO (*to Iago*)
              Go on.

IAGO   I'll bring Cassio here and with clever questions
              I'll lure him to prattle.
             (*pointing to the door to the balcony*)
              You, hidden there,
              Observe his manners, his words,
              His jokes and gestures. Be patient
              Or the proof will elude you. Here is Desdemona.
              It's best to pretend . . . I am going.

*Saying, "I am going," he moves away as if to leave, then
stops and comes back to Othello to speak the last word to him.*

              The handkerchief . . .
OTHELLO   Go! I would happily have forgotten it.
                 (*Iago leaves.*)
DESDEMONA (*from the door at left, still near the threshold*)
              God rest you merry, O husband, sovereign of
                 my soul.
OTHELLO (*going toward Desdemona and taking her hand*)

              Thank you, My Lady, give me your ivory hand.

              Warm moisture bedews its soft beauty.
DESDEMONA It is still unaware of the stamp of grief and of
               age.
OTHELLO   And yet the courteous demon of ill counsel
               nests here,
              Illuminating the lovely ivory of this little claw.

              Gently it assumes the attitude of prayer and of
               pious fervor . . .
DESDEMONA And yet with this hand I gave you my heart.
              But I must speak to you again of Cassio.
OTHELLO   Again the pain
              Of my illness attacks me; bandage my forehead.

DESDEMONA (*porgendogli un fazzoletto*)
    A te.

OTELLO   No; il fazzoletto voglio ch'io ti donai.

DESDEMONA   Non l'ho meco.

OTELLO   Desdemona, guai se lo perdi! guai!
    Una possente maga ne ordia lo stame arcano.
    Ivi è riposta l'alta malìa d'un talismano.
    Bada! smarrirlo, oppur donarlo, è ria sventura!

DESDEMONA   Il vero parli?

OTELLO   Il vero parlo.

DESDEMONA   Mi fai paura!...

OTELLO   Che?! l'hai perduto forse?

DESDEMONA   No ...

OTELLO   Lo cerca.

DESDEMONA   Fra poco ...
    Lo cercherò ...

OTELLO   No, tosto!

DESDEMONA   Tu di me ti fai gioco,
    Storni così l'inchiesta di Cassio; astuzia è questa
    Del tuo pensier.

OTELLO   Pel cielo! l'anima mia si desta!
    Il fazzoletto ...

DESDEMONA   È Cassio l'amico tuo diletto.

OTELLO   Il fazzoletto!!

DESDEMONA   A Cassio perdona ...

OTELLO   Il fazzoletto!!!

DESDEMONA   Gran Dio! nella tua voce v'è un grido di
        minaccia!

OTELLO   Alza quegli occhi!

DESDEMONA   Atroce idea!

OTELLO (*prendendola a forza sotto il mento e alla spalla e obbligandola a guardarlo*)
    Guardami in faccia!
    Dimmi chi sei!

DESDEMONA   La sposa fedel d'Otello.

OTELLO   Giura!
    Giura e ti danna ...

DESDEMONA   Otello fedel mi crede.

OTELLO   Impura ti credo.

DESDEMONA   Iddio m'aiuti!

OTELLO   Corri alla tua condanna,
    Di' che sei casta.

DESDEMONA (*fissandolo*)
    Casta ... lo son ...

OTELLO   Giura e ti danna!!!

DESDEMONA   Esterrafatta fisso lo sguardo tuo tremendo,
    In te parla una Furia, la sento e non l'intendo.

DESDEMONA (*handing him a handkerchief*)
Here.

OTHELLO   No, I want the handkerchief I gave you.

DESDEMONA   I haven't it with me.

OTHELLO   Desdemona, woe, if you have lost it! Woe!
A mighty sorceress disposed its secret weave.
It contains the lofty magic of a talisman.
Take care! To lose it, or to give it away, is
terrible misfortune!

DESDEMONA   Are you speaking the truth?

OTHELLO   I speak the truth.

DESDEMONA   You frighten me! ...

OTHELLO   What?! Have you lost it perhaps?

DESDEMONA   No ...

OTHELLO   Look for it.

DESDEMONA   In a little while ...
I'll look for it ...

OTHELLO   No, at once!

DESDEMONA   You are teasing me,
This way you ward off the question of Cassio;
This is the cleverness of your thinking.

OTHELLO   By heaven! My soul is aroused!
The handkerchief ...

DESDEMONA   Cassio is your beloved friend.

OTHELLO   The handkerchief!!

DESDEMONA   Forgive Cassio ...

OTHELLO   The handkerchief!!!

DESDEMONA   Great God! Your voice is a menacing cry!

OTHELLO   Raise those eyes!

DESDEMONA   Horrible idea!

OTHELLO (*seizing her by the chin and the shoulder and
forcing her to look at him*)
Look me in the face!
Tell me who you are!

DESDEMONA   Othello's faithful wife.

OTHELLO   Swear!
Swear and damn yourself ...

DESDEMONA   Othello believes me faithful.

OTHELLO   I believe you impure.

DESDEMONA   God help me!

OTHELLO   You are running to your damnation,
Say that you are chaste.

DESDEMONA (*fixing him with her eyes*)
I am ... chaste ...

OTHELLO   Swear and damn yourself!!!

DESDEMONA   Terrified, I look into your fearful gaze,
A Fury speaks in you; I hear it and don't
understand it.

Mi guarda! il volto e l'anima ti svelo; il core
infranto
Mi scruta ... io prego il cielo per te con questo
pianto.
Per te con queste stille cocenti aspergo il suol.

Guarda le prime lagrime che da me spreme il
duol.

OTELLO   S'or ti scorge il tuo dèmone un angelo ti crede

E non t'afferra.

DESDEMONA   Vede l'Eterno la mia fede!

OTELLO   No! la vede l'inferno.

DESDEMONA   La tua giustizia impetro,
Sposo mio!

OTELLO   Ah! Desdemona! Indietro! indietro! indietro!!

DESDEMONA   Tu pur piangi?!... e gemendo freni del cor lo
schianto
E son io l'innocente cagion di tanto pianto!...

Qual è il mio fallo?

OTELLO (*cupo*)
E il chiedi?... Il più nero delitto
Sovra il candido giglio della tua fronte è scritto.

DESDEMONA   Ahimè!

OTELLO   Che? non sei forse una vil cortigiana?

DESDEMONA   Ciel! No ... no ... pel battesmo della fede
cristiana!...

OTELLO   Che?...

DESDEMONA   Ah!... non son ciò che esprime quella parola
orrenda.

OTELLO (*mutando d'un tratto l'ira nella più terribile calma
dell'ironia, prende Desdemona per mano e la conduce alla
porta d'onde entrò*)
Datemi ancor l'eburnea mano, vo' fare
ammenda.
Vi credea (perdonate se il mio pensiero è fello)

Quella vil cortigiana che è la sposa d'Otello.

*Otello sforza con un'inflessione del braccio, ma senza scom-
porsi, Desdemona ad escire. Poi ritorna verso il centro della
scena nel massimo grado dell'abbattimento.*

OTELLO (*voce soffocata*)
Dio! mi potevi scagliar tutti i mali
Della miseria, della vergogna,
Far de' miei baldi trofei trionfali
Una maceria, una menzogna ...
E avrei portato la croce crudel
D'angoscie e d'onte
Con calma fronte
E rassegnato al volere del ciel.
Ma, o pianto, o duol! m'han rapito il miraggio

Look at me! I reveal my face and my soul to
you; examine
My broken heart . . . with these tears I pray
to heaven for you.
For you I sprinkle the ground with these
burning drops.
Look at the first tears that grief presses from
me.

OTHELLO   If your devil glimpses you now he believes
you an angel
And does not seize you.

DESDEMONA   The Eternal One sees my loyalty!

OTHELLO   No! Hell sees it.

DESDEMONA   I implore your justice,
My husband!

OTHELLO   Ah! Desdemona! Away! Away! Away!

DESDEMONA   You weep too? . . . and moaning, hold back the
breaking of your heart
And I am the innocent cause of such
weeping! . . .
What is my wrong?

OTHELLO (*grimly*)
You ask it? . . . The blackest crime
Is written on the white lily of your forehead.

DESDEMONA   Alas!

OTHELLO   What? Aren't you perhaps a base strumpet?

DESDEMONA   Heaven! No . . . no . . . by my baptism in the
Christian faith! . . .

OTHELLO   What?

DESDEMONA   Ah! . . . I am not what that horrible word
expresses.

OTHELLO (*his wrath suddenly changing into a more terrible,
ironic calm, he takes Desdemona by the hand and leads her
to the door where she came in*)
Give me your ivory hand again. I want to make
amends.
I thought you (forgive me if my thought is
wicked)
That base strumpet who is Othello's wife.

*Without losing his composure Othello bends his arm and
forces Desdemona to leave. Then he comes back to the center
of the stage in the deepest stage of dejection.*

OTHELLO (*in a choked voice*)
God! You could have hurled at me all the ills
Of poverty, of shame,
Made of my bold, triumphal trophies
A ruin, a falsehood . . .
And I would have carried the cruel cross
Of anguish and shame
With a serene brow
Resigned to the will of heaven.
But, O tears, O grief! They have taken from me
the mirage

Dov'io, giulivo, l'anima acqueto.
Spento è quel sol, quel sorriso, quel raggio
Che mi fa vivo, che mi fa lieto!
Tu alfin, Clemenza, pio genio immortal

Dal roseo riso,
Copri il tuo viso
Santo coll'orrida larva infernal!
Ah! Dannazione!
Pria confessi il delitto e poscia muoia!
Confession! Confession!...
        (*Entra Jago.*)
La prova!...

JAGO (*indicando l'ingresso*)
Cassio è là!

OTELLO   Là?! Cielo! Oh gioia!!
        (*con raccapriccio*)
Orror!... Supplizî immondi!!

JAGO   Ti frena! Ti nascondi.

Conduce rapidamente Otello nel fondo a sinistra dove c'è il vano del verone. Jago, appena condotto Otello al verone, corre verso il fondo del peristilio.

JAGO (*incontra Cassio che esita ad entrare*)
Vieni; l'aula è deserta.
T'inoltra, o Capitano.

CASSIO   Questo nome d'onor suona ancor vano
Per me.

JAGO   Fa cor, la tua causa è in tal mano
Che la vittoria è certa.

CASSIO   Io qui credea di ritrovar Desdemona.

OTELLO (*nascosto*)
(Ei la nomò.)

CASSIO   Vorrei parlarle ancora,
Per saper se la mia grazia è profferta.

JAGO (*gaiamente*)
L'attendi;
(*conducendo Cassio accanto alla prima colonna del peristilio*)
E intanto, giacchè non si stanca
Mai la tua lingua nelle fole gaie,
Narrami un po' di lei che t'innamora.

CASSIO   Di chi?

JAGO (*sottovoce assai*)
Di Bianca.

OTELLO   (Sorride!)

CASSIO   Baie!...

JAGO   Essa t'avvince
Coi vaghi rai.

CASSIO   Rider mi fai.

JAGO   Ride chi vince.

CASSIO (*ridendo*)
In tai disfide per verità,
Vince chi ride. Ah! ah!

Where, rejoicing, I still my spirit.
Extinct is that sun, that smile, that radiance
That makes me alive, that makes me happy!
And you, finally, Clemency, pious, immortal
    spirit
Of the rosy laughter,
Cover your holy face
With the horrible, hellish apparition!
Ah! Damnation!
Let her first confess the crime and then die!
Confession! Confession! . . .
        (*Iago enters.*)
The proof!

IAGO (*pointing to the entrance*)
    Cassio is there!

OTHELLO   There? Heaven! Oh, joy!!
        (*with horror*)
    Horror! . . . Foul torments!

IAGO   Restrain yourself! Hide.

He quickly leads Othello to the back, at left, where there is the door of the balcony. As soon as he has led Othello to the balcony, Iago runs toward the end of the courtyard.

IAGO (*meeting Cassio, who hesitates to come in*)
    Come, the hall is deserted.
    Come inside, Captain.

CASSIO   That honored word still rings in vain
    For me.

IAGO   Take heart, your cause is in such hands
    That your victory is certain.

CASSIO   I thought I would find Desdemona here.

OTELLO   (*hidden*)
    (He spoke her name.)

CASSIO   I would like to speak to her again,
    To know if my pardon has been proclaimed.

IAGO (*gaily*)   Wait for her;
    (*leading Cassio next to the first column in the court*)
    And meanwhile, as your tongue
    Never wearies of gay tales,
    Tell me a little of her whom you love.

CASSIO   Of whom?

IAGO (*in a very low voice*)
    Of Bianca.

OTHELLO   (He smiles!)

CASSIO   Foolishness! . . .

IAGO   She ensnares you
    With her lovely glances.

CASSIO   You make me laugh.

IAGO   He laughs who wins.

CASSIO (*laughing*)
    In such duels, in truth,
    He wins who laughs. Ha! Ha!

JAGO (*ridendo*)
                    Ah! ah!
OTELLO (*dal verone*)
                    (L'empio trionfa, il suo scherno m'uccide;

                                        (*con disperazione*)
                    Dio frena l'ansia che in core mi sta!)
CASSIO   Son già di baci
                    Sazio e di lai.
JAGO   Rider mi fai.
CASSIO   O amor' fugaci!
JAGO   Vagheggi il regno d'altra beltà.
                    Colgo nel segno?
CASSIO   Ah! ah!
JAGO   Ah! ah!
OTELLO   (L'empio m'irride, il suo scherno m'uccide;
                    Dio frena l'ansia che in core mi sta!)
CASSIO   Nel segno hai côlto.
                    Sì, lo confesso.
                    M'odi ...
JAGO (*assai sottovoce*)
                    Sommesso parla. T'ascolto.

Jago conduce Cassio in posto più lontano da Otello.

CASSIO   Jago, t'è nota
                    La mia dimora ...
                            (*Le parole si perdono.*)
OTELLO (*avvicinandosi un poco e cautamente per udir ciò
    che dicono*)
                            (Or gli racconta il modo,
                            Il luogo e l'ora ...)
CASSIO (*sempre sottovoce*)
                    ... da mano ignota ...

Le parole si perdono ancora.

OTELLO   (Le parole non odo ...
                    Lasso! udir le vorrei! Dove son giunto!!)

CASSIO   Un vel trapunto ...
JAGO   È strano! è strano!
OTELLO   (D'avvicinarmi Jago mi fa cenno.)

Passa con cautela e si nasconde dietro le colonne.

JAGO   Da ignota mano?
                            (*forte*)
                    Baie!
CASSIO   Da senno.
                    (*Jago gli fa cenno di parlar ancora sottovoce.*)
                    Quanto mi tarda
                    Saper chi sia ...
JAGO (*guardando rapidamente dalla parte d'Otello, fra sè*)
                    (Otello spia.)
                            (*a Cassio ad alta voce*)

IAGO (*laughing*)
        Ha! Ha!

OTHELLO (*from the balcony*)
        (The villain's triumphant; his contempt kills
           me;
           (*with desperation*)
        God curb the anxiety that is in my heart!)

CASSIO
        I am already sated
        With kisses and poems.

IAGO
        You make me laugh.

CASSIO
        O fleeting loves!

IAGO
        You dream of the reign of another beauty.
        Have I struck home?

CASSIO
        Ha! Ha!

IAGO
        Ha! Ha!

OTHELLO
        (The villain mocks me, his contempt kills me;
        God curb the anxiety that is in my heart!)

CASSIO
        You've struck home.
        Yes, I confess it.
        Hear me . . .

IAGO (*in a very low voice*)
        Speak softly. I'm listening to you.

Iago leads Cassio to a place farther from Othello.

CASSIO
        Iago, you know
        My house . . .
           (*The words are lost.*)

OTHELLO (*coming a little closer, cautiously, to hear what they say*)
        (Now he's telling him the manner,
        The place and the time . . .)

CASSIO (*still in a low voice*)
        . . . by an unknown hand . . .

The words are lost again.

OTHELLO
        (I can't hear the words . . .
        Alas! I want to hear them! What have I come
           to!!)

CASSIO
        An embroidered handkerchief . . .

IAGO
        It's strange! It's strange!

OTHELLO
        (Iago motions me to come closer.)

He moves cautiously and hides behind the columns.

IAGO
        By an unknown hand?
           (*louder*)
        Nonsense!

CASSIO
        Truly.
        (*Iago motions to him to speak softly still.*)
        How eager I am
        To know who it is . . .

IAGO (*looking quickly toward Othello, to himself*)
        Othello is watching.
        (*to Cassio in a loud voice*)

L'hai teco?

CASSIO (*estrae dal giustacuore il fazzoletto di Desdemona*)
Guarda.

JAGO (*prendendo il fazzoletto*)
Qual meraviglia!
            (*a parte*)
(Otello origlia.
Ei s'avvicina
Con mosse accorte.)
            (*a Cassio scherzando*)
Bel cavaliere, nel vostro ostel,
Perdono gli angeli l'aureola e il vel.

Mette le mani dietro la schiena perchè Otello possa osservare il fazzoletto.

OTELLO (*avvicinandosi assai al fazzoletto, dietro le spalle di Jago e nascosto dalla prima colonna*)
(È quello! è quello!
Ruina e morte!)

JAGO   (Origlia Otello.)

OTELLO (*a parte sottovoce*)
(Tutto è spento! amor e duol.
L'alma mia nessun più smuova.)

JAGO (*a Cassio indicando il fazzoletto*)
Questa è una ragna
Dove il tuo cuor
Casca, si lagna,
S'impiglia e muor.
Troppo l'ammiri,
Troppo la guardi;
Bada ai deliri
Vani e bugiardi.
Questa è una ragna, ecc.

CASSIO (*guardando il fazzoletto che avrà ritolto a Jago*)

Miracolo vago
Dell'aspo e dell'ago
Che in raggi tramuta
Le fila d'un vel,
Più bianco, più lieve
Che fiocco di neve
Che nube tessuta
Dall'aure del ciel.

JAGO   Questa è una ragna, ecc.

CASSIO   Miracolo vago ...
Più bianco, più lieve
Che fiocco di neve,
Che nube tessuta
Dall'aure del ciel.
Miracol, miracolo vago!

OTELLO (*nascosto dietro la colonna e guardando di tratto in tratto il fazzoletto nelle mani di Cassio*)
(Tradimento, tradimento, tradimento,

            You have it with you?
CASSIO (*takes Desdemona's handkerchief from his doublet*)
            Look.
IAGO (*taking the handkerchief*)
                What a marvel!
                    (*aside*)
                (Othello's listening.
                He's approaching
                With cautious movements.)
                    (*to Cassio, joking*)
                Handsome knight, in your dwelling,
                The angels lose halo and veil.

*He puts his hands behind his back so that Othello can see
the handkerchief.*

OTHELLO (*coming very close to the handkerchief, behind
    Iago's back, still hidden by the first column*)
                (That's the one! That's the one!
                Ruination and Death!)
IAGO   (Othello's listening.)
OTHELLO (*partly in a whisper*)
                (All is dead! Love and grief.
                No one can move my soul any more.)
IAGO (*to Cassio, pointing to the handkerchief*)
                This is a cobweb
                In which your heart
                Falls, complains,
                Is entangled and dies.
                You admire it too much,
                You look at it too much;
                Beware of vain
                And false ravings.
                This is a cobweb, etc.
CASSIO (*looking at the handkerchief, which he has taken back
    from Iago*)
                Lovely miracle
                Of the spool and the needle
                That changes into rays
                The threads of a cloth,
                Whiter, lighter
                Than a snowflake,
                Than a cloud woven
                From the sky's breezes.
IAGO   This is a cobweb, etc.
CASSIO   Lovely miracle . . .
                Whiter, lighter
                Than a snowflake,
                Than a cloud woven
                From the sky's breezes.
                Miracle, lovely miracle!
OTHELLO (*hidden behind the column and looking from time
    to time at the handkerchief in Cassio's hand*)
                (Betrayal, betrayal, betrayal,

La tua prova, la tua prova
Spaventosa mostri al Sol.)
CASSIO   Miracolo vago!
OTELLO   Tradimento!
JAGO   Troppo l'ammiri.
OTELLO   Tradimento!
JAGO   Bada! Bada!

Otello sarà ritornato nel vano del verone; colpo di cannone; rispondono dal Castello.

JAGO   Quest'è il segnale che annuncia l'approdo
              Della trireme veneziana. Ascolta.
              (*squilli da varie parti*)
              Tutto il castel co' suoi squilli risponde.

              Se qui non vuoi con Otello scontrarti,
              Fuggi.
CASSIO   Addio.
JAGO   Va.

Cassio esce velocemente dal fondo.

OTELLO (*avvicinandosi a Jago*)
              Come la ucciderò?
JAGO   Vedeste ben com'egli ha riso?
OTELLO   Vidi.
JAGO   E il fazzoletto?
OTELLO   Tutto vidi.
VOCI LONTANE Evviva!
              Alla riva! Allo sbarco!

OTELLO   È condannata.
              Fa ch'io m'abbia un velen per questa notte.
VOCI (*più vicine*)
              Evviva! Evviva il Leon di San Marco!
JAGO   Il tosco no, val meglio soffocarla,
              Là, nel suo letto, là, dove ha peccato.
OTELLO   Questa giustizia tua mi piace.
JAGO   A Cassio Jago provvederà.
OTELLO   Jago, fin d'ora
              Mio Capitano t'eleggo.
JAGO   Mio Duce, grazie vi rendo.
              Ecco gli Ambasciatori.
              Li accogliete. Ma ad evitar sospetti
              Desdemona si mostri a quei Messeri.

OTELLO   Sì, qui l'adduci.

Jago esce dalla porta di sinistra. Otello s'avvia verso il fondo per ricevere gli Ambasciatori.
   Entrano Jago, Lodovico, Roderigo, l'araldo, Desdemona con Emilia, dignitarî della Repubblica Veneta, gentiluomini e dame, soldati, trombettieri, poi Cassio.

	You display your proof, Your frightful proof to the Sun.)
CASSIO	Lovely miracle!
OTHELLO	Betrayal!
IAGO	You admire it too much.
OTHELLO	Betrayal!
IAGO	Take care! Take care!

Othello goes back to the door of the balcony; a cannon shot;
shots are returned from the castle.

IAGO	That is the signal to announce the landing Of the Venetian trireme. Listen. (*trumpet blasts from several directions*) The whole castle answers with its trumpet blasts. If you don't want to encounter Othello here, Flee.
CASSIO	Good-by.
IAGO	Go.

Cassio goes out quickly at the back.

OTHELLO (*coming over to Iago*)	How will I kill her?
IAGO	You saw clearly how he laughed?
OTHELLO	I saw.
IAGO	And the handkerchief?
OTHELLO	I saw everything.
DISTANT VOICES	Hurrah! To the shore! To the landing!
OTHELLO	She is condemned. See that I have a poison for tonight.
VOICES (*closer*)	Hurrah! Long live the Lion of St. Mark!
IAGO	Poison, no. Better to smother her, There, in her bed, there, where she has sinned.
OTHELLO	I like this justice of yours.
IAGO	Iago will see to Cassio.
OTHELLO	Iago, starting now I name you my Captain.
IAGO	My General, I give you my thanks. Here are the Ambassadors. Receive them. But, to avoid suspicion, Let Desdemona show herself to those gentlemen.
OTHELLO	Yes, bring her here.

Iago goes out through the door at left. Othello goes toward
the back to receive the Ambassadors.
Enter Iago, Lodovico, Roderigo, the herald, Desdemona
with Emilia, dignitaries of the Venetian Republic, gentlemen
and ladies, soldiers, trumpeters, then Cassio.

TUTTI   Viva! Evviva! Viva il Leon di San Marco!
             Evviva, evviva, ecc.

LODOVICO (*tenendo una pergamena avvoltolata in mano*)
             Il Doge ed il Senato
             Salutano l'eroe trionfatore
             Di Cipro. Io reco nelle vostre mani
             Il messaggio dogale.

OTELLO (*prendendo il messaggio e baciando il suggello*)
             Io bacio il segno della Sovrana Maestà.
             (*Poi lo spiega e legge.*)

LODOVICO (*avvicinandosi a Desdemona*)
             Madonna,
             V'abbia il cielo in sua guardia.

DESDEMONA   E il ciel v'ascolti.

EMILIA (*a Desdemona, a parte*)
             (Come sei mesta!)

DESDEMONA (*ad Emilia, a parte*)
             (Emilia! una gran nube
             Turba il senno d'Otello e il mio destino.)

JAGO (*a Lodovico*)
             Messere, son lieto di vedervi.

Lodovico, Desdemona e Jago formano crocchio insieme.

LODOVICO   Jago, quali nuove?... ma in mezzo a voi non
             trovo Cassio.

JAGO   Con lui crucciato è Otello.

DESDEMONA   Credo che in grazia tornerà.

OTELLO (*a Desdemona rapidamente e sempre in atto di
         leggere*)
             Ne siete certa?

DESDEMONA   Che dite?

LODOVICO   Ei legge, non vi parla.

JAGO   Forse che in grazia tornerà.

DESDEMONA   Jago, lo spero;
             Sai se un verace affetto io porti a Cassio ...

OTELLO (*sempre in atto di leggere, ma febbrilmente a
        Desdemona, sottovoce*)
             Frenate dunque le labbra loquaci ...

DESDEMONA   Perdonate, signor ...

OTELLO (*avventandosi contro Desdemona*)
             Demonio taci!!

LODOVICO (*arrestando il gesto d'Otello*)
             Ferma!

TUTTI   Orrore! Orrore!

LODOVICO   La mente mia non osa
             Pensar ch'io vidi il vero.

OTELLO (*all'araldo, con accento imperioso*)
             A me Cassio!

L'araldo esce.

JAGO (*ad Otello a bassa voce*)
             (Che tenti?)

ALL   Hurrah! Hurrah! Long live the Lion of St. Mark!
      Hurrah, hurrah, etc.

LODOVICO (*holding a rolled parchment in his hand*)
      The Doge and the Senate
      Greet the triumphant hero
      Of Cyprus. I convey to your hands
      The Doge's message.

OTHELLO (*taking the message and kissing the seal*)
      I kiss the symbol of the sovereign Majesty.
      (*Then he unrolls it and reads.*)

LODOVICO (*approaching Desdemona*)
      My lady,
      May heaven keep you.

DESDEMONA And may heaven listen to you.

EMILIA (*to Desdemona, aside*)
      (How sad you are!)

DESDEMONA (*to Emilia, aside*)
      (Emilia! A great cloud
      Disturbs Othello's wisdom and my destiny.)

IAGO (*to Lodovico*)
      Sir, I am happy to see you.

Lodovico, Desdemona, and Iago form a group together.

LODOVICO Iago, what news? . . . But I do not find Cassio in
      your midst.

IAGO   Othello is angry with him.

DESDEMONA I believe he will return to favor.

OTHELLO (*to Desdemona quickly as he continues reading*)

      Are you certain of it?

DESDEMONA What do you say?

LODOVICO He is reading, he isn't speaking to you.

IAGO   Perhaps he will return to favor.

DESDEMONA Iago, I hope so;
      You know that I am truly fond of Cassio . . .

OTHELLO (*still reading, but in a low, feverish voice, to
  Desdemona*)
      Then restrain your talkative lips . . .

DESDEMONA Forgive me, My Lord . . .

OTHELLO (*hurling himself at Desdemona*)
      Be silent, you devil!!

LODOVICO (*arresting Othello's gesture*)
      Stop!

ALL   Horror! Horror!

LODOVICO My mind doesn't dare
      Believe that what I saw was true.

OTHELLO (*to the herald, in a commanding tone*)
      Bring Cassio to me!

The herald goes out.

IAGO (*to Othello in a low voice*)
      (What are you attempting?)

OTELLO (*a Jago sottovoce*)
      (Guardala mentre ei giunge.)
CORO   Ah! triste sposa!
LODOVICO (*si avvicina a Jago e gli dice a parte*)
      Quest'è dunque l'eroe? quest'è il guerriero
      Dai sublimi ardimenti?
JAGO (*a Lodovico alzando le spalle*)
      È quel ch'egli è.
LODOVICO   Palesa il tuo pensiero.
JAGO   Meglio è tener su ciò la lingua muta.
OTELLO (*che avrà sempre fissato la porta*)
      (Eccolo! È lui!
            (*Appare Cassio.*)
                  (*a Jago*)
      Nell'animo lo scruta.)
OTELLO (*ad alta voce a tutti*)
      Messeri! Il Doge ...
            (*a parte a Desdemona*)
      (Ben tu fingi il pianto.)
            (*ad alta voce a tutti*)
      Mi richiama a Venezia.
RODERIGO   (Infida sorte!)
OTELLO   E in Cipro elegge
      Mio successor colui che stava accanto
      Al mio vessillo, Cassio.
JAGO (*fieramente e sorpresso*)
      (Inferno e morte!)
OTELLO (*continuando e mostrando la pergamena*)
      La parola Ducale è nostra legge.
CASSIO (*inchinandosi ad Otello*)
      Obbedirò.
OTELLO (*rapidamente a Jago ed accennando a Cassio*)
      (Vedi?... Non par che esulti l'infame.)

JAGO   (No.)
OTELLO (*ancora ad alta voce a tutti*)
      La ciurma e la coorte ...
            (*sottovoce a Desdemona*)
      (Continua i tuoi singulti ...)
            (*a tutti*)
      E le navi e il castello
      Lascio in poter del nuovo Duce.
LODOVICO (*additando Desdemona che s'avvicina
supplichevole*)
      Otello, per pietà la conforta o il cor le intrangi.

OTELLO (*a Lodovico e Desdemona*)
      Noi salperem domani.
   (*Afferra Desdemona furiosamente. Desdemona cade.*)
            (*a Desdemona*)
      A terra!... e piangi!

   *Otello avrà, nel suo gesto terribile, gettata la pergamena al
suolo, e Jago la raccoglie e legge di nascosto.*

OTHELLO (*to Iago in a low voice*)
>>(Watch her when he arrives.)

CHORUS   Ah! Unhappy wife!

LODOVICO (*comes to Iago and says to him, aside*)
>>Is this then the hero? This the warrior
>>Of sublime daring?

IAGO (*to Lodovico, shrugging*)
>>He is what he is.

LODOVICO   Reveal what you are thinking.

IAGO   Better to keep my tongue dumb on that score.

OTHELLO (*who has been staring at the door*)
>>(Here he is! It is he!
>>>>(*Cassio appears.*)
>>>>>>(*to Iago*)
>>Stare into his soul.)

OTHELLO (*in a loud voice, to all*)
>>Gentlemen! The Doge ...
>>>>(*aside to Desdemona*)
>>(You feign weeping well.)
>>>>(*in a loud voice to all*)
>>Recalls me to Venice.

RODERIGO   (Treacherous fortune!)

OTHELLO   And elects as my successor
>>In Cyprus the man who stood beside
>>My banner, Cassio.

IAGO (*fiercely, surprised*)
>>(Hell and death!)

OTHELLO (*continuing to display the parchment*)
>>The Doge's word is our law.

CASSIO (*bowing to Othello*)
>>I shall obey.

OTHELLO (*quickly to Iago, indicating Cassio*)
>>(You see? ... The villain doesn't seem to
>>>>rejoice.)

IAGO   (No.)

OTHELLO (*again in a loud voice to all*)
>>The crew and the troops ...
>>>>(*in a low voice to Desdemona*)
>>(Continue your sobbing ...)
>>>>(*to all*)
>>And the ships and the castle
>>I leave in the power of the new General.

LODOVICO (*pointing to Desdemona, who approaches pleadingly*)

>>Othello, have pity, comfort her or you will
>>>>break her heart.

OTHELLO (*to Lodovico and Desdemona*)
>>We'll sail tomorrow.
>>(*He seizes Desdemona furiously. Desdemona falls.*)
>>>>(*to Desdemona*)
>>To the ground! ... And weep!

*In his terrible gesture, Othello has thrown the scroll on the
floor. Iago picks it up and reads it secretly.*

Emilia e Lodovico sollevano pietosamente Desdemona.

DESDEMONA   A terra!... sì ... nel livido
             Fango ... percossa ... io giacio ...
             Piango ... m'agghiaccia il brivido
             Dell'anima che muor.
             E un dì sul mio sorriso
             Fioria la speme e il bacio
             Ed or ... l'angoscia in viso
             E l'agonia nel cor.
             Quel Sol sereno e vivido
             Che allieta il cielo e il mare
             Non può asciugar le amare
             Stille del mio dolor.

EMILIA   (Quell'innocente un fremito
             D'odio non ha nè un gesto,
             Trattiene in petto il gemito
             Con doloroso fren.
             La lagrima si frange
             Muta sul volto mesto;
             No, chi per lei non piange
             Non ha pietade in sen.)

CASSIO   (L'ora è fatal! un fulmine
             Sul mio cammin l'addita.
             Già di mia sorte il culmine
             S'offre all'inerte man.
             L'ebbra fortuna incalza
             La fuga della vita.
             Questa che al ciel m'innalza
             È un'onda d'uragan.)

RODERIGO   (Per me s'oscura il mondo,
             S'annuvola il destin,
             L'angiol soave e biondo
             Scompar dal mio cammin.)

LODOVICO   (Egli la man funerea
             Scuote anelando d'ira,
             Essa la faccia eterea
             Volge piangendo al ciel.
             Nel contemplar quel pianto
             La carità sospira,
             E un tenero compianto
             Stempra del core il gel.)

DESDEMONA   (E un dì sul mio sorriso
             Fioria la speme e il bacio,
             Ed or ... l'angoscia in viso
             E l'agonia nel cor.
             A terra ... nel fango ...
             Percossa ... io giacio ...
             M'agghiaccia il brivido
             Dell'anima che muor ...)

DAME   Pietà! Pietà! Pietà!
             Ansia mortale, bieca,
             Ne ingombra, anime assorte in lungo orror.
             Vista crudel!
             Ei la colpì! Quel viso santo, pallido,

Emilia and Lodovico pityingly lift up Desdemona.

DESDEMONA To the ground! . . . Yes . . . in the livid
Mire . . . beaten . . . I lie . . .
I weep . . . and the shudder of my dying soul
Chills me.
And one day in my smile
Hope and a kiss blossomed
And now . . . anguish in my face
And agony in my heart.
The serene, bright Sun
That gladdens sky and sea
Cannot dry the bitter
Drops of my grief.

EMILIA (That innocent one makes no gesture
Or shudder of hatred,
She checks the moan in her breast
With mournful restraint.
Her tears start
Silently on her sad face;
No, whoever does not weep for her
Has no mercy in his breast.)

CASSIO (The hour is decisive! A thunderbolt
On my path indicates it.
The climax of my fate
Is offered to my inert hand.
Drunken fortune presses on
The race of life.
This wave that lifts me to heaven
Is a hurricane's wave.)

RODERIGO (The world darkens for me,
My destiny is clouded;
The blond, tender angel
Disappears from my path.)

LODOVICO (He shakes his gloomy hand,
Gasping with anger,
She turns her ethereal face,
Weeping, toward heaven.
Observing those tears,
Charity sighs,
And a tender compassion
Melts the chill of the heart.)

DESDEMONA (And one day in my smile
Hope and a kiss blossomed
And now . . . anguish in my face
And agony in my heart.
On the ground . . . in the mire . . .
Beaten . . . I lie . . .
The shudder of my dying soul
Chills me . . .)

LADIES Mercy! Mercy! Mercy!
Mortal, grim anxiety
Obstructs them, souls long obsessed in horror.
Cruel sight!
He struck her! That sainted, pale, innocent

Blando, si china e tace e piange e muor.
Piangon così nel ciel lor pianto gli angeli
Quando perduto giace il peccator.

CAVALIERI   Mistero! Mistero! Mistero!
Quell'uomo nero è sepolcrale, e cieca
Un'ombra è in lui di morte e di terror!
Strazia coll'ugna l'orrido
Petto! Gli sguardi figge immoti al suol.
Poi sfida il ciel coll'atre pugna, l'ispido
Aspetto ergendo ai dardi alti del Sol.

JAGO (*avvicinandosi a Otello che si sarà accasciato su d'una
sedia*)
Una parola.

OTELLO   E che?

JAGO   T'affretta! Rapido
Slancia la tua vendetta! Il tempo vola.

OTELLO   Ben parli.

JAGO   È l'ira inutil ciancia. Scuotiti!
All'opra ergi tua mira! All'opra sola!
Io penso a Cassio. Ei le sue trame espia.
L'infame anima ria l'averno inghiotte!

OTELLO   Chi gliela svelle?

JAGO   Io.

OTELLO   Tu?

JAGO   Giurai.

OTELLO   Tal sia.

JAGO   Tu avrai le sue novelle questa notte.
(*ironicamente a Roderigo*)
(I sogni tuoi saranno in mar domani
E tu sull'aspra terra.)

RODERIGO (*a Jago*)
(Ahi triste!)

JAGO   Ahi stolto! stolto!
Se vuoi, tu puoi sperar; gli umani,
Orsù! cimenti afferra, e m'odi.

RODERIGO   T'ascolto.

JAGO   Col primo albor salpa il vascello.
Or Cassio è il Duce.
Eppur se avvien che a questi accada
sventura ...
(*toccando la spada*)
Allor qui resta Otello.

RODERIGO   Lugubre luce d'atro balen!

JAGO   Mano alla spada!
A notte folta io la sua traccia vigilo,
E il varco e l'ora scruto; il resto a te.
Sarò tuo scorta. A caccia! a caccia!
Cingiti l'arco!

RODERIGO   Sì! t'ho venduto onore e fè.

JAGO   (Corri al miraggio! Il fragile tuo senno
Ha già confuso un sogno menzogner.
Segui l'astuto ed agile mio cenno,

Face is bent, silent; she weeps and dies.
So the angels in heaven weep their tears
When the sinner lies lost.

GENTLEMEN   Mystery! Mystery! Mystery!
That black man is tomblike, and in him
There is a blind shadow of death and terror!
With his nails he rends
His fearful breast! His eyes are motionless, fixed
    on the ground.
Then with his grim fist he defies heaven, raising
His rough visage to the high rays of the Sun.

IAGO (*approaching Othello, who has slumped on a chair*)
A word.

OTHELLO   What?

IAGO   Make haste. Unleash your vengeance
Rapidly. Time flies.

OTHELLO   You are right.

IAGO   Anger is idle chatter. Bestir yourself!
Raise your eyes to the task! To the task only!
I think of Cassio. Let him expiate his plots
And the grave swallow his foul, guilty soul.

OTHELLO   Who is to tear it from him?

IAGO   I.

OTHELLO   You?

IAGO   I swore.

OTHELLO   So be it.

IAGO   You will have news of him tonight.
(*ironically to Roderigo*)
(Your dreams will be on the sea tomorrow,
And you on the harsh land.)

RODERIGO (*to Iago*)
(Ah, how sad I feel!)

IAGO   Ah, fool! Fool!
If you wish, you can hope; come,
Grasp human boldness, and listen to me.

RODERIGO   I am listening to you.

IAGO   The ship sails at the break of dawn.
Now Cassio is the Commander.
And yet, if it should happen that misfortune
    befall him . . .
(*touching his sword*)
Then Othello remains here.

RODERIGO   Doleful light of a grim lightning!

IAGO   Hand on your sword!
At dead of night I will watch his path,
I'll observe the place and the hour; the rest is
    up to you.
I will be your sentry. To the hunt! To the hunt!
Take up your bow!

RODERIGO   Yes! I have sold you my honor and loyalty.

IAGO   (Hasten to your mirage! Your fragile intelligence
Has already confused a false dream.
Follow my sly and quick indication,

Amante illuso, io seguo il mio pensier.)

RODERIGO   (Il dado è tratto! Impavido t'attendo,
Ultima sorte, occulto mio destin.
Mi sprona amor, ma un avido, tremendo
Astro di morte infesta il mio cammin.)

OTELLO (*ergendosi e rivolto alla folla, terribilmente*)
Fuggite!

TUTTI   Ciel!

OTELLO (*slanciandosi contro la folla*)
Tutti fuggite Otello!

JAGO (*a tutti*) Lo assale una malia
Che d'ogni senso il priva.

OTELLO (*con forza*)
Chi non si scosta è contro me rubello.

LODOVICO (*fa per trascinare lontano Desdemona*)
Mi segui ...

VOCI (*di dentro*)
Evviva!

DESDEMONA (*scogliendosi da Lodovico e accorrendo verso
Otello*)
Mio sposo!

OTELLO (*terribile, a Desdemona*)
Anima mia ti maledico!

TUTTI   Orror!...

*Desdemona, fra Emilia e Lodovico, esce. Tutti escono
inorriditi.*

OTELLO   Fuggirmi io sol non so!... Sangue! Ah!
(*sempre affannoso*)
L'abbietto pensiero!... ciò m'accora!
(*convulsivamente, delirando*)
Vederli insieme avvinti ... il fazzoletto!...

Ah! ah! ah!...
(*sviene*)

JAGO   (Il mio velen lavora.)

VOCI (*interno*)
Viva Otello!

JAGO (*ascoltando le grida*)
L'eco della vittoria ...

VOCI   Evviva, viva!

JAGO   ... porge sua laude estrema.

Osserva Otello disteso a terra tramortito.

VOCI   Evviva!

JAGO   Chi può vietar che questa fronte prema
Col mio tallone?

VOCI (*interno e più vicino*)
Evviva! Evviva Otello! Gloria
Al Leon di Venezia!

JAGO (*ritto e con gesto d'orrendo trionfo, indicando il corpo
inerte d'Otello*)
Ecco il Leone!...

VOCI   Viva! viva! viva Otello!

Deluded lover, I follow my thought.)

RODERIGO (The die is cast! Fearless, I await you,
Ultimate fate, my hidden destiny.
Love spurs me on, but an avid, terrible
Star of death infests my path.)

OTHELLO (*rising and addressing the crowd, in a terrible voice*)
Begone!

ALL Heaven!

OTHELLO (*hurling himself at the crowd*)
Flee from Othello, all of you!

IAGO (*to all*) A spell attacks him
That robs him of all feeling.

OTHELLO (*vigorously*)
He who does not leave is a rebel against me.

LODOVICO (*starts to draw Desdemona away*)
Follow me . . .

VOICES (*within*)
Hurrah!

DESDEMONA (*freeing herself from Lodovico and running
toward Othello*)
My husband!

OTHELLO (*fearsome, to Desdemona*)
My soul, I curse you!

ALL Horror! . . .

*Desdemona goes out between Lodovico and Emilia. All go
out, horrified.*

OTHELLO Only I cannot flee from myself! . . . Blood! Ah!
(*still gasping*)
The despicable thought! . . . That distresses me!
(*convulsively, raving*)
To see them together, embracing . . . the handkerchief! . . .

Ah! Ah! Ah!
(*faints*)

IAGO (My poison is working.)

VOICES (*within*)
Long live Othello!

IAGO (*listening to the shouts*)
The echo of victory . . .

VOICES Hurrah! hurrah!

IAGO . . . offers its last praise.

He observes Othello lying senseless on the ground.

VOICES Hurrah!

IAGO Who can prevent me from pressing my heel
On that forehead?

VOICES (*within and nearer*)
Hurrah! Long live Othello! Glory
To the Lion of Venice!

IAGO (*erect, with a gesture of horrible triumph, pointing to
Othello's inert body*)
There is the Lion! . . .

VOICES Hurrah! Hurrah! Long live Othello!

ATTO QUARTO

La camera di Desdemona: letto, inginocchiatoio, tavolo,
specchio, sedie; una lampada arde appesa davanti all'im-
magine della Madonna che sta al disopra dell'inginocchiatoio.
Porta a destra. Un lume acceso sul tavolo. È notte. Desde-
mona, Emilia.

EMILIA   Era più calmo?

DESDEMONA   Mi parea. M'ingiunse
              Di coricarmi e d'attenderlo. Emilia,
              Te ne prego, distendi sul mio letto
              La mia candida veste nuziale.
              (*Emilia eseguisce.*)
              Senti. Se pria di te morir dovessi
              Mi seppellisci con un di quei veli.

EMILIA   Scacciate queste idee.

DESDEMONA   Son mesta tanto, tanto.
       (*sedendo macchinalmente davanti allo specchio*)
              Mia madre aveva una povera ancella
              Innamorata e bella;
              Era il suo nome
              Barbara. Amava
              Un uom che poi l'abbandonò, cantava

              Una canzone: la canzon del Salice.
                 (*ad Emilia, parlante*)
              — Mi disciogli le chiome —
              Io questa sera ho la memoria piena
              Di quella cantilena:
              "Piangea cantando
              Nell'erma landa,
              Piangea la mesta.
              O Salce! Salce! Salce!
              Sedea chinando
              Sul sen la testa!
              O Salce! Salce! Salce!
              Cantiamo! cantiamo! il Salce funebre
              Sarà la mia ghirlanda."
                 (*ad Emilia, parlante*)
              — Affrettati; fra poce giunge Otello. —
              "Scorreano i rivi fra le zolle in fior,
              Gemea quel core affranto,
              E dalle ciglia le sgorgava il cor
              L'amara onda del pianto.
              Salce! Salce! Salce!
              Cantiamo! cantiamo!
              Il Salce funebre sarà la mia ghirlanda.
              Scendean gli augelli a vol dai rami cupi

              Verso quel dolce canto.
              E gli occhi suoi piangean tanto, tanto,
              Da impietosir le rupi."
       (*a Emilia, levandosi un anello dal dito; parlando*)

ACT FOUR

Desdemona's bedroom: bed, prie-dieu, table, mirror, chairs;
a lamp is burning, hanging in front of the image of the Ma-
donna that stands above the prie-dieu. A door at right. A
lighted lamp on the table. It is night. Desdemona, Emilia.

EMILIA   Was he calmer?

DESDEMONA   He seemed so to me. He bade me
Go to bed and await him. Emilia,
Please spread out on my bed

My white nuptial gown.
         (*Emilia obeys*)
Listen. If I should die before you,
Bury me with one of those veils.

EMILIA   Banish these ideas.

DESDEMONA   I am sad, very sad.
     (*sitting down mechanically before the mirror*)
My mother had a poor maidservant,
Beautiful and in love;
Her name was
Barbara. She loved
A man who later abandoned her, she used to
     sing
A song: the Willow Song.
(*to Emilia, in a speaking voice*)
— Loosen my hair —
This evening my memory is filled
With that dirge:
"She wept, singing,
On the lonely heath,
The sad girl wept.
O Willow! Willow! Willow!
She sat, hanging
Her head on her breast!
O Willow! Willow! Willow!
Let us sing! Let us sing! The funereal willow
Shall be my garland."
(*to Emilia, in a speaking voice*)
— Hurry; Othello is coming shortly. —
"The brooks flowed among the flowering fields,
That broken heart moaned,
And her heart released from her eyelids
The bitter wave of tears.
O Willow! Willow! Willow!
Let us sing! Let us sing!
The funereal willow shall be my garland.
The birds came flying down from the dark
     branches
Toward that sweet song.
And her eyes wept so much, so much
They would have moved stones to pity."
   (*to Emilia, taking a ring from her finger; in a speaking tone*)

Riponi quest'anello.
                    (*alzandosi*)
Povera Barbara!
                    (*parlante*)
Solea la storia
Con questo semplice suono finir:
"Egli era nato per la sua gloria,
Io per amar ..."
                    (*ad Emilia, parlante*)
Ascolta. Odo un lamento.
                    (*Emilia fa qualche passo.*)
Taci. Chi batte a quella porta?...

EMILIA   È il vento.

DESDEMONA   "Io per amarlo e per morir ...
Cantiamo! cantiamo!
Salce! Salce! Salce!"
Emilia, addio. Come m'ardon le ciglia!
È presagio di pianto.
Buona notte.
                    (*Emilia si volge per partire.*)
Ah! Emilia, Emilia, addio,
            (*Emilia ritorna e Desdemona l'abbraccia.*)
Emilia, addio!

Emilia esce.

DESDEMONA   (*all'inginocchiatoio*)
Ave Maria, piena di grazia, eletta
Fra le spose e le vergini sei tu,
Sia benedetto il frutto, o benedetta,
Di tue materne viscere, Gesù.
Prega per chi adorando a te si prostra,

Prega pel peccator, per l'innocente
E pel debole oppresso e pel possente,

Misero anch'esso, tua pietà dimostra.
Prega per chi sotto l'oltraggio piega
La fronte e sotto la malvagia sorte;
Per noi tu prega
Sempre e nell'ora della morte nostra,
Prega per noi, prega per noi, prega.
Ave Maria ...

*Resta ancora inginocchiata e appoggiando la fronte sull'-
inginocchiatoio ripete mentalmente l'orazione di cui non
s'odono che le prime e le ultime parole.*

Nell'ora della morte.
Ave!... Amen!

Si alza e va a coricarsi.

*Alla prima nota comparirà Otello sulla soglia di una porta
segreta. Si avanza. Depone una scimitarra sul tavolo. S'arresta
davanti alla face, titubante se spegnerla o no. Guarda Desdemona. Spegne la face. Movimento di furore. Si avvicina al
letto. S'arresta. Rialza le cortine, contempla Desdemona che
dorme. Dà un bacio a Desdemona; altro bacio; un altro ancora.*

Put this ring away.
                    (*rising*)
Poor Barbara!
                    (*speaking tone*)
The story used to end
With this simple tune:
"He was born for his glory,
I to love . . ."
                    (*to Emilia, speaking voice*)
Listen. I hear a moan.
                    (*Emilia takes a few steps.*)
Be silent. Who is knocking at that door? . . .

EMILIA   It is the wind.

DESDEMONA   "I to love him and to die . . .
Let us sing! Let us sing!
Willow! Willow! Willow!"
Emilia, good-by. How my eyelids burn!
It is a presentiment of weeping.
Good night.
                    (*Emilia turns to leave.*)
Ah! Emilia, Emilia, good-by,
(*Emilia comes back to Desdemona and embraces her.*)
Emilia, good-by!

Emilia goes out.

DESDEMONA (*at the prie-dieu*)
                    Hail Mary, full of grace, chosen
                    Are you among brides and maidens,
                    O blessed one, may the fruit be blessed
                    Of your maternal womb, Jesus.
                    Pray for those who prostrate themselves before
                         you, adoring,
                    Pray for the sinner, for the innocent,
                    For the weak and oppressed and for the
                         mighty,
                    Also wretched, display your mercy.
                    Pray for those who bow their heads beneath
                    Outrage and evil destiny;
                    Pray for us
                    Always and in the hour of our death,
                    Pray for us, pray for us, pray.
                    Hail Mary . . .

*She remains still kneeling, resting her forehead against the
prie-dieu, mentally repeats the prayer of which we hear only
the first and last words.*

                    At the hour of death.
                    Hail! . . . Amen!

She rises and goes to bed.

*At the first note Othello appears on the threshold of a secret
door. He comes forward. He sets a scimitar on the table. He
stops in front of the torch, hesitant whether to extinguish it or
not. He looks at Desdemona. He puts out the torch. A furious
gesture. He comes over to the bed. He stops. He lifts the curtains and gazes at the sleeping Desdemona. He gives Desdemona a kiss; another kiss; and still another.*

DESDEMONA (*si desta*)
          Chi è là?...
                    (*si alza*)
          Otello?

OTELLO   Sì. Diceste questa sera
          Le vostre preci?

DESDEMONA   Orai ...

OTELLO   Se vi sovviene
          Di qualche colpa commessa che attenda
          Grazia dal ciel, imploratela tosto.

DESDEMONA   Perchè?

OTELLO   T'affretta! Uccidere non voglio
          L'anima tua.

DESDEMONA   D'uccider parli?

OTELLO   Sì.

DESDEMONA   Pietà di me, mio Dio.

OTELLO   Amen.

DESDEMONA   E abbiate pietà voi pure.

OTELLO   Pensa a' tuoi peccati.

DESDEMONA   Mio peccato è l'amor.

OTELLO   Perciò tu muori.

DESDEMONA   E perchè t'amo m'uccidi?...

OTELLO   Ami Cassio.

DESDEMONA   No! sull'anima mia!!

OTELLO   Quel fazzoletto ch'io ti donai gli desti.

DESDEMONA   Non è vero!

OTELLO   Nella sua man lo vidi.

DESDEMONA   Io rea non sono!

OTELLO   Confessa!

DESDEMONA   Giuro!

OTELLO   Bada allo spergiuro ...
          Pensa che sei sul tuo letto di morte.

DESDEMONA   Non per morir.

OTELLO   Per morir tosto.

DESDEMONA   Aita!
          Cassio non amo ... ch'ei qui venga ... ei parli.

OTELLO   Muto è per sempre.

DESDEMONA   Cielo! Morto?

OTELLO (*freddo*)
          Morto.

DESDEMONA   Son perduta!... ei tradito!

OTELLO (*con forza*)
          E pianger l'osi?

DESDEMONA   Otello ... non uccidermi ...

OTELLO   Tu invano ti difendi.

DESDEMONA (*con disperazione*)
          Ch'io viva ancor ...

OTELLO   Giù! cadi, giù, cadi, prostituta!

DESDEMONA   Pietà!

DESDEMONA (*waking*)	
	Who is there? . . .
	(*rising*)
	Othello?
OTHELLO	Yes. Did you say
	Your prayers this evening?
DESDEMONA	I prayed . . .
OTHELLO	If you remember
	Some sin you have committed that awaits
	Forgiveness from heaven, implore it at once.
DESDEMONA	Why?
OTHELLO	Make haste! I don't want to kill
	Your soul.
DESDEMONA	You speak of killing?
OTHELLO	Yes.
DESDEMONA	Have pity on me, God.
OTHELLO	Amen.
DESDEMONA	And you too have pity.
OTHELLO	Think of your sins.
DESDEMONA	My sin is love.
OTHELLO	For that you die.
DESDEMONA	You kill me because I love you? . . .
OTHELLO	You love Cassio.
DESDEMONA	No! On my soul!!
OTHELLO	You gave him that handkerchief I gave you.
DESDEMONA	That is not true!
OTHELLO	I saw it in his hand.
DESDEMONA	I am not guilty!
OTHELLO	Confess!
DESDEMONA	I swear!
OTHELLO	Beware of perjury . . .
	Think, you are on your deathbed.
DESDEMONA	Not to die.
OTHELLO	To die at once.
DESDEMONA	Help!
	I do not love Cassio . . . let him come here . . .
	let him speak.
OTHELLO	He is silent forever.
DESDEMONA	Heaven! Dead?
OTHELLO (*coldly*)	
	Dead.
DESDEMONA	I am lost! . . . He, betrayed!
OTHELLO (*fiercely*)	
	And you dare weep for him?
DESDEMONA	Othello . . . do not kill me.
OTHELLO	You defend yourself in vain.
DESDEMONA (*in desperation*)	
	Let me still live . . .
OTHELLO	Down! Fall! Down! Fall, prostitute!
DESDEMONA	Pity!

OTELLO   Muori!!
DESDEMONA   Ch'io viva questa notte ...
OTELLO   No!
DESDEMONA   Un'ora ...
OTELLO   No!
DESDEMONA   Un istante.
OTELLO   No!
DESDEMONA   Sol ch'io dica un'Ave.
OTELLO   È tardi!

La soffoca.

DESDEMONA (*grido*)
            Ah!

Emilia dal di fuori bussa alla porta.

OTELLO (*contemplando il corpo inerte di Desdemona*)
            Calma come la tomba.
EMILIA (*picchia di nuovo*)
            Aprite! aprite!
OTELLO (*trabalzando*)
            Chi è là! Chi batte!
EMILIA (*picchia ancora*)
            Signor mio ... ven prego,
            Lasciate ch'io vi parli ... Aprite!
OTELLO (*aprendo*)
            Emilia! che avvenne?
EMILIA (*entrando*)
            Un gran delitto!
            Cassio uccise Roderigo.
OTELLO   E Cassio?
EMILIA   Vive.
OTELLO   Cassio vive!!
DESDEMONA (*dal letto*)
            Ingiustamente ... uccisa ingiustamente ...
EMILIA (*accorrendo al letto*)
            Chi geme là?... Orror!
DESDEMONA   Muoio innocente ...
EMILIA   Gran Dio! Chi fu? chi fu?
DESDEMONA   Nessuno ... io stessa ... al mio
            Signor mi raccomanda ...
            Muoio innocente ... Addio ...
                        (*muore*)
OTELLO   O mentitrice! io l'uccisi.
EMILIA   Assassino!
OTELLO   Fu di Cassio la druda. A Jago il chiedi.
EMILIA   A Jago?!
OTELLO   A Jago.
EMILIA   Stolto!! e tu il credesti?
OTELLO (*fa per avventarsi contro Emilia*)
            Negarlo ardisci?

OTHELLO   Die!!
DESDEMONA   Let me live this night . . .
OTHELLO   No!
DESDEMONA   An hour . . .
OTHELLO   No!
DESDEMONA   A moment.
OTHELLO   No!
DESDEMONA   Let me say only an Ave Maria.
OTHELLO   It is late!

He smothers her.
DESDEMONA (*crying out*)
                Ah!

Emilia knocks at the door from outside.

OTHELLO (*contemplating the inert body of Desdemona*)
                Still as a tomb.
EMILIA (*knocking again*)
                Open! Open!
OTHELLO (*starting*)
                Who is there? Who knocks?
EMILIA (*knocking again*)
                My Lord . . . I beseech you,
                Let me speak to you . . . Open!
OTHELLO (*opening*)
                Emilia! What is happening?
EMILIA (*entering*)
                A great crime.
                Cassio killed Roderigo.
OTHELLO   And Cassio?
EMILIA   He lives.
OTHELLO   Cassio lives!!
DESDEMONA (*from the bed*)
                Unjustly . . . killed unjustly . . .
EMILIA (*running to the bed*)
                Who is moaning there? . . . Horror!
DESDEMONA   I die innocent . . .
EMILIA   Great God! Who was it? Who was it?
DESDEMONA   No one . . . I myself . . . Commend me
                To by lord . . .
                I die innocent . . . Farewell . . .
                        (*dies*)
OTHELLO   O liar! I killed her.
EMILIA   Murderer!
OTHELLO   She was Cassio's mistress. Ask Iago.
EMILIA   Iago?!
OTHELLO   Iago.
EMILIA   Fool!! And you believed him?
OTHELLO (*starting to assault Emilia*)
                You dare deny it?

EMILIA   Non ti temo.

OTELLO (*la afferra*)
                Bada!

EMILIA (*si svincola e corre verso la porta gridando
    disperatamante*)
                Olà! Soccorso! Aiuto!
                Otello uccise Desdemona!

Entrano Lodovico, Cassio e Jago.

TUTTI (*tranne Otello ed Emilia*)
                Quai grida!
                    (*vedendo Desdemona*)
                Orrore! Orror!

EMILIA (*a Jago*)
                Jago, smentisci quel vile assassino.
                Hai tu creduto Desdemona infida?
                Parla!

JAGO   Tal la credea.

OTELLO   Quel fazzoletto
                Che un dì le diedi, a Cassio essa donava.

EMILIA   O potenza divina!

JAGO (*ad Emilia*)
                Taci!

EMILIA   No! tutto divelo!

JAGO   Taci!

EMILIA   No! Costui
                Dalla mia man quel fazzoletto svelse
                A viva forza.

CASSIO   E nella mia dimora trovai quel vel.

MONTÀNO (*entrando con gente armata ed indicando Jago*)
                Roderigo morente mi svelò di quest'uom l'arti
                    nefande.

OTELLO (*a Jago*)
                Ah! discolpati!!

JAGO (*fuggendo*)
                No.

LODOVICO   Ferma.

MONTÀNO   S'insegua.

Alcuni escono inseguendo Jago.

LODOVICO e CASSIO
                Afferratelo!

OTELLO (*slanciandosi per afferrar la spada*)
                E il ciel non ha più fulmini?!...

LODOVICO   La spada a me!

OTELLO   Tant'osi?! Niun mi tema
                S'anco armato mi vede. Ecco la fine
                Del mio cammin ... Oh! Gloria! Otello fu.
                (*lascia cadere la spada, va presso al letto,
                    contemplando Desdemona*)
                E tu ... come sei pallida! e stanca, e muta, e
                bella,

EMILIA   I do not fear you.

OTHELLO (*seizing her*)
         Beware!

EMILIA (*frees herself and runs toward the door, shouting desperately*)
         Ho there! Help! Help!
         Othello has killed Desdemona!

Lodovico, Cassio, and Iago enter.

ALL (*except Othello and Emilia*)
         What are these shouts!
            (*seeing Desdemona*)
         Horror! Horror!

EMILIA (*to Iago*)
         Iago, contradict that base murderer.
         Did you believe Desdemona unfaithful?
         Speak!

IAGO   So I believed her.

OTHELLO   That handkerchief
         That I once gave her, she gave to Cassio.

EMILIA   O divine powers!

IAGO (*to Emilia*)
         Be silent!

EMILIA   No! I will reveal everything!

IAGO   Be silent!

EMILIA   No! He tore
         That handkerchief from my hand
         By main force.

CASSIO   And I found that handkerchief in my house.

MONTANO (*entering with armed men and pointing to Iago*)
         Dying, Roderigo revealed this man's vile
            plottings to me.

OTHELLO (*to Iago*)
         Ah! prove your innocence!!

IAGO (*fleeing*)
         No.

LODOVICO   Stop.

MONTANO   Pursue him.

Some men go out, pursuing Iago.

LODOVICO and CASSIO
         Seize him!

OTHELLO (*rushing forward to seize his sword*)
         Has heaven no more thunderbolts?! ...

LODOVICO   Give me that sword!

OTHELLO   You dare? Let no one fear me
         Even seeing me armed. This is the end
         Of my road . . . Oh! Glory! Othello is dead.

(*drops the sword, goes to the bed, contemplating Desdemona*)
         And you . . . how pale you are! And weary, and
         silent, and beautiful,

Pia creatura nata sotto maligna stella.
Fredda come la casta tua vita, e in cielo assorta.
Desdemona! Desdemona!... Ah!... morta! morta!
morta!
(*estraendo furtivamente dalle vesti un pugnale*)
Ho un'arma ancor!
(*si ferisce*)

CASSIO   Ah! ferma!

LODOVICO e MONTÀNO
Sciagurato!

OTELLO   Pria d'ucciderti ... sposa ... ti baciai.
Or morendo ... nell'ombra in cui mi giacio ...
Un bacio ... un bacio ancora ...
Ah!... un altro bacio ...

Muore.

Cala la tela.

Sainted creature born under a malign star.
Cold as your chaste life, and borne up to heaven.
Desdemona! Desdemona! . . . Ah! . . . Dead!
Dead! Dead!
(furtively drawing a dagger from his garment)
I still have a weapon!
(wounds himself)

CASSIO   Ah! Stop!

LODOVICO and MONTANO
Wretched man!

OTHELLO   Before killing you . . . wife . . . I kissed you.
Now, dying . . . in the darkness where I lie . . .
A kiss . . . a kiss again . . .
Ah! . . . Another kiss . . .

He dies.

The curtain falls.

Falstaff

Boito sent Verdi the outline for the libretto of *Falstaff* at the beginning of July 1889. The composer was at Montecatini, a favorite spa of his. His reaction to Boito's work was promptly enthusiastic: "Excellent! Excellent! . . ." Before writing this first letter, Verdi had taken the trouble to reread *The Merry Wives of Windsor* and the *Henry* plays in which the character of Falstaff appears; so he was in a position to appreciate and praise Boito's skillful, sensitive job of cutting, patching, and telescoping. Far more than in the case of *Otello*, the librettist had to summon all his ingenuity in order to turn the sprawling, thickly populated original work into a sprightly, neatly constructed text for music.

A day later, however, Verdi's caution tempered his original enthusiasm. He considered the project with a more practical eye and wrote Boito again: "When one comes down to earth . . . doubts and discouragements arise. In sketching *Falstaff*, did you ever think of the enormous number of my years? I know that you will answer, exaggerating the condition of my health, good, excellent, robust . . . Nevertheless . . ."

Boito replied with a respectful, cogently argued letter, not only insisting on Verdi's good health but also on the composer's notorious industry: "You have a great desire to work; this is an unquestionable proof of health and power . . . All your life you've wanted a good comic opera subject . . . Instinct is a good adviser. There is only one way to conclude better than with *Otello*, and that is to end victoriously with *Falstaff*. After having made the outcries and laments of the human heart resound, to end with an enormous outburst of hilarity!"

Verdi answered by return mail. "Dear Boito, Amen. And so be it; Let us then do *Falstaff!*"

As usual, Verdi began at once to make suggestions. The third act worried him. He was not sure about the wedding of Anne and Fenton. Again, with diplomatic patience, Boito reassured him: "Fenton and Anne must marry. That love of theirs appeals to me. It serves to make the whole play more fresh and more compact. That love should constantly enliven the whole, so that I would almost like to eliminate the duet of the two lovers. In every ensemble scene that love is present in its own way . . . Their part, even without the duet, will be highly effective . . . The way you sprinkle sugar on a cake, I would like to sprinkle that merry love over all the play, without concentrating it in one point."

The collaboration moved much more easily and rapidly than it had with *Otello*. By March 1890, Verdi had completed the first act. In September 1892, the whole opera was finished except for some tinkering, which continued through the rehearsals and after the first performance.

When he began composing the work, Verdi swore Boito to secrecy. "I am writing the opera to pass the time," he said more than once. Not even the publisher Ricordi was informed until he absolutely had to be. At last the whole musical world learned that a new Verdi opera was on its way. Boito, even before the music was complete, began to discuss scenery with

the designer Hohenstein. And librettist, composer, and publisher started listening to singers with a future *Falstaff* cast in
mind. Boito and Ricordi were determined that the première
should be given at La Scala. Verdi thought the theater too big
and personally disliked its impresario. He suggested the
smaller Teatro Carcano and—probably to tease his friends—
even a private première in his Villa Sant'Agata. In the end,
La Scala won out.

Casting presented problems. Victor Maurel, the French
baritone who had been the first Iago, considered the part of
Falstaff his by right. This attitude infuriated Verdi, who
wanted to send Maurel packing. The baritone was made to see
reason. Franco Faccio, the conductor of *Otello*'s première and
Boito's lifelong friend, was dead, a personal loss also for
Verdi. Faccio's successor at La Scala, Edoardo Mascheroni,
conducted the historic first *Falstaff* on February 9, 1893.

The performance (though apparently not entirely to Verdi's
satisfaction) was a triumph. The brilliant audience included
royalty, government officials, critics from all over Europe, and
members of the rising generation of composers, notably Puc-
cini and Mascagni. Verdi was called frequently out on the
stage amid frenzied cheering; he brought Boito out with him
to share the ovation.

Boito's contribution to *Falstaff*'s success can hardly be over-
stated. Without the poet's delicate persuasion, Verdi might
never have written the opera at all. And the excellence of the
text is beyond doubt. As a nonoperatic poet, Boito was at
times heavy-handed or excessively cerebral; but he was a
deft writer of occasional verse, little poems that he often
included in letters to friends. This light touch is always in
evidence in *Falstaff*, and its inspiring effect on the composer
is clear.

After La Scala, *Falstaff* went to other theaters with equal
success. In London, it was reviewed by Shaw, who had
written, on examining the score: "Falstaff is lighted and
warmed only by the afterglow of the fierce noonday sun of
Ernani; but the gain in beauty conceals the loss in heat—if,
indeed, it be a loss to replace intensity of passion and spon-
taneity of song by fullness of insight and perfect mastery of
workmanship . . . Verdi . . . is now, in his dignified com-
petence, the greatest of living dramatic composers. It is not
often that a man's strength is so immense that he can remain
an athlete after bartering half of it to old age for experience . . ."

Despite other strong advocates, headed by Toscanini,
Falstaff in the first decades of this century suffered a decline
in popularity; but in recent years, it has returned firmly to
the repertory, joining the works of the composer's long, fertile,
fierce noonday.

THE PLOT

ACT ONE

At the Garter Inn, the bulky but irrepressible John Falstaff,
a knight fallen upon hard times, seals two letters, both

declaring his love: for Mrs. Alice Ford and for Mrs. Margaret (Meg) Page. After an altercation with Dr. Caius, who complains that Falstaff's henchmen Bardolph and Pistol have robbed him during a drinking bout, Falstaff gives the letters to the henchmen to deliver. They refuse. Falstaff hands the letters to a page, then preaches to the other pair an ironic sermon on the subject of honor, after which he drives them out of the inn.

In the next scene, Alice and Meg meet, with Anne (Alice's daughter) and Mistress Quickly. The two wooed ladies compare their love letters from Falstaff. Amused and indignant, they decide to punish him. Ford, warned by Bardolph and Pistol of Falstaff's wooing, has come to the same decision independently. Ann Ford and young Fenton, in the midst of the confusion, repeat their vows of love. Finally, the ladies send Mistress Quickly off to the Garter Inn to deliver an invitation to Falstaff to visit Mrs. Ford's house, where a trap will be set for him.

ACT TWO

Bardolph and Pistol return to Falstaff, pretending to be penitent. Then Mistress Quickly arrives with messages of love both from Alice and Meg. Falstaff takes both messages at face value and replies that he will visit Alice, as she suggests, between two and three that afternoon. When Quickly has left, Bardolph and Pistol introduce Ford under an assumed name. Offering Falstaff a demijohn of Cyprus wine and a sum of money, Ford asks the fat knight to grant him a favor—to seduce a lady who has spurned his, Ford's, advances. Her name is Alice. If Falstaff succeeds, then perhaps a second lover can hope. Falstaff accepts the presents and the assignment, assuring the visitor that the project is already well under way. The knight is to visit Alice very soon. In fact, he leaves Ford alone in order to prepare for the appointment. In a monologue, Ford gives full vent to his searing jealousy. When Falstaff returns, they go out together, after some polite skirmishing.

In Ford's house, Alice, Meg and Quickly set the trap for Falstaff. Anne is at first sad because she knows her father wants her to marry the despicable Dr. Caius. But when the others reassure her, she joins in the fun. Falstaff arrives, starts to pay court to Alice, but is soon interrupted by Ford's arrival. Falstaff hides first behind a screen, then—with some squeezing—in a laundry hamper. Anne and Fenton exploit the confusion to sing of their love. Ford's search, with the help of Bardolph, Pistol, and others, is intense but fruitless. In the end, the laundry hamper containing Falstaff is emptied into the Thames, beneath the window. Ford, seeing the knight's discomfiture, joins the others in hearty laughter.

ACT THREE

Outside the Garter Inn, warming himself in the sunshine after his dunking, Falstaff drinks some hot wine and reflects on the sad state of the world. Mistress Quickly comes in and is at first received with suspicion. But she delivers Alice's apologies for the mishap and an invitation for the two of them to meet at midnight beneath the Oak of Herne in Windsor Park. Quickly and Falstaff go into the Inn to discuss the tryst further. The others, outside, observe the success of their developing plan for revenge on the fat knight. Finally, Ford promises Anne's hand to Caius, but the promise is overheard by Quickly, who is determined to foil this match.

At midnight, in the moonlit park, Fenton and Anne have a brief moment in which to express again their love. Then Falstaff arrives, and after a short exchange with Alice, is frightened and taunted by strange spirits (his enemies and some local children, all in disguise). When he discovers the identity of his tormenters, he turns on them cleverly, insisting that it is his own wit that makes them witty. Finally, Ford blesses two masked couples. To his amazement, he discovers that he has paired Dr. Caius with the masked Bardolph, and Anne with the unwanted Fenton. Ford good-naturedly accepts the previously rejected son-in-law, and the scene ends with general merriment as Falstaff, followed by the others, declares that everything in the world is jest.

FALSTAFF

libretto by Arrigo Boito

First performed at the Teatro alla Scala
February 9, 1893

CHARACTERS

Sir John Falstaff	*Baritone*
Ford, husband of Alice	*Baritone*
Fenton	*Tenor*
Dr. Caius	*Tenor*
Bardolfo (Bardolph) ⎫ Falstaff's henchmen	*Tenor*
Pistola (Pistol) ⎭	*Bass*
Mrs. Alice Ford	*Soprano*
Nannetta (Anne), her daughter	*Soprano*
Mrs. Quickly	*Mezzo-soprano*
Mrs. Meg Page	*Mezzo-soprano*
The Host of the Garter Inn	
Robin, Falstaff's page	
A page of Ford's	

Burghers and humble people—Ford's servants,
Masquerade of sprites, fairies, witches, etc.

The scene is laid in Windsor during the reign of
Henry IV of England

ATTO PRIMO

PARTE PRIMA

L'interno dell'Osteria della Giarrettiera. Una tavola. Un gran seggiolone. Una panca. Sulla tavola i resti d'un desinare, parecchie bottiglie e un bicchiere. Calamaio, penne, carta, una candela accesa. Una scopa appoggiata al muro. Uscio nel fondo, porta a sinistra. Falstaff è occupato a riscaldare la cera di due lettere alla fiamma della candela, poi le suggella con un anello. Dopo averle suggellate spegne il lume e si mette a bere comodamente sdraiato sul seggiolone.

DR. CAJUS *(entrando dalla porta a sinistra e gridando miniaccioso)*
Falstaff!

FALSTAFF *(senz'abbadare alle vociferazioni del Dr. Cajus, chiama l'oste che si avvicina)*
Olà!

DR. CAJUS *(più forte di prima)*
Sir John Falstaff!

BARDOLFO *(al Dr. Cajus)*
Oh! che vi piglia?

DR. CAJUS *(sempre vociando e avvicinandosi a Falstaff, che non gli dà retta)*
Hai battuto i miei servi!

FALSTAFF *(senza dargli retta, all'oste)*
Oste! un'altra bottiglia di Xeres.

DR. CAJUS
Hai fiaccata la mia giumenta baia,
Sforzata la mia casa.

FALSTAFF
Ma non la tua massaia.

DR. CAJUS
Troppa grazia! Una vecchia cisposa.
Ampio Messere, se fosti venti volte
John Falstaff Cavaliere
Vi forzerò a rispondermi.

FALSTAFF *(con flemma)*
Ecco la mia risposta:
"Ho fatto ciò ch'hai detto."

DR. CAJUS
E poi?

FALSTAFF
L'ho fatto apposta.

DR. CAJUS *(gridando)*
M'appellerò al Consiglio Real.

FALSTAFF
Vatti con Dio. Sta zitto
O avrai le beffe;
Quest'è il consiglio mio.

DR. CAJUS *(ripigliando la sfuriata contro Bardolfo)*
Non è finita!

FALSTAFF
Al diavolo!

DR. CAJUS *(sempre in furia)*
Bardolfo!

ACT ONE

SCENE ONE

Interior of the Garter Inn. A table. An armchair. A bench. On the table, the remains of a meal, numerous bottles and a glass. Inkwell, pens, paper, a lighted candle. A broom propped against the wall. Exit at rear, door at left. Falstaff is busy heating the wax of two letters at the flame of the candle. Then he seals them with a ring. After having sealed them, he extinguishes the light and starts drinking, comfortably stretched out in the armchair.

DR. CAIUS *(entering by the door at left and shouting menacingly)*
Falstaff!

FALSTAFF *(without paying attention to Dr. Caius's vociferations, calls the innkeeper, who approaches)*
Ho there!

DR. CAIUS *(louder than before)*
Sir John Falstaff!

BARDOLPH *(to Dr. Caius)*
Oh! What's got into you?

DR. CAIUS *(still shouting and approaching Falstaff, who pays no attention to him)*
You've beaten my servants!

FALSTAFF *(without paying attention to him, to the host)*
Host! Another bottle of sherry.

DR. CAIUS   You've worn out my bay mare,
Broken into my house.

FALSTAFF   But not your housekeeper.

DR. CAIUS   Too kind of you! A bleary old woman!
Ample Sir, if you were twenty times
John Falstaff, knight,
I would force you to answer me.

FALSTAFF *(with indifference)*
Here is my answer:
"I did what you have said."

DR. CAIUS   And then?

FALSTAFF   I did it purposely.

DR. CAIUS *(shouting)*
I'll appeal to the Royal Council.

FALSTAFF   Go with God. Be quiet
Or you'll have taunts;
This is my counsel.

DR. CAIUS *(resuming his furious outburst, against Bardolph)*
It's not over!

FALSTAFF   Go to the devil!

DR. CAIUS *(still in a rage)*
Bardolph!

BARDOLFO   Ser Dottore!

DR. CAJUS   Tu, ier, m'hai fatto bere.

BARDOLFO   Pur troppo! e che dolore!
> *(si fa tastare il polso dal Dr. Cajus)*
Sto mal. D'un tuo pronostico
M'assisti.
Ho l'intestino guasto.
Malanno agl'osti
Che dan la calce al vino!
> *(mettendo l'indice sul proprio naso enorme
> e rubicondo)*
Vedi questa meteora?

DR. CAJUS   La vedo.

BARDOLFO   Essa si corca rossa così
Ogni notte.

DR. CAJUS *(scoppiando)*
Pronostico di forca!
> *(a Bardolfo)*
M'hai fatto ber, furfante,
> *(indicando Pistola)*
Con lui,
Narrando frasche;
Poi, quando fui ben ciùschero,
M'hai vuotate le tasche.

BARDOLFO *(con decoro)*
Non io.

DR. CAJUS   Chi fu?

FALSTAFF *(chiamando)*
Pistola!

PISTOLA *(avanzandosi)*
Padrone.

FALSTAFF *(sempre seduto sul seggiolone e con flemma)*
Hai tu vuotate le tasche a quel
Messere?

DR. CAJUS *(scattando contro Pistola)*
Certo fu lui. Guardate
Come s'atteggia al niego
Quel ceffo da bugiardo!
> *(vuotando una tasca del farsetto)*
Qui c'erano due scellini del regno
D'Edoardo
E sei mezze-corone.
Non ne riman più segno.

PISTOLA *(a Falstaff, dignitosamente brandendo la scopa)*
Padron, chiedo di battermi
Con quest'arma di legno.
> *(al Dr. Cajus, con forza)*
Vi smentisco!

DR. CAJUS   Bifolco! tu parli
A un gentiluomo!

PISTOLA   Gonzo!

BARDOLPH   Sir Doctor!

DR. CAIUS   Yesterday you made me drink.

BARDOLPH   Unfortunately! And what suffering!
       (has Dr. Caius feel his pulse)
       I'm ill. Help me
       With a diagnosis of yours.
       My intestine is ruined.
       A curse on hosts
       Who put quicklime in the wine!
          *(putting his forefinger on his own enormous
          and reddened nose)*
       You see this meteor?

DR. CAIUS   I see it.

BARDOLPH   It goes to bed, red like this,
       Every night.

DR. CAIUS *(exploding)*
       The diagnosis is the gallows!
          (to Bardolph)
       You made me drink, scoundrel!
          (pointing to Pistol)
       With him,
       Telling idle tales;
       Then, when I was good and tipsy,
       You emptied my pockets.

BARDOLPH *(with decorum)*
       Not I.

DR. CAIUS   Who was it?

FALSTAFF *(calling)*
       Pistol!

PISTOL *(coming forward)*
       Master.

FALSTAFF *(still seated in the armchair and with indifference)*
       Did you empty the pockets of
       That gentleman?

DR. CAIUS *(bursting out, against Pistol)*
       Of course it was he. Look
       How that liar's mug
       Assumes an attitude of denial!
          (emptying a pocket of his doublet)
       Here there were two shillings
       Of the reign of Edward
       And six half crowns.
       Not a sign is left of them.

PISTOL *(to Falstaff, brandishing the broom with dignity)*
       Master, I ask leave to duel
       With this wooden weapon.
          (to Dr. Caius, strongly)
       I give you the lie!

DR. CAIUS   Boor! You're speaking
       To a gentleman!

PISTOL   Dolt!

DR. CAJUS	Pezzente!
PISTOLA	Bestia!
DR. CAJUS	Can!
PISTOLA	Vil!
DR. CAJUS	Spauracchio!
PISTOLA	Gnomo!
DR. CAJUS	Germoglio di mandràgora!
PISTOLA	Chi?
DR. CAJUS	Tu.
PISTOLA	Ripeti!
DR. CAJUS	Sì.

PISTOLA *(scagliandosi contro il Dr. Cajus)*
    Saette!!!

FALSTAFF *(con un cenno frena Pistola)*
    Ehi là! Pistola!
    Non scaricarti qui.
    (chiamando Bardolfo che s'avvicina)
    Bardolfo! Chi ha vuotate
    Le tasche a quel Messere?

DR. CAJUS *(scattando)*
    Fu l'un dei due.

BARDOLFO *(con serenità, indicando il Dr. Cajus)*
    Costui beve, poi pel gran bere
    Perde i suoi cinque sensi,
    Poi ti narra una favola
    Ch'egli ha sognato
    Mentre dormì sotto la tavola.

FALSTAFF *(al Dr. Cajus)*
    L'odi? Se ti capaciti,
    Del ver tu sei sicuro.
    I fatti son negati.
    Vattene in pace.

DR. CAJUS
    Giuro che se mai
    M'ubriaco ancora all'osteria
    Sarà fra gente onesta,
    Sobria, civile e pia.
    (esce dalla porta a sinistra)

BARDOLFO, PISTOLA *(accompagnando buffonescamente sino all'uscio il Dr. Cajus e salmodiando)*
    Amen!

FALSTAFF
    Cessi l'antifona.
    La urlate in contrattempo.
    (Bardolfo e Pistola smettono e si avvicinano
    a Falstaff)
    L'arte sta in questa massima:
    "Rubar con garbo e a tempo."
    (con disprezzo)
    Siete dei rozzi artisti.

BARDOLFO, PISTOLA
    A . . .

DR. CAIUS   Beggar!

PISTOL   Animal!

DR. CAIUS   Dog!

PISTOL   Coward!

DR. CAIUS   Scarecrow!

PISTOL   Gnome!

DR. CAIUS   Mandrake sprout!

PISTOL   Who?

DR. CAIUS   You.

PISTOL   Repeat that!

DR. CAIUS   Yes.

PISTOL *(hurling himself upon Dr. Caius)*
                Thunder and lightning!!!

FALSTAFF *(with a gesture restrains Pistol)*
                Hey there, Pistol!
                Don't go off here.
                     (calling Bardolph, who approaches)
                Bardolph! Who emptied
                The pockets of that gentleman?

DR. CAIUS *(exploding)*
                It was one of the two.

BARDOLPH *(calmly, pointing to Dr. Caius)*
                This man drinks, then from his great drinking
                He loses his five senses.
                Then he tells you a fable
                That he dreamed
                While he slept under the table.

FALSTAFF *(to Dr. Caius)*
                You hear him? If you grasp that,
                You're sure of the truth.
                The deeds are denied.
                Go off in peace.

DR. CAIUS   I swear that if ever
                I get drunk again at the tavern
                It will be amid honest,
                Sober, civil and devout people.
                     (exits through the door at left)

BARDOLPH, PISTOL *(clowningly accompanying Dr. Caius to the exit and intoning)*
                Amen!

FALSTAFF   Stop the antiphon.
                You're shouting it in the wrong time.
                     (Bardolph and Pistol stop and approach Falstaff)
                Art lies in this rule:
                "To steal with grace and rhythm."
                     (with contempt)
                You're crude artists.

BARDOLPH, PISTOL
                A . . .

FALSTAFF *(impone silenzio)*
>
> Ssss.
> *(si mette ad esaminare il conto che l'oste*
> *avra portato insieme alla bottiglia di Xeres)*
> "6 polli: 6 scellini.
> 30 giarre di Xeres: 2 lire.
> 3 tacchini . . ."
> *(a Bardolfo, gettandogli la borsa, e si rimette*
> *a leggere lentamente)*
>
> Fruga nella mia borsa.
> "2 fagiani. Un'acciuga."

BARDOLFO *(estrae dalla borsa le monete e le conta sul tavolo)*
>
> Un mark, un mark, un penny.

FALSTAFF Fruga.

BARDOLFO Ho frugato.

FALSTAFF Fruga.

BARDOLFO *(gettando la borsa sul tavolo)*
>
> Qui non c'è più uno spicciolo.

FALSTAFF *(alzandosi)*
>
> Sei la mia distruzione!
> Spendo ogni sette giorni dieci ghinee!
> Beone!
> So che se andiamo, la notte,
> Di taverna in taverna,
> Quel tuo naso ardentissimo
> Mi serve da lanterna;
> Ma quel risparmio d'olio
> Tu lo consumi in vino.
> Son trent'anni che abbevero
> Quel fungo porporino!
> *(a Bardolfo)*
> Costi troppo . . .
> *(a Pistola)*
> E tu pure.
> *(gridando)*
> Oste! un'altra bottiglia.
> *(a Bardolfo e Pistola)*
> Mi struggete le carni.
> Se Falstaff s'assottiglia
> Non è più lui,
> Nessun più l'ama; in quest'addome
> C'è un migliaio di lingue
> Che annunciano il mio nome!

PISTOLA *(acclamando)*
>
> Falstaff immenso!

BARDOLFO *(acclamando)*
>
> Enorme Falstaff!

FALSTAFF *(guardandosi e toccandosi l'addome)*
>
> Quest'è il mio regno.
> Lo ingrandirò.

BARDOLFO Immenso Falstaff!

PISTOLA Enorme Falstaff!

FALSTAFF *(imposes silence)*
>Sssh.
>>*(turns to examining the bill that the host will have brought together with the bottle of sherry)*
>"6 chickens: 6 shillings.
>30 jars of sherry: 2 pounds.
>3 turkeys . . ."
>>*(to Bardolph, throwing him his purse, and resuming reading slowly)*
>Rummage in my purse.
>"2 pheasants. An anchovy."

BARDOLPH *(takes coins from the purse and counts them on the table)*
>One mark, one mark, one penny.

FALSTAFF   Search.

BARDOLPH   I've searched.

FALSTAFF   Search.

BARDOLPH *(throwing the purse on the table)*
>Here, there's no longer a tiny coin.

FALSTAFF *(rising)*
>You're my destruction!
>I spend ten guineas every seven days!
>Drunkard!
>I know that if we go, at night,
>From tavern to tavern,
>That most glowing nose of yours
>Serves me as a lantern;
>But that saving on oil
>You consume in wine.
>For thirty years I've been soaking
>That purplish mushroom!
>>*(to Bardolph)*
>You cost too much . . .
>>*(to Pistol)*
>And you too.
>>*(shouting)*
>Host! Another bottle.
>>*(to Bardolph and Pistol)*
>You're wasting my flesh.
>If Falstaff grows thin
>He is no longer himself,
>No one loves him any more; in this paunch
>There are a thousand tongues
>That announce my name!

PISTOL *(hailing)*
>Immense Falstaff!

BARDOLPH *(hailing)*
>Enormous Falstaff!

FALSTAFF *(looking at himself and touching his paunch)*
>This is my realm.
>I shall enlarge it.

BARDOLPH   Immense Falstaff!

PISTOL   Enormous Falstaff!

FALSTAFF	Ma è tempo d'assottigliar l'ingegno . . .
BARDOLFO, PISTOLA	
	Assottigliamo.
	(tutti e tre in crocchio)
FALSTAFF	V'è noto un tal, qui del paese
	Ch'ha nome Ford?
BARDOLFO	Sì.
PISTOLA	Sì.
FALSTAFF	Quell'uom è un gran borghese . . .
PISTOLA	Più liberal d'un Creso!
BARDOLFO	È un Lord!
FALSTAFF	Sua moglie è bella.
PISTOLA	E tien lo scrigno.
FALSTAFF	È quella!
	O amor! Sguardo di stella!
	Collo di cigno!
	E il labbro?! un fior!
	Un fior che ride.
	Alice è il nome, e un giorno
	Come passar mi vide
	Ne' suoi paraggi, rise.
	M'ardea l'estro amatorio nel cor.
	La Dea vibrava raggi
	Di specchio ustorio
	(pavoneggiandosi)
	Su me, su me, sul fianco baldo,
	Sul gran torace,
	Sul maschio piè, sul fusto saldo,
	Erto, capace;
	E il suo desir in lei fulgea
	Sì al mio congiunto
	Che parea dir:
	"Io son di Sir John Falstaff."
BARDOLFO	Punto.
FALSTAFF	*(continuando la parola di Bardolfo)*
	E a capo. Un'altra——
BARDOLFO	Un'altra!
PISTOLA	Un'altra!
FALSTAFF	E questa ha nome: Margherita.
PISTOLA	La chiaman Meg.
FALSTAFF	È anch'essa de' miei pregi invaghita.
	È anch'essa tien le chiavi
	Dello scrigno.
BARDOLFO, PISTOLA	
	Dello scrigno.
FALSTAFF	Costoro saran le mie Golconde
	E le mie Coste d'oro!
	(facendosi ammirare)
	Guardate. Io sono ancora
	Una piacente estate
	Di San Martino. A voi,

FALSTAFF   But it's time to sharpen our wit . . .

BARDOLPH, PISTOL
            Let us sharpen.
               (all three in a huddle)

FALSTAFF   Do you know a certain man, here in the town,
            Who has the name of Ford?

BARDOLPH   Yes.

PISTOL   Yes.

FALSTAFF   That man is a substantial citizen . . .

PISTOL   More openhanded than a Croesus!

BARDOLPH   He 's a Lord!

FALSTAFF   His wife is beautiful.

PISTOL   And keeps the moneybox.

FALSTAFF   That's she!
            O Love! Star's gaze!
            Swan's neck!
            And her lips?! A flower!
            A flower that laughs.
            Alice is her name, and one day
            As she saw me pass by
            In her neighborhood, she laughed.
            Amatory fancy burned in my heart.
            The Goddess cast rays
            Of a burning mirror
               (swaggering)
            On me, on me, on my bold flank,
            On my great chest,
            On my virile foot, on my solid trunk,
            Erect, capacious;
            And her desire shone in her
            So joined to mine
            That she seemed to say:
            "I am Sir John Falstaff's."

BARDOLPH   Period.

FALSTAFF *(continuing Bardolph's word)*
            And paragraph. Another woman——

BARDOLPH   Another!

PISTOL   Another!

FALSTAFF   And this one has the name Margaret.

PISTOL   They call her Meg.

FALSTAFF   She is also charmed by my merits.
            And she also keeps the keys
            Of the moneybox.

BARDOLPH, PISTOL
            Of the moneybox.

FALSTAFF   They will be my Golcondas
            And my Gold Coasts!
               (showing himself off)
            Look. I am still
            An attractive
            St. Martin's summer. For you:

Due lettere infuocate.
*(dà a Bardolfo una delle due lettere che sono
rimaste sul tavolo)*
Tu porta questa a Meg;
Tentiam la sua virtù.
(Bardolfo prende la lettera)
Già vedo che il tuo naso
Arde di zelo.
(a Pistola, porgendogli l'altra lettera)
E tu porta questa ad Alice.

PISTOLA *(ricusando con dignità)*
Porto una spada al fianco.
Non sono un Messer Pandarus.
Ricuso.

FALSTAFF *(con calma sprezzante)*
Saltimbanco.

BARDOLFO *(avanzandosi e gettando la lettera sul tavolo)*

Sir John, in quest'intrigo
Non posso accondiscendervi.
Lo vieta . . .

FALSTAFF *(interrompendolo)*
Chi?

BARDOLFO   L'Onore!

FALSTAFF *(vedendo il paggio Robin che entra dal fondo)*
Ehi! paggio!
(poi subito a Bardolfo e Pistola)
Andate a impendervi,
Ma non più a me!
(al paggio che escirà correndo colle lettere)

Due lettere, prendi,
Per due signore.
Consegna tosto, corri,
Via, lesto, va! lesto!
Va, va, va, va, va!
(il paggio esce)

FALSTAFF *(rivolto a Pistola e Bardolfo)*
Onore! Ladri!
Voi state ligi
All'onor vostro, voi!
Cloache d'ignominia, quando,
Non sempre, noi
Possiam star ligi al nostro.
Io stesso, sì, io, io,
Devo talor da un lato
Porre il timor di Dio
E, per necessità,
Sviar l'onore, usare
Stratagemmi ed equivoci,
Destreggiar, bordeggiare.
E voi, coi vostri cenci
E coll'occhiata tôrta
Da gatto pardo e i fetidi

Two inflamed letters.
*(gives Bardolph one of the two letters that
have remained on the table)*
You take this to Meg;
Let us try her virtue.
(Bardolph takes the letter)
I see that your nose already
Is glowing with zeal.
(to Pistol, handing him the other letter)
And you take this to Alice . . .

PISTOL *(refusing, with dignity)*
I carry a sword at my side.
I am not a Mister Pandarus.
I refuse.

FALSTAFF *(with contemptuous calm)*
Mountebank.

BARDOLPH *(coming forward and throwing the letter on the
table)*
Sir John, in this intrigue
I cannot oblige you.
It is forbidden . . .

FALSTAFF *(interrupting him)*
By whom?

BARDOLPH Honor!

FALSTAFF *(seeing the page Robin entering at the rear)*
Hey! Page!
(then immediately to Bardolph and Pistol)
Go hang yourselves,
But not on me any longer!
*(to the page, who will then exit, running, with
the letters)*
Two letters—take them—
For two ladies.
Deliver quickly, run!
Away, speedily! Go, speedily!
Go, go, go, go, go!
(the page leaves)

FALSTAFF *(addressing Pistol and Bardolph)*
Honor! Thieves!
You are true
To your honor, you!
You sewers of ignominy, when
We cannot always
Be true to ours.
I myself, yes, I, I,
I must sometimes set aside
The fear of God
And, out of necessity,
Deflect honor, use
Stratagems and equivocations,
Maneuver, tack.
And you, with your rags
And with your crooked glance
Like a leopard's and your fetid

Sghignazzi avete a scorta
Il vostro Onor! Che onore?
Che onor? che onor! che ciancia!
Che baja!
Può l'onore riempirvi la pancia?
No. Può l'onor rimetterti
Uno stinco? Non può.
Nè un piede? No.
Nè un dito? No. Nè un capello? No.
L'onor non è chirurgo.
Che è dunque? Una parola.
Che c'è in questa parola?
C'è dell'aria che vola.
Bel costrutto! L'onore
Lo può sentir chi è morto?
No. Vive sol coi vivi? . . .
Neppure: perchè a torto
Lo gonfian le lusinghe,
Lo corrompe l'orgoglio,
L'ammorban le calunnie;
E per me non ne voglio!
No! non ne voglio, no, no, no!
Ma, per tornare a voi, furfanti,
Ho atteso troppo,
E vi discaccio.

> (prende in mano la scopa e insegue Bardolfo
> e Pistola che scansano i colpi correndo qua
> e là e riparandosi dietro la tavola)

Olà! Lesti! Lesti! al galoppo!
Al galoppo! Il capestro
Assai bene vi sta!
Lesti, lesti, lesti!
Al galoppo, al galoppo!
Ladri! ladri! ladri! ladri!
Via di qua, via di qua,
Via di qua!

> (Bardolfo fugge dalla porta a sinistra. Pistola
> fugge dall'uscio del fondo, non senza essersi
> buscato qualche colpo di granata, e Falstaff
> lo insegue).

PARTE SECONDA

Giardino. A sinistra la casa di Ford. Gruppi d'alberi nel centro della scena. Alice, Nannetta, Meg, Mrs. Quickly, poi Mr. Ford, Fenton, Dr. Cajus, Bardolfo, Pistola. Meg con Mrs. Quickly da destra. S'avviano verso la casa di Ford, e sulla soglia s'imbattono in Alice e Nannetta che stanno per escire.

MEG *(salutando)*
      Alice.
ALICE *(salutando)*
      Meg.
MEG   Nannetta.

Sniggerings have as escort
Your Honor? What honor?
What honor? What honor? What nonsense!
What foolishness!
Can honor fill your belly?
No. Can honor replace
A shinbone for you? It cannot.
Or a foot? No.
Or a finger? No. Or a hair? No.
Honor is not a surgeon.
What is it then? A word.
What is there in this word?
There is some air that flies.
Fine benefit! Can one who is dead
Feel honor?
No. Does it live only with the living? . . .
Not even: because wrongly
Flattery swells it,
Pride corrupts it,
Slanders infect it;
And, for myself, I want none of it!
No! I want none of it, no, no, no!
But, to get back to you, rogues,
I've put up with too much,
And I dismiss you.
*(takes the broom in hand and chases Bar-
dolph and Pistol, who dodge the blows, run-
ning here and there and taking refuge behind
the table)*
Hey, there! Quickly! Quickly! At a gallop!
At a gallop! The noose
Suits you very well!
Quickly, quickly, quickly!
At a gallop, at a gallop!
Thieves! Thieves! Thieves! Thieves!
Away from here, away from here,
Away from here!
*(Bardolph escapes through the door at left.
Pistol escapes by the exit at the rear, not
without having received some broom blows,
and Falstaff pursues him).*

SCENE TWO

*Garden. At left, Ford's house. Groups of trees in the center
of the stage. Alice, Anne, Meg, Mrs. Quickly, then Mr. Ford,
Fenton, Dr. Caius, Bardolph, Pistol. Meg, with Mrs. Quickly,
from the right. They go toward Ford's house, and on the
threshold they encounter Alice and Anne, who are about to
come out.*

MEG *(greeting her)*
Alice.

ALICE *(greeting her)*
Meg.

MEG
Anne.

ALICE *(a Meg)*
          Escivo appunto
          Per ridere con te.
          (a Mrs. Quickly)
          Buon dì, comare.

QUICKLY   Dio vi doni allegria.
          (accarezzando la guancia di Nannetta)
          Botton di rosa!

ALICE *(a Meg)*
          Giungi in buon punto.
          M'accade un fatto
          Da trasecolare.

MEG   Anche a me.

QUICKLY *(che parlava con Nannetta, avvicinandosi con curiosità)*
          Che?

NANNETTA *(pure avvicinandosi)*
          Che cosa?

ALICE *(a Meg)*
          Narra il tuo caso.

MEG   Narra il tuo.

NANNETTA Narra, narra.

QUICKLY   Narra, narra.

ALICE *(a tutte in crocchio)*
          Promessa di non ciarlar.

MEG   Ti pare?!

QUICKLY   Oibò! Vi pare?

ALICE   Dunque: se m'acconciassi

          A entrar nei rei
          Propositi del diavolo, sarei
          Promossa al grado
          Di Cavalleressa!

MEG   Anch'io!

ALICE   Motteggi!

MEG *(cerca in tasca: estrae na lettera)*
          Non più parole.
          Chè qui sciupiamo
          La luce del sole.   .
          Ho una lettera.

ALICE *(cerca in tasca)*
          Anch'io.

NANNETTA, QUICKLY
          Oh! !

ALICE *(dà la lettera a Meg)*
          Leggi.

MEG *(scambia la propria lettera con quella d'Alice)*
          Leggi.
              (leggendo la lettera d'Alice)
          "Fulgida Alice! amor t'offro . . ."
          Ma come?! Che cosa dice?
          Salvo che il nome

ALICE *(to Meg)*
>I was just coming out
>To laugh with you.
>>*(to Mrs. Quickly)*
>Good day, gossip.

QUICKLY God give you merriment.
>>*(caressing Anne's cheek)*
>Rosebud!

ALICE *(to Meg)*
>You arrive at a good moment.
>A thing has happened to me
>That is startling.

MEG Also to me.

QUICKLY *(who was speaking with Anne, approaching with curiosity)*
>What?

ANNE *(also approaching)*
>What thing?

ALICE *(to Meg)*
>Tell your tale.

MEG Tell yours.

ANNE Tell, tell.

QUICKLY Tell, tell.

ALICE *(to all, in a group)*
>Promise not to gossip.

MEG The idea!

QUICKLY Oh, my, the idea!

ALICE Well then: if I were prepared
>To enter into the evil
>Designs of the devil, I would be
>Promoted to the rank
>Of Knight's lady!

MEG I too!

ALICE You're joking!

MEG *(seeks in her pocket, takes out a letter)*
>No more words.
>For here we're wasting
>The sunlight.
>I have a letter.

ALICE *(seeks in her pocket)*
>I too.

ANNE, QUICKLY
>Oh! !

ALICE *(gives the letter to Meg)*
>Read.

MEG *(exchanges her own letter for Alice's)*
>Read.
>>*(reading Alice's letter)*
>"Radiant Alice! I offer you love . . ."
>What? What does he say?
>Except for the name

La frase è uguale.

ALICE *(cogli occhi sulla lettera che tiene in mano, ripete la lettura di Meg)*
"Fulgida Meg! amor t'offro . . ."

MEG *(continuando sul proprio foglio la lettura d'Alice)*
" . . . amor bramo."

ALICE   Qua Meg, là Alice.

MEG   È tal e quale.
"Non domandar perchè,
Ma dimmi:"

ALICE   " . . . t'amo."
Pur non gli offersi cagion.

MEG   Il nostro caso è pur strano.
(Tutte in un gruppo addosso alle lettere, confrontandole e maneggiandole con curiosità)

QUICKLY   Guardiam con flemma.

MEG   Gli stessi versi.

ALICE   Lo stesso inchiostro.

QUICKLY   La stessa mano.

NANNETTA   Lo stesso stemma.

ALICE, MEG   " . . . sei la gaia comare,
Il compar gaio
Son io, e fra noi due
Facciamo il paio."

ALICE   Già.

NANNETTA   Lui, lei, te.

QUICKLY   Un paio in tre.

ALICE   "Facciamo il paio
In un amor ridente
Di donna bella
E d'uom appariscente."

NANNETTA, MEG, QUICKLY
" . . . appariscente."

ALICE   "E il viso tuo
Su me risplenderà
Come una stella, come una stella
Sull'immensità."

TUTTE *(ridendo)*
Ah! ah! ah! ecc.

ALICE *(continua e finisce)*
"Rispondi al tuo scudiere,
John Falstaff Cavaliere."

QUICKLY   Mostro!

MEG   Mostro!

NANNETTA   Mostro!

ALICE   Mostro!

NANNETTA, MEG, QUICKLY
Mostro!

ALICE   Dobbiam gabbarlo.

NANNETTA   E farne chiasso.

The sentence is identical.

ALICE *(with her eyes on the letter she holds in her hand, repeats Meg's reading)*
"Radiant Meg! I offer you love . . ."

MEG *(continuing on her own page Alice's reading)*
" . . . I desire love."

ALICE   Here "Meg"; there "Alice."

MEG   It's exactly the same.
"Do not ask why,
But say to me:"

ALICE   " . . . I love you."
Yet I offered him no motive.

MEG   Our situation is truly odd.
(All in a group, over the letters, comparing them and handling them with curiosity)

QUICKLY   Let us look with calm.

MEG   The same verses.

ALICE   The same ink.

QUICKLY   The same hand.

ANNE   The same coat of arms.

ALICE, MEG   " . . . you are the merry wife,
The merry groom
Am I, and between the two of us
Let us make a couple."

ALICE   Indeed.

ANNE   He, she, you.

QUICKLY   A couple in three.

ALICE   "Let us make a couple
In a joyous love
Of a beautiful woman
And a man who is striking."

ANNE, MEG, QUICKLY
" . . . striking."

ALICE   "And your countenance
Will shine upon me
Like a star, like a star
Upon the immense firmament."

ALL *(laughing)*
Ha, ha, ha! *etc.*

ALICE *(continues and concludes)*
"Reply to your squire,
John Falstaff, Knight."

QUICKLY   Monster!

MEG   Monster!

ANNE   Monster!

ALICE   Monster!

ANNE, MEG, QUICKLY
Monster!

ALICE   We must mock him.

ANNE   And make a fuss about it.

ALICE   E metterlo in burletta.

NANNETTA   Oh! oh! che spasso!

QUICKLY   Che allegria!

MEG   Che vendetta!
                 (*rivolgendosi or all'una ora all'altra, tutte in
                 crocchio cinguettando*)

ALICE   Quell'otre! quel tino!
                 Quel Re delle pancie,
                 Ci ha ancora le ciance
                 Del bel vagheggino.
                 Quell'otre! Quel tino! *ecc.*
                 E l'olio gli sgocciola
                 Dall'adipe unticcio
                 E ancora ei ne snocciola
                 La strofa e il bisticcio!
                 Lasciam ch'ei le pronte
                 Sue ciarle ne spifferi,
                 Farà come i pifferi
                 Che sceser dal monte.
                 Vedrai che se abbindolo
                 Quel grosso compar,
                 Più lesto d'un guindolo,
                 Più lesto, *ecc.*
                 Lo faccio girar.

QUICKLY (*ad Alice*)
                 Quell'uom è un cannone!
                 Se scoppia ci spaccia,
                 Se scoppia, *ecc.*
                 Un flutto in tempesta
                 Gittò sulla rena
                 Di Windsor codesta
                 Vorace balena.
                 Ma qui non ha spazio
                 Di farsi più pingue;
                 Ne fecer già strazio
                 Le vostre lingue.
                 Tre lingue più allegre
                 D'un trillo di nacchere,
                 Che spargon più chiacchiere
                 Di sei cingallegre.
                 Tal sempre s'esilari
                 Quel bel cinguettar.
                 Così soglion l'ilari
                 Così, *ecc.*
                 Comari ciarlar.

NANNETTA (*ad Alice*)
                 Se ordisci una burla
                 Vo' anch'io la mia parte.
                 Se ordisci, *ecc.*
                 Conviene condurla
                 Con senno, con arte.
                 L'agguato ov'ei sdrucciola
                 Convien ch'ei non scerna.
                 Già prese una lucciola
                 Per una lanterna.

ALICE   And put him to ridicule.

ANNE   Oh! oh! What fun!

QUICKLY   What merriment!

MEG   What vengeance!
                (addressing first one, then another, all the
                women, in a group, chattering)

ALICE   That wineskin! That tub!
                That King of bellies,
                Still has the chatter
                Of the handsome swain.
                That wineskin! That tub! *etc.*
                And oil drips
                From his greasy corpulence
                And he still rattles off
                A strophe and a pun about it!
                We'll let him spout
                His ready chatter,
                He'll act like the pipers
                Who came down from the mountain in vain.
                You'll see that if I trick
                That gross gentleman,
                Faster than a reel,
                Faster, *etc.*
                I'll make him spin.

QUICKLY *(to Alice)*
                That man is a cannon!
                If he explodes, he'll kill us,
                If he explodes, *etc.*
                A wave in a storm
                Cast on the beach
                Of Windsor this
                Voracious whale.
                But here he has no space
                To make himself fatter;
                Your tongues already
                Have torn him to pieces.
                Three tongues, merrier
                Than a trill of castanets,
                That spread more chatter
                Than six great tits.
                Let that fine twittering
                Always be exhilarated.
                Thus do the gay
                Thus, *etc.*
                Wives chatter.

ANNE *(to Alice)*
                If you plan a jest
                I want also my share.
                If you plan, *etc.*
                It's best to conduct it
                With wisdom, with skill.
                It's best for him not to glimpse
                The ambush where he trips.
                He has already
                Been deceived by appearances.

Che il gioco riesca
Perciò più non dubito;
Per coglierlo subito
Bisogna offrir l'esca.
E se i scilinguagnoli
Sapremo adoprar,
Vedremo a rigagnoli,
Vedremo, *ecc.*
Quell'orco sudar.

MEG Un flutto in tempesta
Gittò sulla rena
Di Windsor codesta
Vorace balena,
Di Windsor, *ecc.*
Quell'uom è un cannone,
Se scoppia, ci spaccia.
Colui, se l'abbraccia,
Ti schiaccia Giunone.
Ma certo si spappola
Quel mostro a un tuo cenno
E corre alla trappola
E perde il suo senno.
Potenza d'un fragil
Sorriso di donna!
Scienza d'un agile
Movenza di gonna!
Se il vischio l'impegola
Lo udremo strillar.
E allor la sua fregola,
La sua fregola,
Vedremo, vedremo svampar.

Escono in gruppo da sinistra; ma di tratto in tratto se ne
vedrà taluna fra gli alberi del fondo, senza che si accorgono
gli uomini, che entrano vivamente da destra: Ford, seguito dal
Dr. Cajus, poi Bardolfo, poi Pistola, poi Fenton. Tutti in
gruppo parlano a Ford a bassa voce, brontolando.

DR. CAJUS È un ribaldo, un furbo, un ladro,
Un furfante, un turco, un vandalo;
L'altro dì mandò a soqquadro
La mia casa e fu uno scandalo.
Se un processo oggi gl'intavolo
Sconterà le sue rapine.
Ma la sua più degna fine
Sia d'andare in man del diavolo.
È un ribaldo, *ecc.*
E quei due che avete accanto
Genti son di sua tribù
Non son due stinchi di santo
Nè son fiori di virtù.

BARDOLFO Falstaff, sì, ripeto, giuro,
Sì, ripeto, giuro,
(Per mia bocca il ciel v'illumina)
Contro voi, John Falstaff rumina

Therefore I no longer doubt
That the game will succeed;
To catch him promptly
We must offer the bait.
And if we know how to use
Our tongue-strings,
We'll see, in streams,
We'll see, *etc.*
That ogre sweat.

MEG   A wave in a storm
Cast on the beach
Of Windsor this
Voracious whale,
Of Windsor, *etc.*
That man is a cannon;
If he explodes, he'll kill us.
He, if he embraces her,
Would crush Juno for you.
But surely that monster
Will be reduced to pulp at your signal
And will run to the trap
And lose his senses.
The power of a fragile
Smile of a woman!
The art of an agile
Movement of a skirt!
If the bird-lime catches him
We'll hear him yell.
And then his ardor,
His ardor,
We'll see, we'll see cool off.

They go out in a group at left; but from time to time one of them will be seen among the trees in the rear, without their being noticed by the men, who enter energetically from the right: Ford, followed by Dr. Caius, then Bardolpho, then Pistol, then Fenton. All in a group, speak softly to Ford, grumbling.

DR. CAIUS   He's a rascal, a sly one, a thief,
A rogue, a Turk, a vandal;
The other day he turned my house
Upside down and it was a scandal.
If I bring a lawsuit against him today
He'll pay for his robberies.
But his most worthy end
Would be to fall into the devil's hand.
He's a rascal, *etc.*
And those two you have beside you
Are people of his tribe,
They are far from being saints,
Nor are they prizes of virtue.

BARDOLPH   Falstaff, yes, I repeat, I swear
Yes, I repeat, I swear
(May heaven enlighten you through my mouth),
Against you, John Falstaff is pondering

Un progetto alquanto impuro.
Son uom d'arme e quell'infame
Più non vo' che v'impozzangheri;
Non vorrei, no, escir dai gangheri
Dell'onor per un reame.
Messer Ford, l'uom avvisato
Non è salvo che a metà
Tocca a voi d'ordir l'agguato
Che l'agguato stornerà.
Tocca a voi, *ecc.*

FENTON   Se volete, io non mi perito
Di ridurlo alla ragione
Colle brusche o colle buone
Colle brusche o colle buone,
E pagarlo al par del merito,
Pagarlo, *ecc.*
Mi dà core e mi solletica,
(E sarà una giostra gaia, gaia),
Di sfondar quella ventraia
Iperbolico-apoplettica.
Col consiglio o colla spada
Se lo trovo al tu per tu,
Se lo trovo, *ecc.*
O lui va per la sua strada,
O l'assegno a Belzebù.
Se lo trovo, *ecc.*

ALICE, NANNETTA, MEG, QUICKLY *(allontanandosi)*
Quell'otre! Quel tino!
Quell'otre, *ecc.*

FORD   Un ronzio di vespe e d'avidi
Calabron brontolamento,
Un rombar di nembi gravidi
D'uragani è quel ch'io sento.
Il cerèbro un ebro allucina
Turbamento di paura;
Ciò che intorno a me si buccina
È un susurro di congiura.
Parlan quattro ed uno ascolta;
Qual dei quattro ascolterò?
Qual dei quattro, *ecc.*
Se parlaste uno alla volta,
Se parlaste, *ecc.*
Forse allor v'intenderò
Forse allor, *ecc.*

PISTOLA   Sir John Falstaff già v'appresta,
Sir John Falstaff già v'appresta,
Messer Ford, un gran pericolo.
Già vi pende sulla testa
Qualche cosa a perpendicolo.
Messer Ford, fui già un armigero
Di quell'uom dall'ampia cute;
Or mi pento e mi morigero
Per ragioni di salute.
La minaccia or v'è scoperta,

A highly impure plan.
I'm a man of arms and I don't want
That infamous man to besmirch you further;
I wouldn't like to leave the bounds
Of honor for a kingdom.
Master Ford, a man warned
Is only half saved.
It's up to you to plan the trap
That will deflect the trap.
It's up to you, *etc.*

FENTON   If you like, I have no scruples
About making him see reason
With harsh means or with mild,
With harsh means or with mild,
And paying him as he deserves,
Paying him, *etc.*
I'm encouraged and I'm tickled
(And it will be a merry, merry joust),
To demolish that bag of guts,
Hyperbolic apoplectic.
With advice or with my sword,
If I find him, face-to-face,
If I find him, *etc.*
Either he'll go on his way,
Or I'll deliver him to Beelzebub.
If I find him, *etc.*

ALICE, ANNE, MEG, QUICKLY *(dispersing)*
That wineskin! That tub!
That wineskin, *etc.*

FORD   A buzzing of wasps
And a grumbling of greedy hornets,
A rumbling of clouds laden
With hurricanes is what I hear.
A delirious agitation of fear
Bewilders my brain;
What is being trumpeted around me
Is a hum of conspiracy.
Four speak and one listens;
To which of the four shall I listen?
To which of the four, *etc.*
If you spoke one at a time,
If you spoke, *etc.*
Perhaps then I would understand you,
Perhaps then, *etc.*

PISTOL   Sir John Falstaff is already fixing for you,
Sir John Falstaff is already fixing for you,
Master Ford, a great danger.
Already something perpendicular
Is hanging over your head.
Master Ford, I was formerly an esquire
Of that man with the ample skin;
Now I repent and I mend my ways
For reasons of health.
The threat is now clear to you.

Or v'è noto il ciurmador.
State all'erta! all'erta! all'erta!
State all'erta, *ecc.*
Qui si tratta dell'onor.
Or v'è noto, *ecc.*

FORD *(a Pistola)*
Ripeti.

PISTOLA *(a Ford)*
In due parole:
L'enorme Falstaff vuole
Entrar nel vostro tetto,
Beccarvi la consorte,
Sfondar la cassa forte e . . .
E . . . sconquassarvi il letto.

DR. CAJUS   Caspita!

FORD   Quanti guai!

BARDOLFO *(a Ford)*
Già le scrisse
Un biglietto . . .

PISTOLA *(interrompendo)*
Ma quel messaggio abietto
Ricusai.

BARDOLFO   Ricusai.

PISTOLA   Badate a voi!

BARDOLFO   Badate!

PISTOLA   Falstaff le occhieggia tutte
Che sieno belle o brutte,
Pulzelle o maritate.

BARDOLFO   Tutte!

PISTOLA   Tutte!

BARDOLFO, PISTOLA
Tutte!

BARDOLFO   La corona che adorna
D'Atteòn l'irte chiome
Su voi già spunta.

FORD   Come sarebbe a dir?

BARDOLFO   Le corna.

FORD   Brutta parola!

DR. CAJUS   Ha voglie voraci il Cavalier.

FORD   Sorveglierò la moglie.
Sorveglierò il messere.

Rientrano da sinistra le quattro donne.

FORD   Salvar vo' i beni miei
Dagli appetiti altrui.

FENTON *(vedendo Nannetta)*
(È lei.)

NANNETTA *(vedendo Fenton)*
(È lui.)

Now the swindler is known to you.
Be on guard! On guard! On guard!
Be on guard, *etc.*
Here it's a question of honor.
Now he is known to you, *etc.*

FORD *(to Pistol)*

Repeat.

PISTOL *(to Ford)*

In two words:
The enormous Falstaff wants
To enter beneath your roof,
To catch your wife,
Stave in your strongbox and . . .
And . . . shatter your bed.

DR. CAIUS   Goodness!

FORD   How many calamities!

BARDOLPH *(to Ford)*

Already he's written her
A note . . .

PISTOL *(interrupting)*

But that despicable message
I refused.

BARDOLPH   I refused.

PISTOL   Watch out for yourself!

BARDOLPH   Watch out!

PISTOL   Falstaff ogles them all,
Whether they're beautiful or ugly,
Maidens or married.

BARDOLPH   All!

PISTOL   All!

BARDOLPH, PISTOL
All!

BARDOLPH   The crown that adorns
The shaggy locks of Acteon
Is already sprouting on you.

FORD   What might that mean?

BARDOLPH   Horns.

FORD   Ugly word!

DR. CAIUS   The Knight has voracious desires.

FORD   I'll keep watch over my wife.
I'll keep watch over the gentleman.

The four women come in again from the left.

FORD   I want to save my belongings
From the appetites of others.

FENTON *(seeing Anne)*
(It's she.)

ANNE *(seeing Fenton)*
(It's he.)

FORD *(vedendo Alice)*
          (È lei.)
ALICE *(vedendo Ford)*
          (È lui.)
DR. CAJUS *(a Ford, indicando Alice)*
          (È lei.)
MEG *(ad Alice, indicando Ford)*
          (È lui.)
ALICE *(alle altre, a bassa voce, indicando Ford)*
          S'egli sapesse! . . .

NANNETTA   Guai!
ALICE   Schiviamo i passi suoi.
MEG   Ford è geloso?
ALICE   Assai!
QUICKLY   Zitto!
ALICE   Badiamo a noi.

*Alice, Meg e Quickly escono da sinistra. Resta Nannetta.
Ford, Dr. Cajus, Bardolfo e Pistola escono da destra. Resta
Fenton.*

FENTON *(fra i cespugli, verso Nannetta, a bassa voce)*
          Pst, pst, Nannetta.
NANNETTA *(mettendo l'indice al labbro per cenno di silenzio)*
          Ssssss.
FENTON   Vien qua.
NANNETTA   Taci. Che vuoi?
FENTON   Due baci.
NANNETTA   In fretta.
FENTON   In fretta.

Si baciano rapidamente presso il gruppo d'alberi.

NANNETTA   Labbra di fuoco!
FENTON   Labbra di fiore! . . .
NANNETTA   Che il vago gioco
              Sanno d'amore.
FENTON   Che spargon ciarle,
              Che mostran perle,
              Belle a vederle,
              Dolci a baciarle.
                   (tenta di abbracciarla)
              Labbra leggiadre!
NANNETTA *(difendendosi e guardandosi attorno)*
              Man malandrine!
FENTON .   Ciglia assassine!
              Pupille ladre!
              T'amo!
                   (fa per baciarla ancora)
NANNETTA   Imprudente. No . . .
FENTON   Sì, due baci.
NANNETTA *(si svincola)*
              Basta.

FORD *(seeing Alice)*
       (It's she.)

ALICE *(seeing Ford)*
       (It's he.)

DR. CAIUS *(to Ford, pointing to Alice)*
       (It's she.)

MEG *(to Alice, pointing to Ford)*
       (It's he.)

ALICE *(to the other women, in a low voice, pointing to Ford)*
       If he were to know! . . .

ANNE	Beware!
ALICE	Let us avoid his steps.
MEG	Is Ford jealous?
ALICE	Very!
QUICKLY	Hush!
ALICE	Let's watch out for ourselves.

Alice, Meg and Quickly go off at left. Anne remains. Ford, Dr. Caius, Bardolph and Pistol go off at right. Fenton remains.

FENTON *(among the bushes, toward Anne, in a low voice)*
       Pst, pst, Anne.

ANNE *(putting her forefinger to her lip in a signal for silence)*
       Ssssh.

FENTON	Come here.
ANNE	Hush. What do you want?
FENTON	Two kisses.
ANNE	In haste.
FENTON	In haste.

They kiss rapidly near the group of trees.

ANNE   Lips of fire!

FENTON   Flower lips! . . .

ANNE   Which know the lovely
       Game of love.

FENTON   That strew prattle,
       That display pearls,
       Beautiful to see,
       Sweet to kiss.
         (tries to embrace her)
       Charming lips!

ANNE *(defending herself and looking around)*
       Roguish hands!

FENTON   Murderous lashes!
       Thieving pupils!
       I love you!
         (starts to kiss her again)

ANNE   Foolhardy. No . . .

FENTON   Yes, two kisses.

ANNE *(frees herself)*
       Enough.

FENTON   Mi piaci tanto!

NANNETTA   Vien gente.

Si allontanano l'uno dall'altro.

FENTON *(cantando, si nasconde fra gli alberi sempre guardan-*
do Nannetta)
                Bocca baciata non perde ventura . . .

NANNETTA   Anzi rinnova come fa la luna,
                Come fa la luna.

Entrano nuovamente Alice, Meg, Mrs. Quickly. Nannetta in
fondo.

ALICE *(alle altre)*
                Falstaff m'ha canzonata.

MEG   Merita un gran castigo.

ALICE   Se gli scrivessi un rigo? . . .

NANNETTA *(riunendosi al crocchio, con disinvoltura)*
                Val' meglio un'ambasciata.

ALICE   Sì.

NANNETTA   Sì.

QUICKLY   Sì.

NANNETTA   Sì.

ALICE *(a Quickly)*
                Da quel brigante tu andrai . . .
                (riflettendo)
                Lo adeschi all'offa
                D'un ritrovo galante con me.

QUICKLY   Quest'è gaglioffa!

NANNETTA   Che bella burla!

ALICE   Prima, per attirarlo a noi
                Lo lusinghiamo.

NANNETTA   E poi? . . .

ALICE   E poi
                Gliele cantiamo in rima.

QUICKLY   Non merita riguardo.

ALICE   È un bove.

MEG   È un uomo senza fede.

ALICE   È un monte di lardo.

MEG   Non merita clemenza.

ALICE   È un ghiotton che scialacqua
                Tutto il suo aver nel cuoco.

NANNETTA   Lo tufferem nell'acqua.

ALICE   Lo arrostiremo al fuoco.

NANNETTA   Che gioia!

ALICE   Che allegria!

MEG, QUICKLY   Che gioia!

TUTTE   Che gioia, che gioia, che gioia!

MEG *(a Quickly)*
                Procaccia di far bene
                La tua parte.

FENTON   I like you so much!

ANNE   People are coming.

They move away from each other.

FENTON *(singing, hides among the trees, still looking at Anne)*

      A kissed mouth doesn't lose luck . . .

ANNE   Rather it's renewed, as the moon is,
      As the moon is.

Again Alice, Meg, Mrs. Quickly enter. Anne remains in the rear.

ALICE *(to the others)*
      Falstaff has mocked me.

MEG   He deserves a great punishment.

ALICE   If I were to write him a line? . . .

ANNE *(joining the group, nonchalantly)*
      Sending a message is better.

ALICE   Yes.

ANNE   Yes.

QUICKLY   Yes.

ANNE   Yes.

ALICE *(to Quickly)*
      You will go to that brigand . . .
        (pondering)
      You snare him with the bribe
      Of an amorous encounter with me.

QUICKLY   This is a saucy trick!

ANNE   What a beautiful joke!

ALICE   First, to draw him to us
      We flatter him.

ANNE   And then? . . .

ALICE   And then
      We'll settle our score with him.

QUICKLY   He deserves no consideration.

ALICE   He's an ox.

MEG   He's a man without faith.

ALICE   He's a pile of lard.

MEG   He deserves no clemency.

ALICE   He's a glutton who squanders
      All his substance on the cook.

ANNE   We'll plunge him into the water.

ALICE   We'll roast him on the fire.

ANNE   What joy!

ALICE   What merriment!

MEG, QUICKLY   What joy!

ALL   What joy, what joy, what joy!

MEG *(to Quickly)*
      Take care to play well
      Your part.

QUICKLY *(accorgendosi di Fenton che gira nel fondo)*

        Chi viene?

MEG   Là c'è qualcun che spia.

Escono rapidiamente da destra Alice, Meg, Mrs. Quickly.

FENTON *(tornando accanto a Nannetta)*

        Torno all'assalto.

NANNETTA *(come sfidandolo)*

        Torno alla gara.

        Ferisci!

FENTON   Para!

Si slancia per baciarla: Nannetta si ripara il viso con una mano che Fenton bacia e vorrebbe ribaciare; ma Nannetta la solleva più alta che può e Fenton ritenta invano di raggiungerla colle labbra.

NANNETTA   La mira è in alto.

        L'amor è un agile

        Torneo, sua corte

        Vuol che il più fragile

        Vinca il più forte.

FENTON   M'armo, ti guardo.

        T'aspetto al varco.

NANNETTA   Il labbro è l'arco.

FENTON   E il bacio è il dardo.

        Bada! la freccia

        Fatal già scocca

        Dalla mia bocca

        Sulla tua treccia.

           (le bacia la treccia)

NANNETTA *(annodandogli il collo colla treccia, mentre egli la bacia)*

        Eccoti avvinto.

FENTON   Chiedo la vita!

NANNETTA   Io son ferita

        Ma tu sei vinto.

FENTON   Pietà! Pietà!

        Facciamo la pace

        E poi . . .

NANNETTA   E poi?

FENTON   Se vuoi,

        Ricominciamo.

NANNETTA   Bello è quel gioco

        Che dura poco.

        Basta.

FENTON   Amor mio!

NANNETTA   Vien gente. Addio!

           (fugge da destra)

FENTON *(allontanandosi cantando)*

        Bocca baciata non perde ventura.

NANNETTA *(di dentro rispondendo)*

        Anzi rinnova come fa la luna . . .

QUICKLY (*noticing Fenton, who is wandering in the background*)

    Who's coming?

MEG   There's someone spying there.

Alice, Meg, Mrs. Quickly go off rapidly at right.

FENTON (*coming back to Anne's side*)

    I return to the attack.

ANNE (*as if challenging him*)

    I return to the contest.
    Strike!

FENTON   Parry!

He rushes to kiss her. Anne shields her face with one hand, which Fenton kisses and would like to kiss again; but Anne raises it as high as she can, and Fenton tries again in vain to reach it with his lips.

ANNE   The aim is high.
    Love is a lively
    Joust; its court
    Decrees that the more fragile
    Defeat the stronger.

FENTON   I arm myself; I look at you.
    I await you at the pass.

ANNE   The lip is the bow.

FENTON   And the kiss is the arrow.
    Mind! the fatal
    Arrow already flies
    From my mouth
    On your braid.
        (*kisses her braid*)

ANNE (*entwining his neck with the braid, while he kisses it*)

    There you are, bound.

FENTON   I sue for my life!

ANNE   I am wounded,
    But you are conquered.

FENTON   Mercy! Mercy!
    Let's make peace
    And then . . .

ANNE   And then?

FENTON   If you like,
    Let's begin again.

ANNE   That game is beautiful
    Which lasts a short time.
    Enough.

FENTON   My love!

ANNE   People are coming. Farewell!
        (*flees at right*)

FENTON (*going away, singing*)

    A kissed mouth doesn't lose luck.

ANNE (*from within, replying*)

    Rather it's renewed, as the moon is . . .

FENTON   Bocca baciata non perde ventura,
                    Non perde ventura.
NANNETTA   Come fa la luna.

Rientrano dal fondo Dr. Cajus, Bardolfo, Ford e Pistola.
Fenton si unisce poi al crocchio.

BARDOLFO (*a Ford*)
                    Udrai quanta egli sfoggia
                    Magniloquenza altera.
FORD   Diceste ch'egli alloggia . . .
                    Dove?
PISTOLA   Alla "Giarrettiera."
FORD   A lui mi annuncierete,
                    Ma con un falso nome,
                    Poscia vedrete come
                    Lo piglio nella rete.
                    Ma . . . non una parola.
BARDOLFO   In ciarle non m'ingolfo.
                    Io mi chiamo Bardolfo.
PISTOLA   Io mi chiamo Pistola.
FORD   Siam d'accordo.
BARDOLFO   L'arcano custodirem.
PISTOLA   Son sordo e muto.
FORD   Siam d'accordo tutti.
BARDOLFO, PISTOLA
                    Sì.
FORD   Qua la mano.

Dal fondo rientrano Alice, Nannetta, Meg e Mrs. Quickly.
DR. CAJUS (*a Ford*)
                    Del tuo barbaro diagnostico
                    Forse il male è assai men barbaro.
                    Ti convien tentar la prova
                    Molestissima del ver,
                    Ti convien, *ecc.*
                    Così avvien col sapor ostico
                    Del ginepro o del rabarbaro;
                    Il benessere rinnova
                    L'amarissimo bicchier.
                    Ma quei due che avete accanto
                    Genti son di sua tribù,
                    Non son due stinchi di santo,
                    Nè son fiori di virtù.
                    Ma quei due, *ecc.*
BARDOLFO (*a Ford*)
                    Messer Ford, un infortunio
                    Marital in voi s'incorpora.
                    Se non siete astuto e cauto
                    Quel Sir John vi tradirà,
                    Se non siete, *ecc.*
                    Quel paffuto plenilunio
                    Che il color del vino imporpora
                    Troverebbe un pasto lauto

FENTON   A kissed mouth doesn't lose luck,
Doesn't lose luck.

ANNE   As the moon is.

*Re-enter from the rear Dr. Caius, Bardolph, Ford and Pistol.
Fenton then joins the group.*

BARDOLPH *(to Ford)*
You'll hear how much haughty
Magniloquence he displays.

FORD   You said he lodges . . .
Where?

PISTOL   At the "Garter."

FORD   You will announce me to him,
But with a false name;
Then you will see how
I catch him in the net.
But . . . not a word.

BARDOLPH   I don't become involved in chatter.
My name is Bardolph.

PISTOL   My name is Pistol.

FORD   We are agreed.

BARDOLPH   We'll keep the secret.

PISTOL   I'm deaf and dumb.

FORD   We are all agreed.

BARDOLPH, PISTOL
Yes.

FORD   Here's my hand on it.

From the rear re-enter Alice, Anne, Meg and Mrs Quickly.

DR. CAIUS *(to Ford)*
Perhaps the sickness is far less barbarous
Than your barbarous diagnosis.
It's best for you to try
The very troublesome test of the truth,
It's best for you, *etc.*
So it happens with the nasty taste
Of juniper or of rhubarb;
The very bitter glass
Restores well-being.
But those two you have beside you
Are people of his tribe;
They are far from being saints,
Nor are they prizes of virtue.
But those two, *etc.*

BARDOLPH *(to Ford)*
Master Ford, a marital
Mishap is being embodied in you.
If you aren't astute and cautious
That Sir John will betray you,
If you aren't, *etc.*
That plump full moon
That the color of wine empurples
Would find a lavish meal

Nella vostra ingenuità.
Messer Ford, l'uom avvisato
Non è salvo che a metà.
Tocca a voi d'ordir l'agguato
Che l'agguato stornerà.
L'uom avvisato, *ecc.*

PISTOLA *(a Ford)*

Voi dovete empirgli il calice
Tratto, tratto interrogandolo
Per tentar se vi riesca
Di trovar del nodo il bandolo,
Per tentar, *ecc.*
Come all'acqua inclina il salice
Così al vin quel Cavalier.
Scoverete la sua tresca,
Scoprirete il suo pensier.
La minaccia or v'è scoperta,
Or v'è noto il ciurmador,
Sì, state all'erta, all'erta, all'erta,
Qui si tratta dell'onor.
La minaccia, *ecc.*

ALICE *(a Meg)*

Quell'otre! Quel tino!
Quel Re delle pancie
Ha ancora le ciance
Del bel vagheggino!
Quell'otre! Quel tino!
Vedrai che se abbindolo
Quel grosso compar . . .
Più lesto d'un guindolo
Lo faccio girar.
Più lesto, *ecc.*
Quell'otre, *ecc.*

NANNETTA *(ad Alice)*

Se ordisci una burla
Vo' anch'io la mia parte,
Conviene condurla
Con senno e con arte.
Quell'otre! Quel tino!
E se i scilinguagnoli
Sapremo adoprar
Vedremo a rigagnoli
Quell'orco sudar.
Vedremo, *ecc.*
Quell'otre, *ecc.*

MEG *(ad Alice)*

Vedrai che a un tuo cenno
Quel mostro si spappola
E perde il suo senno
E corre alla trappola.
Qul mostro! Quel mostro!
Se il vischio lo impegola
Lo udremo strillar,
E allor la sua fregola

In your ingenuousness.
Master Ford, the warned man
Is only half saved.
It's up to you to plan the trap
That will deflect the trap.
The warned man, *etc.*

PISTOL *(to Ford)*

You must fill his goblet
Gradually, questioning him,
To see if you succeed
In finding the key to the question.
To see if, *etc.*
As the willow bends to the water,
So that Knight does to wine.
You will find out his intrigue,
You will discover his thought.
The threat is now clear to you.
Now the swindler is known to you,
Yes, be on guard, on guard, on guard,
Here it's a question of honor.
The threat, *etc.*

ALICE *(to Meg)*

That wineskin! That tub!
That King of bellies,
Still has the chatter
Of the handsome swain.
That wineskin! That tub!
You'll see that if I trick
That gross gentleman . . .
Faster than a reel
I'll make him spin.
Faster, *etc.*
That wineskin, *etc.*

ANNE *(to Alice)*

If you plan a jest
I want also my share.
It's best to conduct it
With wisdom and with skill.
That wineskin! That tub!
And if we know how to use
Our tongue strings
We'll see in streams
That ogre sweat.
We'll see, *etc.*
That wineskin, *etc.*

MEG *(to Alice)*

You'll see that at a signal from you
That monster will be reduced to pulp
And lose his senses
And run to the trap.
That monster! That monster!
If the bird lime catches him
We'll hear him yell,
And then his ardor

Vedremo svampar.
E allor, *ecc.*
Quell'otre, *ecc.*

QUICKLY   Tre lingue più allegre
D'un trillo di nacchere,
Che spargon più chicchiere
Di sei cingallegre.
Quell'otre! Quel tino!
Tal sempre s'esilari
Quel bel cinguettar,
Così soglion l'ilari
Comari ciarlar.
Così soglion, *ecc.*
Quell'otre, *ecc.*

FENTON *(fra sè)*
Qua borbotta un crocchio d'uomini,
C'è nell'aria una malìa,
C'è nell'aria una malìa.
Là cinguetta un stuol di femine,
Spira un vento agitator.
Ma colei che in cor mi nomini,
Dolce amor, vuol esser mia!
Noi sarem come due gemine
Stelle unite in un ardor.

FORD *(a Pistola)*
Tu vedrai se bene adopera
L'arte mia con quell'infame;
E sarà prezzo dell'opera
S'io discopro le sue trame.
Tu vedrai, *ecc.*
E sara prezzo dell'opera
Lo sventare le sue trame.
Se da me storno il ridicolo
Non avrem oprato invan,
Se l'attiro nell'inganno
L'angue morde il cerretan.
Se l'attiro, *ecc.*

Ford, Dr. Cajus, Fenton, Bardolfo, Pistola escono.

ALICE   Qui più non si vagoli . . .
NANNETTA *(a Quickly)*
Tu corri all'ufficio tuo.
ALICE   Vo' ch'egli miagoli
D'amore come un micio.
(a Quickly)
È intesa.
QUICKLY   Sì.
NANNETTA   È detta.
ALICE   Domani.
QUICKLY   Sì. Sì.
ALICE *(salutando)*
Buon dì, Meg.

We'll see cool off.
And then, *etc.*
That wineskin, *etc.*

QUICKLY   Three tongues merrier
Than a trill of castanets,
That spread more chatter
Than six great tits.
That wineskin! That tub!
Let that fine twittering
Always be exhilarated,
Thus do the gay
Wives chatter.
Thus do, *etc.*
That wineskin, *etc.*

FENTON *(aside)*

Here a group of men is grumbling.
There is an enchantment in the air,
There is an enchantment in the air.
There a swarm of females is twittering,
A conspiratorial wind blows.
But she who calls my name in her heart,
Sweet love, wants to be mine!
We shall be like two twin
Stars joined in one ardor.

FORD *(to Pistol)*

You'll see if I use well
My skill with that scoundrel;
And if I discover his plots
It will be the price of my work.
You'll see, *etc.*
And the destroying of his plots
Will be the price of my work.
If I deflect ridicule from myself,
We will not have worked in vain,
If I draw him into the deceit,
The serpent bites the charlatan.
If I draw him, *etc.*

Ford, Dr. Caius, Fenton, Bardolph, Pistol leave.

ALICE   Let us dawdle here no longer.
ANNE *(to Quickly)*
You hasten to your task.
ALICE   I want him to mew
With love like a kitten.
(to Quickly)
It's understood.
QUICKLY   Yes.
ANNE   It's bespoken.
ALICE   Tomorrow.
QUICKLY   Yes. Yes.
ALICE *(saying goodbye)*
Good day, Meg.

QUICKLY   Nannetta, buon dì.

NANNETTA   Addio.

MEG   Buon dì.

NANNETTA   Buon dì.

MEG   Buon dì.

ALICE *(trattenendo ancora le altre)*
              Vedrai che quell'epa
              Terribile e tronfia
              Si gonfia,
              Si gonfia, si gonfia.

NANNETA, MEG
              Si gonfia, si gonfia.

QUICKLY   Si gonfia.

ALICE, NANNETTA, MEG, QUICKLY
              E poi crepa.

ALICE   Ma il viso mio
              Su lui risplenderà . . .
              Come una stella . . .

NANNETTA   Come una stella . . .

TUTTE   Come una stella
              Sull'immensità!
              Ah! ah! ah! ah! *ecc.*

Si accomiatano e s'allontanano ridendo.

ATTO SECONDO

PARTE PRIMA

L'interno dell'Osteria della Giarrettiera. Una tavola. Un gran seggiolone. Una panca. Sulla tavola i resti d'un desinare, parecchie bottiglie e un bicchiere. Calamaio, penne, carta, una candela accesa. Una scopa appoggiata al muro. Uscio nel fondo, porta a sinistra.

Falstaff è adagiato nel suo gran seggiolone al suo solito posto bevendo il suo Xeres. Bardolfo e Pistola verso il fondo accanto alla porta di sinistra.

BARDOLFO, PISTOLA *(battendosi con gran colpi il petto, in atto di pentimento)*
              Siam pentiti e contriti.

FALSTAFF *(volgendosi appena verso Bardolfo e Pistola)*
              L'uomo ritorna al vizio,
              La gatta al lardo . . .

BARDOLFO, PISTOLA
              E noi torniamo al tuo servizio.

BARDOLFO *(a Falstaff)*
              Padron, là c'è una donna
              Che alla vostra presenza
              Chiede d'esser ammessa.

FALSTAFF   S'inoltri.

Bardolfo esce da sinistra e ritorna subito accompagnando Mrs. Quickly.

QUICKLY   Anne, good day.

ANNE   Goodbye.

MEG   Good day.

ANNE   Good day.

MEG   Good day.

ALICE *(keeping the others longer)*
>You'll see that belly,
>Terrible and pompous,
>Swells,
>Swells, swells.

ANNE, MEG   Swells, swells.

QUICKLY   Swells.

ALICE, ANNE, MEG, QUICKLY
>And then bursts.

ALICE
>But my countenance
>Will shine upon him . . .
>Like a star . . .

ANNE   Like a star . . .

ALL
>Like a star
>Upon the immense firmament!
>Ha! ha! ha! ha! *oto.*

They take leave of one another and go away, laughing.

ACT TWO

SCENE ONE

The interior of the Garter Inn. A table. An armchair. A bench. On the table, the remains of a meal, numerous bottles and a glass. Inkwell, pens, paper, a lighted candle. A broom propped against the wall. Exit at rear, door at left.

Falstaff is settled in his great armchair in his usual place, drinking his sherry. Bardolph and Pistol are toward the rear, next to the door at left.

BARDOLPH, PISTOL *(striking their chests with great blows, in a gesture of repentance)*
>We're penitent and contrite.

FALSTAFF *(barely turning toward Bardolph and Pistol)*
>Man returns to his bad habit,
>The cat to the lard . . .

BARDOLPH, PISTOL
>And we return to your service.

BARDOLPH *(to Falstaff)*
>Master, there's a woman outside
>Who asks to be admitted
>To your presence.

FALSTAFF   Let her come in.

Bardolph goes off at left and returns at once, accompanying Mrs. Quickly.

QUICKLY *(inchinandosi profondamente verso Falstaff il quale è ancora seduto)*
    Reverenza!

FALSTAFF   Buon giorno, buona donna.

QUICKLY   Reverenza!
    (avvicinandosi con gran rispetto e cautela)
    Se vostra grazia vuole,
    Vorrei, segretamente,
    Dirle quattro parole.

FALSTAFF   T'accordo udienza.
    (a Bardolfo e Pistola, rimasti nel fondo a spiare)
    Escite.
    (escono da sinistra facendo sberleffi)

QUICKLY *(facendo un altro inchino ed avvicinandosi più di prima)*
    Reverenza!
    (esitando)
    Madonna Alice Ford . . .

FALSTAFF *(alzandosi e accostandosi a Quickly premuroso)*
    Ebben?

QUICKLY   Ahimè! Povera donna!
    Siete un gran seduttore!

FALSTAFF *(subito)*
    Lo so. Continua.

QUICKLY   Alice sta in grande agitazione
    D'amor per voi;
    Vi dice che ebbe la vostra lettera,
    Che vi ringrazia
    E che suo marito esce sempre
    Dalle due alle tre.

FALSTAFF   Dalle due alle tre.

QUICKLY   Vostra Grazia a quell'ora
    Potrà liberamente
    Salir ove dimora
    La bella Alice.
    Povera donna! le angoscie sue
    Son crudeli!
    Ha un marito geloso!

FALSTAFF *(rimuginando le parole di Quickly)*
    Dalle due alle tre.
    (a Quickly)
    Le dirai che impazïente
    Aspetto quell'ora.
    Al mio dover non mancherò.

QUICKLY   Ben detto.
    Ma c'è un'altra ambasciata
    Per Vostra Grazia.

FALSTAFF   Parla.

QUICKLY   La bella Meg (un angelo
    Che innamora a guardarla)
    Anch'essa vi saluta
    Molto amorosamente,

QUICKLY *(bowing deeply toward Falstaff, who is still seated)*

> My respects!

FALSTAFF Good day, good woman.

QUICKLY My respects!
> *(approaching with great respect and caution)*
> If your Grace wishes,
> I'd like, privately,
> To say a few words to you.

FALSTAFF I grant you audience.
> *(to Bardolph and Pistol, who have remained
> at the rear to spy)*
> Go out.
> *(they exit at left, making grimaces)*

QUICKLY *(making another bow and coming closer than before)*

> My respects!
> *(hesitating)*
> Madam Alice Ford . . .

FALSTAFF *(rising and coming closer to Quickly eagerly)*
> Well?

QUICKLY Alas! Poor woman!
> You're a great seducer!

FALSTAFF *(promptly)*
> I know. Continue.

QUICKLY Alice is in great agitation
> Out of love for you;
> She tells you that she received your letter,
> That she thanks you,
> And that her husband always goes out
> From two until three.

FALSTAFF From two until three.

QUICKLY Your Grace at that hour
> Can freely
> Go up where
> The beautiful Alice lives.
> Poor woman! Her torments
> Are cruel!
> She has a jealous husband!

FALSTAFF *(turning Quickly's words over in his mind)*
> From two until three.
> *(to Quickly)*
> You will tell her that I await
> That hour impatiently.
> I shall not fail in my duty.

QUICKLY Well said.
> But there's another message
> For your Grace.

FALSTAFF Speak.

QUICKLY The beautiful Meg (an angel
> Who inspires love to look at her)
> Also sends you greeting
> Very lovingly;

Dice che suo marito
È assai di rado assente . . .
Povera donna!
Un giglio di candore e di fè!
Voi le stregate tutte.

FALSTAFF Stregoneria non c'è.
Ma un certo qual mio
Fascino personal . . .
Dimmi: l'altra sa
Di quest'altra?

QUICKLY Oibò! La donna nasce scaltra.
Non temete.

FALSTAFF *(cercando nella borsa)*
Or ti vo' remunerar . . .

QUICKLY Chi semina grazie,
Raccoglie amor.

FALSTAFF *(estraendo una moneta e porgendola a Quickly)*
Prendi, Mercurio-femina.
(congedandola col gesto)
Saluta le due dame.

QUICKLY M'inchino.
(esce da sinistra)

FALSTAFF Alice è mia!
Va, vecchio John,
Va, va per la tua via.
Questa tua vecchia carne
Ancora spreme
Qualche dolcezza a te.
Tutte le donne ammunitate
Insieme si dannano per me!
Buon corpo di Sir John,
Ch'io nutro e sazio,
Va, ti ringrazio.

BARDOLFO *(entrando da sinistra)*
Padron, di là c'è
Un certo Mastro Fontana
Che anela di conoscervi;
Offre una damigiana
Di Cipro per l'asciolvere
Di Vostra Signoria.

FALSTAFF Il suo nome è Fontana?

BARDOLFO Sì.

FALSTAFF Bene accolta sia
La fontana che spande
Un simile liquore!
Entri.
(Bardolfo esce)
Va, vecchio John, per la tua via.

Mr. Ford, travestito, entra da sinistra preceduto da Bardolfo che si ferma all'uscio e s'inchina al suo passaggio, e seguito da Pistola il quale tiene una damigiana. Pistola e Bardolfo restano nel fondo. Ford tiene un sacchetto in mano.

She says that her husband
Is very rarely absent . . .
Poor woman!
A lily of innocence and faith!
You bewitch them all.

FALSTAFF   There's no witchcraft.
But a certain sort
Of personal fascination of mine . . .
Tell me: does the one know
About this other one?

QUICKLY   Oho! Woman is born sly.
Do not fear.

FALSTAFF *(searching in his purse)*
Now I want to reward you . . .

QUICKLY   Whoever sows favors,
Reaps love.

FALSTAFF *(taking out a coin and handing it to Quickly)*
Take this, female Mercury.
(dismissing her with a gesture)
Greet the two ladies.

QUICKLY   I bow.
(leaves at left)

FALSTAFF   Alice is mine!
Go, old John,
Go, go along your way.
This old flesh of yours
Still squeezes out
Some sweetness for you.
All women, in mutiny,
Damn themselves together for me!
Good body of Sir John,
That I nourish and sate,
Go, I thank you.

BARDOLPH *(entering from the left)*
Master, outside there's
A certain Master Fountain
Who longs to know you;
He offers a demijohn
Of Cyprus wine for the breaking
Of your Lordship's fast.

FALSTAFF   His name is Fountain?

BARDOLPH   Yes.

FALSTAFF   Let the fountain
That sheds such liquor
Be properly received!
Have him come in.
(Bardolph goes out)
Go, old John, along your way.

*Mr. Ford, disguised, enters at left, preceded by Bardolph,
who stops on the threshold and bows as Ford passes him,
followed by Pistol, who is holding a demijohn. Pistol and Bardolph remain in the rear. Ford is holding a little sack in his
hand.*

FORD *(avanzandosi dopo un grande inchino a Falstaff)*
　　　　　　　Signore, v'assista il cielo!

FALSTAFF *(ricambiando il saluto)*
　　　　　　　Assista voi pur, signore.

FORD *(sempre complimentoso)*
　　　　　　　Io sono, davver, molto indiscreto,
　　　　　　　E vi chiedo perdono,
　　　　　　　Se, senza ceremonie,
　　　　　　　Qui vengo e sprovveduto
　　　　　　　Di più lunghi preamboli.

FALSTAFF　　Voi siete il benvenuto.

FORD　　　　In me vedete un uom
　　　　　　　Ch'ha un'abbondanza grande
　　　　　　　Degli agi della vita;
　　　　　　　Un uom che spende e spande
　　　　　　　Come più gli talenta
　　　　　　　Pur . . . pur di passar mattana.
　　　　　　　Io mi chiamo Fontana!

FALSTAFF *(andando a stringergli la mano con grande cor-
dialità)*
　　　　　　　Caro signor Fontana!
　　　　　　　Voglio fare con voi
　　　　　　　Più ampia conoscenza.

FORD　　　　Caro Sir John, desidero
　　　　　　　Parlarvi in confidenza.

BARDOLFO *(sottovoce a Pistola nel fondo, spiando)*
　　　　　　　Attento!

PISTOLA *(sottovoce a Bardolfo)*
　　　　　　　Zitto!

BARDOLFO　Guarda! Scommetto!
　　　　　　　Egli va dritto nel trabocchetto.

PISTOLA　　Ford se lo intrappola.

BARDOLFO　Zitto!

PISTOLA　　Zitto!

FALSTAFF *(a Bardolfo e Pistola, i quali escono al cenno di
Falstaff)*
　　　　　　　Che fate là?
　　　　　　　　(a Ford, col quale è rimasto solo)
　　　　　　　V'ascolto.

FORD　　　　Sir John, m'infonde ardire
　　　　　　　Un ben noto proverbio popolar:
　　　　　　　Si suol dire
　　　　　　　Che l'oro apre ogni porta,
　　　　　　　Che l'oro è un talismano,
　　　　　　　Che l'oro vince tutto.

FALSTAFF　　L'oro è un buon capitano
　　　　　　　Che marcia avanti.

FORD *(avvicinandosi verso il tavolo)*
　　　　　　　Ebbene . . .
　　　　　　　Ho un sacco di monete
　　　　　　　Qua, che mi pesa assai.

FORD *(advancing, after a great bow to Falstaff)*
> Sir, may Heaven assist you!

FALSTAFF *(returning the greeting)*
> May it assist you also, Sir.

FORD *(still obsequious)*
> I am, truly, very indiscreet,
> And I beg your pardon,
> If, without standing on ceremony,
> I come here, also without
> Longer preambles.

FALSTAFF You are welcome.

FORD
> In me you see a man
> Who has a great abundance
> Of the comforts of life;
> A man who spends and squanders
> However he most cares to
> So long . . . so long as his whim passes.
> My name is Fountain!

FALSTAFF *(going to shake his hand with great cordiality)*

> Dear Mister Fountain!
> I want to become
> Better acquainted with you.

FORD
> Dear Sir John, I wish
> To speak to you in confidence.

BARDOLPH *(in a low voice to Pistol, in the rear, spying)*
> Pay attention!

PISTOL *(in a low voice to Bardolph)*
> Hush!

BARDOLPH
> Look! I bet
> He goes straight into the snare.

PISTOL Ford is trapping him.

BARDOLPH Hush!

PISTOL Hush!

FALSTAFF *(to Bardolph and Pistol, who go out at Falstaff's sign)*

> What are you doing there?
> *(to Ford, with whom he has remained alone)*
> I am listening to you.

FORD
> Sir John, a well-known folk saying
> Inspires me with boldness:
> It is generally said
> That gold opens every door,
> That gold is a talisman,
> That gold conquers everything.

FALSTAFF
> Gold is a good captain
> Which marches ahead.

FORD *(approaching toward the table)*
> Well then . . .
> I have a sack of gold pieces
> Here, which weighs me down greatly.

                    Sir John, se voi volete
                    Aiutarmi a portarlo.

FALSTAFF *(prende il sacchetto e lo depone sul tavolo)*
                    Con gran piacer . . .
                    Non so, davver,
                    Per qual mio merito, Messere . . .

FORD   Ve lo dirò.
                    C'è a Windsor una dama,
                    Bella e leggiadra molto,
                    Si chiama Alice; è moglie
                    D'un certo Ford . . .

FALSTAFF   V'ascolto.

FORD   Io l'amo e lei non m'ama;
                    Le scrivo, non risponde;
                    La guardo, non mi guarda;
                    La cerco e si nasconde.
                    Per lei sprecai tesori,
                    Gittai doni su doni,
                    Escogitai, tremando,
                    Il vol delle occasioni.
                    Ahimè! tutto fu vano!
                    Rimasi sulle scale,
                    Negletto, a bocca asciutta,
                    Cantando un madrigale.

FALSTAFF *(cantarellando scherzosamente)*
                    "L'amor, l'amor
                    Che non ci dà mai tregue,
                    Finchè la vita strugge."

FORD   " . . . strugge."

FALSTAFF   "E come l'ombra . . ."

FORD   " . . . che chi fugge . . ."

FALSTAFF   " . . . insegue . . . "

FORD   "E chi l'insegue . . ."

FALSTAFF   " . . . fugge."

FORD   "L'amor!"

FALSTAFF   "L'amor!"

FORD   "L'amor!"

FALSTAFF   "L'amor!"

FORD   E questo madrigale
                    L'ho appreso a prezzo d'or.

FALSTAFF   Quest'è il destin fatale
                    Del misero amator.

FORD   "L'amor, l'amor
                    Che non ci dà mai tregue . . ."

FALSTAFF *(interrompendo)*
                    Essa non vi diè
                    Mai luogo a lusinghe?

FORD   No.

Sir John, if you care
To help me carry it.

FALSTAFF *(takes the sack and sets it on the table)*
With great pleasure . . .
I don't know, really,
Through what merit of mine, Sir . . .

FORD
I will tell you.
In Windsor there's a lady,
Very beautiful and charming.
Her name is Alice; she's the wife
Of a certain Ford . . .

FALSTAFF
I'm listening to you.

FORD
I love her and she doesn't love me.
I write her; she doesn't answer;
I look at her, she doesn't look at me;
I seek her, and she hides.
For her I squandered treasures,
I cast gifts after gifts,
I contrived, trembling,
The snatching of opportunities.
Alas! All was in vain!
I was left outside on the stairs,
Neglected, empty-handed,
Singing a madrigal.

FALSTAFF *(singing softly, in a joking manner)*
"Love, love
That never gives us respite,
Until life is consumed."

FORD
" . . . consumed."

FALSTAFF
"It's like the shadow . . ."

FORD
" . . . that when a man flees . . ."

FALSTAFF
" . . . it pursues him . . ."

FORD
"And when a man pursues it . . ."

FALSTAFF
" . . . it flees."

FORD
"Love!"

FALSTAFF
"Love!"

FORD
"Love!"

FALSTAFF
"Love!"

FORD
And this madrigal
I learned at the cost of gold.

FALSTAFF
This is the fatal destiny
Of the wretched lover.

FORD
"Love, love
That never gives us respite . . ."

FALSTAFF *(interrupting)*
She never gave you
Any occasion to flatter yourself?

FORD
No.

FALSTAFF   Ma infin,
Perchè v'aprite a me?

FORD   Ve lo dirò:
Voi siete un gentiluomo
Prode, arguto, facondo,
Voi siete un uom di guerra,
Voi siete un uom di mondo . . .

FALSTAFF *(con gesto d'umiltà)*
Oh!

FORD   Non v'adulo, e quello
È un sacco di monete:
Spendetele! Spendetele!
Sì, spendete e spandete
Tutto il mio patrimonio!
Siate ricco e felice!
Ma, in contraccambio, chiedo
Che conquistiate Alice!

FALSTAFF   Strana inguinzion!

FORD   Mi spiego:
Quella crudel beltà
Sempre è vissuta
In grande fede di castità.
La sua virtù importuna
M'abbarbagliava gl'occhi,
La bella inespugnabile
Dicea: Guai se mi tocchi!
Ma se voi l'espugnate,
Poi, posso anch'io sperar;
Da fallo nasce fallo
E allor . . . che ve ne par?

FALSTAFF   Prima di tutto,
Senza complimenti, Messere,
Accetto il sacco. E poi
(Fede di cavaliere;
Qua la mano!)
    (stringendo forte la mano a Ford)
Farò le vostre brame sazie.
Voi, la moglie di Ford
Possederete.

FORD   Grazie!

FALSTAFF   Io son già molto innanzi;
(Non c'è ragion ch'io taccia
Con voi) fra una mezz'ora
Sarà nelle mie braccia.

FORD *(come un urlo)*
Chi?

FALSTAFF *(con calma)*
Alice. Essa mandò dianzi
Una . . . confidente.
Per dirmi che quel tanghero
Di suo merito è assente
Dalle due alle tre.

FORD   Dalle due alle tre . . .

FALSTAFF   But, in short,
                 Why are you confiding in me?

FORD   I'll tell you:
                 You are a gentleman,
                 Bold, clever, eloquent,
                 You are a man of war,
                 You are a man of the world . . .

FALSTAFF *(with a gesture of humility)*
                 Oh!

FORD   I'm not flattering you, and that
                 Is a sack of gold pieces:
                 Spend them! Spend them!
                 Yes, spend and squander
                 All my patrimony!
                 Be rich and happy!
                 But, in return, I ask
                 That you conquer Alice!

FALSTAFF   Strange command!

FORD   I'll explain:
                 That cruel beauty
                 Has always lived
                 With great belief in chastity.
                 Her troublesome virtue
                 Dazzled my eyes;
                 The unconquerable beauty
                 Would say: Woe if you touch me!
                 But if you conquer her,
                 Then I can also hope.
                 Sin is born from sin
                 And then . . . What do you think?

FALSTAFF   First of all,
                 Without any ceremony, Sir,
                 I accept the sack. And then
                 (A Knight's honor;
                 Here's my hand!)
                     (shaking Ford's hand hard)
                 I'll have your desires sated.
                 You shall possess
                 Ford's wife.

FORD   Thank you!

FALSTAFF   I'm already quite advanced;
                 (There's no reason why I should be
                 Silent with you) within half an hour
                 She will be in my arms.

FORD *(like a cry)*
                 Who?

FALSTAFF *(calmly)*
                 Alice. She sent earlier
                 A . . . confidante.
                 To tell me that that boor
                 Of a husband of hers is absent
                 From two until three.

FORD   From two until three . . .

Lo conoscete?

FALSTAFF   Il diavolo se lo porti
All'inferno con Menelao suo avolo!
Quel tanghero, quel tanghero!
Vedrai, vedrai, vedrai,
Vedrai, vedrai!
Te lo cornifico netto, netto!
Se mi frastorna
Gli sparo una girandola
Di botte sulle corna!
Quel messer Ford è un bue,
Un bue, vedrai, *ecc.*
Ma è tardi.
Aspettami qua.
Vado a farmi bello.
    (piglia sil sacco di monete ed esce dal fondo)

FORD   È sogno? o realtà? . . .
Due rami enormi
Crescon sulla mia testa.
È un sogno?
Mastro Ford! Mastro Ford! Dormi?
Svegliati! Su! . . . ti desta!
Tua moglie sgarra
E mette in mal'assetto
L'onor tuo, la tua casa
Ed il tuo letto!
L'ora è fissata,
Tramato l'inganno;
Sei gabbato e truffato! . . .
E poi diranno
Che un marito geloso
È un insensato!
Già dietro a me
Nomi d'infame conio
Fischian passando;
Mormora lo scherno.
O matrimonio: inferno!
Donna: demonio!
Nella lor moglie
Abbian fede i babbei!
Affiderei
La mia birra a un Tedesco,
Tutto il mio desco
A un Olandese lurco,
La mia bottiglia d'acquavite
A un Turco,
Non mia moglie a sè stessa.
O laida sorte! Quella brutta parola
In cor mi torna:
Le corna!
Bue! Capron! le fusa torte!
Ah! le corna! le corna!
Ma non mi sfuggirai!
No! sozzo! reo!

Do you know him?

FALSTAFF   The devil take him
To hell with Menelaus, his ancestor!
That boor, that boor!
You'll see, you'll see, you'll see,
You'll see, you'll see!
I'll cuckold him neatly, neatly!
If he disturbs me
I'll fire a Catherine wheel
Of blows on his horns!
That Master Ford is an ox,
An ox, you'll see, *etc.*
But it's late.
Wait for me here.
I'm going to make myself handsome.
    *(takes the sack of gold pieces and goes out at
    the rear)*

FORD   Is it a dream? Or reality? . . .
Two enormous branches
Are growing on my head.
Is it a dream?
Master Ford! Master Ford! Are you asleep?
Awake! Up! . . . Rouse yourself!
Your wife is straying
And putting in a bad way
Your honor, your house
And your bed!
The time is set,
The deceit is plotted;
You are mocked and tricked! . . .
And then they'll say
That a jealous husband
Is a fool!
Already behind my back,
Names of infamous invention
They whistle, passing by;
Contempt is murmuring.
O matrimony: inferno!
Woman: demon!
Let simpletons have faith
In their wives!
I would entrust
My beer to a German,
All my table
To a gluttonous Dutchman,
My bottle of brandy
To a Turk:
Not my wife to herself.
O foul fate! That ugly word
Comes back to my heart:
Horns!
Ox! Billy goat! Faithlessness!
Ah! horns! horns!
But you shall not elude me!
No! Polluted man! Guilty man!

Dannato epicureo!
Prima li accoppio
E poi li colgo,
Li accoppio, li colgo, *ecc.*
Io scoppio!
Vendicherò l'affronto!
Laudata sempre sia
Nel fondo del mio cor
La gelosia.

FALSTAFF *(rientrando dalla porta del fondo. Ha un farsetto*
nuovo, cappello e bastone.)
                  Eccomi qua. Son pronto.
                  M' accompagnate un tratto?

FORD   Vi metto sulla via.

Si avviano: giunti presso alla soglia fanno dei gesti com-
plimentosi per cedere la precedenza del passo.

FALSTAFF	Prima voi.
FORD	Prima voi.
FALSTAFF	No, no. Sono in casa mia.
	Passate.
FORD	Prego . . .
FALSTAFF	È tardi.
	L'appuntamento preme.
FORD	Non fate complimenti . . .
FALSTAFF	Passate!
FORD	Prego!
FALSTAFF	Passate!
FORD	Prego!
FALSTAFF	Ebben . . .
	Passiamo insieme!
FORD	Passiamo insieme!

    Falstaff prende il braccio di Ford sotto il suo ed escono a
braccetto.

PARTE SECONDA

    Una sala nella casa di Ford. Ampia finestra nel fondo. Porta
a destra, porta a sinistra e un'altra porta verso l'angolo di
destra nel fondo che riesce sulla scala. Un'altra scala nell'an-
golo del fondo a sinistra. Dal gran finestrone spalancato si vede
il giardino. Un paravento chiuso sta appoggiato alla parete
di sinistra accanto ad un vasto camino. Armadio addossato
alla parete di destra. Un tavolino, una cassapanca. Lungo le
pareti un seggiolone e qualche scranna. Sul seggiolone un
liuto. Sul tavolo dei fiori.
    Alice, Meg, poi Quickly. Poi Nannetta.

ALICE   Presenteremo un bill
                 Per una tassa
                 Al parlamento,
                 Sulla gente grassa.

> Damned epicure!
> First I pair them
> And then I catch them,
> I pair them, I catch them, *etc.*
> I'm exploding!
> I'll avenge the insult!
> Praised be forever,
> From the bottom of my heart,
> Jealousy.

FALSTAFF *(re-entering from the door in the rear. He has on a new doublet, with hat and cane.)*
> Here I am. I'm ready.
> Will you accompany me a bit?

FORD   I'll put you on your way.

They start off. When they have reached the threshold, they make obsequious gestures, to give each other precedence in going out.

FALSTAFF   You first.

FORD   You first.

FALSTAFF   No, no. I'm in my own house.
            Pass.

FORD   Please . . .

FALSTAFF   It's late.
            The appointment is pressing.

FORD   Don't stand on ceremony.

FALSTAFF   Pass!

FORD   Please!

FALSTAFF   Pass!

FORD   Please!

FALSTAFF   Very well . . .
            Let us pass together!

FORD   Let us pass together!

Falstaff takes Ford's arm under his own and they go out arm in arm.

SCENE TWO

A room in Ford's house. A broad window in the rear. Door at right, door at left, and another door toward the corner at right in the rear leading to the stairway. Another stairway in the left rear corner. Through the great opened window the garden is seen. A closed screen is propped against the left wall, next to a huge fireplace. A wardrobe is set against the right wall. A little table, a chest bench. Against the walls, an armchair and some stools. On the armchair, a lute. Some flowers on the table.

Alice, Meg, then Quickly, then Anne.

ALICE   We'll present a bill
            In Parliament
            For a tax
            On fat people.

QUICKLY *(entra dalla porta a destra ridendo)*
        Comari!

ALICE *(accorrendo con Meg verso Quickly, mentre Nannetta ch'è entrata anch'essa resta triste in disparte)*
        Ebben?

MEG   Che c'è?

QUICKLY   Sarà sconfitto!

ALICE   Brava!

QUICKLY   Fra poco gli farem la festa!

ALICE, MEG   Bene!

QUICKLY   Piombò nel laccio a capo fitto.

ALICE   Narrami tutto, lesta.

MEG   Lesta.

ALICE   Lesta.

QUICKLY   Giunta all'Albergo della Giarrettiera
        Chiedo d'esser ammessa
        Alla presenza del Cavalier,
        Segreta messaggera.
        Sir John si degna
        D'accordarmi udienza,
            (voce grossa)
        M'accoglie tronfio
        In furfantesca posa:
            (contraffacendo Falstaff)
        "Buon giorno, buona donna."
            (contraffacendo sè stessa)
        "Reverenza."
        A lui m'inchino
        Molto ossequiosamente,
        Poi passo alle notizie ghiotte.
        Lui beve grosso
        Ed ogni mia massiccia
        Frottola inghiotte.
        Infin, per farla spiccia,
        Vi crede entrambe
        Innamorate cotte
        Delle bellezze sue.
            (ad Alice)
        E lo vedrete presto, presto,
        Presto ai vostri piè.

ALICE   Quando?

QUICKLY   Oggi, qui,
        Dalle due alle tre.

MEG   Dalle due alle tre.

ALICE *(guardando l'oriolo)*
        Son già le due!

MEG   Dalle due alle tre.

ALICE   Dalle due alle tre.

QUICKLY *(all'una)*
        Dalle due alle tre.
            (all'altra)
        Dalle due alle tre.
            (a tutte e due)

QUICKLY (*enters from the door at right, laughing*)
Gossips!

ALICE (*running with Meg toward Quickly, while Anne, who
has also come in, remains to one side, sadly*)
Well?

MEG   What's new?

QUICKLY   He'll be defeated!

ALICE   Good for you!

QUICKLY   In a little while we'll fix him!

ALICE, MEG   Good!

QUICKLY   He plunged headlong into the noose.

ALICE   Tell me everything, quickly.

MEG   Quickly.

ALICE   Quickly.

QUICKLY   Having arrived at the Garter Inn,
I ask to be admitted
To the Knight's presence
As a private messenger.
Sir John condescends
To grant me an audience,
    (*heavy voice*)
He receives me pompously,
In a knavish attitude:
    (*imitating Falstaff*)
"Good day, good woman."
    (*imitating herself*)
"My respects."
I bow to him
Very obsequiously,
Then I go on to the juicy news.
He drinks deeply
And swallows my every
Huge tale.
Finally, to make it brief,
He believes both of you
Madly enamored
Of his beautiful qualities.
    (*to Alice*)
And you will see him soon, soon,
Soon at your feet.

ALICE   When?

QUICKLY   Today, here,
Between two and three.

MEG   Between two and three.

ALICE (*looking at the clock*)
It's two already!

MEG   Between two and three.

ALICE   Between two and three.

QUICKLY (*to one woman*)
Between two and three.
    (*to the other*)
Between two and three.
    (*to both*)

Dalle due alle tre!
ALICE *(correndo subito all'uscio del fondo e chiamando)*
Olà! Ned! Will!
(a Quickly)
Già tutto ho preparato.
(torna a gridare dall'uscio verso l'esterno)

Portate qui la cesta del bucato.
QUICKLY   Sarà un affare gaio!
ALICE   Nannetta, e tu non ridi?
Che cos'hai?
(avvicinandosi a Nannetta ed accarezzando-la)
Tu piangi? . . . Che cos'hai?
Dillo a tua madre.
NANNETTA *(singhiozzando)*
Mio padre . . .
ALICE   Ebben?
NANNETTA   Mio padre . . .
ALICE   Ebben?
NANNETTA   Mio padre . . .
(scoppiando in lagrime)
Vuole ch'io mi mariti
Al Dottor Cajo!
ALICE   A quel pedante?
QUICKLY   Oibò!
MEG   A quel gonzo!
ALICE   A quel grullo!
NANNETTA   A quel bisavolo!
ALICE   No! no!
MEG, QUICKLY   No!
TUTTE   No, no, no, no!
NANNETTA   Piuttosto lapidata viva . . .
ALICE   Da una mitraglia
Di torsi di cavolo.
QUICKLY   Ben detto!
MEG   Brava!
ALICE   Non temer.
NANNETTA *(saltando di gioja)*
Evviva! Col Dottor Cajo
Non mi sposerò!

Intanto entrano due servi portando una cesta piena di bian-cheria.

ALICE *(ai servi)*
Mettete là.
Poi, quando avrò chiamato,
Vuoterete la cesta
Nel fossato.
NANNETTA   Bum!

                  Between two and three.

ALICE *(running at once to the door in the rear and calling)*
                  Ho there! Ned! Will!
                  (to Quickly)
                  I've already prepared everything.
                  (starts shouting again from the door, toward
                  the outside)
                  Bring the laundry hamper here.

QUICKLY   It'll be a merry business!

ALICE   Anne, you're not laughing?
                  What's wrong with you?
                  (approaching Anne and caressing her)

                  You're crying? . . . What's wrong with you?
                  Tell your mother.

ANNE *(sobbing)*
                  My father . . .

ALICE   Well?

ANNE   My father . . .

ALICE   Well?

ANNE   My father . . .
                  (bursting into tears)
                  Wants me to be married
                  To Doctor Caius!

ALICE   To that pedant?

QUICKLY   Oho!

MEG   To that dolt!

ALICE   To that fool!

ANNE   To that ancestor!

ALICE   No! No!

MEG, QUICKLY No!

ALL   No, no, no, no!

ANNE   Rather stoned alive . . .

ALICE   By a volley
                  Of cabbage stalks.

QUICKLY   Well said!

MEG   Good for you!

ALICE   Don't fear.

ANNE *(jumping with joy)*
                  Hurrah! I won't marry
                  Doctor Caius!

    *Meanwhile two manservants enter, carrying a hamper full
of laundry.*

ALICE *(to the servants)*
                  Put it there.
                  Then, when I have called,
                  You will empty the hamper
                  Into the ditch.

ANNE   Boom!

ALICE *(a Nannetta)*
    Taci.
    (ai servi che escono)
    Andate.

NANNETTA   Che bombardamento.

ALICE   Prepariamo la scena.
    (corre a pigliare una sedia e la mette presso al tavolo)
    Qua una sedia.

NANNETTA *(corre a pigliare il liuto e lo mette sul tavolo)*
    Qua il mio liuto.

ALICE   Apriamo il paravento.

Nannetta e Meg corrono a prendere il paravento, lo aprono dopo averlo collocato fra la cesta e il camino.

ALICE   Bravissime! Così!
    Più aperto ancora.
    Fra poco s'incomincia
    La commedia!
    Gaie comari di Windsor!
    È l'ora!
    L'ora d'alzar la risata sonora!
    L'alta risata
    Che scoppia, che scherza,
    Che sfolgora, armata
    Di dardi e di sferza!
    Gaie comari! festosa brigata!
    Sul lieto viso
    Spunti il sorriso,
    Splenda del riso
    L'acuto fulgor!
    Favilla, favilla incendaria
    Di gioia nell'aria,
    Di gioia nel cor.
    (a Meg)
    A noi!
    Tu la parte farai
    Che ti spetta.

MEG *(ad Alice)*
    Tu corri il tuo rischio
    Col grosso compar.

QUICKLY   Io sto alla vedetta.

ALICE *(a Quickly)*
    Se sbagli ti fischio.

NANNETTA   Io resto in disparte
    Sull'uscio a spiar.

ALICE   E mostreremo
    All'uom che l'allegria
    D'oneste donne
    Ogni onestà comporta.
    Fra le femine
    Quella è la più ria
    Che fa la gattamorta.

ALICE *(to Anne)*

> Hush.
> *(to the servants, who go out)*
> Go.

ANNE   What a bombardment.

ALICE   Let's set the scene.

> *(runs to fetch a chair and places it near the table)*
> A chair here.

ANNE *(runs to fetch the lute and puts it on the table)*

> My lute here.

ALICE   Let's open the screen.

Anne and Meg run to fetch the screen. They unfold it, after having placed it between the hamper and the fireplace.

ALICE   Very good! Like that!

> Still more open.
> In a little while
> The play begins!
> Merry wives of Windsor!
> This is the hour!
> The hour to raise resounding laughter!
> The loud laughter
> That explodes, that jokes,
> That flashes, armed
> With darts and with the lash!
> Merry wives! Festive company!
> Let the smile blossom
> On the happy face,
> Let the bright blaze
> Of laughter shine!
> Spark, the incendiary spark
> Of joy in the air,
> Of joy in the heart.
> *(to Meg)*
> It's our turn!
> You will play the part
> That is yours.

MEG *(to Alice)*

> You're running your risk
> With the hefty gentleman.

QUICKLY   I'll stand watch.

ALICE *(to Quickly)*

> If you err, I'll hiss at you.

ANNE   I'll stay to one side

> At the door, to observe.

ALICE   And we'll show

> Mankind that the merriment
> Of honest women
> Implies full honesty.
> Among females,
> She is the most evil
> Who acts the most slyly.

NANNETTA, MEG
          Gaie comari di Windsor . . .

Intanto Quickly va alla finestra del fondo, guardando sulla strada.

ALICE, NANNETTA, MEG
          Gaie comari di Windsor,
          È l'ora, *ecc.*

QUICKLY *(avvicinandosi alle altre)*
          Eccolo! È lui!

ALICE   Dov'è?

QUICKLY   Poco discosto.

NANNETTA   Presto.

QUICKLY   ´ A salir s'avvia.

ALICE *(a Nannetta, indicando l'uscio a sinistra)*
          Tu di qua.
                    (a Meg, indicando l'uscio di destra)
          Tu di là. Al posto!

NANNETTA *(esce correndo da sinistra)*
          Al posto!

MEG *(esce correndo da destra)*
          Al posto!

QUICKLY *(esce dal fondo)*
          Al posto!

Alice sola. Poi Falstaff. Alice si sarà messa accanto al tavolo, avrà preso il liuto toccando qualche accordo.

FALSTAFF *(entra con vivacità; vedendo che Alice sta suonando si mette a cantarellare)*
          "Alfin t'ho colto, raggiante fior . . .
          T'ho colto! . . ."
                    *(prende Alice pel busto. Alice cessa di suon-
                    are e si alza deponendo il liuto sul tavolo)*

          Ed or potrò morir felice.
          Avrò vissuto molto
          Dopo quest'ora di beato amor.

ALICE   O soave Sir John!

FALSTAFF   Mia bella Alice!
          Non so far lo svenevole,
          Nè lusingar, nè usar
          Frase fiorita,
          Ma dirò tosto
          Un mio pensier colpevole.

ALICE   Cioè?

FALSTAFF   Cioè: vorrei che Mastro Ford
          Passasse a miglior vita . . .

ALICE   Perchè?

FALSTAFF   Perchè? Lo chiedi?
          Saresti la mia Lady
          E Falstaff il tuo Lord!

ANNE, MEG
          Merry wives of Windsor . . .

Meanwhile Quickly goes to the window in the rear, looking out on the street.

ALICE, ANNE, MEG
          Merry wives of Windsor,
          This is the hour, *etc.*

QUICKLY *(approaching the other women)*
          There he is! It's he!

ALICE   Where is he?

QUICKLY   Not far away.

ANNE   Hurray.

QUICKLY   He's about to come up.

ALICE *(to Anne, pointing to the door at left)*
          You, this way.
              (to Meg, pointing to the door at right)
          You, that way. To your place!

ANNE *(leaves, running, at left)*
          To our place!

MEG *(leaves, running, at right)*
          To our place!

QUICKLY *(goes out, at the rear)*
          To our place!

Alice, alone. Then Falstaff. Alice will have sat near the table and will have picked up the lute, plucking a few chords.

FALSTAFF *(enters vivaciously; seeing that Alice is playing, he starts singing softly)*
          "At last I've picked you, radiant flower . . .
          I've picked you! . . ."
              (takes Alice by the waist. Alice stops playing and stands up, putting the lute down on the table)
          And now I can die happy.
          I will have lived much
          After this hour of blissful love.

ALICE   O sweet Sir John!

FALSTAFF   My beautiful Alice!
          I don't know how to act sentimental,
          Or flatter, or use
          Flowery phrases,
          But I will say at once
          A guilty thought of mine.

ALICE   Namely?

FALSTAFF   Namely: I'd like Master Ford
          To pass on to a better life . . .

ALICE   Why?

FALSTAFF   Why, You ask?
          You would be my Lady,
          And Falstaff, your Lord!

ALICE   Povera Lady inver!

FALSTAFF   Degna d'un Re. T'immagino
           Fregiata del mio stemma,
           Mostrar fra gemma e gemma
           La pompa del tuo sen . . .
           Nell'iri ardente
           E mobile dei rai
           Dell'adamante,
           Col picciol piè nel nobile
           Cerchio d'un guardinfante
           Risplenderai più fulgida
           D'un ampio arcobalen.

ALICE   Ogni più bel giojel mi nuoce
           E spregio il finto idolo d'or.
           Mi basta un vel legato in croce,
           Un fregio al cinto
               (*si mette un fiore nei capelli*)
           E in testa un fior.

FALSTAFF (*per abbracciarla*)
           Sirena!

ALICE (*fa un passo indietro*)
           Adulator!

FALSTAFF   Soli noi siamo
           E non temiamo agguato.

ALICE   Ebben?

FALSTAFF   Io t'amo!

ALICE (*scostandosi un poco*)
           Voi siete nel peccato!

FALSTAFF (*avvicinandola*)
           Sempre l'amor l'occasione azzecca.

ALICE   Sir John!

FALSTAFF   Chi segue vocazion non pecca.
           T'amo!
           E non è mia colpa . . .

ALICE (*interrompendolo e scherzando*)
           Se tanta avete vulnerabil polpa . . .

FALSTAFF   Quand'ero paggio
           Del Duca di Norfolk
           Ero sottile, sottile, sottile,
           Ero un miraggio
           Vago, leggiero,
           Gentile, gentile, gentile.
           Quello era il tempo
           Del mio verde aprile,
           Quello era il tempo
           Del mio lieto maggio.
           Tant'era smilzo,
           Flessibile e snello
           Che sarei guizzato
           Attraverso un anello.
           Quand'ero paggio
           Ero sottile, *ecc.*

ALICE   A poor Lady, indeed!

FALSTAFF   Worthy of a King. I picture you
                 Adorned with my coat of arms,
                 Displaying between one gem and another
                 The splendor of your bosom . . .
                 In the glowing
                 And shifting iris
                 Of the magnet's rays,
                 With your tiny foot in the noble
                 Circle of a farthingale
                 You will shine more radiant
                 Than a broad rainbow.

ALICE   Even the loveliest jewel hurts me,
                 And I despise the false idol of gold.
                 A veil tied in a knot is enough for me,
                 A buckle at my waist,
                     (puts a flower in her hair)
                 And a flower on my head.

FALSTAFF *(about to embrace her)*
                 Siren!

ALICE *(takes a step backward)*
                 Flatterer!

FALSTAFF   We are alone
                 And we don't fear an ambush.

ALICE   Well?

FALSTAFF   I love you!

ALICE *(moving away slightly)*
                 You are in a state of sin!

FALSTAFF *(approaching her)*
                 Love always seizes the occasion.

ALICE   Sir John!

FALSTAFF   He who follows his vocation doesn't sin.
                 I love you!
                 And it's not my fault . . .

ALICE *(interrupting him and joking)*
                 If you have so much vulnerable flesh . . .

FALSTAFF   When I was the page
                 Of the Duke of Norfolk
                 I was slim, slim, slim,
                 I was a mirage,
                 Lovely, light,
                 Tender, tender, tender.
                 That was the time
                 Of my green April,
                 That was the time
                 Of my happy May.
                 I was so slender,
                 Flexibile and thin,
                 That I could have slipped
                 Through a ring.
                 When I was the page
                 I was slim, *etc.*

ALICE	Voi mi celiate.
	Io temo i vostri inganni.
	Temo che amiate . . .
FALSTAFF	Chi?
ALICE	Meg.
FALSTAFF	Colei?
	M'è in uggia la sua faccia.
ALICE	Non traditemi John . . .
FALSTAFF	Mi par mill'anni
	D'averti fra le braccia.
	(rincorrendola e tentando d'abbracciarla)
	T'amo . . .
ALICE *(difendendosi)*	
	Per carità!
FALSTAFF *(la prende traverso il busto)*	
	Vieni!
QUICKLY *(dall'antisala gridando)*	
	Signora Alice!
FALSTAFF *(abbandona Alice e rimane turbato)*	
	Chi va là?
QUICKLY *(entrando e fingendo agitazione)*	
	Signora Alice!
ALICE	Che c'è?
QUICKLY *(rapidamente ed interrotta della foga)*	
	Mia signora! C'è Mistress Meg,
	E vuol parlarvi, sbuffa,
	Strepita, s'abbaruffa . . .
FALSTAFF	Alla malora!
QUICKLY	E vuol passar
	E la trattengo a stento . . .
FALSTAFF	Dove m'ascondo?
ALICE	Dietro il paravento.

Falstaff si rimpiatta dietro il paravento. Quando Falstaff è nascosto, Quickly fa cenno a Meg che sta dietro l'uscio di destra: Meg entra fingendo d'essere agitatissima. Quickly torna ad escire.

MEG	Alice! che spavento!
	Che chiasso! Che discordia!
	Non perdere un momento,
	Fuggi! . . .
ALICE	Misericordia!
	Che avvenne?
MEG	Il tuo consorte vien
	Gridando: "accorr'uomo!"
	Dice . . .
ALICE *(a bassa voce)*	
	Parla più forte.
MEG	Che vuol scannare un uomo!
ALICE	(Non ridere.)
MEG	Ei correva

ALICE	You are teasing me.
	I fear your deceits.
	I fear that you love . . .
FALSTAFF	Whom?
ALICE	Meg.
FALSTAFF	She?
	Her face is unpleasant to me.
ALICE	Don't betray me, John . . .
FALSTAFF	It seems a thousand years to me
	That I've wanted to have you in my arms.
	(chasing her and trying to embrace her)
	I love you . . .

ALICE *(defending herself)*
For heaven's sake!

FALSTAFF *(grasps her by the waist)*
Come!

QUICKLY *(from the antechamber, shouting)*
Mistress Alice!

FALSTAFF *(lets go of Alice and remains upset)*
Who goes there?

QUICKLY *(entering and pretending alarm)*
Mistress Alice!

ALICE   What is it?

QUICKLY *(rapidly and interrupted by her impetuosity)*
My lady! Mistress Meg is here,
And wants to speak to you. She's huffing,
Shouting, squabbling . . .

FALSTAFF	Damnation!
QUICKLY	And she wants to come in,
	And I am restraining her barely . . .
FALSTAFF	Where can I hide?
ALICE	Behind the screen.

Falstaff conceals himself behind the screen. When Falstaff is hidden, Quickly signals to Meg, who is outside the door at right. Meg enters, pretending to be greatly upset. Quickly goes out again.

MEG	Alice! What a fright!
	What a racket! What quarreling!
	Don't waste a moment:
	Flee! . . .
ALICE	Mercy!
	What's happened?
MEG	Your husband is coming,
	Shouting: "After the man!"
	He says . . .

ALICE *(in a low voice)*
Speak louder.

MEG	That he wants to cut a man's throat.
ALICE	(Don't laugh.)
MEG	He was running,

        Invaso da tremendo
        Furor! Maledicendo
        Tutte le figlie d'Eva!
ALICE   Misericordia!
MEG   Dice che un tuo ganzo
        Hai nascosto;
        Lo vuole ad ogni costo
        Scoprir . . .

QUICKLY (*ritornando spaventatissima e gridando più di prima*)

        Signora Alice! Vien Mastro Ford!
        Salvatevi!
        È come una tempesta!
        Strepita, tuona, fulmina,
        Si dà dei pugni in testa,
        Scoppia in minaccie
        Ed urla . . .

ALICE (*avvicinandosi a Quickly, a bassa voce e un poco allarmata*)

        (Dassenno oppur da burla?)
QUICKLY   Dassenno.
        Egli scavalca
        Le siepi del giardino . . .
        Lo segue una gran calca
        Di gente . . . è già vicino . . .
        Mentr'io vi parlo ei valca
        L'ingresso . . .

FORD (*di dentro urlando*)
        Malandrino! !

Falstaff agitatissimo avrà già fatto un passo per fuggire dal paravento, ma udendo la voce dell'uomo torna a rimpiattarsi: Alice con una mossa rapidissima lo chiude nel paravento in modo che non è più veduto.

FALSTAFF   Il diavolo cavalca
        Sull'arco d'un violino! !

FORD (*entra dal fondo gridando a chi lo segue*)
        Chiudete le porte!
        Sbarrate le scale!
        Seguitemi a caccia!
        Scoviamo il cignale!

Entrano correndo il Dr. Cajus e Fenton.

FORD (*a Cajus*)

        Correte sull'orme,
        Sull'usta.
        (*a Fenton*)
        Tu fruga negli anditi.

Bardolfo e Pistola irrompono nella sala gridando, mentre Fenton corre a sinistra.

BARDOLFO, PISTOLA
        A caccia!

FORD (*a Bardolfo e Pistola indicando la camera a destra*)

                Invaded by a terrible
                Fury! Cursing
                All the daughters of Eve!

ALICE   Mercy!

MEG   He says that you've hidden
                Your lover;
                He wants at all costs
                To discover him . . .

QUICKLY *(returning, very frightened, and shouting more than*
   before)
                Mistress Alice! Master Ford's coming!
                Escape!
                He's like a storm!
                He's raging, thundering, fulminating,
                He's striking his head with his fists,
                He's exploding in threats
                And shouts . . .

ALICE *(approaching Quickly, in a low voice and a bit alarmed)*

                (Really or is this a joke?)

QUICKLY   Really.
                He's climbing over
                The garden's hedges . . .
                A great crowd of people
                Is following him . . . He's already near . . .
                As I speak to you, he's crossing
                The threshold . . .

FORD *(from within, shouting)*
                Robber! !

*Highly agitated, Falstaff will already have taken a step, to
escape from the screen; but hearing the man's voice, he goes
back and hides again. With a very rapid movement, Alice
closes him in the screen in such a way that he isn't seen.*

FALSTAFF   The devil rides
                On a violin's bow! !

FORD *(enters from the rear, shouting to those following him)*
                Shut the doors!
                Block the stairs!
                Follow me hunting!
                We'll rouse the boar!

Enter, running, Dr. Caius and Fenton.

FORD *(to Caius)*
                Run, on his tracks,
                On the scent.
                  (to Fenton)
                You search the corridors.

*Bardolph and Pistol burst into the room, shouting, while
Fenton runs off to the left.*

BARDOLPH, PISTOL
                To the hunt!

FORD *(to Bardolph and Pistol, pointing to the bedroom at
right)*

Sventate la fuga!
Cercate là dentro!

Bardolfo e Pistola si precipitano nella camera coi bastoni levati.

ALICE *(affrontando Ford)*
Sei dissennato?
Che fai?

FORD *(vedendo il cesto)*
Che c'è dentro quel cesto?

ALICE   Il bucato.

FORD *(ad Alice)*
Mi lavi! ! rea moglie!

Consegna un mazzo di chiavi al Dr. Cajus che poi esce correndo dall'uscio di sinistra.

FORD   Tu, piglia le chiavi,
Rovista le casse!
          (ancora ad Alice)
Ben tu mi lavi!
          (dà un calcio alla cesta)
Al diavolo i cenci!
          (gridando verso il fondo)
Sprangatemi l'uscio del parco!
          *(estrae furiosamente la biancheria dalla cesta,
          frugando e cercando dentro e disseminando i
          panni sul pavimento)*
Camicie . . . gonnelle . . .
Or ti sguscio, briccon!
Strofinacci! Via! . . . Via! . . .
Cuffie rotte! Ti sguscio . . .
Lenzuola . . . Berretti da notte . . .
Non c'è . . .
          (rovescia la cesta)

ALICE, MEG, QUICKLY *(guardando i panni sparsi)*
Che uragano!!

FORD   Cerchiam sotto il letto,
Nel forno, nel pozzo,
Nel bagno, sul tetto,
In cantina . . .
          (correndo e gridando, esce dalla porta a sinistra)

ALICE   È farnetico!

QUICKLY   Cogliam tempo.

ALICE   Troviamo modo
Com'egli esca.

MEG   Nel panier.

ALICE   No, là dentro non c'entra,
È troppo grosso.

FALSTAFF *(sbalordito, ode le parole d'Alice, avendo aperto con cautela il paravento. Sbuca e corre alla cesta)*
Vediam;
Sì, c'entro, c'entro.

ALICE   Corro a chiamare i servi.
          (esce)

                              Prevent the flight!
                              Search in there!

*Bardolph and Pistol hasten into the bedroom, with clubs
upraised.*

ALICE *(confronting Ford)*
                              Have you lost your senses?
                              What are you doing?

FORD *(seeing the basket)*
                              What is there inside that basket?

ALICE   The laundry.

FORD *(to Alice)*
                              You do my washing!! Guilty wife!

*He hands a bunch of keys to Dr. Caius, who then goes out,
running, through the door at left.*

FORD   You, take the keys,
                              Ransack the chests!
                                 (again to Alice)
                              You do my washing well!
                                 (gives the hamper a kick)
                              To the devil with the rags!
                                 (shouting toward the rear)
                              Bar the gate of the park for me!
                                 *(furiously takes the linen from the hamper,
                                 rummaging and searching inside and scatter-
                                 ing the garments on the floor)*
                              Shirts . . . skirts . . .
                              Now I'll husk you, rascal!
                              Dishcloths! Away! . . . Away! . . .
                              Torn caps! I'll husk you . . .
                              Sheets . . . Nightcaps . . .
                              He's not here . . .
                                 (overturns the hamper)

ALICE, MEG, QUICKLY *(looking at the scattered garments)*
                              What a hurricane!!

FORD   Let's search under the bed,
                              In the oven, in the well,
                              In the bath, on the roof,
                              In the cellar . . .
                                 *(running and shouting, he goes out through
                                 the door at left)*

ALICE   He's raving!

QUICKLY   Let's seize the moment.

ALICE   Let's find a way
                              How he can escape.

MEG   In the basket

ALICE   No, he won't fit in there;
                              He's too big.

FALSTAFF *(amazed, hears Alice's words, having cautiously
     opened the screen. He comes forth and runs to the hamper)*
                              Let's see:
                              Yes, I fit, I fit.

ALICE   I'll run and call the servants.
                                 (exits)

MEG *(fingendo sorpresa)*
    Sir John! Voi qui? Voi?

FALSTAFF *(entrando nella cesta)*
    T'amo! Amo te sola . . .
    Salvami! salvami!

QUICKLY *(a Falstaff, raccattando i panni)*
    Svelto!

MEG   Lesto!

QUICKLY   Svelto!

MEG   Svelto!

FALSTAFF *(accovacciandosi con grande sforzo nella cesta)*
    Ahi! Ahi! Ci sto . . .
    Copritemi . . .

QUICKLY *(a Meg)*
    Presto! colmiamo il cesto.

Fra tutte e due con gran fretta ricacciano la biancheria nel cesto. Attendono a nascondere Falstaff sotto la biancheria, mentre Nannetta e Fenton entrano da sinistra.

NANNETTA *(sottovoce e con cautela, a Fenton)*
    Vien qua.

FENTON   Che chiasso!

NANNETTA *(avviandosi al paravento)*
    Quanti schiamazzi!
    Segui il mio passo.

FENTON *(la segue)*
    Casa di pazzi!

NANNETTA   Qui ognun delira
            Con vario error.
            Son pazzi d'ira . . .

FENTON   E noi d'amor.

Nannetta lo prende per mano, lo conduce dietro il paravento e vi si nascondono.

NANNETTA   Seguimi. Adagio . . .

FENTON   Nessun m'ha scorto.

NANNETTA   Tocchiamo il porto.

FENTON   Siamo a nostr'agio.

NANNETTA   Sta zitto e attento.

FENTON *(abbracciandola)*
    Vien sul mio petto!

NANNETTA   Il paravento
            Sia benedetto!

FENTON   Sia benedetto!

DR. CAJUS *(urlando di dentro)*
    Al ladro!

FORD *(urlando di dentro)*
    Al pagliardo!

DR. CAJUS *(entra, traversando di corsa la sala)*
    Squartatelo!

MEG *(feigning surprise)*
> Sir John! You here? You?

FALSTAFF *(entering into the hamper)*
> I love you! I love you alone . . .
> Save me! Save me!

QUICKLY *(to Falstaff, collecting the garments)*
> Hurry!

MEG   Fast!

QUICKLY   Hurry!

MEG   Hurry!

FALSTAFF *(crouching with great effort down into the hamper)*
> Ouch! Ouch! I'm in . . .
> Cover me . . .

QUICKLY *(to Meg)*
> Hurry! Let's fill the basket.

The two of them, with great haste, cram the laundry back into the basket. They are busy hiding Falstaff under the linen, as Anne and Fenton enter at left.

ANNE *(in a low voice and with caution, to Fenton)*
> Come here.

FENTON   What a racket!

ANNE *(approaching the screen)*
> So much brawling!
> Follow my footsteps.

FENTON *(follows her)*
> House of madmen!

ANNE   Here each one raves
> With a different delusion.
> They're mad with wrath . . .

FENTON   And we, with love.

Anne takes him by the hand, leads him behind the screen, and they hide there.

ANNE   Follow me. Slowly . . .

FENTON   No one glimpsed me.

ANNE   We're reaching the port.

FENTON   We're at our ease.

ANNE   Be quiet and careful.

FENTON *(embracing her)*
> Come to my breast!

ANNE   May the screen
> Be blessed!

FENTON   May it be blessed!

DR. CAIUS *(shouting, from within)*
> After the thief!

FORD *(shouting, from within)*
> After the libertine!

DR. CAIUS *(enters, crossing the room, running)*
> Quarter him!

FORD *(entra di corsa, mentre Bardolfo e Pistola corrono da destra con gente del vicinato. Quickly e Meg rimangono accanto alla cesta dove c'è Falstaff nascosto.)*
Al ladro!
(a Pistola, che incontra)
C'è?

PISTOLA   No.

FORD *(a Bardolfo)*
C'è?

BARDOLFO   Non c'è, no.

FORD *(correndo, cercando e frugando nella cassapanca)*
Vada a soqquadro la casa.

DR. CAJUS *(dopo aver guardato nel camino)*
Non trovo nessuno.

Bardolfo e Pistola escono da sinistra.

FORD   Eppur giuro
Che l'uomo è qua dentro.
Ne sono sicuro,
Sicuro, sicuro!

DR. CAJUS   Sir John! Sarò gaio
Quel dì che ti veda
Dar calci a rovaio!

FORD *(slanciandosi contro l'armadio e facendo sforzi per aprirlo)*
Vien fuora, furfante!
O bombardo le mura!

DR. CAJUS *(tenta aprire l'armadio colle chiavi)*
T'arrendi!

FORD   Vien fuora! Codardo!
Sugliardo!

BARDOLFO, PISTOLA *(entrano dalla porta di sinistra, di corsa)*
Nessuno!

FORD *(a Bardolfo e Pistola, mentre continua a sforzare l'armadio col Dr. Cajus)*
Cercatelo ancora!
T'arrendi! Scanfardo!

Bardolfo e Pistola ritornano subito d'onde erano venuti. Ford riesce finalmente ad aprire l'armadio.

FORD   Non c'è!!

DR. CAJUS *(aprendo a sua volta la cassapanca)*
Vien fuora! Non c'è!!
(gira per la sala sempre cercando e frugando)
Pappalardo! Beòn!
Bada a te!

FORD *(come un ossesso aprendo il cassetto del tavolino)*
Scagnardo! Falsardo!

DR. CAJUS   Scagnardo!

FORD   Scagnardo!

DR. CAJUS   Falsardo!

FORD   Briccon!

FORD *(enters running, as Bardolph and Pistol run in at right,
with people of the neighborhood. Quickly and Meg remain
by the hamper where Falstaff is hidden.)*
>After the thief!
>>*(to Pistol, whom he runs into)*
>Is he there?

PISTOL   No.

FORD *(to Bardolph)*
>Is he there.?

BARDOLPH   He's not there. No.

FORD *(running, searching, and rummaging in the chest bench)*
>Let the house be turned upside down.

DR. CAIUS *(after having looked into the fireplace)*
>I can't find anyone.

Bardolph and Pistol go off at left.

FORD   And yet I swear
>That the man is in here.
>I'm sure of it,
>Sure, sure!

DR. CAIUS   Sir John! I'll be merry
>On that day that sees you
>Kicking in the air!

FORD *(hurling himself on the wardrobe and making efforts to
open it)*
>Come out, scoundrel!
>Or I'll bombard the walls!

DR. CAIUS *(tries to open the wardrobe with the keys)*
>Surrender!

FORD   Come out! Coward!
>Repulsive man!

BARDOLPH, PISTOL *(enter by the door at left, running)*
>Nobody!

FORD *(to Bardolph and Pistol, as he continues forcing the
wardrobe with Dr. Caius)*
>Hunt for him some more!
>Surrender! Chamber pot!

*Bardolph and Pistol go back immediately to whence they
came. Ford finally succeeds in opening the wardrobe.*

FORD   He's not there!!

DR. CAIUS *(opening, in his turn, the chest bench)*
>Come out! He's not there!!
>>*(wanders around the room, still searching and rummaging)*
>Glutton! Drunkard!
>Watch out!

FORD *(like one obsessed, opening the drawer of the table)*
>Yelper! Liar!

DR. CAIUS   Yelper!

FORD   Yelper!

DR. CAIUS   Liar!

FORD   Rogue!

DR. CAJUS, FORD
    Scagnardo! Falsardo! Briccon!

Nannetta e Fenton sempre dietro il paravento si saran fatte
moine durante il frastuono. Si danno un bacio sonoro. In
questo punto è cessato il baccano e tutti sentono il susurro
del bacio.

FORD *(sottovoce, guardando il paravento)*
    C'è.

DR. CAJUS C'è.

FORD *(avviandosi pian piano e cautamente al paravento)*
    Se t'agguanto!

DR. CAJUS *(come sopra)*
    Se ti piglio!

FORD   Se t'acciuffo!

DR. CAJUS Se t'acceffo!

FORD   Ti sconquasso!

DR. CAJUS T'arronciglio
    Come un can!

FORD   Ti rompo il ceffo!

DR. CAJUS Guai a te!

FORD   Prega il tuo Santo!

QUICKLY *(accanto alla cesta, a Meg)*
    Facciamo le viste
    D'attendere ai panni;
    Pur ch'ei non c'inganni
    Con mosse impreviste.

DR. CAJUS Guai a te! Guai!

FORD   Guai!

MEG *(accanto alla cesta, a Quickly)*
    Facciamogli siepe
    Fra tanto scompiglio.
    Ne' giuochi il periglio
    È un grano di pepe.

FORD   Se alfin con te m'azzuffo!
    Se ti piglio!

DR. CAJUS Guai!

QUICKLY Fin'or non s'accorse
    Di nulla; egli può
    Sorprenderci forse,
    Confonderci no.

DR. CAJUS Se t'agguanto!

FORD   Se t'acceffo!

MEG   Il rischio è un diletto
    Che accresce l'ardor,
    Che stimola in petto
    Gli spiriti e il cor.

QUICKLY Egli può sorprenderci, *ecc.*

DR. CAJUS Se t'acciuffo!

BARDOLFO *(rientrando da sinistra)*
    Non si trova.

DR. CAIUS, FORD
> Yelper! Liar! Rogue!

Anne and Fenton, always behind the screen, will have done some billing and cooing during the uproar. They exchange a loud kiss. At this point the din has stopped and all hear the sound of the kiss.

FORD *(in a low voice, looking at the screen)*
> He's there.

DR. CAIUS   He's there.

FORD *(moving softly and cautiously to the sccreen)*
> If I catch you!

DR. CAIUS *(doing the same)*
> If I seize you!

FORD   If I grab you!

DR. CAIUS   If I snap you up!

FORD   I'll shatter you!

DR. CAIUS   I'll hook you
> Like a dog!

FORD   I'll smash your mug!

DR. CAIUS   Woe betide you! Woe!

FORD   Pray to your Saint!

QUICKLY *(beside the hamper, to Meg)*
> Let's pretend
> To take care of the clothes;
> Provided he doesn't trick us
> With unforeseen moves.

DR. CAIUS   Woe betide you! Woe!

FORD   Woe!

MEG *(beside the hamper, to Quickly)*
> Let's act as a hedge for him
> In the midst of so much confusion.
> In games, danger
> Is a peppercorn.

FORD   If I finally scuffle with you!
> If I catch you!

DR. CAIUS   Woe!

QUICKLY   So far he hasn't realized
> Anything; he can
> Perhaps surprise us,
> But not confound us.

DR. CAIUS   If I catch you!

FORD   If I snap you up!

MEG   Risk is a pleasure
> That increases ardor,
> That stimulates in the breast
> Spirits and heart.

QUICKLY   He can surprise us, *etc.*

DR. CAIUS   If I grab you!

BARDOLPH *(re-entering at left)*
> He can't be found.

PISTOLA *(rientrando con Bardolfo ed alcuni del vicinato)*
Non si coglie.

FORD *(a Bardolfo, Pistola e loro compagni)*
Psss . . . Qua tutti.
L'ho trovato.
(indicando il paravento)
Là c'è Falstaff
Con mia moglie.

BARDOLFO   Sozzo can vituperato!

DR. CAJUS, PISTOLA
Zitto!

FORD   Zitto!
Urlerai dopo!

DR. CAJUS   Zitto! Zitto!

FALSTAFF *(sbucando colla faccia)*
Affogo!

QUICKLY *(ricacciando giù Falstaff)*
Sta sotto, sta sotto!

DR. CAJUS, FORD, PISTOLA
Zitto! zitto!

FALSTAFF   Affogo!

FORD   Là s'è udito
Il suon di un bacio.

MEG   Or questi s'ensorge.

QUICKLY *(abbassandosi e parlando a Falstaff sulla cesta)*
Se l'altro ti scorge
Sei morto.

FALSTAFF *(sotto la biancheria)*
Son cotto!

BARDOLFO   Noi dobbiam pigliare il topo
Mentre sta rodendo il cacio.

MEG   Sta sotto, sta sotto!

QUICKLY   Sta sotto, sta sotto!

FORD   Ragoniam.

FENTON *(a Nannetta)*
Bella! ridente!
Oh! come pieghi
Verso i miei prieghi,
Verso i miei prieghi
Donnescamente!
Come ti vidi
M'innamorai,
E tu sorridi
Perchè lo sai.

NANNETTA *(a Fenton)*
Mentre quei vecchi
Corron la giostra,
Noi di sottecchi
Corriam la nostra.
L'amor non ode

PISTOL *(re-entering with Bardolph and some people of the neighborhood)*
>He can't be caught.

FORD *(to Bardolph, Pistol and their companions)*
>Ssssh . . . Here, all of you.
>I've found him.
>>*(pointing to the screen)*
>Falstaff is there
>With my wife.

BARDOLPH   Filthy, disgraced dog!

DR. CAIUS, PISTOL
>Hush!

FORD   Hush!
>You'll shout afterward!

DR. CAIUS   Hush! Hush!

FALSTAFF *(his face emerging)*
>I'm drowning!

QUICKLY *(pushing Falstaff down again)*
>Stay down, stay down!

DR. CAIUS, FORD, PISTOL
>Hush, hush!

FALSTAFF   I'm drowning!

FORD   There was heard there
>The sound of a kiss.

MEG   Now this one rises up.

QUICKLY *(crouching and speaking to Falstaff over the hamper)*
>If the other one glimpses you,
>You're dead.

FALSTAFF *(under the linen)*
>I'm cooked!

BARDOLPH   We must catch the mouse
>While it's gnawing the cheese.

MEG   Stay down, stay down!

QUICKLY   Stay down, stay down!

FORD   Let's use our reason.

FENTON *(to Anne)*
>Beautiful! Laughing!
>Oh! how you bend
>Toward my pleas,
>Toward my pleas
>In a womanly way!
>When I saw you
>I fell in love,
>And you smile
>Because you know it.

ANNE *(to Fenton)*
>While those old men
>Run their tourney,
>We stealthily
>Run ours.
>Love doesn't hear

                         Tuon nè bufere,
                         Vola alle sfere
                         Beate e gode.

FORD   Colpo non vibro
                         Senz'un piano di battaglia.

BARDOLFO, PISTOLA, GENTE DEL VICINATO
                         Bravo!

DR. CAJUS   Un uom di quel calibro
                         Con un soffio ci sbaraglia!

FORD   La mia tattica maestra
                         Le sue mosse pria registra.
                         (a Pistola e a due compagni)
                         Voi sarete l'ala destra.
                         (a Bardolfo e al Dr. Cajus)
                         Noi sarem l'ala sinistra.
                         (agli altri)
                         E costor con piè gagliardo
                         Sfonderanno il baluardo.

BARDOLFO, PISTOLA, GENTE DEL VICINATO
                         Bravo, bravo, generale!

DR. CAJUS   Aspettiam un tuo segnale.

BARDOLFO, PISTOLA, GENTE DEL VICINATO
                         Bravo, bravo, *ecc.*

FENTON   Già un sogno bello
                         D'Imene albeggia,
                         Un sogno bello, *ecc.*

NANNETTA   Lo spiritello
                         D'amor volteggia,
                         Lo spiritello, *ecc.*

FALSTAFF *(sbucando)*
                         Che caldo!

MEG   Sta sotto!

FALSTAFF   Mi squaglio!

QUICKLY   Sta sotto!

MEG   Il ribaldo vorrebbe
                         Un ventaglio.

FALSTAFF *(supplicante col naso fuori)*
                         Un breve spiraglio,
                         Non chiedo di più.

QUICKLY   Ti metto il bavaglio
                         Se parli.

MEG *(ricacciando Falstaff sotto la biancheria)*
                         Giù!

QUICKLY   Giù! giù! giù!

MEG   Giù! Giù!

NANNETTA   Tutto delira,
                         Sospiro e riso.
                         Sorride il viso
                         E il cor sospira.
                         Dolci richiami d'amor.

Thunder or storms,
It flies to the blissful
Spheres and rejoices.

FORD   I won't deal a blow
Without a battle plan.

BARDOLPH, PISTOL, PEOPLE OF THE NEIGHBORHOOD
Good for you!

DR. CAIUS   A man of that caliber
Can rout us with a puff!

FORD   My master tactic
First registers its moves.
        (to Pistol and to two companions)
You will be the right flank.
        (to Bardolph and to Dr. Caius)
We will be the left flank.
        (to the others)
And they, with vigorous foot,
Will knock down the rampart.

BARDOLPH, PISTOL, PEOPLE OF THE NEIGHBORHOOD
Good for you! Good, general!

DR. CAIUS   We await a signal from you.

BARDOLPH, PISTOL, PEOPLE OF THE NEIGHBORHOOD
Good for you! Good, etc.

FENTON   Already a beautiful dream
Of Hymen is dawning,
A beautiful dream, *etc.*

ANNE   The little sprite
Of love is flitting.
The little sprite, *etc.*

FALSTAFF *(emerging)*
What heat!

MEG   Stay down!

FALSTAFF   I'm melting!

QUICKLY   Stay down!

MEG   The scoundrel would like
A fan.

FALSTAFF *(pleading, with his nose emerging)*
A little air hole,
I ask no more.

QUICKLY   I'll put a gag on you
If you talk.

MEG *(pushing Falstaff back down beneath the linen)*
Down!

QUICKLY   Down! Down! Down!

MEG   Down! Down!

ANNE   Everything is delirious,
Sigh and laughter.
The face smiles,
And the heart sighs.
Sweet calls of love.

Sì, t'amo, t'amo, t'amo!

FENTON   Fra quelle ciglia
Veggo due fari
A meraviglia
Sereni e chiari.
Dimmi se m'ami?
T'amo! t'amo!

FORD *(al Dr. Cajus accostando l'orecchio al paravento)*
Senti,
Accosta un po' l'orecchio!

DR. CAJUS *(a Ford, accostando l'orecchio al paravento)*
Sento, sento.

PISTOLA   Ma fra poco il lieto giuoco
Turberà dura lezion.
Egli canta, ma fra poco
Muterà la sua canzon.

GENTE DEL VICINATO
S'egli cade più non scappa,
Nessun più lo può salvar.
Nel tuo diavolo t'incappa
Che tu possa stramazzar!

BARDOLFO   È la voce della donna
Che risponde al cavalier.

MEG   Parliam sottovoce
Guardando il Messer
Che brontola e cuoce
Nel nostro panier,
Che brontola, *ecc.*

QUICKLY   Costui s'è infardato
Di tanta viltà,
Che darlo al bucato
È averne pietà.
Che darlo, *ecc.*

FORD   Che patetici lamenti!!
Su quel nido d'usignuoli
Scoppierà fra poco il tuon.

DR. CAJUS   Sento, intendo
E vedo chiaro
Delle femmine,
Delle femmine gl'inganni.

FORD *(agli altri)*
Zitto! A noi!

FALSTAFF *(sbucando e sbuffando)*
Ouff! Cesto molesto!

ALICE *(rientra e si avvicina alla cesta)*
Silenzio!

FORD   Quest'è il momento.
Zitto! Attenti!

FALSTAFF *(sbucando)*
Protesto!

MEG, QUICKLY   Che bestia restìa.

Yes, I love you, I love you, I love you!

FENTON   Through those lashes
I see two beacons
Wondrously
Serene and limpid.
Tell me that you love me?
I love you! I love you!

FORD *(to Dr. Caius, putting his ear close to the screen)*
Listen,
Put your ear a little closer!

DR. CAIUS *(to Ford, putting his ear close to the screen)*
I hear, I hear.

PISTOL   But shortly a severe lesson
Will disturb the happy play.
He sings, but shortly
He'll change his song.

PEOPLE OF THE NEIGHBORHOOD
If he falls, he won't run off again.
No one can save him any more.
You and your devil are meeting:
May you fall headlong!

BARDOLPH   It's the woman's voice
Which answers the Knight.

MEG   Let us speak softly,
Looking at the gentleman
Who is grumbling and stewing
In our basket,
Who is grumbling, *etc.*

QUICKLY   He has besmirched himself
With so much wickedness,
That to give him to the laundry
Is to have pity on him.
That to give him, *etc.*

FORD   What pathetic laments!!
Over that nightingales' nest
Shortly thunder will burst.

DR. CAIUS   I hear, I understand,
And I see clearly
The deceits of females,
Of females.

FORD *(to the others)*
Hush! It's our moment!

FALSTAFF *(popping up and huffing)*
Uff! Annoying basket!

ALICE *(re-enters and approaches the hamper)*
Silence!

FORD   This is the moment.
Hush! Pay attention!

FALSTAFF *(popping up)*
I protest!

MEG, QUICKLY What an uneasy animal.

FORD   Attenti a me.

FALSTAFF   Portatemi via!

DR. CAJUS   Dà il signal.

MEG, QUICKLY   È matto furibondo!

FALSTAFF *(si nasconde)*
                Aiuto!

FORD   *Uno . . .*

FALSTAFF   Aiuto!

FORD   *Due . . .*

FALSTAFF   Aiuto!

FORD   *Tre.*
                (rovesciando il paravento)

DR. CAJUS   Non è lui!!

Nannetta e Fenton nel rovesciarsi del paravento rimangono scoperti e confusi.

ALICE, MEG, QUICKLY
                È il finimondo!

BARDOLFO, FORD, PISTOLA, GENTE DEL VICINATO
                Sbalordimento!

NANNETTA, FENTON, DR. CAJUS
                Ah!

FORD *(a Nannetta con furia)*
                Ancora nuove rivolte!
                (a Fenton)
                Tu va pe' fatti tuoi!
                L'ho detto mille volte:
                Costei non fa per voi.

Nannetta sbigottita fugge. Fenton esce dal fondo.

BARDOLFO *(correndo verso il fondo)*
                È là! Ferma!

FORD   Dove?

PISTOLA   Là! sulle scale.

FORD   Squartatelo!

DR. CAJUS, BARDOLFO, PISTOLA, GENTE DEL VICINATO
                A caccia!

QUICKLY   Che caccia infernale!

Tutti gli uomini salgono a corsa la scala del fondo.

ALICE *(scampanellando)*
                Ned! Will! Tom! Isäac!

Nannetta rientra con quattro servi e un paggetto.

ALICE   Rovesciate quel cesto
                Dalla finestra nell'acqua del fosso . . .
                Là! presso alle giuncaie
                Davanti al crocchio
                Delle lavandaie.

NANNETTA, MEG, QUICKLY
                Sì, sì, sì, sì!

FORD	Pay attention to me.
FALSTAFF	Take me away.
DR. CAIUS	He's giving the signal.
MEG, QUICKLY	He's raving mad!

FALSTAFF (*hides*)
> Help!

FORD	*One . . .*
FALSTAFF	Help!
FORD	*Two . . .*
FALSTAFF	Help!
FORD	*Three.*

> (*overturning the screen*)

DR. CAIUS   It's not he!!

Anne and Fenton, at the overturning of the screen, remain discovered and bewildered.

ALICE, MEG, QUICKLY
> It's the end of the world!

BARDOLPH, FORD, PISTOL, PEOPLE OF THE NEIGHBORHOOD
> Amazement!

ANNE, FENTON, DR. CAIUS
> Ah!

FORD (*to Anne, furiously*)
> Still new rebellions!
>> (*to Fenton*)
> You go on about your business!
> I've said it a thousand times:
> This girl's not for you.

Anne, dismayed, flees. Fenton goes out at the rear.

BARDOLPH (*running toward the rear*)
> He's there! Stop!

FORD	Where?
PISTOL	There! On the stairs.
FORD	Quarter him!

DR. CAIUS, BARDOLPH, PISTOL, PEOPLE OF THE NEIGHBORHOOD
> To the hunt!

QUICKLY   What an infernal hunt!

All the men climb the stairway in the rear, running.

ALICE (*ringing the bell*)
> Ned! Will! Tom! Isaac!

Anne comes back in with four manservants and a page.

ALICE   Empty that basket
> From the window into the water of the ditch . . .
> There! near the beds of rushes
> In front of the group
> Of washerwomen.

ANNE, MEG, QUICKLY
> Yes, yes, yes, yes!

NANNETTA *(ai servi che s'affaticano a sollevare la cesta)*
C'è dentro un pezzo grosso.

ALICE *(al paggetto, che poi esce dalla scala nel fondo)*

Tu chiama mio marito;
(a Meg, mentre Nannetta e Quickly stanno a
guardare i servi che avranno sollevata la
cesta)
Gli narreremo
Il nosto caso pazzo.
Solo al veder
Il Cavalier nel guazzo,
D'ogni gelosa ubbìa
Sarà guarito.

QUICKLY *(ai servi)*
Pesa!

ALICE, MEG *(ai servi che sono già vicini alla finestra)*
Coraggio!

NANNETTA   Il fondo ha fatto *crac!*

NANNETTA, MEG, QUICKLY
Su!

ALICE *(la cesta è portata in alto)*
Trionfo!

NANNETTA, MEG, QUICKLY
Trionfo! Ah! Ah!

ALICE   Che tonfo!

NANNETTA, MEG
Che tonfo!

La cesta, Falstaff e la biancheria capitombolano giù dalla
finestra. Ford e gli altri uomini rientrano. Alice vedendo Ford
lo piglia per un braccio e lo conduce presso la finestra: im-
mensa risata di tutti.

TUTTI   Patatrac!

ATTO TERZO

PARTE PRIMA

Un piazzale. A destra l'esterno dell'Osteria della Giarret-
tiera coll'insegna e il motto: Honni soit qui mal y pense. *Una*
panca di fianco al portone. È l'ora del tramonto. Falstaff è
seduto sulla panca, meditabondo. Si scuote ad un tratto, dà
un gran pugno sulla panca e rivolto verso l'interno dell'osteria
chiama l'Oste.

FALSTAFF   Ehi! Taverniere!
(pensieroso e di pessimo umore)
Mondo ladro. Mondo rubaldo.
Reo mondo!
(entra l'Oste)
Taverniere: un bicchier
Di vin caldo.

ANNE *(to the servants who are laboring to lift the hamper)*
        A big piece is in there.

ALICE *(to the page, who then goes out by the stairway in the*
   rear)
        You, call my husband!
           (to Meg, as Anne and Quickly are watching
           the servants, who will have lifted the ham-
           per)
        We'll recount to him
        Our mad situation.
        Merely at seeing
        The Knight in the pool,
        He will be cured
        Of every jealous fear.

QUICKLY *(to the servants)*
        It's heavy!

ALICE, MEG *(to the servants, who are already near the window)*
        Take heart!

ANNE   The bottom went *crack*!

ANNE, MEG, QUICKLY
        Raise it!

ALICE *(the hamper is raised up high)*
        Triumph!

ANNE, MEG, QUICKLY
        Triumph! Ha! Ha!

ALICE   What a splash!

ANNE, MEG   What a splash!

*The hamper, Falstaff and the linen plunge down from the
window. Ford and the other men re-enter. Alice, seeing Ford,
takes him by the arm and leads him over to the window: immense laughter from all.*

ALL   Bang!

ACT THREE

SCENE ONE

*A yard. At right the outside of the Garter Inn, with its sign
and the motto:* Honi soit qui mal y pense. *A bench beside the
entrance. It is the hour of sunset. Falstaff is seated on the
bench, pensive. He arouses himself abruptly, brings his fist
down hard on the bench and, turning toward the interior of
the tavern, he calls the Host.*

FALSTAFF   Hey! Innkeeper!
           (thoughtful and in the worst humor)
        Thieving world. Rascally world.
        Evil world!
           (the Host enters)
        Innkeeper: a glass
        Of hot wine.

L'Oste riceve l'ordine e rientra.

FALSTAFF   Io, dunque, avrò vissuto
             Tant'anni, audace e destro
             Cavaliere, per essere portato
             In un canestro
             E gittato al canale
             Coi pannilini biechi,
             Come si fa coi gatti
             E i catellini ciechi.
             Che se non galleggiava
             Per me quest'epa tronfia
             Certo affogavo.
             Brutta morte. L'acqua mi gonfia.
             Mondo reo. Non c'è più virtù.
             Tutto declina.
             Va, vecchio John, va,
             Va per la tua via; cammina
             Finchè tu muoia.
             Allor scomparirà la vera
             Virilità dal mondo.
             Che giornataccia nera.
             M'aiuti il ciel!
             Impinguo troppo.
             Ho dei peli grigi.

Ritorna l'Oste portando un gran bicchiere di vino caldo.
Mette il vassojo sulla tavola, poi rientra nell'osteria.

FALSTAFF   Versiamo un po' di vino
             Nell'acqua del Tamigi.

Beve sorseggiando ed assaporando. Si sbottona il panciotto,
si sdraia, ribeve a sorsate, rianimandosi poco a poco.

FALSTAFF   Buono. Ber del vin dolce
             E sbottonarsi al sole,
             Dolce cosa! Il buon vino
             Sperde le tetre fole
             Dello sconforto, accende
             L'occhio e il pensier, dal labbro
             Sale al cervel e quivi risveglia
             Il picciol fabbro
             Dei trilli; un negro grillo
             Che vibra entro l'uom brillo
             Trilla ogni fibra in cor,
             L'allegro etere al trillo
             Guizza e il giocondo
             Globo squilibra una demenza
             Trillante! E il trillo
             Invade il mondo!!!

QUICKLY *(avvicinandosi e interrompendo Falstaff)*
             Reverenza. La bella Alice . . .

The Host receives the order and goes back in.

FALSTAFF   So then, I have lived
              So many years, a bold and skillful
              Knight, to be carried
              In a basket
              And thrown into the ditch
              With the dirty clothes,
              The way they do with cats
              And with blind puppies.
              So that, if this puffed belly
              Didn't float for me,
              I would surely have drowned.
              Ugly death. Water swells me up.
              Evil world. There's no virtue any more.
              Everything's declining.
              Go, old John, go,
              Go on your way; walk on
              Until you die.
              Then true virility
              Will disappear from the world.
              What a bad, black day.
              May heaven help me!
              I'm growing too fat.
              I have some gray hairs

*The Host comes back, bringing a big glass of hot wine. He
places the tray on the table, then re-enters the tavern.*

FALSTAFF   Let's pour a little wine
              Into the water of the Thames.

*He drinks, sipping and savoring. He unbuttons his waist-
coat, stretches out, drinks again in sips, gradually recovering
his spirits.*

FALSTAFF   Good. To drink some sweet wine
              And unbutton oneself in the sun:
              Lovely thing! Good wine
              Dispels the grim nonsense
              Of dejection, kindles
              The eye and the thought; from the lip
              It rises to the brain and there wakens
              The little smith
              Of trills; a black cricket
              That hums within the tipsy man,
              Every fiber of the heart trills;
              The gay air, at the trill,
              Flashes and a trilling
              Madness unbalances the merry
              Globe! And the trill
              Invades the world!!!

QUICKLY *(approaching and interrupting Falstaff)*
              My respects. The beautiful Alice . . .

FALSTAFF *(alzandosi e scattando)*
    Al diavolo
    Te con Alice bella!
    Ne ho piene le bisaccie!
    Ne ho piene le budella!

QUICKLY   Voi siete errato . . .

FALSTAFF   Un canchero!!
    Sento ancor le cornate
    Di quell'irco geloso!
    Ho ancor l'ossa arrembate
    D'esser rimasto curvo,
    Come una buona lama
    Di Bilbào, nello spazio
    D'un panierin di dama!
    Con quel tufo! E quel caldo!
    Un uom della mia tempra,
    Che in uno stillicidio
    Continuo si distempra!
    Poi, quando fui ben cotto,
    Rovente, incandescente,
    M'han tuffato nell'acqua.
    Canaglie!!!

 Alice, Meg, Nannetta, Mr. Ford, Dr. Cajus, Fenton sbucano dietro una casa a sinistra, or l'uno or l'altro spiando, non visti da Falstaff, e poi si nascondo, poi tornano a spiare.

QUICKLY   Essa è innocente,
    Essa è innocente,
    Prendete abbaglio.

FALSTAFF   Vattene!!

QUICKLY *(infervorata)*
    La colpa è di quei fanti
    Malaugurati! Alice piange,
    Urla, invoca i santi.
    Povera donna!! V'ama.
    Leggete.

 Estrae di tasca una lettera. Falstaff la prende e si mette a leggere.

ALICE *(nel fondo sottovoce agli altri, spiando)*
    Legge.

FORD *(sottovoce)*
    Legge.

NANNETTA Vedrai che ci ricasca.

ALICE   L'uomo non si corregge.

MEG *(ad Alice, vedendo un gesto nascosto di Mrs. Quickly)*
    Nasconditi.

DR. CAJUS Rilegge.

FORD   Rilegge.
    L'esca inghiotte.

FALSTAFF *(rileggendo ad alta voce e con molta attenzione)*

FALSTAFF *(rising and snapping)*
>To the devil
>With you and beautiful Alice!
>I have a pack full of you!
>I have a belly full of you!

QUICKLY You are mistaken . . .

FALSTAFF A pox!!
>I can still feel the horn thrusts
>Of that jealous ogre!
>I still have aching bones
>From having remained curved
>Like a good blade
>From Bilbao, in the space
>Of a lady's basket!
>With that stuffiness! And that heat!
>A man of my temperament
>Who, in a constant
>Trickle, becomes distempered!
>Then, when I was well roasted,
>Searing, incandescent,
>They plunged me into the water.
>Swine!!!

Alice, Meg, Anne, Mr. Ford, Dr. Caius, Fenton now emerge behind a house at left, first one spying, then the other, unseen by Falstaff. Then they hide, then they come out to spy again.

QUICKLY
>She is innocent,
>She is innocent,
>You're making a mistake.

FALSTAFF Go away!!

QUICKLY *(filled with fervor)*
>The fault is of those wicked
>Servants! Alice weeps,
>Screams, calls on the saints.
>Poor woman!! She loves you.
>Read.

She takes a letter from her pocket. Falstaff takes it and starts to read.

ALICE *(in the rear, in a low voice, to the others, spying)*
>He's reading.

FORD *(in a low voice)*
>He's reading.

ANNE You'll see: he'll fall again.

ALICE Man is incorrigible.

MEG *(to Alice, seeing a secret gesture from Mrs. Quickly)*
>Hide.

DR. CAIUS He's rereading.

FORD He's rereading.
>He's swallowing the bait.

FALSTAFF *(rereading aloud and with great attention)*

"T'aspetterò nel parco Real,
A mezzanotte.
Tu verrai travestito
Da Cacciatore nero
Alla quercia di Herne."

QUICKLY   Amor ama il mistero.
Per rivedervi Alice
Si val d'una leggenda
Popolar. Quella quercia
È un luogo da tregenda.
Il Cacciatore nero
S'è impeso ad un suo ramo.
V'ha chi crede
Vederlo ricomparir . . .

FALSTAFF *(rabbonito prende per un braccio Mrs. Quickly, e
s'avvia per entrare con essa nell'osteria)*
Entriamo.
Là si discorre meglio.
Narrami la tua frasca.

QUICKLY *(incominciando il racconto della leggenda con mis-
tero, entra nell'osteria con Falstaff)*
Quando il rintocco della
Mezzanotte . . .

FORD *(dal fondo)*
Ci casca.

QUICKLY   . . . cupo si sparge
Nel silente orror,
Sorgon gli spirti
Vagabondi a frotte . . .

ALICE *(avanzandosi con tutto il crocchio, comicamente e mis-
teriosamente ripigliando il racconto di Mrs. Quickly)*
Quando il rintocco
Della mezzanotte
Cupo si sparge
Nel silente orror,
Sorgon gli spirti
Vagabondi a frotte
E vien nel parco
Il nero Cacciator.
Egli cammina
Lento, lento, lento,
Nel gran letargo
Della sepoltura.
S'avanza livido . . .

NANNETTA   Oh! che spavento!

MEG   Sento già il brivido
Della paura!

ALICE *(con voce naturale)*
Fandonie che ai bamboli
Raccontan le nonne
Con lunghi preamboli,
Per farli dormir.

"I'll wait for you in the Royal Park
At midnight.
You will come disguised
As the Black Huntsman
To the oak of Herne."

QUICKLY   Love loves mystery.
To see you again, Alice
Is using a folk
Legend. That oak
Is a witching place.
The Black Huntsman
Hanged himself from one of its boughs.
There are those who believe
They see him reappear . . .

FALSTAFF *(pacified, takes Mrs. Quickly by the arm and moves
to enter the tavern with her)*
Let us go inside.
There one converses better.
Tell me your tale.

QUICKLY *(beginning the story of the legend mysteriously, enters
the tavern with Falstaff)*
When the tolling of
Midnight . . .

FORD *(from the rear)*
He's falling for it.

QUICKLY   . . . grimly spreads
In the silent horror,
The wandering spirits
Rise in bands . . .

ALICE *(advancing with the whole group, comically and myster-
iously taking up the narration of Mrs. Quickly)*
When the tolling
Of midnight
Grimly spreads
In the silent horror,
The wandering spirits
Rise in bands
And into the park comes
The Black Huntsman.
He walks
Slowly, slowly, slowly,
In the great lethargy
Of the grave.
He advances, livid . . .

ANNE   Oh, what a fright!

MEG   I already feel the shudder
Of fear!

ALICE *(in a natural voice)*
Idle tales that grandmothers
Tell babies
With long preambles
To make them go to sleep.

Vendetta di donne
Non deve fallir.

NANNETTA, MEG

Vendetta di donne
Non deve fallir.

ALICE (*ripigliando il colore del racconto*)

S'avanza livido
E il passo converge
Al tronco ove esalò
L'anima prava.
Sbucan le Fate.
Sulla fronte egl'erge
Due corna lunghe, lunghe,
Lunghe . . .

FORD

Brava!
Quelle corna
Saranno la mia gioia!

ALICE

Bada! tu pur ti meriti
Qualche castigoia!

FORD

Perdona . . . Riconosco
I miei demeriti . . .

ALICE

Ma guai se ancor ti coglie
Quella mania feroce
Di cercar dentro
Il guscio di una noce
L'amante di tua moglie.
Ma il tempo stringe
E vuol fantasia lesta.

MEG

Affrettiam.

FENTON

Concertiam la mascherata.

ALICE

Nannetta.

NANNETTA

Eccola qua!

ALICE (*a Nannetta*)

Sarai la Fata
Regina delle Fate,
In bianca vesta,
Chiusa in candido vel,
Cinta di rose.

NANNETTA

E canterò parole armoniose.

ALICE (*a Meg*)

Tu la verde sarai
Ninfa silvana.
E la comare Quickly . . .
Una befana.

NANNETTA (*allegramente*)

A meraviglia!

Comincia a scendere la sera e resterà una penombra di crepuscolo.

ALICE

Avrò con me dei putti
Che fingeran folletti
E spiritelli
E diavoletti

| | Women's revenge
Must not fail. |
| ANNE, MEG | Women's revenge
Must not fail. |

ALICE *(resuming the tone of the story)*
He advances, livid,
And his step is directed
To the trunk where
His depraved soul breathed its last.
The Fairies emerge.
On his brow he bears
Two long horns, long,
Long . . .

| FORD | Good for you!
Those horns
Will be my joy! |

| ALICE | Mind you! You also deserve
Some punishment! |

| FORD | Forgive me . . . I recognize
My faults . . . |

| ALICE | But woe to you if again
That fierce mania seizes you
To hunt inside
A walnut shell
For your wife's lover.
But time is pressing
And demands lively imagination. |

| MEG | Let's hasten. |

| FENTON | Let's plan the masquerade. |

| ALICE | Anne. |

| ANNE | Here she is! |

ALICE *(to Anne)*
You will be the Fairy
Queen of the Fairies,
In a white dress,
Enveloped in a white veil,
Girded with roses.

| ANNE | And I shall sing harmonious words. |

ALICE *(to Meg)*
You will be the green
Wood Nymph.
And Gossip Quickly . . .
A witch.

ANNE *(merrily)*
Wonderful!

Evening is beginning to fall and a semidarkness of dusk will remain.

| ALICE | I'll have some children with me
Who'll pretend to be sprites
And little spirits
And little devils |

                                        E pipistrelli
                                        E farfarelli.
                                        Su Falstaff camuffato
                                        In manto e corni
                                        Ci scagliermo tutti.

NANNETTA, MEG, FENTON
                                        Tutti! tutti!

ALICE   E lo tempestermo
                                        Finch'abbia confessata
                                        La sua perversità.
                                        Poi ci smaschereremo
                                        E pria che il ciel raggiorni,
                                        La giuliva brigata
                                        Se ne ritornerà.

MEG   Vien sera. Rincasiam.

ALICE   L'appuntamento
                                        È alla quercia di Herne.

FENTON   È inteso.

NANNETTA   A meraviglia!
                                        Oh! che allegro spavento!

ALICE, NANNETTA, FENTON *(scambievolmente)*
                                        Addio.

MEG *(ad Alice e Nannetta)*
                                        Addio.

*Alice, Nannetta e Fenton s'avviano per uscire da sinistra.
Meg da destra.*

ALICE *(a Meg, gridando)*
                                        Provvedi le lanterne.

*In questo momento Mrs. Quickly esce dall'osteria: vedendo
Ford e Dr. Cajus parlare segretamente, si ferma ad origliare
sulla soglia.*

FORD *(al Dr. Cajus, sottovoce)*
                                        Non dubitar,
                                        Tu sposerai mia figlia.
                                        Rammenti bene
                                        Il suo travestimento?

DR. CAJUS   Cinta di rose,
                                        Il vel bianco e la vesta.

ALICE *(di dentro a sinistra gridando)*
                                        Non ti scordar le maschere.

MEG *(di dentro a destra gridando)*
                                        No, certo.
                                        Nè tu le raganelle!

FORD *(continuando il discorso col Dr. Cajus)*
                                        Io già disposi
                                        La rete mia.
                                        Sul finir della festa
                                        Verrete a me col volto ricoperto

                                        Essa dal vel,
                                        Tu da un mantel fratesco

And bats
And little butterflies.
On Falstaff disguised
In cloak and horns,
We'll all hurl ourselves.

ANNE, MEG, FENTON
All! All!

ALICE   And we'll pummel him
Until he has confessed
His perversity.
Then we'll unmask ourselves
And before the sky dawns
The gay party
Will come home again.

MEG   Evening is coming. Let's go home.

ALICE   The meeting place
Is at the oak of Herne.

FENTON   It's agreed.

ANNE   Wonderful!
Oh, what merry fright!

ALICE, ANNE, FENTON *(to one another)*
Goodbye.

MEG *(to Alice and Anna)*
Goodbye.

Alice, Anne and Fenton start off, to exit at left; Meg, at right.

ALICE *(to Meg, shouting)*
You provide the lanterns.

At this moment Mrs. Quickly comes out of the tavern. Seeing Ford and Dr. Caius talking secretly, she stops on the threshold to eavesdrop.

FORD *(to Dr. Caius, in a low voice)*
Have no doubts:
You will marry my daughter.
Do you remember well
Her disguise?

DR. CAIUS   Girded with roses,
White veil and dress.

ALICE *(from within, at left, shouting)*
Don't forget the masks.

MEG *(from within, at right, shouting)*
No, of course not.
Nor you, the rattles!

FORD *(continuing his conversation with Dr. Caius)*
I have already arranged
My net.
Toward the end of the festivity
You will both come to me with your faces
    covered:
She by the veil,
You, by a friar's habit;

E vi benedirò
Come due sposi.

DR. CAJUS *(prendendo il braccio di Ford ed avviandosi ad*
escire da sinistra)
Siam d'accordo.

QUICKLY *(sul limitare dell'osteria, con gesto accorto verso i due*
che escono)
Stai fresco!
(esce rapidamente da destra)
Nannetta! Ohè!
Nannetta! Ohè!

NANNETTA *(di dentro)*
Che c'è? Che c'è?

QUICKLY   Prepara la canzone della Fata.

NANNETA *(di dentro)*
È preparata.

ALICE *(di dentro a sinistra)*
Tu, non tardar.

QUICKLY *(di dentro, più lontano)*
Chi prima arriva,
Aspetta.

Si è fatta notte.

PARTE SECONDA

Il Parco di Windsor. Nel centro, la gran quercia di Herne.
Nel fondo, l'argine d'un fosso. Fronde foltissime. Arbusti in
fiore. È notte. Si odono gli appelli lontani dei guardia boschi.
Il parco a poco a poco si rischiarirà coi raggi della luna.

Entra Fenton.

FENTON   Dal labbro il canto
Estasïato vola
Pei silenzi notturni
E va lontano
E alfin ritrova
Un altro labbro umano
Che gli risponde
Colla sua parola.
Allor la nota
Che non è più sola.
Vibra di gioia
In un accordo arcano
E innamorando
L'aer antelucano
Con altra voce
Al suo fonte rivola.
Quivi ripiglia suon,
Ma la sua cura
Tende sempre ad unir
Chi lo disuna.
Così baciai
La disïata bocca!

> And I will bless you
> As a bride and groom.

DR. CAIUS *(taking Ford's arm and starting to go off with him at right)*
> We're agreed.

QUICKLY *(at the threshold of the tavern, with a sly gesture toward the two, who leave)*
> That's what you think!
> *(exits rapidly at right)*
> Anne, hey!
> Anne, hey!

ANNE *(from within)*
> What is it? What is it?

QUICKLY Prepare the Fairy's song.

ANNE *(from within)*
> It's prepared.

ALICE *(from within, at left)*
> You: don't be late.

QUICKLY *(from within, farther off)*
> Whoever arrives first
> Will wait.

Night has fallen.

SCENE TWO

Windsor Park. In the center, the great oak of Herne. In the rear, the bank of a ditch. Very thick boughs. Flowering shrubs. It is night. The distant calls of the forest guards can be heard. The park will gradually be illuminated by the rays of the moon.

Fenton enters.

FENTON From the lips the song
> Flies, in ecstasy,
> Through the nocturnal silences
> And goes far,
> And finally discovers
> Another human lip
> That replies to it
> With its word.
> Then the note
> Which is no longer alone
> Vibrates with joy
> In a secret chord
> And bewitching
> The antelucan air
> With another voice
> Flies back to its source.
> There it regains sound,
> But its concern
> Tends always to unite
> Who disunites it.
> Thus I kissed
> The desired mouth!

Bocca baciata
Non perde ventura . . .

NANNETTA *(di dentro lontana, avvicinandosi)*

Anzi rinnova come fa la luna . . .
Come fa la luna.

FENTON   Ma il canto muor
Nel bacio che lo tocca.

Entra Nannetta, vestita da Regina delle Fate. Fenton l'abbraccia. Alice, entrando improvvisamente trattiene Fenton. Alice non mascherata porta sul braccio una cappa nera ed una maschera.

ALICE *(obbligando Fenton ad indossare la cappa)*
Nossignore!
Tu indossa questa cappa.

FENTON *(aiutato da Alice e Nannetta)*
Che vuol dir ciò?

NANNETTA   Lasciati fare.

Mrs. Quickly segue Alice: ha una gran cuffia e manto grigio da befana, un bastone ed un brutto ceffo di maschera.

ALICE *(porgendo la maschera a Fenton)*
Allaccia.

Fenton si aggiusta la cappa e la maschera.

NANNETTA *(rimirando Fenton)*
È un fraticel
Sgusciato dalla Trappa.

ALICE *(frettolosa ed aiutando Fenton ad allacciare la maschera)*
Il tradimento
Che Ford ne minaccia
Tornar deve in suo scorno
E in nostro aiuto.

FENTON   Spiegatevi.

ALICE   Ubbidisci presto e muto.
L'occasione come viene scappa.
(a Mrs. Quickly)
Chi vestirai da finta sposa?

QUICKLY   Un gaio ladron nasuto
Che abborre il Dottor Cajo.

MEG *(accorrendo dal fondo, vestita con veli verdi e mascherata, ad Alice)*
Ho nascosto i folletti
Lungo il fosso.
Siam pronte.

ALICE *(origliando)*
Zitto . . .
Viene il pezzo grosso.

NANNETTA   Via! . . .

ALICE   Via! . . .

A kissed mouth
Doesn't lose luck . . .

ANNE *(from within, far off coming nearer)*
Rather it's renewed
As the moon is . . .
As the moon is.

FENTON   But the song dies
In the kiss that touches it.

*Enter Anne, dressed as the Queen of the Fairies. Fenton
embraces her. Alice, entering suddenly, restrains Fenton. Not
masked, Alice is carrying over her arm a black cloak and a
mask.*

ALICE *(making Fenton put on the cloak)*
No, sir!
You put on this cloak.

FENTON *(assisted by Alice and Anne)*
What does this mean?

ANNE   Let us do it.

*Mrs. Quickly follows Alice. She has a great bonnet and a
gray witch's cloak, a stick, and the mask of an ugly face.*

ALICE *(handing the mask to Fenton)*
Fasten this.

Fenton arranges the cloak and the mask.

ANNE *(looking Fenton over)*
He's a little monk
Who's slipped away from La Trappe.

ALICE *(in haste, and helping Fenton fasten the mask)*
The betrayal
That Ford threatens us with
Must rebound to his disgrace
And in our aid.

FENTON   Explain.

ALICE   Obey promptly and silently.
Opportunity flees as it comes.
(to Mrs. Quickly)
Whom will you dress as the false bride?

QUICKLY   A merry, big-snouted thief
Who detests Doctor Caius.

MEG *(running in from the rear, dressed in green veils and
masked: to Alice)*
I've hidden the sprites
Along the ditch.
We're ready.

ALICE *(listening)*
Hush . . .
The big fellow's coming.

ANNE   Away! . . .

ALICE   Away! . . .

MEG   Via! . . .
QUICKLY   Via! . . .

Tutte fuggono con Fenton da sinistra. Dal fondo a destra,
quando suona il primo colpo di mezzanotte entra Falstaff con
due corna di cervo in testa ed avviluppato in ampio man-
tello.

FALSTAFF   Una, due, tre, quattro,
                Cinque, sei, sette botte,
                Otto, nove, dieci, undici,
                Dodici. Mezzanotte.
                (vedendo la quercia di Herne)
                Quest'è la quercia. Numi,
                Proteggetemi! Giove!
                Tu per amor d'Europa
                Ti trasformasti in bove;
                Portasti corna. I Numi
                C'insegnan la modestia.
                L'amore metamorfosa
                Un uom in una bestia.
                (Alice comparisce nel fondo a sinistra)
FALSTAFF *(ascoltando)*
                Odo un soave passo!
                Alice! Amor ti chiama!
                (avvicinandosi ad Alice)
                Vieni! l'amor m'infiamma!
ALICE *(avvicinandosi a Falstaff)*
                Sir John!
FALSTAFF   Sei la mia dama!
ALICE   Sir John!
FALSTAFF   Sei la mia damma!
ALICE   O sfavillante amor!
FALSTAFF *(afferrandola)*
                Vieni!
                Già fremo e fervo!
ALICE *(sempre evitando l'abbraccio)*
                Sir John!
FALSTAFF   Sono il tuo servo!
                Sono il tuo cervo imbizzarrito.
                Ed or piovan tartufi,
                Rafani, finocchi!!!
                E sien la mia pastura!
                E amor trabocchi!!
                Siam soli . . .
ALICE   No . . . Qua nella selva densa
                Mi segue Meg.
FALSTAFF   È doppia l'avventura!
                Venga anche lei!
                Squartatemi
                Come un camoseio a mensa!!
                Sbranatemi!!! Cupido
                Alfin mi ricompensa!

MEG   Away! . . .
QUICKLY   Away! . . .

All the women flee, with Fenton, at left. From the rear, at right, when the first stroke of midnight sounds, enter Falstaff with two stag's horns on his head, and wrapped in an ample cloak.

FALSTAFF   One, two, three, four,
             Five, six, seven strokes,
             Eight, nine, ten, eleven,
             Twelve. Midnight.
                  (seeing the oak of Herne)
             This is the oak. Cods,
             Protect me! Jove!
             You, out of love for Europa,
             Transformed yourself into a bull;
             You wore horns. The Gods
             Teach us humility.
             Love metamorphoses
             A man into an animal.
                  (Alice appears in the rear, at left)

FALSTAFF *(listening)*
             I hear a soft footstep!
             Alice! Love calls you!
                  (approaching Alice)
             Come! Love inflames me!

ALICE *(approaching Falstaff)*
             Sir John!

FALSTAFF   You are my lady!

ALICE   Sir John!

FALSTAFF   You are my hind!

ALICE   O sparkling love!

FALSTAFF *(seizing her)*
             Come!
             Already I tremble and blaze!

ALICE *(still avoiding the embrace)*
             Sir John!

FALSTAFF   I am your slave!
             I am your frisky stag.
             And now let truffles rain,
             Radishes, fennel!!!
             And let them be my pasturage!
             And let love overflow!!
             We're alone . . .

ALICE   No . . . Here in the thick forest
             Meg is following me.

FALSTAFF   The adventure is double!
             Let her come too!
             Quarter me
             Like a chamois at table!!
             Tear me limb from limb!!! Cupid
             Is repaying me at last!

              Io t'amo!, io t'amo!
              Io t'amo!, t'amo!

MEG *(di dentro)*
              Aiuto!!!

ALICE *(fingendo spavento)*
              Un grido! Ahimè!

MEG *(dal fondo, senza avanzare: non ha la maschera)*
              Vien la tregenda!
              (fugge)

ALICE   Ahimè! Fuggiamo!

FALSTAFF *(spaventato)*
              Dove?

ALICE   Il ciel perdoni al mio peccato!
              (fugge da destra rapidamente)

FALSTAFF *(appiattandosi accanto al tronco di quercia)*
              Il diavolo non vuol
              Ch'io sia dannato.

NANNETTA *(di dentro)*
              Ninfe! Elfi! Silfi!
              Doridi! Sirene!
              L'astro degl'incantesimi
              In cielo è sorto.
              Sorgete! Ombre serene!
              (comparisce nel fondo fra le fronde)

VOCI DI DONNE *(molto lontane)*
              Ninfe! Silfi! Sirene!

FALSTAFF *(gettandosi colla faccia contro terra lungo disteso)*

              Sono le Fate.
              Chi le guarda è morto.

    Entrano Nannetta vestita da Regina delle Fate, Alice; alcune Ragazzette vestite da Fate bianche e da Fate azzure: Falstaff sempre disteso contro terra, immobile.

ALICE *(sbucando cautamente da sinistra con alcune Fate)*
              Inoltriam.

NANNETTA *(sbucando a sinistra, con altre Fate e scorgendo Falstaff)*
              Egli è là.

ALICE *(scorge Falstaff e lo indica alle altre)*
              Steso al suol.

NANNETTA   Lo confonde il terror.

    Tutte si inoltrano con precauzione.

LE FATE   Si nasconde.

ALICE   Non ridiam!

LE FATE   Non ridiam!

NANNETTA *(indicando alle Fate il loro posto, mentre Alice parte rapidamente da sinistra)*
              Tutte qui, dietro a me . . .
              Cominciam . . .

LE FATE   Tocca a te.

I love you! I love you!
I love you! I love you!

MEG *(from within)*
Help!!!

ALICE *(feigning fright)*
A cry! Alas!

MEG *(from the rear, without advancing; she hasn't her mask)*
The witch pack is coming!
(runs off)

ALICE   Alas! Let us flee!

FALSTAFF *(frightened)*
Where?

ALICE   May heaven forgive my sin!
(flees at right, rapidly)

FALSTAFF *(flattening himself against the trunk of the oak)*
The devil doesn't wish
That I be damned.

ANNE *(within)*
Nymphs! Elfs! Sylphs!
Nereids! Sirens!
The star of enchantments
Has risen in the sky.
Rise! Serene shades!
(she appears in the rear among the boughs)

WOMEN'S VOICES *(very far off)*
Nymphs! Sylphs! Sirens!

FALSTAFF *(flinging himself full length with his face against the ground)*
It's the Fairies.
Whoever looks at them is a dead man.

Enter Anne dressed as Queen of the Fairies, Alice, some little girls dressed as White Fairies and Blue Fairies. Falstaff is still lying on the ground, motionless.

ALICE *(emerging cautiously from the left with some Fairies)*
Let's move forward.

ANNE *(emerging at left, with other Fairies, and perceiving Falstaff)*
He's there.

ALICE *(glimpses Falstaff and points him out to the others)*
Stretched out on the ground.

ANNE   Terror confounds him.

They all come forward cautiously.

THE FAIRIES   He's hiding.

ALICE   Let's not laugh!

THE FAIRIES   Let's not laugh!

ANNE *(pointing out their places to the Fairies, while Alice goes off rapidly, at left)*
All here, behind me . . .
Let's begin . . .

THE FAIRIES   It's up to you.

*Le piccole Fate si dispongono in cerchio intorno alla loro
Regina: le Fate più grandi formano gruppo a sinistra.*

LA REGINA DELLE FATE (NANNETTA)
        Sul fil d'un soffio etesio
        Scorrete, agili larve,
        Fra i rami un baglior cesio
        D'alba lunare apparve.
        Danzate! e il passo blando
        Misuri un blando suon,
        Le magiche accoppiando
        Carole alla canzon.

Danzetta lenta e molle delle piccole Fate.

LE FATE   La selva dorme e sperde
        Incenso ed ombra; e par
        Nell'aer denso un verde
        Asilo in fondo al mar.

LA REGINA DELLE FATE (NANNETTA)
        Erriam sotto la luna
        Scegliendo fior da fiore,
        Ogni corolla in core
        Porta la sua fortuna.
        Coi gigli e le vïole
        Scriviam de' nomi arcani,
        Dalle fatate mani
        Germoglino parole.
        Parole alluminate
        Di puro argento e d'or,
        Carmi e malìe. Le Fate
        Hanno per cifre i fior.

LE FATE (*mentre le piccole Fate vanno cogliendo fiori*)
        Moviamo ad una ad una
        Sotto il lunare albor,
        Verso la quercia bruna
        Del nero Cacciator.
        Verso la quercia bruna, *ecc.*

NANNETTA   Le Fate hanno
        Per cifre i fior.

*Tutte le Fate, colla Regina, mentre cantano s'avviano lenta-
mente verso la quercia. Dal fondo a sinistra sbucano: Alice
mascherata, Meg da ninfa verde colla maschera, Mrs. Quickly
da befana, mascherata. Sono precedute da Bardolfo vestito
con una cappa rossa, senza maschera, col cappuccio abbassato
sul volto e da Pistola da satiro. Seguono: il Dr. Cajus in cappa
grigia, senza maschera, Fenton in cappa nera, colla maschera,
Ford senza cappa, nè maschera. Parecchi borghesi in costumi
fantastici chiudono il corteggio, e vanno a formare gruppo a
destra. Nel fondo altri mascherati portano lanterne di varie
foggie.*

BARDOLFO (*intoppando nel corpo di Falstaff e arrestando con
   un gran gesto le Fate*)
        Alto là!

The little Fairies arrange themselves in a circle around their Queen; the older Fairies form a group at left.

THE QUEEN OF THE FAIRIES (ANNE)
> On the breath of an Ethesian breeze,
> Scamper, agile phantoms,
> Among the boughs a bluish glow
> Of lunar dawn has appeared.
> Dance! And let a soft sound
> Measure your soft tread,
> Coupling the magic
> Dances to the song.

Slow and gentle little dance of the little Fairies.

THE FAIRIES
> The forest sleeps and scatters
> Incense and shadow; and it seems
> In the thick air a green
> Refuge at the bottom of the sea.

THE QUEEN OF THE FAIRIES (ANNE)
> Let us wander beneath the Moon,
> Choosing flower from flower,
> Each corolla in its heart
> Bears its good fortune.
> With lilies and violets
> Let us write mysterious names;
> From our enchanted hands
> Let words blossom.
> Words illuminated
> In pure silver and gold,
> Songs and spells. The Fairies
> Have flowers as their letters.

THE FAIRIES (*as the little Fairies go picking flowers*)
> Let us move, one by one,
> Beneath the lunar glow,
> Toward the dark oak
> Of the Black Huntsman.
> Toward the dark oak, *etc.*

ANNE
> The Fairies have
> Flowers as their letters.

All the Fairies, with the Queen, as they sing, move slowly toward the oak. From the rear, at left, appear: Alice, masked; Meg, as a green nymph with a mask; Mrs. Quickly, as a witch, masked. They are preceded by Bardolph, dressed in a red cloak, without a mask, with a hood pulled down over his face, and by Pistol, as a satyr. They are followed by Dr. Caius in a gray cloak without a mask; Fenton in a black cloak, with a mask; Ford without cloak or mask. Numerous villagers in fantastic costumes bring up the rear of the procession and go to form a group at right. In the rear other maskers carry lanterns of various shapes.

BARDOLPH (*stumbling over Falstaff's body and stopping the Fairies with a broad gesture*)
> Halt there!

PISTOLA *(accorrendo)*
                    Chi va là?

FALSTAFF   Pietà!

QUICKLY *(toccando Falstaff col bastone)*
                    C'è un uomo!

ALICE, NANNETTA, MEG
                    C'è un uom!

LE FATE   Un uom!

FORD *(che sarà accorso vicino a Falstaff)*
                    Cornuto come un bue!

PISTOLA   Rotondo come un pomo!

BARDOLFO   Grosso come una nave!

BARDOLFO, PISTOLA *(toccando Falstaff col piede)*
                    Alzati olà!

FALSTAFF *(alzando la testa)*
                    Portatemi una grue!
                    Non posso.

FORD   È troppo grave.

QUICKLY   È corrotto!

LE FATE   È corrotto!

ALICE, NANNETTA, MEG
                    È impuro!

LE FATE   È impuro!

BARDOLFO *(con dei gran gesti da stregone)*
                    Si faccia lo scongiuro!

ALICE *(in disparte a Nannetta, mentre il Dr. Cajus si aggira
come chi cerca qualcuno. Fenton e Quickly nascondono
Nannetta colle loro persone)*
                    Evita il tuo periglio.
                    Già il Dottor Cajo ti cerca.

NANNETTA   Troviamo un nascondíglio.
                    *(s'avvia con Fenton nel fondo della scena,
                    protetta da Alice e da Quickly)*

QUICKLY   Poi tornerete lesti
                Al mio richiamo.

Nannetta, Fenton, Quickly scompaiono dietro le fonde.

BARDOLFO *(continuando i gesti di scongiuro sul corpo di Falstaff)*
                    Spiritelli! Folletti!
                    Farfarelli! Vampiri!
                    Agili insetti
                    Del palude infernale!
                    Punzecchiatelo!
                    Orticheggiatelo!
                    Martirizzatelo!
                    Coi grifi aguzzi!

*Accorrono dal fondo velocissimi alcuni ragazzi vestiti da
Folletti, e si scagliano su Falstaff: altri Folletti, spiritelli, diavoli, sbucano da varie parti. Alcuni scuotono crepitacoli, alcuni
hanno in mano dei vimini: molti portano delle piccole lanterne
rosse.*

PISTOL *(running up)*
> Who goes there?

FALSTAFF   Mercy!

QUICKLY *(touching Falstaff with her stick)*
> There's a man!

ALICE, ANNE, MEG
> There's a man!

THE FAIRIES   A man!

FORD *(who will have run up close to Falstaff)*
> With horns like an ox!

PISTOL   Round as an apple!

BARDOLPH   Big as a ship!

BARDOLPH, PISTOL *(touching Falstaff with their foot)*
> Stand up! Ho!

FALSTAFF *(raising his head)*
> Bring me a crane!
> I can't.

FORD   He's too heavy.

QUICKLY   He's rotten!

THE FAIRIES   He's rotten!

ALICE, ANNE, MEG
> He's impure!

THE FAIRIES   He's impure!

BARDOLPH *(with great gestures like a wizard)*
> Let exorcism be made!

ALICE *(to one side, to Anne, as Dr. Caius wanders around as if looking for someone. Fenton and Quickly hide Anne with their bodies)*
> Avoid your danger.
> Doctor Caius is already seeking you.

ANNE   Let's find a hiding place.
> *(goes off with Fenton at the rear of the stage, shielded by Alice and by Quickly)*

QUICKLY   Later you will return promptly
> At my summons.

Anne, Fenton, Quickly disappear behind the boughs.

BARDOLPH *(continuing the exorcism gestures over the body of Falstaff)*
> Spirits! Sprites!
> Butterflies! Vampires!
> Agile insects
> Of the infernal swamp!
> Sting him!
> Benettle him!
> Torture him!
> With your sharp snouts!

From the rear some children dressed as Sprites come running up, very fast, and they fling themselves on Falstaff. Other Sprites, little spirits, devils, emerge from various places. Some are shaking rattles; some have willow staves; many are carrying little red lanterns.

FALSTAFF *(a Bardolfo)*
          Ahimè . . . tu puzzi
          Come una puzzola.
SPIRITI, FOLLETTI, DIAVOLI *(adosso a Falstaff spingendolo e*
facendolo ruzzolare)
          Ruzzola, ruzzola, ruzzola, ecc.

I Folletti più vicini gli pizzicano le braccia, le guancie, lo
fustigano coi vimini sulla pancia, lo pungono con ortiche.

ALICE, MEG, QUICKLY
          Pizzica, pizzica, pizzica,
          Stuzzica, spizzica, spizzica,
          Pungi, spiluzzica,
          Pungi, spiluzzica,
          Fin ch'egli abbai!

I più piccoli Folletti gli ballano intorno, alcuni gli montano
sulla schiena e fanno sgambetti: Falstaff vorrebbe difendersi
ma non può muoversi.

FALSTAFF   Ahi! ahi! ahi! ahi!
Frastuono di crepitacoli.
SPIRITI, FOLLETTI, DIAVOLI
          Scrolliam crepitacoli,
          Scarandole, nacchere!
          Di schizzi e di zacchere
          Quell'otre si macoli.
          Meniam scorribandole,
          Danziamo la tresca,
          Treschiam le faràndole
          Sull'ampia ventresca.
          Zanzàre ed assilli,
          Volate alla lizza
          Coi dardi e gli spilli!
          Ch'ei crepi di stizza,
          Ch'ei crepi, ecc.
Cessa il frastuono.
ALICE, MEG, QUICKLY
          Pizzica, ecc.
FALSTAFF   Ahi! ahi! ahi! ahi!
ALICE, MEG, QUICKLY, LE FATE
          Cozzalo, aizzolo
          Dai piè al cocuzzolo!
          Strozzalo, strizzalo!
          Strozzalo, strizzalo!
          Gli svampi l'uzzolo!
          Pizzica, pizzica,
          L'unghia rintuzzola!
          Pizzica, ecc.
SPIRITI, FOLLETTI, DIAVOLI
          Ch'ei crepi, ecc.
FALSTAFF   Ahi! ahi! ahi! ahi!
SPIRITI, FOLLETTI, DIAVOLI
          Ruzzola, ruzzola, ecc.

FALSTAFF *(to Bardolph)*
   Alas . . . you stink
   Like a skunk.

SPIRITS, SPRITES, DEVILS *(upon Falstaff, pushing him and making him roll)*
   Roll, roll, roll, *etc.*

The nearest Sprites pinch his arms, his cheeks; they whip him on the belly with their willow staves; they prick him with nettles.

ALICE, MEG, QUICKLY
   Pinch, pinch, pinch,
   Prod, nibble, nibble,
   Sting, peck,
   Sting, peck,
   Until he yelps!

The smaller Sprites dance around him. Some climb on his back and swing their legs. Falstaff would like to defend himself but he cannot move.

FALSTAFF Ouch, Ouch! Ouch! Ouch!
Din of rattles.

SPIRITS, SPRITES, DEVILS
   Let us shake rattles,
   Clappers, castanets!
   With spurts and splashes
   Let that wineskin be stained.
   Let us lead raids,
   Let us dance and mime,
   Let us dance farandoles
   On the broad paunch.
   Mosquitoes and flies,
   Fly to the jousting
   With arrows and pins!
   Let him burst with vexation,
   Let him burst, *etc.*

The din ceases.

ALICE, MEG, QUICKLY
   Pinch, *etc.*

FALSTAFF Ouch! Ouch! Ouch! Ouch!

ALICE, MEG, QUICKLY, THE FAIRIES
   Butt him, goad him,
   From the feet to the crown!
   Strangle him, wring him out!
   Strangle him, wring him out!
   Let his urge cool off!
   Pinch, pinch,
   Dull your claws!
   Pinch, *etc.*

SPIRITS, SPRITES, DEVILS
   Let him burst, *etc.*

FALSTAFF Ouch! Ouch! *etc.*

SPIRITS, SPRITES, DEVILS
   Roll, roll, *etc.*

ALICE, MEG, QUICKLY, LE FATE
>   Pizzica, pizzica, *ecc.*

FALSTAFF   Ahi!

Ford, Dr. Cajus. Pistola e Bardolfo alzano Falstaff e lo obbligano a star ginocchioni.

DR. CAJUS, FORD
>   Cialtron!

BARDOLFO, PISTOLA
>   Poltron!

DR. CAJUS, FORD
>   Ghiotton!

BARDOLFO, PISTOLA
>   Pancion!

DR. CAJUS, FORD
>   Beòn!

BARDOLFO, PISTOLA
>   Briccon!

DR. CAJUS, BARDOLFO, FORD, PISTOLA
>   In ginocchion!

FORD   Pancia ritronfia!

ALICE   Guancia rigonfia!

BARDOLFO   Sconquassa-letti!

QUICKLY   Spacca-farsetti!

PISTOLA   Vuota-barili!

MEG   Sfonda-sedili!

DR. CAJUS   Sfianca-giumenti!

FORD   Triplice mento!

Bardolfo prende il bastone di Quickly a dà una bastonata a Falstaff.

BARDOLFO, PISTOLA
>   Di' che ti penti!

ALICE, MEG, QUICKLY
>   Di' che ti penti!

FALSTAFF   Ahi! ahi! mi pento!

TUTTI GLI UOMINI
>   Uom frodolento!

LE DONNE   Di' che ti penti!

Pistola, prendendo il bastone da Bardolfo dà un'altra bastonata a Falstaff.

FALSTAFF   Ahi! ahi! Mi pento!

TUTTI GLI UOMINI
>   Uom turbolento!

LE DONNE   Di' che ti penti!

Bardolfo riprende il bastone e colpisce nuovamente Falstaff.

FALSTAFF   Ahi! ahi! mi pento!

GLI UOMINI   Capron! Scroccon! Spaccon!

FALSTAFF   Perdon!

ALICE, MEG, QUICKLY, THE FAIRIES
> Pinch, pinch, *etc.*

FALSTAFF   Ouch!

Ford, Dr. Caius, Pistol and Bardolph pull Falstaff up and force him to stay on all fours.

DR. CAIUS, FORD
> Lout!

BARDOLPH, PISTOL
> Poltroon!

DR. CAIUS, FORD
> Glutton!

BARDOLPH, PISTOL
> Big belly!

DR. CAIUS, FORD
> Drunkard!

BARDOLPH, PISTOL
> Rogue!

DR. CAIUS, BARDOLPH, FORD, PISTOL
> On all fours!

FORD   Puffed-up paunch!

ALICE   Swollen cheek!

BARDOLPH   Bed smasher!

QUICKLY   Doublet splitter!

PISTOL   Barrel emptier!

MEG   Chair breaker!

DR. CAIUS   Mare destroyer!

FORD   Triple chin!

Bardolph takes Quickly's stick and gives Falstaff a beating.

BARDOLPH, PISTOL
> Say that you repent!

ALICE, MEG, QUICKLY
> Say that you repent!

FALSTAFF   Ouch! Ouch! I repent!

ALL THE MEN   Fraudulent man!

THE WOMEN   Say that you repent!

Pistol, taking the stick from Bardolph, gives Falstaff another beating.

FALSTAFF   Ouch! Ouch! I repent!

ALL THE MEN   Turbulent man!

THE WOMEN   Say that you repent!
Bardolph takes the stick back and strikes Falstaff again.

FALSTAFF   Ouch! Ouch! I repent!

THE MEN   Billy goat! Sponger! Boaster!

FALSTAFF   Pardon!

BARDOLFO *(colla faccia vicinissima a quella di Falstaff)*
    Riforma la tua vita!

FALSTAFF   Tu puti d'acquavita!

ALICE, MEG, QUICKLY
    Domine fallo casto!

GLI UOMINI   Pancia ritronfia!

FALSTAFF   Ma salvagli l'addomine.

LE FATE   Pizzica, pizzica, pizzica!

ALICE, MEG, QUICKLY
    Domine fallo guasto!

GLI UOMINI   Pancia ritronfia!

FALSTAFF   Ma salvagli l'addomine.

LE FATE   Pizzica, stuzzica, pizzica.

MEG, ALICE, QUICKLY
    Fallo punito Domine!

GLI UOMINI   Vuota-barili!

FALSTAFF   Ma salvagli l'addomine.

LE FATE   Pizzica, pungi, spilluzzica!

GLI UOMINI   Sfianca-sedili!

FALSTAFF   Ma salvagli l'addomine.

LE FATE   Pizzica, pizzica, pizzica!

GLI UOMINI   Globo d'impurità!
    Rispondi.

FALSTAFF   Ben mi sta.

DR. CAJUS, BARDOLFO, FORD, PISTOLA
    Monte d'obesità!
    Rispondi.

FALSTAFF   Ben mi sta.

DR. CAJUS, BARDOLFO, FORD, PISTOLA
    Otre di malvasia!
    Rispondi.

FALSTAFF   Così sia.

BARDOLFO   Re dei panciuti!

FALSTAFF   Va via, tu puti.

BARDOLFO   Re dei cornuti!

FALSTAFF   Va, via, tu puti.

DR. CAJUS, BARDOLFO, FORD, PISTOLA
    Furfanteria!

FALSTAFF   Ahi! Così sia.

DR. CAJUS, BARDOLFO, FORD, PISTOLA
    Gagliofferia!

FALSTAFF   Ahi! Così sia.

DR. CAJUS, BARDOLFO, FORD, PISTOLA
    Furfanteria! Gagliofferia!

FALSTAFF   Ahi! ahi! ahi! ahi!

BARDOLPH *(with his face very close to Falstaff's)*
                    Reform your life!
FALSTAFF   You stink of brandy!
ALICE, MEG, QUICKLY
                    Lord, make him chaste!
THE MEN   Puffed-up paunch!
FALSTAFF   But save his abdomen.
THE FAIRIES   Pinch, pinch, pinch!
ALICE, MEG, QUICKLY
                    Lord, make him desolate!
THE MEN   Puffed-up paunch!
FALSTAFF   But save his abdomen.
THE FAIRIES   Pinch, goad, pinch.
MEG, ALICE, QUICKLY
                    Punish him, Lord.
THE MEN   Barrel emptier!
FALSTAFF   But save his abdomen.
THE FAIRIES   Pinch, sting, peck!
THE MEN   Chair breaker!
FALSTAFF   But save his abdomen.
THE FAIRIES   Pinch, pinch, pinch!
THE MEN   Globe of impurity!
                    Answer.
FALSTAFF   It serves me right.
DR. CAIUS, BARDOLPH, FORD, PISTOL
                    Mountain of obesity!
                    Answer.
FALSTAFF   It serves me right.
DR. CAIUS, BARDOLPH, FORD, PISTOL
                    Wineskin of Malmsey!
                    Answer.
FALSTAFF   So be it.
BARDOLPH   King of the paunchy!
FALSTAFF   Go away, you stink.
BARDOLPH   King of cuckolds!
FALSTAFF   Go away, you stink.
DR. CAIUS, BARDOLPH, FORD, PISTOL
                    Knavery!
FALSTAFF   Ouch! So be it.
DR. CAIUS, BARDOLPH, FORD, PISTOL
                    Loutishness!
FALSTAFF   Ouch! So be it.
DR. CAIUS, BARDOLPH, FORD, PISTOL
                    Knavery! Loutishness!
FALSTAFF   Ouch! Ouch! Ouch! Ouch!

BARDOLFO *(con veemenza)*
                    Ed or che il diavolo
                    Ti porti via!
                    (nella foga del dire gli casca il cappuccio)

FALSTAFF *(rialzandosi)*
                    Nitro! Catrame! Solfo!!!
                    Riconosco Bardolfo!
                    *(incalzando violentemente Bardolfo che
                    retrocede)*
                    Naso vermiglio!
                    Naso bargiglio!
                    Puntùta lesina!
                    Vampa di resina!
                    Salamandra! *Ignis fatuus!*
                    Vecchia alabarda! Stecca
                    Di sartore! Schidion
                    D'inferno! Aringa secca!
                    Vampiro! Basilisco!
                    Manigoldo! Ladrone!
                    Ho detto. E se smentisco
                    Voglio che mi si spacchi
                    Il cinturone!
TUTTI   Bravo!
FALSTAFF   Un poco di pausa.
                    Sono stanco.

QUICKLY *(sottovoce a Bardolfo, col quale poi scompare dietro
gli alberi)*
                    Vieni. Ti coprirò
                    Col velo bianco.
FORD   Ed or, mentre vi passa
                    La scalmana,
                    Sir John, dite:
                    Il cornuto chi è?
MEG *(ironicamente a Falstaff)*
                    Chi è?
ALICE *(ironicamente a Falstaff)*
                    Chi è?
MEG   Chi è?
ALICE   Chi è?
                    (smascherandosi)
                    Vi siete fatto muto?
FALSTAFF *(stendendo la mano a Ford)*
                    Caro Signor Fontana . . .
ALICE *(interponendosi)*
                    Sbagliate nel saluto.
                    Quest'è Ford, mio marito.
QUICKLY *(ritornando)*
                    Cavaliero . . .
FALSTAFF   Reverenza.
QUICKLY   Voi credeste
                    Due donne così grulle,

BARDOLPH *(vehemently)*
        And now let the devil
        Carry you off!
            (in the impetuosity of his speech his hood falls off)

FALSTAFF *(standing up again)*
        Nitre! Pitch! Sulphur!!!
        I recognize Bardolph!
            (violently pursuing Bardolph, who steps backward)
        Vermilion nose!
        Wattled nose!
        Pointed awl!
        Resin flame!
        Salamander! Will-o'-the-wisp!
        Old halberd! Tailor's
        Stick! Spit
        Of hell! Dried herring!
        Vampire! Basilisk!
        Ruffian! Thief!
        I've spoken. And if I take it back,
        I want my belt
        To break!

ALL   Bravo!

FALSTAFF   A bit of rest.
        I'm tired.

QUICKLY *(in a low voice to Bardolph, with whom she then disappears behind the trees)*
        Come. I'll cover you
        With the white veil.

FORD   And now, while your whim
        Passes,
        Sir John, say:
        Who is the one with horns?

MEG *(ironically, to Falstaff)*
        Who is it?

ALICE *(ironically, to Falstaff)*
        Who is it?

MEG   Who is it?

ALICE   Who is it?
        (unmasking herself)
        Have you been struck dumb?

FALSTAFF *(extending his hand to Ford)*
        Dear Mister Fountain . . .

ALICE *(coming between them)*
        You're mistaking the greeting.
        This is Ford, my husband.

QUICKLY *(returning)*
        Sir Knight . . .

FALSTAFF   My respects.

QUICKLY   You believed
        Two women were so silly,

Così citrulle,
Dar darsi anima e corpo
All'Avversiero,
Per un uom vecchio,
Sùdicio ed obeso . . .

MEG, QUICKLY
Con quella testa calva . . .

ALICE, MEG, QUICKLY
E con quel peso!

FORD   Parlan chiaro.

FALSTAFF   Incomincio ad accorgermi
D'esser stato un somaro.

ALICE   Un cervo.

FORD   Un bue.

TUTTI   Ah! ah!

FORD   E un mostro raro, ah! ah!
Un cervo, un bue, ah! ah!

ALICE   Un bue, un cervo, *ecc.*

CORO   Un mostro, raro, ah! ah!

FALSTAFF   Ogni sorta di gente dozzinale
Mi beffa e se ne gloria;
Pur, senza me costor
Con tanta boria
Non avrebbero
Un briciolo di sale.
Son io, son io, son io
Che vi fa scaltri.
L'arguzia mia crea
L'arguzia degli altri.

TUTTI   Ma bravo!

FORD   Per gli Dei! Se non ridessi
Ti sconquasserei!
Ma basta. Ed or
Vo' che m'ascoltiate.
Coronerem la mascherata bella
Cogli sponsali
Della Regina delle Fate.

Il Dr. Cajus e Bardolfo vestito da Regina delle Fate col viso coperto da un velo, s'avanzano lentamente tenendosi per mano. Il Dr. Cajus ha la maschera sul volto.

FORD   Già s'avanza il corteggio
Nuziale. È dessa!

FALSTAFF, CORO
Attenti!

FORD   Ha il serto virginale.
Circondatela, o Ninfe!

Bardolfo e il Dr. Cajus si portano nel mezzo: le Fate grandi e piccole li circondano. Alice presenta Nannetta e Fenton che

So foolish,
That they would give themselves body and soul
To Satan
For an old man,
Filthy and obese . . .

MEG, QUICKLY
                With that bald head . . .

ALICE, MEG, QUICKLY
                And with that weight!

FORD   They speak clearly.

FALSTAFF   I begin to realize
                That I was an ass.

ALICE   A stag.

FORD   An ox.

ALL   Ha! ha!

FORD   And a rare monster, ha! ha!
                A stag, an ox, ha! ha!

ALICE   An ox, a stag, *etc.*

CHORUS   A rare monster, ha! ha!

FALSTAFF   Every sort of commonplace person
                Taunts me and boasts of it;
                And yet, without me, they
                With all their vainglory
                Wouldn't have
                A pinch of saltiness.
                It is I, it is I, it is I
                Who make you clever.
                My cleverness creates
                The cleverness of the others.

ALL   Why, good for you!

FORD   By the gods! If I weren't laughing,
                I'd shatter you.
                But enough. And now
                I want all of you to listen to me.
                We'll crown the beautiful masquerade
                With the wedding
                Of the Queen of the Fairies.

*Dr. Caius and Bardolph, dressed as Queen of the Fairies
with his face covered by a veil, come forward slowly, hand in
hand. Dr. Caius has a mask on his face.*

FORD   The nuptial procession is advancing
                Already. It is she!

FALSTAFF, CHORUS
                Pay attention!

FORD   She wears the virginal garland.
                Surround her, O Nymphs!

*Bardolph and Dr. Caius stand in the center. The Fairies,
big and small, surround them. Alice presents Anne and Fen-*

saranno entrati: Nannetta è tutta coperta da un gran velo
celeste: Fenton ha la maschera e la cappa.

ALICE   Un'altra coppia
             D'amanti desïosi
             Chiede d'essere ammessa
             Agli augurosi
             Connubi!

FORD   E sia.
             Farem la festa doppia!
             Avvicinate i lumi.
             Il ciel v'accoppia.

I Folletti guidati da Alice si avvicinano a Bardolfo ed al
Dr. Cajus: Alice prenderà in braccio il più piccolo dei ragaz-
zetti che sarà mascherato da spiritello, e fara in modo che la
lanterna che tiene in mano illumini in pieno la faccia di Bar-
dolfo appena questi resterà senza il velo che lo nasconde. Un
altro spiritello guidato da Meg illuminerà Nannetta e Fenton.

FORD   Giù le maschere e i veli.
             Apoteòsi!

TUTTI *(tranne Dr. Cajus, Ford, Bardolfo)*
             Ah! ah! ah! ah!

DR. CAJUS *(riconoscendo Bardolfo, immobilizzato dalla sor-*
presa)
             Spavento!

FORD *(sorpreso)*
             Tradimento!

FALSTAFF, PISTOLA, CORO
             Apoteòsi!

FORD *(vedendo l' altra coppia)*
             Fenton con mia figlia!!!

DR. CAJUS *(esterrefatto)*
             Ho sposato Bardolfo!

TUTTI *(tranne Nannetta, Fenton, Ford, Dr. Cajus, Bardolfo)*
             Ah! ah!

DR. CAJUS   Spavento! Spavento!

TUTTI *(tranne Nannetta, Fenton, Ford, Dr. Cajus, Bardolfo)*
             Vittoria! Evviva! Evviva!

FORD *(ancora sotto il colpo dello stupore)*
             Oh! meraviglia!

ALICE *(a Ford)*
             L'uom cade spesso
             Nelle reti ordite
             Dalle malizie sue.

FALSTAFF *(avvicinandosi a Ford con un inchino ironico)*
             Caro buon Messer Ford,
             Ed ora, dite:
             Lo scornato chi è?

FORD *(accenna al Dr. Cajus)*
             Lui.

ton, who will have come in. Anne is completely covered by a
great blue veil; Fenton is wearing mask and cloak.

ALICE   Another couple
                  Of yearning lovers
                  Asks to be admitted
                  To the propitious
                  Marriage rite!

FORD   So be it.
                  We'll make a double feast!
                  Bring the lights closer.
                  May heaven unite you.

The Sprites, led by Alice, approach Bardolph and Dr. Caius.
Alice will pick up in her arms the smallest of the little boys
who is disguised as a sprite and she will hold him in such a
way that the lantern he bears in his hand illuminates fully the
face of Bardolph, as soon as the latter will remain without the
veil that hides him. Another sprite, led by Meg, will illu-
minate Anne and Fenton.

FORD   Off with masks and veils.
                  Apotheosis!

ALL *(except Dr. Caius, Ford, Bardolph)*
                  Ha! ha! ha! ha!

DR. CAIUS *(recognizing Bardolph; stock-still with surprise)*

                  Horrors!

FORD *(surprised)*
                     Treachery!

FALSTAFF, PISTOL, CHORUS
                  Apotheosis!

FORD *(seeing the other couple)*
                  Fenton with my daughter!!!

DR. CAIUS *(terrified)*
                  I've married Bardolph!

ALL *(except Anne, Fenton, Ford, Dr. Caius, Bardolph)*
                  Ha! ha!

DR. CAIUS   Horrors! Horrors!

ALL *(except Anne, Fenton, Ford, Dr. Caius, Bardolph)*
                  Victory! Hurrah! Hurrah!

FORD *(still under the effects of his amazement)*
                  Oh! wonder!

ALICE *(to Ford)*
                  Man often falls
                  In the nets placed
                  By his tricks.

FALSTAFF *(approaching Ford, with an ironic bow)*
                  Dear, good Master Ford,
                  And now, say:
                  Who's been dishorned?

FORD *(nods toward Dr. Caius)*
                  He.

DR. CAJUS *(a Ford)*
          Tu.

FORD   No.

DR. CAJUS   Sì.

BARDOLFO *(a Ford e Cajus)*
          Voi.

FENTON *(accenna pure al Dr. Cajus e Ford)*
          Lor.

DR. CAJUS *(mettendosi con Ford)*
          Noi.

FALSTAFF   Tutti e due!

ALICE *(mettendo Falstaff con Ford e il Dr. Cajus)*
          No! Tutti e tre!
             (a Ford, mostrando Nannetta e Fenton)
          Volgiti e mira
          Quell'ansie leggiadre.

NANNETTA *(a Ford, giungendo le mani)*
          Perdonateci, o padre.

FORD   Chi schivare non può
          La propria noia
          L'accetti di buon grado.
          Facciamo il parentado
          E che il ciel vi dia gioia.

TUTTI *(tranne Ford, Falstaff e il Coro)*
          Evviva!

FALSTAFF   Un coro e terminiam la scena.

FORD   Poi con Sir John Falstaff,
          Tutti, andiamo a cena.

TUTTI *(tranne Ford)*
          Evviva!

FALSTAFF, poi TUTTI
          Tutto nel mondo è burla.
          L'uom è nato burlone,
          Burlone, burlone, *ecc.*
          Nel suo cervello ciurla
          Sempre la sua ragione,
          Sempre, sempre, *ecc.*
          Tutti gabbati!
          Tutti gabbati, *ecc.*
          Irride
          L'un l'altro ogni mortal,
          Ma ride ben,
          Ride ben chi ride
          La risata final.
          Tutto nel mondo, *ecc.*

DR. CAIUS *(to Ford)*
You.

FORD No.

DR. CAIUS Yes.

BARDOLPH *(to Ford and Caius)*
Both of you.

FENTON *(also nods toward Dr. Caius and Ford)*
They.

DR. CAIUS *(joining Ford)*
Us.

FALSTAFF Both!

ALICE *(putting Falstaff with Ford and Dr. Caius)*
No! All three!
    (to Ford, indicating Anne and Fenton)
Turn and look
At those lovely ardors.

ANNE *(to Ford, clasping her hands)*
Forgive us, O father.

FORD He who cannot evade
His own vexation
Must accept it willingly.
Let us create this kinship
And may heaven give you joy.

ALL *(except Ford, Falstaff and the Chorus)*
Hurrah!

FALSTAFF A chorus and we'll end the scene.

FORD Then, with Sir John Falstaff,
We'll go, all of us, to supper.

ALL *(except Ford)*
Hurrah!

FALSTAFF, then ALL
Everything in the world is jest.
Man is born a jester,
Jester, jester, *etc.*
In his mind, his reason
Is wavering always,
Always, always, *etc.*
All mocked!
All mocked, *etc.*
All mortals
Taunt one another,
But he laughs well,
He laughs well who has
The last laugh.
Everything in the world, *etc.*